上海交通大學
百年报刊集成

第一辑（1896—1949）

学 术 学 科

综合卷（第二册）

上海交通大学
档案文博管理中心 编

上海交通大學出版社
SHANGHAI JIAO TONG UNIVERSITY PRESS

目　录

《南洋季刊》简介

该刊 1926 年 1 月 15 日创刊于上海，系季刊，由南洋大学出版部和南洋公学同学会共出版发行。本书收录了 1926 年出版的第一卷，共四期，分别为创刊号、电机工程号、经济和机械工程号。停刊时间及原因不详。

该刊以介绍学术、弘扬学校精神为重心，内设学术、专著、文苑、记载、附载等栏目。“学’栏目主要刊登比较专业的学术性文章，如探究电力事业发达之掌故，论述无线电对于事效用的重要性，研究英国现行所得税制度等。“专著”栏目则有很多实际经验的记载，震华电机制造厂的实习记，苏州胥门发电厂一瞥等，也有聚焦于对水电工程等实际科学题的研究，如同步换流机与同步电动发电机在实习应用上的比较等。“文苑”栏目主要刊文学作品，包括游记、诗歌、散文等，如《北游吟草》《游张家口赐儿山记》等。“记载”栏目要记载了学校的一些重大事件以及同学会、校友会、会员、理事题名等重要内容。附载栏主要刊载一些调查报告、述略等内容，如工程心理调查报告、四库全书述略等。

该刊对于学术内容的介绍，比较侧重于理工科，如电气、机械、经济等方面，文学方面涉内容不多，同时也有一些学校的珍贵图像资料，对研究学校校史具有一定的参考价值。

NANYANG QUARTERLY

創刊號

本期要目

民國十五年一月十五日

南洋大學出版部南洋公學同學會同發行

中華郵政特准掛號認為新聞紙類

南洋大學出版部南洋公學同學會同發行

南洋季刊創刊號目錄

（民國十五年一月發行）

圖　　畫

發刊辭

學　　術

文 苑

記 載

雜 俎

本校新建體育館

本校新建調養室

師範班同學攝影（紀事閱本刊盍簪記）

（後行）沈叔逵　張師石　黃涵之　潘若梁　張雲搏　（陳景韓）

（前行）趙瑞侯　孟純生　朱燏之　張惕銘　傅緯平　林賞齋

（此照為陳景韓君所攝故陳君不在照內）

交通部南洋大學學生會全體攝影

發刊辭

本校之有定期出版物，由來已久；先後繼起，非止一種：有提倡科學者，有介紹工程者，有研究經濟者，亦有專以傳布學校及校友消息爲事者：而其所自出之組織亦不一：或爲學術團體，或爲校友會，或爲同鄉會，或爲遊藝性質之集會。出版物之內容既常不能兼容並包，表示吾南洋大學之精神，而其經費資料，又每以組織較小，苦於不易維持。於是乎校內外師生校友，本共同合作之精神，盡工程，經濟，科學等探討研究之所得，羣策羣力，以介紹學術傳布消息爲職志，而剏辦一我校空前之出版物：此南洋季刊之所以應運而興也。

十三年夏，本校經濟學會有經濟學報之刊行；不兼年而工程學會亦以工程學報問世。此二者，雖皆出於同學方面之努力，其內容固頗有價值。一二年來，兩學會均以財力不足，不能早日繼續出版。去年十月，校中爰有出版委員會及出版部之組織。委員會掌學校出版物之規劃，出版部司出版事業之進行。嗣後卽復商得校友會同意，共同發行南洋季刊南洋旬刊二種：前者主介紹學術，後者重傳布消息；而以發揚學校精神論，季刊之責任尤重大。

校中既以較完全之組織，較充裕之財力，決定發行季刊，於是同學方面各種團體，如工程學會，經濟學會，學生會、南洋學會，國樂研究社，南洋歌社等等，均各先後推舉編輯員，共同加入；工程經濟兩學會，且以舊備用之稿併入季刊發表。十一月一日，旬刊首期出版，頗受校友之歡迎，委員會，出版部乃更進行特約撰述校審員之聘請，及稿件之徵求與編輯。十二月杪，倉卒員付印，此南洋季刊乃得於今年一月，在國內出版界中露其頭角。

本刊之主旨，固可以「介紹學術」四字概括之，然就工程，經濟，科學三者分別而言，則本刊之態度有可爲讀者告者：(一)工程則主張工程學術，工程事業，工程教育之國化；(二)經濟則注重歐西經濟學說之介紹，我國固有經濟思想之研究，以及經濟學上理論事實之有關交通事業者，(三)科學則當提倡科學精神與科學方法以拯救今日國困襲，混亂，偏激之思想。

本刊所具之宗旨，所抱之態度，所懸之鵠的，具如上述。但編輯同人，學識淺薄，心餘力絀，本校教職員及同學，又皆以校課繁重，不克致全力於著述；本刊之能否饜讀者諸君之望，是在海內外學者之不吝指教焉！

編輯者言

本刊既幸告竣，編輯同人猶有願爲讀者告者，謹略貢數語於下：

一，本刊內容本擬分門別類，以醒眉目。茲因本期所載，篇數既多，品類尤衆，故祇就大體上分學術文藝，紀載，雜俎四類，至各類中各篇先後之次序，或視稿件收到之遲早，或視內容之性質而定，至不一律。匆遽編印，不得不如此，幸 讀者諒之。

一，本期所載各篇，或爲著論，或爲迻譯，或爲紀述，或爲調査，或爲研究，或爲考據，類皆極有價値，不俟贅言。惟編輯同人，學識譾陋，才力有限，倘蒙當世明達，錫以南針，惠以宏著，不勝欣幸。

一，本期封面圖樣，承同學陳琦君繪畫，徵稿事宜，得工程學會代表費福燾君襄助不少，茲特聲明誌謝。至校內外惠稿諸校友，本刊同人，亦甚願於此謹致謝意。

電力事業發達之掌故

李熙謀

電之在今日,其能力之宏,應用之繁,經濟力之偉大,與世界任何事業比,當無有出其右者.電力事業發達最早者,應推電報.繼之者為電燈電話.自電動機發明後,則一切工業製造,又為電力之發展地.今日電力事業,可分為下列數項:

(一) 電力運輸,有電力鐵道,電車,電動輪艦等.

(二) 電力交通,有電話,電報,無綫電信,電傳影相等.

(三) 電力化學,有鍊銀,鍊銅,化鋼,冶鐵,提鎂鉀及鈉,製燐,製炭精,及鉀綠化合物,電鍍等.

(四) 電力工業,有採鑛,製造,建築等.

(五) 電力醫療,有愛克司光與鐳等.

(六) 日用電力,有街衢,工廠,戲院,住宅,及公共會所之電燈,電扇,電爐,電力烹飪等.

據美國地質測量局報告,一九二四年美國全國發電廠出售電力,合值拾叁萬三千五百拾萬金元.發電廠之資產,約合陸拾陸萬萬金元.全年之內,全國人民於發電事業之投資,約增拾萬萬金元.若以電話,電報,電力鐵道,電機製造等之資本,統合計之,則美國全國電力事業之總資產,約值壹百陸百萬萬餘金元.吾國今日駭人聽聞之巨額國債,據最近調查,約合國幣拾陸萬萬元.若以美金一元,合國幣一元八角計,則美國電機事業一項之企業投資,已超過吾國國債拾八倍有餘.其經濟力之偉大,與其將來之發展,於此可見一斑.

又美國『發電廠年鑑』及『郵政指南』二書,關於近年美國人民利用電力之程度,記載甚詳.謂凡鄉村市集,居留人數在五千以上者,必有電力供給.全國七千餘萬人口中,享有使用電力之便利者,占百分之九十餘.即以工程事業閉塞如吾國,而沿滬甯滬杭二路綫所經之區域,及水陸交通便利之都市,皆有發電廠以供電火.杭蘇甯嘉,津滬武漢等巨埠,且有用電力以工作製造者.全國電報局所,已增至千局左右.電話用戶,已達九萬餘,則電力事業應用之普遍,亦可概見.

考電力事業之發達,實肇始於千八百三十一年弗拉臺(Farapry)感應電流之發見.迄今不及百年,較之土木,建築,機械,汽機等工程,均爲後起.然數十年來,歐美人士研究電學者才智輩出.數年數十年間,必有非常之進步.今日電力事業,在工程界之重要位置,已爲盡人皆知之事實.然探本窮源,電之有今日,非由華而太(Volta)弗拉臺,墨克司威而(Maxwell)輩,孜孜矻矻,窮微探賾,爲之先導,曷克臻此.水源木本,已往事蹟,不可不記,俾明電學發達之由來,事非偶然.他山之石,可以攻玉.科學幼稚如吾國,或足以資借鏡也.

電學發達歷史,可分爲二大時期.第一期爲靜電發達時期,第二期爲動電與磁電發達時期.二時期間,固無截然之界限.且經弗拉臺,凱而文(Kelvin)輩之研究,第二時期中靜電之進步,亦甚可觀.史籍所載,電之發現,遠在西歷前六百年.當時希臘人已知凡琥珀松脂等物,受毛絨物磨擦後,則羽毛落葉敗草等,均被吸引.英文「電」字,乃希臘文「琥珀」字之轉借.蓋所以示凡物體受磨擦後吸引他物者,均與琥珀具同樣之特性也.吾國史乘,凡關雷電等記載,都屬神秘,於科學無補.惟黃帝用指南車,爲時獨早.故天然磁之發見,遠在希臘人發見電之前.差足自豪.惜無繼起者,故外此無聞也.

歐洲文化,一盛於希臘,再盛於羅馬.羅馬衰,全歐分裂,文物蕩然.至文藝復興,始漸恢復舊觀.中間歷千餘年,科學發展,毫無可紀,而電學亦同遭劫難.迄十六世紀末,英人奇而白(Gilbert)始續絕學.奇氏身任皇室御醫,以其餘暇,專攻格致.於磁電尤致力焉.奇氏製電針,凡與琥珀同類之物,一經磨擦移近電針,均能吸動之.千六百年,發表其傑著「磁性物及地球爲大磁石」一書,實爲近世磁電著作之濫觴.此後磁電學之研究進步,皆由奇氏啓其端.

繼奇氏而起者,在英有鮑哀而(Boyle),葛萊(Stephen Grary),加頓(Cantoan),開文狄許(Cavendish),在美有弗蘭克林(Franklin),在德有高士(Gauss),在法有柯倫姆(Coulomb),巴澳爽(Poisson).雖年代有先後而要皆一時名士.鮑氏以研究所得,斷定荷電體間之吸引,爲物體間之公同作用,而非任一荷電體之單獨引力.一七二九年,葛萊分物質爲傳電與非傳電二類,稱物體之傳電者曰導體,物體之不傳電者曰絕電體.杜揮(Du Fay)則發見電有「玻璃性」與『琥珀性』之不同.凡磨擦而得之電,與玻璃受磨擦後所生之電相同者,即屬玻璃性,若與琥珀受磨擦後所生之電相同者,則屬琥珀性.蓋即近世所稱陽電陰電或正負電之分也.同性之電則相拒,異性之電則相引.杜氏實創二流說之鼻祖.弗蘭克林在美,亦以探求電理著稱.弗氏之紙鳶試驗,證明天空間暴風驟雨時之雷電,與由磨擦而得之電爲同本一源之物.弗氏不以杜揮二流說爲然,故創一流說.其說謂電無分陽陰與正負.所別者有餘與不足耳.電有餘,如水在高山,有傾下之勢,即二流說之陽與正也.電不足,如澤陷深谷衆流灌注,即二流說之陰與負也.故陽爲有餘之狀態,陰爲不足之狀態而電之本體原無陰陽正負之分也.在十八世紀中,二流說與一流說,各有信崇,無可軒輊.一七五三年,加頓發見靜電感應,是爲取電之第三法.希臘人之磨擦法,第一法也.加氏以A導體,移近B荷電體時,則A體與B接近之一端即起與B異性之電,而較遠一端,起與A同性之電.此種現象,謂之靜電感應.開文狄許繼起,研究更進,於電之陰陽性狀外,兼及質量與發生之力之關係蓋自哲理探討而進於科學研究矣.開氏於(一)蓄電量之測定,(二)電荷間與距之關係,(三)通感體於蓄電量之影響諸問題,都有發明.法人好學理,於力數理電學,造詣獨高.柯倫姆巴澳爽,拉柏拉司(Lap.ace)尤其著者.柯氏與開文狄許均從事於電荷間引力拒力之研究.柯氏以螺力秤(Torsion balance)直接測定,開氏以同心二圓球間接推證,而結果相同,即今吾人皆知之

公理『二電荷間之引力或拒力與電荷之乘積爲正比與距之平方爲反比』是也.近世電學書籍所稱巴澳爽公式,

$$Div.A=\frac{dAx}{dx}+\frac{dAy}{dy}+\frac{dAz}{dz}=4\pi\rho$$

與拉柏拉司公式,

$$Div.A=\frac{dAx}{dx}+\frac{dAy}{dy}+\frac{dAz}{dz}=0$$

均爲巴氏拉氏攻治數理電學之功績,皆所以通電荷與電荷周圍發生電力線之關係者也.

當是時,靜電感應發電機,雷頓瓶蓄電器,均已先後發明,學者極盛.然所研究探討者終未出乎靜電範圍以外也.一七九九年,華而太製電池成功,因以得電流,遂開電學上之新紀元.第二時期磁電動電之研究亦於此發軔.華氏分導體爲二類:金屬與炭精爲第一類,水與其他液質導體爲第二類.以第一類中,任何二金屬使之接觸,即起電勢而生電流.若欲增高電勢,法以二金屬置於第二類導體中,分爲一組,組與組相連.電勢即隨之而增.設金屬不置于第二類導體中,則雖連而電勢不增,是乃華氏製成電池之原則也.一八〇〇年尼古森(Wm. Nicholson)以銀與鋅置水中,通以電,有氣泡上升,乃即輕養二氣.是爲電解之冶,一八〇三年,諜威(Dovy)以電解法得純粹之鉀與鈉,爲電解冶金之第一人.電之效能既繁.研究者衆,而所得結果自富.歐司德(Oersted)於一八一九年得電流周圍發生磁場之現象.若電荷周圍發生電場然.翌年,法人安培(Ampere)以其酷好學理之天性,推算電流量與由電流而發生磁力之關係.所得結果,爲『二電流間所起之磁力與電流量之乘積及流之長度爲正比與距之平方爲反比.』此律已成磁電學上不磨之公例.世稱之別華薩槐(Biot-Savart)定律.

$$df=\frac{m}{r^2}\bar{I}\,\mathrm{Sin}\theta\,dl$$

乃安氏所得結果特例之一耳.同時談威,奧拉谷（Arago），施得琴(Sturgeon）諸,均發見電流之磁感力凡以荷電之線繞於鋼或鐵上,則此鋼或鐵頓成強有力之磁鐵.是乃人造磁鐵（即電磁鐵）之始近世製造電機,非用電磁鐵以造磁場,則不能得巨量之電力.故電磁鐵之發明,亦電機發達史上一重要功績也.自電流發生磁場之理明,學者聞風興起,昔之泥於電與磁者風馬牛不相及者,今則恍然於二者有至密切之關係矣.

一八二〇年以後,實爲研究磁電學全盛時代.奧拉谷,弗拉臺,均先後得實驗結果:凡帶電導線置於磁場內,則導線即能自由繞磁極而旋轉.此種現象,爲發明近代電動機之先導.他若西培克（Seebeck）配而休(Peltier)歐姆(Ohm),均各有發明.然綜觀前後數百年間,爲近代電力事業之第一功臣,則舍弗拉臺莫屬.弗氏自一八二五年起,至一八三一年止歷六載之久,而感應電流之試驗,方告成功.弗氏以銅碟旋轉於磁場內,以導線之二端,接於線之外緣及中心,則導線內即有電流.更證明凡導線與磁場有相對之運動時,或導線內包圍磁場之密度變更時,則導線內均起電流.因歐司德之發明,則知磁場可由電而起.因弗氏之發明,則更知電亦可由磁而生.磁與電循環相生之理,於是乎大著.弗氏不滿於法國學者「相距作用」之說,乃創力線說.凡主「相距作用」之說者,則曰物體在異空間,亦能相引,如日之於地.地之於月,無介體之必要.弗氏則謂二物體間發生引力或拒力,必須第三體爲之介否則違背機械原則.故二電相引,則中間必生力線.二磁相引,中間亦起磁力線.力線者,即介體中因電力或磁力而所起之狀態也.弗氏更證明凡電之由摩擦或靜電感應,磁電感應,電池而得者,均爲同體同性之一物.繼弗氏而起者,英有凱而文（Kelvin,）墨克司威而,海維塞愛(Heaviside)美有亨利(Henry,)莽斯(Morse),德有漢姆化滋（Helmholtz）黑滋(Hertg)一八三七年頃亨利,漢姆化滋均發見蓄電器上,二電消和時,爲高週率通盪現象.一八五三年,凱而文以數理證明二氏所見之準確.凱氏於靜電學,則發明投影法,以計算蓄電量.

及發明靜電電荷計,電壓計等.於海電收發機件,則有懸鏡電流計等,謂海電之成功,半由凱氏,亦無不可.然得弗拉臺之心傳,續弗氏電磁學說之正統者,則爲墨克司威而.墨氏與弗氏同其浩博,然弗重實驗,其所著「電學實驗研究」三巨册,無一非實驗之結果.墨好推演,所著「數理磁電學」,滿紙數學公式.墨氏蓋融合英法二學派而爲一者也.墨氏能道前人所不能道.前此之學者謂電流僅能起於導體內.墨氏則謂通感體中,亦起電流.惟導體內電流,爲繼續無間之流.而通感體內之電流,僅俄頃間之流耳.一八六三年墨氏發表其傑作曰「磁電場之動力說」證明磁電場經流空際,亦能傳送電力,導線非必需之物.而光亦爲磁電力之一種.當時學者,太半懷疑其說.至一八八七年,墨氏發表學說之時,已二十四年,黑洲始以實驗證明墨氏學說之非妄,而舉世方翕然嚮從焉.自黑氏而後,研究磁電學之致用者衆,故電力事業發達極速.尤以葛拉姆(Gramme)西門子(Siemens)等改良發電機之構造,愛迪生(Edison)之計劃發電及電力輸送與分佈,電動機與貝爾(Bell)電話之發明爲重要.電報之試驗,爲時甚早.一八三七年,茅斯始告成功.電力事業中,直接食墨克司威而學說之賜者,則爲馬可尼發明之無線電信.自譚化來(De Fe-rest)三極眞空管發明,應用于電話電報及無線電信極廣,前程效用,未可限量.近代各項電力事業之類別,已如篇首所舉.而當代學者所研究之電子說,氣體低壓傳導,電子發射,愛克司光分析等,太半尚在科學研究時代.於電力事業,無甚大關係,故不備述焉.

吾國水泥事業之概況

施孔懷

一,導言. 二,水泥之發明及進化略史. 三,水泥原料之比例. 四水泥之製造方法. 五,吾國水泥廠之詳情. 六,吾國水泥每年之總產額. 七,十五年來吾國水泥進口價値之一瞥, 八,今後吾國水泥工業之預測.

一,導言　自英人阿司庭 Joseph Aspdin 於千八百二十四年發明水泥後,各國人士,無不震駭,歎爲人工戰勝天然.豈知百年來,經學者之精研搜求,盡量供獻,降至今日,舉凡長橋大廈,禦水避火之工程,無不惟水泥是賴.其故緣水泥建築,堅固耐久,火不能燬,水不能濡,水陸相宜,歲修省費,故自水泥發明後,建築界爲之別開生面.吾國工程實業,序屬後進,然於水泥事業,尙能逐漸發達.爰本所知,著述是篇,爲國人告焉

二,水泥之發明及進化略史　千七百五十六年,英國土木工程師史墨頓 John Smeaton 受英國國會之聘,於英國海峽礁石處建一燈塔,以便航行;始用木材,爲風雨侵蝕,未能經久;繼用灰砂,然在水中,不能凝結.因發明凡含黏土之石灰石,煅燒後,遠勝純粹石灰石水泥之發明,此爲嚆矢.然煅燒後,磨成細粉,能成極強之材料,則史氏未之知也.至千七百九十六年,英人派克 Joseph Parker 始發明之,名爲羅馬水泥.於水泥之發明,更進一步矣.千八百二十四年,阿司庭專利英國水泥事業.製造方法,用黏土及石灰石爲原料,置之窰中煅燒,再行磨細,即成水泥.其名稱之謂巴德郎 portland 水泥者,因水泥和水凝結後,色作黃灰,有似英國巴德郎地方所產之石色故也.水泥之發明,雖歸功於阿司庭,然其煅燒溫度,未至開始鎔化程度,（約在華氏三千度左右）此點與水泥之凝結密度及強固等性質至有關係,卒於千八百二十五年,爲英人富而司脫 James Frost 發明水泥之製造,於是完善.德人有鑒

於水泥之可貴,急起直追,於千八百五十二年,在司達丁 Stettin 地方,創辦一水泥製造廠,研究試驗,不遺餘力,應用科學方法,製造更精更良之水泥,故至今日,每談水泥,輒引德產爲標準.是故水泥之發明,當歸功英人,繼長增高,精進不已,則德人之力也.

三,水泥原料之比例　製造水泥之原料,爲石灰石與黏土.然欲所製之水泥,質地高上,凝結循規,強度超等,非將原料妥爲配合不可.有時各廠雖據同一原理配合原料,然所成之水泥,其成份並不脗合.其故常因石膏之加入或煤灰與水泥塊混合,或煅燒時吸收空氣中之炭養二,種種關係而其最大原因,則爲原料質地之不盡相同.美人米突 Richard K. Meade, 曾本其試驗結果,及顧慮上述情形,寫成下列原料配合之公式,式中%爲百分之記號.

$$\frac{\text{石灰石}}{\text{黏土}}=\frac{(\%\text{矽石加}\%\text{鐵養加}\%\text{礬土在黏土內者})\text{乘四減}(\%\text{炭酸鈣在黏土內者})}{(\%\text{炭酸鈣在石灰石內者})\text{減}(\%\text{矽石加}\%\text{鐵養加}\%\text{礬土在石灰石者})\text{乘四}}$$

設下表爲黏土及石灰石以百分計之成份.

	矽石	鐵養	礬土	炭酸鈣	炭酸鎂
黏土	一九、〇六	一、一四	四、四四	六九、二四	四、二一
石灰石	二、一四	〇、四六	一、〇〇	九四、三五	二、一八

配合時將各成份代入公式,計石灰石與黏土爲二九•三二與七九•九五之比,即用百份黏土,須用三六•七份石灰.

四,水泥之製造方法　方水泥事業之初興也,將原料石灰石及黏土,依成份配合,磨成糊漿,製成磚塊,置之直窰中煅燒,然後細磨爲粉,水泥遂成.此法名爲間斷法.燃煤較省,惟製造遲緩,工值浩大,故已有棄而不用之趨勢.今所盛行者爲接續法.法將磨細之生料,通入旋窰,所煅燒之水泥塊,轉入水泥磨磨細,其機械俱屬自動,費煤甚多.接續製法,分乾濕兩種,乾法需費較省,濕法用煤較多,惟成份易於配準.採用時,須視原料之性質而定.美國盛產天然水泥石,故乾法應用甚廣.如原料爲石灰石及黏土,則以濕法爲宜.今將二法

之製造程序附列於後以供參考

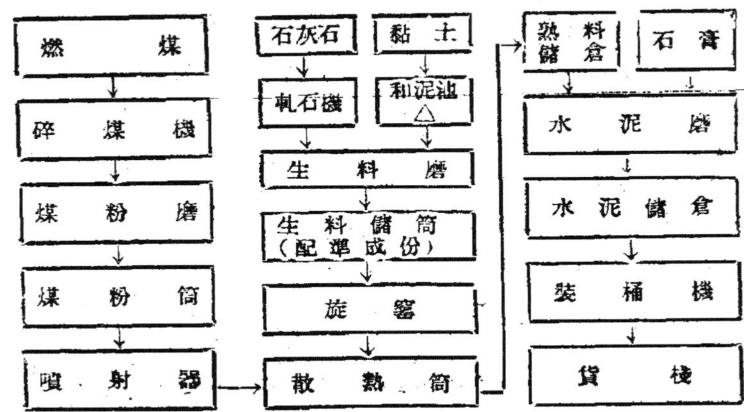

在此處加入定量之水

濕法製造水泥之程序

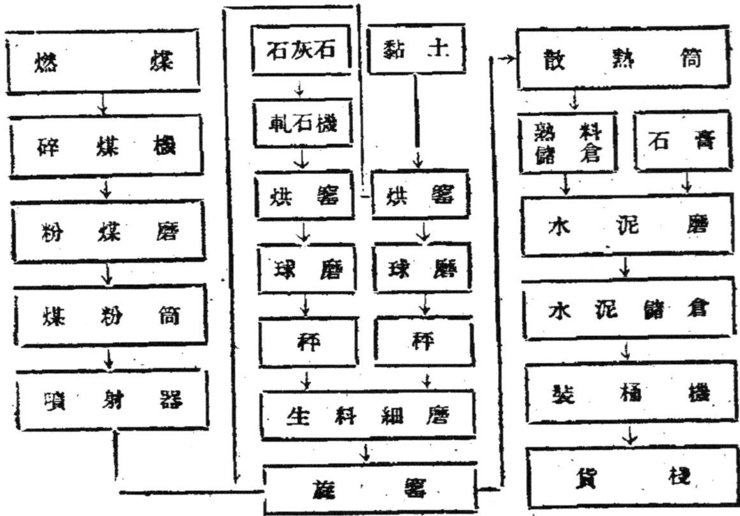

乾法製造水泥之程序

上述程序,非一定不易,常因原料之性質,機器之佈置而更改所加石膏,其作用在延緩水泥之凝結,加入量不可過百分之三.

五,吾國水泥廠之詳情　吾國因政府之不加提倡,及工商實業之不甚振興,水泥事業,於前清光緒二十七年,始行發軔,吾國國人管理之水泥廠凡六,即啓新洋灰公司,華記湖北水泥公司,廣東士敏土廠,濟南水泥公司,中國水泥公司,及上海水泥公司等是.每廠情形詳述如下.

啓新洋灰公司,位置在直隸唐山,當京奉鐵路之衝,交通便利.東達秦皇島,西南可至天津,將水泥運輸別埠.創辦於光緒二十七年.初爲開灤礦務局所經營,光緒三十四年,售與啓新洋灰公司.資本四百萬兩.原料石灰石及黏土在廠之附近開採,煤則取給於開灤礦務局,石膏購自中南部.廠分新舊二部,舊廠用蒸汽轉動旋窰,窰凡二,長百尺,採乾法製造水泥,新廠有長百五十尺之旋窰二,用電力轉動,製造則採用濕法.開第三廠裝置長二百二十尺之旋窰二,亦採用濕法,尚在計劃之中.產額每桶以三百七十五磅計,每日可出三千桶.運銷中國北部,上海,福州,香港,及南洋羣島等處.商標爲馬牌.每桶約五元五角.

華記湖北水泥公司,位置在湖北大冶,鄰近大冶輪埠.所出水泥,由輸送機運至江邊輪舶,機係架定橋梁,繞以繩索,此往彼來,極形便利.組織於前清宣統二年.開工四年,虧耗甚多,遂歸併於啓新洋灰公司,改今名.資本一百萬兩,近來頗獲利.廠之附近,石灰石與黏土,甚爲豐富.煤則購自開灤礦務局.採用乾法製造.機器來自德國,原動力用蒸汽機,每日可產一千二百桶.運銷中國中部九江,安慶及上海等處.商標塔牌.每桶約五元五角.

廣東士敏土廠,在廣東省城東隅珠江南岸.於光緒三十四年,爲清政府所設立.民國成立,廣東政府管理之.於民國元年,租與士敏土廠,年納租金三十六萬四千五百元.原料石灰石採自珠江上游距廠五十里之石礦.黏土於下游距廠十二里之沙島運來,石膏取給吾國中部.煤由開灤礦務局及台灣供給.用間斷法構造.有八直窰四烟突.製造時加赤鐵礦少許,以增水泥之色.每日可產五百桶.惟因連年戰事頻仍,兼之原料不甚豐富,每日平均祇出二百桶.全銷本地,尚不敷應用.

濟南水泥公司,在山東濟南.規模較小,資本為二十萬元.廠之附近,石灰石及黏土原料豐富.煤亦盛產.所用機器,購自德國.窰為直立式.採用間斷法製造.產額每日二百五十桶.供濟南及鄰近建築之需.

中國水泥公司,位於江蘇句容縣之龍潭鎮.交通便利,陸則滬甯鐵路,道經廠前,水則可由便民河輸入長江.組織於民國十年,十三年開工.資本一百萬元.原料石灰石黏土及燃煤,廠之附近產額甚豐.原動力用七百四馬力之直立式蒸汽機,直接拖動五百二十基羅瓦脫之交流電機,再由一百五十四馬力之馬達兩座,轉動生料磨及水泥磨.有氣壓機三座,引擎生料從生料磨至儲筒,再由儲筒至旋窰.電燈電力,由八十四馬力之黑油引擎及六十基羅瓦脫之交流電機供給.上項機器,購自英德二國.工程師聘德人.採用濕法製造.每日可產五百桶.運銷江甯鎮江無錫常州一帶.商標為泰山牌.質地經上海公共租界工部局試驗合格,給予證書.比重為三、一.凝結起點須二點五十分.終點須三點五十五分.淨水泥拉力,七天後每方吋六百二十七磅,二十八天後每方吋七百五十三磅,一分水泥,三分黃砂,七天後每方吋二百二十七磅,二十八天後每方吋三百三十九磅.

上海水泥公司,位於上海龍華,交通有黃浦江及滬杭鐵路之便.發起於民國七年,十三年開工.資本二百萬元.原料石灰石採自浙江之湖州,黏土來自青浦之佘山,煤則取給於開灤礦務局.機器購自德國.原動力用透平發電機,工程師為德人.應用濕法製造.每日出一千二百桶.銷售上海及滬杭路一帶.商標為象牌.價格每桶約五元五角.質地經上海公共租界工部局試驗合格,給予證書.比重為三、一.凝結起點須二點鐘,終點須三點二十五分.淨水泥拉力,七天後每方吋六百二十二磅,二十八天後每方吋七百二十磅.一分水泥,三分黃砂,七天後每方吋二百十九磅,二十八天後每方吋三百十二磅.

此外吾國自設之水泥廠,在建築而尚未開工者,有河南水泥廠,及無錫太湖水泥公司.後者交通便利,規模宏大.石灰石及黏土,鄰近盛產,煤須取給開灤或賈汪或長興,機器購自德國.用濕法製造.每日可產二千桶.

其非吾國創辦而設在吾國本部或邊境者,有山東業興會社,舊爲德人所創,歐戰時,日人取而代之,改今名.每日產三百桶,供青島建築之用.有英人在香港及澳門所設立之青洲洋灰公司,商標爲黑鱷牌及青洲牌.每日產二千桶,運銷廣東.每桶約六元五角.有法人所經營之海防洋灰公司,商標爲黑龍牌.日出二千桶,銷售吾國南部.

六,吾國水泥每年之總產額　每桶以三百七十五磅計,各水泥廠每月之產量,列表如下.

廠名	每月產量	廠名	每月產量
啓新洋灰公司	九萬桶	濟南水泥公司	七千五百桶
華記湖北水泥公司	三萬六千桶	中國水泥公司	一萬五千桶
廣東士敏土廠	一萬五千桶	上海水泥公司	三萬六千桶

由此表計算,吾國水泥每年之總產額,爲二百三十九萬四千桶,爲日本每年產額之百分之四十.

七,吾國十五年來水泥進口價值之一瞥　歷年來,吾國所產之水泥,不敷應用,仰給於日本香港及安南等地.茲據海關報告,將最近十五年來水泥進口之價值,列表如下.(并附圖表)

宣統二年	一九八七三六七兩	宣統三年	八四六八一三兩
民國元年	五〇七,〇七九兩	民國二年	六〇八,二一一兩
民國三年	九一一,八〇三兩	民國四年	六九四,〇四六兩
民國五年	九六四,一〇四兩	民國六年	七九一,四四六兩
民國七年	九五三,八二〇兩	民國八年	一,六一二,三五一兩

民國九年　一,八六〇,一七〇兩　民國十年　三,六五六,四八七兩

民國十一年　三,九七七,三五七兩　民國十二年　三,二五〇,九五四兩

民國十三年　二,〇七三,八五五兩

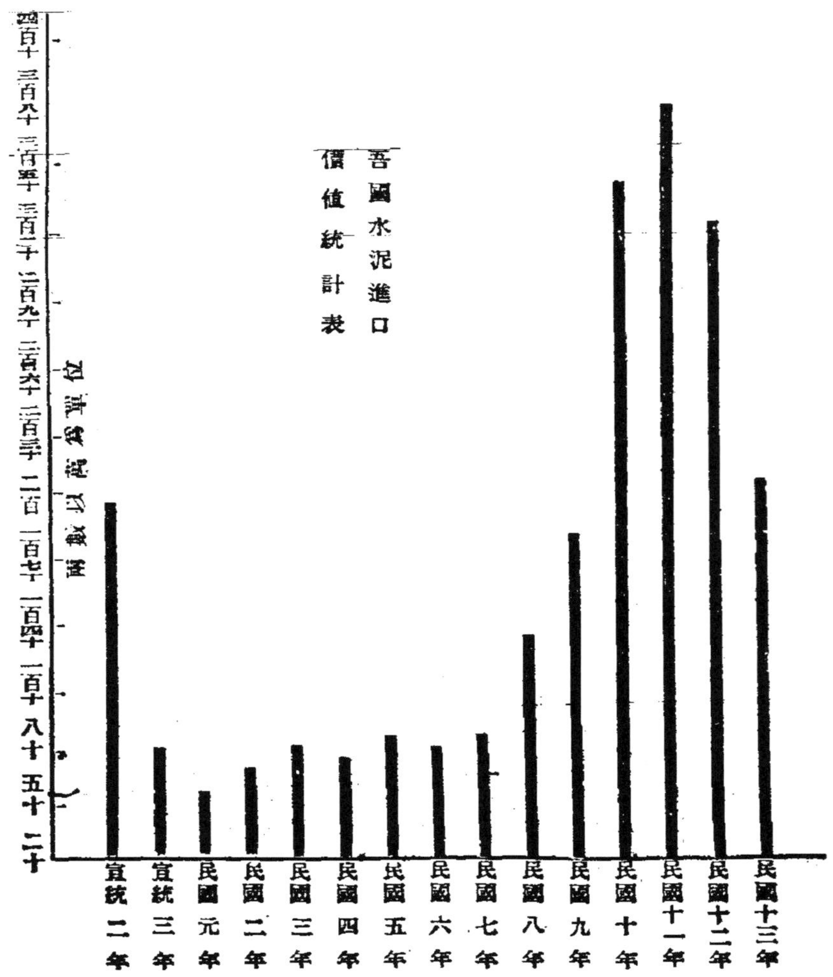

觀統計圖表,知宣統二年水泥輸入甚多.自宣統三年至民國七年,八年之中,進口無多增減.從民國八年起,年有增加.至民國十一年激增至三百九十七萬七千三百五十七兩.十二年稍減,十三年又形減少.想係中國及上海兩水泥公司出貨所致.

八,今後吾國水泥工業之預測 吾國自改元以來,兵亂頻仍,一切工商實業及國家大計,原有狀態,尚難維持,遑論發展.惟亂極則治,事理之常.行見反紛擾爲治平,由停滯而建設.爲時不遠.水泥事業,其將隨此時機由幼稚而勃興,可斷言也.蓋吾國城市,除少數通商大埠外,大都湫隘簡陋.刷新改良,急不容緩.陰溝之添設,自來水之供給,糞穢之排洩,電燈電話之應用,路政之改良,橋梁之建築,及其他一切市政之設施,在在需用水泥.此水泥之應用於市政工程,而其事業之發達可期者一也.國家之富強,全賴實業之發達,吾國天產豐富,惜因時局屢變,不克集資辦廠,致生貨輸出,熟貨輸入,有如花之於布,絲之於綢,鐵之於鋼,羊毛之於嗶嘰絨;利源外溢,漏巵孰甚.欲挽回利權,舍開工廠,其道未由.然欲使工廠之建築,堅久避火,非用水泥不可.此水泥之應用於工廠建築而其事業之發達可期者二也.江河者,吾人資以灌溉田園,排洩雨水,航行舟楫,利至溥也.然連年江河汎濫,潰決時聞,若黃河之於豫魯,白河滹沱河之於幽燕,湘江沅江之於三湘七澤,淮河之於蘇皖,珠江閩江之於粵閩,災禍之作,損失鉅萬.今欲去其患而資其利,其有賴於水泥建築之閘壩.此水泥之應用於水利工程,而其事業之發達可期者三也.且夫社會人口,日益繁密,以有限之田產,供無限之糧食,其勢不能.植林之地,轉植稻黍,事有必至.若是則建築所需之材木,將必代以水泥.例如鐵路所需之枕木,俢矣甚夥,歐美已有代以鋼骨混凝土之舉.况吾國所產之材木,質地脆弱,不能供主要建築之用.所用者,多係外來,其有資於水泥者更切.此隨民食及經濟之趨勢,而吾國水泥事業之發達可期,尤屬彰明較著者也.總之,水泥爲吾國發展工商業所必不可少之材料.國內現有之廠,已供不給需.將來水泥廠之年須增加,蓋可想見.其能利用豐富之原料,製造精良之水泥,供國民之應用,減外貨之輸入,藉免外人之投資越俎,以達吾國實業由國人創辦而管理之目的,是所望於國人之協力經營者也.

英國現行所得稅制度之研究

沈奏廷

國家稅源有二.曰直接稅.曰間接稅.田賦房捐.直接稅也.關稅貨捐.間接稅也.按稅源之優劣.視各種條件而定.條件之最要者.莫彈性若.稅之有彈性者.能隨國庫之需求而增減.無彈性者.則往往背道而馳.例如一國在戰爭時期.貨源減少.海關進口稅亦因而缺乏.國家正需財孔殷之時,而稅源頓減.此其缺乏彈性故也.直接稅則不然.其徵稅之根據.非無定之貨物.乃固定之財產.非買賣之貨價.乃盈餘之收入,一有急需.即可高其稅率.以增稅收.此直接稅之所以爲可恃之稅源也.國家欲鞏固其財政.非先有可恃之稅源不可.視國庫之需要.得隨時增損.自由伸縮.然後內可應行政之需求.外可作戰爭之後盾.富國在此.強國亦在此.乃者關稅自主聲浪.甚囂塵上.雖自主之目的.在保護國內之幼稚實業.與排斥外貨之侵凌.然當局目標.亦未始非在增加收入.以充國庫.第不知此種間接稅源.和平時固無問題.戰爭時實多困難.欲根本鞏固中國財政.必先自整理直接稅着手.目下政局俶擾.國步愈艱.整理國稅.無暇顧及.然將來大局底定.整理必不容緩.蓋厲兵秣馬,固爲國防之根本.而鞏固財政.亦爲對外之要圖.愚以爲整理中國稅源.目光不當在間接稅.蓋間接稅無彈性.不足恃也.至中國之直接稅.其制又陋而不平.耕田一畝者.納稅一元.耕百畝者.納稅百元.無累進法以爲升降.担負至不公允.整理之方.非實行所得稅制不可.按所得稅除富有彈性外.尚有下列數種優點.

(一)稅率可以累進.貧者免之.小康者稅之.富者重稅之.犧牲担負.至爲公允.

(二)凡有進款至一定限度以上者.必須納稅.故負担均平.不致有一部分人

納稅一部分人漏稅之弊.

(三) 稅之僅加于一種資產者.往往此種資產脫售時.非抑價不可.抑價後.新產主反得免稅.而稅永爲舊產主之一種支出.若行所得稅制.則各種進益.皆須課稅.新產主自無要求抑價之理由.

所得稅既有此種優點.吾國苟能實行之.其利蓋有不勝言者.然所得稅制,頗緒紛繁.非有極精確之研究.不能爲將來整理稅制之助.考所得稅發明極早.而行之成效最著者,莫如英國.爰特詳考英國現行所得稅制度.以貢吾同志.而爲他日整頓中國直接稅之圭臬.實行中國所得稅之臂助.想必爲學者所歡迎也.英國所得稅.約分五種.一爲 A 類. Schedule A 不動產所得屬之.二爲B類. Schedule B 土地佔有所得屬之.三爲C類 Schedule C 公債利息所得屬之.四爲 D 類.Schedule D 營業及其他所得屬之.五爲E 類 Schedule E 各種辛金所得屬之.

所得稅之蠲免

所得稅有種種蠲免.茲列舉如次.

(一) 賺得所得之蠲免 Earned Income Relief. 凡所得由勞心力而獲者.曰賺得所得.賺得所得之十分之一.准免所得稅.但每人以二百鎊爲限.例如某人年賺三百鎊.則政府祇于其二百七十鎊上徵稅.若此人年賺三千鎊.則政府祇于其二千八百鎊上徵稅.此二百七十鎊或二千八百鎊.名曰應課所得. Assessable Income

(二) 個人之蠲免 Personal allowance. 然實際上政府並不卽於應課所得上徵稅.凡未婚者或鰥居者.於其應課所得中.准有一百三十五鎊免徵所得稅.例如有人年賺三百鎊.而年稚未婚.或妻死鰥居.則三百鎊減去三十鎊之賺得所得之蠲免,復減去一百三十五鎊之個人之蠲免.則應納稅之所得額.當僅爲一百三十五鎊.此一百三十五鎊.名曰應稅所得. Taxable Income

（三）結婚之蠲免 Marriage Allowance- 凡已婚者得於其應課所得中.有二百二十五鎊之免稅.倘其妻另有賺得進款.而進款在五十元以上者.復得有四十五鎊$\left(\frac{9}{10}\times 50=45\text{鎊}\right)$之免稅.例如有人年賺六百鎊.則其應課所得.當爲五百四十鎊.減去二百二十五鎊之結婚蠲免.則餘三百十五鎊.而六百鎊中尙有其妻一百鎊之賺得所得在內.故又得減去四十五鎊.所餘爲二百七十鎊.此數始爲其應稅所得.（故此人雖年賺六百鎊.而納稅時祗須以二百七十鎊計算.以視我國農民.年耕田四五畝.而必須畝畝納稅者.待遇優劣.蓋可想見矣.）

（四）子女之蠲免 Children's allowance- 有子女者其家庭負担必較多.故有一女或一子者.得于其所得內有三十六鎊之免稅.有子或女一人以上者則蠲免額分配如下.（甲）其中一子或一女.仍視爲獨子或獨女.家庭以此子故或此女故.得有三十六鎊免納所得稅（乙）餘子或餘女以人數計.每人在家庭得二十七鎊之免稅.然有時子女中有不能據以爲免稅理由者.計有下列兩種.

一.子女年在十六歲以上者.（然在正式學校內肄業者.不在此限.）.

二.子女已在外任事.年獲薪金四十鎊以上者.（但學校奬金.不能作一例看待.）

此種蠲免.頗爲糾紛.請設下例以明之.某人年獲所得計一千鎊.有子女四人.其中二女.一年六歲.一年十五歲.其中二男.一年八歲.一年十七歲十七歲者在正式學校肄業.年獲奬金一百鎊.長女（十五歲者）在外任事.年獲薪金八十鎊.今欲知此人應稅所得之數目.則必先除去其結婚蠲免二百二十五鎊.所餘爲七百七十五鎊.（1000－225＝775鎊）子女四人中.惟長女不能豁免.其餘三人.應有豁免.總額爲七十.鎊（36＋27＋27＝70鎊）故從七百七十五鎊中.尙須減去七十鎊.然後所餘者爲七百零五鎊.此數始得視爲此人之應稅所得.（按年十六歲以上而

在正式學校肄業之子女.仍與十六歲以下者視同一例.足見英國政府.重視教育.吾國苟實行所得稅.此種優點.當採納之.)

(五) 親戚依賴之蠲免 Allowances For Dependent Relatives. 親戚之依賴者分兩種.一則爲家庭服一種職務.而非自願依賴或不得不依賴者.如爲鰥夫代持家務者是.一則以老弱疾病.不得不依賴者.前者每人許在該家庭所得額內.減去六十鎊.然後計稅.後者每人許減二十五鎊.然後計稅.(按此種親戚.皆不得已而發生依賴者.中國家庭中依賴之親戚特多.若年老之父母祖父母等.按我國習慣.總視爲不得已之依賴.足爲要求蠲除所得稅之充足理由.反之若大家庭內.數世同堂.兄弟皆以依賴爲生活.此種依賴.萬不能視爲出于不得已.非特不能蠲稅.愚謂且應加稅.以示懲戒.加稅理由有三.一爲社會的.一爲政治的.一爲財政的.社會的理由維何.曰大家庭增長依賴性.消磨國民獨立精神.並損壞節儉與互助諸道德.足爲全社會之害.加其稅所以懲之也.政治的理由維何.曰家庭既大.一切概由家長主持.國令不達.韓非子曰.家大而國小.可亡也大家庭之不利于政治如此.加其稅亦所以懲之也.財政的理由維何.曰依賴生活.減少生產.苟無大家庭制.則弟兄必外出服務.服務必有薪金政.府可于其薪金上.亦徵所得稅.今不能徵得.即爲政府之損失.加稅取償.固自有理也.)

(六) 保險之蠲免 Allowance For Life Assurance Premium. 凡保人壽險者.于所得稅上亦有若干蠲免.第以保險時期與各人進款之不同.分爲四種蠲免法.茲列于下.

(甲) 每年所得一千鎊以下者.不論保險何年起始.每鎊保險費.蠲所得稅二先令三辨士.(現行所得稅率之半)

(乙) 保險在一九一六年後起始者.不論每年所得幾何每鎊保險費.蠲所得稅二先令三辨士.

（丙）年進款一千鎊以上二千鎊以下.其保險在一九一六年前起始者.每鎊保險費蠲所得稅三先令四辨士半.（即現行稅率四分之三）

（丁）年進款二千鎊以上者.保險苟自一九一六年以前開始每鎊保險費.得蠲四先令六辨士.（即全稅率）

但尚有數種限制.應附帶注意者.

一,按鎊蠲稅之保險費.不得超過所得額全數之六分之一.例如有人年獲所得一千八百鎊.而其每年付出之保險費.則爲三百二十鎊.在此種情形內.其保險費祇得作三百鎊計.

二,倘保險額于人死時約一次付齊者.按鎊蠲稅之保險費.只限于保險額百分之七計算.譬有保險額一千鎊.則蠲免祇限于七十鎊上之所得稅.

三,倘保險額不擔保于人死時一次付齊者.則按鎊蠲稅之保險費.以百鎊爲限.

四,一九一六年後之保險非人死時一次付足者.不得蠲免所得稅（按英所得稅制.稅富蠲貧.而保險蠲免.反與所得額俱增者何也.蓋稅制規定(一)按鎊蠲稅之保險費.不得逾所得全數六分之一.（二）保險額苟不於人死時一次付足.則按鎊蠲稅之保險費.以百鎊爲限.然所得多者保險額必大.今加以限制.則一部分保險費.勢必不得蠲稅.以視保險額較小而全數保險費皆得蠲稅者.寧不厚薄不均耶.是以政府規定蠲稅率與所得額俱增.富者每鎊得較貧者多蠲此正所以均其不均.非厚于富而薄于貧也.英國保險事業極形發達.人民視人壽保險爲一種儲蓄.故政府免稅以獎勵之.所以培養儲蓄之習慣也.吾國保險事業.既未發達.人民對于人壽保險.又乏信仰.故此種儲蓄.在目下情狀之下.無由獎勵.惟儲蓄不限于保險.凡他種支出.確有真正儲蓄惟賫者.亦當在獎勵之列.吾國苟實行所得稅,則愚謂保險以外之儲蓄.在一定限制下當竭力以蠲稅獎勵之.略仿英國保險蠲稅之制.以蠲免一般真能儲蓄者.庶幾儉德得以培養.民生前途所關非淺.泰西各國.常寓政治社會經濟等目的于其徵稅制度保險蠲稅.卽爲一例.吾國亟宜起而效之也.)

現行所得稅稅率（附加稅稅率）

前會計年度內（一九二四年至一九二五年）所得稅稅率爲每鎊四先令六辨士.照所得稅條例.第一二百二十五鎊得照率折半納稅.故設有人年獲四百鎊.除去個人蠲免一百三十五鎊後.尚得二百六十五鎊.卽爲其應稅所得,其納稅實數.當爲三十四鎊六先令四辨士.

（225×2鎊3先令十40×4鎊6先令＝25鎊6先令4辨士十9鎊＝34鎊6令先4辨士

所得稅制度目的,首在免貧稅富.各項蠲免.前旣述之矣.然此爲免貧之道.而非稅富之方.凡減收于貧戶者.必取償于富戶.而後稅制乃平.國用乃足英政府之於所得稅外.復徵附加稅者.意在斯耳.按附加稅條例.凡年獲所得二千鎊以上者.應于所得稅外復稅之.是爲附加稅.附加稅依不規則之累進法計徵茲錄如下.

所得額	稅率（每鎊）
(一) 第一二千鎊	無
(二) 次五百鎊	一先令六辨士
(三) 次五百鎊	二先令
(四) 次一千鎊	二先令六辨士
(五) 次一千鎊	三先令
(六) 次一千鎊	三先令六辨士
(七) 次一千鎊	四先令
(八) 次一千鎊	四先令六辨士

(九) 次一萬二千鎊……………………五先令

(十) 次一萬鎊……………………………五先令六辨士

(十一) 總所得額三萬鎊以上者……一律六先令

以上所述.皆依據所得稅制度全體而言.茲請分述各種所得稅之詳細徵收法.以爲更進一步之研究

(一) A類所得稅(不動產)

此類所得稅乃從不動產之所得中徵收.試以房屋爲例.以明此稅之徵收法.房產所得.即租金是.因房屋時需修理.故租金全數.不能視爲徵稅之根據.必先減去每年法定修理費.而後稅之,始稱公允.一九二三年至一九二四年之法定修理費.規定如下.

1, 租金總額(百鎊以下者) 法定修理費(當租金幾分之幾)

四十鎊以下者………………………四分之一

四十鎊以上百鎊以下者…………五分之一

2. 租金總額(百元以上者) 法定修理費

等于百鎊者…………………………二十鎊

百鎊以上者…………………………A,百鎊以內每鎊五分之一(二十鎊)
B,百鎊以上每鎊六分之一

倘修理費爲租戶所出.則租主不能有修理費之蠲免.應照租金全數納稅.但修理費由房主租戶各担若干時.房主仍得按上述法定率蠲稅.舉例如次.設有租主年得租金一百四十鎊.租戶出修理費九鎊.餘爲租主自出.則租主之應稅所得.當爲一百二十一鎊.算法如下.

$(140+9)-(20+49\times 1/6)=149-28=121$鎊

苟修理費統歸租戶担負.則租主必須在一百四十鎊上(倘租金仍舊)納稅.而不能享蠲免之利矣.

房租所得稅.平時不向房主徵收.概由租戶代納.惟稅到期而屋空閒時.則始向房主追繳.租戶代納之稅.往往于下次付租金時扣除之.

房主住主同一人時.則房主于納所得稅時.應報告其屋每年能獲之租金.然後減去修理費地租及建屋費之利息等.以爲納稅之根據.蓋房屋無論出租或自住.在政府眼光中.均視爲一種所得.出租則得租金.租金之爲進益人盡知之.自住則免出租金.免出租金.按所得稅條例.亦爲進益.何以言之.曰建屋須款.款能生利.苟此款不用以建住屋.而用以經商業.則年獲盈餘.必須納稅.今以用以建屋故.未有盈餘.幷以建屋以備自住故.未有租金.然政府之稅.不能因是而漏免也.是以房屋之自住者.仍須納稅.

土地亦爲不動產之一種.故歸A類收稅.稅法與房產相同.卽依據土地年入租金.減去修理費.（當租金八分之一.）而由租戶代納.例如某人有田百畝.年入租金九十鎊.則除去八分之一之修理費.（計十一鎊五先令）而餘應稅所得七十八鎊十五先令.按每鎊四先令六辨士徵所得稅.則此人應納之稅.計爲十七鎊十四先令四辨士半.此數應由租戶代納.于租金內扣之（按所得稅皆由付款者代繳.是謂截源Stoppage at Source所以防漏稅也.稅係租主所出.租戶無爲避稅之理.隱漏之弊.可以免除.他如營業所得稅.稅係租得稅.亦皆稅其源.而非稅其主者多.均所以杜隱漏也.）

（二）B類所得稅（俗稱農夫稅）

此類所得稅.爲租用他人田地所得上之稅.如農人之租田樹穀.租地植樹.租園種果等.除付租金與租主外.常有餘利可獲.因有此種餘利.故得徵收此類所得稅.此稅極爲簡單.其根據非農夫之實獲盈餘.乃爲一種法定所得額.適等于其租金全數.然租地之非用於農事者.則等于其租金三分之一.例如某農夫租地五十畝.年納租金每畝一鎊半.二十五畝用於農墾.餘二十五畝作農事以外之用.則其應納所得稅幾何.可答如下,

$$\left(25\times 1,5+\frac{1}{3}\times 25\times 1,5\right)\times 4s6d=(37,5+14,5)\times 4s6d=52.\times 4s6d=11\text{鎊}14\text{先令}$$

照上列算法此農人應納所得稅十一鎊十四先令.

（三）C類所得稅（利息）

此類所得稅爲公債利息等所得上之稅.大都於付息前將稅預先扣除.亦有不扣除者.稅法簡單,不復贅述.

（四）D類所得稅

此類所得稅.包含最廣,如營業所得.外國債券利息.外國股票紅利等均屬之.其中以營業所得稅爲最重要.而於我國經濟狀況.亦最有關係.爰詳述于左.他稅之屬于此類者.恕不縷贅.

營業所得稅者.根據營業上之盈餘而徵收者也.然所謂盈餘者.非普通商人賬上所記之盈餘.而有特別標準在焉.按標準而計之盈餘與普通盈餘大不相同.增減損益.大有出入.普通視爲支出者.按所得稅規則.往往不得視爲支出.普通視爲收入者.按所得稅規則.往往不得視爲收入.英政府規定盈餘上應增應減之支收款項如次

(甲) 資本上之收支款項（一）開辦費資本利息.集資費用.改良或添置資產費用等.普通除末項外.往往視爲出款.而入損益賬內.但於呈報所得稅額時.均應一一加入盈餘計算.（二）購入之股票漲價.倘所漲之價.視爲進益.而已記入損益賬時.則于呈報所得稅額之際.得自盈餘減去.

(乙) 個人之支出款項　個人者指營業主人而言.個人之支出.當然不能視爲營業上費用.倘已入損益賬時.于報稅之際.應將支出各款加入盈餘.例如業主家內之房租電燈費等是.

(丙) 與營業無關之支出款項　凡非營業上所須支出之款項.均屬之.苟已支出而已入損益賬時.于報稅之際.應向盈餘加上.

(丁) 已除去所得稅之利息及其他收支款項（一）如付出之款先將所得稅扣去而後付者.于報稅時.應加入盈餘.（二）凡收入之款.已經扣去所得稅者.于報稅時.應從盈餘減去.

(戊) 準備金（一）凡付出之款.充作準備金以防放賬不穩等虞者.于報稅時.應加入盈餘.（二）若放賬果已不能收回.則不能收回之數.應從準備金

或盈餘減去.

普通商家賬上所載裁之餘.加入上述之各種增減.即成爲所得稅制所欲知之盈餘.是之謂釐正盈餘. Adjusted Income 請設一詳晰之例.以明上述各條之應用.

某業某年獲利三千元.其賬上之收支.得下列數項.（1）付股東利息一百元（2）收已扣去所得稅之地租十元.（3）付已扣去所得稅之借款利息十五元（4）付房租三百元（5）付準備金二百元同時删去呆賬五十元（6）付股東薪水五百元房金二百元問此店是年之釐正所得幾何

應加入盈餘之款項

股東利息一百元（甲）　借款利息十五元（丁）

準備金一百五十元（戊）　股東薪水及房金七百元（乙）

共九百六十五元

應自盈餘減去之款項

地租十元（丁）

故從叁千元上加九百六十五元.後減十元.結果爲三千九百五十五元是爲此店是年之釐正所得.（其中房租三百元爲店基租金.係營業上必付之出款.應視爲營業上一種費用.不得加入盈餘.）

每年釐正所得.仍非是年徵收所得稅之根據.蓋英國會計年度.定爲自四月六日起.至翌年四月五日止.而所得額報告.必須于五月或六月內送呈政府.是本年盈餘.皆在未可知之數也.然則如何而可.曰舉前三年之釐正所得而平均之.結果即爲本年應稅所得額.此之曰法定所得 Statutary Income 政府即根據法定所得而徵所得稅.倘年終結賬.盈餘實數較法定所得有多少時.稅法仍不得變更.多則政府旣不能額外再徵.少則亦不能請求政府減稅.要皆以法定所得爲根據.而無關係乎實獲盈餘也.至若新營業之未滿三

載以上者.則又將如何計算其法定所得耶.曰.是亦有條例在.請分述如左.

(一) 在第一不完全會計年度內.按其第一年釐正所得.徵一部分所得稅.

(二) 在第一完全會計年度內.按其第一年釐正所得.徵收是年度之所得稅.第二完全會計年度亦如之.

(三) 在第三完全會計年度內.將第一年及第二之年釐正所得平均之.結果即爲法定所得.按此徵稅.

(四) 在第四完全會計年度內.將上三年之釐正所得平均之.而復徵稅.以後與舊營業無異.統採三年平均之法.

前列四則.可設例以明之.

某商人于一九二一年開始營業.其各年釐正後之盈餘如下.

1921:300鎊1922:400鎊1923:鎊500鎊1924:600鎊

(1) 會計年度(自四月六日起至翌年四月五日止) (2)法定所得或應稅所得

1. 1920—1921 ······ $300\times\frac{1}{4}=75$鎊

2. 1921—1922: ······ 300鎊

3. 1922—1923: ······ 300鎊

4. 1923—1924 ······ $\frac{(300+400)}{2}=350$鎊

5. 1924—1925 ······ $\frac{300+400+500}{3}=400$鎊

根據三年平均法而納稅.與根據每年釐正所得而納稅.其間大有出入.例如某業今年虧本.照理今年不應有稅.然因其前三年賺錢.以三年平均法計.今年仍須納稅.苟此業繼續進行.則所碍尙小.蓋今年之稅雖徵.他年可望免除.損于此可償于彼也.推苟此業以虧本而停閉.則所納之稅.不能取償于他年.三年平均法.寧不甚欠公允耶.政府知之.故定有償還已繳所得稅之例.即業營停閉前三年中所納之稅.倘與根據每年釐正所得計算之稅不同.而業主因以受損時.得于停業後六年以內.請求政府償還逾限之數.設例如下.

某業各年釐正盈餘有如下列.而是業已于一九二四年停閉.（盈餘以鎊計算）1918: 580 1919: 590; 1920: 600 1921 560 1922, 460 1923: 580. 1924: 680.

按三年平均法計稅	稅率	應納之所得稅
年份 (1921—22) $\frac{580+590+600}{3}=590$	6先令	58鎊1先令
(1922—23) $\frac{590+600+560}{3}=583$	5先令	46鎊17先令6辨士
(1923—24) $\frac{600+560+460}{3}=540$	4先令6辨	33鎊8先令3辨士
總計1713鎊		138辨6先令9辨士
(1924—25) $\frac{560+460+580}{3}=533$	4先6辨	32鎊1先令3辨年
		170鎊8先令

按每年釐正所得計稅	稅率	應納之稅
年份 (1921—22) $\frac{1}{2}\times560+\frac{1}{2}\times460=510$	6先令	36鎊9先令
(1922—23) $\frac{1}{2}\times460+\frac{1}{2}\times580=520$	5先令	33 ,, 2 ,, 6辨士
(1923—24) $\frac{1}{2}\times580+\frac{1}{4}\times680=630$	4先令6辨士	51 ,, 34 ,, 9 ,,
總計1660		121鎊16先令3辨士
(1924—25) $\frac{1}{2}\times680=340$	4先令6辨士	9鎊2先令3辨士
		130鎊18先令6辨士

按第一法計稅.則稅數爲一百七十鎊八先令.按第二法計算.則僅得稅一百三十鎊十八先令六辨士.相差三十九鎊九先令六辨士之多.前數（百七十鎊八先令）爲該業已繳之稅;後數（百三十鎊十八先令六辨士）爲該業應繳之稅.故該業既于一九廿四年停歇.則得請求政府退還三十九鎊九先令六辨士之逾限額.（因會計年度不與營業年度相符.故第二表中計

算每年度之修正所得.以兩年之修正所得二分而加之.是之謂裂賬 Splitting of accounts 若營業年度亦自四月六日起(開賬)至翌年四月五日止.(結賬)則無用裂賬矣.

若營業之繼續進行者.則雖遇損失而負本年不應納之稅時.仍得取償于他年.前既已述及之矣.故如遇此種情形.業主似不必急急請政府退還其損失.請舉例以明之. 某業每年修正後之盈虧如左

1918年贏600鎊	1923年虧400鎊
1919 ,, ,, 500鎊	1922 ,, 贏200鎊
1920 ,, ,, 700鎊	1923 ,, ,, 400鎊

I. 按常例計稅法	II 虧本時當求補償之計稅法
1921—22 $\frac{600+500+700}{3}=600$鎊	$600-400=200$鎊
1922—23 $\frac{500+700-400}{3}=267$鎊	$\frac{500+700+0}{3}=400$鎊
1923—24 $\frac{700+200-400}{3}=166$鎊	$\frac{700+0+200}{3}=300$鎊
1924—25 $\frac{200+400-400}{3}=600$鎊	$\frac{0+200+400}{3}=200$鎊
共計1100鎊	共計1100鎊

英國所得稅條例.凡本年虧折而仍須納稅者.其虧折額得由法定所得減去.而後計稅.此卽虧折時當求補償之法也.倘照此計稅.則本年虧折額.卽不能再與他年之盈虧平均矣.故上列二表.總數相同.可見該業或當求補償其虧損,或任其自然而取償于他年.其果無以異也.然有時二者亦大有出入焉.何以言之.稅率趨減時.則以當求補償法爲較愈.稅率趨增時.則以分期取償爲較愈.試就上表證明之(以鎊改元藉便計算而原則不變)

(一) 設稅率逐年漸增

一九二一年至二二年(二角) 一九二二年至二三年(三角) 一九二三

年至二四年(四角) 一九二四年至二五年(五角)

$ 600×0.2=$ 120	$ 200×0.2=$ 40
$ 267×0.3= 80.1	$ 400×.0.3=$ 120
$ 166×0.4= 66.4	$ 300×0.4=$ 120
$ 67×0.5= 33.5.	$ 200×0.5=$ 380
共納稅$ 300.00	共納稅$ 380

故第二法（即當求補償法）當較第一法多納八十元之稅.其爲不利也明矣.

(二) 設稅率逐年漸減

$ 600×0.5=$ 300	$ 200×0.5=$ 100
$ 267×0.4=106.80	$ 400×0.4=$ 160
$ 166×0.3=49.80	$ 300×0.3= 90
$ 67+0.2= 13.40	$ 200×0.2= 40
共納$ 470.00	共納$ 390

第二法較第一法少納八十元.故較爲有利.

又若營業衰落.盈餘有逐年遞減之勢.則亦以當求補償一法爲較愈.總之兩法孰得孰失.惟在商人善自謀之.

業主易人時.法定所得額（即由三年平均而得者）亦不能變更.但苟以特種原因.盈餘以易人而頓減.則新業主始得請求按實發證正盈餘計納所得稅.

營業所得稅大都徵于盈餘未派之前.如公債利息然.先稅而後付者也.然有時亦有按各業主所分得之淨利而分別徵稅者.

E類所得稅（辛金）

辛金者即工資薪水等.勞心力而得者也.辛金所得稅徵收法.與營業所得稅完全不同.今年應徵之稅.恆以上年所入辛金爲根據.倘今年所入較上

年爲少.則納稅者可向政府追還已納之逾限稅額.反之今年所入較上年爲多則政府亦得追徵不足之稅額.此其與營業稅不同之要點也.

辛金上可免所得稅者.有下列數項.要皆與其職務有直接關係者也.（一）旅居費（因職務外出所費者.但必須減去其在家原應支出之日常費用）（二）保證金之利息（三）營業費（如會計師納于會計師公會之費）（四）養老儲蓄費

凡職員所得辛金.雇主每年必須作一次之報告.送呈政府.政府備有報告紙.按式填寫可耳.惟職員之薪金在一百五十鎊以下而他處並無職務者.不必報告.

有時職員辛金.每星期付一次.則雇主對于此種職員.亦不必代具報告.應由本人自行報告之.此項辛金.一年分四季徵稅.所有各種蠲免數目.亦分四季計核.譬有工人每季得工資一百鎊.而其全年應豁免者爲三百二十鎊.則分季蠲稅.每季應爲八十鎊.故其一季應稅所得.僅二十鎊也.但若第二季因職務減少.祇得工資七十鎊.則蠲免額超過納稅者之所得額.爾時非特不必納稅.且所差十鎊上之所得稅.得于下季納稅時扣除之.

各類所得稅之性質及計算法.既詳述於前矣.茲尚有應加考慮者.即財產之逐年損耗是也.請陳其計算法如下.

財產逐年損耗之計算法

財產往往有逐年損耗.不能久持其原有價值者.如機器.如器械.經用既久.必致敗壞.故必設基金以爲預防.而後可置新機械以替之.計所得稅時.此項損失.應逐年算入.而與以豁免.然後公允.計算之法.不外二種.

（一）逐年由財產原價減若干成以免之.

（二）由原價減去各年之蠲免額.所餘之價.逐年減若干成以免之.

(一)

(按原價百分之四計算)

財產原價	10.000鎊
第一年蠲免額	400鎊
第二年 ,,	400鎊
第三年 ,,	400鎊
第三年新置財產	1000鎊
第四年產價	11000鎊
第四年蠲免額	440鎊
第四年賣出舊產	2000鎊 2000鎊
第四年新置財產	3000鎊
第五年產價	12000鎊
第五年蠲免額	480鎊
至第五年之總蠲免額	2120鎊

(二)

(按原價百分之六計算)

財產原價	10.000鎊
第一年蠲免額	600
第二年產價	9400
第二年蠲免額	564
第三年產價	8836

第三年豁免額……………………………………………………530

8306

第三年新置產價……………………………………………………1000

第四年產價……………………………………………………9306

第四年豁免額……………………………………………………558

第五年產價……………………………………………………8748

第五年豁免額……………………………………………………525

第六年產價……………………………………………………8223鎊

(餘可類推)

第二法較第一法爲可取.因其不計入已免稅之數也.

倘營業無利.財產損窳豁免額超過法定所得時.則超過之數得逐年累積.遇獲利多時扣除之.其法如下:

年份	法定所得	應得豁免額	已得豁免	未得豁免
1	700鎊	600鎊	600鎊	——
2	500鎊	564鎊	500鎊	64鎊
3	450鎊	530鎊	450鎊	140鎊(64＋80)
4	500鎊	558鎊	500鎊	193鎊(140＋58)
5	650鎊	525鎊	650鎊	73鎊(193＋525-650)
6	800鎊	493鎊	566鎊	——

機器等物之已陳舊者.往往脫售之.苟受損失.亦可於所得中扣除.而得免所得稅之權利.例如

機價 2000鎊

賣價 400

1600鎊（此數可于是年所得額中除去而後計稅）

倘該機已經用數年.逐年損蝕已有免稅者.則免稅之一部分.必須由原價上減去.例如

機器原價……………2000鎊

第一年蠲免…………80鎊 1920鎊

第二年 ,,……………………77鎊 1843鎊

第三年 ,,……………………………73鎊 1770鎊

第四年賣價……………………………………700鎊

是年應免所得稅之數…… ……………………1070鎊

所得稅繳納法及繳納之時期

各類所得稅.其繳納法及繳納時期各各不同.共有三種.分述于下.

(一) 一次繳足至遲以一月一日爲期者

B 類所稅（佔地者苟從事農業則不在此限）

C 類所得稅

D 類所得稅（非賺得所得）

(二) 分二期繳納者（第一期本會計年度一月一日止第二期次年度七月一日止）

A 類所得稅

B 類所得稅（佔地人從事于農業者）

D 類所得稅（各種營業所得）

上類所得稅（惟工人之工資每星期一付者不在此限）

(三) 分四季繳納者（四月五日至七月五日爲第一季 七月五日至十月五日爲第二季餘類推）

工人工資每星期一付者均按此法納所得稅

結論

英國所得稅制之精密.於此可見一斑矣.其間不知幾費經營.幾費擘畫.始克臻此.考稅制之要點有二.曰公平.曰普遍.所得稅根據納稅能力.而高下其負担.可謂公平矣.復有附加稅以輔助之.其公平之優點益彰.所得稅以各類收入爲根據.無此漏彼薄彼厚此之弊.與單一稅原則.適成反比.可謂普遍矣.又已徵稅者弗使再稅.未徵稅者弗使漏稅.顧慮周詳.絕無重複遺漏之虞.此其利一也.稅所得之數.而不稅財產之價.其中得免估價之弊.而避美國產業稅估價不公允之憾.我國田賦亦以產價爲根據.而田畝之大小不同.政府未令清丈也.肥瘠各異.官廳未嘗明辨也.若推行所得稅.則田畝雖不丈.肥瘠雖不辨.而稅制反良.負擔反均.上可以裕國用.下可以紓民困.此其利二也惟所得稅制範圍廣而組織繁.非有適當之社會狀況以助之推行.難免困難若會計之改良也.人口之統計也.教育之普及也.公司式營業之推廣也.皆與推行所得稅制度.具有密切之關係.一旦大局底定.自不難一一舉而理之.所幸先進國已示我以模型.與我以圭臬.仿而行之.在自勉耳.夫我亦嘗試行所得稅制矣.然力之所及.乃少數之公共機關辦事員.收入僅達華幣八千元之譜.以付徵稅員之薪金.猶嫌不敷.寧非空前之笑柄耶.國事蜩螗.夫復何言.改革振興.俟諸異日.世有關心于中國前途者.其亦注意于吾國稅制之將來.而有以見教否乎.

空隙與完全擠縮在蒸汽循環上之利弊論

張 陰 煊

工程目的在乎運用天然力能.有媒介物而後得運用,此自然之理也.運用貴乎連續持久,持久之道無他,媒介物之循環耳.媒介物之循環,恃乎二大要素:(一)體質上適于受授熱能之媒介物,(二)能接運力能而不傳熱之器具.今日此二要素之存在者已不一而足,是籍所謂蒸汽循環,其所根據之二要素:即今日最普通之蒸汽,以及內藏活塞之圓筒(註1)是也.

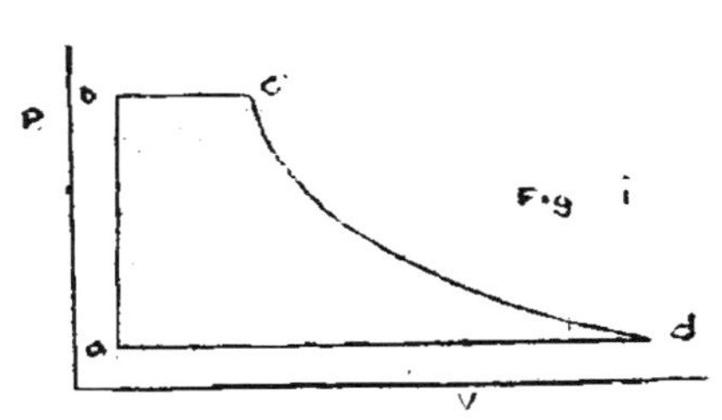

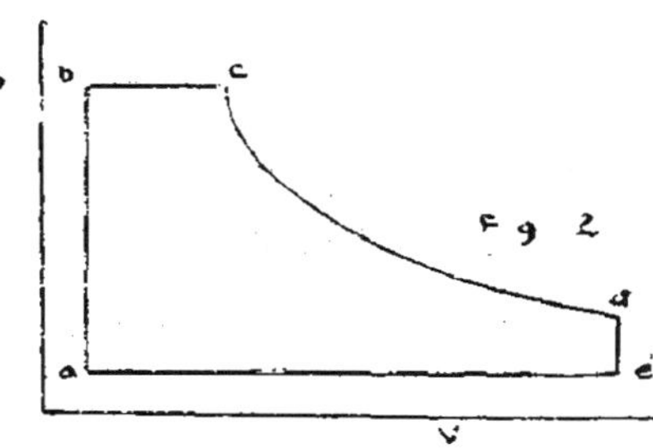

蒸汽循環凡二,曰克洛捷斯循環,曰梁鐸循環.克洛捷斯循環者,如第一圖之壓力容積表上所示之一種循環 a b c d. 梁鐸循環者,如第二圖所示之循環 a b c d e.

圓筒分二種,曰有空隙圓筒,曰無空隙圓筒,空隙(Cearance)容積,于各種循環上關係不爲不大而與此有連帶關係者,厥惟擠縮(C mpression).今請論其利弊如次.

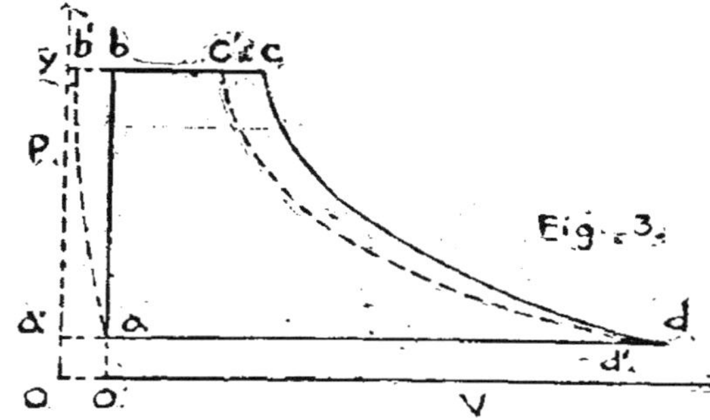

(一)克洛捷斯循環

無空隙圓筒者,其筒塞在每擊終止時塞面與筒蓋相碰,而使塞面筒蓋之間全無空隙.進汽門既開,蒸汽即進迫筒塞前行,至進汽門復關閉時,蒸汽佔容積 b c（第三圖,）割斷蒸汽於c.內熱能變化膨脹開始,汽壓因而跌落,筒塞繼續前行,及 d,乃止.時筒內汽壓已與背壓相等.此所謂膨脹之完全者也.是時出汽門開,蒸汽放出,同時筒塞回行,至筒塞面復碰筒蓋,蒸汽放盡而止.此種外放之汽入冷凝器化成液體而復入鍋爐蒸發,再成壓力 o'b 蒸蒸汽,遂完畢一循環 a b c d.

無空隙圓筒事實上難于存在,今日存在之圓筒類皆具此空隙,俾筒塞于每擊終止時筒蓋與塞面之間留一空隙,以避碰擊.進汽門既開,蒸汽先充滿此項空隙容積 b b'（第三圖,）而後進迫筒塞.設進汽容積與前者（放進無空隙圓筒者）相同,則割斷蒸汽於 c',容積 c c' 等于容積 b b',等于充滿空隙之生汽容積.于是開始膨脹如前,至膨脹完全時,其經過變化可以c' d' 一線代表之.出汽門開,蒸汽逃放,筒塞回轉,至 a 而止.是時出汽門即閉,餘汽乃充滿空隙,其容積爲 a a' 等于空隙容積,而其壓力爲 o' a,與背壓相等.此項蒸汽將于生汽進筒時沿 a b' 增高其壓力,至b',與進筒之生汽壓力相等,而其容積則擠縮至 y b'.至于 a b' 乃一等能線也.(Energy Balance Liue')如是遂完成一循環 ab' c' d'.

今觀第三圖,實線圖代表一循環之成于無空隙圓筒內者,虛線圖代表一循環之成于有空隙圓筒內者,二圖相較,顯見實線之循環,筒塞所接運之力能爲 abcd,而虛線循環,筒塞所接運之力能爲 b c' d' a,其相差爲 c' c d d'.足證有空隙圓筒于克洛捷斯循環爲不利.

無空隙圓筒在理論上較勝于有空隙圓筒既如上述,而此種空隙,事實上又不能絕滅,則改進之策當在他途.今試以有空隙圓筒之出汽門不在完成筒塞還擊(Return Stroke)a 處關閉,而提早于筒塞回轉之中途 e 處（第四圖）關閉.自 e 至 a,筒塞即擠縮禁閉筒內之蒸汽,于是汽壓沿 e b 線逐漸增高至 b 而止,筒內汽壓適與筒外鍋爐壓相等,易言之此時空隙已滿裝如筒外同壓之蒸汽,此所謂完全擠縮也 (Complete Compress ion.) 進汽門開筒外蒸汽可立卽追動筒塞而不必先事充滿空隙.設所進之蒸汽容積仍與前相同.蒸汽割斷於 c,所進之蒸汽容積bc,與第三圖之 b c 完全相同,易言之此時蒸汽割斷及所進之蒸汽容積完全與在無空隙圓筒者相同.雖然,無空隙筒內之膨漲線爲cd',而此時之膨漲線爲 c d,因前者膨漲開始時之容積爲bc,而後者爲 b c,加空隙容積 b b',等于 b' c.故克洛捷斯循環于有空隙圓筒,而用完全擠縮者,在割斷蒸汽時,筒內之蒸汽可分二部:(一) 充滿空隙之蒸汽其容積自 b' o 量起等于 b b'.壓力與鍋爐壓力相同,沿 be 線而膨漲.(二) 鍋爐放進之蒸汽,其容積自 b o' 量起等于 b c,沿 c d' 線而膨漲,筒塞行動至任何一處,筒內之蒸汽容積可以 m r 一線表之.設筒塞在 g 之時,筒內蒸汽容積等于空隙之蒸汽容積 mo,加鍋爐放進之蒸汽容積np,共計容積 m g (no 等于pg.) 故混合之膨漲線爲cd.筒塞回轉,出汽門開,蒸汽卽外放,至 e 而出汽門閉,禁閉之蒸汽復沿eb線而被筒塞擠縮,至汽壓 o' b 時而完成一循環bcde.若圓筒不有空隙,並不用完全擠縮,則此循環當爲abcd' (與第三圖實線者相等.)

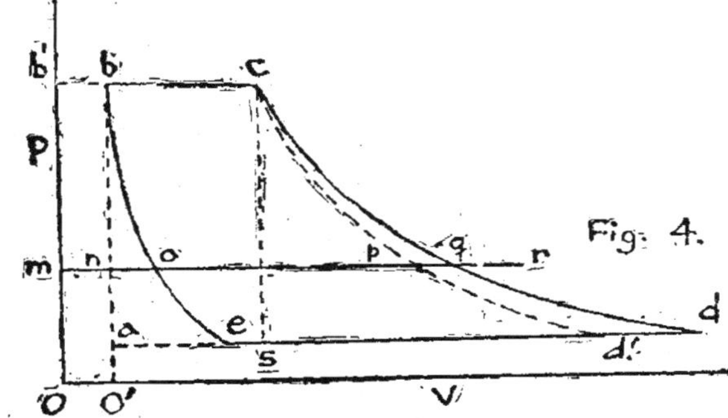

今以兩圖相較,bcde少于 abcd'有用力能,a b e,而多乎 abcd'有用力能 c d d' 但 abe等于c d d' (因a b e乃活塞授與空隙蒸汽之力能,cds乃空隙蒸汽會同進筒生汽授與活塞之力能,而c d's 乃進筒生汽獨自授與活塞之力

能，cds減cd's等于cdd'，即空隙蒸汽授與活塞之力能，故abe等于cdd'．所得適償所失，足證bcde等于abcd'．故完全擠縮于有空隙之克洛捷斯循環上，對于空隙之損失有補還之功，此利益之所在也．

（二）梁鏗循環

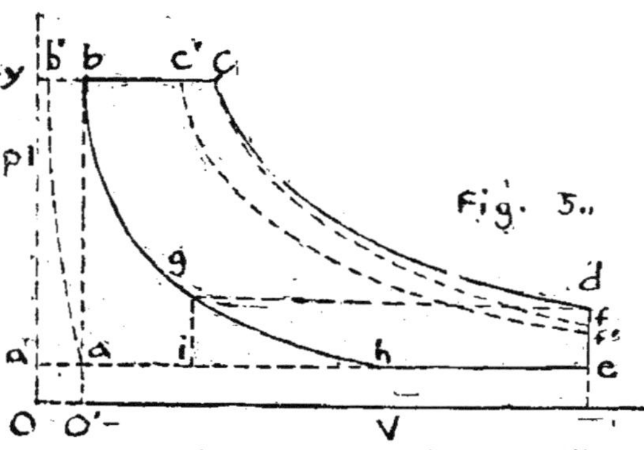

梁鏗循環用于無空隙圓筒者，為abcfe（第五圖，）用于有空隙圓筒者，為ab'c'ef'，損失于空隙者等于c'cff'．用于有空隙圓筒而復用完全擠縮者如第五圖bcdehg在蒸汽割斷c之後，空隙之蒸汽沿b h 而膨脹，鍋爐放進之蒸汽沿cf而膨脹，兩汽相合，沿cd而膨脹，至d筒內蒸汽即行逃放筒外由圖上觀之，空隙之蒸汽沿bh膨脹時，自b至g之膨脹，蒸汽內含熱能，確移運于筒塞，自g至h之膨脹，此項熱能不過加高逃放筒外之蒸汽速度，無絲毫移運于筒塞，故自g至h，在擠縮時筒塞所給于禁閉蒸汽之力能hgi在此種循環上決不能在膨脹時盡行歸還，是故每一個循環，須失力能h g i．

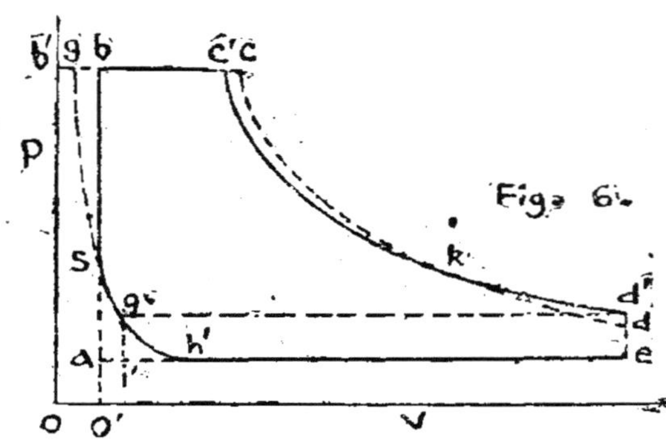

今試以不完全擠縮觀之，假設出汽門不在h（第五圖）關閉而在h'（第六圖）關閉，自h'至s禁于筒內之蒸汽即被擠縮，在筒塞還擊終了時

空隙汽壓等于o's,在開始循環之時放進之蒸汽須先沿b'g自s填擠空隙蒸汽至g,而後始迫動筒塞,其所填去之容積,等于bg,至割斷蒸汽c'之時總共放進之蒸汽容積,等于gc' 沿c'd',而膨脹.若不有此項填擠,則蒸汽割斷當在C'沿cd而膨脹.如此顯見損失于此種空隙之填擠者等c'ckc',而于得之于此項填擠者,等于d'rdd'.筒塞至d出汽門已開,在gh'膨脹線上,自g'至h'之膨脹蒸汽未稍移運任何力能于筒塞,力能h'g'i',于擠縮時筒塞所給于蒸汽者未克收回萬一,是又損失也.總計損失于此種不完全擠縮及圓筒空隙者等于[(c'ckc'+h'g'i')—d'kdd'].

今復以完全擠縮之梁踏循環（第五圖）與不完全擠縮者（第六圖）相併而比較之,如第七圖顯見完全擠縮者bcdehg雖多得c'cdd'而失去更大之力能如hgbg'h'是故完全擠縮于有空隙之梁蹉循環,殊爲不利,而任何擠縮,較低于完全擠縮者較爲勝算至若bb's乃空隙之損失也.

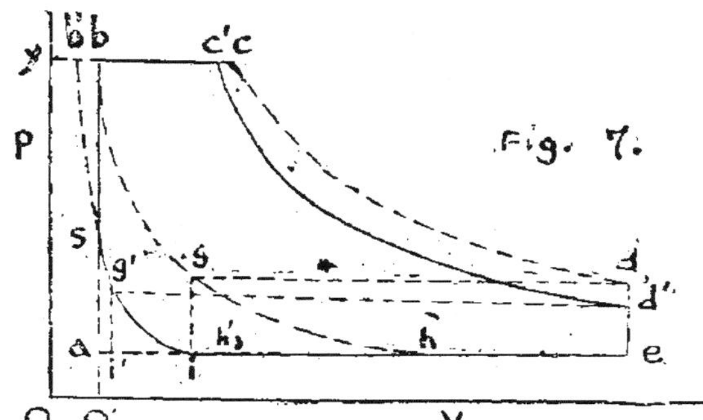

按今日存在之來往行動蒸汽機,其圓筒無一不具空隙,而其所運用之循環,類皆梁踏式.觀乎上述各節,可知于校正線門時擠縮何以不能過高之理矣.

(註1) 現今應用之圓筒類皆導熱.但玆便于立論起見假作不傳熱論.

THE DESIGN OF A REINFORCED CONCRETE FLOATING DOCK FOR SERVICE ON UPPER YANGTZE RIVER

By H. K. Chow (周厚坤) *S.B.; S.B.; S.M.*

INTRODUCTION

The present dock has been designed for the service of steamers on Upper Yangtze River, i.e., the stretch of Yangtze River between Chunking of Szechuen and Ichang of Hupeh, a distance of 350 miles. The character of the current in this part of the River is entirely different from that below Ichang. The stream below Ichang may be swift during high water season, but nothing can be compared with the whirl, the rapid, and the roar of the Yangtze Gorges above Ichang. Steam navigation in this section was always considered impossible until in 1900 when the British gunboats Woodcock and Woodlark made their historical trip up the gorges as far as Chunking. But the honor of commercial navigation belonged to s/s Shutung (蜀通) of the Szechuen Steam Navigation Co. The owners of this high power vessel, it is gratifying to record, were Chinese, showing in an unmistakable way how enterprising the Chinese are. It was all pioneering work and the risk of investment was great, but the enterprising Chinese business man forced it through with courage, thus opening up the way for the steam navigation of Upper Yangtze to the present day which is now assuming large proportions.

There are now to the writer's knowledge over forty vessels, large and small, plying between Ichang ang Chunking. The number is growing each year, and, if it not were for the never-ending warfare in the Szechuen province, the number might have increased to one hundred, since the opening of the River. The reason for such expansion, in spite of political difficulties is not far to seek. The junk traffic, which was the sole means of passenger and goods transportation, was slow, costly and, above all, risky. It used to be for a junk to spend three months for the upward trip, while carrying a crew of one hundred, and on that trip no one knew when and where the vessel might run against a rock or be sucked in by the cavitating forces of the whirl-pool. Naturally such mood of transportation must be veay costly, and freight for cotton yarns was sometimes as high as eighty dollars per bale. Even to this day the larger portion of the goods traffic is still carried in junks, the steam boats being unable to furnish the entire tonnage.

Szechuen is a very large province, baving an area equal to Japan and a population greater than British Isles. The whole province is not hilly. although aurrounded by lofty mountains, and possesses large expanses of flat agricultural land well intersected by irrigating canals. The agricultural or forest products of the land are enormous. Here is a place where natural resources are almost inexhaustible, but, unlike the seaboard provinces, have not been much exploited alike by Chinese and foreigners. But the Americans, with their characteristic business foresight, have been and are paying a great deal of attention. Japan has not lagged behind, with great Britain a close third. With their gunboats acting as convoys in case of bandit trouble, the shipping companies of these nationals are not only eking out a living but are actually making a profit,- with troubles and difficulties here and there of course. It is therefore not too much to predict that, with the return of peace and the suppression of banditry in the province, there will be a wonderful expansion of shipping business in this section of Yangtze where steam navigation as constructed with junk is not only safer but more economical. To the writer's mind that day is not very far if it is remembered that the country has already been under disorder for the last fourteen years, and a reaction to settle down is bound to come, just as it has happened in Mexico.

LOCATION OF THE FLOATING DOCK

Shipping requires ships, and ships, like evertyhing else, deteriorate with time and under service. More so it is with ships in this service which require more care in handling ank more repair every year for two reasons. Firstly, in order to cut down dead-weight and to give more room to propelling machinery and space for cargo, the scantlings for these ships are usually light. That means they are comparatively frail structurally, and the non-rigidity of the hull and the high speed of the machinery induce vibration to a degree that is hard on the structure, in consequence of which, frequent repairs have become necessary. Secondly, the navigating channel is full of under-water rocks, landslides here and there, and rock banks every-where. The current is so swift that even with the greatest care of the best pilot, the vessel is liable to founder and holes in the hull after a trip are of common occurrence rather than exceptions. A good-sized repair shop at each or both ends of the channel is of great importance and should be welcome by all shipping interests.

Enquiries made by the writer among the ship owners comfirmed the need of such a shop. As the matter stands now, when a hole is made into a hull it is patched with bags of cement; repairs of a very limited charcter are made by the small shops having a few pieces of machine tools. For big repairs and the annual overhauling,—these steamers invariably come to Shanghai to dock. No where along the whole Yangtze River below Chunking is there any facility for docking the steamers and making the necessary repairs in a first class way. In making this round trip, the ships of the Chi-King (吉慶) Class, i.e. 165 feet long, 26 feet beam, and 250 tons dead-weight burned coal to the value of $5,000. The loss of freight during the trips is very large indeed. It is therefore seen that if these repairs could be undertaken in Ichang or Chunking the saving to the shipping interests will come to large figures.

The question arises as to where the floating dock should be located, Ichang or Chunking. It is the writer's belief that the location at Ichang should be chosen, for the following reasons: Firstly, since all the shipping companies have their managing headquarters in Ichang, this location is preferable from business point of view. Secondly, Ichang is comparatively near to Hankow where supplies of metal and other materials can be drawn in large quantities and at reasonable prices. Thirdly, for the same reason, skilled labor can be more easily obtained. Fourthly, there is a regular shipping service between Hankow and Ichang (with a type of boat smaller than those on the Shanghai Hankow run), thus insuring good communication. Finally, the seasonal fluctuation of water in the River is much smaller at Ichang than at Chunking, 60 feet against 100 feet. A floating dock must move with the changing level of water. The difficulty of managing a floating vessel in a place where over night the water level may change twenty feet is too obvious, and a location which will minimise such difficulty should be selected. Reasons one to four are commercial while the final one is technical.

CHOICE OF TYPE OF DOCK

Having fixed the location of the plant, the next consideration is the selection of type of dock. The selection should be based upon the following considerations,

(1) It must be a floating structure.

(2) It must be as economical as consistent with strength.

(3) It must be easy to handle.

(1) A floating structure is selected because the rise and fall of water in this part of Yangtze is easily 50 to 60 feet. A graving dock such as those in Kiangnan Docks has to rest on solid foundations well piled, has to be provided with side walls 70 feet to 80 feet high. and an entrance gate of like depth under enormous hydraulic pressure during high water season. The capacity of the pumping machinery must also be unusually large in order to cope with the very large volume of water to be pumped out. Not only is the initial cost enormous, but also the operating expenses will be very high. And from engineering point of view the writer doubts if a graving dock of such depth in comparision with its length and breadth has ever been designed, constructed, and successfully run for a seasonal fluctuating water head of 50 to 60 feet. The engineering difficulties are tremendous.

Nor the idea of a slipway can be entertained. Slipways, to be practical, can not have inclinations greater than 1 in 13, or 1 in 20, the latter being the usual slope. For a tide range of ten feet at the seaboard, this means a length of 200 feet excluding the portion under water below the lowest tide. But here we have an annual variation of water level of 60 feet. If the same slope is maintained throughout, and if the slipway is for service all the year round, it must have length of over 1200 feet. Not only is the cost prohibitive for such a structure, but also the engineering difficulties will be very great when we remember the treacherous nature of the Yangtze silt forming the banks

Hence, the only other alternative is a floating dock. Docks of this type new in China, although quite common in the foreign countries especially in England where at Southampton a 60,000 tons dock was this year completed. The only floating dock in China to the writer's knowledge is the one owned by the Yangtze Engineering Works of Hankow, now defunct. It is 80' × 25', constructed of steel and can dock vassels up to 200 tons. The structure is, however, frail, and its capacity is too small for Ichang-Chunking boats.

(2) The design must be as economical as consistent with strength. This requirement is, as a matter of fact, common to all engineering designs. For what is the use of having a structvre that is over-strong and very expensive. There is the double waste of capital and material. Moreover in a floating structure, too much material means greater dead-weight, and less carrying load. In this case, the measure of efficiency is the minimum of first cost per ton of maximum weight of ship to be lifted.

(3) It must be easy to handle. The writer's frist design was one of the self docking type consisting of three sections each 33' long, 45' wide and 5' deep with appropriate side walls. It was felt, however, that in view of the swift current in the stream, it would not be safe to have three separate sections, the joining of which was a difficult task at best. Moreover since these steamers are of light construction for the same power and tonnage, any yielding of one section of the dock relative to others will throw an unusual strain upon the hull, a procedure to which the owners would have good reason to object. The final design as shown in the accompanying drawings consists of one piece pontoon and two side walls integral with it, giving a rigidity quite necessary under the conditions of river current and hull construction of the steamers. The handling is thus rendered simple.

DETERMINATION OF GENERAL DIMENSIONS

Having selected the type of floating dock, the next step is to determine the general dimensions. These should suit the size and tonnage of ships now existing and those which may be built during the life of the dock. It became necessary to make enquiries at shipyards that make a specialty of building these boats, as well as from the owners of these ships.

The design of early steamers followed the suggestions of Captain Plant,

River Inspector, Chinese Maritime Customs, whose recommendations concerning the construction and fitting of Upper Yangtze Steamers in so far as it related to sizes and speed were as follows:

"Limit of Size.-The dimensions of steamer for running at all stages of the river, when steam navigation is possible should not exceed:

Length	...	...	...	210 feet o.A.
Breadth	...	...	...	35 feet moulded
Depth	...	...	...	$9\frac{1}{4}$ feet moulded.

"Speed.- The speed of the steamers should not be less than as follow:

Steamers under 80 ft. in length	...	...	10 knots
Steamers of lengths 80 to 130 feet	...	...	11 "
Steamers of lengths 130 to 210 feet	...	...	12 "

"These are the minimum speeds for safe navigation through races, whirlpools, and minor rapids, but are insufficient to push up over the main rapids without having recourse to warping.

"Vessels intended to proceed over the main rapids under their own steam must have considerably more power than that provided for in these recommendations."

The above recommendations were published in 1917 by the Coast Inspector of the Chinese Maritime Customs. The boats built in accordance with these recommendations were all good-sized ones. The docking weight might be easily 600 tons. But more recently the tendency is towards smaller sizes as is shown by the following list:

隆茂	length	200'	巴東	length	71'
江慶	"	200'	其川	"	153'
新蜀通	"	200'	慶和	"	150'
福源	"	200'	其平	"	138'
大來喜	"	200'	其南	"	120'
雲陽	"	200'	其來	"	120'
宜陽	"	200'	福來	"	140'
宜仁	"	200'	夷陵	"	150'
吉慶	"	165'	夷賓	"	150'
江源	"	81'			

The above is only a partial list, but indicates in a clear way the tendency of designers towards small sizes.

The newest addition to the fleet of steamers for service on Upper Yangtze is s/s "Fushun" (富順) built by John I. Thorny-croft and Co., Ltd., of Southampton, England. It embodies the best practice in design and construction of this type of ship and the very modern equipment in propelling machinery. It is a boat of moderate size and the dimensions agree very closely with the recommendations as to size of the Chinese naval architects in the Kiangnan Docks who have had extensive experience with the design and construction of this class of vessel. The hull particulars of Fushun are as follows:

Length overall	147'-8'
Breadth moulded	28'
Depth	8'-6"
Mean draught	6'
Deadweight carrying capacity on 5' draft about	100 tons
" " " " 6' " "	200 "
Cargo space measurement	23,000 ft.
Designed speed, loaded	13.5 knots
Actual speed, loaded	13.9 "

It is thus seen that while 200' steamers were popular, the more moderate sizes 120'-150' are the rule of the day. The reason is of course found in the better manoeuvering qualities of the smaller steamers in negotiating around the sharp bends in this part of the River.

We must therefore reasonably assume that the steamers to be docked will be of the 120'-150' class. It is good business wisdom to look ahead, and also to cater to the requirements of a majority of steamers instead of spending large sums of money just to handle the peaks only, i.e., in this case, the large sizes, which, owing to the frail construction as stated above, are depreciating badly and will disappear in less than ten years time. For a steamer of 140 feet length, the beam will be 27 ft., draft 6 ft. The total displacement in cubic feet, assuming a block coefficient of 0.7, will be 140 x 27 x 6 x .7 = 15876. At 35 cu. ft. of water = 1 ton, the displacement will be 455 tons. Allowing 70% of displacement to be the weight of hull, machinery, equipment and fittings, in other words, the docking weight in light condition will be about 455 x .7 = 320 tons. With due allowance for docking larger steamers, a lifting capacity of 500 tons is provided for. Length.- If the steamers to be docked are 120 - 150 feet long, then a length of 120 feet for the dock will be sufficient. When the 150 feet steamers are berthed, an overhang of 15 feet at either end is permissible in practice. Breadth.- These boats being of shallow draft, and of limited length, are usually broad - beamed. Allowing 6 feet on either side for the side walls and again 4 feet on either side a for working room and shoring, and 30 feet for maximum beam of the boats, then the total breadth will be 50 feet Depth.- The determination of this dimension requires considerable study, and is closely related to the type of structure as well as the material used in its construction. If steel is used, then the dead-weight is smaller, aed the depth of the pontoon proper can be made less. on the other hand if reinforced concrete is used, as in this case it is, then the dead-weight is more, and depth of the pontoon proper must be increased in order to secure additional displacement for the increased weight. After several preliminary calculations, a depth of 8 feet was selected, due regard being given to the available data for four reinforced wharf pontoons under service conditions at the Tayeh Works and Mines, Han Yeh Ping Iron & Coal Co. (see below).

Total Height of the dock.- The height of the structure should fulfill two purposes: (a) The height of the steamers up to the strength deck for shoring purposes. (b) The height should be such that in case of complete flooding of all compartment in the pontoon through accident the water tight side walls should afford sufficient buoyancy to keep the structure floating. A height above deck of 18 feet has been selected.

Here then we have a structure with the followingm aximu mdimensions: Length 120', Breadth 50' and Total Height 17' - 2"+8' = 25' - 2".

DETAILED DESIGN

Reinforced concrete pontoons in China are scarce, and of the reinforced concrete floating dock there is none. It would have been entirely an innovation and the design thus rendered difficult and uncertain, if it not were for the fact that in the Tayeh Works and Mines, there were at the wharf four reinforced concrete pontoons for shipping purposes since 1919. These pontoons have been entirely satisfactory under service conditions as to river current and inclement weather and are still giving as good a service as when new. This is attributable to the monolithic character of the structure, and to the fact that the concrete is water proof so that, unlike wood and steel, needs no painting to protect the under water portions from the attacks of elements. No repair on the under-water portion has been found necessary. Buttressed by these fine performance records the writer did not hesitate to design a floating dock based along general lines on the existing pontoons. For no test can ever be better than placing the structure under actual working conditions and observing the results thereof, which, when satisfactory, can be applied to subsequent designs of a similar nature with imbrovements or modifications as called for from time to time. It would be rash on the part of the designer to undertake something absolutely novel, but if he is guided by the favorable results of similar structures, though not identical, the course so pursued is not at all risky. In fact progress in engineering demands that some such steps be taken in order that the usefulness of the data may receive wider application.

Lack of space does not allow full description of all details. Only salient features can described here. It will be observed, (Plate I), that the pontoon proper is divided into six chambers or compartments four of 25' x 36' and two of 25' x 48'. There is inter-communication between the compartments but the flow of water is rather restricted. This is important for trimming and stability purposes. The strength of the pontoon (see plate II) is given longitudinally by seven top and bottom girders, each 24" x 8", spaced 8'-4" apart; and transversely by eleven top and bottom girders each 20" x 6", spaced 6' apart; and the whole skeleton is covered or united by a continuous slab of 4" thick corresponding to the plating of a steel floating dock. There are diagonal bracings for all the girders and the usual fillets and haunches at intersections of different members; also columns at stated intervals.

The superstructure consists of two side walls each 6' x 18' x 120'. The strength part consists transversely of vertical latticed columns 4' wide 8" thick spaced 12' apart; and the cover part consists of wooden planking 2" thick. The whole superstructure is caulked to make it watertight.

There are two electric pumps, one on each side, located above the pontoon deck, of such power and capacity as to empty the entire contents of water in

5 hours. There are the usual bo la ds and capstans for mooring the dock, flooding valves for sinking the dock; inclinometer for keeping the dock in trim while rising and falling.

WEIGHT, CAPCACITY AND EFFICIENCY

Total Weight in long tons:

Concrete parts	595
Steel bars	51
Wooden parts	79
Pumping and Mooring Equipment	10
	735 tons

Lifting Capacity:

Volume of the pontoon proper 8'50'x120' ... 48,000 cu. ft.

Force of buoyancy when immersed 8' $= \frac{48,000}{35}$ 1,337 tons

Net lifting capacity = 1337 - 735 ... ... 602 „

Efficiency of the Dock $\frac{602}{1337}$ ... ... 45 %

STABILITY

Stability is that property of a floating body in a liquid which, when the body is displaced by any external moment, tends to return to its former position. The degree of stability is measured to the metacentric height at varying depths of immersion, and is found by substracting the distance between the center of gravity and center of buoyancy from the distance betwean the latter aad the metacenter. In symbolic form, it can be stated as follows:

$$GM = BM - BG = \frac{I}{V} - BG \text{ or } (I - BG \times V)/V$$

where GM is the metacentric hight; I is moment of inertia of the water plane about the longitudinal axis; V is the volume of immersion up to that water plane; BG, the distance between the center of gravity and center of buoyancy. In the case of a floating dock where water is admitted into the interior of the vessel, the equation is modified as follows:

$$GM = (I - GB \times V - \Sigma i)/V$$

where Σi = summation of moment of inertia of interior contained water

Reinforced Concrete Floating Dock

Plate I

Designed By H. K. Chow

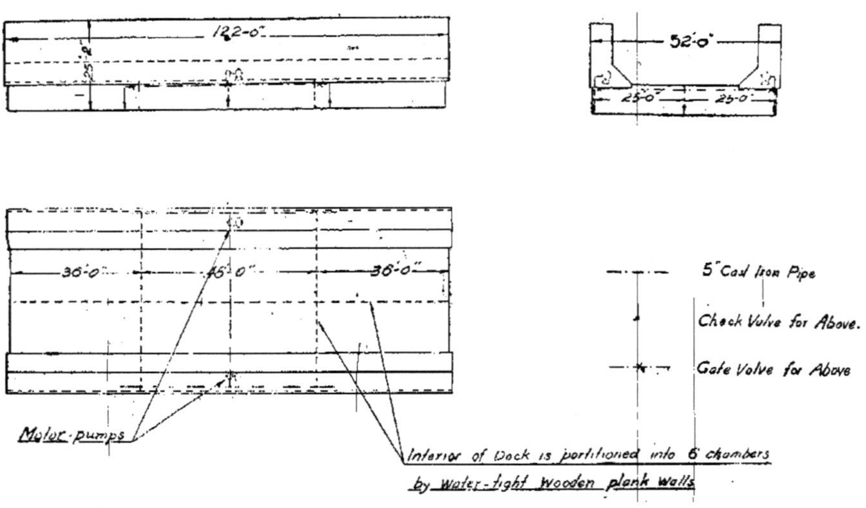

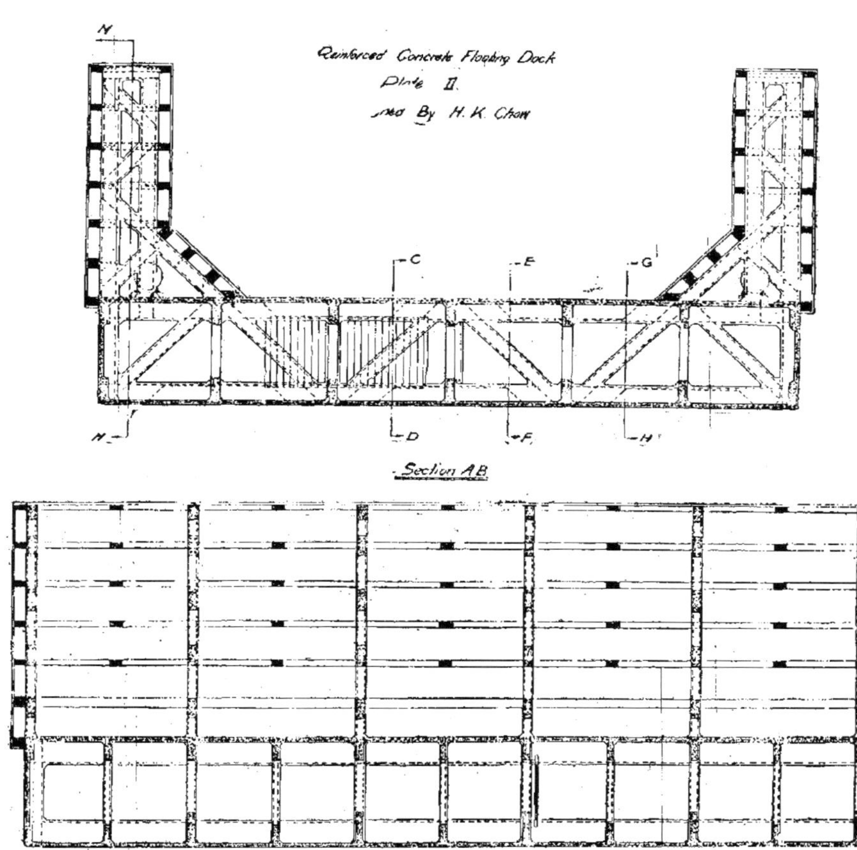
Reinforced Concrete Floating Dock
Plate II.
By H. K. Chow
C
E
G
N
N
D
F
H
Section A.B.
Section M.N.

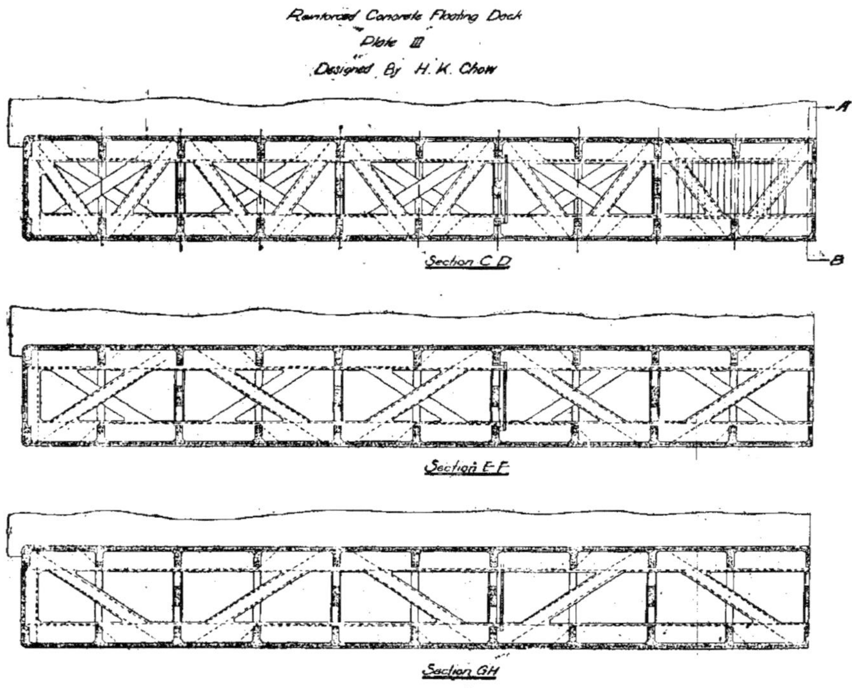
Reinforced Concrete Floating Dock
Plate III
Designed By H. K. Chow
A
B
Section C D
Section E-F
Section GH

surfaces. With a ship on a floating dock, the stability of the ship must also be taken into consideration, and I, GB, V and Σi of the equation are the combined expressions for ship and floating dock.

It will be seen that a vessel like a floating dock rising and falling during docking operation has its I, V, GB, and Σi constantly changing so that its stability also constantly changes and must be carefully watched. The stability, as a rule, is greatest when the deck of the pontoon is above water, and very much smaller when the side walls are deeply immersed for accomodating the ship, and is smallest when the ship just emerges from water. Data are available showing that for a floating dock large enough to lift a ship of 12,000 tons, the combined metacentric height of ship and dock varies from 16 feet when operations are commenced, to a minimum of 3 feet when the bottom of the ship just clears the water, and then to a maximum of 74 feet when the operation is complete. For any new design along orthodox lines, therefore, we only need to figure the metacentric height at this worst condition.

CALCULATION OF STABILITY

Assume the worst condition of service viz., a ship of 500 tons deadweight is docking and the ship is just emerging from water. The amount of water still remaining in pontoon is 1337 - (500 + 735) = 102 tons, and may be assumed to be in the four end compartments 2 feet deep. The water plane will be a horizontal section through the two side walls, and I will be I_0+Ay^2, the symbols having the usual meanings.

$$I=I_0+Ay^2=\frac{1}{12}Ah^2+Ay^2=2A\left(\frac{h^2}{12}+y^2\right)$$

Here A = 8'x122', h = 8', y = 22'. Substituting these values into the equation,

$$I=2\times8\times122\left(\frac{8^2}{12}+22^2\right)=1956\times489.3=980\,000\ \text{ft.}^4$$

$$\Sigma i=4\left(\frac{25\times36\times25^2}{12}\right)=187{,}500\ \text{ft.}^4$$

$$I-\Sigma i=980{,}000-187{,}500=792\,500\ \text{ft}^4$$

Assume a combined center of gravity of ship and dock to be 2 feet above, and center of buoyancy 3.8 feet below the top of the pontoon. Then $\overline{GB}$ = 5.8'

$$GM=(I-\Sigma i-GB\times V)/V=\frac{792{,}500-5.8\times 48{,}000}{48{,}000}$$

$$=\frac{792{,}500-278{,}000}{48{,}000}=\frac{514\,500}{48\,000}\doteq 10.7 \text{ feet.}$$

This high stability even at this worst condition is explained by:

(1) The low center of gravity of the dock on account of the wooden side wall planking and heavy concrete pontoon.

(2) The low center of gravity of this type of ship common on this part of Yangtze, which demands shallow draft, broad beam, heavy propelling machinery.

(3) The low combined conter of gravity of dock and ship.

(4) The ample width of the dock itself.

ECONOMICS OF THE STRUCTURE

There remains the question of economy of the structure. As stated at the beginning of this paper, the dock has been designed with a view to economy. An ideal structure of this type, from the point of view of strength, would be constructed entirely of steel, but the cost will be probibitive. Since the undertaking is new without precedent to follow, investors will hesitate to sink in large sums of money. The writer has been repeatedly told that a first class repair yard with a floating dock can not be got up for less than 300,000 taels. This is a very big sum in this part of the world, and its mere mention cools the enthusiasm and stifles the thought of any man who may be contemplating such undertaking. The writer's views are, however, different, and he believes that where the best can not be had, the second best should always be encouraged and prosecuted, and where investors are skeptical and yet the demand for a new project is insistent, a plan requiring the least amount of money should always be adopted. This explains the selection of reinforced concrete as the main material of construction, and timber, for the planking of the side walls. The latter is used partly to correct the unusual heavy weight of the reinforced concrete and partly to substitute the form timber for the bottom of the pontoon, always remembering that the cost of wooden form in reinforced concrete construction is a big item. There is no objection to the use of timber on side walls, because it is nearly all the time above water and is therefore not subject to the deleterious effects thereof, and when damaged can be easily repaired. A complete wooden structure, however, can not be safely recommendded apart from the high initial cost, owing to the difficulty of making joints in timber, and the lack of experienced builders to construct it. Such structures have long become obsolete.

The estimates of cost of material and labor have been made to the smallest item, and has been found to be $14,800 for material and 2,200 for labor, totaling $17,000. This does not include cost for pumping and mooring equipments. If 10% is allowed for incidentals then the above figure becomes $18,700. The following unit prices have been assumed (July, 1925); all being in Mexican dollars, the material delivered at Taych.

Material	Description	Unit Price
Portland Cement *		4.78 per bbl.
Yellow sand	Coarse granules	3.30 per 100 cu.tf.
Gravel	not over 1" size	4.00 ,,
Steel Bars *	Corrugated	100.00 per long ton
Steel wire *	1/10" diam.	0.15 per lb.
Oregon pine board *	2" thick	20.00 per 100 sq.ft.
,, ,, beams *	8"x10"	70.00 per 100 ft.
,, ,, ,,	4"x4"	15.00 ,,
,, ,, ,,	5"x10"	44.00 ,,
Big Chinese Firs	Circ = 2 Chinese ft.	10.00 per pc.
Small ,, ,,	,, = 1.3 ,, ,,	1.20 ,, ,,
Small Pine sticks		0.30 per pc.
Wire Nails	2" to 5" long	10.00 per 100 lb.
Square nails	5" long	10.00 per 100 lb.
Bolts and Nuts	$\frac{3}{4}$" dia, 24", 20", 16". long	0.35 pes pc.
Hemp	Low grade	0.15 per lb.
Wood Oil		0.30 ,,
Heavy Wood Oil		0.40 ,,
Coal Tar		0.05 ,,

Items with an asterik * can not be obtained locally at Ichang and a percentage might have to be added to the above prices which were ruling at Tayeh. Such increase in cost has already been allowed for under "incidentels."

It must be noted however, that the total cost of $18,700 does not include fess to the naval architect, profit to the contractor, and expenses chargeable to supervision.

RECAPITULATION

(1) The number of steamers on the Upper Yangtze is growing rapidly. (2) There is a demand for a repair shipyard which, as a condition precedent, must have a floating dock. (3) Such a dock should be located in Ichang. (5) A reinforced concrete floating dock of 600 tons liftng capacity can be constructed at a cost about Mex $20,000. (5) The design as submitded possesses ample stability and strength.

原動力學發明家傳略

茅以新譯

湯姆生——能力不滅律 (Benjamin Thompson)

卡腦特——汽機效率之理論 (Nicolas L. S· Carnot)

馬爾——熱力與工作之關係 (Julius R. Mayer)

柯而丁——熱力與工作之關係 (Ludevig A. Co'ding)

加而——熱力學 James P. Joule)

斯透金——電與熱力工作 (William Sturgeon)

原動力廠,乃現世文明之基礎.凡百事業,如鐵路,電車,汽車,城市之電燈,電力,及建築等,皆先有原動力然後可以發展.原動力之基本學,爲熱力學.以無論蒸汽,油機等,皆因熱力之關係,方能發力,發電.熱力學之發明,在十九世紀.至今不過百年,已有如許之成績.其進步之速,可謂鷩人矣!然而發明者雖辛苦經營,爲後人造福,後之人則常忽略而不注意.有作爲之青年,必讀大人物與發明家之傳略,以爲奮發之模範.此本篇所由作也.

湯姆生　一七五三年,富蘭克林在英國接受皇家學會所贈之金牌,所以稱揚其發明避電針之功也.同時湯姆生亦生於美國麻省之小村中.湯姆生初爲學徒,暇時曾在哈佛大學讀課.次爲小學教員.次又在軍營中爲少佐.湯姆生卽起始學槍砲與火藥.不久美國獨立.湯姆生被稱爲不熱心者,乃渡大西洋往英國.派爲移民局書記.又回美國爲陸軍中佐.又往歐洲巴維利亞爲選帝侯.十餘年內,其總部在麥立西.一七九一年,爲羅馬教皇之伯爵.湯姆生在麥立西所作之事中,監督製造軍火亦其一.湯姆生卽於此處研究得摩擦生熱之理.湯氏取一鋼塊,以一萬磅力壓於鐵板上,另加二馬力以轉動鋼塊,速率爲每分鐘三十二轉.二小時半後,所發生之熱足能合十八磅四分三之水熱至沸點.湯氏謂此所發生之熱,與九枝四分之三寸直經之臘燭所有者相同.湯氏當即將此事報告於皇家學會.但無人注意之.此時湯氏始創皇家學院.所以獨行其志也.老年在巴黎.死于一八一四年.享年六十一歲.湯氏以前,能力不滅論亦有人提過.但至湯氏方確實證明.工作可以生熱.能力不滅論,方有穩固之基礎.其後又有達威氏者取冰二塊,互相摩擦,冰卽融化.亦所以證摩擦之力能變爲熱也.

卡腦特 卡腦特之名,在熱力學上可謂最重要者矣.一百年前,一八二四年時,卡氏卽發刊一熱力雜誌.凱爾文公爵稱爲科學上之新紀元.實言之卡腦特之聲名,全由此雜誌而來!初出時,銷行甚少,社會亦不甚注意.但至卡氏死後,此雜誌乃成爲科學上之重要成績.許多科學家皆用以參考焉.卡腦特之父爲法國革命時期之重要人物.卡氏于一七九六年生于盧森堡.初入小學,後入專門學校其時社會有名數學家,皆在此校.卡氏此時雖未能與拿破崙同爲戰爭,亦在守備隊中爲工程師.一八一九年,調至尼黎.一八二六年,升爲將軍.明年,告退.五年後,死于虎列拉病.時年僅三十六歲.卡氏死後,幾于埋沒不聞.幸一八三六年,專門學校雜誌中,刊其一文.述熱之理論.因此少年凱爾文公爵更事追求,卒成蓋世有名之科學家.至今各熱力學書本中,皆詳述卡腦特氏之汽機效力,與其循環法,爲熱力學之最要部分.卡氏死後,有人搜尋其記事簿之草算,卒發現熱乃動之一種理論.卡氏早死非僅世界上少一偉大科學家,卽熱力理論,亦因遲數年方得發佈.

與卡氏同時者,有克萊布龍亦在專門學校讀書.嗣在俄國從事市政.後又回至法國.曾創築鐵路,橋梁,及機車甚多.又賽格因發明繩橋,與細管鍋爐.賽格因又曾著一文.論如熱卽力,則蒸汽自鍋爐中出時必較多于至凝冷器時.因汽缸工作之力,卽取自此蒸汽也.同時尚有一德國少年學者莫爾.習化學與醫學.作一文論熱之性質.其言曰:「化學原質五十四種以外,尚有一居間之物,名之曰力.力可以動作,化學引力,電,光,磁,等.且能互相轉變.」此爲一八三七年之事,亦甚可疑矣.

馬爾 馬爾生于一八一四年.習醫生.一八四二年,爲船中醫生.即作一文論宇宙間之力.于人體之熱.與外界之熱與力之關係.敍述尤詳.稱爲當時之先進.謂爲熱力之祖.未始不當.馬氏曾求得熱與力之等數.其法乃從同壓同溫度之空氣中求之.

柯爾丁 馬爾之文發表後一年,丹麥工程師柯爾丁亦著一文.論力更詳盡.柯氏曾作試驗二百餘次.結論謂增加一磅水之溫度一攝氏度,須作工一一四八呎磅（按此數雖不精確.然已甚近.正確之數.應爲一四〇〇呎磅）柯氏尙有其他論文不少.

加而 以上所述數人之事略.尙不能及加而之重要.加而曾致力于實驗十想,二年,其結果可謂熱力學中之最重要者.加氏爲一研究最精確之學者.其一八四三,五,七,九,之數次論文.將舊有之熱質理論,完全推翻.而設立一新思新紀元.其重要可以想見.加氏生于一八一八年耶蘇節.幼時受教于家中.曾習數學於達爾頓.達氏乃創原子論者.獲益不淺.達氏設立文學哲學會.加氏後即爲會中之圖書館員,書記.至最後乃爲會長.達氏與加氏發明新學理之多,不可勝計.市人立銅像以紀念之.其時有斯透金者,與加而爲同鄉.發明軟鐵電磁與轉路器.加而曾與之同作軟鐵電磁之試驗.一八三八年發表.一八四三年,加而作磁電之熱力論文.宣讀時,僅有欲睡之聽衆六人.一八四七年之論文.在牛津宣讀.加氏因得與凱爾文公爵晤面.一八四九年,加而宣讀其熱之等數.謂增加一磅水之溫度法氏一度,須工作七七二呎磅.（按此數不甚準確.應爲七七八呎磅.）三十年來.賴以作種種之計算.相傳凱爾文與加而一次同在一會場中,加而宣讀其論文,凱爾文頻以爲謬誤.但愈聽愈見其獨到之處,卒未起立反對.僅會後與之討論而已.自此二人之交益深.斯透金與克勞修之研究尙在此後一二年.後人之論加而.斯透金.克勞修與凱爾文四人.稱爲近世原動力機器原理之祖.而加而之功爲尤大焉.加而一八五〇年爲皇家學會會員受有奬牌.曾自謙曰:「吾僅作一二小文,何能爲？」一八八九年死於本鄉.

上海法商電氣公司參觀紀載

世界最大提士引擎電力廠

提士引擎四座

發電量一萬 K. V. A.

楊樹仁

上海法商電氣公司 (Chmpagnie Francaise de Tramways et d' Eclairage Electrique de Shanghai) 在1906年集資本三百萬法郎在巴黎組織專營上海法租界區域內電車電燈,及自來水事業.其後營業順利,添招股份,十足資本增至八百萬法郎.現該廠正從事擴張,設立新廠,增購電機.再增一千二百萬法郎之資本,務使其新計劃,能於1925年內實現.該廠原有1500 H. P.蘇爾壽提士引擎兩座.新添3600 H. P.一座.再訂購同樣引擎一座,將於明年裝設,使總共馬力有一萬零二百匹.電車生意近年非常興盛.霞飛路上雙軌,已舖至善鐘路.自來水事業,該公司亦謀發展.在黃浦江邊董家渡建一抽水廠,增設儲水塔二座.一在董家渡,一在丁家灣,可供每日用水量四萬cnbic meters

新廠在呂班路底,盧家灣電車之終點在焉;與舊有蒸汽機廠相對立於徐匯岸旁.廠房佔地約二畝半,用鋼骨三和土建築.落成於1922年十二月.同時裝置瑞士蘇爾壽提士引擎二座,共計有三千馬力.

蘇氏兄弟公司 (Sulzer Freres Societe Anonyme, Winerthur, Suisse) 製造提士引擎 (Diesel Engine) 素負盛名.在中國頗受歡迎.近年向該廠訂購引擎者頗多.蘇氏提士引擎,直接發電機,生三相交流電.發電機乃飛輪式,爲瑞士 Oerlikon 公司所造.提士引擎速率甚低,每分鐘僅一百五十轉.故交流電機欲得五十波率,(50 cycles) 即須載有四十個磁極 (poles) 旋動磁場之對徑,於是不得不大如飛輪焉.

新添設之3600 H.P.提士引擎亦爲蘇氏兄弟公司所造,速率更低,每分鐘僅有一百二十五轉.此機有六個氣筩,筩之口徑爲760 m.m.而Stroke length爲1020 m.m.(約合30 by 49 inches.)此機已在製造地點試用,所耗油量甚少.據廠中報告每馬力僅須黑油(Crude oil)百分之四十二磅.(0.42 pound of oil per brake Horsepower delivered)速率節制機爲飛輪式,(Fly-wheel Type governor).支配油量,並調制氣壓.開機時,用八十五磅空氣壓力.發動以後,則用七十一磅氣壓.

新機所聯接之發電機,爲法國巴黎某公司所造,(The Creusot Works of Messrs Schneiger & Company)亦爲飛輪式,電壓爲五千二百Volts能量爲三千三百 K. V. A.電機之一端裝有直流勵磁機.用一百十Volts,電壓,送電流至磁場圈線之內.

晚間最高電量爲4000 K. W.,日間廠中發電僅供電車耗用,只須600 K. W.故廠中裝有350 K. W. Rotary Converter變流機三座.使交流電變成高壓(550-Volt)直流電.

廠中高壓交流電,不經變壓器,即由二萬米達(20 Kilometres)地線直達六個變壓器站.再由六萬米達之露天銅線,傳送至十五個變壓器小站.以一百十volts低壓供燈用,二百Volts供電力用.

本級同學二十人,於十一月十九日下午一時,由教授謝宅山先生領往該新廠參觀.對面舊有蒸汽力廠,地旁徐匯小溪河水不足供鍋爐及凝冷器之用.但營業順利,急須擴充,以應需求,不得不拋棄舊廠,添造新屋.設立提士引擎電力廠.其新計畫擬在1925年內備有馬力一萬零二百.總電量一萬K. V. A.云.

該廠所用油料,係亞細亞殼牌提士引擎油(Diesel oil).油裝在長筒內,淨重五百六十磅.一噸油(計四筒)照市價值銀三十兩左右.據該廠工程師云每度電力須耗油三百十grams計合千分之六百八十四磅(310grams of oil per k.w.hr.).茲將可靠紀載錄下,以資留心電力事業者之參考焉:

原有資本	8,000,000 法郎
添增資本	12,000,000 法郎
總共資本	20,000,000 法郎

廠屋　　在1922年落成,為鋼骨三合土建築物,分三層.

工程師　五人皆法人.

機匠　　十八.工資分每月四十元,三十元,及二十六元三級.

現在馬力總數	6,600 H.P.
1925年將有馬力總數	10,200 H.P.
現在需用電力（最高限度）	4,000K.W.
（最低限度）	600 K.W.
耗用油量平均數	310 grams per k.w.hr.

燈用電費	13 Tls.cents per k.w.hr
熱用電費	6 Tls. cents per k.w.hr.
日間 Power facfor	80%—75%
晚間 Power facfor	95%

開機費時三分鐘併車費時六分鐘（min. for parallel operation）

1 unit 3600H.P. Diesel Engine

2 units 1500H. P. ,, ,,

1 unit 3300 K.V.A. Generator — 5200—volts—125R.P.M.

Exciter voltage: 110—volt;570 —amp.

2 units 1200 K.V.A. Generator — 5200--Volts—150 R.P.M

Exciter voltage: 110—volt; 200—amp.

3 units Rotary converter— 550.volts, 633—amp. 1000 R.P.M.

Diesel Engine made by Sulzer Fre'res societe Anonyme, Winterthur, Suisse.

Generators made by Ateliers de Constr. Oerl.kon. stisse.

Creusot Works of Messrs. Schneiner & co.

日晷及時差

朱鼎元

滗園所置日晷,係平面式.茲將其原理,製法,時差,及校正之法,爲中學學生略述之.

原理

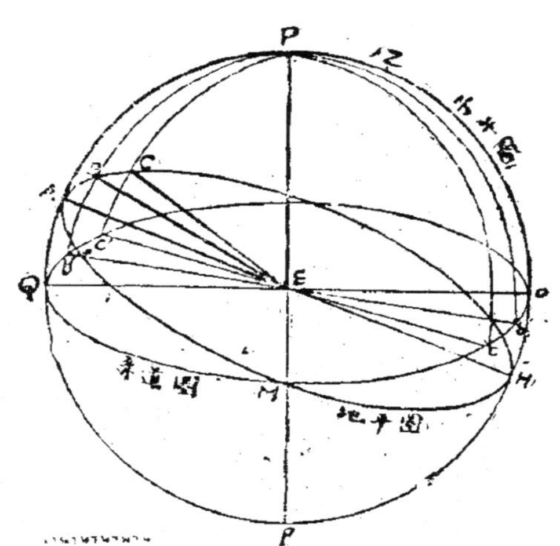

地球繞日一週爲一年,自轉一週爲一日.日過本處子午圈爲正午,至次日復過子午圈時,即一日也.其間分爲二十四小時,故日行十五度,爲時一小時也.設右圖爲一透明之球PP與地軸平行,P爲北極.QMA爲赤道圈,z爲本處天頂,AMH爲本處地平圈.AZP爲經過天頂與北極之赤經圈,即本處之子午圈也.將赤道圈分爲二十四等份,如b,c,等處,即ab,bc,諸弧各爲十五度也.

作bPb', cPc',諸赤經圈,日過aZP子午圈時,即爲本處之正午.其時PE線之日影,落於赤道圈上者爲EQ線.落於地平圈上者爲EA線,故EA線卽平面日晷上正午時之痕也.日過BPb'赤經圈時,卽下午一時,（因ab=15°）其時PE線之日影,落於赤道圈上者爲EB'線落於地平圈上者爲EB線.故EB'線卽下午一時之痕也.同例,EC線卽下午二時之痕.Qb'及b'c'諸弧,顯係各爲十五度.AB及AC諸弧,可從BAP弧三角求得之.因PAB爲直角,PA弧等於本處之緯度,∠APB=15°故用弧三角之公式

正切AB＝正切APB.正弦AP

卽　正切AB＝正切15°.正弦本處緯度

正切AC＝正切30°.正弦本處緯度

………………………………………

求得AB,AC,諸弧之度數,卽可據以作晷面矣.

製法

作一指時針與地軸平行,用鐵片或木片爲之.其厚可自四分之一英寸至半英寸,其斜度等於本處之緯度.例如上海之緯度約爲32°12',則作A角爲32°12',也（如圖甲）將時針置於平面上使其垂面與平面正交,針端直指正北,則與地軸平行矣.

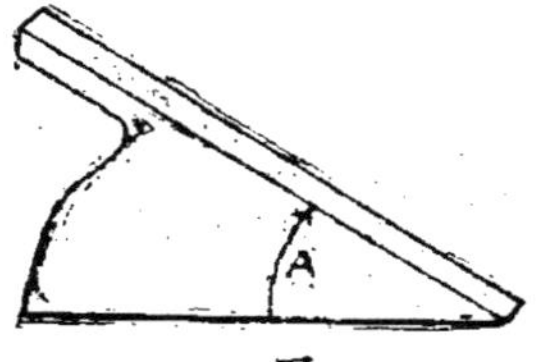

甲

指時針左右二棱之垂面與平面之交線.卽正午線,如（乙圖）aba'b'二線卽正午線也.其餘各時之線與正午線之交角,可用上述公式求之.如以上海緯度32°12'爲例,則得

緯　度	下午一時 上午十一時	下午二時 上午十時	下午三時 上午九時	下午四時 上午八時	下午五時 上午七時
31° 12'	7° 54'	16° 39'	27° 23'	41° 54'	62° 39'

自a點起,依表中角度,向右分之,卽下午各時之線.自a'點起,依表中角度,向左分之,卽上午各時之線也.每時之間,可復分爲四分或二分,上午之時,

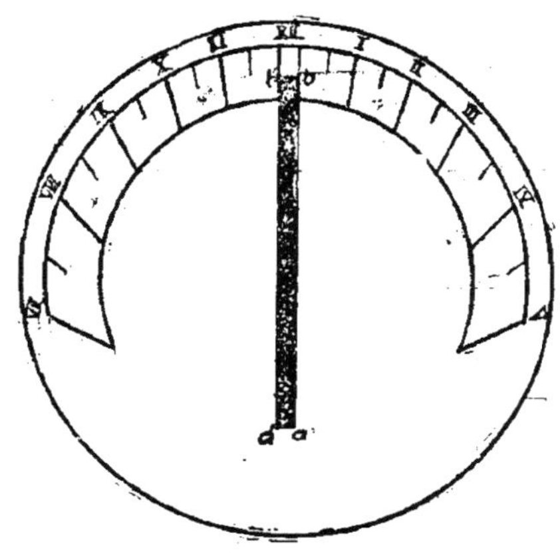

視左棱之日影下午之時,視右棱之日影.製成之後安置本處子午線上.用水平儀以驗其平否,測北辰以定午線之向（即正北之向）或用磁針以定之,但不能正確耳.

時差

日晷之時與時鐘之時,每歲僅有四次相合,其餘均不盡符.蓋日晷之時爲「視時」,時鐘之時爲「平時」.太陽二次過同一子午線之時間爲一日,然其時間之長短,實不一律.故天文家名之曰「太陽視日.」二十四等分之,名曰「視時.」太陽視日之不齊一,乃大不使用也.天文家因取週歲太陽視日之實數而平均之名爲「太陽平日.」二十四等分之,名爲「平時.」時鐘之時,即平時也.（天文家測恆星以定之）

視日長短不一之故,其理有二.

（一）地球繞日之軌道乃橢圓形,距日有遠近.距日近時,地球繞日之速率頓增,故人之視日每日東行之弧較大.而本處午線過日心,至其再過,所歷之時較平均日爲長.距日遠時,則反是.其長短較平均日之差,或正或負最多時可差八分餘.

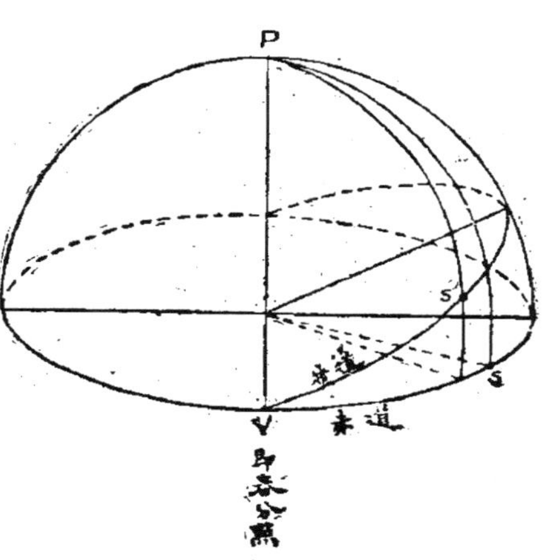

（二）地球繞日之速率不均,固足令每日之長不等.即使其均,而每日之長仍不等.因日躔爲黃道,黃道與赤道斜交故也.如上圖設天空有二日.

一爲黃日,循黃道依眞日之平均速率東行,一爲赤日,循赤道亦依眞日之平均速率東行,二日同在春分點(卽黃赤道之交點)起行,黃日至s'時,赤日至s''. 所行之弧vs'與vs''相等,惟s'與s''殊不同在一赤經圈上,故不能同時過一子午線,其相差之數,有正有負,最多時約十分鐘,惟春秋分冬夏至日,則s'與s''同在一赤經圈上,無差.

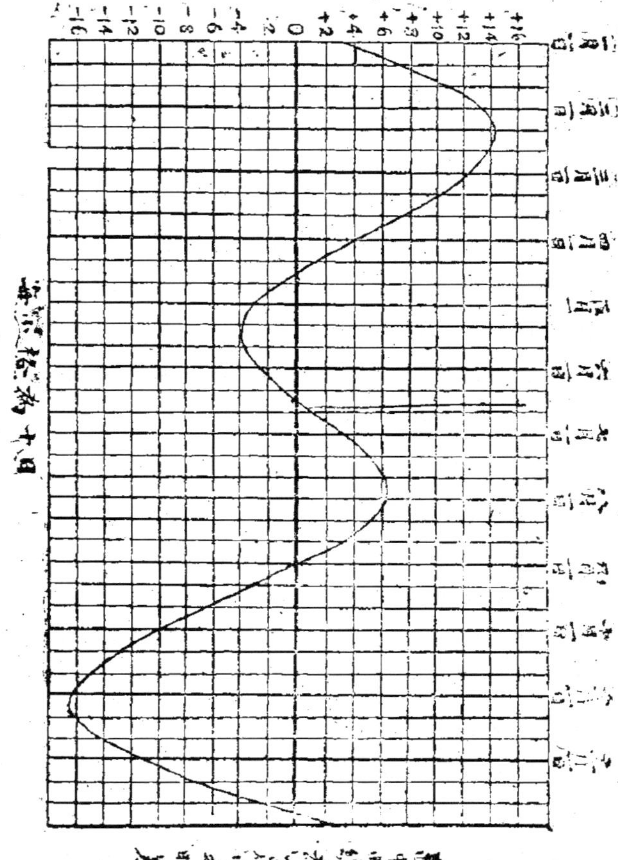

綜以上二種原因,視時與平時之差可自＋14分至－16分,統謂之時差.

校正

航海通書(Nautical Almanac)中,詳列每日格林威治正午視時化平時所應增減之數,中央觀象書亦列每日太陽過北京子午線之平時,均可據以推本處本日視時化平時所應增減之數,時差之數,逐年微有不同,故歷家每年各有其表,但其差既小,則一年之表,作普通多年之用亦可.

上圖乃將一歲之時差.繪成曲線.從此亦可得每日時差之略數.亦足爲校正日晷時之用.圖中時差作＋號者.應加於視時.作－號者.應從視時減去.即得平時也.觀圖又可見一歲僅有四次無差.約在四月十五日六月十四日,九月一日,十二月二十五日也.

惟日晷之時.終以近午時爲準.過早過晚.蒙氣差甚大.校正更難.

不兌現紙幣應如何兌現

諫　　初

當戰爭緊急之時.國家財政.常感困難.非稅制優良.如英國之所得稅者.則稅往往不能增.非人民饒足.如合衆國之富而多金者.則債往往不能舉.無已.惟有發行紙幣.以濟眉急.此所以戰爭之後,一國之金融必亂.如俄如德.其著例也.此類戰時發行之紙幣.並無準備.故不兌現.人民以強迫行使,不得不用.其實一片花紙.毫無價值之可言.政府以之購物,不啻向人民賒買.或與向人民借錢無異.所付紙幣,不過政府所出之允付票據而已.然此種票據.爲無期的.非可與六十日期三十日期之商業票據比也.惟其無期.弊竇斯生.人民知其不能兌現也.羣起疑慮之心.然以強迫行使,又不能拒而不用.於是提高物價.爲其惟一之保安法.物價高即紙幣之價低.紙幣遂賤於金幣.而金幣爲所驅逐.換言之,即金紙之間.發生一種差額.此差額與商業票據貼現時預扣之利息,可謂性質相同.惟一爲有期的.所扣之數不多.一爲無期的.應扣之數無限.故濫發之紙幣.嘗有跌至一文不值.其明證也.考紙幣之價格.全賴信用或兌現以爲維持.戰時所發之紙幣.旣不兌現,又無充分之信用擔保.其必跌價也審矣.顧其跌價也,有步驟焉.無兌現之機會.無信用之担保.此僅跌價之起因耳.其始也價雖日漸看跌.尚無一落千丈之勢.繼被人民察覺.知幣值日降.今日之值十元者,二三日後或祗值五六元不等.乃爭購物品,不事儲蓄.今日收入,即今日用出.於是金錢流通愈速,物價愈昂,幣價益跌.如是輾轉經月.紙幣之値,急轉直下,莫能阻遏.故吾謂無信用與不兌現,僅跌價之起因.無恐懼心與預防心以輔佐之,紙幣之購買力,縱有減少,終尚可作較久之維持.蓋使紙幣跌價者,發軔固爲商人,繼起猶在大衆.前者知紙幣之不能兌現,且乏擔保,故高物價以防損失,而後者僅見紙幣日就跌落,乃思隨收隨用,以換較穩之貨物.其於紙幣之來源性質,且恐泰半莫之知,莫能言也.是可知紙幣跌價約可分爲三期:一爲商人開始提高物價時期,一爲人民察覺幣價不穩減少儲蓄時期,一爲物價飛騰,紙幣充斥市場時期.此三時期內紙幣之價不一.即同一時期,價亦不一.卒至江河日下,釀成戰後俄德之恐慌.此則最可懼者也.

紙幣之害,受之最深者,固爲人民,而影響尤大者,莫如政府.蓋政府之收入,亦係紙幣.紙幣價跌,即政府之購買力減.上月徵集之稅,預計足供本月之用者,以購買力之減縮,不敷或竟達數十萬.此種損失,將何以彌縫之?故曰,政府所受之影響尤大也.政府即不爲人民利益計,而爲維持自身計,亦當設法整理,收回跌價紙幣,以固金融.此各國政府之所以於增幣之後,必須厲行減幣也.收回紙幣,或須增稅,或須減政,必有餘款,始可兌現.今假定餘款有着,則兌現似頗易易.然有二種情形,應注意焉.請申述之.

一,紙幣跌價未久者

上述紙幣跌價,可大別爲三時期.足見其跌價之經過時間,有已久未久之分.跌價未久,則紙幣未發前之債權債務關係尚在.換言之,紙幣未發或未跌時所負之債,此時大部未還.債權者日盼紙幣價漲,冀免其借款之損失.例如甲借乙洋一百元,在紙幣未跌價時交付.嗣紙幣自一元跌至九角,苟政府即於此時兌現,并照紙幣市價付給,則一百元之紙幣,兌現時只可取得九十元.此時乙償甲款,亦祇須交付九十元.是一借一還,甲已蒙十元之損失.其損失之由來,則政府照市價兌現故也.故在此種情形內,據經濟學者之意,以府爲政府收回紙幣,應照票面價兌現,以免與債務者以利,與債權者以損也.

二, 紙幣跌價已久者

紙幣跌價,已經過長時間者,則一切出入,皆以已跌價之紙幣計算,紙幣之原値十元者,入吾手時已祇作五元計價.苟斯時政府宣告兌現,并照面價(十元)付給,則我嚮之作五元收入者,今竟能兌十元之現金.非特無損,且蒙大利.我之不應得利,正猶債權者之不應受損.政府固不當無故損人,亦不必無故利人.又如有人向友借洋百元,其友以紙幣付之.此人盡用此款以購貨.貨價以金計算,共値六十元五角.是百元紙幣,業已跌去三十九元五角矣.後政府宣告兌現,亦照紙幣面價付給,則向之値六十元五角者,今又値一百元矣.倘此債務者能將借來之紙幣留而不用,(此實際必無者,不然,又奚用借爲?)則至此時,彼固仍可以原幣償其友.或持向政府兌現,處換現金百元以還之.第彼業已用以買物矣.物价祇値金元六十元五角.今苟將此物再行售出,至多亦僅値六十元五角之紙幣.(蓋此時金紙同一價値,故原値紙價一百元,金價六十元五角者.今以紙計,亦僅値六十元五角矣.)是借時祇得六十元五角之權利,而償時須負一百元之義務,而蒙三十九元五角之損失矣.其害於債務者,寗不大耶?故在此種情形內,據經濟學者之說,政府收回紙幣,應照市價付給.

雖然,跌價已久未久之分,亦難言矣.設某幣跌價已三閱月,由一元跌至八角.有人於第二月內向銀行稱貸三萬元,其時一元適値九角,是三萬元祇値二萬七千元也.假令至第三月終,政府宣告兌現,因跌價未久,故照面价付給.是二萬七千元須作三萬元金价償還矣.債權者受三千元之利,債務者受三千元之損.一利一損,豈得謂平.又如長期借款,借時紙价一元,値金价六角.閱五年紙幣更跌,一元祇値金三角.設此時政府有力兌現,惟以跌价已久,僅照市價付給.是借時爲六角,償時付三角足矣.寗不與債務者以利,與債權者以損耶?第此爲特別情形而言也.政府兌現,不能隨特別情形以爲轉移,而應視平均趨勢以定方針.苟隨特別情形以爲轉移,則借款時有一元祗值九角金幣者,有一元祗值八角金幣者,有一元祗值七角五分金幣者.按第一種情形,應照紙幣面價百分之九十兌現.按第二種情形,應照百分之八十兌現.按第三種情形,應照百分之七五兌現.始得無益無損,各稱公允.然實際上萬不可能也.故當視平均之趨勢,跌價之久暫而定兌現之方針.苟照面價兌現,而損多益少,則卽採用市價.照市價兌現,而損多益少,則卽採用面價.是在政府詳加考察,權衡利害,以大多數之利益爲依歸.而不以一部分之損益爲從違.大都考察之根據.仍以跌價久暫爲標準.跌價未久.羣情均望復原者,宜用面價兌現.跌價已久,民已習爲固然者,宜用市價兌現.此通例也.

然此就理論言也,實際上必不若是之簡易.有國家困窮,雖連年增稅減政,而仍無充分餘款以兌現者.有紙幣發行太濫,價已一落千丈,政府雖力事撙節,仍不能全數收回者.則折價收回,終較不收回爲愈.折價收回,或損在一時,損及一部分.遷延而不收回.則損在將來,而害及全體矣.此德之所以發行任頓馬克 Rentenmarck 以收回其紙馬克也.（按一九二三年一任頓馬克值一萬萬萬(1 000,000,000,000.) 紙馬克是蓋照市價兌現者也）反之國庫充盈,儘有餘力以兌現,則雖跌價已久,政府常願用面價兌現,所以維持其信用也.故十九世紀初葉,英政府發行紙幣以充戰費,幣價跌至百分之六十.（卽百鎊祗值金六十鎊左右）而一八一五年,拿破崙敗後,英國商業漸盛,卒能照面價兌現,以維固政府之信用.英國綠背劵亦然.發行至四萬三千三百萬之巨.物價指數自一八六〇年至一八六五年五年之間,自一〇〇增至二二〇.卽綠背劵二百二十元祗值現金一百元.是跌價至百分之四五.四五矣.而卒以工商發達,得於一八七九年,宣告綠背劵與金幣並價行使.是發行後閱十有九年,仍以面價兌現者也.此皆視政府財力之盈虛,以定兌現之方針.跌價久暫非所計矣.

不特此也,政府於兌換時猶須防投機者之漁利.我國之銅元票,與濫發之銅元,其著例也.苟銅元多而價跌一元可兌四百枚,或四百枚之銅元票.政府如有意收回,宜告二百銅元兌現金一元,則販夫小卒,似可大蒙其恩矣.不知操縱其間,有市儈焉,聞有兌換消息,將盡力以賤價收買銅元,即稍昂其價,亦願收受而販夫小卒,未之知也.見收買之價稍昂,且欲爭向兌換.詎知大利之在市儈手乎.彼以賤價兌進,政府則以高價向之收回,是繼富而非濟窮也耗財而非恤民也.故政府果有力收回銅幣,則寧用市價付現.此又與銀元紙幣之兌現不同也.

紙幣跌價之爲害,舉世殆咸知之矣.故歐戰時英美兩國皆以租稅公債爲挹注.英國戰費,租稅佔四分之一,公債佔四分之三.美國戰費,租稅佔三分之一.公債佔三分之二.良以欲免紙幣之危險,與夫收回之困難,惟有另闢途徑,不發無擔保之紙幣而已.與其受困於後,莫若慎之於先.英美戰時財政,洵不可及哉,雖然,非平日稅制完善,工商發達,又曷克臻此？法國創巨痛深,紙幣日跌兌現無方,羅掘俱窮,此則最可憂者也.然則平日財政,可不加之意乎.

我國鬃業之回顧

From Economic Monthly

施彥聖

鬃爲製刷原料.歐戰以前.波蘭芬蘭輸出最多,我國次之.芬蘭產鬃質堅不易撓曲.製刷最宜.華鬃除四川產品外.要皆質地柔軟.每年輸出約計海關銀四百四十萬兩.此大戰前之商情也.戰時我國輸出最多.年計海關銀約五六百萬兩.戰後銷路不暢.降至四百五十萬兩.但一九二二年仍升至六百二十萬兩.其時銷數達六萬七千擔.

國內各地,多畜牧豕.是以猪鬃產地.幾徧國中.年產若干頗難核算.約數爲十萬擔.三分之二銷售外國.餘供國內之用.其中百分之九十爲黑鬃.產於滿洲及華北一帶者計三萬五千擔.產於揚子流域者計二萬五千擔.而產於廣東者計一萬五千擔.百分之十爲白鬃.產於河南及四川等省.

天津輸出最多.漢口重慶次之.

輸出擔數

	一九一八年	一九一九年	一九二〇年	一九二一年	一九二二年
天津	二〇二六五	一五一七八	一八八〇二	一四一七八	二〇七二四
漢口	一七一七四	一三七七七	一五六五一	七八四〇	一五四一〇
重慶	一五一二五	一一二八五	一〇一六三	一〇〇〇八	一四六七九
九龍	一六四一	二五四	四〇七	一四二	一八九
其餘	一〇二三九	一一二五三	一三九一八	九九一一	一七六二五
統計	六四四五四	五三九二七	五八九四一	四二〇七九	六七六二七

天津附近爲各莊.爲鬃業之中心.凡鬃之產於滿洲東蒙古熱河朝陽直隸及山西各地者.悉運輸至此.以便轉送各處.中有一小部分.運送大連牛莊.由此直接運往歐美.晚近洋商在奉天境內設立鬃場數處.專營清潔及分類等事.將來鬃業之發達.或能駕天津而上之.

天津產鬃.大別爲三種.卽高尖鬃青鬃及毛鬃是.其長度高尖鬃達四五英寸.青鬃凡二三英寸.毛鬃品類最雜.色澤尤繁.如須運往外洋.必重爲分類裝置.上貨長凡二又四分一英寸達五英寸.長短相等之鬃.搜集裝納於一箱.其次者長短不齊.均在三英寸之下.市價僅及上貨之半.

漢口亦爲鬃業之中心.冬季銷貨最旺.凡湖南四川河南山西諸省.委貨悉於此時交卸.概由各行預先訂約承受.訂合同時.先付貨價二成.餘俟交貨時付清.

鬃之分類以長短爲標準每差半英寸列爲一類上貨價值約較次貨高出海關銀八十兩.一九二二年四月份公報載二寸鬃每擔售銀五十兩.二寸半鬃一百五十五兩.三寸鬃二百卅五兩.三寸半鬃三百十兩.

河南鬃質地最劣.色白.較黑鬃爲短.銷路不甚旺.年僅二千擔.運往漢口

者.不問長短一并裝置箱中.二英寸者佔二成五.二英寸半者如之.三英寸者一成五.其餘三成五或爲三英寸五英寸不等.

川鬃質地純良.爲各鬃之冠.富彈性而具色澤.白鬃品質之優.舉國無與倫比.每年出產統計.黑鬃約萬五千或二萬擔.白鬃約萬五六千擔.假道重慶輸出者計萬擔.其餘并運澳口.本地所用者.僅極短之鬃.

白鬃產於榮昌隆昌,合江,及瀘州,諸地.黑鬃則川省各地.無不產之.成都重慶附近所產尤豐.

雲南貴州鬃亦假道川省輸運外省.雲貴產鬃.有生熟二種.生鬃以長短或所含水分或雜質之多寡.再分爲原莊,提莊,尖子,及飛尾,四種.

出口公司購就熟鬃.再行分類.再用麻囊布捆紮.厚凡二英寸.每箱可容一擔.箱底墊以油紙或錫紙.每箱內鬃之長短分配.悉遵商業習慣.法詳下列甲乙二表.

(甲) 白鬃種類

鬃之長短	甲	乙	丙	丁	戊	己
五寸半或較長	百成					
五寸四一		四十成				
五寸		六十成				
四寸半或四三			四十成			
四寸或四一			六十成			
三寸半				五十成		
三寸四三				五十成		
三寸					五十成	
二寸四一					五十成	
三寸四三或較短						百成

(乙) 黑鬃種類

纜之長短	甲	乙	丙	丁
二寸	二十成	二十成	廿五成	三十成
二寸四一	五成	十成	十五成	廿五成
二寸半	十五成	十成	十二成	廿成
二寸四三	八成	八成	十一成	十五成
三寸	八成	八成	十成	十成
五寸四三	廿二成	廿二成	十三成	
六寸	廿二成	廿二成	十四成	
共計	百成	百成	百成	百成

（完）

電氣傳影之新發明

趙曾珏

電氣之在二十世紀,洵有一日千里,愈演愈巧之勢.昔日所理想而不能實現者,今乃漸成事實.世界文明,人羣進化,電氣實具豐功.最近美國電話電報公司（The American Telephone & Telegraph Co.）及西方電氣公司(Western Electric Co.)得試驗成功,以電話線傳達照片.益徵電氣之萬能.本年五月十九號下午,在美國屋海屋省之克利夫蘭城（Cleveland, Ohio State）所攝七寸長之照片,在五分鐘內,而由電綫傳至紐約城.實爲電氣界極有價值之發明.

傳影之法頗爲簡捷.凡普通照相之軟片,悉可用以傳遞.傳達之時,以已攝過之軟片插于傳遞機內,由圓桶轉動之.當軟片盤旋之際.乃以一縷強光引射于軟片上,成爲一細點.軟片盤旋于此光點之下,一若留聲機唱片之迴旋于發音針下.當光線射經軟片之際,因軟片色澤之深淺,而定其光度之強弱.傳遞照片之主要器械.爲傳影電池 (Photoelectric Cell),後當詳述.此電池置于已經軟片之光線內,一依光度之強弱,而變更其電流之力量.如照中白晰之處,則光綫易過而電流乃增強.如照中黑暗之處,光線不易經過,電流乃轉弱.惟電池所生之電甚微,不能傳過長距離之電綫;故須以直流電眞空管放大器（D. C. Vacuum Tube Amplifier）放大之,然後經眞空管調波器（Vacuum Tube Modulator）調節之,而達于電話線上傳至收影之一端.

收影之端,乃以一未經攝過之軟片,盤旋轉動於一縷光線之下.光度之強弱乃由電話線傳來之電流而變更.惟收影及發影兩端之軟片,均須轉運于同樣之速度（另以一特製之節制機節制之,）然光度能隨電流而變更.電流能隨光度而轉強弱,則全恃傳影電池,又名光之活瓣(Light Valve).

傳影電池頗似兩極眞空管 (2-electrode Vacuum Tube). 其作用乃由海時 (Heinrich Hertz) 于一八八七年發現.海時曾發明電浪, (Electric Waves) 實爲無綫電之祖師.彼于試驗電浪之時,覺火花(Electric spark)生于鋅質火花隙上 (Zinc spark gap),如以某種亮光照之,其發生較在暗中爲易.後乃考得此種現狀,乃由于火花片所發射之電子(Electrons),經紫微光 (Ultra-Violet Light) 照之,可增其四周眞空之傳導度 (Conductivity). 金屬物,如鈉及鉀,經普通光綫照之,亦呈此現象.惟其他金屬則須紫微光照之,始呈同樣之現象.

傳影電池之兩電極 (Electrodes) 置于眞空器內.其一極乃以鈉或鉀所製,他極則以任何傳導體製之.當光力射于鈉或鉀極上,電子乃由第一極而發射于眞空中.如第二極上加以正電壓 (Positive Potential), 電子遂吸引至彼端而成電流.惟電子之量悉依光力而變動,故電流之強弱亦隨光度之強弱而變更.惟變更之電每嫌太弱,故須以放大器增強之,而後傳出.此爲傳影電池在發影一端之作用.在收影之端,其作用適相反.蓋收影之際,先有電流,而後變更光度,而後由此變動之光射于未經攝過之軟片上.光度之深淺隨發影端所傳之電而變動.收影軟片經此一度之照射,乃加以沖晒,一若普通已攝之軟片.而發影端之影像乃重現.

電傳照片之術頗合實用.不特其所傳之影明晰,且傳遞便捷,各種電話綫均可採用.且歷經試驗,此法可行之于無綫電中.此次成功,倍而式.(Bell System)電話工程師實費數載之經營.至于將來之發展,全賴社會之需要.惟目前所預定之用途已屬不鮮.例如傳達工程上之圖樣及商務文契上之花押等.他若犯人及罪魁等之照片,均可立時(不過數分鐘)傳遞,使無逃法網,則又能助法律之進行矣.

是篇譯自一九二四年八月號美國科學雜誌(The Scientific American).惟爲便利讀者了解起見,文字方面略有更動.讀者如參看原文,當知其不盡相同也. 譯者附誌

無線電對於軍事上效用之重要

方子衛

軍用通信法.以有效力的組織爲要.人皆知之.以下所論.乃用無綫電報電話以補充或代替以前所用之方法.至於舊時通信法.可分爲二大類.一爲可見之信號.如燈號旗語等.二爲有綫電報電話用暫時或永久電綫相接者.

『可見信號』之唯一利益爲適便.但其所達之距離甚短.且近敵處.易爲所見.轉爲炮火之的.故其用有限.

陸綫電報電話.則不爲距離所限.可於小面積內與多處接綫.並可組織一中央接綫處.如商用電報電話然.

陸軍總司令部必常設於一適中地點.電綫則可埋於地下.如此可不爲敵之炮火所燬.且可避免暴風.及其他意外之損壞.但軍事行動時.得安然埋於地下之機會甚少.故不得不設法架置於沿途便利之樹枝,或木桿上.因此常受外界損害.而有中斷之虞.

無綫電報電話由無形之路徑.以供軍事通信.苟有完全可恃而又便於

攜帶之機具.則可免去陸綫法之弊.蓋通信之兩端.既不用人工接綫.無論何地均可設立通信.而收同等之效果.

如軍艦與潛艇在海洋中.可用暗碼互通信息.蓋軍艦潛艇關係軍事.至重且大.萬一遇敵.即可發信求援於鄰近軍艦.他若空中飛機與陸地.飛機與飛機.船隻與海岸.軍車與大本營.炮場與測量台.及中隔敵軍勢力之兩端.或天然阻隔間之通信.無一不可.

雖然.使敵方亦設一無綫電收信機.則信號不將被抄錄而洩漏秘密乎.此不難以密碼或更換電浪長度.及單向法.俾不與敵方相同等方法以解決之也.且軍事通信重在迅速.若敵方不能解釋詞意.而立即報告於相當關係部分者.過後雖知亦歸無用矣.

凡兩軍交鋒.常決勝於主將指揮之靈敏與否.欲指揮靈敏.全賴消息靈通.無綫電利用空中以太(Ether)傳播電浪達於四方.無長途傳導綫.祇須雙方有兩副機器而已.其便利於軍事.誠非有綫電所能比擬.且軍用無綫電較陸地收發商報之無線電尤爲簡單.全副收報機一馬負之可以捷足而驅.若于主將所在地設較大之無線電台.而以較小之電台分配於前敵重要地點.則主將雖離前敵千里.其發號施令.或報告前敵軍情.瞬息間.可以立至.他如對於海軍方面.昔日兩艦談話.晝用旗語.夜用燈語.且其效能僅限於數十里之內.百里之外非所能也.若大霧迷天.山島中梗.則旗語燈語.失其效力.近日三四萬噸之巨艦.可以配置能及一二千里信號之無線電機.大海反足以增加其發信距離.山島亦不能阻礙之.海軍多一無線電機.不啻多一耳目也.

哲學與科學之定義

蘇　民

易言形而上者謂之道.形而下者謂之器.解之者曰莊周論道術裂而後有方術.形上之學.道術也.形下之學.方術也.道術則無所不統.方術則各明一

理.盡力於道術,得其全者曰儒.致功於方術,得其偏者曰伎.儒,哲學也.伎,科學也.愚謂邃古之談哲學者,莫備於易.繫辭伏羲氏之王天下焉.仰則觀象於天,俯則觀法於地.觀鳥獸之文,與地之宜.近取諸身.遠取諸物.於是始作八卦.以通神明之德.以類萬物之情.夫曰通神明之德者,形上之學.即所謂道也.類萬物之情者,形下之學.即所謂器也.故下文云作結繩而爲網罟.以佃以漁.蓋取諸離.伏羲氏歿.由神農黃帝以至於堯舜.所謂通神明.類萬物.遞演而遞進.故神農氏作.斲木爲耜.揉木爲耒.耒耜之利.以教天下.蓋取諸益.神農氏歿.黃帝堯舜氏作.刳木爲舟.剡木爲楫.舟楫之利.以濟不通.蓋取諸渙.服牛乘馬.引重致遠.以利天下.蓋取諸隨.斷木爲杵.掘地爲臼.臼杵之利.萬民以濟.蓋取諸小過.弦木爲弧.剡木爲矢.弧矢之利.以威天下.蓋取諸睽.此則制器取象而爲形下之學.且不啻與後世科學家以歸納試驗之機能.亦既班班可考矣.繫辭又言黃帝堯舜通其變,使民不倦.神而化之,使民宜之.通變神化,皆爲形上之道.而一切形形色色.均包含於道體之中,而莫或外也.大學言致知在格物.物格而后知止.是通乎道者,變其體即足以致用.非謂形而下者之必不能通乎道也.宋儒釋格物致知之義.言所謂致知在格物者,言欲致我之知.在即物而窮其理也.蓋天下之人,莫不有知,而天下之物.莫不有理.惟其理有未窮.故其知有不盡.是以必使學者即凡天下之物.因其已知之理而益窮之.以求至乎其極.至於用力之久.而一旦豁然貫通.則衆物之表裏精粗無不到.而我心之全體大用無不明.是則道術之中,方術備也.是說焉.非即盡力於道術,得其全者曰儒之謂乎.孔子讀易.韋編三絕.而於物無所不通.此則物格知止之學,惟孔子有之.可謂科學之導師.而實則哲學家之先進也.斯賓塞之言曰世所謂下學,不備之學也.科學,偏備之學也.哲學,全備之學也 Knowledge of Lowest Kind is un-unified Knowledge. Science is Partially unified Knowledge. Philosophy is completely unified Knowledge. 蓋科學之原理,無不出於哲學.及其日趨於精微,乃離哲學而獨立.是說焉,非即致功於方術,得其偏者曰伎之謂乎.今則儒之與伎,姑不具論.而科學之實自哲學而分.哲學之包含科學所有,詢不誣謬.試再分別論之.

論語言志於道.據於德.依於仁.游於藝.所謂道者,天道也.地道也.人道也.通天地人之謂儒.萬事萬物之殊,以一理貫之.此道之所以大也.德訓爲得.有得於心.則萬事萬物之理,融會貫通.而不喪其所守.仁訓爲愛.人孰不愛其身.推己之心以及於人.知盡人之可愛.更推而至於造物生生不息之義.知禽獸草木.皆宜遂其生機,而不可故事戕賊.是即孟氏所謂親親而仁民.仁民而愛物也.藝之包含者甚廣.朱氏以禮樂射御書數釋之.未足盡其所有也.農圃醫卜.皆屬於藝.近今卜筮之書不多見.而農醫兩門,且別爲專科.著書立說.發揮新理.視爲重要之科學.而當時則目之爲小道.然則即萬事萬物之理,融會貫通.而不喪其所守.其所謂德.即其所謂道,志於道.據於德.依於仁.游於藝.茲四端者所謂道術之中,有方術.而科學之原理,無不出於哲學也.孔子不爲科學家言.故兩童子論日而不贊一詞.樊遲請學稼.而曰不如老農.顧其謂曾子曰,吾道一以貫之.一者,理也.萬事萬物衆矣.雖不必強其異者而使之同.然以我之知.研究事物之理而會其通.則即小以見大.因微以知著.考之近時,科學進步,一日千里.究其所以如此者,亦無非即其已知之理而益窮之.於是物質文明遂日新月異而歲不同.溫故知新之說.不啻爲科學家發其覆.然孔子則並非爲科學家言也.其意若曰,齊家治國平天下之道廣矣.即一名一物之微.足以致我之知者,皆當盡力研究,變而通之.神而化之.有得於心,而能發前人之所未發者,即可以爲人師.此哲學之定義也.

社會事變之推遷.莫不有自然之現象.即其自然之現象而研究之.以求其眞理之所在.眞理既明.實用亦隨之而見.故科學之方法.以闡然現象,爲研究之材料.以增進知識爲指歸.故洛紂培根弗蘭西斯培根之徒之言曰.非格物何以致知.吾當精吾歸納之術.竭吾試驗之能.以闡自然界之秘蘊而已.
If knowledge can only be obtained by researches I shall sharpen my inductive

reasoning and supplement it with experiments so that I may plunge in to the secrecy of nature. 夫引經据典.以推勘事物之理.較若可信矣.顧不加之以實驗.則過去事物之通理.仍為一己之意象.準確與錯誤.無由而判斷.洪範之言五行也.水曰潤下.火曰炎上.木曰曲直.金曰從革.土爰稼穡.潤下作鹹.炎上作苦.曲直作酸.從革作辛.稼穡作甘.此則有科學之原理存也.中土之人.沿用其說而未聞有實驗之者.是以知其然而不知其所以然.夫空氣可以製礮.行之於天然界已不知其幾千萬年.而得之於試驗室.不過晚近事耳.(見科學通論)於此可見吾國人向無實驗之學也.雖然實驗之原始.根基於觀念.觀念之發生.根基於事物.苟無事物以為佐證.則其觀念.即為懸揣虛擬而無科學之價值.如重力之發明始於墜果.汽機之發明始於蒸汽之動壺蓋.苟不善用其觀念.則蘋果之墜.壺蓋之動.亦在莫知所以然之數.厄斯台特於講室中以銅線導電.線下磁針忽自轉動.因悟磁針引電之理.後人闡其義蘊.遂造成今日橫繞地球二百五十周之電線.蓋為學之要.在發展學者之本能.與以適當之訓練.使事物之新理.用正確之方法.為獨立之研究.即哲學家所謂因其已知之理而益窮之.以求至乎其極之意.故即其自然之現象而研究之.以求其真理之所在.真理既明.實用亦隨之而見.此科學之定義也.

四庫全書述畧

杜定友

四庫全書為我國最近最富之智識府庫.因部數太少.又多零落不全.國人能讀能用是書者.固甚尠.即明瞭是書之概略者.亦不多.吾友杜君定友.游學歸來.固留心國故.近於百城坐擁牙籤檢點之暇.著四庫全書述略一篇.明白簡要.誠人人必讀之文.爰為序而布之.紹興柴騁陸.

源流第一

我國藏書.代稱盛典.自秦火而還.民間典籍.蕩然無存.册府之藏.不絕如

錄.〔漢興,改秦之敗,大收篇籍,廣開獻書之路.迄孝武世,書缺簡脫,禮壞樂崩.於是建藏書之策,置寫書之官.下及諸子傳說,皆充祕府.至成帝時,以書頗散亡,使謁者陳農求遺書於天下.詔光祿大夫劉向校經傳諸子詩賦,步兵校尉任宏校兵書,太史令尹咸校數術,侍醫李柱國校方技.每一書已,向輒條其篇目,撮其指意,錄而奏之.會向卒,哀帝復使向子侍中奉車都尉歆,卒父業.歆於是總羣書,而奏其七略.〕㊀是爲中國目錄學之始祖.書凡三萬三千〇九十卷.後經王莽之亂,焚燒無遺.

東漢光武中興,篤好文雅.肴班固校書東觀,編漢書藝文志.固乃本七略刪繁就簡,以備篇册.並〔詔諸儒正定五經,刊於石碑.爲古文,篆,隸,三體書法,以相參檢.樹之學門,使天下咸取則焉.〕㊁其時有辟雍,東觀,蘭台,石室,宣明,鴻都,諸藏,蔚爲大觀.今七略已亡,漢志猶存.撫覽殘篇,尙可追念古代國家藏書嘉惠士林之盛.惜其書經長安之亂,焚蕩泯盡.

其後魏有中經新簿.晉有四部目錄.王儉依七略,而撰七志.阮孝緒參校官簿,更爲七錄.隋初,牛弘上表,請開獻書之路,從之.唐代藏書,盛於開元.其著錄者,凡五萬三千九百十五卷.唐之學者,自爲之書,又二萬八千四百六十九卷.可謂盛矣.

後唐長興三年二月,中書門下,奏請刊刻九經,以廣流傳.〔敕令國子監集博士儒徒,將西京石經本,各以所業本經句度,鈔寫註出,子細看讀.然後顧召能彫字匠人,各部隨帙刻印板,廣頒天下.〕㊂又五代時馮道始奏請官鏤板印行監本五經.是爲官書頒佈之始.

宋初三館,有書萬餘卷.後改建爲崇文院.倣開元四部錄,爲崇文總目.慶曆初成書,凡三萬〇六百六十九卷.淳熙四年,祕書少監陳騤等以中興館閣藏書,前後搜訪.部帙漸廣.仿崇文總目類次.凡四萬四千四百八十六卷.嘉定十三年,又得一萬四千九百四十三卷.㊃

金元藏書,無足述者.

明永樂五年，命解縉纂集類書，爲文獻大全．已而嫌其未備，乃命姚廣孝等重修．書成，凡二萬二千九百三十七卷，賜名永樂大典．依韻編例最爲浩博㊄是爲官編類書巨著之一．其影響於中國文化至巨．惜今全書散亡．至當時藏書，以文淵閣爲最．約二萬餘部，近百萬卷，刻本十三，抄本十七．㊅

清滿族入關．未遑文治，康熙命儒臣廣羅羣籍，分別門類統爲一書．曰圖書集成．初由陳夢雷編纂，繼由蔣廷錫重加編校〔凡欽定三千餘卷，增圖數十萬言．圖繪精審，攷定詳悉．列爲六編，析爲卅二典．其部六千餘，其卷一萬．〕㊆

總觀歷代藏書，卷帙浩繁．上行下效，推稱盛事．祕閣中書，其動機雖不免於文飾，而影響文化，亦云至巨．永樂大典圖書集成，尤爲空前巨製，關係學術至乾隆初年卽詔令搜集中外遺書，校勘十三經二十一史，以編布黌宮，嘉惠後學．又開館編修綱目，三編通鑑輯覽及三通諸書．又整藏舊板書籍，宋金元明版本，彙爲天祿琳瑯，藏於昭仁殿．〔凡藝林承學之士所當戶誦家絃者，既已薈萃各備．〕㊇是皆受歷代莊書刊書之影響也．而影響最大者，莫若四庫全書．

乾隆以〔康熙所修圖書集成，全部兼收並錄，極方策之大觀．引用諸書編者率屬因類取裁，勢不能悉載全文，使閱者沿流溯源，一一徵其來處．今內府藏書插架，不爲不富，然古今來著作之手，無慮數千百家．或逸在名山，未登柱史，正宜及時採集，彙送京師，以彰千古同文之盛．〕㊈是搜集四庫全書之始也．

又以永樂大典蕪雜不當因有纂修之議．林謂〔乾隆三十八年，癸巳正月．安徽學政朱筠，奏搜採永樂大典及提要之法，遂得旨允行．命出內府所藏祕籍，分司校閱……再按李光地年譜，載康熙二十六年，光地奏秦漢以後，經壞東崩．六經雖經宋儒闡明，然永樂間所修大典，未免蕪雜疏漏．宜大徵天下之士，蒐羅羣書，討論編纂．然則搜採永樂大典，修輯全書之舉，光地已發於先〕㊉

乾隆因命校永樂大典，並成八韻示意，序曰「翰林院署庋有永樂大典一書，蓋自皇史宬移貯者，初不知其名也。比以搜訪遺籍，安徽學政朱筠以校錄是書為請，廷議允行。奏既上，勅取首函以進。見其採掇蒐羅，極為浩博。且中多世不經見之書，雖原冊亡什之一，固不足為全體累也。第彼則部區函，寧雜貪多務得，細大不捐，而編韻分字，踳駁不倫。由當時領書局者，惟一姚廣孝，因而濫引緇流，遂其猥瑣之識，雅俗並陳，舉釋典道經，悉為闌入。其奚當於古柱下史，藏書之義乎？因命內廷大學士等為總裁，揄選翰林官三十人，分司校勘。先為發凡起例，俾識所從事。蕪者芟之，龐者釐之，散者裒之，完善者存之。已流傳者弗再登，言二氏者在所擯。取精擇醇，依經史子集為部次。俟其成，付之剞劂。當以四庫全書名之。夫「四庫」之目，始於荀勗，而盛於唐時。自來志藝文者，大都以是為準。較原書斤斤於韻字之末者，純駁何啻霄壤。於以廣金匱石室之儲，用嘉來學，詎非萬世書林之津逮，而表章闕佚之餘，為之正其名而訂其失，又詎非是書之大幸乎！」⑪是則四庫全書纂編之源流及其動機，已具見於此矣。

---

① 班固 漢書藝文志序

② 馬端臨 文獻通考卷一百十四經籍考

③ 王溥 五代會要卷八經籍

④ 見 欽定續文獻通考卷一百四十一經籍

⑤ 聞北京大學圖書館長袁同禮先生著有關於永樂大典一文

⑥ 張廷玉 明史藝文志一

⑦ 圖書集成雍正四年序

⑧ 乾隆三十七年正月四日諭 見四庫全書總目卷首下倣此

⑨ 仝上

⑩ 林鶴年 四庫全書表文箋釋卷二第七頁

⑪ 乾隆御製詩四集卷十一

指意第二

清以異族入主中國.奠定之初,未遑文治.後經康熙六十一年之建設,雍正十三年之整飭,而逮乾隆六十年太平之治.得以優遊於藝林.故一開博學鴻詞科,再開陽城馬周科,三開經學科.雖云崇獎文學,亦所以收拾漢士大夫之心.至如四庫全書之修纂,五經試題之更改,皆不免有粉飾張皇之意.㊀明因遷京,而纂永樂大典.康熙欲消弭異族之見,而編圖書集成,其意亦在斯乎?清初文字之獄頻興,㊁其拑制言論之自由,至矣盡矣.乃尤慮民間著述尚有譏貶朝廷者,故大搜羣書.假石文稽古之美名,而逞秦政焚書之故智.證之光宣間,章一山喻長霖之奏議,謂〔四庫全書告成已百卅餘年,海內文字孳亂滋多,歐化西來,經涂益闢.曾奏請續開四庫全書館,明定宗旨,力排異議,以齊一天下之耳目,庶幾邪說或可稍熄.〕㊂則其編纂四庫全書之意旨,概可想見.當時藏書之家,昧於榮利,爭相趨奉.以至慷慨激昂之作,悉遭燒燬湮滅之例.然因此以保存諸家之說,而垂永久者,亦不可勝算.於我國文化學術,亦大有功焉.

據乾隆本旨,則謂〔方今文治光昭,典籍大備.恐名山石室,儲蓄尚多.用是廣為蒐輯,俾無遺佚.冀以闡疑補闕.所有進到各遺書,並交總裁等同永樂大典內現有各種,詳加核勘,分別刊鈔.擇其中有益於世道人心者,壽之梨棗,以廣流傳.餘則選派謄錄,彙繕成編,陳之冊府.其中有俚淺訛謬者,止存書名,彙為總目,以彰右文之盛.此採擇四庫全書之本旨也.〕㊃其言之成理,持之有故.雖為文飾之詞,亦足見搜羅之廣,典藏之盛.

茲採擇表文數聯,以見其內容意旨之一斑.

〔惟全書之浩博實括羣言,合衆手以經營條遂竣成……經崇世教貴實徵而賤虛談.史繫人心削誣詞而存公論.選諸子百家之粹博收而不悖聖賢.懲十八九集之非歸汰而需拘門戶.上沿虞夏咸挹海以求珠.下採元明各披沙而見寶……包千齡而建極道出於天.綜百氏以歸型言表諸聖……六千籤琛分圭合延閣儲珍二百卷部次州居崇文列目.水四瀛而山五嶽侔此壯觀前千古而後萬年無斯巨帙!」

㊀參攷　劉法曾清史纂要第七十三至七十四頁

㊁參攷　捫蝨談虎客近世中國秘史第一編第卅五至一百〇四頁

㊂林鶴年　四庫全書表文箋釋自敍

㊃乾隆三十八年五月十七日諭

職官第三

四庫全書館,以乾隆三十八年開館,職官凡三百五十六人,鈔錄凡千五百八.玆略舉如右,以見盛況.

總裁官　皇六子多羅質郡王　永瑢等二十八人

總纂官　文淵閣直閣事兵部侍郎　紀昀等三人

提調官　日講起居注官司經局洗馬　夢吉等三十一人

協勘總目官　文淵閣校理原任洗馬候補侍講　劉權之等七人

纂修官　日講起居注又淵閣校理左春坊左庶子　邵晉涵等五十三人

天文算法纂修官　欽天監中官　郭長發等三人

收掌官　翰林院筆帖　安盛額等三十八人

總閱官　經筵講官禮部尚書兼管樂部太常寺鴻臚寺事務　德保

覆校官　中允銜翰林院編修　王燕緒等四人

分校官　日講起居注官右春坊右中允　張曾勷等一百八十人

篆隸分校官　翰林院庶吉士　王念孫等二人

繪圖分校官　工部員外郎　門應兆

編文責簽考證官　候補國子監司業　王太岳等二人

督催官　翰林院編修　祥慶

監造官　內部府郎中兼佐領　劉淳等三人

修纂時,每書發交館臣首貼一紙.翰林院儲存底本,往往見之.其式如下:

第　　卷底本　十　頁

武英殿於　　月　　日發出

分校處於　　月　　日發出　　處發交謄錄　　寫成

十　頁於　　月　　日收到寫本於　　月　　日校畢交覆

收訖

覆校處於　　月　　日收於　　月　　日　　覆校畢交

殿

此卷計　萬　千　百　十　字

連前共交過　　萬　千　百　十　字

〔按右式所載收發校謄錄等名目開報時皆設有專官.總校分校,以翰林編檢爲之.又有繕書處總校官分校官,則翰林六部郞中主事內閣中書國子監學錄皆有其人.至繕書處收掌官,則中科中書國子監典簿學正等.武英殿收掌官,僅各部筆帖式,無大臣也〕㊀

㊀ 葉德輝　書林清話卷九第十至十一頁

編校第四

自開館搜訪遺書,各省進到者,絡繹不絕.當時進書情形極爲踴躍.表文云:〔十行丹詔徧徵汲古之家七,錄緗囊廣啓獻書之路.遂經斷簡出自大航,雜卦殘篇發從老屋.錦帆捩舵孟家東洛之船,玉軑飛軨吳氏西齋之軸.鱗排玉字多王粲之所未聞,筍束金繩卒張華之所莫識.〕車水馬龍,可謂盛矣!

所有進到之書.如係絕本.則鈔錄後,發還原人.俾保其世守.凡藏書滿百種以上者,稱爲藏書之家.即將其姓名,附載於各書提要之末,以示不忘.其進書六七百種以上者,賚賞古今圖書集成一部,以爲好古之勸.其進百種以上者,贈內府爲印佩文韻府一部.其他各書,均有御題詩文於卷首,交還原獻書

入,以爲紀念.㊀

至於採購手續,命羣臣〔取其歷代傳作留書,內有闡明性學治法,關繫世道人心者,自當首先購覓.至若發揮傳注,攷覈典章,旁暨九作百家之言,有裨實用者,亦應備爲甄擇.又如歷代名人,洎本朝士林宿望,向有詩文專集.及近時沈潛經史,原本風雅,如顧棟高陳祖范任啓運沈德潛輩,亦各著成編.並非勦說卮言可比.均應概行査明.在坊肆者,或是爲給價.客藏者.或官爲裝印.其有未經鐫刊,祇係鈔本存留者,不妨繕錄副本.……先將各書敍列目錄注係某朝某人所著？書中要旨何在？簡明開載,具摺奏聞.候彙齊後,令廷臣檢覈.有堪備閱者,再開單行知取進.庶幾副在石渠,用儲一覽.從此四庫七略,益昭美備.〕㊁

各書收到後,均一一辨厥妍媸,嚴爲去取.其上者,悉登編錄罔致遺珠.其次者,亦長短兼臚,見瑕瑜之不掩.其有言非立訓義或違經,則附載其名,兼匡厥繆.至於尋常著述,未越羣流,雖咎譽之咸無,究流傳之已久,準諸家著錄之例,亦併存其目以備考核.㊂其中有明季諸人書集,詞意牴觸朝廷者,則盡行銷燬.但亦有祇改一二語,而不忍並從焚棄,致令湮沒不彰者.若其人品誼未醇,而其建一言陳一musiwas,切中利病有裨時政者.亦不可以人廢言.其中詳加釐訂,然費斟酌.故云〔筆削權衡,務求精當.使綱舉目張,體裁醇備,足爲萬世法,即後之好論辨者,無從置議,方爲盡善.〕㊃但此亦片面之詞,書中有應收而不收,有不應收而收者.有應改而不改,有不應改而改者,亦頗足訾議.

每書提編之後,必將大旨評於簡端.奏問裁奪.其應鈔應刊,亦次第呈閱乾隆親爲批覽.故表文曰〔凡皆詞臣之奏進,誤點丹黃一經聖主之品題立分黑白.……凡茲獨斷,咸稟睿裁.懿此闓情,實孚公義.〕

當時編纂諸臣,頗極忙碌.所謂〔程材效技各一一而使吹,累牘連篇遂多多而益辦.香霏䜿惡擁書何止百城,潘積嚼嚌剏業甯惟兩屋？……鯨鐘力警啓蓬館以晨登,鵠籥嚴關焚藜膏以夜繼.〕㊄其間情形概可想見矣.

㊀見乾隆三十八年五月十四日十七日及三十九年二十五日諭

㊁乾隆三十七年正月四日諭

㊂四庫全書總目凡例三

㊃乾隆四十六年二月十五日諭

㊄見表文

纂次第五

四庫全書編校次弟,先校天祿琳瑯舊藏之書,以擇其善本.次校圖書集成,擇其未經採錄,而實在流傳已久,尚可裒輯成編者.次校永樂大典.因原編體例,以韶編次,先已割裂全文,首尾難期貫串.但因當時採撫甚博,其中或有古書善本,世不恆見者,則就各門彙訂,可以湊合成部者,以廣名山石室之藏.次校各省呈進之書,嚴覈貶以定去取,此校書之次弟也.

纂書,先纂四庫全書薈要.於全書中,擇其尤醇者;經一百七十三種,史七十種,子八十二種,集一百三十九種.所取纂精,視全書不及十之三.每書前均有提要,凡一萬二千册.八年而成.凡二分,一貯大內摛藻堂,己亥告成.一貯御園味腴書室.庚子告成.次纂四庫全書總目提要.總目之中於經史子集內,外著錄存目二種各書條下,俱經撰有提要.將一書原委撮舉大凡.并詳著書人世次爵里,可以一覽了然.較之崇文總目蒐羅既廣,體例加詳.惟提要於各書內容,多語焉不詳,是其缺點.(逐篇奏御,仰承親定.告成之曰,彙爲總目二百卷,其中考辨繁賾,引徵明確,可爲學海津梁.)㊀次纂四庫全書簡明目錄以(四庫全書總目提要多至萬餘種,卷帙甚繁.將來鈔刊成書,繙閱頗爲不易自應於提要之外,另刊簡明書目一篇.……俾學者由書目而尋提要,由提要而得全書)㊁書成,都二百卷.此纂書之次第也.

㊀欽定皇朝通志卷一百〇五第一頁

㊁乾隆三十九年七月二十五日諭

類例第六

四庫全書卷帙浩繁.編列目錄例先分類.乾隆以〔從來四庫書目,自以經史子集爲綱領,裒輯分儲,實古今不易之法〕㊀故四庫全書即以經史子集四部爲編例.四部之首,各冠以總序.撮述其源作正變,提綱絜領.四部之下,復分四十四類.各類首亦冠以小序,詳述其分合改併之原因.各書之下,復〔一一撰爲提要.分之,則散併諸編.合之,則共爲總目.每書先列作者之爵里,以論世知人.次考本書之得失,權衆說之異同,以及文字增刪.篇帙分合,皆詳爲訂辨,巨細不遺.〕㊁其各部書籍,則依撰述年代列次,然亦間多出入.初纂臣以先列〔欽定〕〔御製〕各書,冠於各部之首,爲請.諭曰:〔四庫全書內,惟集部應以本朝御製詩文集冠首.至經史子三部,仍照例編次不必全以本朝官書爲首.今若於每部內又特標聖義諸名目,雖爲尊崇起見,未免又多增義例……至朕題四庫諸書詩文,若亦另編卷首,將來排列,轉在列聖欽定諸書之前,心尤未安.雖纂校諸臣尊君之意,爲竟似四庫全書之輯,端爲朕詩文而設者然,朕不爲也.〕㊂所言排列次序,自不適於今日.而當時之審愼用詳.可以見矣.

四庫全書計分四部,經史子集.經部分十類.史部分十五類.子部分十四類.集部分五類.其流別繁碎者,又分子目.小學爲三子目.地理爲九子目.傳記爲五子目.政書爲六子目.術數爲六子目.藝術錄譜爲四子目.雜家爲五子目.詞曲爲四子目.使條理分明.類例清晰.其大綱如左:

四庫全書總目

門目

一　經部

1. 易類	卷一至六	存目	卷七至十
2. 書類	卷十一至十二	存目	卷十三至十四
3. 詩類	卷十五至十六	存目	卷十七至十八
4. 禮類		存目	卷二十三至二十五

(1)周禮 卷十九

(2)儀禮 卷二十

(3)禮記 卷二十一

(4)三禮通義卷二十二

(5)通禮 又

(6)雜禮書 又

5. 春秋類 卷二十六至二十九 存目 卷三十至三十一

6. 孝經類 卷三十二 存目 卷三十二

7. 五經說義類卷三十三 存目 卷三十四

8. 四書類 卷三十五至三十六 存目 卷三十七

9. 樂類 卷三十八 存目 卷三十九

10.小學類 存目 卷四十三至四十四

(1)訓詁 卷四十

(2)字書 卷四十一

(3)韶書 卷四十二

二 史部

1. 正史類 卷四十五至四十六 存目 卷四十六

2. 編年類 卷四十七 存目 卷四十八

3. 記事本末類卷四十九 存目 卷四十九

4. 別史類 卷五十 存目 卷五十

5. 雜史類 卷五十一 存目 卷五十二至五十四

6. 詔令奏議類卷五十五 存目 卷五十六

7. 傳記類 存目 卷五十九至六十四

(1)聖賢 卷五十七

(2)名人 又

(3)總錄上	又		
(4)總錄下	卷五十八		
(5)雜錄	又		
8. 史鈔類	卷六十五	存目	卷六十五
9. 載記類	卷六十六	存目	卷六十六
10.時令類	卷六十七	存目	卷六十七
11.地理類		存目	卷七十二至七十八
(1)總志	卷六十八		
(2)都會郡縣	卷六十八		
(3)河渠	卷六十九		
(4)邊防	卷六十九		
(5)山川	卷七十		
(6)古蹟	卷七十		
(7)雜記	卷七十		
(8)遊記	卷七十一		
(9)外記	卷七十一		
12職官類	卷七十九	存目	卷八十
13政書類		存目	卷八十三至八十四
(1)通制	卷八十一		
(2)典禮	卷八十二		
(3)邦計	卷八十二		
(4)軍政	卷八十二		
(5)法令	卷八十二		
(6)營建	卷八十二		
14.目錄類		存目	卷八十七

(1)經籍 卷八十五

(2)金石 卷八十六

15.史評類 卷八十八 存目 卷八十九至九十

三 子部

1. 儒家類 卷九十一至九十四 存目 卷九十五至九十八

2. 兵家類 卷九十九 存目 卷一百

3. 法家類 卷一百一 存目 卷一百一

4. 農家類 卷一百二 存目 卷一百二

5. 醫家類 卷一百三至四 存目 卷一百五

6. 天文算法類 存目 卷一百七

(1)推步 卷一百六

(2)算書 卷一百七

7. 術數類 存目 卷一百十至十一

(1)數學 卷一百八

(2)占候 卷一八百

(3)相宅相墓卷一百九

(4)占卜 卷一百九

(5)命書相書卷一百九

(6)陰陽五行卷一百九

8. 藝術類 存目 卷一百十四

(1)書畫上 卷一百十二

(2)書畫下 卷一百十三

(3)琴譜 卷一百十三

(4)篆刻 卷一百十二

(5)雜技 卷一百十三

9. 譜錄類　　存目　卷一百十六

(1)器用　卷一百十五

(2)食譜　卷一百十五

(3)草木蟲魚 卷一百十五

(4)雜物　卷一百十五

10.雜家　　存目　卷一百十四五三十四

(1)雜學　卷一百十七

(2)雜考　卷一百十八至十九

(3)雜說　卷一百二十至二十二

(4)雜品　卷一百二十三

(5)雜纂　卷一百二十三

(6)雜編　卷一百二十三

11.類書類　卷一百三十五至三十六 存目　卷一百三十七至三十九

12.小說家　　存目　卷一百四十三至四十四

(1)雜事　卷一百四十至四十一

(2)異聞　卷一百四十二

(3)瑣語　卷一百四十二

13.釋家類　卷一百四十五　存目　卷一百四十五

14.道家類　卷一百四十六　存目　卷一百四十七

四　集部

1. 楚辭類　卷一百四十八　存目　卷一百四十八

2. 別集類　卷一百四十八至七十三 存目　卷一百七十四至八十五

3. 總集類　卷一百八十六至九十一 存目　卷一百九十二至九十四

4. 詩文評類　卷一百九十五至九十六 存目　卷一百九十七

5. 詞曲類　卷一百九十八至九十九 存目　卷二百

右四庫全書門目，凡四部四十四類，五十一子目。於從前部次，類多釐訂。庶閱者可以即目求類，即類求書。惟分類書籍，殊多出入。檢查書籍，亦非易易也。故年學誠有曰（部次條別，將以辨章學術，考鏡源流，非深明於道術精微羣言得失之故者，不足與此。）

㊁乾隆三十八年二月十一日諭

㊂四庫全書總目凡例

㊃乾隆四十六年二月十三日諭

化工新志

徐名材

西國工商盛興，得力于利用科學，此其義人人知之。顧吾國講求實學，亦且四五十年，而夷考其實，迄未大獲效用。舊傳藝術，進步未見；新創事業，失利頻聞。碩學相望，而謀生匱絀；富源徧地，而舉國憂貧。衡諸外邦，榮枯迥異。同一不龜手之藥，或以霸，或不免于洴澼絖。豈真西人對于科學，獨得神祕，踰淮成枳，易地勿良耶。東瀛提倡實學，略先于我，而利用厚生，獲效與西國無殊。獨吾國學者為環境所困宥，乏相當之工具，匱碌碌難以展布。達識之士，不察本原，行且以學術為贅旒，而不屑措意。朕端已兆，堪為隱憂。人方學競，我已後人，廢學空談，寧復有幸。記者竊外國之盛況，久深臨淵羨魚之思，慨來日之大難，益增久病蓄艾之想。輒于課暇，集近年來工業新進步若干則，一一考察其本末，諦究其原委，撮取要端，敍述梗概，冀供國人之參證。說理不求高深，措辭惟期共曉。庶使讀者瀏覽之餘，不徒增益異聞，足資茶餘酒後之談助，亦可以窺見西人實學致用之真精神，而知吾國今日欲爭存于世界，舍急起直追，實力提倡無異術也。

一　談人造絲

人造絲輸入日增，漸為國人所注目。絲織界既有限制攙用之約，而浙省又復抽特別捐以資抵制,爲維持原料計,固不得不出于此.但人造絲究用何法製成,過去之經過及未來之趨勢何若,當亦留心國產者所欲聞也.

織物原料,以絲毛棉麻爲主,效用各異,並行不悖.絲毛取材動物,內含淡質.棉麻係植物品,爲纖維質組成.其成分與絲毛截然不同,一經化學方法除去雜質,再加相當藥劑,可以溶化成液.復以壓力穿過微孔,引曳成絲.溶液除去,纖維復舊,紡紗爲線,質等棉紗,色澤鮮明,光逾眞絲.世以其由人工製成,因通稱爲人造絲,實則論其性質,與眞絲迥不相侔也.

人造絲之發明,遠在一千八百八十四年.法人謝鐸諾 (Chardonnet) 首先創製,旋在瑞法兩國先後設廠,沿襲至今,是爲第一法.後六年有載沛氏 (Despeisses) 復發明以銅養及阿麻尼亞溶液製絲法,呈請專利,未及核准而去世.七年後復有英人寶利 (Pauly) 獲得專利,世遂稱爲寶利法,是爲第二種.一千九百十二年,經英人葛祿士 (Cross) 等發明,以炭硫,爲化藥,亦可製成人造絲.嗣後復有德人醋酸法.故現在市上人造絲,實有四種.其製造手續,可分四步:第一步溶棉成液,所用方藥各法互異.第二步壓入微孔,俾成細絲.第三步經過化藥,復成纖維.第四步洗淨烘乾紡紗成線.各法不同之點,約如下表:

	成絲前所用溶液	成絲後經過之藥劑
1.	硫酸及硝酸	酸,鹼,及硫化鈉等液
2.	銅養及阿麻尼亞	酸液或鹼液
3.	苛性鈉及炭硫	硫酸,及硫酸鈉溶液.
4.	純醋酸及無水醋酸	水

至于紡染等法,大概相同.出品質地,亦復不相上下.原料或用製紙之木粕,或用棉子上附着之短棉,均可收效.惟第三法若用棉製,色較暗,不如用木爲宜也.

現在四法之中,以第三法爲最通行,占美國出產百分之八十六,進步亦較他法爲獨速.請略述製造大概以例其餘.先製濃鹼液,浸木粕其中,約一小時取出,搾去餘鹼,割成碎塊,儲置數時,俾其成熟.次封置臥桶中,以高壓注入炭硫,液.桶能旋轉,二三小時後水粕硬如橡皮,色變橙黃.復輸入拌合機,略加淡鹼,使成溶液,安置多時,漸起分解作用,硫質減去,而纖維質加增,再以濾機提去雜質,方成純淨溶液.紡絲機置有多孔之模,模以白金爲之,孔大約千分寸之二三,溶液經高壓通過微孔,注入硫酸鈉及硫酸溶液中,硫質化去,纖維質卽硬結成絲.次置玻錠上以清水洗淨,入烘房烘乾,復轉繞木棍上,以數絲成數十絲絞結成線.檢定等級,漂白烘乾,卽成商品,每束長三千碼,每箱十磅.製造手續,大概如是.第出品靭力之強弱,與外觀之優劣,在在與化製方法有關,一不審愼,卽成廢物.炭硫,質毒,又易炸發,偶爾洩漏,便成巨患.故製造之時,非徒賴優美之機械,兼須有精密之化驗,使各步經過,適合需要,無過中不及之弊,而後能得優良結果也.

人造絲光澤較眞絲爲佳,而柔軟略遜,尤以遇水則靭力減少爲一大缺點.第以成本低廉之故,織品暢銷,用途甚廣,絲帶花邊等品用此織造無論已.巾襪衣服之常須洗滌者,亦多以此爲之.至與棉絲等交織之品,耐用殆與眞絲無殊.辨別之法,最簡者有二:分散織品纖維,抽少許燒之.其灰黑而蜷曲,其臭如燒毛髮,爲眞絲之證.反是者爲人造絲.置織品于苛性鈉溶液中,（含苛性鈉一分水九分）而熱之.眞絲約十分時卽消溶.人造絲至雖經久亦不變.至品質較低者遇濕卽脹,故以織品纖維含口中,約一分鐘許,而試其易否撕斷.亦足爲辨認人造絲之一法.

人造絲之產額一九二四年已達一萬四千萬磅.美占百分之二十七.英德各占十七.意占十三.法占九.其餘諸國合占十七.數載以來,突飛進步.卽以美國論,五年間增至六倍.疇之恃德法輸入者,現已自給有餘.再就歷來產量列表比較,近年增進之速,更可概見.

一九一二年	1,100,000磅

一九一六年	5,475,000磅
一九二〇,,	10,250,000 ,,
一九二四,,	38,750,000 ,,

照此推算,去年產量當達五千五百萬磅.今年或可達七千五百萬磅.其發達正未有艾也.

據外人調查,人造絲產量已超過真絲遠甚.吾國絲產,素無精確統計.此言或未必可靠.但人造絲價廉物美.足以濟真絲所不及.進步甚速,前途殊未易量.吾人欲維持絲業,是否賴禁止購用所能收效,可以不辯自明.是則審察世界趨勢.謀抵制之方策,提倡人造絲工業誠爲不可緩之舉矣.但人造絲製造繁複,非有偉大資本不能經營.美國各廠大者歲產三千萬磅,小者亦三十萬磅,資本動輒數十百萬.以今日國內情況,安能步其後塵.且國人仿辦大規模工業,成者寥寥.而敗者接踵.彼普通工業,尙如是,而况此新式事業日在進步之中者,締造艱難,奚啻十倍,又安能保其獲利如操劵耶.吾國爲蠶絲祖國.卓著盛名.彼法日諸邦後來居上,甯有異術.惟其以學理之研究,爲改良之導師.故能出品日精.銷路日廣.吾若能效用其法,神而明之.蠶桑繅織.各究其精不難恢復失地.重執全世界絲業之牛耳.正可以以我所有,易其所無,交易互市,各得其利.人造絲雖盛,庸何傷.焉用懼又焉用禁.

2. 葡萄乾與工業

美國西部諸省,盛植葡萄.製乾輸出,歲錄巨量,尤以銷英國及坎拿大者爲多.近來忽有澳州製品.出而與爭,三年前輸入英國者不及百噸,前年竟增至五千噸.英人且有增加外貨稅率以保護殖民地工業之說,循是以往,美產將無立足地.業此者大起恐慌.乃有利用爲工學原料之計畫.試驗之初.困難百出.乾葉雜砂甚多,磨機及節水機等不出數日,即損蝕不堪復用.幾經研究.改用特別堅鋼以造機械方有成效.現規模最大之廠,日可出酒精二百萬格侖.效用之廣,固不待言.其釀造時所發生之炭酸氣,用藥烘乾後壓入鐵桶亦可供種種利用.製冰冷藏.使用亞麻尼亞法發生冷氣,炭氣凝結,性等于冰可以代用,兵艦儲食,非此不可.油漆房屋,用工甚費.新法代以氣壓噴霧器.可收事半功倍之效.炭酸氣與油漆不生化合作用,利尤勝于空氣.製造牛油,易致酸化,用炭氣可保持久乾.洗衣服,易致火患,用炭氣可免危險.類此者尚多不勝枚舉.此外酒石可製化學藥品,蒸渣酵母可爲牛羊飼料.以葡萄乾一微物而效用如此,固非吾人所及料.以一銷路日蹙之商品.而忽成爲一重要工業原料,尤非經多人之辛苦研究不爲功.四五年來美人推銷葡萄乾于吾國,不遺餘力,美女紙盒,充斥市肆而國人亦復視爲珍品.爭相購用,又孰知其乃受商戰影響,不能不以吾國爲尾閭耶.

3. 汽油供給問題

汽車之發明迄今不過三十年,而現用車數幾達三千萬輛之多,其進步之速,殆非意料所及,而各國之中,尤以美爲巨擘,其發達經過,約如下表.

	一八九九年	一九〇九年	一九一九年
工廠資本	5,769,000	173,837,000	1,802 302,000 元
乘車產量	37,00	127,731	1,657,652
貨車產量	,,	3,255	316,364
出品歲值	4,748,000	249,202,000	2,506,834,000 元
傭資總值	1,616,000	58,173,000	813,731,000 元
用車約數	10000	400,000	7,559,000

近十年來增進尤速,今日人口僅一億零,而用車總數已達二千萬輛,平均已五人合用一車,此後不能繼續增加,固無疑義.但即以全世界三千萬輛計,所需汽油已達三百五十兆桶之多,較之十五年前殆三十倍.若何能供給此多量汽油,誠世界上一大問題矣.三十年來汽車業之突進固由機械之進步.亦實賴有適量汽油以供給之.經過變遷,不一而足.國人習見汽車.不以爲奇,而對于汽油來源,多未熟知,略述始末,以資考證,不徒見西人之物盡其利.

無微不至,亦足徵其推究學理,無往而不收效也.

汽油製造原料,實爲石油內含多種物質,輕重各異,輕者易沸,蒸溜時先化爲氣,過冷凝結,是爲汽油.次輕者沸化較遲,是爲火油.曩時火油爲燃燈所必需,銷用甚廣,而汽油僅供洗衣化學等用,需額有限,供過于求,幾等廢物.自汽車發明後銷量大增,而火油受電燈之影響,需要乃大減.經此變遷,業製造者不能不以增進汽油產量爲急務,而石油蒸溜之所獲適合汽油用者乃極有限,不能任意增加,其困難可知.二十五年來產額增進,具如下表.

一八九九年	6 680,000 桶
一九〇九年	12,900,000 桶
一九一九年	94,234,690 „
一九二四年	213,300,000 „

以產量與車數扯計,昔時每車得六百餘桶,現在僅約十二桶,汽油缺少,可以概見.但以現時產額與二十五年前較,增進逾三十倍,其成績已可驚矣.考其增進原因,約有三端:

(一) 曩時提煉石油,僅用普通蒸溜法,汽油產量不達原料什之一.後得裂化蒸溜 (Cracking) 之法,可以分解火油,使成較輕物質,汽油產量,增至原料什之三.邇後發明者日衆,此類方法之見諸實用者,不下四十餘種之多,在美之二十.

國雖全國五百餘廠中,用新法者僅三之一.歲產汽油,用此增進者,當達百分

(二) 美國中部諸省,地下煤氣甚多,掘井採取,用爲天然燃料.氣中較重物質,質同汽油,加以高壓,或用相當溶液,均可提取.第油質略輕,沸化較易,攙合重質汽油,方適實用.一九一一年產量僅二十七萬桶,一九二一年增至十一兆桶,占汽油產額百分之八.因之輕質火油亦可供汽車燃料之用,其額量增進,又當百分之三四也.

(三) 昔時汽油燃點,約以三百至三百五十度爲衡,近因汽車機械之進步,稍重汽油,亦可利用,標準燃點,已增至四百三十七度.汽油產量之增進,此

亦一大原因也.

現在汽車產額,突進未已,而汽油供給,勢不能隨之而增,利用重油,已達極點,改造機械,不易收效,煤氣產量,亦復日減,此項來源,非可久恃.就此三項而論,尙存增加希望者,僅有裂化之一途,其原料將仍惟石油是賴.美國歲產石油達五百五十兆桶,占世界產額三分之二,估計地下儲藏,僅九千二百兆桶,已不足二十年之需,而世界產藏,強半操諸英人之手,合波斯緬甸及南美在內,油地之爲英人節制者,幾達全量四之三,此外法之于南歐,日之于薩哈里,亦競以占據油地爲務,而美所能控制者,僅一墨西哥.一旦油藏告罄,飛機潛艇,失其效用,汽車停駛,交通受困,而新式戰艦所需之燃料油,亦復無從取給,勢非束手待斃不止,此美國人士所以視汽油供給爲切膚問題,而急謀解決之方,而法德諸國之得油地較少者,亦莫不以研求代用品爲急務也.

十載以來,研究結果,略有實效,將來希望,可得而言.向來高壓裂化之法,僅能分解中質之油,蒸溜油脚及油質之過重者,只可供燃料之用.若能化成汽油,產量可以陡增,此法現已發明,正在試用之中,一也.

美國西部頁岩(Shale)甚多,所含油量,倘七八倍于石油,提煉方法,已獲專利者多不勝數,製成汽油亦優良合用.雖產地荒僻,經營惟艱,現時尙無大利可圖,異時油產告罄,或竟代之而興,二也.

取煤膠（俗稱柏油）蒸溜之,可得本純(Benzene)等質參合汽油,亦可代用.惟產額較之汽油,僅達百分之三,染料原料,又惟此是賴,即舉歲產烟煤悉供製造煤膠之需,所獲亦不過什一,將來希望殊有限,三也.

酒精熱力較汽油稍遜,但攙合等量汽油,而另加少許本純等品,普通汽車皆能利用,其結果且較獨用汽油爲佳,而原料又富,含糖質或纖維質之植物品,皆可爲釀造之用.目前所用者,如糖蜜,如甘藷,如玉蜀黍,如鋸屑,雖產額有定量,未能作無限之增加.而自炭化鈣（俗稱電石）製酒精之法,久已發明,石灰及炭,供給甚多,又可取之無窮,爲異日代替汽油之一法,四也.

法國境內獨少油產,對此問題尤為注意,至前年乃有貝琦氏(Bergius)法之發明.取煤屑煤膠之類,和油少許,調成薄漿,置二三百倍高壓器中,通入輕氣,熱至攝氏四百度,化合而成黑液,蒸溜之後,可得汽油百分之十五,若以重質黑油為原料,汽油產量,達百分之八十,較常法增七八倍云.現正在試驗中,異時告成,則世界煤產皆可為汽油原料,其便利為何如,五也.

德以化學名于時,亦有人造石油(Synthol)之發明,先用煤質製成常用煤氣,(Water gas)復加輕氣在一百五十倍氣壓之下,熱至四百度,佐以鹼性鐵劑之力,化合成液,質同汽油,可以參用.此法亦在試用中.又用同樣煤氣置四百氣壓下熱之,加以鋅養等媒化劑,可以製成木精,(Methanol)成本低廉,較舊法由木料蒸溜而得者,不及三之一,質同酒精,亦可代氣油之用,六也.

由此觀之,未來之汽油供給問題,雖解決未竟全功,而成效已略可覩,異時時勢推移,究以何法為中堅,雖現在未能預測,而石油儲量未竭之前,定有他種汽油出而代興,使社會不至感供給之缺乏,固無疑義.彼西人以汽車之利便,既不能棄而不用,飛機運輸,又方興未艾,而關係國防之主要品物,更不甘一二國之壟斷,其處心積慮以求一當,固無足怪.獨念京滬各埠,汽車盛行,人多樂用,而多量汽油,滿載而來,復為對外貿易增一重漏卮,為可慨耳.

（待續）

秤杆秤錘之小科學

旦 里

吾人日常所用以權貨物之輕重者曰秤,曰天平,小者曰等子.(俗作戥)近更有舶來之彈簧秤及平臺秤,細至毫釐,巨若萬鈞,用以權衡重輕,買賣兩方各無異議.蓋用之者皆已萬分信託造秤之人.其自身從未稍加研究.惟造秤者大概抄襲成法.只顧當然,以獲得營業餘利為目的.學理固毫不知,且亦不暇及此.至於用秤之人,原不乏學問高明之士.然或不屑為此細碎瑣說.習識粗淺者又無程度討論之.現在且里所說之小科學,乃即人人處處時時刻刻所見所用之秤杆秤錘加以研究.須知該器之發明遠在數千年前.社會應用亦數千年.而人不屑論之.讀此文者或許以尚不荒謬.且里幸矣.本篇所舉長短輕重之例悉用營造尺及斤兩錢分,取其通俗也.

秤杆概用堅固木料爲之.取其內構勻淨,木質輕巧.又木係一種遍地皆產之料,擇取又頗便利.秤杆之大小視輕重之限制爲比較.譬如稱三斤者其杆木可以細小.稱二百斤者其杆木自必粗大.至於小式等子.其杆以象牙或獸骨爲之,意取裝飾華美而已.通用之秤杆自以木質爲價廉而適用.大都長二尺左右.（茲所謂尺乃部頒之營造尺,等於部定公尺之三一五.）式如圓柱,取其便利.其對徑最大約三分.（按營造尺十寸爲尺,十分爲寸）現時造秤人所作者大抵兩端粗細不等.往往秤鈎處圓徑最大.由此向秤尾逐漸細小.木之種類甚多.原價隨其堅實勻淨之度爲高低.檀木棗木松木樟木等價各不同.秤杆自身重量,極有關係.故木之比重,必須考明.秤錘概用堅重之金屬.古時亦有以石或泥土爲之者.其本旨在取其質不易消散,使錘重得永遠保守勿變.現時都用鐵質.蓋亦以鐵爲一種不易消散之質料而價又廉也.鐵之比重每立方寸六兩.錘形近代幾一律.

漢書律歷志云:「權者銖兩斤鈞石也.所以稱物平施.知輕重也.本起於黃鐘之重.一龠容千二百黍重十二銖.兩之爲兩.二十四銖爲兩.十六兩爲斤.三十斤爲鈞.四鈞爲石.」又云:「職在太行,鴻臚掌之.」稗史類編云:「皇祐新樂圖有銖秤.其圖幹十分.二十四銖爲一兩正.一面有星.一繫.一盤.如民間金銀等子者.其錘形如環.」（繫即提繩.盤即秤鈎之替.）

歐美各國則近代皆已訂爲法律,異常嚴厲.不但依其長短輕重,建鑄標本數份,分別藏諸政府,慎重保存.且又從而限定在何等天氣,何等空氣中,始合標準.可謂詳確矣.

今日習用之秤杆秤錘爲圖於次:

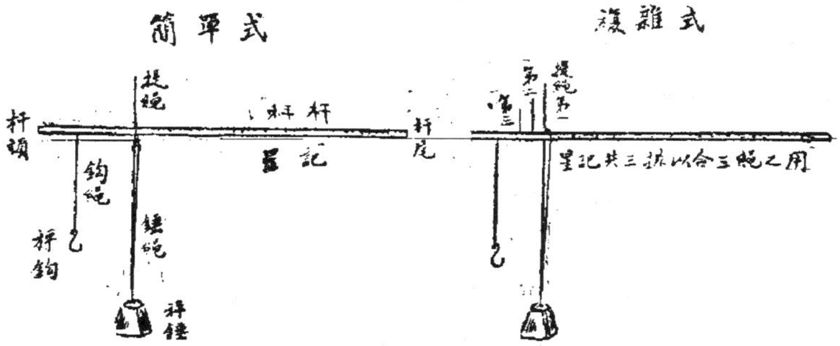

造秤者只顧當然,彼蓋由所謂法碼以及粗淺尺碼規矩相傳而來.其造法係不計杆之分量精粗繩之輕重長短.繩眼應在何處,星記用何資料.有時亦頗合式,惜不常見.亦不易究其底蘊.彼所持以爲製造者,只有相沿認爲標準之法碼若干個耳.以科學論之.自有許多差誤之處.嘗若造一三斤之秤,以最簡單式論之,造者令木匠刨一木杆.粗細隨匠人手術之便而定長短亦隨匠之意度.尺寸略有長短不計焉.杆成之後,提繩眼隨匠意於某處穿之.鈎繩眼亦然.至繩配就時,將現成之鐵鈎置鈎繩端鈎上掛法碼三斤.乃擇一合宜之鐵錘隨便於近杆尾處掛之.如得平衡,則三斤之星記已得.名之曰三斤點.更將錘繩移向「二斤法碼掛鈎得平衡之處」掛之.得二斤點之星記.類推可得無斤點（卽〇點）及兩點之星記.欲無斤點（亦卽無兩點）之星記適起於提繩直線下者,（如圖）造者往往用他種重物（銅皮灌鉛）或鐵鈎加重,置近杆端處卽可.如將三斤點二斤點間平均分置星記,則一兩半兩等皆能看出.造者多用銅絲作星點,鑽細眼於杆面,用錘將銅絲輕輕打入,全體打好,用剉剉光,⋯面呈頗匀淨之星記一排.複雜式者,其星記排數視提繩數.至於銅星共重若干,造者不暇計較也.最後較準.在乎加減輕重於錘或鈎或杆端或竟謬加至杆尾.此種秤杆秤錘絕不可信託.

萬事起於無關重要日常細瑣之間.與吾人性格亦至有關係.諺有不禮

確,安能令一切作爲之眞正愼妥乎.秤杆秤錘其小焉者耳.

造秤用材料之各種法重列次:

棗木每立方寸重五錢半.

澆鐵每立方寸重六兩.

熟銅每立方寸重六兩九錢.

鉛每立方寸重九兩.

麻繩(能安全抵抗五斤重量者)每丈重一兩.

上舉重量不能恰合各種材料.上表係一班研究所得之實錄藉作布算之根據云爾.

簡單式秤之計算　三斤秤　秤杆一律對徑三分.長二十寸.爲最簡單

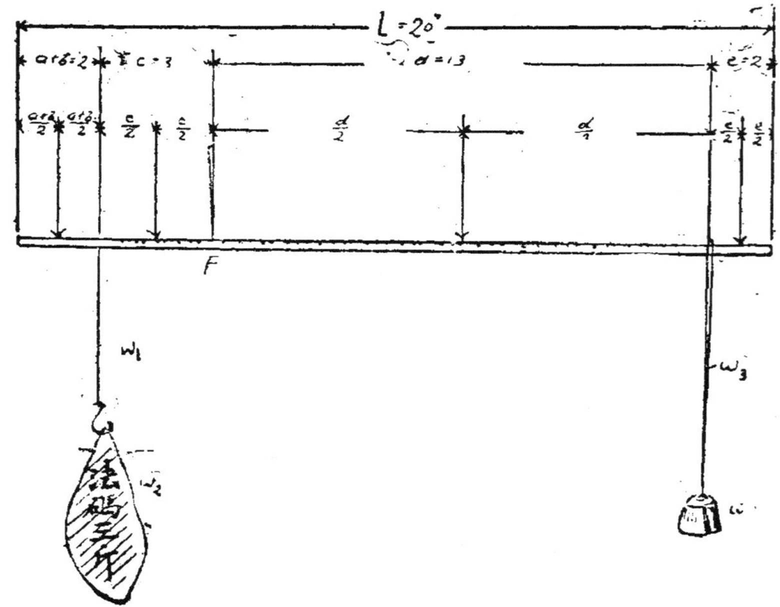

秤杆既係一律三分對徑,以棗木而言,只須求其體積爲若干立方寸.即

可求得秤杆之重量．

$0.3\times0.3\times\frac{3.1416}{4}\times20=1.41372$立方寸，$\times0.55$兩$=0.778$兩爲杆之自重．

計 a+b 一段杆重 $\frac{1}{10}\times0.778$兩，着力於（a+b）$\frac{1}{2}$之處，離F四寸．

c　一段杆重 $\frac{3}{20}\times0.778$兩，着力於$\frac{c}{2}$之處，離F一寸半．

d　一段杆重 $\frac{13}{20}\times0.778$兩，着力於$\frac{d}{2}$之處，離F六寸半．

e　一段杆重 $\frac{1}{10}\times0.778$兩，着力於$\frac{e}{2}$之處，離F十四寸．

鉤繩 W_1重半錢卽0.05兩，　　着力之處，離F三寸．

鐵鉤 W_2重二兩卽2.00兩，　　着力之處，離F三寸．

鏢繩 W_3重半兩卽 0.5兩，　　着力之處，離F十三寸．

法碼　重三斤卽 48兩，　　着力之處，離F三寸．

鐵錘之分量應以下法推之　　惟已知其離F十三寸．

鐵錘之壓掛，可任取相宜之點．留e段者相宜之點所在耳．

$$4\times\frac{1}{10}\times0.778+1\cdot5\times\frac{3}{20}\times0.778+(0.05+2+48)\times3=6.5\times\frac{13}{20}\times0.778$$

$$(0.5+W_4)13+14\times\frac{1}{10}\times0.778$$

$$W_4=\frac{0.778\left(\frac{4}{10}+\frac{4.5}{20}-\frac{6.5\times13}{20}-\frac{14}{10}\right)+50.05-6.5}{13}=\frac{39.66}{13}=3.05\text{兩}.$$

由此可知，若於離F十三寸處壓掛3.55兩，(3.0.5+05=3.55兩) 可合法碼三斤平衡．現可將三斤點記於離F十三寸處．惟不得用銅星．因銅星有重．用之與上算相亂．再求無斤點或無兩點．此點應在F之左或右或正在提繩垂線之下．

$$3(W_1+W_2)+\left(\frac{1}{10}+\frac{3}{20}\right)\times 0.778=X\times 3.55+\frac{e+d}{L}\times 0.778.$$

$$3\times 2.05+\frac{1}{4}\times 0.778=X\times 3.55+\frac{3}{4}\times 0.778.$$

$$X=\frac{6.15+0.1945-.5835}{3.55}=1.623\text{寸}.$$ 此數前有+（加號）點應在F右.

鐵錘壓於F之右1.623寸處.乃該三斤秤之無兩點.此秤係對徑一律之木杆.自無斤點（即無兩點）至三斤點,共佔杆長13—1.623寸,卽11.377寸.如將11.377寸匀分爲爲四十八份,各置號記.則此秤能稱至兩數.將11.377寸匀分爲九十六份,各置記號則此秤能稱至半兩數.此小科學之三斤秤也.

由前觀之,如號記用銅星則算式複雜.如杆尾爲最小徑.漸大至杆首爲最大徑.則複雜又加.如造秤人只顧限數之法碼平正,而謬加極重物於秤首或尾之極短部份,以求一點之準者則此秤鮮能隨處確實可靠.至於複雜式之三提繩秤,且里擬于下次逐漸說明之.再此三斤秤之e段部份,尙可利用以稱較三斤爲重之物.因11.377÷96=0.1185,2÷0.1185=16.88.有16.88個半兩.卽八兩有零.是秤雖號三斤,于必要時三斤半亦可稱也.

六十年來中國交通四政大事年表

趙祖康

年份	路政	電政	郵政	航政
清同治元年 1862				
二年 1863	上海英美商人向蘇撫李鴻章請築上海蘇州間鐵路不准			
三年 1864				
四年 1865				曾國藩設江南造船廠於上海 英商設立廣東香港澳門輪船公司
五年 1866	上海英商怡和洋行始築淞滬鐵路			左宗棠設船政局於福州
六年 1867				英商太古公司成立
七年 1868				
八年 1869				
九年 1870				
十年 1871				
十一年 1872				李鴻章奏辦輪船招商局
十二年 1873				
十三年 1874		兩江總督沈葆楨奏言電報之利奉旨飭辦未行		
光緒元年 1875				日本郵船會社始航行上海橫濱間
二年 1876	淞滬鐵路成 收回淞滬鐵路旋以不適用毀之		驛站之外設文報局	
三年 1877				英商怡和公司成立

四年 1878			發行郵票	
五年 1879		直督李鴻章始招丹麥人承辦大沽天津間電報		
六年 1880	劉銘傳請辦鐵路	李鴻章奏辦津滬陸線合由丹商大北公司承辦		招商局歸還官款自是純爲商股
七年 1881	唐胥鐵路成	津滬線竣工上海招商股八十萬元英商東洋電話公司始設電話於上海租界		設大沽船塢
八年 1882		津滬線改爲官督商辦		
九年 1883				將招商局向旗昌洋行抵銀五百二十五萬兩
十年 1884		設京津陸線 設徐口海線（廣東徐聞至瓊島）		
十一年 1885				
十二年 1886				
十三年 1887				
十四年 1888	津（沽）閻（莊）路成			
十五年 1889				
十六年 1890				
十七年 1891				
十八年 1892				
十九年 1893				
二十年 1894				
二十一年 1895	法人索築廣西龍州至越南河內鐵路拒之仍爭辦			日本大阪商船公司駛入長江航路

二十二年 1896	李鴻章赴俄議密約結中俄加西尼條約許俄西比利亞鐵路通過東三省 許景澄與俄訂東清鐵路合同 訂龍州鐵路合同 派盛宣懷爲鐵路大臣 盧漢鐵路盧保段開工 設鐵路公司於上海		大清郵政局成立隸於總理衙門歸稅務處管理總稅務使赫德兼領總郵政使	
二十三年 1897	德人索膠濟膠沂兩路敷設權允之 盛宣懷與比公司簽訂盧漢借款合同 東清鉄路開工			
二十四年 1898	盛宣懷與比公司續訂盧漢借款合同 胡燏芬與滙豐銀行訂關內外鐵路借款合同債額英金二百三十萬磅 奏請復修之淞滬路成歸併滬寧路辦理 總理各國事務衙門奏定興辦鐵路次第不准商人請辦枝路 廣州灣租約中允准法人修築赤安鐵路			公布內地水路航行章程
二十五年 1899	訂東清鐵路合同	盛宣懷奏准附設電話於天津電報局是爲官辦電話之始		與英訂長江內港行輪章程
二十六年 1900		因敷設上海大沽間海綫借外款二十一萬磅 丹商大北公司乘拳亂設滬烟沽正綫事後由政府收回		

		丹麥人濮爾生乘拳亂設天津北塘塘沽等處電話		
二十七年 1901		濮氏又設北京電話		派員議辦通商行船條約
二十八年 1902	岑春煊與華俄道勝銀行訂正太鐵路新約債額法金四千萬法郎 道清鐵路開工	電報改歸官辦商股仍舊設電政大臣		與英續訂通商行船條約
二十九年 1903	盛宣懷與英中英公司簽訂滬寧鐵路借款合同債額英金三百二十五萬磅 滬寧鐵路開工 盛宣懷與比電車公司訂汴洛鉄路借款合同債額法金四千一百萬法郎 與比訂滇越鐵路條約 與俄訂定東三省採伐鐵路枕木區域三處 制定鐵路章程並禁止以鐵路為抵押而借款	政府設電話局於廣東		與美日訂通商行船條約 日本郵船公司開始航行長江一帶
三十年 1904	汴洛鐵路開工 停辦粵漢鐵路工程 與葡訂廣澳鐵路合同	收回濮氏所設之北京電話	由六關項下每年指撥協款七十二萬兩	
三十一年 1905	正太鐵路開工 盛宣懷與英國福公司簽訂道清鐵路借款合同債額英金八十萬磅收回道清鉄路 京綏鐵路京張段開工詹天佑總其事 向美收回粵漢鐵路價美金六兆七千五百萬元 岑春煊向香港英官廳借收回粵漢	直督袁世凱聘意國葛拉斯等為教習調選上海電局學生至天津學習無線電報十月畢業因在海圻等四艦安設電機令學生實習並在南苑天津保定行營設機通報 收回濮氏所設之天津等處電話		浙紳規辦滬紹輪船公司

		鐵路贖設權借款 一百十萬磅		
三十二年 1906	京漢鐵路全路通車 政府允撥官款助吉紳辦吉長鐵路 江蘇自辦蘇省鐵路	設郵傳部電政（電報電話等）始歸部直轄 淞人設淞滬無線電局	設郵傳部郵政管權仍歸總理衙門掌握 河南奉裁驛站	江南造船廠改為官督商辦
三十三年 1907	外部與英人訂蘇杭甬借款造路章程兩路股東開會抗拒 外部與中英銀公司議定蘇杭甬鐵路交涉分借款造路為兩事 梁敦彥與德華銀行及英國華中公司訂立津浦鐵路借款合同債額英金五百萬磅 那桐等與日南滿鐵路株式會社訂新奉鐵路借款協約債額日金三十二萬元吉長鐵路借款協約債額日金二百五十萬元 關內外鐵路展長至奉天稱京奉鐵路 道清鐵路成 中英合辦九廣鐵路簽押開工借款英金一百五十萬磅 川漢鐵路改歸商辦			
	募款借債贖回京漢全路管理權 滬寧鐵路成 津浦鐵路開工 正太鐵路成 汴洛鐵路成 定鐵路地稅章程	改電報總局為電政局商股收歸國有 部辦太原上海廣東等處電話		

三十四年 1908	蘇杭甬鐵路借用英款一百五十万鎊約簽押改名滬杭甬 向匯豐銀行匯理銀行借收回京漢路款五百萬鎊 借商款贖京漢鐵路預定一千萬兩應募僅數萬元			
宣統元年 1909	滬寧鐵路更訂辦事章程撤廢總管理處以華人爲總辦 吉長鐵路開工 京綏鐵路京張段成 江蘇滬嘉路成 浙江杭嘉路成	贖回上海英商匯中旅館私設之無線電台附設於上海電報局 收回德人所辦津沽電話		
二年 1910	京綏路展築張綏段 准廣東自辦廣澳鐵路 與日訂借收回京漢路款二百二十萬元 徐世昌等與德華銀行華中公司訂津浦鐵路續借款合同債額英金四百八十萬磅 向英借收回京漢鐵路借款六十七萬磅	各省電報官線局所改歸部辦 訂定各省電話暫行章程規定部辦省辦商辦權限	陸軍部始將驛站移交郵傳部接管	與俄訂松花江貿易航行條約
三年	廢滬杭甬借英款約 長株鐵路通車 廣九鐵路成 宣示鐵路政策幹路改歸國有 粵漢川漢鐵路取消商辦借英德法美四國銀行款六百萬磅	海軍部收買德國西門子廠在南京北京借地試驗之無線電報	外交部（前總理衙門）始將郵政局移交郵傳部直轄	

1911	因收川漢鐵路爲國有川民開保路會議決罷市罷課以抵制 派端方帶兵查辦端誘拘保路會會長股東會長諮議局議長等監禁之 向日本正金銀行借贖京漢路款日金一千萬元			
民國元年 1912	朱啓鈐訂借惠華銀行津浦路墊款英金九十萬零四百餘磅 吉長鐵路全路通車 南潯鐵路向日借款五百萬元 周學熙等與比國鐵路電車合股公司訂隴秦豫海鐵路借款英金一千萬磅	南京無線電台吳淞無線電局因軍興破毀北京無線電局歸交部通接管 並購設同式無線電台一座於張家口	改郵傳部爲交通部 六關停解郵政經費	江南造船廠改歸海軍部直轄管理
二年 1913	公布中國鐵路總公司條例 蘇路（滬嘉綫）收歸國有 津浦鐵路全路通車 湘路（粵漢路湘段及三佛支線湘股）收歸國有 中日鐵路聯絡 與日本訂滿蒙鐵路合同 梁士詒等與法比鐵路公司訂同成鐵路借款合同債額英金一千萬磅 熊希齡等與英華中公司訂浦信鐵路借款合同債額英金三百萬磅	分設電政管理局十三處於各行政區域劃一章程 交通部與海陸軍參謀等部會議訂購無線電台八座分設內地邊疆各適中之處 又與馬可尼合組無線電報公司資本中英各半		大沽船塢歸海軍部改名造船所
	晉路（同浦線）收歸國有 皖路收歸國有			

三　年 1914	川路（川漢路川段）收歸國有 浙路（甬嘉線）收歸國有 公布民業鐵路條例 政府議築長城外鐵路 與英俄訂東清鐵路附屬地內行政權協約 熊希齡等與中法實業銀行訂欽渝鐵路借款額法金六萬萬法郎又墊款一萬萬法郎 周自齊與中英公司訂寧湘鐵路借款合同債額英金八百萬磅 交通部向美國借二百萬元以還京張鐵路借款並購鐵路車輛 周自齊等與英寶林公司訂沙興鐵路借款合同債額英金一千萬磅		宣布實行分全國為廿一郵政區每區各設管理局一所 加入萬國郵會派奉天天津上海廣東等埠管理局為直接互換局	
四　年 1915	鄂路（粵漢線川漢線鄂段）收歸國有 北京環城鐵路成 江西南潯路竣工通車 頒布專用鐵路暫行條例 京綏路張綏段築至大同 公布民業鐵路法 周學熙等與日本正金銀行訂四鄭鐵路借款合同債額日金五百萬元	中日訂接水電合同	郵政獲利自本年始	中國郵船公司成立
五　年 1616	曹汝霖與美國裕中公司訂株欽周襄鐵路借款合同 周學熙與俄亞銀行訂濱黑路借款五千萬羅布			

六年 1917	派員參與中日鐵路聯運會議 曹汝霖與日改訂吉長鐵路借款細目合同增債額爲日金六百五十萬元 向日訂南潯鐵路借款二百卅萬元	向日訂漢口水電公司借款一百萬元		
七年 1918	章宗祥與日訂濟順高徐州鐵路借款二千萬元 曹汝霖與正金銀行訂四鄭鐵路短期借款日金二百六十萬元 向日訂南潯鐵路借款十萬元 向日訂吉會鐵路借款一千萬元 中日兩國決定滿蒙鐵路借款	與日桑訂電信借款二千萬元 與日訂電話借款增資合同七百萬元 與英訂無線電借款六十萬元 與英訂無線電借款三百萬元	收回日人所轄青島郵政局	江南造船廠與美國航務部訂承造運艦十二艘 與美訂造船借款一千萬元
八年 1919	向日訂京綏鐵路借款三百萬元 施肇曾與比國公司訂隴秦豫海路第二次短期借郎款法金二千萬法 曾毓雋與南滿鐵道會社訂借四洮路借款日金四千五百萬元	與英商馬可尼公司訂無線電借款訂七十萬磅	辦理郵政儲金 直隸郵區分爲二區	
九年 1920	加入萬國交通大會 施肇曾訂隴秦豫海比荷借款法金一萬五千萬法郎荷幣五千萬弗魯令 曾毓雋訂借四洮短期借款一千三百七十万元		特派專員出席日斯巴尼亞萬國郵會博議大會 在華俄國郵局撤銷 京津間試行飛機郵便	公布航海條例
十年	京綏路全路告成 交通部與內國銀團訂車輛借款六百萬元 向英借滄石鐵路款一千萬元	加入外國電報公約 與美商訂無綫電借款美金四百六十萬元	東三省郵區分爲二區 交通部派郵政專門委員赴華盛頓會議 簽字萬國郵約	

1921	向中美公司訂粵漢鐵路湘鄂段借款八十五萬元 張志潭與中英公司訂京奉鐵路唐榆雙軌借款英金五十萬鎊銀元二百萬元		

附註

本表爲拙作『收回交通權芻議』之第三節.一二節見南洋旬刊.第四節『從利權得失觀劃分中國近世交通史之時期』即從本表所得之結論,擬於下期季刊或第二卷旬刊上發表.

本表暫自清同治元年始至民國十年止.起自同治者,同治以前新式交通事業之史績較少故也.終於民國十年者,數年來交通四政之紀述,成書者少,蒐羅爲難,查考不便.且四五年來又成一新局面,路之所以藏拙也.

本表雖統四政,特重鐵路,尤注意於各路借款.固因作者所見,局於一隅,亦以鐵路借款於我交通利權之得失,至有關係耳.

作者對於交通事業素無研究.此表倉卒編成,參考不多,紕漏矛盾,知所不免,幸讀者教之.

參考書

交通紀實（民國五年交通部編）

五十年來中國之交通（葉恭綽著見最近之五十年）

鐵路借款提要（民國十一年交通部張恩煌編）

五十年來中國大事表（黃炎培沈琦編見最近之五十年）

中國鐵路史講義（關賡麟著）

中國鐵路史（曾鯤化著）

交通史（王倬著商務出版）

中國年鑑（商務出版）

經濟侵略下之中國（漆樹芬著）

遊張家口賜兒山記

傅煥光

張家口爲西北重鎭.拱衞京師.屛蔽塞北.據庫倫多倫等處交通運輸之要點.百貨輻輳.商務繁盛.疊嶂層巒.左右環繞.形勢險要.爲用兵必爭之地也.其市場城郭.列次盆底.南北長十餘里.東西半之.北部地勢較高.曰上堡.南部較窪.曰下堡.中以通橋界焉.民國十四年五月九日.察哈爾舉行.教育實業展覽會.予適代表綏遠實業廳.徵集出品.來此與會.十日午後.公餘有暇.聞賜兒山之勝.偕直隸安次王君哲明往遊焉.山在直屬萬全縣西二里許.山麓可通車馬.自下仰望.寺宇煇煌.歷歷可數.加以巖石重翠.葱鬱可愛.遊人至此.精神一爽.山水怡人.誠不虛語.乃沿坡上登.約半里許.過一亭.題曰眺遠綿邈.行數十武.至覽雲亭.則雲泉寺已迎面矣.寺之原始.代遠無可稽攷.明初始名雲泉.滄桑屢刧.屢廢屢復.今復煥然.殆山川靈秀之氣所鍾.不可湮沒.抑亦地處控要.易得都人士之觀感乎.寺之結構.大體分內中外三院.依山建築.環植叢檜.風景殊勝.入寺門爲外院.中爲眞武殿.左右祠龍王文殊.中院乃一廣庭.中有古柳.槎枒壓臥.數百年物也.後有水洞冰洞.前有廡廊.可坐以眺遠.內院爲觀音如來.觀音殿北向.與廟口劇台遙對.如來冰洞眞武諸殿均東向.如來殿後有澹然亭.其下泉水滴瀝.亭東南爲普佛寺.又東南出院外數十武.有亭翼然.與覽雲亭等相掩映.此下層三院結構之大略也.於中院拾級以登.好事者用崖石磨刻西山曉翠.紫塞靈湫等題.此層廊迴曲折.殿宇參差.最南爲三仙聖母.據水洞上.北有靜室三楹.遊憩所也.又上爲凌霄殿.三元殿.忠義宮.分配左右.少偏北爲老君殿.此上中二層結構之大略也.凌霄殿東南有藥王殿.三王廟.雲泉寺最高處也.余已登雲霄之殿.環顧羣山.俯視塵寰.童山屛峙.蜿蜒磅礴.瑰瑋雄奇.氣象崢嶸.十餘萬家.鱗次釜底.山溝狹淺.河流沙積.環山農民.耕至山腰.不植一樹.山巔岩石纍纍.寸草不生.一遇霪雨.山洪暴漲.流沙挾石.擁

搪澎湃.萬馬奔馳.勢莫能禦.田廬湮沒.村集爲墟.去年大水.水上齊屋.積沙滿街.高與樓等.人民流離.損失不貲.山人爲我言之.不寒而慄.余讀楊夢熊通橋碑記.有自明成化迄乾隆甲午.其間修復不下數十次.碑皆冲失無考.張垣水患.蓋由來久矣.余初蒞此.見山勢之雄奇.市廛之繁盛.深爲居民喜.至觀其伏處釜底.水災頻仍.又不禁爲之懼.而彼野心家又欲肆其陰謀.爭此尺寸土以爲快.余竊謂謀張垣之安全莫如延請水利工程專家考察水量.相度地勢.鑿渠開河.引水出口.又請森林專家將山麓旱地.督勸人民改種果樹.山上多種適宜林木.以節水流.二途并進.則張垣之水災既可戢.而外患亦庶可預防乎.北來六旬.未嘗一遊山水之勝.今偶登臨.不禁感慨係之.願發展西北實業者三致意焉.歸寓記此.

按張家口俗稱東口.爲塞北通商要埠.所有商市一切情形.已於京綏遊記詳述之矣.予於本年三月間因公復赴張垣.逗留一星期之久.其賜兒山,元寶山,東高山,朝陽洞各勝蹟.又未能前往瞻覽.傅君有心人也.此次藉展覽會之便.得遊賜兒山.周覽玩賞.並以爲記.予未能追隨左右不免有望塵莫及之感.且傅君對於張垣水害.圖謀安全之策.尤具灼見.欽佩莫名.然以張垣形勢言之.適當元寶山水勢之衝.而通橋尤爲西流急湍之地.歷年沖淹.已非一次.加之近來商市發達.所修怡安福壽各街.以及車站.均在河漕窪下建築.以致去年山洪暴發.不可遏止.總計淹沒財產房廬.損失約六百餘萬元.男女死者亦在五百餘名之多.慘狀可憫其咎誰在.予曾循河履勘.得知河流由元寶山來.經東太平山麓.西南流貫通橋.以目力測之.上游之河漕.高於車站附近商市.在五十丈以上.是山洪一發.勢必被害.況去年淹沒時.竟將河身改流.直衝通橋之南.愈形危險.當即將危險情形.遍陳當局.雖蒙采納.一時尚難實行.未幾復有消冰水冲斷橋梁之虞.張都統遂聘巡京綏路陳工程師.撥款興修.惟此項工程.非詳加勘測通盤計畫.不能收圓滿之效.若圖目前一時之安.則將來水患仍恐無補.以予管見所及.應於上游劈寬河身.俾水勢來源平緩.下游則多開渠道.分殺水勢.並可藉以灌溉田畝.振興農業.至於石橋可全行拆毀改造無孔之鐵橋.兩傍加以石壩.以免山洪暴發.不致再有壅塞泛濫之虞.約計此項工程需洋二十餘萬元.如當道能毅力實行.可期一勞永逸.而商市人民.則沾惠不淺矣.今讀傅君遊張家口賜兒山記有感.附注數言.願留心張垣水患者.俾得萬一之助耳. 周頌堯附識

丙寅俱樂部徵啓

蘇　民

蓋聞竹秀靈巖.不僅孤生之賞.苔棲幽石.每託同岑之歡.況吾儕以萍聚而論交.就儒酸而得契.青氈食志.白日勞形.跡等磨驢.聞慚野鶴.歎浮生之若夢.須因物以消愁.蘭亭有修禊之文.洛下結吟詩之社.雅人深致.自古爲然.用是會集同人.部開俱樂.羊羔不設.但煮新茶.鶴俸分捐.各奏游藝.或按變聲而讀曲.或研古譜而彈棋.或喜臨池.學米顛之奔放.或工沒骨.寫倪迂之精神.有時効淳于之滑稽.葫盧淺笑.有時作東山之高會.絲竹怡情.凡所以豁羈愁.暢逸興者.皆儒林之韻事.文士之消閒也.有開必先.敢託引喤之雅.隨感而應.載賡伐木之章.

秋　草

（用王漁洋秋柳韻）

墨　隱

秋原一望盪吟魂.莽莽平蕪接玉門.寂寞黃沙深沒跡.淒涼青塚遠留痕.宵征蟋蟀鳴荒磧.夕下牛羊認舊村.無限江山付鶗鴂.美人遲暮不須論.

窺鏡還疏雨點霜.西窗舊夢隔池塘.梁空歸燕曾營壘.扇撲流螢欲上箱.蘆岸維舟傷白傅.蕭皋秋黯憶思王.六朝金粉飄零盡.莫問當年碎錦坊.

窈窕山阿薜荔衣.楚臺人去雨雲非.玉鈎斜畔遺紅淚.金谷園中拾翠稀.集澤驚鴻猶肅肅.繞籬瘦蝶故飛飛.撫絃一奏迷陽曲.目極天涯壯志違.

扶醉登樓枉獨憐.綠波春水渺於煙.斧柯未假嗟滋蔓.杼軸全空待寄棉.征馬而今肥上廐.勞人自昔感華年.浮生悟徹榮枯理.故國新愁到酒邊.

北游吟草

張景良

余遭母喪之百日.憂傷憔悴.弱不能支.友人程君自粵來.瞿然曰.子何憊也.清帝遁津.故宮開放.長安春暮.燕乳絮飛.盍駕言出游.以寫憂乎.余曰諾.明日遂行.

滬寧車中

久泯簪纓想.常深風木思.何圖遭世亂.未盡烏鳥私.強事登程去.悲為逐夢遲.有衣嗟游子.無復密縫時.

過徐州

黃運分流處.英雄自古多.不聞雍門奏.猶憶大風歌.枌社神常祀.桓山惡不磨.無如豐澤畔.當道臥長蛇.

清故宮

重重閬闠靜無譁.此是先朝皇帝家.鑪鼎無烟留獸炭.罘罳有跡認羊車.梁高燕落空巢土.風冷鹿銜上苑花.最是關心銘座語.宸章多半被塵遮.

北海瓊華島

雕甍碧瓦隱迢迢.柳樹陰中度玉橋.百級樓臺臨福地.千章槐柏蔽塵囂.銅亭聳峙迎紅日.磚塔崢嶸刺絳霄.北轉徐穿石窟下.清風水榭木蘭橈.

太和中和保和三殿

青鎖丹墀塵已生.雲龍叠叠任縱橫.風高采蝶簷頭戲.日暮烏鴉殿角爭.帝運三台推既盡.天威咫尺儼無存.沈沈黃屋皆陳跡.眼見銅駝委棘荊.

居庸關

憑山據險設雄關.爲界華夷故作閑.萬騎南來差可禦.二龍北去未曾還.峯巒崔崒層雲上.城堞逶迤遠霧閒.捷徑洞穿八達嶺.青龍橋畔水潺湲.

張家口

闤闠恍如雲.漢蒙此通驛.成群急載來.毛骨與齒革.孰云塞外荒.或殘滋黍稷.西北去萬里.羅羅有軌迹.大地棄不治.人少自多石.救國不先兵.惟患民生瘠.所望秉國者.厲行實邊策.

別京中諸友

我是閒雲不繫身.遨游到處結眞因.十年續做京華夢.兩脚踏殘上苑春.囊底無投方訝老.杖頭有挂幾忘貧.沙蟲猿鶴且休問.歸食故鄉新夏蓴.

菩薩蠻　別情

京華相見頭皆白.飛揚意氣今猶昔.車笠見交情.挑燈話不勝.離多嗟會少.惆悵長亭道.游興已闌珊.倦飛鳥欲還.

商務印書館發行

各大雜誌

革新內容　削減定價

（國內定戶郵費不計）

本館發行各雜誌，內容豐富，供應各方面需要，每年銷數在二百萬册以上，茲爲益求精起見，十五年起內容大加刷新，除婦女 英文兩種，增加篇幅，東方 英語已照新價發售不再改訂外，餘均一律削價，使讀者負擔格外減輕，預定概免郵費，十四年內預定未滿之小說世界每二册，繼續贈閱一册，兒童世界每一册繼續贈閱一册。

名稱	全年册數	零售價目	零售郵費	預定全年價目 國內	預定全年價目 國外	版式（英寸）
東方雜誌	24	每册一角二分五釐	國內二分 國外八分	三元	四元六角	6⅞×9⅞
教育雜誌	12	每册一角	國內二分 國外八分	一元二角	二元	6⅞×9⅞
學生雜誌	12	每册一角	國內二分 國外八分	一元二角	二元	6½×9⅝
少年雜誌	12	每册八分	國內一分 國外四分	九角六分	一元四角	5⅜×7⅞
兒童世界	50	每週一册 每册三分	國內半分 國外二分	一元五角	二元四角	5⅝×7½
兒童畫報	24	月出二册 每册六分	國內半分 國外二分	一元四角四分	一元八角	5⅜×7½
婦女雜誌	12	每册二角	國內二分 國外八分	二元四角	三元二角	6⅝×9⅝
小說月報	12	一角五分	國內二分 國外八分	一元八角	二元六角	6½×9⅞
小說世界	10	每週一册 每册六分	國內一分 國外四分	三元	四元六角	5¼×7¼
英文雜誌	12	每册二角	國內一分 國外四分	二元四角	二元八角	6×9
英語週刊	50	每週一册 每册三分	國內半分 國外二分	一元五角	二元四角	6⅝×9⅝

〈預定半年價照全年折半〉

學 校 記 載

民國十四年本校大事記(摘錄南洋旬刊第七期)

祖 康 編

一月

本年起,機械科科長周子競先生兼任教務長.淩校長暫兼鐵路管理科科長.教員徐君陶先生兼任中學主任. 聘杜礎雲先生為圖書館主任,杜光祖,唐謀伯,張幼涵三先生為教授.

八日 部令去年畢業生派赴各局所實習者一百人.

十一日 江浙二次戰事發生.提前給放寒假.

二月

四日 淩校長晉京,接洽庚款進行及增加上海電報局協款事.

五日 開學.

十六日 本日起,大中學各級補行上學期大考.

三月

本月起,校中每月得增加上海電報局協撥經費二千元.

四日 大中學聯席教務會議議決,改良助教職務及待遇案;提倡學生課外服務案;學生參觀旅行案.

九日 大中學各班恢復晨操.

十一日 呈部請將校外地畝出售,購入校西地畝.二十七日,部令照准.

二十三日 開孫中山先生追悼大會於大禮堂.請章太炎先生等演說.

二十五日 大中學聯席教務會議議決,增設中學生選科指導員案,又大學各級試行指導員制案.

二十七日　事務會議開會.重要議案如下,(一)收回吳淞商船校舍案,(二)規定本校校徽校色校歌校聲案,(三)舉行本校三十週紀念案

四月

一日　本日起,照章放春假七天.大學學生旅行赴杭州閘口等處參觀各工廠.

五日　行植樹典禮,植樹二百餘株.

十八日　舉行全校運動會.結果溫錫東君得個人錦標.

二十五日　東方八大學聯合運動會在南京東南大學舉行.結果本校列第五.

二十八日　美國圖書館專家鮑士偉博士來校參觀.

二十九日　大中學聯席會議議決增加體育教課案.

五月

八日　小學童子軍十七人,舉行二十四小時徒步旅行.

九日　國恥紀念,停課茹素一天.

十六日　發出請求分撥庚款正式說帖,並分寄各董事.

二十二日　華東三大學英語演說競賽會在本校舉行.本校學生邱祜聯君得第一.

二十七日　大中學聯席教務會議議決,中學二年級增加理科一門案又工程科轉入管理科學生應概入管理科一年級第一學期案.

三十日　五卅事起,附屬中學學生陳虞欽君死之.學生罷課.教職員全體加入上海教職員聯合會.

六月

三十日　校長晉京報告滬案經過,並接洽財部補助費

七月

一日　本日起,放暑假.假期內,圖書館員姚大霖先生派赴南京暫圖書

館學.校長在京請添道路科及汽車科,部令照准.

三日　本日起至九日止大學部四年級生舉行畢業攷試.部派滬甯路局長沈叔玉先生來校監攷.

十六日　大學部行畢業禮,授學位,

二十一日　本日及二十二日,大學部招攷一年級新生.

二十四日　本日及二十五日.中學部招攷一年級新生及各級插班生

三十一日　事務會議開會,討論變通攷查學生操行辦法等案.

八月

七日　部令本屆畢業生分發各路練習者四十八人.

十六日　部令淩校長兼任吳淞商船學校籌備處主任.

二十二日　部令知財政部,准於金案餘款內撥給本校補助費.(此款迄未領到)

二十四日　教授李振吾先生赴京出席電報改用國音字母會議,

九月

十五日　本日起,中學部四年級生補行畢業攷試.

十六日　上午,行開學禮.本學期新聘王爾綱丁西崙兩先生爲教授,何志競聶賓彬兩先生爲中學英文教員,方則庭先生爲中學學監,趙祖康先生爲校長室辦事.鐵路管理科科長由該科教授俞行修先生兼任.本學期起,學生穿制服.

二十三日　本日起,大中學各班一律補行學期攷試.

三十日　大中學各班一律上課.

十月

二日　秋節放假.

六日　淩校長召集選派畢業生留學評定會.結果,上學年大學畢業生潘世宜楊恆二人當選.

七日　組織出版演講兩委員會.

十日　國慶放假.上午在大禮堂行慶祝典禮.

十一日　小學童子軍舉行十週紀念會.

十四日　孔誕放假.

十六日　本校體育行政委員會登報聲明,並正式通知華東大學體育聯合會,宣告退出八大學體育聯合會.同時學生會發表退出宣言.

二十一日　組織大學出版部

二十四日　胡適之博士來校演講.

二十九日　小學童子軍參加全滬聯合大露宿四天.

三十一日　庚子賠款委員會派員來校,調查實況.

十一月

十六日　大學電機科續開無線電報收發班.

二十二日　上午,開陳（廣欽）吳（恆慈）二君追悼會.下午,爲陳君舉殯安葬.

二十六日　校務會議議定採用校徽及學生帽章等案.

二十八日　中學各級及大學一年級在大禮堂舉行國文比賽.

十二月

五日　下午二時起,行體育館調養室落成禮.馬湘伯先生蒞會演說.附屬中學補行畢業式.

十七日　淩校長宣布大中學各級國文比賽應行給獎名單,計得獎者章作霖沈孝明朱世通君等八十七人.

二十二日　冬節放假.

二十三日　雲南起義紀念放假.

南洋學會之今昔觀

徐鐘淮

余於民國四年暑假考入本校附屬小學時,南洋學會方創立未久而南洋學會之名已膾炙人口.所出版之學生雜誌尤遠近馳名,紙貴一時.其後會務幾經興革,屢有變遷.先後會員不下千人.歷史深長,前程遠大.爰作斯篇,所以誌既往,示方來.惟倉猝成篇,未暇詳加攷索,舛誤之處,統希閱者正之.　編者識

一, 南洋學會之緣起

本會發起於民國三年.先是上中院同學感於本校精神之渙散,情誼之澆薄,舍功課而外,無復聯絡,乃有組織學會之提議.是年十二月三十日.在上院國文教室開籌備會,討論大綱,選舉參議員.是後擬定草章,徵集會員.定名爲南洋學會,於翌年一月十三日成立.

二, 南洋學會之歷史

本會于四年一月十三日在大禮堂開成立大會.張君時雨.傅君煥光當選爲正副會長.淩君鴻勛,柴君福沅,張君孝安等被舉爲重要職員.諸君悉本會發起人.宏謀遠慮,壓錫元勳.

本會初成立時.會員約百二十人.其後陸續報名入會者又五十餘人.以上院樓下九號爲本會辦事室.未幾,公舉唐前校長爲本會名譽會長,各教職員亦有爲名譽會員者.既得當局者之提倡.益以辦事人之熱心.會務進行乃蒸蒸日上.

本會初分言語,編輯,游藝三部.每月至少有常會兩次.例有中西語演說或辯論.并請名人演講或佐以各種餘興.趣味濃深,裨益匪淺.編輯部專以編輯雜誌爲務.更有營業部,任印刷發行等事.第一期學生雜誌於是年六月出版,不久即銷售一空.良以材料豐富,爲當時我校唯一之出版物,亦最爲社會

所推崇也。

民國五年爲本會全盛時代。會員達四百餘人。各部皆極積進行，不遺餘力。六年秋，柴君福沅繼爲會長，連任三載，厥功尤偉。是時編輯部改爲出版部，分編輯，印刷，發行三科。言語部最爲發達，成績卓著。九年秋，學會改組。取消會長制，代以幹事會。舉彭所君爲幹事長。是年冬，發起南洋商業公司，招股開辦，組織董事會，專司其事。進行有序，規模粗具，此爲本會販賣部之嚆矢。

十年秋爲本會中興時代。理事長張君延祥擘劃周詳，熱心會務。徵求新會員，共得四百五十餘人。會務分編輯，出版，言語，技術，遊藝，營業諸部。遊藝部尤爲當時所重視。該部自八年秋即大加擴充。初分文藝，造像，音樂，彈碁，書畫，金石，英文，幻術八股。繼改打字，攝影，檯球，參觀四股。至是又分爲新劇，崑曲，中樂，西樂，京劇，幻術六股。歷任部長如陶天杏，徐馥雲，柴志明諸君皆一時翹楚是年十二月二十九日，舉行慶祝元旦遊藝會，極有精彩是夕，全校師生同處一堂，融融之樂，前所未有。技術部亦分照相，打字，騎術等股。并舉行攝影比賽。今之照相，打字，國樂三部及學生會之檯球部，皆胚胎於此。其後各部屢有變遷。先後總幹事彭君無荒，曾君麗順，皆能不辭艱苦，力策進行。

十三年秋，又恢復會長制。吳君慶源爲會長。將販賣部所設之營業公司大加整頓。煥然一新。照相股，國樂股皆竭力擴充，進步可驚。翌年春，舉行暗室開幕禮。照相比賽則以五卅停課延至本學期舉行。嗣以遊藝部與學生會之游藝部重複，技術部長之位久虛。乃將照相，打字，國樂三股悉改爲部。共有照相，打字，國樂，編輯及販賣五部。

三，　南洋學會之現狀

本會成立以來兩度采用會長制，取其能統一事權也。泄會務愈趨愈繁，一人之精力有限，會長制已不適用於今日。本學期開學後，乃更改用委員制。卽以各部部長爲委員，俾分工合作，進行便利。除原有之照相，國樂，打字，編輯。販賣諸部外，復增設書畫，弦樂，棋奕三部。於十一月二十五日在大禮堂開全體大會,通過新訂章程,改選各部職員.是日,凌竹銘(鴻勛)校長周明誠(銘,)柴芷湘(福沅)諸先生皆蒞會演說,勉勵有加.後發給照相比賽獎牌,復佐以餘興盡歡而散.

十二月二十四日,本會假大禮堂映演著名電影「董幃警夢」及芬蘭領事贈映之該國風景,運動影片.觀衆達五百餘人.夜深始散.

本會自改組以來,會員均須入部.(如照相部部員等)致舊有會員被擯者不少.嗣以本會志在調劑精神,聯絡感情,爰於十二月內大舉徵求會員.結果計得普通會員(不入各部爲部員)二百餘人,連舊有會員都凡三百四十人,洵盛事也.現復定於一月八日假小學禮堂舉行同樂大會,慶祝新年.玆再將各部最近情形,分述於后.

(一)照相部　照相部原名照相股.創于民國九年.其先因陋就簡,幾於消滅.至十年改隸技術部,始大加整頓,漸次擴充.因歷任部長之熱心,故成績亦特著.現有暗室一間,布置適宜.十月間舉行照相比賽一次,藉以引起研究之興趣,並與滬上諸著名照相館訂定優待章程.現有部員三十人.

(二)打字部　打字部原名打字股.初與照相股同隸技術部.先後購打字機兩架,一置西宿舍,一置上院.部員凡四十人.分兩組練習.近復請校中打字教習金開文先生按時教授.以期進步迅速.

(三)國樂部　國樂部成立於民國十年,以提倡國粹爲宗旨.中備有笙弦管樂二十餘器,以供練習之需.現有部員三十人,分甲乙兩組.請大同樂會柳堯章先生爲教授成績已頗可觀.

(四)書畫部　琴棋書畫古號四藝.高尚之藝術亦日用之技能.本會有鑑於斯,久有提倡之意.故特增設書畫,弦樂,棋奕三部.惟以弦樂部需款浩繁,棋奕部又無固定地點,一時皆難實現.書畫部業經籌備就緒,報名者已達四十餘人.定於一月十三日開成立大會,討論進行方針.幷擬請書畫名家爲教授,藉資指導.

(五)編輯部　南洋學報十一年停刊.本學期職員選齊後,方趕編袖珍記事冊,不日卽可出版.

(六)版賣部　本會之設版賣部,所以便利同學而藉此輔助會中經費也.初用股東制定名南洋營業公司.會中得分潤餘利若干.迨五卅案起,曾由該公司經理部議決,將全部生財悉數捐出.本學期重行組織,廢股東制.並改今名.

四，結　論

本會成立十有一年.慘澹經營,漸著成績.祇以經濟拮据,未能盡力擴充藝者吾校祇有本會唯一團體.且係師生合,作薈萃全校精華,當然發展致易惟本會既有此深長之歷史,已著之成績.瞻前顧後,豈能恝然.本學期改章以來,進行不遺餘力.凡所以利會員,娛同學者罔弗積極,爲謀.惟會務之發達,胥賴羣策羣力.語云:「聚流成河」又曰「衆擎易舉」所盼集思廣益,共圖建樹,豈獨本會之幸,抑亦吾校之光也.

附本會現行組織大綱暨現任委員及各部職員題名

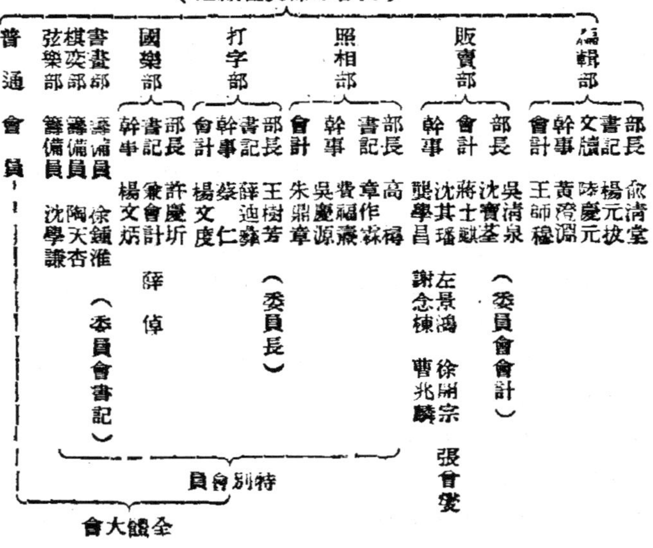

南洋大學技擊部十三年來發達史

技擊部

吾校之有技擊始自遜清宣統二年.校長唐公鑒於旅順遼陽二役.日人以刺擊勝強俄.而回審本國虛弱之風.久而成俗.長此因循.勢將爲人魚肉.爰創是部.以便諸同學課餘練習.冀達自衞衞人之旨.正式成立.於玆十有三載.已紀可頌.爰將本部發達史表而出之.俾知歷年上下孤心苦詣,經營不易.而益思有以光大之.使國粹藉以不亡也.

按我校之始有技擊.並未正式聘請教師.時有外國教授試驗機車.中院同學向君紹洪以雙手承之.車不能動.後稔知其得力於南拳.校長遂請其任教練.學習者不下數十人,厥後學者愈多.向君以課務不克兼顧.乃專聘本埠精武體育會劉振聲張富有趙連和三先生教授北拳.此我校有技擊之濫觴也.

民國元年春.上院同學穆郞君介紹浙江溫州某寺高僧.倉演肅謙兩師先後來校教授蝦蟆功.約半載.當倉演肅謙未來時.部員練習在雨操場.迨倉演肅謙來校.適校外商船學校遷移吳淞.該校房屋甚多.且極幽靜.故技擊同學咸遷入之.至是始得一專練所.而技擊部亦正式成立.舉正副部長黃君照臨李君鴻儒主其事.定規則.備器械.製服裝.限名額.凡入部者.須具有勇敢強毅之體魄.經教師選驗.然後入部.非復昔日之目爲具文也.

民國二年春.同學中多有復學北拳者.乃由部長黃君介紹濟南劉震南先生授心意六合門拳法.同時王芝祥上將軍介紹燕京李存義先生授形義功.此功盛行於北京.士大夫多喜習之.亦爲拳術上乘惜數月即中止.是歲夏.劉師因事遠遊.校長復聘湖南劉世傑先生授白水功.

三年春.世傑先生得軍界要職.復請震南先生來校.入部者接踵.先生拳宗心意六合.譽滿大江南北.足跡半天下.生平義俠軼事甚多.惜不暇詳述.其

勤於職務.熱心教授.尤有足多.藉先生之力.本部得有今日也.至學習之法.可分爲間架動作及用法三步.循序漸進.不可躐等.先生循循善誘.按步教導.領人入室.其年十月.攝影搏擊六張.陳列巴拿馬博覽會.復定學習四年成績優良者.給予證書.以示獎勵.是年部長仍爲黃照臨君.

四年春.本校大運動會加入技擊一項.同學以平日練習有素.故得大顯身手.唐校長更對衆演講.鼓吹斯道.當時徐匯道上.車水馬龍.本部之名.遂播傳衆口.斐然有聞矣.部長仍爲黃君照臨.

五年夏.部長黃照臨畢業.得心意六合門云.是歲部長爲張孝友君.

六年春.學校舉行二十週紀念大會.紀念之末日.首節爲技擊表演.觀者如堵.先小學而後中院上院.愈演愈妙.拳脚兼施.刀鎗並舉.有令人目不暇給之勢.其中以鮑君國寶劉君畯傑對子爲最有精采.一時觀者皆贊美不絕.鮑君後流學美利堅.彼邦人士.深服其武藝.優禮備至.大爲祖國光.此豈偶然哉.是年部長即鮑君也得技擊畢業證書者.有張孝友鮑國寶伍淵諸君.

七年春.入部者增至五十名.是歲唐公發起湘賑遊藝大會.本部表演以葉舒瑤君之醉八仙.蕭蒐張其學.兩君之單刀.遂爲最精采.部長爲張令綵葉舒瑤二君.

八年春.入部者增至七十名.三月十二日之夜.校長唐公召全體部員在大禮堂.諄諄訓辭.以唐荊川陸桴亭諸先輩相勉.唐公冀望之殷.於此可見.部員於是益加奮勵.是年夏.全國學生憤國事日非.外交棘手.相繼罷課.本校同學每晨向國旗行禮後.本部部員即至雨操場練習.自是雞鳴殘月.常見刀光劍影.飛舞於大學之西.輒欲以書生報國.效宗法於少林.是年秋.應上海青年會等團體之請.表演於滬上者數次.名乃益彰.是歲部長爲張令綵君.葉舒瑤君得畢業證書者亦爲張葉二君.

九年春.入部者增至百名.參與學校集會與滬上各團體之請求表演者數次.是歲部長金詠君.朱維銓君.朱君辦事熱心.捨己爲公.曉風夜月.常率本

部健兒.舞劍弄棍.以是人才更多造就.更以部員日增.規模漸大.乃修改章程.添置器械.氣象煥然.蓬勃直上.

十年春.本校改組大學.張主任劍心.鑒於立教之不可缺.竭力提倡之.於是本部益形發達.入部者增至二百餘人.共分甲,乙,丙,丁,四組.甲組以舊部員組織之.練習器械及對搏應變之法.乙組以中院四年級學生組織之.丙組以中院三年級與二年級學生組織之.丁組以中院一年級學生組織之.乙組至丁組.按其年齡體格.授以相當拳術.復有月試以察部員之勤惰.分組錦標比賽.以資鼓勵.是歲秋.學校開懇親會.本部以張公竭力提倡.故表演節目.較歷年倍之.我武維揚.一時稱盛.是歲部長爲朱維銓君.鮑錫瑤君.畢業者有吳維翰君.李果能君.湯輔仁君三人.

十一年春.應滬江大學化裝演講團之請.赴錫表演.演者具有蛟躍螭騰雲合鳥逝之概.大得彼邑人士之歡迎.一時報紙揄揚.譽滿梁溪.是歲新闢技擊部會集室.室中陳列各種器械.拳術圖解等.庶幾同學觀之.一觸目而形勢昭然.更設閱書部.藏古今拳術經集.俾部員課餘揣摩.以資研究.復鑒於勇力亦拳家所須.故設沙袋棒手.部員咸能以恆心持之.敏力赴之.是歲部長爲邱褚驊君.左景鴻君.畢業者.爲費福燾君.高渭初君.陸定一君.

十二年.本部部員稍減.分爲甲乙二組練習.夏.發行十周紀念册.周遍中外.至今各省來函購閱者不絕.秋.部員又增.議决編輯技擊叢刊.是歲部長爲華君壽奎.朱君瑞節.二君才能並長.熱心爲公.極多設施.畢業者.有華壽奎.朱瑞節.邱褚驊三君.

十三年.技擊叢刊第一集.撫寄拳壽備進行.由吳維翰君主其事.侯毓慶君爲編輯.侯君精拳術.擅文學.更能爲公不倦.竭半載心力.是刊始成.惜天忌高才.未及出版.而侯君已長逝.然則侯君與斯刊.同一不朽矣.是年.淩公竹銘來長校務.徐公君陶主任中院.二公於本部提倡不遺餘力.定中院一年級同學須一律加入本部.於是部員益衆.精神益振.是歲.部長春季爲吳君維翰.劉君世

恆.秋季爲劉君世恆.盧君之謙.

十四年,技擊叢刊第一集.燕青拳發行.計五萬餘言.翼飛脛走.社會爭購.按.是刊之成.財力兩方.不藉旁助.洵非易事.是歲一切設施.有興無廢.此現在之情形也.部長春季爲陶君忠澄.滕君修祺.秋季爲劉君世恆.費君福熊.

綜觀以往.我校技擊部之創始篳路藍縷.經營非易.迄今規模完備.成歐績卓然.前途誠無限量.夫國技式微極矣.前代文弱成風.鄙斯道爲末技.今者化東盛.華驚西學.乞鄰之械.喪家之寶.幸賴識時君子.抱殘守缺.奔走提倡.斯道得不滅.是誠剝復消長之好現象也.吾願先民之國技.並中華民國而同長吾不願先民之國技.隨二十世紀而同斬.邦人君子.其亦知所興乎.

同學會紀載

一. 過去一年中之事業　　鶴陸

南洋公學同學會章程,十餘年來,未曾修改.民國十三年三月,重行釐訂.改董事爲理事.一面選舉新理事.一面仍由舊董事維持會務.十四年三月十五日.假大東旅社.舉行年會聚餐.新舊同學到者百餘人.本會會員人數衆多,散在各地.辦理選舉,頗非易事.至四月三十日方開匭檢票.得票最多者爲凌竹銘.沈叔逵.黃任之.胡敦復.張叔良.張松亭.吳稚暉.章伯初.張菊生.王寶清.張雪樓.唐君.張菊生.張雪樓二君辭職.胡敦復.吳稚暉二君不在上海.由次多數之林康侯張貢九張延祥徐君陶四君遞補.改推張菊生君爲名譽會長.並互選章伯初君爲會長,王寅清,張松亭二君爲書記.張延祥君爲會計.公推林康侯君爲基金監,柴芷湘君爲編輯員.同時並將會所由上海三馬路兆福里遷至二馬路平樂里.友聲第十四期趕印出版.八月五日,常務理事會議決捐建科學館贈送母校以爲學校三十周年之紀念.並定募捐辦法.現正在努力提倡中.九月二十七日,乙卯級畢業十周紀念之日彝台建築落成舉行開幕禮.該級同學並邀觀禮諸同學在校聚餐.十月,友聲第十五期出版.十一月,與母校合辦南洋旬刊及季刊.友聲停止刊行.十二月,理事會議決按照會章畢業同學每級互選一人爲議董.應從速實行.本會除上海總會外,各地設分會尤以北京留美兩分會爲最大.均另有記錄,不贅於此.

二. 理事暨職員題名

理事	章宗元（伯初:會長）	王永禮（寅清:書記）
	張孝安（松亭:書記）	張延祥（會計）
	林祖溍（康侯:基金監）	淩鴻勛（竹銘）
	沈慶鴻（叔逵）	黃炎培（任之）
	張世鎏（叔良）	張廷金（貢九）
	徐佩璜（君陶）	
編輯員	柴福沅（芷湘）	

三. 永久會員題名錄

1張元濟	2曾鯤琮	3曾宗鑑	4章宗祥	5陳杜衡	6張世鎏
7章宗元	8陸銘盛	9王聲澳	10潘保同	11李復幾	12曾懋介
13王傳熊	14徐恩第	15楊耀麟	16莊銘九	17鄧福培	18郎國楨
19周恭良	20湯天棟	21周淑壽	22周文炯	23劉元濟	24陶庭耀

25虞順懋　26周承恩　27徐維明　28沈慶鴻　29徐維霞　30周承錫
31邢　城　32潘銘新　23盛同孫　34趙曾珏　35凌鴻勛　36歐陽銘
37吳玉麟　38陸法曾　39謝　仁　40鍾　鍔　41李熙謀　42朱善培
43張一鵬　44黃　炎　45楊耀文　46周　銘　47顧維精　48裘維裕
49朱鼎元　50范永增　51梁樹釗　52周　仁　53周增奎　54項康原
55黃慶瀾　56梁嵩齡　57劉清蘭　58陳大啓　59張孝安　60蔡邦霖
61鄭鼎錫　62席德柄　63席德懋　64楊繡瓚　65王　璧　66陳仁愷
67黃炎培　68余建復　69徐恩元　70張　晉　71胡端行　72楊　毅
73鈕因辭　74王懷曾　75龔寶琳　76俞希稷　77盤珠衡　78楊培琫
79許復陽　80黃家齊　81李大中　82王大鈞　83潘　尹　84趙鴻鈞
85周善同　86林汝耀　87郭祖濤　88葉達前　89陳廣沅　90葛學瑄
91諸水本　92鄭　泗　93茅以新　94毋本敏　95孫家璧　96陳　璋
97葉大根　98張　峻　99梁朌致　100尤寅照　101許應期　102李純圭
103武書常　104姚爾昌　105徐新陸　106夏全綬　107林祖湑　108王永禮
109徐恩曾　101張樹源　111陳體榮　112丁紫芳　113葛吉生　114盛逸銘
115梁汝湑　116戴麟書

四. 籌建科學館先聲

母校新建築圖書館落成之後,體育館調養室繼之,現又先後告竣矣,同學會理事諸君以科學關係重要,未可偏廢,爰於上年八月五日常務理事會通過議案一件,擬就母校三十周年鑑會,向全體同學募捐建築圖書館一所贈送母校藉留永久紀念,其辦法大略擬訂如次:

一　建築費以募足五萬元爲最低限度.

一　科學館內的留餘室,作爲同學會事務室.

一 捐款以（南洋卅周紀念）六字爲標題.南字捐五百元.洋字捐二百元.卅字捐一百元.周字捐五十元.紀字捐二十五元.念字捐十元.

一 以每班爲一隊.分隊募捐.由京會先推正隊長一人,再由滬會推副隊長一人,向各該班同學勸募.歷屆同學名單由滬會印發.

一 募捐擬由京會.滬會及各地分會全體職員共同列名發起.

一 捐款人全體題名館內,以垂紀念.

一 由京.滬兩會職員票選保管捐款及籌備建築委員七人.委員不以兩會職員爲限.

盍簪記

張景良

中國之有師範學校,自南洋公學始.清季朝廷以興國之本.首在教育.武進宮保盛公宣懷.奏設於上海鄉之徐家匯.以何公嗣焜爲總理.張公煥綸爲總教習.招各省學者肄業其中.講求教法.編纂教本.吾同學先後來者.計七十餘人.一堂濟濟.相得益彰.迨乎六年期滿.遂各星散.今忽忽三十年.或仕,或師,或農或商,或主論壇,或事武備.而不幸者則委世事而去.追懷舊雨.能不依依.同學沈君叔逵.攄懷舊之雅意.發思古之幽情.爰於民國十四年十一月二十九日,集旅滬者.宴會於母校西偏之新第.來者爲張君惕銘,朱君樌之,孟君蒓孫.趙君瑞侯,張君實摶,傅君緯平,潘君若梁,黄君涵之,林君植齋.陳君景韓及景良計十有二人.晤言一室.清酒百觴.滄桑世變.故舊情長.景良叨陪末座.追憶前芳.不勝百感.爲賦一章.幸有以教之.

菁菁者莪.陰雨膏之.言念君子.薄言采之.(興也)

勻勻原田.有收有穫.言念君子.其始播百穀.(興也)

瞻彼四方.道阻且長.睠懷我友.日不能忘.(賦也)

君子有酒.聚話滄桑.一堂濟濟.樂且無央.(賦也)

校友要訊

校友消息已隨時登載南洋旬刊.惟讀本刊者未必皆見旬刊,又旬刊零星散,不便保存.擷錄大要.以姓字筆畫繁爲次,彙載於此,用便審覽.

王 王裕光君 畢業於康南耳大學後,在紐約鋼鐵建築公司服務二年.去年九月歸國.

王維尹君(志莘) 曾赴紐約專習銀行學.去春畢業後,游歐洲.秋歸國

王崇植君 在杭州任教職.現兼任本校教授,並主編上海醒獅週刊之科學特刊.

宋 宋慶生君 去夏自費赴美,入普渡大學機械科四年級肄業.

余 余肅謙君(公儼) 客秋應清華學校聘,任該校工程主任.

車 車志城君(耕南) 去春任膠海關監督秘書.現在京奉鐵路會計科辦事.

李 李 錚君(鐵中) 上年十一月二十一日,在申與楊竹雲女士結婚.

李文灝君(希顏) 在上海東亞銀行服務.去年十一月十九日結婚.

李大鵬君 現入本薛佛尼大學研究院,研究運輸學.

李 青君 在坎拿大鐵路公司任職.

杜 杜光祖君 現任本校教授.去年十二月三十一日,在本埠與鄭女士結婚.聞女士即同學鄭祖彝君之令妹云.

沈 沈元慶君(伯衍) 現回校,在文牘股及出版部辦事.

沈炳麟君 仍在美國西屋電廠實習.

周 周延鼎君(君梅) 十四年十月十五日,在上海慕爾堂與張芷英女士結婚.

金 金士城君 與同學徐芝田君等合辦中南機器建築公司於上海愛多亞路五十號.

金 濤君 現在美國某汽車公司實習.

吳 吳遂模君 向在美國西屋電廠實習.現已回國.

吳保豐君 向在西屋公司實習.現入密歇根大學研究院肄業.

范 范本中君 在美國加城實習研究鐵路電氣號誌.

茅 茅以新君 去夏畢業于普渡大學校.七月入坎拿大鐵路公司實習.

俞 俞汝鑫君（恕菴） 現入哈佛大學肄業.

梁 梁汝緒君（濟猛） 向在江浦經營農墾.現寓上海北京路慶泰里同濟號

殷 殷受宜君 在美國加城實習,研究鐵路電氣號誌.

殷文友君 現入哈佛大學肄業.

袁 袁濬昌君 交通部派赴法國調查交通事業.並即充駐法調查員.

袁丕烈君 現在美國費城盤得文機車公司實習.

韋 韋國英君（伯和） 任本埠招商局公學教習.已多年.

韋國鈴君（仲懷） 赴美留學.已回國.現在交通部任職.

韋國傑君（叔達） 在膠濟鐵路服務.本屆該路局會同本校保舉留生.君名與其列.上年十二月三十一日.在青島與楊玉如女士結婚.

桂 桂銘敬君（恕兼） 現任廣東公路局技士.並廣東大學教授.去冬十二月八與.陳美瑰女士結婚.

徐 徐芝田君（蘇生） 與同學金君等合辦中南機器建築公司.

徐恩培君 仍在哈佛大學肄業

徐恩曾君 去夏由美回國.現任南市自來水公司工程師.

陳 陳廣沅君（贊清） 現在意里諾大學任職.

陳體榮君 現入哈佛大學研究院肄業

陳　章君 在美國奇異電氣公司實習.現任同學會分會圖書委員會主任.

陳士鈞君　部派吳淞無線電局實習.現兼任上海招商局公學教職.

陸　陸法曾君（富如）　在西門子公司任職.客冬赴安慶裝設電燈.

曹　曹鳳山君　現入哈佛大學肄業

許　許應期君　現在哈佛大學研究院肄業.

程　程本臧君　現在波斯頓都文機器公司實習.

程本厚君　現在美國盤得文機車公司實習.

傅　傅煥光君（志章）　向在東南大學及昆蟲局服務.現任綏遠實業廳任科長之職.

高　高君湘君　去夏得法學碩士位於密歇根大學.現在福特汽車公司任職.

盛　盛祖江君　留美多年,現已回國.

張　張延祥君　與同學支,呂諸君合組新中公司.去年十一月二十二日,與彭潤菊女士結婚.

張時雨君（澍丞）　在天津順直水利委員會任職.去秋悼亡.

張承緒君　仍在美國西屋電廠實習.

鈕　鈕因梁君　已得碩士學位於康南耳大學.現入費城盤得文機車公司實習.

單　單基乾君　現在美國密歇根電話公司實習.

惲　惲　震君　向在鄭州豫豐紗廠任職.現在東南大學任電磁學教授,並主編上海醒獅週刊之科學特刊.

孫　孫雲霄君　現任長沙工業專門學校教授.去秋與褚女士在嘉興結婚

楊　楊錫鏐君（右辛）　向在東南建築公司任職.現與友人合辦凱泰公司於上海北蘇州路三十號.

楊毅君（華臣）　前膠濟鐵路四方機廠廠長,調任總務處考工課課長.

楊淥暉君　向在上海工部局工程處任事,旋入京.現已回滬矣.

楊瑞德君　向在杭州工業專門學校任電機科長之職.現改就嘉興緯成絲織公司機械電機工程師.

鄒 鄒忠曜君　去秋由美回國.現任愼昌洋行工程師.

趙 趙以曜君（鳳威）　向在交通部任職.十四年秋調入育才科辦事.

趙玉森君（瑞侯）　師範班老同學.工詩古文詞.現寓本埠大沽路中國內地麵粉公會.

葉 葉家垣君　去年十二月六日.在廣州與羅璧君女士結婚.

劉 劉振淸君（劍菴）　向在母校服務.現任蘇州電燈廠工程師.十四年十月十二日,在上海與張慧瑩女士結婚.現寓蘇州鈕家巷十七號.

蔡 蔡承新君　現入哥侖比亞大學肄業.

蔣 蔣以鐸君（達黴）　現任鄭州豫豐紗廠土木科主任.客冬曾赴東三省游歷.

錢 錢德新君（介夫）　向任海門中學教務主任現並代理校長.

聶 聶溥儒君（靜齋）　向在交通部任職.十四年秋調入育才科辦事.

蘇 蘇祖修君　與乃兄祖圭在上海江西路四十三號,開辦亞美公司,經營電機事業,仿造一切小機件.

龐 龐元浩君（贊臣）　曾赴美經營商業.現主持龍華龍章造紙廠.

顧 顧惟精君（心一）　交通部技士兼電報局工程師.十四年秋調任育才科教務主任.

顧希孟君　現在杭州郵局帳務處任職.

南洋一覽稿

柴福沅芷湘甫擬

福沅離校三年.今春復歸故壘.校長淩公以福沅在校時日較長,情形熟悉,命撰南洋一覽,綜述既往,用示方來,意至善也.福沅才識庸愚,筆尤不達.搜求載籍,網羅軼聞,竭半年之力,始克脫稿.篇幅繁重,印刷爲難.入秋趙君祖康乃撮要刪繁,更爲概況一書,已付手民.淩公以一覽原稿應用非便,繙檢尙佳,囑分期印入季刊餘葉.掩胔埋骨,同此仁心.錄副既盡,用誌一言.次列四點.幸注意焉.十四年冬日,福沅識.

一, 本書標目爲篇.敍事貫串.既殊本末,亦異編年.溯古及今,期盡原委.

二, 本書敍述始於創設.截至今夏.秋冬興革,不著於錄.

三, 事實發生,向少記載.考證詳確,實所難冀.如有謬誤,當更訂正.

四, 附載季刊,自爲欄格.分印八期二年可盡.彙編改訂,另自成書.

目次

校名之變更及其年代

南洋公學	七年（清光緒二十三年至二十九年）
上海商務學堂	一年（光緒二十九年至三十年）
商部高等實業學堂	二年（光緒三十一年至三十二年）
郵傳部上海高等實業學堂	五年（光緒三十三年至宣統三年）
南洋大學堂	一年（宣統三年至民國元年）
交通部上海工業專門學校	九年（民國元年至十年）
交通大學上海學校	一年（民國十年至十一年）
交通部南洋大學	民國十一年起

沿革

瀛海大通,神州多故.甲午以還,國勢益弱,朝野上下忧於強鄰之壓迫,思,力圖富強以振之.時勢所趨,競尚新學.盛杏蓀先生宣懷有志興學.適督辦招商電報二局.頗有盈餘.乃奏請設南洋公學於上海.請光緒二十三年,假徐家匯民房開辦.奏派何梅生先生嗣焜爲總理.設師範院.有志之士舍棄舉業,來學於斯.故當時學生,舉人廩貢爲多,秋,設外院.派師範生輪流教之.二十四年購地百餘畝,建築校舍,是爲中院.是年冬,派學生六人留學日本.意氣奮發,慷慨請行,志甚壯也,二十六年,添建上院,並設譯書院於虹口.譯印東西實學書籍,風行一時.嚴幾道先生復之原富尤負盛名.二十七年春,何梅生先生以盡瘁校務.積勞致疾卒.張菊生先生元濟繼任爲總理.當時風氣未開,招生不易乃設附屬小學爲升學之預備.又設特班爲應經濟特科之預備.主其事者蔡子民先生元培也.是年冬,張菊生先生辭職.勞玉初乃宣,沈子培曾植.汪芝房鳳藻,三先生相繼爲總理.二十九年春,師範院特班均裁撤.劉葆良樹屏,張筱圖鶴齡,張讓三美翊,三先生相繼爲總理.是爲南洋公學時代.計七年.二十九年八月,改名上海商務學堂.仍由招商電報二局撥款辦理.三十年,二局改隸商部.本校因亦隸商部,是年秋,盛杏蓀先生,張讓三先生均相繼辭職.

三十一年,廢總理提調之稱,奏派楊杏城先生士琦爲監督.改校名曰商部高等實業學堂.三十二年,設商務鐵路兩專科.是年冬,招商電報二局改隸郵傳部.又改名郵傳部高等實業學堂.計隸屬商部時期.不足二年.

光緒三十三年春,郵傳部派楊頤卿先生文駿爲監督.秋,改派唐蔚芝先生文治爲監督.自是監督始常川駐校辦事.三十四年,設電機專科.並陸續添建金工,木工,電機等廠.時郵傳部擬併路電各科於唐山路礦學堂,而改本校爲商船學堂,嗣以遷移不便,乃仍其舊.但於本校添設船政科,造就航海駕駛人材.唐蔚芝先生在校,竭力提倡國學,歷十餘年不輟.宣統三年秋,移船政各班於校外,另設商船學堂.至民國元年,遂離本校而獨立.武昌起義,全國響應,本校學生組織義勇軍.同時改校名爲南洋大學堂.翌年夏,復歸交通部,改名交通部工業專門學校.民國四年,鑒於體育之不能普及.實行強迫運動並創辦童子軍.六年四月,舉行二十週年紀念大會.展覽成績表演藝術.如荼如火,甚盛事也.同時幷發起建築圖書館藉留紀念.七年春,設鐵路管理科.九年秋,唐蔚芝先生辭職.淩竹銘先生鴻勛,張劍心先生鑄相繼代理校長.十年夏,改組交通大學.自光緒三十三年至是.先後約十五年.均以工業專門學校性質直隸於交通部.其間惟光復時曾一用南洋大學堂之名.爲時實不及一年也.

交通大學爲合併唐山工業專門學校.北京郵電學校.交通傳習所,及本校之總名.當時爲劃一學科起見,移本校鐵路管理科於北京.土木科於唐山.另設機械科.唐山工業專門學校之鐵路機械科亦併入焉.大學設董事會.推名流十九人爲校董.校長駐京辦事.各地設正副主任.葉玉甫先生恭綽被推爲大學校長.張劍心先生爲上海學校主任.淩竹銘先生副之.十年秋,發起籌建三大建築.三大建築者,學生會集室.體育館.調養室也.校長主任及諸董事先生均熱心提倡,踴躍輸將.今體育館圖書室已先後落成.十一年夏,取消董事會.秋,本校復與北京唐山二校分立,自改組大學至是,爲交通大學時代計一年.

民國十一年秋,改名交通部南洋大學.移併於北京之鐵路管理科仍回本校續辦.盧孔生先生炳田,陳芳齋先生杜衡相繼長校.十三年冬,復任淩竹銘先生爲校長,內崇實事,外圖發展,本校前途正未可量也.

附本校大事記

清光緒二十二年丙申（西歷一八九六）

冬,大理寺少卿盛宣懷奏由招商局電報局盈餘項下,年撥銀十萬兩,設南洋公學於上海,造就新學人材,奉旨允准.派盛宣懷爲南洋公學督辦

光緒二十三年丁酉（西歷一八九七）

春,督辦盛宣懷奏派何嗣焜爲南洋公學總理.

聘張煥綸爲總教習.

假徐家匯民房,開辦南洋公學.

設師範院,陸續考取學生四十名.

三月初六日開學.

秋,設外院,考取學生一百二十名,派師範生輪流教之.

聘美國福開森博士爲監院.

光緒二十四年戊戌（西歷一八九八）

春,設中院,錄取學生二十名.（該項學生由外院高級生選拔充之.嗣後外院生遞升中院.外院取消.）

夏,總教習張煥綸辭職.

聘李維格爲提調.

購地一百餘畝於徐家匯北,建築校舍.

冬,派學生六名赴日本留學.(此後逐年派遣學生出洋留學.)

光緒二十五年已亥(西歷一八九九)

夏,中院校舍落成.

提調李維格辭職,伍光建繼之.

秋,購校南民地爲擴充計.

冬,開第一次運動會.

光緒二十六年庚子(西歷一九〇〇)

春,上院校舍落成.

夏,北洋大學學生避拳匪亂來就本校,遂添設鐵路班.並增中院班數.

秋,設譯書院於上海虹口.譯印東西教育政治經濟各書.並考取學生一百二十名,附屬該院.肄習日本文語.聘張元濟爲譯書院主任.

光緒二十七年辛丑(西歷一九〇一)

春正月,總理何嗣焜卒.張元濟繼之

設附屬小學.以師範生陳懋治爲主任.二月初一日開學.

設特班.招學生一百二十名,爲應經濟特科之預備.聘蔡元培爲主任.教員王丹孫及師範生趙從蕃爲教員.

夏,中院第一次畢業.(此後逐年舉行畢業.)

總理.張元濟辭職.勞乃宣繼之.未幾辭職.沈曾植繼之

設政治科.由師範生及中院之高級生選入之.

秋,醇親王載灃使德歸國,便道來校參觀.

冬監院福開森辭職.

光緒二十八年壬寅(西歷一九〇二)

春總理沈曾植,辭職.汪鳳藻繼之.

冬,除師範院及附屬小學外各班學生,同時因事散學.

總理汪鳳藻辭職.劉樹屏繼之.

提調伍光建辭職.張美翊繼之.

散學之各班學生.除特班外均歸校.

光緒二十九年癸卯（西曆一九〇三）

春,裁撤師範院.

總理劉樹屏辭職.提調張美翊兼任.

改政治科爲商科.

夏,小學第一次畢業.（此後逐年舉行畢業.）

秋八月,改校名爲上海商務學堂.

冬,張鶴齡爲總理.

招商電報兩局改隸北洋,經費驟絀.

光緒三十年甲辰（西曆一九〇四）

春,總理張鶴齡辭職.提調張美翊兼任.

小學主任陳懋治辭職,教員林祖縉繼之.

招商電報兩局改隸商部.本校亦改隸商部.

秋,督辦盛宣懷辭職.

冬,提調兼總理張美翊辭職.

光緒三十一年乙巳（西曆一九〇五）

春,商部奏派楊士琦爲監督.

改校名爲商部高等實業學堂.

聘伍光建爲教務長.

秋,監督楊士琦晉京.王清穆代之.

教務長伍光建辭職.教員馮琦繼之.

光緒三十二年丙午（西歷一九〇六）

春,設商務專科.

監督楊士琦回校.

秋,設鐵路專科.

冬,附屬小學校舍落成.

招商電報兩局改隸郵傳部.本年亦改隸郵傳部.並改名郵傳部上海高等實業學堂.

光緒三十三年丁未（西歷一九〇七）

春,監督楊士琦辭職,楊文駿繼之.

三月,因時疫傳染停課.

夏,商務專科畢業.

秋,監督楊文駿辭職.

郵傳部奏派唐文治為監督.常川駐校辦事.

光緒三十四年戊申（西歷一九〇八）

春,改委梁業為教務長.並委李聯珪為國文科長.

遵教育部定章,改高等預科及中院各班為中學.五年畢業.

秋,設電機專科.

宣統元年己酉（西歷一九〇九）

夏,鐵路科第一次畢業.（此後逐年舉行畢業.）

教務長梁業辭職,胡棟朝繼之.

各省咨送學生來校.

設船政科.

添購校後民地,設金工廠.

宣統二年庚戌（西歷一九一〇）

春,就中院後餘地添建宿舍.

建築電機試驗室.

全校減膳助安徽賑捐.

舊同學組織同學會,設總會於上海.北京分會同時成立.

夏,教務長胡棟朝辭職.

收通學生.

聘美國謝而屯爲電機科科長.

冬,選派學生赴南京,參與全國體育大會.

建築木工廠.

聘辜鴻銘爲教務長.

附屬小學開十週紀念會.

宣統三年辛亥（西歷一九一一）

春,聘拳術教師授學生技擊

小學主任林祖溍辭職.教員沈慶鴻繼之.

江淮水災,全校減膳助賑.

購地於吳淞.建商船學堂校舍.

購本校東南之民地房屋.添建宿舍.

校外宿舍落成.

夏,電機科第一次畢業.（此後逐年舉行畢業.）

秋,商船學堂成立.聘夏孫鵬爲主任.招生百餘人.

電機科科長謝而屯介紹畢業生八名,赴美國電廠實習.（本校學生赴外國工廠實習.自此始.）

教務長辜鴻銘辭職.

九月,武昌起義,江蘇響應,本校學生組織義勇軍.

改校名爲南洋大學堂.時南北未統一,經費無着,提招商電報兩局存款充之.

十月,遵用陽歷.放年假.

中華民國元年（壬子）（西歷一九一二）

春,因經費艱窘,徵收學費.

聘胡詒穀爲中學科長.

監督改稱校長.

商船學堂離本校獨立

夏,中學五年級四年級同時畢業,自是中學四年畢業,小學三年畢業.並增設專門預科一級.

本校歸交通部直轄,改名交通部上海工業專門學校.

改鐵路科爲土木科,電機科爲電氣機械科.

中學科長胡詒穀辭職,徐經邦繼之.

民國二年（癸丑）（西歷一九一三）

復聘胡棟朝爲土木科科長.

改訂章程.

夏,建白毓　烈士紀念碑於校園,

民國三年（甲寅）（西歷一九一四）

春,教職員學生一律着制服.

秋,添招中學初年級生一班.

得巴拿馬博覽會第一大獎章.

民國四年（乙　）（　歷一九一五）

春,聘美國萬特克爲土木科科長.

添聘體育專門教員,實行強迫運動.

學生組織南洋學會,刊行雜誌.（自此學生集會始盛.）

夏,參與遠東運動會,中學學生李大星列本國第一.

建築材料試驗廠.

冬,建築養息所及教員宿舍,

辦童子軍,聘英國培克斯爲團長,英國李思廉及小學教員沈維楨副之.

民國五年（丙辰）（西歷一九一六）

春,得北京專門以上學校賽會一等獎.

夏,交通銀行停止匯兌,經費支絀.

冬,爲本校創始人盛宣懷開追悼會.

交通部開交通會議,庶務員阮惟和代表赴京.

民國六年（丁巳）（西歷一九一七）

夏四月,開二十週年紀念大會三日.

民國七年（戊午）（西歷一九一八）

春,設鐵路管理科.

中學科長徐經邦兼任鐵路管理科科長.

二十週年紀念圖書館開工建築.

夏,建築無線電試驗室.

建築西宿舍.

民國八年（己未）（西歷一九一九）

秋,建築鍋爐室.

冬十月,圖書館落成.

民國九年（庚申）（西歷一九二〇）

春三月,圖書館開幕.

冬,校長唐文治辭職,部派教員凌鴻勛代理校長.

鐵路管理科第一次畢業.（此後每年夏舉行畢業.）

民國十年（辛酉）（西歷一九二一）

春,鐵路管理科科長兼中學科長徐經邦辭職,教員徐廣德繼任鐵路管理科科長.李松濤繼任中學科長.

夏五月,小學開二十週年紀念會.

交通部提出閣議議決,合併交通部唐山工業專門學校,北京郵電學校,交通傳習所,及本校改組交通大學.本校改名交通大學上海學校.校長駐京辦事,各地設主任及副主任.

設交通大學董事會.推徐世章,葉恭綽,鄭洪年,梁士詒,嚴修,張謇,唐文治,沈琪,孫鴻哲,王景春,關賡麟,劉景山,陸夢熊,劉成志,鄺孫謀,黃鎬知,周詒春,榮宗錦,簡照南十九人爲董事.

任命葉恭綽爲交通大學校長.

派張鑄爲交通大學上海學校主任.凌鴻勛爲副主任.

添設機械科.聘美國狄克生爲科長.

土木科移併唐山學校.唐山學校之鐵路機械科移併本校.

鐵路管理科移併北京學校.北京學校之郵電班移併本校.

中學科長改稱中學主任.

建築機械試驗室.設翻砂廠,鍛鐵廠.

秋,派教授張廷金代理副主任

發起籌建學生會集室,體育館,調養室三大建築.

民國十一年（壬戌）（西歷一九二二）

夏,任命陸夢熊爲交通大學校長.

取消董事會.

派張廷金爲上海學校主任.

校長陸夢熊辭職.關賡麟繼任校長.

秋本校復與北京唐山二校分立.改名交通部南洋大學.

任命盧炳田爲校長.

聘前主任張廷金爲教務長.中學主任李松濤兼任事務長.

移併北京之鐵路管理科遷回上海,繼續開辦.

聘教授胡仁源爲鐵路管理科科長.

民國十二年（癸亥）（西歷一九二三）

夏五月,任命陳杜衡為校長.

聘顧惟精為教務長,取消事務長.

聘教授周仁為機械科科長.

為本校創始人盛宣懷立銅像.

民國十三年(甲子)(西歷一九二四)

夏,體育館調養室開工建築.

冬十二月,派教授淩鴻勛為校長.

民國十四年(乙丑)(西歷一九二五)

春,教務長顧惟精辭職,機械科科長周仁兼任教務長.

鐵路管理科科長胡仁源辭職,鐵路管理科科長由校長暫兼.

中學主任李松濤辭職,聘教員徐佩璜為中學主任.

添設工程股.

夏,五卅事起,附屬中學學生陳虞欽死之.

徐家匯初名徐家厙,明徐文定公居此,因以得名.地處上海城西十二里.其北曰樓家厙,西北曰法華鎮.本校校址適介三者之間.清光緒二十二年,假民房開辦南學公學.二十四年,始購地百餘畝,建築校舍.二十五年購校南民地.宣統元年,復購校北民地設各工廠.三年,購本校東南民房,改建宿舍.其後於校西校北陸續添置.現計有地約一百九十畝.校址四周環以小溪.溪外皆農田,平疇四望,一碧無際.地勢清曠空氣新鮮.又以去上海市遠,故甚幽靜.

保持交通四政特別會計案（轉載）

吾國之有交通事業,垂五十年.設立專部以來.亦且二十年.顧一語及交通與國家社會之關係.殆鮮有眞知之者.交通之需要不啻菽粟水火,爲人生日用所不可或缺.彼世界先進諸國,其交通發達之程.遠過吾國千百倍.猶且孜孜進行,日新月異.而吾國今日,幾並舊有之事業而不克保持.此誠政府與國民所宜引爲大感者也.吾國自前清宣統三年以後,博采東西各國之先例,確立交通事業之基礎.以交通事業含有營業性質也,故不能無獨立之資金.而資金之營運不能無精密之計劃也.於是有特別會計制度.查交通事業施行特別會計,各國法律均有規定.其最著者,如德國之新憲法第九十二條載明,鉄道之預算及決算,雖爲總預算總決算之一部,但當視爲獨立經濟企業而管理之.鉄道經費,當合鐵道公債之償金及利子,由其自已收入中支付之,並當設立鉄道公積金.償金及公積金之額,並公積金之用途,以特別法律定之.又如日本會計法第三十條載明,遇有特別需要不能援據本法者,得設特別會計.其鉄道會計法第一條,並明白規定,因經營鐵道事業而設固定資本及據置運轉資本,凡營業上之收入及其附屬之雜收入,許充鐵道事業之用,立特別會計各等語.蓋以官營業之會計,異乎普通官署.故依據經濟原理,自成爲完善精密有系統之會計.雖與普通會計劃分.仍以普通會計法爲根據.（本部現行國有鐵路會計條例,即依據我國普通會計法第三十四條,「凡特別事項不能依據本法者得設立特別會計」之規定,）隸屬於國家財政系統之內,受國家法律之監督者也.其所以必須與普通會計劃分,另行計算者.譬諸經商之人,必將營業帳目與家用劃分爲二,乃能得正確之贏虧,而便於處理.若更與人合資,尤非另立帳目不可.交通事業既含營業性質,所有款項帳目,自不能與普通政費等視.且官營事業.間或招商附股,尤有與普通會計劃分之必要.特別會計所以必須設立者,一也.官營事業,本以利國便民爲主旨．營利猶屬第二義．惟無論如何，必有可恃之資金，乃能推行盈利．今使政府對於某項事業，投資若干，則該項事業卽恃此款以爲營運，不能任意挪移，且某項事業之收入，必先儘充該事業維持及擴充費之用．尤不能任意提撥．若視同普通財源，聽政府之流用，事業旣歸停頓．損失更難數計．此特別會計所以必須設立者，二也．吾國官營事業方在萌芽，兼以國家財政困難，政府對於官營業之資金，未能有所供給．僅就該管事業之收入，酌盈劑虛．自謀發展．倘無特別會計以保其固有之資金，何所恃以爲營運．矧此等事業創設之初．什九皆出於借用外債，非有確實保障，且無以維持信用，而息外人之責言．故就吾國情形言之，官營事業尤有采用特別會計之必要．此特別會計所以必須設立者，三也．綜而論之，特別會計之制度，本不僅適用於交通之機關．凡屬國家營業，皆有採用之必要．特以吾國交通事業創設較早，采用較先，故此種意義，世人尙未能明瞭．實則特別會計之條例，及其施行之手續，列帳之辦法，較普通會計尤爲嚴密．所有款項帳目，事前有預算．事後有決算．皆照例咨交法定機關審核．且每歲有會計統計報告刊行中外，出入之間，予天下以共見，初非如議者所云云也．然而十三年來，所謂特別會計者．不過空存其名．且以輿論不察之影響，此種制度，殆已破壞無遺．歷年交通收入，未旣能專備交通事業之用，復以交通債款供軍政兩費之流用．近年軍人，更習以提用路款爲事．京漢一路，每歲額提在千萬元以上．其他各路局進款各電局進款，公然提用及截留者，爲數猶復不貲．營業收入而外，更須重利借貸，以應其誅求．甚或由軍事長官，逕向商家訂借鉅款，以交通收入爲抵押而責以償還．總計截至民國十三年止，所有各方挪用及截留之款，不下一萬八千萬元，若更將所負利息合併計算，當在二萬五千萬元以上，皆交通事業之命脈．所恃以爲營運者也．向使特別會計保持不墜，以此巨款淸償舊債，負担自可減輕．抑或建設新業，利益亦難數計．今則鐵路方面，資金告匱，債台高築．不惟未成之工，無從進行．卽此已成之工，亦漸頹廢．甚至日用材料，未能付價．職工薪資，未能支給，橋梁傾朽,車輛殘破,運輸停頓,日夕堪虞.至於電政借款,既經政府挪用,歷年收入,又爲各省截留.利息延期,久不克付.綫路窳敗,無法展修.所謂國家交通事業者除航政尚未萌芽.郵政尚可保持者外,數十年來辛苦經營,猶在幼稚時代之路電兩政,已入於破產之域.循此以往,不出數年,各路綫悉歸隳壞.爾時國家社會所感受之困難,恐有非筆墨所能形容者矣.近者,畿輔軍興,運輸停滯,商民奔走呼籲,若不終日.此特暫時現象耳.而猶若此.倘各工程同時傾頹,各通訊機關胥歸停頓,其爲痛苦,又當如何,修復之工既非旦夕可蕆,而以今日政府之窮匱,恐亦無如許財力也.是故居今日而言交通,先求維持現狀,其次乃議治本.而要之以保持特別會計爲第一事.特別會計之眞精神,在乎保存交通事業之收入,供交通事業之支出,兼以已成事業之盈利,爲未成事業之資金.誠使各方悉能諒解,相與維持,基礎既立,徐圖進行.夫而後凡百事業,咸與交通事業相因而發達.將來交通事業.收入增多,所有營業贏餘,除塡償債款,擴充產業,提供公積而外,自可以其純益爲國庫之補助,若猶是剜肉醫瘡,殺雞求卵,不惟交通事業委地以盡,卽其他新建設,亦必隨以淪胥.言念及此,焦悚何極,況吾國交通事業,多有外資關係,方今共管之說,未絕於耳.我不自謀,將有越俎而代之者.其禍之中於國家,尤非所忍言者矣.本部職掌所在,此中利害,知之較悉.見死不救,心誠未忍.相應提出保持交通四政特別會計議案,敬請公決施行.

編者案.此文係去年三月交通部提交善後會議議案之一.轉載於此.以供關心交通事業者之參攷.

中國工程學會出版物

工程

第一號要目

杭州浙江實業銀行新屋之建築……李屋身
感應電動机之製造……周琦
漢口電車路軌道商榷書……謝仁
五十年來電氣事業之進步……錢昌祚
膠濟鐵路近況工程報告……顧烈斐士

第二號要目

氣艇運輸……錢昌祚
蘇州電氣廠工程狀況……陸法曾
提士引擎在工業上之應用……王崇植
材料試驗報告（一）磚頭……淩鴻勛等
美國無線電事業概況……陳章

第三號要目

中國工人與工業前途……惲震
創辦化學工廠之管見……陳調父
南通保坍工程意見書……宋希尚
上海工部局停止電力問題……王崇植
孫嘉圖案評判報告……淩鴻勛

第四號要目

中國電机製造廠之創辦計畫……周琦
無線電波前進之新解說……倪尚達
安徽石碌永濟橋建築之經過……庾宗溎等
山西水利狀況……曹瑞芝
Light Waves & Others L.A. Hawkins.

每册大洋二角　　預定六册大洋一元郵費外加

寄售處　上海商務印書館　上海中華書局　上海世界書局

總辦事處　上海江西路四十三號B字

介紹

北京交通日報

——交通界唯一之日刊——

內有交通新聞一欄專載國內外

交通界重要消息及言論著作

為關心交通事業研究交通學術者不可不看之日報

定　價：北京——每月大洋六角，每季大洋一元六角

半年大洋三元，全年大洋五元八角

外埠——每月大洋七角五分，每季大洋二元

半年大洋三元八角，全年大洋七元二角

定閱處：北京宣外米市胡同三十二號交通日報館

電報掛號一八七三

南洋季刊創刊號

民國十五年一月十五日出版

編輯處 上海南洋大學出版部
發行處 上海南洋大學出版部
印刷者 中國印刷廠
代售處 上海商務印書館　中華書局　世界書局
北京宣武門外米市胡同廿二號交通日報館莫葵卿
天津南開大學薛桂綸
廣州廣東大學桂銘敬
青島膠濟鐵路局機務處胡粹士
南京河海大學吳馥初
美國 L. S. Wang, 185 Fairmount Ave., Hyde Park. Mass., U. S. A.

本刊價目表

定價		每期郵費	
每期	大洋二角	本埠	一分
		外埠	二分
每年	大洋八角	國外	四分

本刊廣告刊例

全面	封面裏頁及底面裏外頁	實洋十五元
	尋常地位	實洋十元
半面	封面裏頁及底面裏外頁	實洋八元
	尋常地位	實洋六元

南洋季刊

第二期

電機工程號

要目預告

（以稿件已到者爲限）

南洋季刊社職員錄

（民國十四年至十五年）

◉南洋大學出版部◉

編輯股　趙祖康（總編輯）　柴福沅（編輯）　王瑞虎（編輯）

事務股　曹毓琮（會計）　王永禮（印鑄）　邵禹襄（廣告）　沈元慶（書記）

◉南洋公學同學會編輯員◉

柴福沅

◉南洋大學學生團體選派編輯員◉

衛　杼（學生會）　費福燾（工程學會）　薛椿蔭（經濟學會）

徐鍾淮（南洋學會）　衛　杼（國樂研究社）　史鵬展（技擊部）

許延輝（軍樂隊）

※　※　※　※　※　※

南洋季刊投稿簡章

一　本刊除聘請特約撰述員担任撰述稿件外校內外無論何人倘有投稿均所歡迎

二　本刊分通論工程經濟科學文藝交通事業工商調查校聞紀要同學會紀聞校友要訊新著述評遊記雜俎等門但投稿者得投寄合於本刊宗旨之任何稿件

三　投寄之稿或自撰或翻譯均可其文體以文言為主但亦待酌用白話或外國文

四　投寄之稿望繕寫清楚並加句讀或新式標點符號能依本刊規定之行格（每面橫行廿五每行三十字）繕寫者尤佳

五　投寄譯稿請附原本如原本不便附寄請將原文題目原著者姓名出版日期及發售書局名稱詳細敘明

六　稿末請註明姓名字住址以便通信至揭載時如何署名聽投稿者自定

七　投寄之稿揭載與否本刊編輯者不能預覆如不揭載得因預先聲明寄還原稿

八　投寄之稿俟揭載後酌酬本刊一期或數期

九　投寄之稿其著作讓仍為著作者所有惟於需要時得由本校其他出版物轉載

十　投寄之稿如已先在他處發布者請預先聲明惟揭載與否由本刊編輯者斟酌

十一　投寄之稿本刊編輯者得酌量增刪之但投稿人不願他人增刪者可於投稿時預先聲明

十二　投稿者請寄上海徐家匯南洋大學出版部

南洋大學出版委員會

及

南洋季刊 特約撰述員 專門校審員

題名錄

出版委員會委員

徐名材　李熙謀　范永增

特約撰述員

張景良　張世鎏　李復幾　胡端行　莫衡

薛次莘　周厚坤　鮑國寶　曹麗順　鈕澤全

薄以新　莊前鼎　方子衛　潘世宜　趙曾珏

陳廣沅　楊立惠　王繩善　謝仁　裘維裕

張峻　李聯珪　黃世祚　沈慶鴻　杜定友

唐慶詒　杜光祖　武晉常　劉麟生　朱鼎元

施孔懷　沈昌　吳維翰　沈維楨

專門校審員

周仁　吳玉麟　俞希稷　李聯珪　王繩善

周銘　徐佩璜　楊培琫　徐佩琨

上海 龍章機器造紙廠 廣告

啓者本公司於前清光緒年間奏明開辦雙龍商標呈部立案專造上等潔白洋連史及雙礬毛邊等紙行銷全國已歷二十餘年出品精良早爲各界所歡迎現在格外加工選料精益求精價目亦格外克己以期答謝 愛國惠顧諸君之雅意欲求完全國貨者請認明雙龍商標以免魚目混珠誤用劣貨如蒙 賜顧請向法租界新永安街敝批發處接洽可也

計開 種類

十五刀 頂字連史　十五刀 雙礬連史　十五刀 礬字連史

十五刀 元字連史　十五刀 特字連史　六五刀 潤字毛邊紙

十　刀 頂字連史　十五刀 餘字連史　四四刀 川連史

十五刀 頭字連史

製造廠 上海龍華路外日暉橋

批發所 上海法租界新永安街

上海
竟成造紙有限公司
KING CHEN PAPER MILL LTD.
上海竟成造紙有限公司
註册商標
金熊紙版
本公司專造中西各種紙張
版紙
包紗紙
書面紙
牛皮紙
毛巾紙
火柴紙
草紙
等類
營業部
法租界天主堂街九十五號
工廠部
新閘大王廟東首蘇州河畔
電話營業部中三五四六 工廠部西四二八九
電報號掛三一三七
總理王叔賢謹啓

NANYANG QUARTERLY

第一卷　電機工程號　第二期

本期要目

民國十五年四月

南洋大學出版部南洋公學同學會同發行

中華郵政特准掛號認爲新聞紙類

上海銀行公會會員

中華匯業銀行

廣告

本銀行奉財政部批准立案額定資本金一千萬元公積金及前期滾存金二百十五萬五千元專營國內外匯兌以及各種存放款項抵押貼現跟單押匯買賣生金銀等一切業務總行在北京京滬兩分行設立已久現又在天津設立分行玆將通匯地點開列於下

國內 北京天津濟南青島漢口南京蘇州無錫杭州溫州九江福州廈門廣州汕頭奉天長春大連等處

國外 倫敦紐約香港新嘉坡孟買東京京都大阪神戶橫濱長崎名古屋門司下關函館小樽朝鮮京城福岡廣島台北等處各界賜顧請駕至福州路五號接洽可也

電話
- 公用電話 中央一九四一
- 經理室 中央五六一五 又一九四六
- 匯兌部 中央五六五一 又二六四七

司徒博牙醫生贈
南洋季刊（第二期）讀者
優待券

上海銀行公會會員銀行

上海 中華懋業銀行廣告

資本 額定國幣一千萬元 實收七百五十萬元

公積金 一百五十四萬元

總行 北京

分行 北京 上海 天津 漢口 濟南 哈爾濱

代理處 本國各省及歐美日本南洋各大商埠

業務 各種銀行業務

儲蓄部 各種外國貨幣一概收存

保管箱 保險堅固取費極廉

鈔票 華中央政府特准發行準備十足在營業時間內隨時兌現

地點 南京路十一號

電話 中央八六四一至八六四四

電報掛號 三一七七

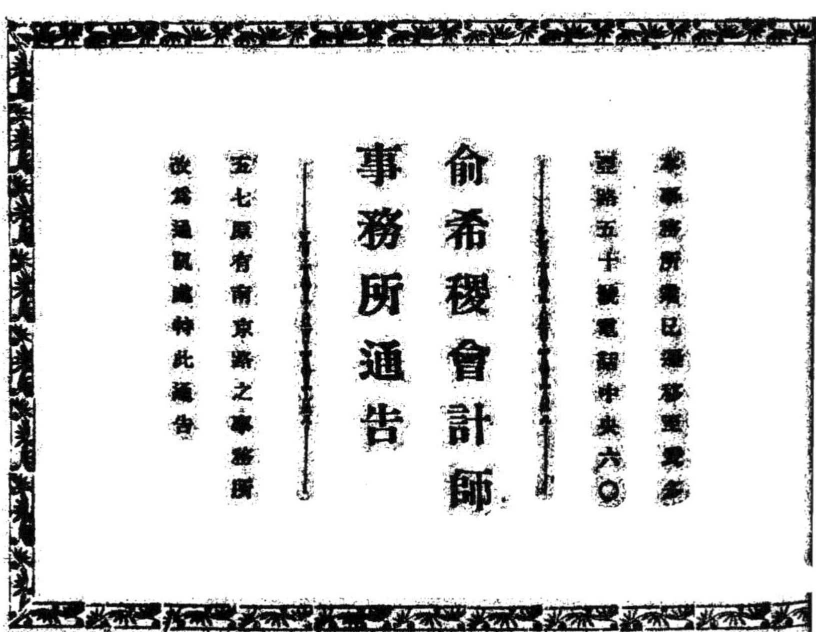

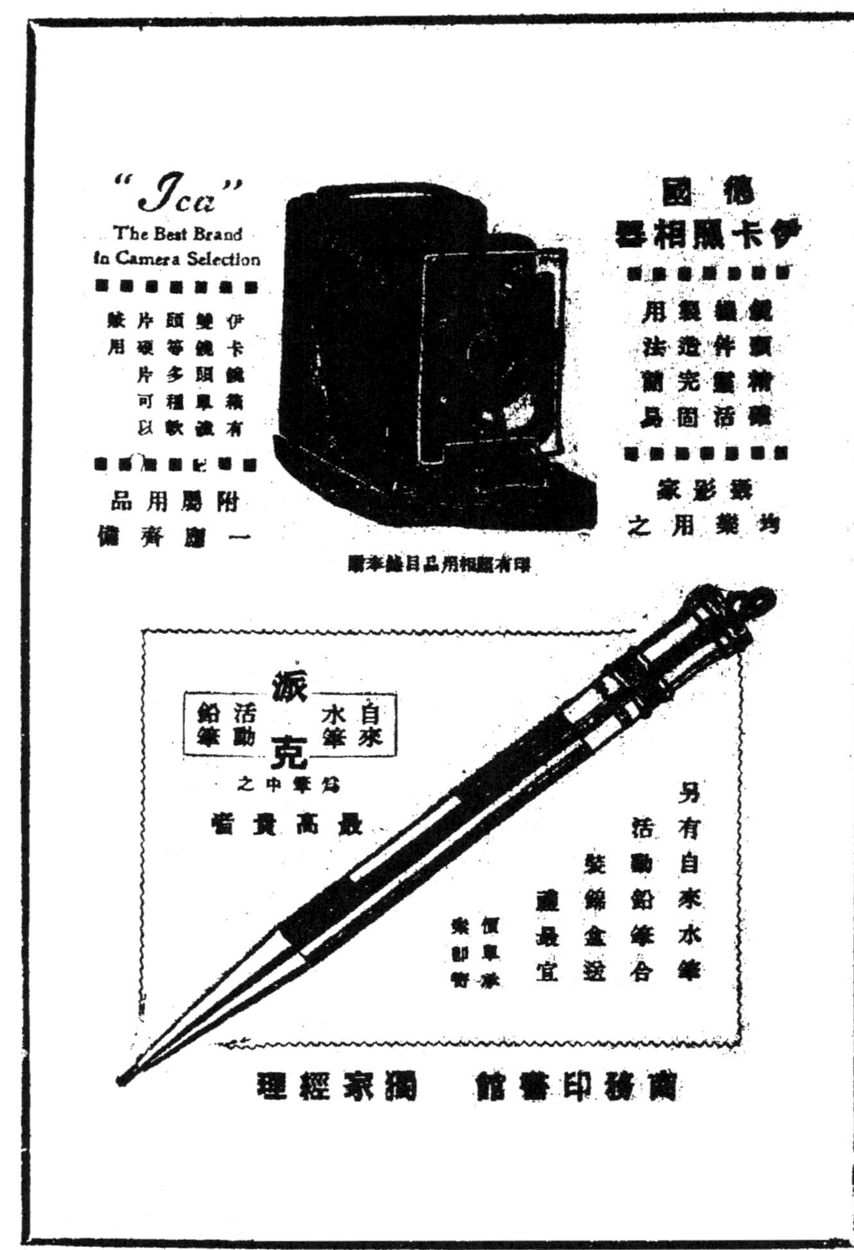
"Ica"
The Best Brand
In Camera Selection
伊卡鏡備有雙鏡頭單鏡頭等多種軟片硬片可以兼用
附屬用品一應齊備
德國
伊卡照相器
鏡頭精巧機件靈活製造完固用法簡易
攝影家均樂用之
另有照相用品目錄奉贈
派克
自來水筆
活動鉛筆
鉛筆中之
最高貴者
另有自來水筆活動鉛筆合裝錦盒送禮最宜
價單承索即寄
商務印書館 獨家經理

南洋大學出版部南洋公學同學會同發行

南洋季刊第一卷第二期電機工程號目錄

（民國十五年四月出版）

插　　圖

編輯者言

專　　著

附　　載

本校旅英校友攝影

張承祜　洪傳炯　李開第　嚴智珠　趙曾珏

本校旅居美國費城校友攝影

本校旅青校友攝影

後排 金雲 孫瑞璋 張漢維 華世忠 奚逸 沈烈炎 郁寅啓·陳靖宇 杜寶田 周仰洛 段世芬 張元霦 姚章桂

中排 高塝 仇建善 鍾文滔 胡端行 楊毅 鄧家駒 鄧益光 王懷曾 張星烺 秦沅 陳非 鄒恩元 朱文鵬

前排 賈存鑑 周乃洪 馮閏模 徐植仁 李爲駿 陳耀奎 朱保邦 朱翹 韓恩炎

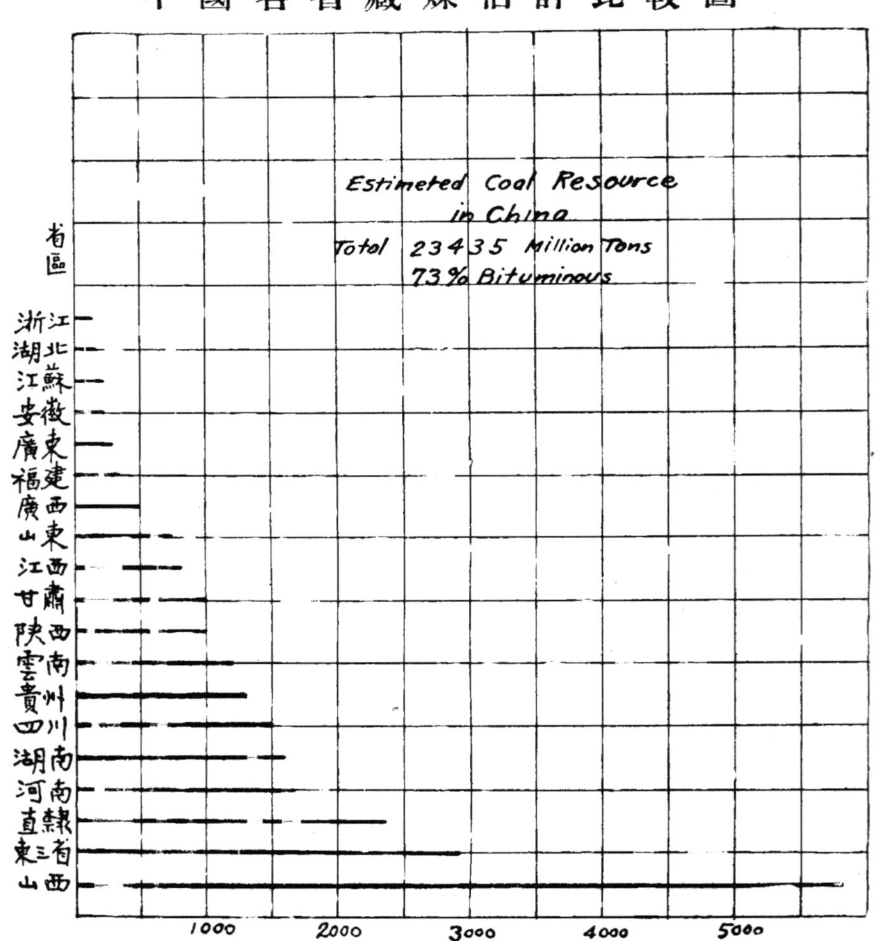
中國各省藏煤估計比較圖
Estimated Coal Resource in China
Total 23435 Million Tons
73% Bituminous
省區
浙江
湖北
江蘇
安徽
廣東
福建
廣西
山東
江西
甘肅
陝西
雲南
貴州
四川
湖南
河南
直隸
東三省
山西
1000
2000
3000
4000
5000
Tons of Coal Millions

拿埃葛拉瀑布之形勢

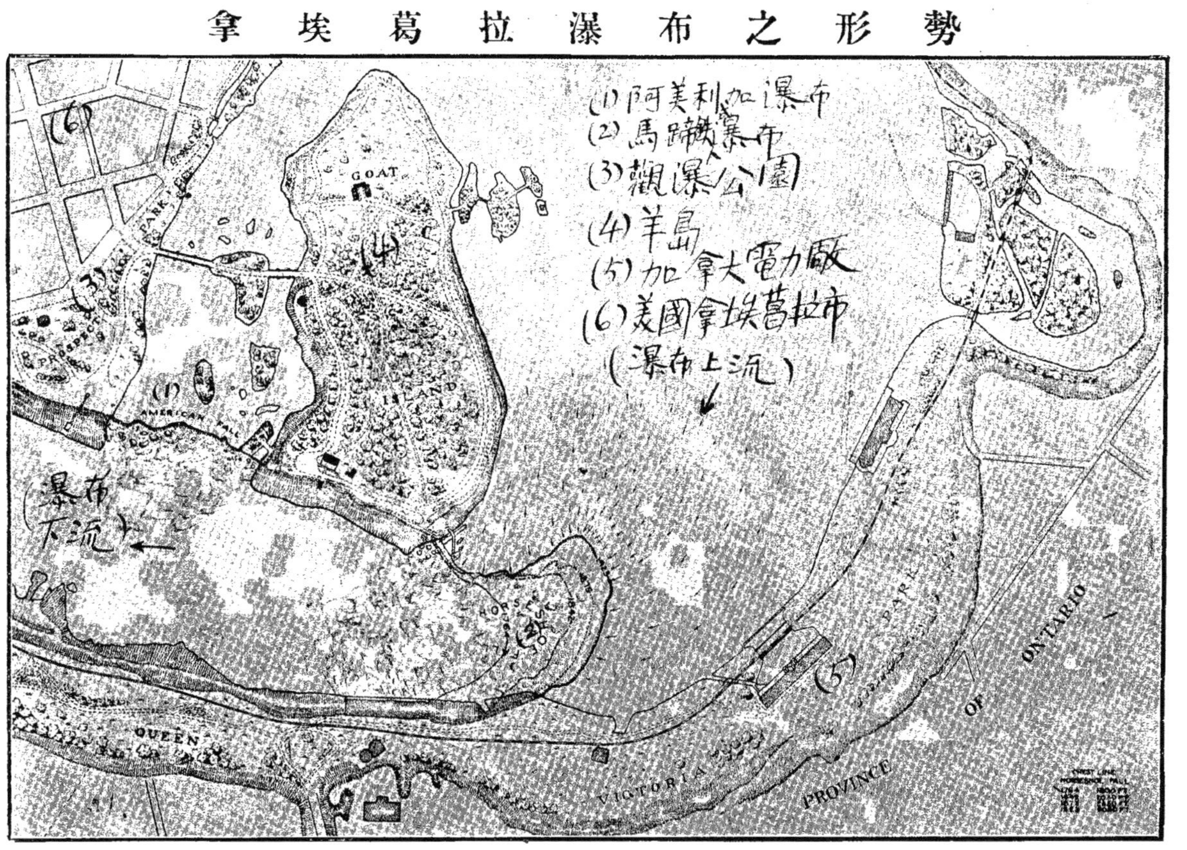

(1)阿美利加瀑布
(2)馬蹄鐵瀑布
(3)觀瀑公園
(4)羊島
(5)加拿大電力廠
(6)美國拿埃葛拉市
(瀑布上流)
(瀑布下流)
GOAT
ISLAND
AMERICAN FALL
PARK
PROSPECT
QUEEN
VICTORIA
PROVINCE
OF
ONTARIO

南洋季刊社職員錄

（民國十四年至十五年）

◉南洋大學出版部◉

編輯股　趙祖康（總編輯）　柴福沅（編輯）　王瑞虎（編輯）

事務股　曹毓琮（會計）　王永禮（印鑄）　邵禹襄（廣告）　沈元慶（書記）

◉南洋公學同學會編輯員◉

柴福沅

◉南洋大學學生團體選派編輯員◉

衛　杼（學生會）　戚其潤（工程學會）　薛椿蔭（經濟學會）

徐鍾淮（南洋學會）　衛　杼（國樂研究社）　史鵬展（技擊部）

許延暉（軍樂隊）

※　※　※　※

南洋大學出版委員會及南洋季刊特約撰述員專門校審員題名錄

◉出版委員會委員◉

徐名材　李熙謀　范永增

◉特約撰述員◉

張景良	張世鎏	李復幾	胡端行	莫　衡
薛次莘	周厚坤	鮑國寶	曹麗順	鈕澤全
茅以新	莊前鼎	方子衞	潘世宜	趙曾珏
陳廣沅	楊立惠	王繩善	謝　仁	裘維裕
張　峻	李聯珪	黃世祚	沈慶鴻	杜定友
唐慶詒	杜光祖	武書常	劉麟生	朱鼎元
施孔懷	沈　昌	吳維翰	沈維楨	

◉專門校審員◉

周　仁	吳玉麟	俞希稷	李聯珪	王繩善
周　銘	徐佩璜	楊培琫	徐佩琨	

編輯者言

本期所載電工著作凡十二篇.其中或屬於研究討論.或屬於載記敍述.計各六篇.雖無電機工程學術上精深之作,要亦足以見近世電工學之大概現世紀爲電學之世紀,甚望讀者因此引起研究電學之興趣.不使法拉台與愛迭生爲西方所獨有也.

此外尚有若干篇如張惠康君之電燈電力廠之估計.壽俊良君之Purdue Engineering Trip 等均爲篇幅所限.不克載入.容後揭登.希作者讀者均加原諒.

附載各篇均甚有價值工程心理調查報告爲本校工程學會調查所得之結果.國中工程學術尚在幼稚時代.工程教育,亦應力求效率之增高.欲圖發展改良,各種調查張本決不可少.此篇其殆工程教育研究之嚆矢歟.

猶有一事.願爲讀者告者.嗣後凡關工程學術之著作,其屬於基本原理及淺近學說者,本刊歡迎其以中文寫成之.其屬於專門研究及高深討論者本刊希望其以外國文寫成之.請言其理.

一國某種事業之發達,甚有賴於此種學術之昌明.國中工程事業之不舉,工程學術之幼稚實負一部份之責任.欲言提倡學術,當先謀學術之獨立.此工程著作應用國文寫成之原則也.然若高深論理.國中一般學習工程者未必注意,而東西各國工程學家或有參考之價值.此所以不妨用外國文行之也.他日者,本刊得成爲中國工程學術昌明之原動力,並得爲廣布高深學理於國外之專門雜誌,則萬幸矣!

本期各稿,於編輯前承吳玉麟李振吾兩先生審閱一過.又得工程學會費福燾君襄助徵稿校勘,均應附此誌謝.至於出版較遲,有勞讀者盼望.編輯同人深滋不安.謹向讀者諸君道歉(康)

THE POWER PROBLEM IN CHINA

BY T. M. WU (吳達模)

Power is considered as the raw material in industrial development. Just as iron and coal are the basic material for almost any kind of industry so is power the necessity for all industries in which mechanical devices are used to secure economical operation and production. In the past, investigations have been made as to both the quality and quantity of coal and iron available for a nation in order to determine and forecast the tendency and possibility of the industrial development of that nation. For the same purpose, similar investigation shouid be made for a raw material that is necessary for all industries power.

In presenting the power problem in China, the entire topic will be divided into two parts: (I) General information and data of the power development at present and (II) the tendency of its future development. Under the first part, there will be given a description of (1) sources of power, (2) power survey in various places and (3) general system of power generation, transmission and distribution and cost. In the second part, a general discussion will be made as to (1) the power market (2) suitable type and capacity of power plants to de constructed, (3) its ownership and management and (4) other activities of central station men.

In China as in other places, there are three sources of power available for power development and these, may be arranged iu the order of their relative importance. At pressnt the most important source of power is coal, owing to its fairly abundant supply and the fact that power development from coal is flexible and economical for the small size plants prevalent in China.

Coal is known to occur in every province in China. Shansi, Chihli, Honan and Three Eastern Provinces contstitute the richest coal bearing regions. According to the recent report of the Geological Survey of China, a minimum estimate of China's wealth in coal is approximately 40 to 50 billion tons, of which about 73% is of bituminous variety. The accompanying chart, Curve 1 shows the coal production in various places in China. The present yearly output is estimated to be about 20 million metric tons. The cost of coal in the mining regions is approximately $2(Mex.) per ton. Due to the inadequate transportation, its cost is increased to as high as $17 per ton, in some large coal consuming cities such as Shanghai.

Water power in China presents many possible opportunities, but up to the present, very little has been done in the way of hydraulic development. This has been due partly to the difficulty of securing sufficient capital and the lack of a market for large blocks of power.

However there are a few hydro-electric plants of small size in operation. In Yunnan, a 600 KW. hydro-electric plant situated at a distance of 30 miles from the city of Yunnanfu is now in operation, the power being transmitted to the market at 22,000 volts. Another station at Yungan, Fukien, of 25 KVA. capacity was completed in 1924 and is now in operation. Still there are many hydro-electric plants in a projected stage. It is stated in the Electrical World, July 5, 1924 that a company has been formed for the purpose of carrying out a project for utilizing the water power of Yalu River to generate electricity. It is proposed to supply energy to operate an electric railway to be built between Mukden and Hsingking.

In Szechuen, far up the Yangtze River, there is a series of rapids from Sufu to Chungking, a distance of 200 miles. The average grade of this part of the river is about 1.5 feet per mile. From calculations as to the volume of the river in this section, it would seem that a vast amount of power would be available. The principal market for this power would be in the neighborhood of Hankow with an average distance of transmission of about 400 miles. Electric development in this neighborhood would facilitate the development of rich resources in Szechuen and the neighboring provinces and could furnish the energy needed in Hankow which is quite a center of indusry,

The third source of power namely, oil and gas, has made very little progress as there are few wells known in China. According to an investigaton, the oil bearing regions in China are Szechuen, Shensi, and Sinkiang and the yearly output of each of these places is not more than 50 tons.

The total number of electrical undertakings in China was 163 at the end of 1920 and is now about 350 indicating an increase of almost 100 percent for a period of three years. Of these installations, there are about 50 works under foreign management, Japan is the most interested of the foreign nations concerned and has invested more than 200,000,000 Yen in the electrical industry of Manchuria alone.

There are in Kwangtung 22 supply companies, including 18 Chinese concerns. which deliver about 12,000 KW. to a connected load of about 3,000,000 lamps or their equivalent. Most of the prime movers are oil engines, only two stations burning coal and only four of these plants exceed 1000 KW.

At the end of 1922, there were in the province of Kiangsu more than 60, in Chekiang 10, in Anhwei 6, and in Fukien 20 electrical power plants, besides a number under construction. Most of these installations are of 50 to 200 KW. capacity, but in almost every case extensions are in progress.

In Hupeh there are 13 and in Hunan 6 power plants. The Hankow Water Works & Electric Light Company, owned by Chinese has a station capacity of 11,200 KW. and the Hanyang Iron & Steel Works has its own generating plant of 5000 KW. capacity. Changsha, the capitol of Hunan, is served by two rival compaies havning a capacity of 1500 KW. each.

In Shangtung there are 9 electrical plants, among these Tsingtau, 1950 KW., Chefoo 500 KW., and Tsinan 375 KW, are the largest stations.

There are five different companies supplying power in Tientsin to approximately a million population, The largest station generating 6500 KW. is owned by the Tientsin Tramways & Light Company. The total connected load in this district is approximately 12,000 KW.

The power station of Peking Chinese Electric Light & Power Company is equipped with 7500 KW. capacity. This company supplies the power for the Peking tramway system which is now in operation. The power is transmitted to various substations at 33,000 volts,

Of 15 stations in South Manchuria. 13 are Japanese owned, but there are Chinese interests therin. About 36,000 KW. is developed and this output is absorbed mainly by industrial and traction loads. The South Manchuria Railway Company is the largest undertaking. It operates a 25 mile tramway system and owns in Darien two power stations of 6000 and 5000 KW. respectively, one in Mukden of 1400 Kw., one in Changchun of 3400 KW. and one in Antung of 8500 KW. capacity, In Fushan and Anshan there are other stations. The Anshan station dovelops 3000 KW. and the Penshihu Iron Works has a 5500 KW. station. In 20 small installations about 10000 KW. is developed.

In Shanghai there are 19 electric power plants with a total capacity of approximately 133 000 KW. The Shanghai Municipal Plant including its Riverside Station and Fearon Road Station is equipped with 13 units of a total capacity of 110,000 KW. The French Tramway & Light Conpany has a station of 3500 KW. cadacity. It is reported that this output will be inereased to 10000 KW. at the end of 1925. The Chinese Merchants' Electric Railway Company has a station of 10000 KW. eapacity to supply power and light in the South District of Shanghai. The most important loads in Shanghai are cotton and flour mills and many other manufacturing industries.

The total electrical power development in China amounts approximately to 300 000 KW. From the above figures, it is noted that over 40% of the total electrical power in China has been developed and utilized in Shanghai and 12% in the Three Eastern Provinces. The balance of China has only about 155,000 KW. of electrical development, indicating a tremendous market for the future development of power.

Due to the limited demand for power as well as the lack of capital, over sixty per cent of the total power plants in China have a station capacity of not exceeding 1000 KW. Most of the plants below 200 KW. capacity are equipped with engine type generators connected either to crude oil engines or belted to reciprocating steam engines. The cost of these plants usually runs as high as $400 to $500 per KW. installed.

Aa a result of free competion in purchasing electrical equipment, both American and European machinery has been extensively used. There are almo t as many 50 cycle systems as 60 ones being operated in Chinese power plants. Th re are still some other older plants using 75 cycle, 45 cycle and 25 cycle circuits, but there is a tendency to change over to either 60 cycle or 50 cycle.

The highest voltage used in power transmission is 33,000 volts. This is used by several companies. Tseng Hwa Company transmits 8000 KW from Changchow to Wusih at this voltage. Another 33 KW. line is operated by the Peking Electric Railway Company. The Linsi Power Plant of the Kailan Mining Administration having a total capacity of 18000 KW. transmits its energy at 30,000 volts to operate the coal mines in the vicinity. The Shanghai Municipal Council Power plants transmtts the power from the Riverside Station to various substations at 22,000 volts. The Tayeh Works of Hanyehping Iorn & Steel Manufacturing Company transmits the energy at 22,000 volts to operate the iron mines at a distance of 18 miles. The third 22,000 volt system is operated by the hydro-electric plant at Yunnan as previously mentioned.

Generally speaking, the central station business in China is very profitable. The annual divident of various companies varies from 8 to 12 per cent as against an average of 7% in the United States. For instance, the capital outlay of the Shanghai Municipal Council, Electrical Department for 1921 amounted to 20,771,489 Taels and on plants actually in operation the capital outlay was 17,654,556 Taels. The return on capital outlay at the end of 1921 on plants in operation was 10.58%, as against 10.34% in 1920. The gross profit of the Department was 1,863,610 Taels and the net profit after provision for interest on loans and depreciation was 1,047,808 Taels.

The average power rate of Chinese operating companies is 3-1/2 cents per Kilowatt hour as against an average figure of 1-1/2 cents in the United States. Comparatively, the powey plants operated by South Manchuria Railway Company sell their power at a lower rate of approximately 1-1/2 to 3 cents for KWH. For small consumers of electric lights it is a usual practice to charge 60 to 70 cents for a 16 candle power lamp per month.

Among all the electrical undertakings, besides the foreign management, power plants are most owned by provincial government and private concerns. A great number of small plants is controlled by a non-technical staff resulting uneconomical investment and operation. Some cities, of moderate size such as Changsha, are usually served by more than one company. As a result of competition, each plant is being operated under an unfavorable condition.

As a summary of the above data of the Chinese Power plants, the following points can be noted:

1. Coal is considered as the chief source of energy and thus steam power plants are extensively used.

2. Total capacity of the Chinese power is approximately 300,000 KW., about 40% of which is developed in Shanghai and 12% in Machuria.
3. There were about 350 electrical undertakings at the end of 1923 and 17% of the cities have been electrified.
4. No standardization has been adopted for electrical systems.
5. Lack of scientific management and spirit of cooperation are some of the causes of failure of small plants.
6. The average power cost is 3-1/2 cent per Kilowatt hour and average dividend is 10% indicating the central station business is very profitable.
7. The capacity of the plants is limited by capital rather than by demand, as indicated by those plants installed by the South Manchuria Railway Co. Smaller plants due to their uneconomical operation and high unit cost of installation should not be encouraged.
8. The number of power plants has doubled during the last three years, indicating the rapid growth of the electrical industry in China. Comparing the total station capacity of the United States, 14,000,000 KW., and that of Japan, 2,000,000 KW., (1922) with respect to the population and territory, the possibilities for electrical development in China are almost without limit.

Knowing the aobve facts concerning the present situation of the central station industry in China, we are now in a position to discuss the possibilities and tendencies of its future development. Through actual investigation, it is a general belief that China possesses rich natural resources. As power is the essential in the development of natural resources, power development varies as the potentialities of industrial development. It is usually a question whether it is justifiable to develop an excessive amount of power for the growth of industry. To answer this question superficially, the relation between power and other industrial developments will be briefly discussed.

One of the fundamental reasons for the location of industrial plants is the proximity of power supply. This factor reduces the initial capital investment of an industrial plant, because no power generating equipment need be supplied. In other words for a plant located in a place where power supply is available, a less capital will be required to do the same amount of business than is needed if it were to install its own power generating plant. This factor is important because it encourages the public to engage in manufacturing industry.

Aside from the financial consideration, the industrial concern usually prefers to purchase power from a central station company due to the cheaper production of power and better service rendered. Power production is at such less cost in a large generating station on account of the economical operation of larger units and a better load factor. A specializied operating staff is maintained in a large central station company, which eliminates as much as possible the interruption of service. These factors together with others such as high power factor, reservet for breakdowns of units, usually make the purchased power more desirable.

The development of water power at Niagara Falls affects the industries in North Amerians. The steel mill-industry and the chemical and metallurgical products from the electrical furnace have sprung forth in this vicinity taking advantage of the cheap and convenient supply of power. The hydro-electric development in Japan electrifies many industries and railroads and makes that country a competitive manufacturer. It ahould be our consideration to develop the water power in the upper part of Yangtse River in order to facilitate transportation between Hankow and the interior of Szechuen and develop other industries in the vicinity. As a further illustration of industrial development due to power supply (in this case of more interest because it is in China) one may note the recent industrial development in South Manchuria.

The type of power plant suited to China depends upon the abundant and adequate supply of fuel. As we have noted from the foregoing statement that water power and oil resources are comparatively rare, while coal is known to occur in every province in China, it is evident that steam power plants will be preferable. The recent development of large and economical steam turbine units has offsest the use of reciprocating engines. The large steam turbine is so economical because, in the first place, since no lubrication is necessary in the parts of the turbine with which the steam comes into contact, a higher degree of superheat is possible with it than with the reciprocating engine, for which cylinder lubrication is necessary. In the second place, when the turbine is used condensing, as it must be for maximum economy, the turbine utilizes the expansive power of the steam down to the highest vacuum which can be devloped.

Curve 2

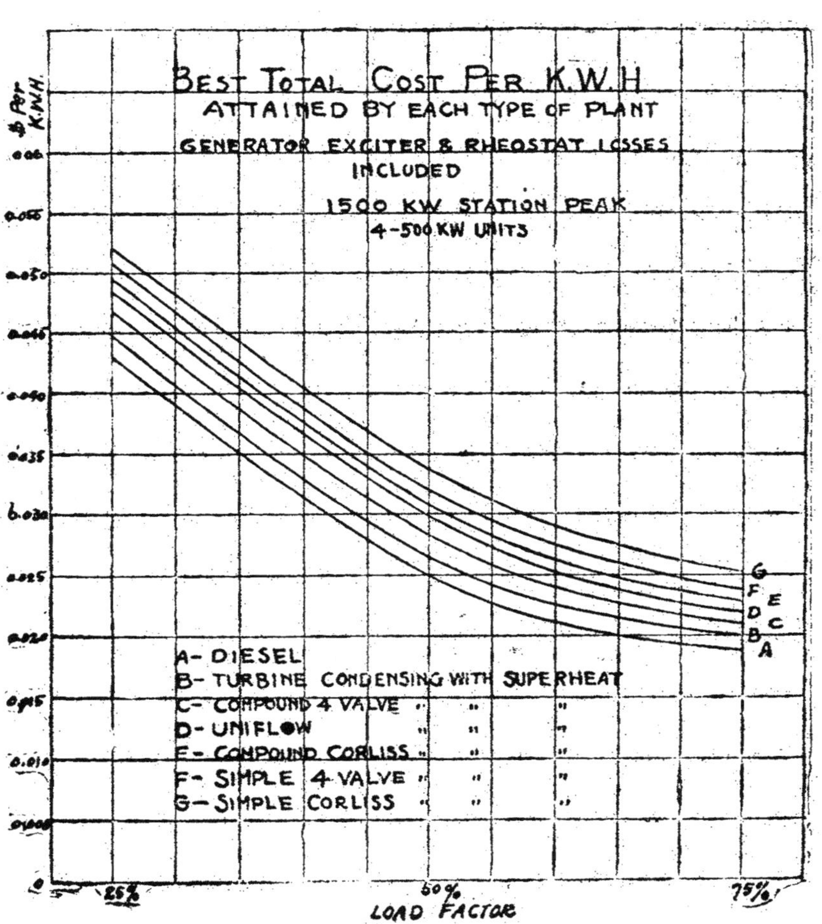

Curve 3

COSTS PER K.W.H FOR ALL TYPES OF UNITS
AT 25% LOAD FACTOR
DIESEL
TURBINE CONDENSING
UNIFLOW CONDENSING
SIMPLE CORLISS CONDENSING
COMPOUND CORLISS CONDENSING
SIMPLE 4 VALVE CONDENSING
COMPOUND 4 VALVE CONDENSING
TURBINE NON-CONDENSING
UNIFLOW NON-CONDENSING
SIMPLE CORLISS NON-CONDENSING
COMPOUND CORLISS NON-CONDENSING
SIMPLE 4 VALVE NON-CONDENSING
COMPOUND 4 VALVE NON-CONDENSING
$ .040
.030
.020
.010
PRODUCTION COST PER K.W.H.
Fuel Coal $7 Per ton 13500 B.T.U. Per lbs
$
.030
.020
FIXED CHARGES PER K.W.H.
5%
$
.060
.050
.040
TOTAL COST PER K.W.H.
DOTTED LINES INDICATE COSTS WITH SATURATED STEAM

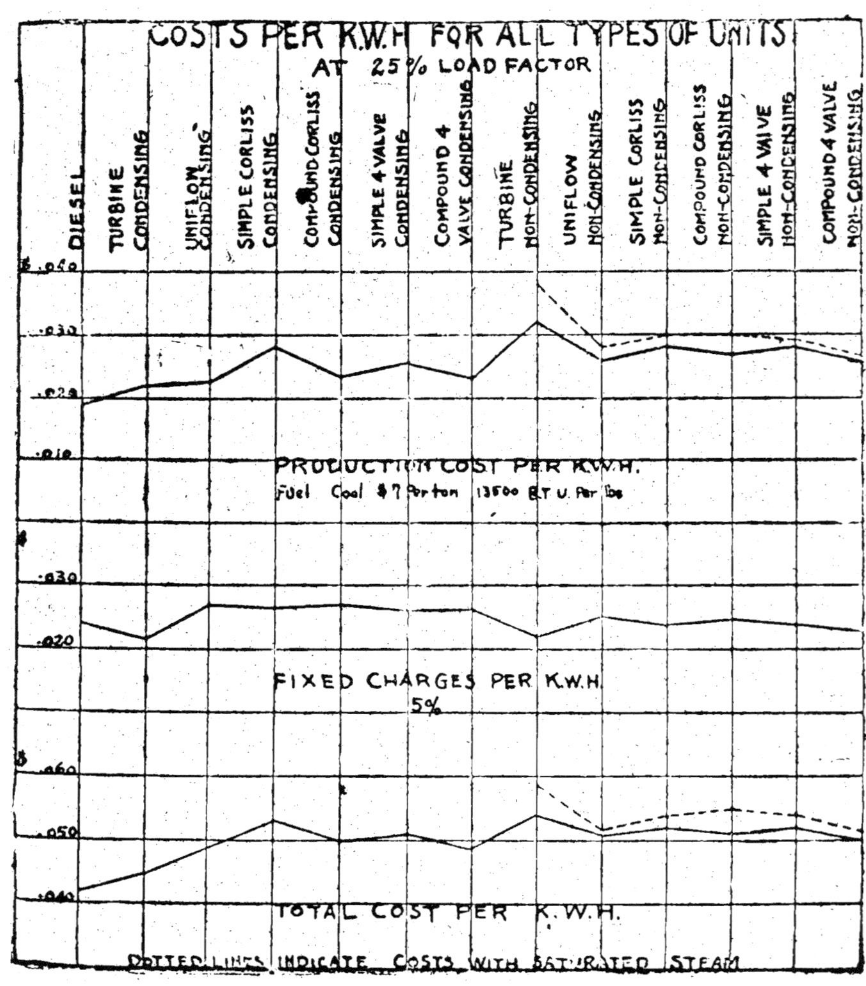

The reciprocating engine can utilize the expansive power of the steam only down to possibly 25 or 26 in vacunm. The largest single unit of steam turbine plant has been built to 60,000 KW. for Colfax station of Duquesne Light Co. Pittsburgh, Pa. This is a 3 cylinder unit, being operated at 265 lbs. steam, 175° superheat and 28.5 inch vacuum. When three cylinders are in operation, the steam consumption is about 10. 93 pounds per kilowatt hour.

Curve 2 shows the best total cost per kilowatt hour attained by each of the following plants:

(a) Diesel

(b) Turbine condensing with superheat

(c) Compound 4 valve condensing with superheat

(d) Uniflow condensing with superheat

(e) Compound corliss condensing with superheat

(f) Simple 4 valve condensing with superheat

(g) Simple corliss condensing with superheat

These curves are reproduced from the report of the N. E. L. A. Prime Movers Committee, 1923. They are made on the basis of a 1500 KW. station peak load with 4-500 KW units and the values are calculated with generator, exciter and rheostat losses included. It is noted from these curves that the most economical installation under all load conditions is the Diesel plant, and the condensing steam turbine plant with superheat comes next.

Curve 3 shows the cost per kilowatt hour for all types of unit at 25% load factor. In this curve, the total cost of each type of unit is split up into two components, production cost and fixed charges which is assumed to be 15%. It should be noted that the fixed charges per KWH of the condensing steam turbine plant is the lowest of all the plants. It means that the first cost of a condensing steam turbine plant is lower than all other types of unit.

It is concluded that to secure the most economical station, the choice of unit will be either Diesel or condensing steam turbine. The slight gain in total cost per KWH of the Diesel units will be offset by the condensing steam turbine unit on account of its lower first cost and less maintenance. For larger units than 500 KW capacity, the steam turbine still proves more economical and satisfactory in operation.

A recent investigation of operating performace of 136 steam generating stations has given the following results:

	B.T.U. per KWH.	Maintenance cost in cents per Kw-Hr.
For stations of 50,000 KW and higher	22,000	0.055
For stations from 15,000 to 50000 KW	27,000	0.078
For stations of 15,000 KW and less	40,000	0.14

It is also found that the total of operating costs and maintenance of a 190,000 KW station was 0.516 cents per KW. hr., whereas the corresponding average costs of 63 smaller stations for substantially the same total annual generation were 1.19 cents per KW. hr. In conclusion, it is mentioned that, as a result of this investigation, they have developed a clear cut picture as to the advantages of using a single large generating station instead of a group of smaller generating stations.

In determining the capacity of a plant, consideration as to the convenience and abundance of coal and water supply together with load conditions should be thoroughly studied. The mouth-of-mine type of plant is considered very desiralbe, as the power can be generated at a cheaper rate, especially when transportation of fuel is difficult, and it can be transmitted over a long distance to various markets where industrial and commercial loads will be served. Plants of very small size should not be encouraged or contemplated on account of its uneconomical operation and high unit cost of installation. It should be noted and remembered by all Chinese industrialists and engineers that the economical use of coal is a very important problem in China. As mentioned before, China's wealth in coal is approximately 40 to 50 billion tons and the present coal consumption is about 20 million tons. If China had the same rate of coal consumption as the U. S. A., that is 640 million tons a year, its coal resource would only last for 70 years.

The saving of fuel can be accomplished by economical design of station, operating system and careful selection of equipment. In the United States, one ton of coal produces 625 KWHrs. in 1919 and 835 Kwhr. in 1923. This improvement in saving of coal is chiefly due to the improvement made on the operating system that is the introduction and practice of super-power and inter connection of power generating systems.

Super-power is the term used to designate the generation of large blocks of power in efficient power stations and transmitting in bulk at very high voltage, such as 220,000 volts, and supplying it through transformers to the present power system for distribution at some lower voltages such as 110,000 volts. Interconnection is the term applied to the parallel operation of two or more power plants on one system or the connecting together of two or more systems to get the benefits arising from this method of operation. Some of the outstanding advnatages of interconnection of systems are as follows:

The tie between power systems permits taking advantage of diversity factors particularly where peak loads occur at different times of the day. When two power systems are tied together, each acts as a reserve for the other thus reducing the amounts of spare capacity carried and accordingly increasing the amount of connected load that can be fed safely from the two systems. This means also a large reduction of coal consumption,

When operating steam and hydraulic plans in parallel the load on the steam plants can be relieved to a large extent during the high water period thus making a direct saving in coal consumption. A further econonmy can be effected by balancing the load and the hours of load between hydraulic and steam plants so that the steam plants will be run at economical load when they are in operation.

The interconnection of systems often permits the postponing by some company of the building of new generating plant thus reducing capital charges.

Super-power and interconnection of syshems would be applicable to China. Although coal occurs in almost every province, large quantity of supply is available in limtied localities. As the Chinese cities and towns are not far apart, especially true in the thickly populated Yangtse valley, a large power generating system would serve both industrial and lighting loads in much better manner and more economically than numerous individual small plants. As the industrial development advances, the rate of coal consumption increases. In developing our natural resources to the fullest extent, it is important to try every means and find out all possibilities in the saving of coal,

As an example, in the United states the big central station with its transmission lines has demonstrated positively and conclusively that it can furnish better service at less cost to the ultimate consumer than can any individual plant. This is particularly true in small towns. This statement is substantial by a report from a representative, showing that in the last ten years, nearly 200 small towns abandoned their individual plants in favor of transmistion line service and that during that period, not one municipelity gave up transmission line service in favor of individual plants.

In connection with the ownership and management of the central station industry, a few points as brught out in the foregoing statement should be criticized. In the first place the municipally and provincially controlled companies should be replaced by customers' ownership. By customers' ownership is meant that the ultimate consumers of the power company are the stockholders of that organization. It is preferable to the Government or individual control due to the following reasosns: (1) It has better management, free from all political and personal influence. The business is on a sound base as the financial sources will not be defrayed for other purposes than for the benefit of that business. (2) The customers' ownership of an industry due to the general interest leads to the gaining good will which is considered as an asset of a public utility company. (3) The public is interest and sympathy with the company's business helps to establish a cooperative spirit between the company and its customers. This means the elimination of some possible difficulties in carrying out the company's plans, such as busines extension and other new policies.

The central station men should give proper and careful consideration to securing information on installation and operation of new stations. A small error in this respect at the early stage is liable to offset the entire plan of a system. For instance the selection of frequency and generating, transmission or distributinge voltage has a great deal to do with economical opeartion. China is now the World's market, full of competitive equipment. It is important that the purchaser should know or consult with the specialist as to the method of operating systems, and the selection of proper equipment. The economical operation of a power system should be considered from the standpoint of fair price as well as satisfactory performance of the equipment purchased.

It is noted thet in some cities of moderate size, lighting load is supplied by more than one company, such as in Changsha, 2-1500KW. stations, 2-2500 KW. station, and two small stations in Chengtu. Still in other localities, the lighting load and industrial load are supplied by different companies, such as the city lighting plant and the cotton mill plant in Chengchow, and a great number of such cases in Shanghai, Hankow and Tientsin. As a result of competition, many companies with an insufficient amount of capital are out of business, and others are barely maintained. Of course, there are many practical difficulties in supplying power to the city market from a single system. These may be due to the monopoly of power cost, inadequate service and management. However' a first consideration should be given to the possibilities of cooperation among the members of enterprises of the same nature. This means not only from the standpoint of mutual benefit but also the putblic relations, such as good will and the common interest in the fuel saving problem.

Men engaged in the central station industry should also take an interest in business other than power supply, such as city transportation, water and gas supply and other public activities. The advantages of controlling business on side lines are usually helpful to the main activity. The addition of operating industrial load in the day time improves the load factor which reduces the cost per Kilowatt hour generated. For a company supplying electricity, water and gas to a city, the management force can secure a maximum efficiency so far as dealing with customers is concerned for the same amount of force would be required whether for one or more lines of work to be handled, such as the collecting of bills and other house appliance service. The operation of several branches of work in public utilities sometimes relieves the financial strain of the organization during the depression of one particular branch of the business. This is especially true when the company is engaged in such businesses as banking and real estate. There is another intangible effect, namely, the public noting the promising future of the enterprise is encouraged to depend upon it for service.

Another important activity of the central station industry is to establish an association to participate in the following functions: (1) to establish standards for power generation, transmission and distribution to be adopted in China, (2) to promote and improve the central station industry by keeping systematic records of operation and management and offering suggestions for research, and (3) to advertise the central station indus ry and teach the public to use more electricity in order to live a better life. Among these, the first function is the most important one and should not be overlooked at present, because a standard system will simplify the problems of interconnection of power sysems, unify the electrical installations for industrial application and offer an easy problem in manufacturing. Periodical conventions of the association offer a good opportunity for members to exchange information and discuss new subjects. Illustrated lectures for the public should be extensively conducted in order to present the technic idea in a form both interesting and instructive.

For the welfare of the country and their own business, the central station men should keep a constant interest in training young men having the necessary fundamental knowledge. A certain number of college graduates should be selected to follow a systematic training in the organization. For the benefit of the operating companies as well as the manutacfurer the latter orgahization usually takes a member of young men evry year to follw a training course involving the general problems in operation, application and designing of power equipment. The operating company should take this advantage and keep constantly in touch with the manufacturers and never miss the opp rtunity of cooperating with them.

To summarize the above discussion, the following points are to be noted:

1. Powar opens market for itself.
2. St am power plan's of large turbine generating units ars preferable.
3. Interconnection and superpower is necessary in China and should be, therefore, encouraged. As coal is the only source of power in China, the saving of fuel is the urgent problem to face in the central station industry.
4. Customer's ownership is more favorable than municipal and government cont ol.
5. Central station men should be specialists.
6. Public interest should be cultivated in order to appreciate the service of the public utility organization.
7. Central station iudustry should be reinforced by other activities, such as gas and water sunply and city transportation.
8. Central station industry is not only a profit making business but also

should take interest in public affairs such as the establishment of association and educational work.

Bibliography

1. Rea's Far Eastern Manual
2. The China Year Book, 1923
3. The Commercial Handbook of China.
4. The Electrical Review, January, 1924.
5. Far Eastern Review, Sept. and Dec. 1924.
6. Electrical World. 1924.
7. N. E. L. A. Prime Movers' Committee's Report, 1923.

震華製造電機廠實習紀

張望良

緒言　諺云百聞不如一見.世間萬事萬物,苟非目擊其實在情況,則雖有善言者,口講指劃,剖析詳盡而聽者對於所聆之事物情狀,終難神會無遺.捫燭扣盤之爲日,常人視爲笑談.盲者尙自喜得計.學問一道,昔人不少求之於書.然卓然特異之作家則常遊歷宇內,周覽河山,於是其文益雄厚奔放,其所見益高人一等.吾儕工程學生,爲學之方,迥異他科.非耳目並用,實地觀察,不得謂爲盡探討之能事.在學校時代,上課聽受,下堂實習.於學理實驗方面,似已能兼顧並進,實則尙不盡然.蓋學校實驗室,不過用以證明基本學理,非可以語工廠之實際設備也.本校機械電機兩試驗室,規模備具.但較之電力廠相差尙遠.舉凡機器之佈置連絡,電氣之管理分配,非目擊者不能悉其所以.是以工程學生,當視工廠實習爲正科之一部,與學校課程相提並論.且工廠設備,盡屬實在,非親歷攷察,安能辨別重輕,爲他日及身服務之準備乎?本年暑假中良由校中介紹,實習於震華電廠.忽忽匝月,未窺全豹.惟聞見所及,不無可紀者,爰就廠中設備方面,述其大概.篇中所載,專爲工程學生,未接近工廠者說法.貽笑方家,未暇計及.讀者諸君,披閱之餘,對於近世中央電力廠之狀況,或可想象於萬一.是則作者區區之意也.

廠史　震華廠創議於民國十一年.奠基於民國十二年,爲華商創辦之股份有限公司.同年夏季裝配機器砌置鍋爐.翌年二月,開機送電於附近鄉鎮.四月,供電至常州.六月初旬,無錫長距離導線,亦告竣通電.計一年之中,即完成擬定計劃.國內大規模工廠,其成立之速,當以震華爲首屈.具見創辦者計劃之周密,進行之積極矣.惟成立伊始,基礎未固,現祇發售電力.其製造一部,尙有待也.

廠中設備.自進煤於爐,至供電於用戶,步驟繁複.茲爲便利筆述起見,分下列三節,依次敍之.

(一) 機房 述關次分配機器位置之大概情形.

(二) 機械動作 述爐鍋透平凝結器等.

(三) 電氣管理 述電氣自發電機至出廠之程序.

(一) 機 房

所稱機房,專指製造電氣所需之房屋而言.廠中附設之打鐵間 Forge shop, 金工間Machiue shop, 及造冰間Refrigerator Room, 不在論列.機房可依其工作性質,分爲四大部如下.

甲 爐鍋間及出灰間 此兩間居機房之後部,分上下層.爐鍋間據於上,出灰間承於下.爐鍋間中,已裝B and W水管式雙汽包爐鍋三座.每座附有進煤機 Chain stoker 省煤器 Economizer 各一副.省煤器上有附帶之去灰機 Ash scraper 一具.第一第二兩爐鍋自開廠以來,交互應用.第三座尚餘總汽管及烟突未竟全功.第四座機件亦已購入.惟擱置未裝,因尚非需要也.二鍋爐合用一烟突.他日,第三第四座裝竣後,將有兩烟突高峙廠中.每座鍋爐有兩灰穴. ash pit. 一出塵灰,一出塊灰.灰穴下接有灰斗,伸入出灰間內.斗之下口,掩以鉛皮蓋.去蓋則灰瀉於地.乃糞除之.出灰間之內部,設有浴盆,通以冷熱水管.便工人之洗浴也.

乙 進水間及水櫃間 緊接鍋爐間之前爲進水間,即澄清鍋爐用水及打水入鍋爐之室也.是室之南半,裝蒸發器Evaporator三具.及附屬之加熱器 Heater, 濾水器 Filter, 馬達小抽水機Small motor-driven water pump等.其北半有馬達轉運之汽鍋用水進水機 Motor-driven feed-water pump 二座,汽輪轉用之汽輪用水進水機Turbine-driven fled-water pump一座.及附屬之加熱器 Heater. 進水間之上爲水櫃間.中有清濁二水櫃.清水供給鍋爐以成汽濁水經澄清手續後,亦入鍋爐.又機房所需之自來水,均直接仰給於濁水櫃

中

丙　汽輪發電機間及凝結器間　汽輪發電機間居機房之前部正中.已裝有汽輪發電機Turbo-generator二部.尚有餘地可供擴充.室之牆壁上敷設鐵軌.架活動吊車一具.起重力量爲一萬二千啓羅格蘭姆 Kilogram 凝結器間卽進水機間及汽輪發電機間之下層.有凝結器 Condenser 二具.每具各正對一汽輪 Turbine. 以接收汽輪之餘汽 Exhausteam. 與凝結器相依者.爲冷水進水機 Circulating-water pump.及凝結水抽水機Hot well pump.又抽水入濁水櫃用之抽水機Water pump二具.與前舉各機.均裝於是室中.

丁　油開關間.電氣分配間.石板間.變壓器間　以上四室.分爲三層.電氣分配間石板間並立於最上層.油開關間居於中.變壓器間位於下.變壓器間置有本廠用變壓器 Transformer 二具.農田戽水用變壓器一具.又無錫常州輸送用高壓變壓器二具.此間用水泥混凝土 Concrete. 更分爲小間.除本廠用二變壓器外.每具各佔一小間.油開關間內.裝有油開關 Oil switch 多只.爲電氣由發電機至分配銅板 Bus bar. 或由分配銅板至各路線所必經之途.室中亦用水泥混凝土.隔成小間二列.小間之大小.以能容油開關爲度.二列小間之中間.留有走道.面走道之小間隔牆上.裝有油開關之開關柄.以司啓閉.電氣分配間.有分配銅板二排.一載三萬三千伏脫電氣.一載六千六百伏脫電氣.石板間背電氣分配間而面汽輪發電機間.中有石板 switch board 九塊.上裝各式量電計Measuremeut instrumeuts紅綠號燈.及本廠用電力電燈線石板之後.裝本廠用之三百八十伏脫分配銅板.電表臺一座.專裝發電機上之總開關.各式電表及管理機關.

機房外形.及其分間中之機器位置.如圖 ：

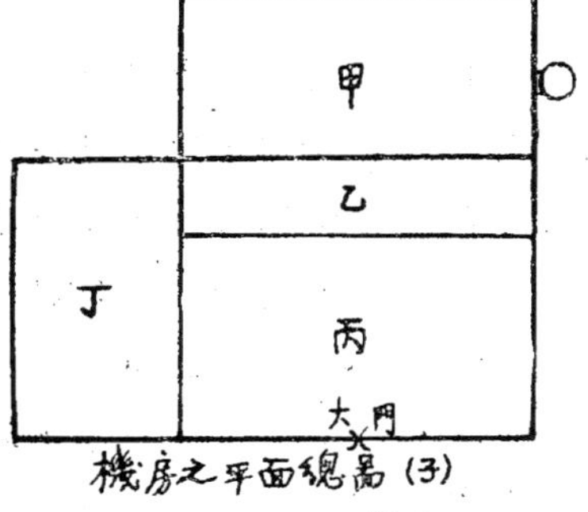

機房之平面總圖（子）

甲.爐鍋間及出灰間
乙.水櫃間及進水機間
丙.汽輪發電機間及凝結器間
丁.電氣分配間石板間油開關間及變壓器間

機房分圖（丑）

1.33000伏脫分配銅板
2.6600 伏脫分配銅板
3.380 伏脫分配銅板
4.給電石板
5.電表檯
)(門

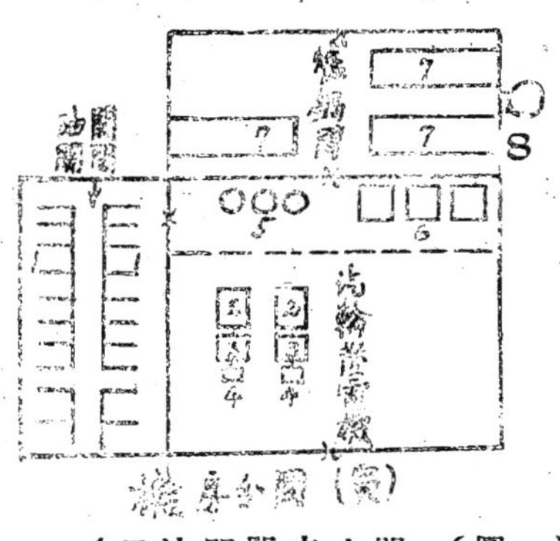

機房分圖（寅）

1.置油開關之小間 （圖一）
2.汽輪
3.更流發電機
4.礪磁機
5.蒸發器三具
6.進水機三具（抽汽水水用）
7.爐鍋三具
)○ 烟突
)(門

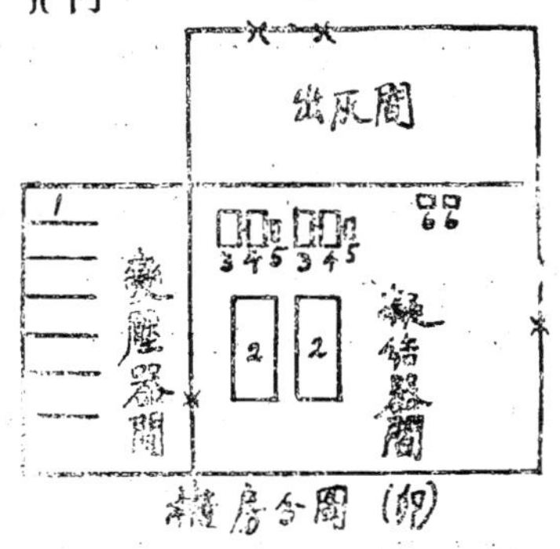

機房分圖（卯）

1.置變壓器之小間
2.凝結器二具
3.小汽輪二具
4.冷水進冷機
5.凝結水抽水機
6.濁鍋抽水機
)(門

(二) 機械動作

機械動作依其作用之差別,而匯納於三種各不相謀之環線circuit中.(甲)燃熱環線Heatiug circuit,(乙)動力環線Motive power circuit(丙)凝冷環線Cooling circuit.此等不同之環線,有如圖二所示.三環線中所需各式機器及其佈置,略如下述.

蒸汽電力廠之機務三環線

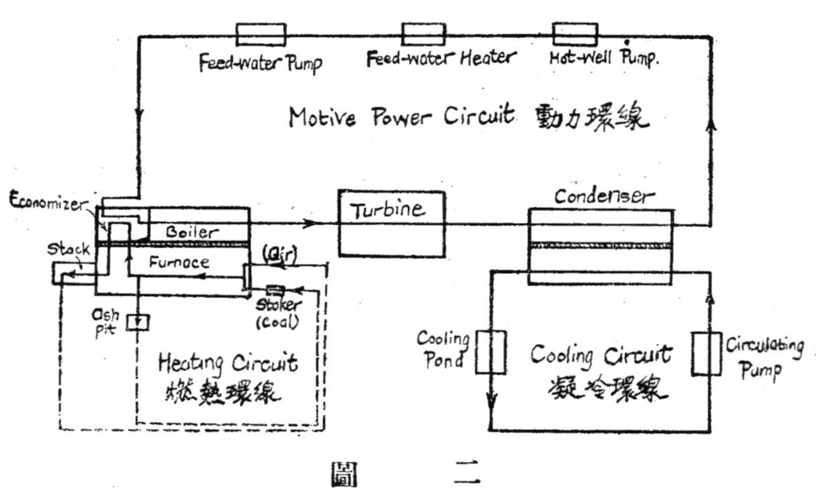

圖　二

甲　燃熱環線　此環線開始於空氣及煤之送入爐膛.空氣中之氧與煤中之炭在進煤機面上化合而生熱.鍋中之水受熱而成汽.導汽入於汽輪,而原動力出矣.空氣與煤化合之後,燼餘之爲固體者,下降於灰斗,在出灰間撤除之.氣體之燼餘,則取道省煤機經烟突而飛散於太空.此環線不能周行無間,故爲斷環線Open circuit.圖中虛線表理想中可連續之途徑也.

氣體餘燼,常取道省煤器.惟當鍋爐生火之際,省煤器尚非需要,而爐內通風須極圓滿,庶火勢易旺,於是另備地道,與省煤器並行,使氣體得由地道不經若何阻碍而入於烟突.省煤器之口,有氣閘Air damper二扇,地道之口,亦有一扇.欲氣入地道.則閉前二扇氣閘,而開後一扇,欲氣入省煤器,則反行之,氣閘開闢之窄闊.可使通風隨之有緩急.例如氣閘大闢,則通風最旺是也.

每具鍋爐前部,有煤斗 Coal hopper 一只.煤用人力送入斗中,因其本身重量,次第落於進煤機上.進煤機上煤層之厚薄,有隔板,可使之隨心所欲.通風不藉機械,而爲自然式Natural draft.故鐵筋混凝土Reinforced concrete築成之烟突,達六十米突Meter之高.突之內徑上爲3.68米突,下爲7.3米突云.

進煤機爲鐵鍊式.組成環形,用二匹馬力之感應馬達 Inducton motor 運行之.鐵鍊於爐端受煤斗落下之煤.因馬達之力,且燃且入爐腹.迨至擋壁 Baffle blate,煤已成灰降於灰斗.馬達與進煤機以減速齒輪Reducing gear爲聯接之媒介.齒輪有速度多種.值班者隨時加減鍊上煤層,或更換齒綸速度以控制燃燒速率 Rate of combustion,使鍋中汽壓,常保規定之數.大抵汽壓變化大者,加減煤層,以左右之小者以齒輪控制之云.

進煤機上原動力,或用馬達,或用汽機.在中央電廠,電氣無時或斷,馬達佔地小而簡潔,頗爲合用.若非日夜工作之廠,汽機較爲適宜.蓋每次生火蒸汽時,用以轉動進煤機之人力,可以稍省至於利用餘汽問題,在中央電廠可不必論也.

乙 動力環線 蒸汽自鍋中出,至汽輪變爲機械力,至凝結器凝爲水此水由凝結水抽水機抽入淸水櫃,由淸水櫃入加熱器,再用汽鍋用水進水機將水打入省煤器,而重進鍋中.此乃動力環線之大概也.

蒸汽在鍋中之壓力,爲每方吋二百磅.經超熱器Superheater溫度升至華氏六百度.此二百壓力及六百溫度之蒸汽,由超熱器升入總汽管Main steam pipe,經水汽分析器 Moisture separator. 而入於汽輪.餘汽Exhuast steam壓力爲 750 密厘米突Mm.眞空.此餘汽自汽輪尾部直入緊接之凝結器,熱氣爲器中冷水所奪而成爲水,至加熱器,則與來自蒸發器之低壓蒸汽相混而略温.再進至省煤器,因烟氣Fluegas之灼熱,水之温度約升近華氏表二百度之數.水汽分析器所分出之水汽Moisture,再經一汽水分離器Automatic steam trap,將水分放於室外.

汽輪餘汽入凝結器而成水,已如上述.但尚有一管可將餘汽自汽輪直放天空,所以備凝結器有障碍難用時,權宜救急,或初開機時.直接放餘汽於天空也.水入汽鍋亦有二途.一經省煤器,前已說及.一則不經省煤器,而直入汽鍋第二途當鍋爐生火或省煤機有損壞時,偶一用之,非常道也.

汽鍋爲B&W水管式每具有兩汽包 Drum, 其受熱面積爲四千五百二十平方呎,超熱器受熱面積爲一千三百二十平方呎.汽包每只長二十二呎半,直徑四呎半.水管二百根,每根長十八呎,圓周四吋.

汽輪爲催進式Impulse type. 蒸汽壓力在汽輪內.分八次遞降,速率則始終不變.故爲單速率多壓位 Siugle velocity, multiple stages.汽輪馬力爲四千六百匹,速度每分鐘三千轉.管理及保險開關 Governor and Emergency valve,皆應用油力繼續器 Oil relay.製造者爲德國克虜伯廠.

凝結器緊接汽輪之下端,器爲管面隔離式Surface condenser.冷水在管中,蒸汽圍管外,二者不相混雜.此種凝結器之主要優點,在凝成之水,可再用於汽鍋,不必另經其他治理手續.器爲德國克虜伯廠造.長四米突直徑二又十分之三米突.寒冷面積爲六百六十平方米突.直徑二十九密厘米突之水管,計一千六百二十五根.冷水三門,由器之一端下方而入.往復於各小管中.最後於他端上方,亦分三門而出.匯於一出水總管而瀉於運河.

凝結水抽水機與冷水進水機同裝一軸上,由一小汽輪轉動之.凝結水雖可由是機直送清水櫃,實則當全廠日夜工作時,凝結水每被送入汽鍋進水機 Feed-water pump, 藉後者之力,重入汽鍋.若後者未克盡量吸收,其剩餘之量,始進水櫃以待取用.

鍋爐所成之汽,經多次之循環工作後,不能全無漏失.但汽輪所需之汽苟負重不變,不能強之減縮.汽鍋用水,須極純潔,於是補充用水問題,必須妥爲解決.震華廠計劃之初,恐內地水源不合汽鍋之用,故於補充汽鍋用水,特備蒸發器爲他廠所罕見.蒸發器共有三具,並立於進水間內.(見圖一寅)鍋水自濁水櫃下瀉,先過一加熱器,與來自蒸發器之少量蒸汽相混和,使水微温,再過一濾水器將水濾淨,乃由抽水機抽入蒸發器中.此抽水機用一匹半馬力之感應馬達運動之.濾清之水,在蒸發器中,與來自汽鍋之蒸汽相遇而蒸發.自水蒸得之汽,與用以蒸發之汽,(此汽本係超熱.至此則其中所含熱氣,稍被奪於水.而成溼汽 Wet steam)除小部份至濁水加熱器外,其餘盡至清水加熱器.與來自清水櫃之冷清水相混合,使復凝爲水,幷提高清水温度,故蒸發器之設,所以使補充之水.先行蒸化一次,以盡除雜質,非若他廠之僅用濾水器爲已足也.

打水入汽鍋之進水機有三.兩用馬達轉運,一用汽輪轉運.馬達轉動之進水機,各有每分鐘八百三十五立脫 Liter 之出水量,馬達能力爲四十基羅瓦特 Kilowatt.汽輪轉運之進水機出水量爲每分鐘一百立方米達.汽輪馬力未詳.平日祗用一具,餘供調換.

省煤機每副合六組而成.共計直立之管八十根,受熱面積二百四十八平方米突.裝於爐鍋與烟突之間.全身被磚砌沒.管中之水,奪烟之熱氣,以增高温度.管之外周,與烟直接相觸.烟灰時常積聚其上,足以減少管之傳熱功用.倘不設法革除,則不數日間,省煤機將大失其效用.是以每省煤器,各附有去灰機一具.機以二匹馬力之馬達轉運之.

丙 凝冷環線 此環線頗爲簡單.即凝結器所需冷水之巡行途徑也.水由冷水進水機.自冷池抽入,經凝結器而回入冷池.

震華廠地臨運河,因即利用運河,作爲冷池.但河身距機房之凝結器間約有六七百碼之遙.爰開鑿二渠,通至凝結器間下層之前後兩方.水自此渠

吸起,由彼渠放出.吸起之水十之七八入於凝結器.餘者供抽氣器及放散軸承Bearing熱氣之用.(詳見後節)

冷水進水機爲離心式Ceutrifugal type,與德國克虜伯廠造八十五匹馬力之寇氏汽輪Curtis turbine相接聯,汽輪之速度爲每分鐘二千一百轉.管理及保險開關,皆利用慣性及彈簧Inertia and Spring作用以行之.蒸汽在寇氏汽輪工作後,或直入凝結器,或入發電機上之大汽輪相助工作,一視發電機發電之多寡,而自行管理.

抽氣器爲喇叭形,利用水力以吸去凝結器中所積存之空氣.冷水自冷水進水機來,經抽氣器而回入進水渠,當水過抽氣器之喇叭頸時,因壓力驟減而急遽衝出.喇叭頸之一部遂成眞空現象.凝結器中之空氣因被吸出,使其中壓力,得以常保其規定之最高眞空度數而利汽輪之工作.

電力廠之機務設備,大概不外上述之三環線.惟廠之大者,因所用機器能力大而速度高,機器上軸承之散熱Bearing cooling,遂成一重要問題.每有散熱不善,致機器不能功作,甚至損壞者.散熱之劑,都爲油類,不僅用以減熱,且可使軸承Bearing潤滑也.聯於發電機之大汽輪,附有特製之機件,使冷油川流不息於軸承之間.此機件之動作,與汽輪同其行止.冷油出自油櫃,經汽輪及相聯發電機之軸承後,回入櫃中.惟回入之熱油,其熱氣不能速行自散.於是用鐵管引冷水盤旋油櫃中,以速其消失.如此則油經櫃後,又可供用矣.當汽輪開關之時,另有小進油機Oil pump一具,用雙汽缸小汽機動之,以促冷油之巡行軸承.蓋當此等時機,特製之進油機件未克應用,不得不別闢蹊徑,以成此工作也.用於油櫃之水,在未至櫃時,先經一銅砂布濾水器,使水濾淨.蓋在油櫃中之盤香水管,僅如指粗.若有沈澱壅積其間,水即難於通行,而易生危險.

冷水進水機所用之小汽輪.其軸承所需之油,注於軸承間油槽中.槽之外圍以冷水細管.以散其熱.管之粗約如鉛筆桿云.

機務方面所有機件,除上述外.尙有抽濁水用之抽水機二具一爲離心式 Centrifugal type. 與七匹半馬力之三相馬達相聯.一爲水筒式 Reciprocating-motion type, 與一雙汽缸汽機相聯.此二抽水機,均自下層進水櫃中抽水入上層之濁水櫃,

(三) 電氣管理

電氣自發電機出,以至應用於各種事業.其徑過程序,可分四步,卽發電Generation,分配Distribution,傳送Transmission,應用Utilization是也.此篇所及,以機房內者爲限.傳送應用二步,付之闕如.其他二步之機件佈置,分述於下.

甲 發電 發電機間中,裝汽輪發電機 Turbo-generator 二部.汽輪爲德國克虜伯廠出品,用聯軸 Coupling 與德國西門子廠所造之更流發電機 Alternator 相連.發電機之前端,裝有勵磁機 Exciter.汽輪之動力,直接由軸柱 Shaft,傳於發電機及勵磁機.機身全部盡行舊沒.其露於外者.僅勵磁機之整流器 Commutator, 及發電機磁場之輸電圈.(用以輸送直流電至發電機磁場之銅圈)所以利空氣之流通,而放散發電機中之熱氣也,

氣輪	4600 H.P.	3000R.P.M.	350° C Temperature
	14Atm. press,	91%Vacuum.	Oil-pressure. Governor
發電機	4000 KV-A.	6600 volts.	350 Amperes,
	3 Phase	Y connection	0.80 Power Factor
	50 Cycle		
勵磁機	23 KW.	110 Volts.	
	209 ampers.	Shunt Winding.	

勵磁用之直流電,自勵磁機出.穿過地板由發電機間之下層,經甲號電氣阻力器Rhostat,而入發電機之磁場.勵磁機之本身磁場中有一乙號電氣阻力器,甲號阻力器用以控制直流電電流量之輸入發電機磁場.乙號阻力

器用以控制礪磁機磁場中之電流量.此二者間接皆用以校正發電機之電壓者也.發電機之電氣導線,出電機後,穿過地板,取道凝結器間,而至油開關 Oil switch,再經閘刀開關 Disconnecting Switch ,乃與 6600－Volt 之分配銅板 Busbar 相聯合.

乙 分配　電氣分配在分配銅板上行之.銅板有屬於發電機,低壓,高壓三種.發電機及高壓之分配銅板,各有二副,以備損壞時之調換.且合佔一室,與他部相隔離.以免危險.若低壓分配銅板,則祇有一副,裝於給電石板 Switch board 之後.

電氣自發電機出,經上節所述之行程.而上發電機分配銅板.此種銅板所受電壓爲6600伏脫.自此銅板引出並行電路六條,兩條至長途輸送用昇級變壓器Step-up transformer.兩條至本廠用降級變壓器Step-dawn transformer 其餘兩條,一至利民紗廠,一至戚墅堰鎮.至昇級變壓器之電路,所經過者有閘刀開關及油開關,至利民紗廠及戚鎮者,亦先經閘刀開關與油開關而出廠至降級變壓器者,經閘刀開關油開關及塞電圈Choke coils.

輸送用變壓器爲蚌殼式Shll type. 器之散熱利用其外廓之皺紋面積 Corrugated surface. 置此器之小間壁上,裝有電扇以盛空氣之流通.其進線爲6600 伏脫,出線爲33000 伏脫.本廠用變壓器亦爲蚌殼式及皺紋散熱面積.二具合置一小間中,有6600 伏脫之進線,及380伏脫之出線.此出線分而爲二,一上低壓分配銅板,一至戽水用之昇級變壓器.器之構造與前者同樣.

至戽水用變壓器之電路,自本廠變壓器來經閘刀開關而入於380伏脫之進線.電壓在此變壓器中,昇至2300 伏脫,經塞電圈,油開關,及閘刀開關而出廠房.此路無特備之分配銅板.僅分爲兩幹線,通至廠之西北兩鄉.

輸送用變壓器上33000伏脫之出線,經塞電圈,閘刀開關,而上高壓分配銅板.自此銅板引出二電路,爲無錫常州之長途輸送路線.出廠之前,各先經閘刀開關,油開關,再經一閘刀開關云.本廠用變壓器上之380伏脫出線,經閘刀開關重負續電器Overload relay，再一開刀開關，而上低壓分配銅板.廠中電力，盡取給於此.於本廠變壓器之380伏脫方面，尙有一中和線Neutral wire 自Y形接線之中和部引出.廠中電燈線，合中和線及一單相力線而成.電力電燈各線皆先經一保險鉛絲Fuse，開刀開關，乃通至應用之處，

各具油開關上.每相Phasc皆附裝一重負續電器，爲電流量反常時之保障.天空雷電，常有襲擊路線之虞.以夏季爲最烈，其防止之方，在33000伏脫及6600伏脫方面者，用角形擒雷器Horn-gap arrester，裝於各自統屬之分銅板上.用於380伏脫者.爲鋁質電池式擒雷器 Aluminium-cell arrester，裝於380伏脫之分配銅板上.

與發電分配二步，互相聯絡.而莫可或離者，爲査察電氣自發電至出廠之狀况襄助此種査察之工具，爲各式量電計Electrical measuument meters.關於發電機之量電計，匯集一檯，簡稱之曰電表檯.用於各路出線者，不論本廠與用戶，其量電計及紅綠號燈，盡分佈於給電石板Switch board上紅號燈示路線有變故發生，綠號燈示平穩無事.給電石板上，尙裝有本廠各路電氣開關.電表檯上有電流計Ammeter電壓計Voltmeter，週率計Frequency meter，電折計. Power factor meter，及電力計Wattmeter等.石板上有電流計，電壓計.電工計#watthour meter等.

出線上之電氣.因其電壓之高，及電流之大，量電計不能徑行接在出線中，以驗電壓之升降.電流之多寡，於是應用電壓變壓器及電流變壓器，以減低電壓電流之成數，使合於量電計之用.此種變壓器，所處之位置，不便一一贅述.可於第三圖中所示各分配銅板及各路線上就而索之.

上述各種電氣導線，其所取之路徑，及一切佈置，作者不文，或有未能條達之處.爰附以下圖.讀者按圖推尋，當能瞭然胸次也.

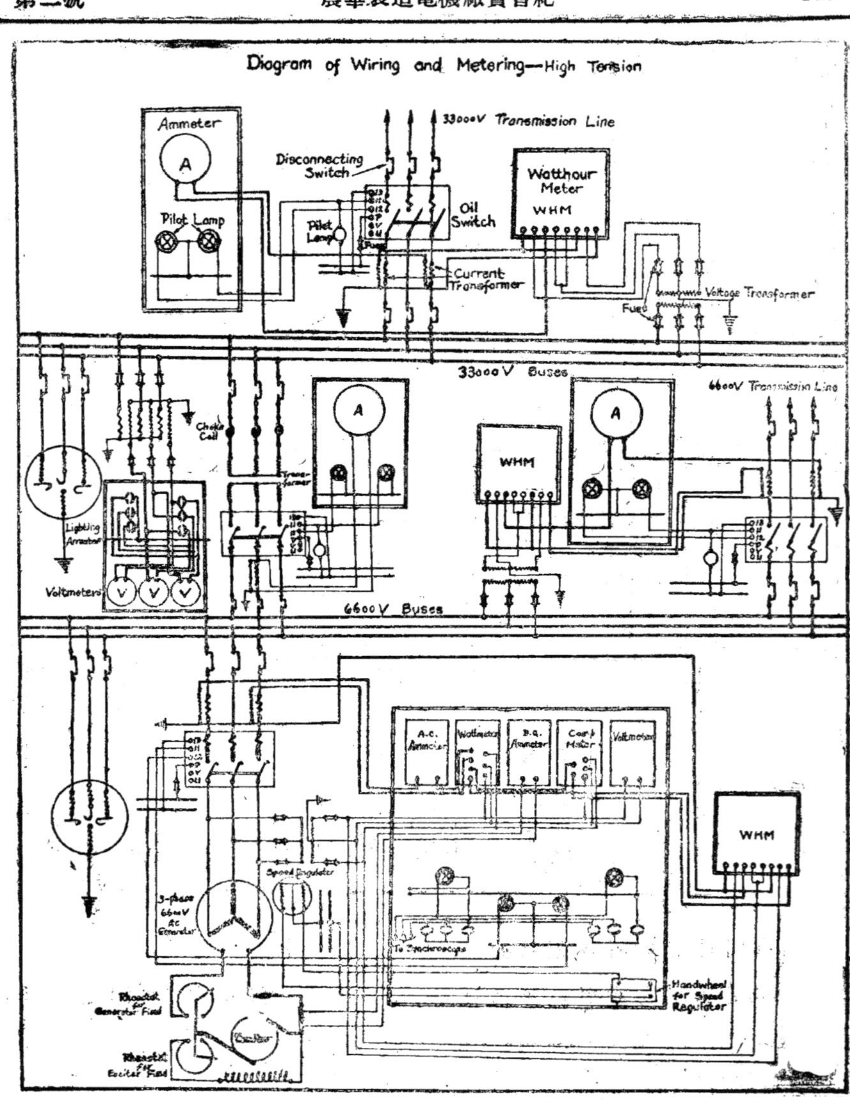
Diagram of Wiring and Metering—High Tension
Ammeter
A
Pilot Lamp
33000V Transmission Line
Disconnecting Switch
Oil Switch
Pilot Lamp
Current Transformer
Watthour Meter
WHM
Voltage Transformer
Fuse
33000V Buses
Choke Coil
Transformer
Lightning Arrester
Voltmeters
6600V Transmission Line
6600V Buses
A.C. Ammeter
Wattmeter
D.C. Ammeter
Voltmeter
Speed Regulator
3-phase 6600V AC Generator
To Synchroscope
Handwheel for Speed Regulator
Rheostat for Generator Field
Rheostat for Exciter Field
Exciter

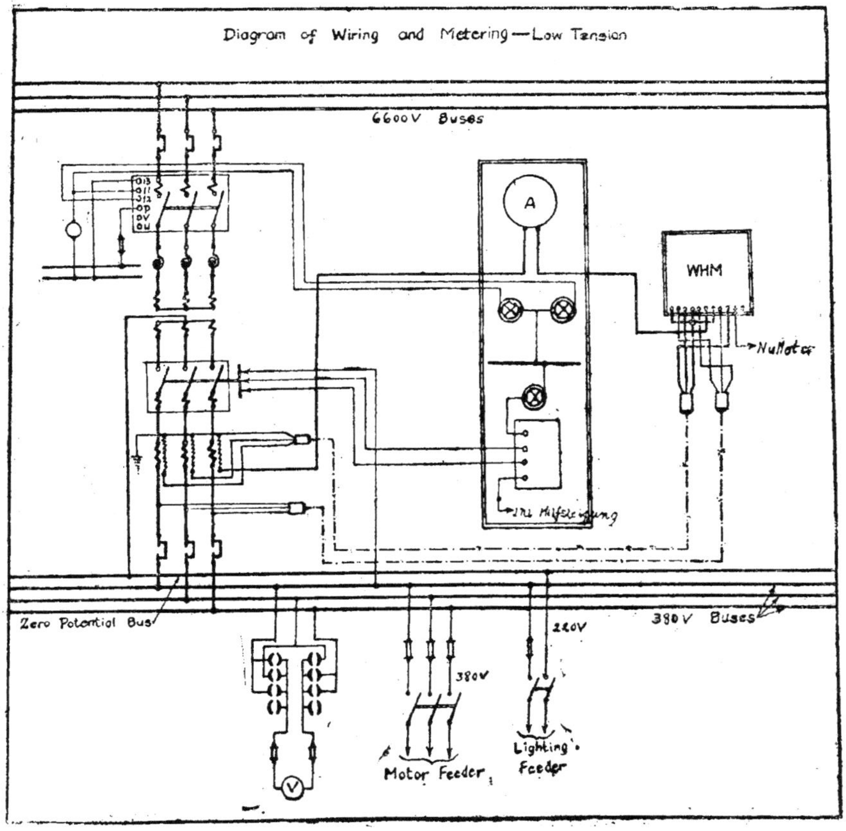

Diagram of Wiring and Metering—Low Tension

此次同往實習者,為張君德載.陸君增福.陸君競智,對與良共四人.廠中待遇優渥.工程師及辦事員等指疑解惑,均懃懃不倦,殊可感也.附誌於此.以誌謝悃.

蘇州胥門發電廠一瞥

鮑錫瑤記

乙丑季冬,予與張君望良,同遊姑蘇之電廠,正值新機間建造之際.並蒙老同學張工程師指導一切.爰就四日中之見聞雜錄以誌鴻爪.

蘇州電廠現有二處;一即棗市橋之胥廠,創辦於民國七年.一即在閶門之舊廠,舊廠本係日人經營,後歸胥廠盤頂.吾等所視者,胥廠之新舊各機及鍋爐也.

胥廠南臨胥江,北鄰郊野,東近通衢,可以直達車站.胥江則遠通大河,故供給水量,源源不絕,便利而純潔.該廠汽鍋用水及所需冷水,皆自此江引入,此種河水,濾清亦便.可免汽鍋內部生沉澱物(Scale)之弊也.

光線充足.爲該廠之特點.佈置亦善.即如目下新建之機間,大部以水門汀造成,軒敞而堅固.惟屋頂等間用木料,非完全禦火(Fireproof)者.

其新機間之門面,加造洋臺以壯瞻觀.屋前則爲新鑿之二水池.凝水器(Condenser)之進水出水兩大管.即終於此點.

佈置新機間之代價

新機間之建設.吾人既樂觀其垂成.其所需費用自所亟欲聞知.且最近之時價尤值得注意.故首將其共費之數錄如下:

一—（裝設新機一切由上海新通公司包辦）

1　新機間（可置兩電機,以期共發 10,000 K.V.A.）——————$30,000

2　新煙囪——————————————$14,000

3　新透平發及附件——————————————$70,000

4 新石板 (Switchboard) ——————————$10,000

5 新汽管(Theam Fiping)——————————$ 8,000

6 冷水鑄鐵管 (Circulating pipesC.I.) ——————————$ 4,500

7 新水池 ——————————$ 6,000

8 歲添自動加煤機三只 (• 於舊鍋爐) ——————————$10,000

9 新添電線(Feederwire)——————————$ 3,000

(用#61/16bare Copper 計價 $300 pur每1000 ft)

10 裝建費 (Erecting cost) ——————————$ 5,000

11 雜費——————————$ 2,000

共需費約 ——————————$162,500

此總數尙係從少數計算者.

兩廠職工人數及經濟情形

工人共數一百六十,月薪自六十元至十六元不等.(學徒不在內)

營業職員共八十五人.

每月開銷共七千元.

每月燒煤一千二百噸.(平均每日四十噸)

資本約計洋一百八十萬元.

胥廠佔地約十畝.

刻下二廠可發電能總數(Total Available Plant Power)如下:——

(A) 4500 K.V.A. 50 Cycle (turbine driven) 由胥廠新機發出.

(B) 2000 K.V.A. 60 Cycle (turbine driven) 由胥廠舊機發出.

(C) 750 K.W. 50 Cycle (turbine driven) 由老廠發出.

(D) 315 K.V.A. Single-Phase (Engine driven) 由胥廠舊機發出.

(E) 375 K.V.A. 3-Phase 50 Cycle (Engine Driven) 由老廠發出.

二廠之鍋爐共有燃煤面積(Heatingsurface) 15,490 Sq.ft.胥廠鍋爐之數凡七.汽壓力爲每方吋二百磅.

二廠煤料之來源爲中興.撫順.開平三處.

胥廠係租地造屋.共租三十年.租費每年需洋二千元.九勝巷之辦事處亦係租地.每年需費八百元.

至於爲異日擴充之計;胥廠已有預備.無虞缺少地盤.蓋其屯煤之場甚廣,足容三千噸煤料也.

該廠售電之價（電燈用）每度(卽Kilowatthour)計洋二角.成本共約一角.煤料價佔其七分也.若照燈數計算,(Flate-rate)則每十六枝光燈一盞,月需洋一元二角,（合四分一夜）若租火表.則每月租費二角,其火表之原價三盎貝者值十五元,而五盎貝者值二十元.其電限表(Current liniter)之價約十三四元.

每日胥廠共發電力(Energy)約八千五百度左右.其最高電能(Peak load)約一千餘基羅瓦特(Kilowatts)

路　線

1. 2300 V.之Feeder共有四路.城中凡三路.城外有一路.另有6600. V.之Eeeder一路通至四鄉,卽木瀆,滸墅關,望亭等處是也.（此路用變壓器自2300 V.變高至6600 V.)

2. 2300 V.之Transmission Wire用#37/13之電線或#6者不等.#(37/14卽用三十七根十四號線所絞成者.)

各電桿之距離,大約一百尺.大都用木桿.電桿之高度平均三十五尺.

3. 變壓器分站(Transformer substation):——

(A) 種類——變壓器之High tension winding爲Three-phase, △-connectec:其Low tension winding爲Three phase, four wire, Y-connected.點燈用,則將2300 V.變至220 V.若爲電力用,則將2300

V.變至 380 V. 同一 2300 V.而能變成兩種不同之低壓力者.蓋若接電燈則將Y式之中心線(Neutral-wire)通出,故能得220V.之壓力也.

(B) 防護之設備——重要之分站,則備有油開關(Oil-switch)其餘則用電鎔線(Fuse),電表等(Metering)自亦皆備有也,

(C) 容量(Cadacity)自 50 K.V.A.至 400 K.V.A.

(D) 製造者——German, westinghouse, sweden, G.E. co.(U.S.A.)及華生.(Chinese)

(E) 鐵扁担(Cross-arm)之長度——2-Wire者三十吋長而 4-Wire者五十吋長.

(F) 低壓部(Low tension)——若爲街燈之用,則用另一出線以便開關.若爲電力之用,則巨大之馬達亦須用另一出線,惟小馬達則不妨,

4. 植電桿之路權(Right of way)——蘇地無須出價購此路權.

5. 路線分布有詳圖可覽.惜未及錄下.其分布之法,足以預防某處傳電路徑之或斷.試舉一例如下.:——

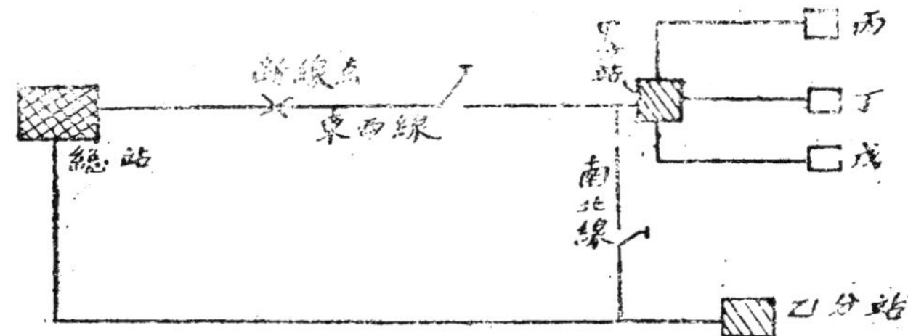

參觀上圖,譬如總站至甲分站之東西線斷則甲,丙,丁.戊需用之電仍可由乙分站旁之南北支線接濟之.不然,則東西線既斷,甲.丙,丁,戊立即同受缺電之累矣.

新機間之觀察

該廠預備擴充,故其汽鍋間與引擎間之佈置係並行式而非魚貫式.略如下圖,可任意使兩部伸張而機器與鍋爐之數可同時並增,略如下圖.

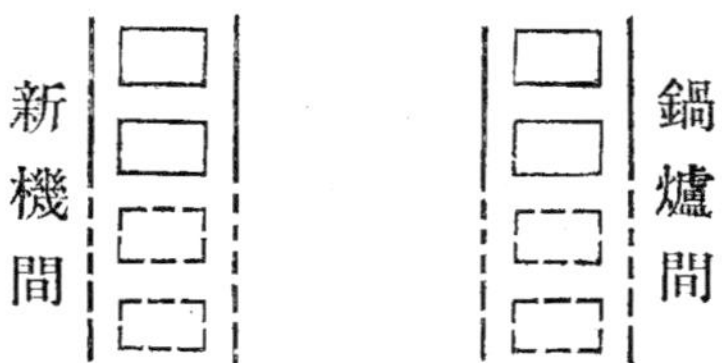

諸鍋爐本係舊物,惟增以自動加煤機而已.（以一小馬達發動之）其鍋爐間亦係將舊屋修理增高者,故其低矮之樑位猶可得見也.

所設之自動加煤機,實祇能節省人工.至於省煤一端,據稱並無幾許也.

鍋爐內之熱量,放散於煙囪者,尙不少,故將裝省煤器 (Economizer)於煙囱之兩旁以收其熱.而加熱器 (Feed water heater) 則可以不裝矣.

機間之下層裝設水管.抽水機並冷油器 (Oil cooler) 及凝水器 (Condenser)等.水管之直徑約二呎,以生鐵鑄成.抽水機之馬達其銅牌(Name-plote)上所載如下:——

Volts = 350　Amp. = 165　Cos φ = 0.88

f = 50 Cycle　Y-connected

R.P.M. = 960　H.P. = 100

機間之上層有已裝成之新發電機連透平一座以及石板等.

其發電機之銅牌所載如下.——

k.V.A. = 4500　Volts = 2300

f = 50 Cycle　Y-connected,　Cos φ = 0.8

Manufacturer: Brown-Boveri co.
Switzerland.

其透平之銅牌所載如下: ——

K.W = 3600 R.P.M. = 3000

Steam press. = 135 K.g./cm^2

Steam temp. = 310°c

Manufacfurer: Brown-Boveri co.

新機間之佈置可於後列二草圖中窺見一斑,惟其大小並不照尺寸耳至於各水管汽管及油管之往來不得不略加說明.

A-B Section

Turbine
Generator
Exciter
Condenser
Oil Cooler
Steam pipe
Base containing oil
Small turbine
Bearing
Fresh air room
For Air pump

A = Packing valve for steam source
B = Valve for starting small turbine
C = Valve for opening the exhaust port before condensing

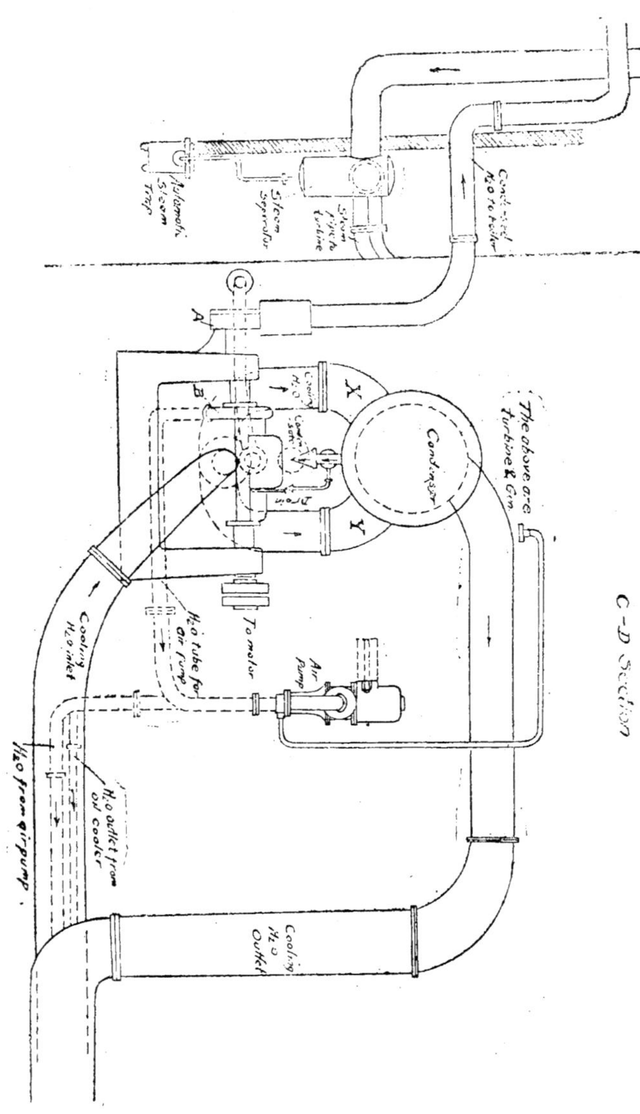
C-D Section
Condenser
To motor
Air Pump
Cooling H2O Outlet
The above are turbine & Gen

參觀 C—D section 圖,可見進水管自通胥江之蓄水池引至 Fump 而由 Pump將冷水分兩大管X Y打至Condenser內. Condenser之出水管乃一在上面之大管直通至另一池內而達胥江.

Condenser之底面中間有管將Condensate下引以通至Pump之A處（ A乃Hot-wellpump)而打至Boiler其Drain Tube,則在Condenser之外面底下.圖中Pump之B處將一部分進來之冷水打至Condenser之Air Pump處.其自Air Pump流出之水則與Oil Cooler之出水管一同匯入通胥江之大出水管.

Oil Cooler之進水管則係進水大管X Y之支流.

Drain Tube 內之水則預先匯入Oil Cooler之出水管中.然後Oil Cooler之出水管再通至出水大管以達出水池中也

參觀A-B Section圖 可見 Oil Cooler（冷油器 ）凡有四管.其二在冷油器之兩端卽爲進水管及出水管.中間二管係油管.其油自Turbine之左端流下至 Oil Cocler, 再自 Oil Cooler 上行至 Turbine 與 Generator 之中間.佈及Turbine全體及Generator之軸承等處.

Turbine 及Generator之底座大而中空,蓋貯潤油之所也.圖中之小Turbine乃用以爲運行潤油之具.當未開大Turbine之前.卽須先開小Turbine之塞門,使油得先行周流於各部耳.

派根廢汽管(Exhaust Pipe For Packing)之地位乃介於Turbine及 Generator之間.此管兩圖中未載.

石板處之觀察

新機間共設石板六座.其五座爲出線之用.而一座則將發電機(Generator) 發出之電引至石板處也.其石板之全部佈置可於後列二草圖中見之

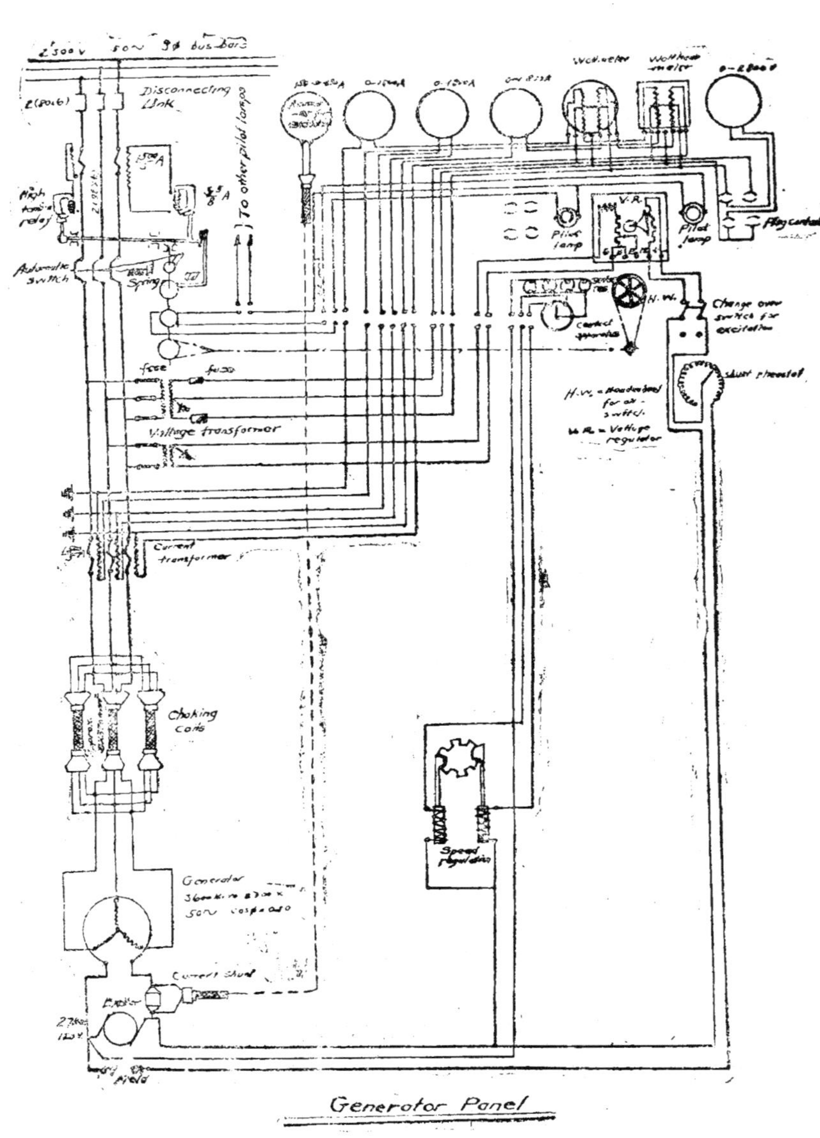

Generator Panel

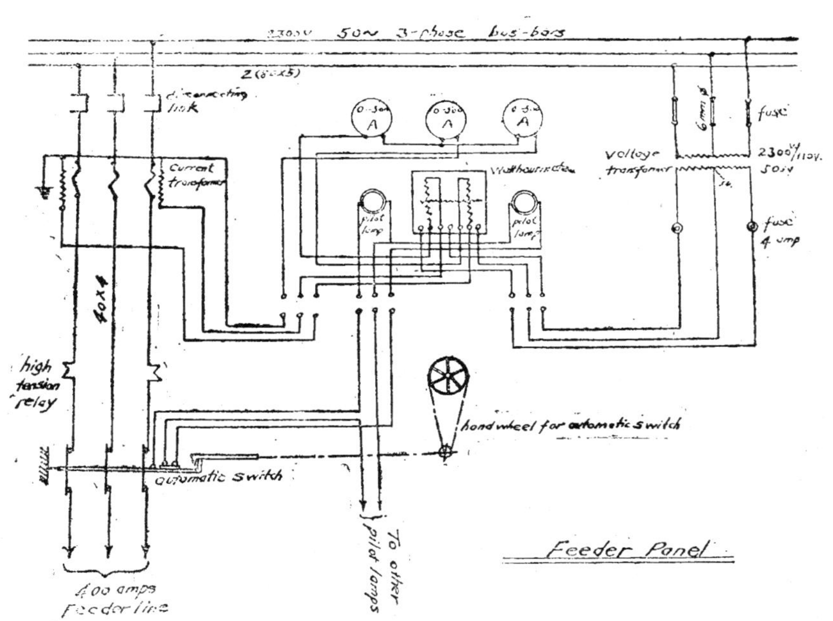

參觀 Generator Panel 圖可見 Generator 所發之電引至配電銅板 (Bus Bars.) 再觀 Feeder Panel 圖（五座中之一）則配電銅板上之電乃引至三相 (3Φ) 出線 (Feeder Line) 也. 該新石板之量電計 (metering) 佈置於石板各座類皆相若以取等勢 (Symmetrical.) 其特點爲高壓處統在樓下.若與人手接近之部則均在樓上.如此則尤爲安全也.

結 論

該廠電燈一項,營業範圍頗廣,統括吳縣全境及四鄉,並無權利旁奪之缺憾.（指並無競爭者或一部分營業權爲他處所攫奪等）然電力一項因用之者少無分營業,蓋電力之售價且不能若電燈之昂也.實則電力之發售可補各處無益諸耗費.(Stand-by toss.) 如此則日夜並皆發送電量.獲益加多鬧現將經營矣.至電車一項,未克舉辦.是蓋由於蘇城街道之狹陋,大有不能囘馬之概,何況此龐重之電車哉.且電車之業往往不能得利.平常電氣公司大都取盈於電燈一項.由此觀之.電車之興辦尚非一時所能談及,必須主路政者.與該公司努力合作,則地方之福增進可期矣.

THE ADVANTAGES OF USING HYPERBOLIC FUNCTIONS IN SOLVING POWER TRANSMISSION PROBLEMS

BY TEE-YUNG CHEN (陳體榮)

(Paper read before C.E.S. annual conference at Syracuse, N.Y. Sept. 5, 1925)

In a real smooth transmission line, the line inductance, condensance, resistance, and leakage are unifoımly distributed along its length. The resistance and inductance of the conductor effect the magnitude and phase position of voltage in proportion to the current flowing at that point. The conductance and susceptance effect those of the current in proportion to the voltage at the point selected. As a result both current and voltage vary in magnitude and phase position along the line.

THE NOMINAL "T" OR "π" LINE........The calculation of a trnsmission line (when it is very short and operated under low frequency or zero frequency) would be very much simple when neglecting both line londensance and leakage. In usual practice, however, it is to consider the line leakage and condensance, tolaly concentrated at the center of the line as T (Fig. I), or one half of the total each being placed at two ends of the line (Fig. 2), as the so-called π. Both of them are termed as nominal in order to distinguish the assumet lumpiness from the real distributed cases. The calculation of π or T is then to start from the generating or the receiving end of the line, by constructing vector diagrams showing the respective magnitudes and phase positions of the voltages and currents in order to get those at the receiving or generating end. Such method is simple and gives resonable degree of acuracy when the line is moderate in length and being operated under low frequency.

When the line is getting longer and longer, the result from the nominal π calculation may deviate much from the actual case, the so-called correction factor due to the lumpiness then becomes appreciable, and should be properly applied to the calculation (This will be discussed in Appendix)

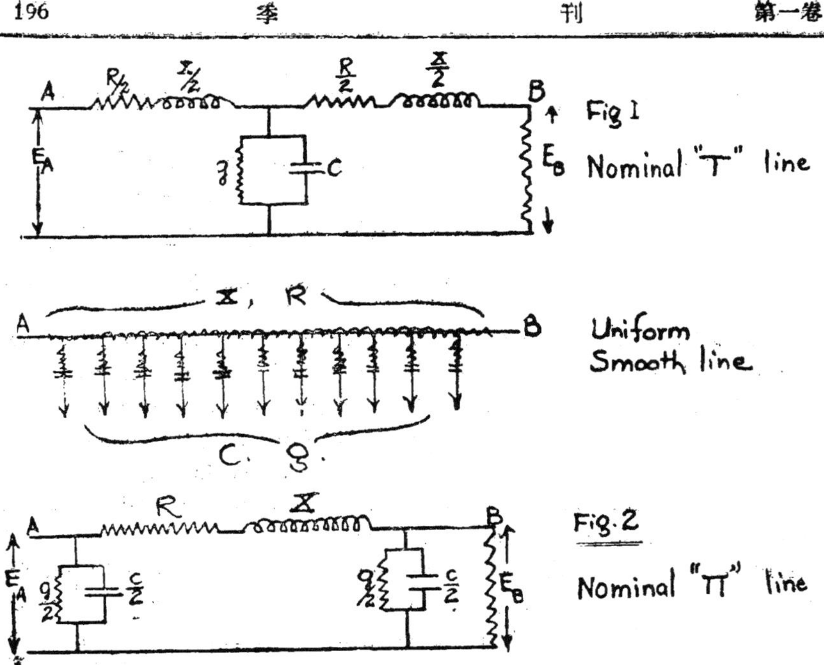

DEVELOPMENT OF TRANSMISSION LINE EQUATIONS..............To study the actual voltage and current distribution along the line, the following equations will be developed:

For unit length of line, let

r = resistance

x = reactance

g = conductance

b = susceptance

Then $z = \text{impedance} = r \pm jx$, and

$y = \text{admittance} = g \pm jb$

In Fig. 3 the plane P_1 P_2 is at a distance 1 from the origin of the line on the left hand. The plane Q_1 Q_2 is at a distance of 1+dl from the origin. Let E and I be the potential and current. Then the potential at Q will be E+dE, where dE is the drop of potential due to the conductor impedance. Since the linear impedance is z, that of the element of conductor is then equal to zdl, and the change in potential from P to Q will therefore be

$$dE = Izdl, \quad \text{or} \quad \frac{dE}{dl} = Iz \quad \cdots\cdots (1)$$

Similarly the current will change between P and Q as

$$dI = Eydl, \quad \text{or} \quad \frac{dI}{dl} = Ey \quad \cdots\cdots (2)$$

Differentiating (1) and (2) with respect to 1, we have

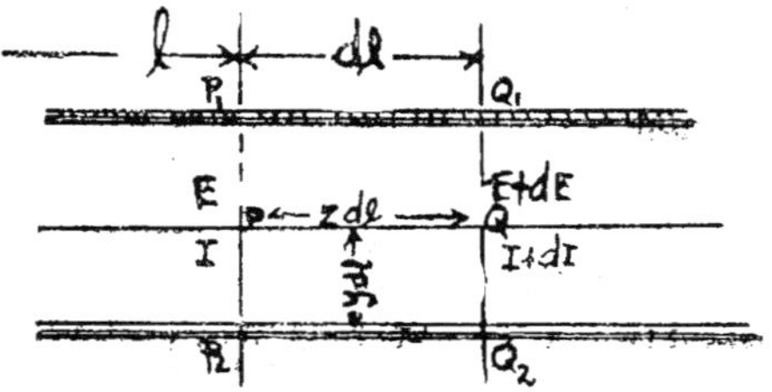

$$\frac{d^2E}{dl^2} = \frac{zdI}{dl} \quad \cdots\cdots (3)$$

$$\frac{d^2I}{dl^2} = y\frac{dE}{dl} \quad \cdots\cdots (4)$$

Substituting (2) in (3) and (1) in (1) in (4) we have

$$\frac{d^2E}{dl^2} = zyE \quad \cdots\cdots (5)$$

and

$$\frac{d^2I}{dl^2} = yzI \quad \cdots\cdots (6)$$

The solution of equation (5) or (6) will contain two arbitrary constants.

$$I = A_1 \in^{(yz)^{\frac{1}{2}}l} - A_2 \in^{-(yz)^{\frac{1}{2}}l} \quad \cdots\cdots (7)$$

and $$E=\frac{(yz)^{\frac{1}{2}}}{y}\left[A_1\epsilon^{(yz)^{\frac{1}{2}}l}+A_2\epsilon^{-(yz)^{\frac{1}{2}}l}\right]\cdots\cdots(8)$$

If we let $\alpha_1=\left[\frac{1}{2}(zy+rg-xb)\right]^{\frac{1}{2}}$ and $\beta_1=\left[\frac{1}{2}(zy-rg+xb)\right]^{\frac{1}{2}}$

then $$I=A_1\epsilon^{+(\alpha_1-j\beta_1)l}-A_2\epsilon^{-(\alpha_1-j\beta_1)l}\cdots\cdots(9)$$

$$E=\frac{\alpha_1-j\beta_1}{y}\left[A_1\epsilon^{+(\alpha_1-j\beta_1)l}+A_2\epsilon^{-(\alpha_1-j\beta_1)l}\right]\cdots(10)$$

when $$\epsilon^{\pm j\beta_1 l}=\cos\beta_1 l\pm j\sin\beta_1 l$$

equation (9) and (10) become

$$I=A_1\epsilon^{\alpha_1 l}(\cos\beta_1 l-j\sin\beta_1 l)-A_2\epsilon^{-\alpha_1 l}(\cos\beta_1 l+j\sin\beta_1 l)\cdots(11)$$

$$E=\frac{\alpha_1-j\beta_1}{y}\left[A_1\epsilon^{+\alpha_1 l}(\cos\beta_1 l-j\sin\beta_1 l)+A_2\epsilon^{-\alpha_1 l}(\cos\beta_1 l+j\sin\beta_1 l\right]\cdots\cdots(12)$$

In erder to determine the constants A_1 and A_2, the length 1 is set at generator end or at receiver end; that is 1=0 or 1=l ength of the line, measured from the left end of the line. At 1=0 $E=E_g$ and $I=I_g$. At 1=length of the line, $E=E_R$ and $I=I_R$. The complete solution of the equations (11) and (12) will not be considered here, into any particular case, but will be left to the later when coming to the using of hyperbolic functions.

In mathmatical calculations, it has been found that equations (11) and (12) require tedious and complicate work, and that they are not easy to be memorized for practical purposes By introducing of hyperbolic functions, they can be reduced to a much more concise form and are convenient to the calculations.

FUNDAMENTAL CONCEPTIONS OF HYPERBOLIC FUNCTIONS……

To study the hyperbolic angle we can compare with the circular angles. Figs. 4 and 5 show the circular angle and hyperbolic angle respectively. the angle AOP in either case can be measured in radiant units.

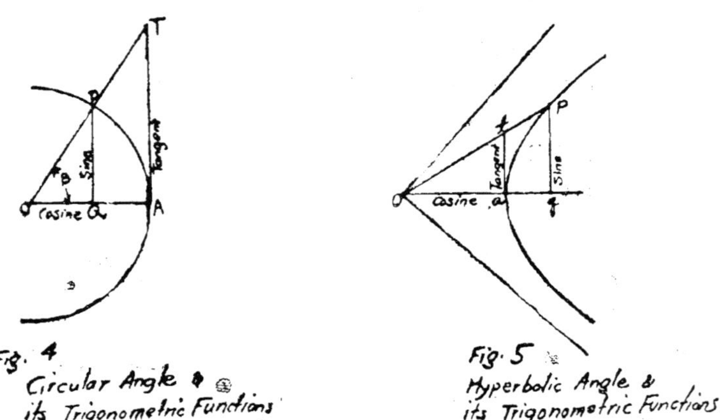

Fig. 4 Circular Angle & its Trigonometric Functions

Fig. 5 Hyperbolic Angle & its Trigonometric Functions

In Figs. 4 and 5, let the radius vector OA be equal to unit length. Draw PQ from the free end of the vector at P, making perpendicular to Oa at Q. Then in circular angle

PQ = Sine of the circular angle AOP, similarly,

pq = sinh of the hyperbolic angle aop.

Again,

OQ = cosine of the circular angle AOP, and

oq = cosh of the hyperbolic angle aop.

Now to find the value of the Tangent, we can carry a perpendicular from the end of the initial radius up to the radius vector or its production as AT or at in Figs. 4 and 5.

For circular angle,

AT = tangent of AOP, and for hyperbolic angle

at = tanh of aop.

To find other functions the same relations in circular trigonometry can be applied. And to show their identification, some of the notable formulas will be mentioned as below:

$\cos^2 B + \sin^2 B = 1$

$\cosh^2 A - \sinh^2 A = 1$

$\sin(A+B) = \sin A \cos B + \cos A \sin B$

$\sinh(A+B) = \sinh A \cosh B + \cos A \sinh B$

$\cos(A+B) = \cos A \cos B - \sin A \sin B$

$\cosh(A+B) = \cosh A \cosh B - \sinh A \sinh B$

Thus it is seen that the hyperbolic functions are not hard to get acquainted with if one is familiar with circular trigonometric functions.

EXPONENTIAL SERIES EXPRESSION FOR HYPERBOLIC FUNCTIONS; In this case we have

$$\sinh \theta = \frac{\epsilon^{\theta} - \epsilon^{-\theta}}{2} = \theta + \frac{\theta^3}{3!} + \frac{\theta^5}{5!} + \frac{\theta^7}{7!} + \cdots\cdots$$

$$\cosh = \frac{\epsilon^{\theta} + \epsilon^{-\theta}}{2} = 1 + \frac{\theta^2}{2!} + \frac{\theta^4}{4!} + \frac{\theta^6}{6!} + \cdots\cdots$$

so $\epsilon^{\theta} = \cosh \theta + \sinh \theta$, and $\epsilon^{-\theta} = \cosh \theta - \sinh \theta$ ......(13)

TRANSMISSION EQUATIONS EXPRESSED IN HYPERBOLIC FUNCTIONS........From the forgoing study we can convert equations (7) and (8) with hyperbolic functions.

Let

$a = \sqrt{yz}$, and $\theta = a\,l$

then equation (7) becomes

$$I = A_1 \epsilon^{\alpha l} - A_2 \epsilon^{-\alpha l} \quad \cdots\cdots(14)$$

Substituting (13) in (14), we have

$$I = A_1 (\cosh \theta + \sinh \theta) + A_2 (\cosh \theta - \sinh \theta)$$

or

$$I = A_3 \cosh \theta + A_4 \sinh \theta \quad \cdots\cdots(15)$$

Similary,

$$E = A_5 \cosh \theta + A_6 \cosh \theta \cdots\cdots(16)$$

Equations (15) and (16) are another expressions of (11) and (12), and they are found more convenient in computation than those expressed in exponential forms.

Next to evaluate the arbitrary constants in (15) and (16), it has been fully demonstrated in the "ARTIFICIAL ELECTRIC LINES" by Dr. A. E. Kennelly, from page 24-35. A brief reference will be shown in the appendix of the paper.

To evaluate equations from data at the generator end, we have

$$I_P = I_A \cosh \theta_1 - \frac{E}{Z} \sinh \theta_1 \cdots\cdots(17)$$

and

$$E_P = E_A \cosh \theta_1 - I_A z_0 \sinh \theta_1 \cdots\cdots(18)$$

These formulas express the potential and current at any point along the line, with distance 1 from the generating end, in terms of E and I, and other line constants.

Similarly the evaluation from the data at the motor end gives

$$I_P = I_B \cosh \theta_2 + \frac{E_B}{Z_0} \sinh \theta_2 \cdots\cdots(19)$$

and

$$E_P = E_B \cosh \theta_2 + I_B z_0 \sinh \theta_2 \cdots\cdots(20)$$

THE MEANING OF THE LINE ANGLE θ ·········The line angle θ, indeed, is a new term to the electrical engineers who are not in accustom of using hyperbolic functions in solving transmission problems. But as matter of fact is not hard to grap the physical meaning; and when getting familiar, with, it will help the engineers a great deal.

Since

$a = \sqrt{yz}$, a linear constant of the line, sometime called the linear hyperbolic angle of the line, the attenuation constant of the line, or the propargation constant; the angle θ is just a pooduct of this constant with the length of the line. Different lines have different constants, and so their line angles are not same for a given length.

The meaning OF THE SURGE IMPEDANCE Z………From equations (7) to (20) we have the term Z which has been called the surge impedance. It is the only impedance offered by the line to its surges. It has been known that the impedance of a uniform wire of indefinitely long is always equal to its surge impedance Z, which expressed in formula is

$$Z_0=\sqrt{\frac{z}{y}} \quad \cdots\cdots(21)$$

The MEANING OF POSITION ANGLE……… When a line terminates a load δ, the position angle at the line end, by definition, is

$$\theta' = \tanh^{-1}\frac{\delta}{z_0}=\delta_B \quad \cdots\cdots(22)$$

while at any point along the line, the positon angle at that point is

$$\delta_P= \theta_P + \theta' \quad \cdots\cdots(23)$$

VOLTAGE, CURRENT and IMPEDANCE ALONG THE LINE IN TERMS OF POSITION ANGLE………It has been shown that the voltage, current and impedance along the line can be conveniently expressed in term of the position angles: Thus

$$\frac{V_P}{V_B}=\frac{\operatorname{Sinh}\delta_P}{\operatorname{Sinh}\delta_B} \quad \cdots\cdots(24)$$

$$\frac{I_P}{I_B}=\frac{\operatorname{Cosh}\delta_P}{\operatorname{Cosh}\delta_B} \quad \cdots\cdots(25)$$

and

$$\frac{Z_P}{Z_B}=\frac{\operatorname{Tanh}\delta_P}{\operatorname{Tanh}\delta_B} \quad \cdots\cdots(26)$$

where δ_P and δ_B are the posiiion angles at any point P and at the far end B oft he line respectivly. By these formulas if we know V, I, and Z at the far end of a given line (the voltage and current conditions at the receving end of a transmission line are generally known in ordinary case), it is easy to find those at any point of the line.

Graphical METHOD OF USING EQUATIONS (17), (18),or (19), (20)……In equations (19) and (20) if we let $I_P = I_A$ and $E_P = E_A$, we have

$$E_A = E_B \cosh\theta_2 + I_L Z_0 \sinh\theta_2 \cdots\cdots(27)$$

$$I_A = I_B \cosh\theta_2 + \frac{E_B}{Z_0} \sinh\theta_2 \cdots\cdots(28)$$

The construction of the voltage equation (27) will be based on E_B as reference line. In Fig. 6, from O we draw E_B the reference vector. $E_B \cosh\theta_2$ will then be drawn in a shorter and in lead to E_B. $E_B \cosh\theta_2$ is the generator voltage when the far end is opened as seen from the equation (27) when $I_B = 0$. The difference between it and E_B is due to the so-called Ferranti effect. Next draw $CP = I_B Z_0 \sinh\theta_2 = Q\angle P^0$, where $\angle P^0$ is the angle between CP and OE_B. The position of the vector CP depends on the character of the load. With unity power factor load at the receiving end, while the power factor is varied, P will move along a line perpendicular to OA. With a constant Kva load, P will move along the arc of a circle drawn from C as a center. In order to keep the generator voltage constant as the load on the line is varied, the point P must follow the arc of a circle from O as a center and having a radius equal to E_A

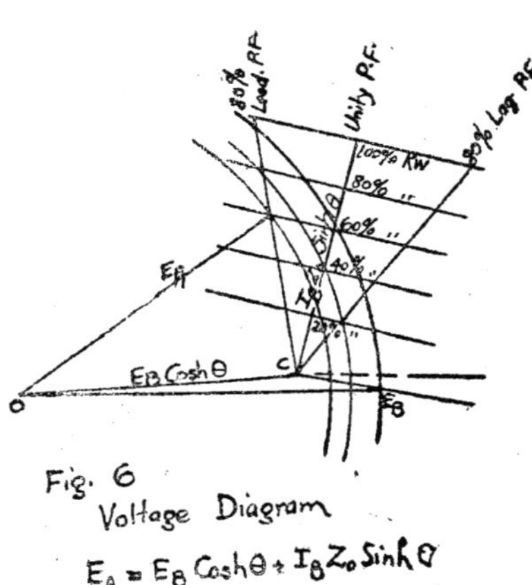

Fig. 6
Voltage Diagram
$E_A = E_B \cosh\theta + I_B Z_0 \sinh\theta$

THE CURRENT DIAGRAM ....

Now we come to the equation (23). As in the voltage diagram E_B will be used as the reference vector. From O draw OO" equal to (Fig. 7)

$$\frac{E_B}{Z_0}\sinh\theta = E_B\, y_0 \sinh\theta$$

This is the charging current taken from the generator when the voltage at the receiving end is E_B. When a load is thrown on B, the current $I_B \cosh\theta$ will be added to the charging current. This component is almost in phase with the recewing current and a listle smaller in magnitude. It is represented by the vector O"P.

with a unity power factor load P will be on the line O"A. With constant power and varying power factor, P will travel along a line perpendicular to O''A. Similarly the locus of P for constant KVA load will be a circle drawn from O'' as a center.

Unity P.F. 80% P.F. Lead 80% P.F. Lag 100% Load 80% 60% 40% 20% $I_B \cos\theta$ $E_B Y_o \sin\theta$ I_A

Fig. 7
Current Diagram
$I_A = I_B \cos\theta + E_B Y_o \sin\theta$

COMBINATION OF CURRENT AND VOLTAGE DIAGRAM......In Fig. 8 we have the combination of the current and voltage diagram. Take OA as unity and 100% load, divide it into 5 parts, as 80%, 60%, 40%... The same case is applied to O''P. Three scales are necessary. These give current, power, and voltage. The constant voltage circles are drawn with O as center.

CONDENSER CAPACITY..........THE condenser capacity to regulate the power factor can be easily determined from the voltage diagram. Thus DA would represent the necessary reactive load to bring back the power factor from 85% to unity at 100% load.

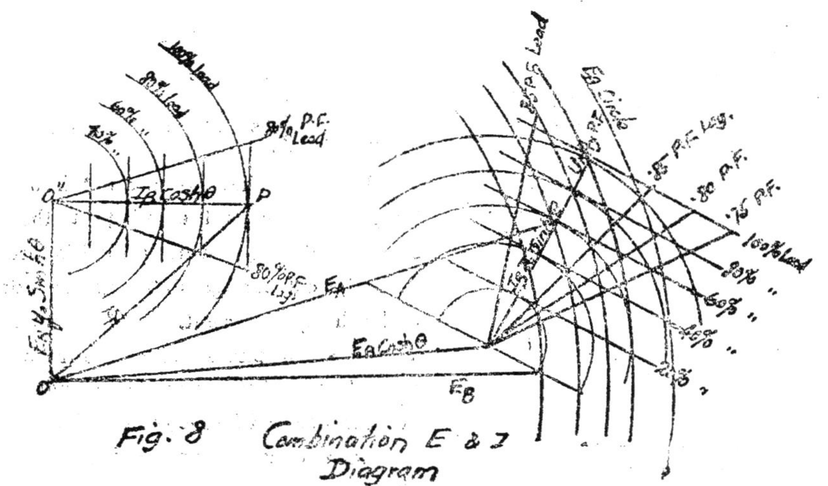

Fig. 8 Combination E & I Diagram

SUMMARY……So far we have discussed the use of hyperbolic functions in solving power transmission problems, it is seen that the changing of equations (11), (12) into (17), (18), (19) and (20) gives the advantages of

(1) Simplicity in calculation,

(2) Easiness in memorizing for practioal use,

(3) Greater facility in finding voltage and current condition at any point of the line by the use of the POSITION ANGLES FORMULAS,

(4) The convenience of the graphical method proving the means to show the characteristic of the particular line at a glance,

and (5) Accuracy in result.

—APPENDIX—

CORRECTION FACTOR………To reduce the nominal T or π into the equivalent one, we have the following formulas.

For the branches, $k=\frac{\tanh\frac{\theta}{2}}{\theta/2}$ For the architrave, $k=\frac{\sinh\theta}{\theta}$

The use of these two formulas is indicated in the following diagrams respectively both for T and π.

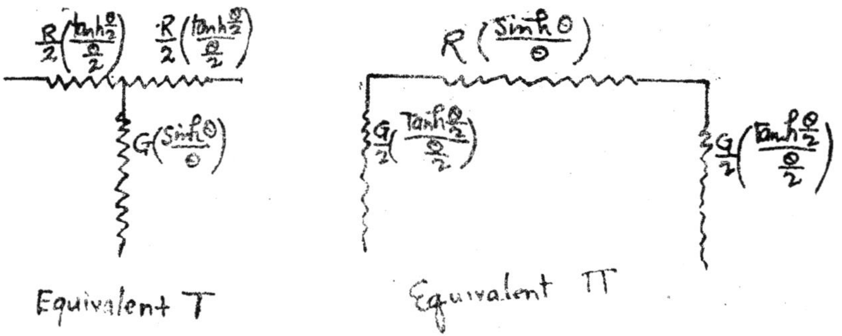

REFERENCE: A: E: Kennelly's (1) Artificial Lines. (2) Application of Hyperbolic Functions in Electrical Engineering (3) Electrical World, May 99, 1925 P 966 (4) Journal A. I. E. E. 1922 P. 795

注：原刊206页为空白页。

美國拿埃葛拉瀑布水電力廠

黎智長

拿埃葛拉瀑布之發現

今日之北美合衆國即昔日北美洲土人所居之地.最初發現拿埃葛拉瀑布(Niagrafalls)者,亦爲此地土人.惟土人視之爲神靈,從而膜拜頂禮,迨乎哥崙布發現新大陸,歐洲人士相率來美,拿埃葛拉瀑布始得在歐洲人眼光中,成爲一種美妙之風景,而以其怒奔呼號之狀,且膺水雷(Thunder of waters)之稱.西歷十七世紀,距今約二百年.法國探險家沙乃(La Salle)曾造船航行拿埃葛拉瀑布以上之湖,於是法國商人及其將士咸往瞻仰,均歎爲世界最大之瀑布.詩人學士從而詠歌贊歎之.名篇巨製蓋不可勝數焉.

拿埃葛拉瀑布最初引用水力

約在西歷一千七百五十七年.有一販皮貨商人名肯卡意爾伊(Ghabert Joncaire)曾在阿美利加瀑布(屬於拿埃葛拉瀑布之一部分名爲American Falls)掘一圓溝約深六英尺.引此水以轉動鋸木機器,約有二十馬力.此種所鋸之木.用以造船,以運皮貨,從下湖以至上湖.如此百年之間用拿埃葛埃瀑布水力之方法.毫無變更進步.至於拿埃葛拉瀑布全境之形勢,閱第一圖可知其概略.

拿埃葛拉瀑布應用水力之進步

西歷一千八百五十二年,拿埃葛拉瀑布始用最新方法利用其水力.其時開導所謂水力運河(Hydraulic Canal.)此河約距阿美利加瀑布半英里.橫過拿埃葛拉市,直至瀑布下流石崖之處.令運河中之水從石崖下落其水力較從前用任何方法得之者爲大.所惜者其時引用水力僅以轉水輪(Water

Whee.)直接銜接於應用之機器.故開運河之資本甚大而應用水力之利益甚小.每不能得利,而資本且難收囘,其時有名勃來揚(Walter Bryant)者,與其同志,損失美金三十萬,卒未成功.又有台好來司(Horace H. Day)諸人,亦共損失美金七十萬,迄無實益.幸有喜俄爾夸夫(Jacob F. Schoellkopf)及其同志,購買此水力運河作試驗之用,不久有一麵粉廠用此水力運河,有九百馬力之多,

拿埃葛拉瀑布應用水力發電

自英國佛那台(Farady)發明電機原理,至葛萊吳(Gramme)方具電機初創之模型,由是改良進步.至美國勃內須(Brush)之電機,方能燃弧光燈不用人力對準燈頭火光.於是西歷一千八百七十九年,觀瀑公園(Prospect Park)用拿埃葛拉瀑布水力轉動電機發電,燃弧光燈,越二年,水輪增至二千馬力,用粗繩接於發電機.蓋此時猶未能用齒輪及橡皮帶,故用繩也.從此以後,拿埃葛拉瀑布之水電力,方出賣爲商業工業之用.不數年美國愛迪生(Thomas Edison)發明電燈,於是拿埃葛拉水電事業益蒸蒸日上.西歷一千八百九十六年,美國水牛城(此城昔爲美國盛產水牛之區,距拿埃葛拉瀑布約數十里)方用拿埃葛拉瀑布之水電力以行電車.其所得電力,凡五千馬力.

拿埃葛拉瀑布水電方廠傳電之艱難

自電氣應用於實業,拿埃葛拉瀑布之水電力愈形發達.然而僅應用於拿埃葛拉瀑布市場究屬有限.且他城之渴望拿埃葛拉瀑布之水電力,實有過於拿埃葛拉瀑布之水電力廠.其故在用煤發電,其電力多少,以煤爲比例故煤價與發電價有連帶之關係.發電愈多,煤價愈漲.其發電之價必日高.則售出之電必不能低廉.供少於求,其價必漲,經濟之原理也.而水力發電則不

然.除投資裝置後,發電用水力,不需資本且人工開銷.尤較用煤生汽者爲省.是以拿埃葛拉瀑布水電力廠恨不能全用此瀑布之水力以滿其所望.然在電力傳送成功之前,曾經許多幻想,冀傳水電力於各城.最初之一法,則以氣筒(Pneumatic Tubes)傳被壓空氣(COmpressed air)至各工廠而發力,至廠則以水輪聯接壓空氣機器.(air Compressors)其他一法,更爲可噱.用排列許多圓軸(Counter Shafting),從發力廠分布於四面八方.此長圓軸用齒輪聯接於水輪各工廠可由此長軸得力.其另一法,雖不經濟似尙可能.其法則造成無數之運河,均從拿埃葛拉瀑布上流之處開掘,各工廠可用此運河之水流以轉運機械.其出水用水管通各廠,以至拿埃葛拉河之下流.各種計畫均曾經各工程師考量多次,卒以財政關係,不能加以試驗.自電力傳送發明以後,於是向之以爲難而不能成者,今而後可以行矣.雖電力傳送已屬可能然必須大資本以爲裝置及保守折舊諸費.其初傳送電力祇數英里,以爲此爲最經濟而可能之距離.拿埃葛拉傳電公司.(The N agra Tockport And Ontario Power Co.)擬用高壓電傳送電力(High Voltage Transmission)於西臘可司城(Syracuse)其欲傳電力於此城者,蓋因此城爲鐵路之中心.易於運輸貿易,工廠甚多,爲售水電力之商塲.然在昔日高壓電力,猶不敢嘗試.蓋高壓電力,用銅線傳導其銅線較傳低壓電者爲細.故銅線較輕.亦較省.然高壓電較低壓電爲危險,故必完全無虞,方可用之.在此時不但工程智識未足且欲聚集如此,大資本以傳送電力.亦不可能也.西歷一千八百九十六年,美國水牛城僅用電力五千馬力.現至十萬馬力.西臘可司城在西歷一千九百零七年所用電力不過爲現今所用者之二十五分之一.(現其每年所用之電力在二萬萬基羅瓦特鐘點以上)蓋美國人民.不畏艱難,前仆後繼,日在努力之中故得臻盛如今日也.此公司在今日傳送電力用六萬弗打(60,000 Volts)高壓電,有二十二萬五千馬力.惟其電線可傳送十一萬弗打高壓電,並能傳送電力五十萬馬力.現此公司傳送電力過一千三百英里高壓電而其投資已過三千萬美金其電線經過紐約省之十七大城有一百四十二城鎭市鄉,人民用之者,約二百萬.第二圖表明現今之高壓電傳送至水牛城.第三圖表明最新之鋼塔用以傳送長途交流電者.

拿埃葛拉瀑布水電力廠之現狀

拿埃葛拉瀑布居今美國紐約省之西北角.拿埃葛拉瀑布市有居民七萬.屬於美國方面.有阿美利加瀑布(American Falls,)實高一百六十七英尺並有馬蹄鐵式瀑布(Horsehoe Falls,)實高一百五十八英尺.平均拿埃瀑拉河在此二瀑布之下,有一百八十英尺.每分鐘有一千五百萬立方英尺之水經瀑布而下落.即每星期有一立方英里之水經此瀑布而下落也.須知拿埃葛拉瀑布水電力廠之設立,並非直接取水於此二大瀑布.蓋一則損壞天然之美景,二則工程設備生許多困難.故此廠之取水.從拿埃葛拉瀑布之上流引為運河,用三合土做成圓筒.接至水電力廠.此圓筒高有三十二尺,速度每分鐘有四百五十萬加倫之水.運河之水.既入廠中,經過水電透平而下落於拿埃葛拉河,此水電力廠共有電力四十五萬馬力.第四圖中可見一斑.其中有最大之水電透平發電機三具.每具有電力七萬馬力,為亞麗斯却澇司公司所造,第五圖之後三電機即是也.此電機為世界最大之發電機云.四十年前全拿埃葛拉瀑布祇有二千馬力,現有水電力一.百四十萬馬力.惟美國與英國互有條約之關係現二國共有水電力一百萬馬力.為已應用者.美國拿埃葛拉瀑布水電力廠本為兩大公司.其用水力以生電力者為拿埃葛拉水電力公司(The Niagra Falls Power Co.)其傳送電力於各處,者為拿埃葛拉傳電公司(The Niagra Lockport And Ontario Power Co.)最近二公司合組,改為水牛城拿埃葛拉東方電力股份公司.(Baffalo, Niagra. and Eastern Power Corporation)共有資本一萬五千萬.據云此猶為最少最經濟之投資云.投資者約一萬五千人,大半居紐約省.而用電力者包含男女老幼.各種職業.第六圖表明分布電力於十七大城之總機關.第七圖表明此公司電力分布之地圖於紐約省之大部分(紐約城在外)

综合卷（第二册） 南洋季刊 第一卷 第二期 电机工程号（1926）

第二圖 高壓電傳送於水牛城

第三圖 最新之鋼塔傳送電力於各處

第四圖 拏埃葛拉水電力廠

第五圖 廠中最大之三水電透平發電機

第六圖 電力傳送及分布總機關

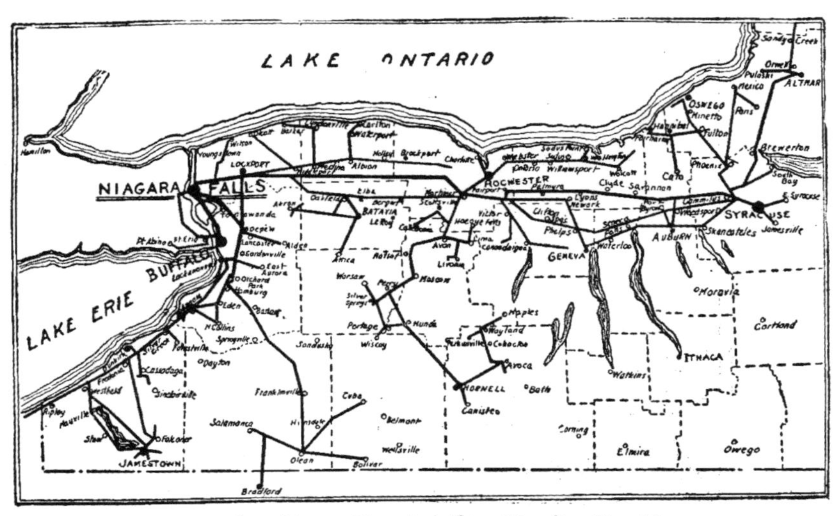

第七圖 電力分布之地圖

第八圖 惠而破兒奔流之狀況

第九圖 美國方面之二大瀑布

拿埃葛拉瀑布水電力廠之功績

此廠所供給之電力,爲居民取光生火,取熱,爲工廠轉動馬達以運機械.電價甚廉,人民便之,此人人所知也.其大功偉績,即在能供給多量電力,而取價極廉.然化學工業之不能在他處製造者,均於應用拿埃葛拉瀑布之地建廠以用此廠之電.如鐵質混合金屬(Ferroalloys)電氣火爐之受軟物(Electric Furnace Abrasives)煉鉛等爲不可能,則最近十年來之汽車工業不能若是之驚人.推其原因,蓋汽車許多要部,須用特別鋼鐵,此種鐵鋼,必與其他金屬相混合以求堅固耐用.此種部分不能在平常翻砂廠爲之,須在打鐵廠爲之,而平常鐵廠之熱度不足,非用電氣火爐不爲功.其他如化學上種種物品如炭等,與汽車工業至關重要.如無電氣火爐之熱度,必無從着手.至於鉛之一物.尤爲重要.蓋其體質較鋼鐵爲輕,而堅固僅次之.若無電氣火爐,他法又不能爲多量之提取.是以無賤價之電力,則汽車之價將二三倍,而出貨之速度將減爲百分之八十.無體輕而價廉之汽車,則世人享受之者,得較現今爲少,自電力化學昌明,爲化學史開一新紀元.蓋電力化學遠勝昔日慢而且貴之化學方法,如造鹹性蘇打(Caustic soca'Naoh,)綠氣(Chlorine,)以及燐質化合物(Phcsphorus Compounds.)或取純粹物質使其獨立,如鈉類(Sodium, Potassium, Calcium, Masnesium)及鋁(Aluminum)等,此種物品,平時振興化學工業,戰時以造戰具.如鉛爲製造飛船要物,綠氣爲戰場要品,皆甚重要者也.

拿埃葛拉瀑布水電力廠未來之希望

拿埃葛拉爲布爲英美分界處.英屬加拿大在其北,北美合衆國在其南.二國互締條約,引用水力.各有限制.是以美國政府於此公司之用水力,亦加以限制,以免與英國加拿大政府抵觸.此廠所發之電力已不足應居民農田工業之所求.又以條約關係不能多用.似將來之發展毫無希望.然美國人之奮鬭精神,決不稍懈.電力廠既不能多取水於上流.於是更想得其他二法,不久或能實行也.第一法因水流已用以生電,下落於拿埃葛拉河,此水沿流數英里,即至惠而破兒奔流.(Whirlpcol Rapids)引此奔流,經過三合土水筒並不過長,至拿埃葛拉河更下流,因是可得電力二十萬馬力.此種計畫,既不多取水於瀑布上流,有違條約於瀑布全部風景,亦無妨害.第二法則擬於馬蹄鐵式瀑布下興辦工程.蓋因馬蹄鐵式瀑布中深而兩旁甚淺.以是水力速度中快而旁緩,若令此瀑布中央及兩旁同深,速度相同,不但可得水力雙倍於現今之水電力,且因現今中流太快,毀壞瀑布水底之石塊,不久馬蹄鐵式瀑布將成虛名.不如設法加以人工改造,不致中疾而旁徐,且可增進此瀑布風景愈形美麗.第八圖表明惠而破兒奔流之狀況.拿埃葛拉瀑布下落成爲拿埃葛拉河,即在此處轉灣,故水勢甚猛.第九圖表明美國方面之阿美利加及馬蹄鐵式二瀑布.阿美利加瀑布下落之水僅全部百分之七.馬蹄鐵式瀑布則有百分之八十.其中部水流之疾於圖可以見之.

餘論

余昔在母校學及水電力廠一科時,有感於我國水電力事業之不發達,常神馳於世界最大之拿埃葛拉瀑布水電力廠不止,今夏從波士頓麻省理工西行至明城亞麗却潑司公司,入學生工程師部實習.便道至拿埃葛拉瀑布,參觀英美二國之水電力廠英國方面聞同學陳君體榮已有著述爰就美國方面貢其所見,以告國人.夫我國天然水力亦至偉大.曩在國內旅行參觀至山西,沿正太鐵路,農民利用水力轉輪以利灌溉者不可勝舉惜其未能利用新法,以轉電機.且較大較深之瀑布,未嘗不可作開煤鑛之原動力.更以四川而論.自古稱三峽之險,行人視爲畏途.長江長九千餘里.上流之瀑布奔流,蓄水甚多.而其下落必深其流必疾.川漢鐵道至今未成.固以國內擾攘,亦以工程艱巨之故.苟能引用水電之力,以開道運石.路途一平,建設自易.其崎嶇之處,可行電氣鐵道.如美國明城至聖保鐵路中,有六百英里用水電力以行電氣鐵路.將來輪軌一通,藉此行電氣鐵路之高壓電,西至宜昌漢口.東至重慶成都,且可爲農工商業之用.又如福建一省,猶之四川.環境多山交通不便.水力之多.恐亦不下於蜀省.苟能應用水力.發電興工,其能利便交通,振興工商,可操左劵也.

奇異公司實習雜記

陳　章

作者小傳

陳君字俊時江蘇吳縣人,民國十年畢業于母校電機科,即在母校任助教一年.民國十二年春在愼昌洋行任職一年.民國十三年夏渡美入普渡大學研究院.十四年六月獲碩士學位.現在美國奇異總公司製造廠實習.陳君素善文,作品散見東方雜誌等.爲人和藹可親.在美時曾爲母校圖書館搜集有價値書籍極多,擬于民國十六年歸國云.

民國十四年六月,余離普渡大學後,在印地安那州之福特威納 (Fort Wayne)城發電廠.名 Indiana Service Corporation 者,實習二月.爲時雖促,頗略窺見發電廠方面之處置.八月,離福城到紐約州之斯乃台城 (Schenectady)之奇異公司實習.工後餘暇.雜記所經歷不特爲有志於電機製造廠實習者之參考,亦將爲余日後之紀念耳. （按此篇祇述余個人在廠之經歷,及試驗科之情形.至於關於奇異公司之規模,製造情況公司組織等等,當另文述之）

入奇異公司之途徑在開明義之前,自當先述入該公司之途徑.該公司每年於三四月間,派人赴國內各大學電機工程及機械工程科接洽關於畢業生入廠問題.先期由各學生之願入者報名,屆期面談.由公司代表,當時記錄會談結果.携歸公司.彙集各大學名單.通盤籌算.約在五月中,通告取入與否,每年所收,即總廠而言雲在四百人以上.至於外國學生之欲入該廠者,手續不同.一切手續均經過國際奇異公司(International General Electric Company)該公司與奇異公司實二而一者也.但爲劃請營業界限起見,凡國外貿易,均由國際公司經手.其專司外國學生者,爲郭克歇爾氏,(R.F. Coggeshall)吾中國同學之入奇異公司者,向以吾母校同學爲多,在先均由謝爾屯科長與奇異公司直接商定,近年此事奇異公司已委責於其在華經理愼昌洋行,凡入該公司之先,類皆由愼昌保荐.而愼昌以本行辦事人情形,較爲熟悉,故每喜荐在行辦事或間接有關係者.而近年愼昌營業清淡,人員不增.母校同學之新進該行者絕少,故母校同學欲直接入奇異者至不易.除在華經理介紹外公司,每年尙收自在美留學界中二三人.其選擇方針,大概亦須得在華經理之間接介紹函件,否則必須能證明一己之父兄或戚族地位,及將來有擴充電力事業之能力者.或在美大學成績優美,由師長特例介紹者.惟中國學生在廠之額,僅五六人.每年空缺,尙止三四人.(因大多在廠不止一年)而各方面自荐欲進該廠者,往往三四十人,是以欲進該廠頗非易易也.

余之入奇異公司,屢逢挫折,雖事微不足述,要亦可爲有志竟成者勸.余於民國十一年在母校任職時,即有志來奇異公司實習.後經謝師介紹,遂得成功定於十二年夏來美就事.忽患病甚久,致不果行.而該位即爲愼昌辦事人某君接替.十二年春,余入愼昌辦事,復以此爲請,得行中同意,惟至夏間,以空額已爲在美留學界佔去.余以久待非計,遂改計先到美讀書,再設法入該公司.到美後即與國際奇異公司郭氏接洽.郭氏以余之舊資格關係,允特別設法.今春即得其准入之函.是余入奇異公司之志先後經三年之久.始得實現,可見成就一事雖微小,如此煞費經營.凡事豈可輕視,書此實以自勉也.

奇異學生工程師試驗科之解釋 奇異學生工程師試驗科（Student Engineers' Testing Course）爲該公司特爲電科畢業生設置,使得電機工程實用經驗,而爲他日爲工程師之備者也.學生在學校中,雖有實驗課程,究嫌規模太小,時間不足.若畢業後,即入工程界任負責之事,仍恐不勝.欲得此種實用經驗,自以試驗爲最佳.因電機工程之工作,約分爲三種一爲計劃（Designing）二爲製造,（Manufacturing）三爲使用.（Operating）而進電機工程界者,以矢志於第三種爲最多.故欲學使用電機方法實習試驗,爲最稱重要.凡一機械,計劃後製造製造之後,出運以前,須經一番詳細試驗,以測該機之能否使用,安穩適當,如預定規例.（Specifications）旣可以擔保出品精良復可以知計劃及製造之是否確當,以及有何改良之處.試驗之時,復可明瞭該機各部份之動作及使用方法機多則必有若干有毛病者,（即不能行動或發生困難之謂,）試驗者,即須設法尋出病之所在.若可以隨時改正者,則隨時補救之,依舊出運.如不能隨時補救,即書明病之所在,送回製造部設法修理後.再行試驗經驗即可於此時得到.因毛病各各不同在尋求病由之時,即將該機內容,詳細考求,不久對於該一種機器,自然應付裕如矣.奇異公司爲世界最大電機製造廠,規模之大,資本之厚.出貨種類之繁,爲近世實業界之巨觀所設學生試驗科.確能使學子得到經驗爲日後負責辦事之預備.其機會之佳,雖非絕無,却爲僅有.

奇異公司設立學生試驗科之用意 奇異公司之設立試驗科,以便學生之方自大學出校者,得有實驗之學識.雖爲電工界造就人材,對於該公司,尤有莫大之效用.其一該公司規模之宏大,人材之衆多,而將來之計劃,猶日在考慮準備之中,今日一輩有經驗之工程師,總分經理,正副主任,小至於分部首領,類皆有數年以至數十年之經驗.時光如駛.老者將物化,少者壯者或他去;若不早日培植人材,以爲之備,他日將有人才缺乏之慮.雖可以向他公司雇用,然猝然授以要職,往往不妥.故試驗科,即所以預儲人材每年由試驗科轉爲普通職員者,約百五十人.(單指總廠而言)此輩大概均擇定一部,久而久之,經驗益富,即可循資格升遷.實爲人材主義之最良法則.(不若我國立實業機關當事者一更,則下至差役,同時被迫去位,遂至數年大功,往往敗之頃刻.)二則奇異公司培植此種人材,以爲他日擴充及保持營業之機會.蓋因凡習於奇異機械者,如無他種原因,自願置備該公司物品,既熟於使用方法,復有感情作用.此輩人材,試驗科畢後,大都分往國內各大電廠任事,十年廿年後,掌買賣大權者,自不在少.則公司所受良好結果,又豈淺鮮.其招收外國學生入試驗科,此尤爲主因.蓋國外學生,大都一二年即出廠,鮮有久留公司中者,故無所謂預儲人材之意,上述二點,乃公司中所以設此試驗科之本意.在學生方面,則視此爲得實習經驗之絕好機會.各種電機原理構造,大致相同,精於此家公司所製造者,必能使用之可無疑義.雖在試驗科之收入較他處略低,而機會甚佳,仍多樂就,至於如我中國同學則除廠家公司之與中國有營業關係者,進去甚非易事也.

試驗之種類　機器之試驗,既爲製造後出運前之一步,則無論各機,大都均須試驗,故所稱試驗部,均散在各廠.屋中特闢一隅,爲試驗之地.而其管理及一切待遇,與製造部各自獨立而不相涉.該試驗科所列試驗種類如下

試驗名稱	星期數(日工)	星期數(夜工)
發電電動合機	一六	一六
發電機及電動機(大號)	一四	一四
發電機及電動機(小號)	一〇	
感應電動機	一〇	一〇
透平商業試驗	一六	一六
透平研究試驗	一〇	一〇
實業控制器甲	八	

實業控制器乙	一〇
特式電鑰板	一二
自働電鑰板	一〇
電壓制定器	三
汽流表	四
電線	六
無線電（收受器）	九
計算	二四
電光試驗室	一二
變壓機	一三（在Pittsfielol分廠）
電機鐵路機件	二四（在 Erie 分廠）

上表爲其大概.其餘尙有例外爲表上所未載者,如無線電強力三極眞空管,及分廠 Lynn 亦可調往.上述日夜工,在同一部中,如做日工,可免夜工,做夜工者亦同.

依上表而言,若將各部試驗做完,勢非三年至四年不可.實則並無人將各部做完者.美國學生,大概留試驗部一年左右,因在進廠前,早有專門何部之成見,則其他較無關係之部,卽可免入.一年或數月後,卽可設法進奇異爲公司普通雇員;或在他處分廠或辦事室任職,或往他處發展.公司方面,亦不甚欲人之久留.因其目的,旣爲營業及儲備人材,招收學生愈多愈佳.舊者不去,新者難進.然居試驗科二年,公司中不致有拒絕之意,至於我中國學生,則情形又略有不同.我中國同學之進奇異者,固皆大概有專門何部之意.國內電機工程之幼稚,人材之缺乏,回國後旣名爲學電,社會上必責以凡關關於電之事業.故其所學習範圍,不宜太狹.雖不免有泛而不精之弊,然爲我國目前計,勢所必然.例如學電力門與無線電門,本屬專門;大概有志於此者,無志於彼.然在中國幼稚之電工界,尙說不到此,仍以兼習二科爲得.此問題極有討論之餘地,上述不過為余個人之意見耳.

工作之時間工資及種種情形 工作時間,日工早七時二十分起,下午四時三十分止.午餐,停半小時.星期六下午停工.夜工,自晚七時起,次晨六時止.午夜停一小時.僅做星期一,二,三,四,五共五夜.在法定工作時間外之工作稱為過時工作.(Overtime work) 工資則試驗部學生,開始六個月,每小時美金五角每,日以八小時又三分二計算,每星期四十八小時,得工資二十四美金,過時工作加百分之五十,為每小時七角五分.時有時無極不一定,且做否本人有自主之權,並不強迫.非待下班人來,不能離去者除外,六月後每小時加至五角五分,在試驗部中,不能再加,夜工較日工加百分之五,此其大較也

試驗部遷調之程序,有如下述.初進第一試驗,一則以不悉情形,二則為安全起見,大概由試驗部長,派入研究透平試驗,或無線電收受器.前者不須技能.只須抄錄表數.(Readings) 後者機件甚小,又無高電壓,非常安全.以後遷調則於本試驗將完之星期一,填入下次願意前往之試驗二種,交部長,部長將全廠各部情形分派,於可能範圍內,排入願入之部.假如同時有二人願意同一位置則以進廠日期先後為標準.惟有時所得,為並未填進者.大概初進時,不易隨願而得.較久則易得矣.因未做過之部數愈少,機會自愈多也.即在同一部之中平常職務,往往不同.依入內學習之經驗起見,自然宜將各職做過.因各職事務不同,所學亦異.但公司為出貨迅速計,不甚願將各人在一部內遷調,致碍出貨.因新手須舊手教導,初時手術遲鈍,在所不免.然此亦看各部工頭性情而異不可以一概論之也.

上工前之經過 余於八月四日抵斯城.五日往見國際奇異公司學生科主任郭氏,略寒暄後,即領余至奇異公司之 Industrial Service 部該處凡公司雇員之進廠離廠,均須經過註册.除填一張關於年歲籍貫及種種箇人瑣事外,再需簽字於一印刷品上,證明同意,凡在公司雇用期內,所有發明之專利權,均歸公司享受.雖余等匆匆一二年,未必能有所發明,而在公司方面,不

得不防,其辦事之周密如此.後至醫院驗身,略事檢驗,醫生簽字後,遂爲公司雇員矣.後即至試驗部見總主任,填單如前.此外復給以標章一,上書以號目余號爲40842.有此則出進廠門,可以自由.小機件三色,爲試驗時之用.試驗講義一卷.該書爲奇異公司自編,關於該公司出品試驗方法,大概述遍.俾便試驗時之參考.書首有深紅黑字數頁均載種種謹愼小心規則,以防觸電意外之虞.並有一紙述明本人已將規則讀過一遍,並允遵守,簽字交進.蓋如此則萬一有意外發生,公司不負法律上之責任矣.

余個人工作生活之情形　余每日約六時起身,盥洗整裝.六時半赴附近飯館早餐.步行至廠,已七時一刻左右.七時二十分上工,至十二時.在廠內餐館午餐,停半小時.四時三十分下工.抵寓約爲五時.洗浴易衣.然後再出,常在左近青年會閱書報,約半小時.乃往餐館晚膳.七時歸家.自七時至九時,看報寫信或譯述文字.九時半就寢.生活異常呆板,其佳處則飲食起居均有定時,身體得益.其弊端則人生有如機器,循環旋轉,客中處此.益覺枯寂,星期六及星期日生活較活潑,然以勞動一星期之後,到星六星日,肢體已疲,宜於休息.若欲於此時努力振作,又有所不能.星期日大概起略遲,購閱一分近五六十頁之紐約時報.下午則或往公園游覽,或在近處散步,或聚數中國同學談天,殊不一定.而余則總於星期日中勉力抽出一二小時,看書或作文,仍覺時間太少也.

奇異學生科之外國學生　全公司之外國學生,常共爲三十五至四十之數.人數常在增減,國數爲二十五國左右其各國人數大概以現在公司營業數量,及將來希望爲衡.歐洲各國,本國電業發達,奇異營業甚小,故額不多.南美各國營業頗佳,日本亦然,故額亦多.（日本約爲四五人左右）中國則以將來希望甚大,故額亦多.現在總廠者.除余外,有趙壽芳,（北京工業奉天電燈廠）吳毓驤（清華麻省理工,）龐德丙（漢口愼昌洋行,）魏毓賢（清華,普渡大學,）四君,十一月起加入單基乾君（南洋,普渡）在Lynn分廠者現有楊鉅君.（南洋.普渡）此外在廠省理工.奇異合作科,中國同學三四人尙不在內.

無線電收受器試驗部之情形 余到廠後首入之部,爲無線電收受器此項收受器.專爲廣播收受器,限於接收廣播電音之用.現在所製造者,爲過量差節收受器.（Super heterodyneset）爲收受器中最近發明而最爲完美者.其靈驗性（Sensitiveness）及選擇性,（Selectivity）可稱獨著.共分八眞空管及六眞空管二種.所用以收集電波者,爲橫呎半縱三呎及十三圈之闌帶形傳受線.(Loop Antenna)天氣高爽之夜,往往可收二三千哩之電音.其一切線路,非常繁複;包含成音週率(Audio Freguency)二級,中間週率二級,（Intermediate freg.)及射電週率(Radio Freq.)一級,再有局部發玻一級.(Local Oscillator）其複雜可知.若在試驗室中桌上.連接起來,必致繁雜至目迷神眩.而廠中製造能將各件及百十根線頭,聚在一極小之鐵匣中.其量度約爲10"×5"×4,"而引出線頭二十根,爲接至各項電池及電量器等之用.匣中復盛以蜜臘.防接頭之因動彈而折斷之虞.製造可稱絕妙.（此項收受器原理較複不及詳論）此項收受器發明家.卽爲發明 Regenerative Circuit之 Armstrong 氏其專利權已買給美國無線電公司(Radio Corporation of America)奇異公司卽爲上述公司之一份子.（其組織情形可參看拙文『美國無線電事業概況』見工程第二期）製造資本甚廉,以專利之故,售價甚貴.依式樣及附件之多少,價格自一百五十美金至五百美金之鉅.盈餘當在過半以上.單指六管式一種,先做四萬具,其數可觀.每具構造靈巧,攜帶便利,裝璜美麗,確爲家庭中極佳之娛樂及裝飾器具.價格雖巨,購者踴躍;蓋美國素豐之家甚多,未有無線電收受器者,果皆欲買,而已有者,亦以一二年前出品陳腐.重新更置故無線電收受器營業.極發達.奇異公司近二年營業略淡.幸有無線電一項以爲挹注.且冬日天電擾亂較少,各廣播站更有佳節目,故九十月間急求出貨,製造特忙.可見美國家庭之富饒.近來日本輸進美國無線電器具額甚鉅若論我中國以千元墨銀（五百美金）購一娛樂品,非豪富不能辦.故此項製造品在中國,奇異公司一時尙無巨量營業之望也.

該項收受器試驗,共分三步.第一步爲Cata Combs 試驗. Cata Combs者,即上述之鐵匣,內裝無數線路,而眞空管卽可於外排列插入者.以其大小如猫,又以其引出線頭甚多,有如猫鬚,故名.先將該匣未裝蜜臘時試驗其Resonance Curve 及 Over-all Amplification Ratio,是否合度,及是否能自行發波.(Oscillate)如有毛病,須尋出病由註明送回修換.如佳,則送出裝臘後再試.第二步爲 Panel 試驗.將該匣連接圍帶傳受線.及電量器,試驗收受二〇〇及五五〇兩波長.因此二波長,爲廣播電音所用波長之上下兩界.能收到此二波,則此器可以擔保凡有廣播電音,均可收到也.第三步爲Cabinet試驗,將Panel裝入木箱中,重新試驗一次,與第二步略同.三步中以第一步最爲有意,在搜尋毛病時可將其線路及構造,詳細研究.此外尙有關於試驗之手續.另有講義發閱.每星期有一小時之演講.有時參觀該器之製造部,極爲有趣.雖區區娛樂小品其製造之繁複,有如此者.

（以上十四年十月止）（未完待續）

上海之電氣供給

（譯自十五年三月十七日出版之 North-China Trade Review）

張 功 煥

工部局管理下之顯著成績　二十五年來穩健之進步　現在狀況與將來

上海工業發達之因雖非一,工部局電氣處,一切制度之改進,實有以致之,今試先略述其過去之歷史,蓋有可以注意之價值在焉.一八九五年前,曾有一私資公司,經營電業)供給有限之電燈用戶,同時並有少數弧光路燈之設置,一八九五年,公司企業,爲工部局所獲,因就裴倫路與餘杭路之轉角建立一發電總站.惜是站之設施.在彼時已嫌太舊式,不合時尚,一再遷延,至一九〇五年,勢不得不另建新廠,以替之.無奈當時計畫甚形簡陋.初未爲他日擴充之準備,不得已將舊有横置式汽機及皮帶轉動式發電機,全數廢除,而易以直接轉動式高速率發電機及水管式鍋爐,緣解决一九〇一年後發生之電氣需求增加問題,舍此固無他法也.重建時,第一期共裝六百啓羅華特直接轉動之並列複式汽機發電機二座.一九〇四年工竣開機,一九〇五年始有第一座渦輪機之訂購.此機能量爲八百啓羅華特.Parsons of Newcastle所造,其發電機部分,則爲 Bruce Peebles & Co. 所造.由是營業發達至速,一九〇六年,既置第二座同能量之渦輪發電機,復購六百啓羅華特Belliss-Peebles汽機直流電機二座,及三百啓羅華特電動變流機一座,專供電車公司電力之用,蓋時正敷設電車之發軔期也.自後繼續添辦及改良.至一九一二年,裴倫路總站之準備電量竟達六千四百啓羅華特,迥非一九〇一年僅具五百七十六啓羅華特電量時所逆料及者矣.

楊樹浦電廠之發展

一九一〇年始籌建楊樹浦新廠其廠基,則數年前已爲工部局所購得一九一三年四月,該廠落成,第一期共裝二千啓羅華特渦輪發電機二座,及水管式鍋爐四座,第二期添置五千啓羅華特渦輪發電機二座,及水管式鍋爐四座,一九一五年,又訂購一萬啓羅華特渦輪發電機二座,五千啓羅華特渦輪發電機一座,及水管式鍋爐八座時適歐洲戰起一萬啓羅華特機二座中之一爲戰事所阻,未能及時應用,其餘二機及新鍋爐間則皆在一九一七年內相繼使用,歐戰將終,電力之需要,增加進步尤速楊樹浦廠,爲社會情形所衝動,乃更事擴充,一九一七年冬,遂有一萬八千啓羅華特渦輪發電機之裝設,翌年,又繼之以同樣渦輪發電機一座,一九二〇年,購二萬啓羅華特渦輪發電機二座,同時並訂購供廠中自用電力三千啓羅華特之渦輪發電機二座,及其鍋爐配件等,至是全廠準備電量,合計之當為十二萬一千啓羅華特即現今所具電量之總數也.目下營業突進未已,不久將添置至少五萬啓羅華特云.

二十年前,斐倫路舊站發電及饋電,係用二千二百伏爾脫電壓,一百周波之單相交流電,分送用戶時,則將電壓壓低至二百伏爾脫,迨該站重建.始改為五十周波之三相交流電,並備三相變壓器變高電壓,用六千六百伏爾脫饋電,以應此範圍廣大之電力需求,此變壓器具,終成斐倫路總站與楊樹浦廠聯絡饋電之關鍵.蓋楊樹浦廠機器,皆發三相五十周波六千六百伏爾脫之交流電.其高架及地底饋電電線,開始卽用六千六百伏爾脫而饋電幹線之埋在地下,亦自彼時始也.後來該廠第二期擴充,為增高長距離饋電效率計,復用變壓器將發電電壓,自六千六百伏爾脫,變高至二萬二千伏爾脫,因是乃一九一九年後地底饋電幹線之表準電壓耳.

人工之省除

據最近所知,在中國境內採用加煤機以供給鍋爐燃燒者,斐倫路總站實為其嚆矢,當時固曾有一部分之議,謂中國工資低廉,機器加煤,斷不能與人力競,不料事有不然,其應用成績殊佳,良以鍋爐之大小,隨工廠規模而增工資雖廉人力加煤,在大規模之工廠,未必一定合算也.

今再試以一九〇五年之斐倫路總站,與一九二五年之楊樹浦發電廠較,準備電量,則已由一千六百啓羅華特,增至十二萬一千啓羅華特,最高負荷,則已由一千〇九十啓羅華特,增至八萬啓羅華特,每日平均發電度數,則已由八千七百啓羅華特小時,增至一百五十萬啓羅華特小時,前之每啓羅華特小時平均耗煤九·四六磅者,今已遞減至一·六七磅.蓋一九〇五年斐倫路總站全年僅耗煤一萬〇六百噸,今則楊樹浦廠,每日須耗煤一千噸排洩煤燼,在二百噸上,是以現代電廠效率之高于規模宏大如楊樹浦廠者.

尤可見一斑矣.

運煤燃燒發電及饋電

楊樹浦廠每日耗煤之多,既如上述.故每次煤船進口,駁運晝夜不輟,廠中自備載重二百噸之貨船十二艘,載重三百噸之鋼甲駁船四艘.及專同拖曳之大汽船二艘,自煤船或承攬煤商之埠起運.皆利賴之,煤既抵廠,起岸時卽同行過磅,因廠備起重輸運機三座,各設有自動之衡秤也.鍋爐間之下層敷有鐵軌,載重五噸之電動矮車.曳數拖車,行駛其上,載煤燼以出廠,至此鉅量之煤燼,間或有人投標承購,但供求相差既遠,屯積爲慮,電氣處因特備載重一百五十噸之鋼甲運船四艘,曳之出吳淞口而傾卸焉.

發電及饋電手續,約略如下,燃煤先從煤船起岸,爲運煤機所輸載,而止於鍋爐間上層之貯煤倉,繼受重心作用,陸續墮入煤斗,經鏈索式或Underfeed式之加煤機,漸入于爐墊,依次燃燒汽鍋盛水,至是受熱成汽,經汽管之導引生器,使汽潛入渦輪,渦輪及電機,因以轉動,廢汽由渦輪出,復經冷水凝結化水後仍注入汽鍋,循環應用.至電機所生電流,先用變壓器將電壓增高至二萬二千伏爾脫,經電閘及地線而達東西北三幹站,繼由各幹站將電壓壓低至六千六百伏爾脫,再饋送滿佈公共租界之各分站,作者草此篇時,其饋域已由楊樹浦進展至虹橋矣,各分站從六千六百伏爾脫,再壓低之電壓,共二種供給小量電力之應用者,爲三百五十伏爾脫供給電燈電扇及電爐之應用者,則爲二百伏爾脫云.

下列統計示一九〇五年與一九二五年兩年營業之比較.

	一九〇五年	一九二五年
已繳資本（銀兩）	八〇〇,〇〇〇	三〇,〇〇〇.〇〇〇
收入（銀兩）	二二四二二七	九二二七〇二七(一九二四)
盈餘（銀兩）	虧三七一七	一四六四一六二(一九二四)

用戶總數	一一六七	三八九三二(一九二五)
啓羅華特負荷	二六五〇	一三九六一三
售出啓羅華特小時	一七七六三二六	二九四三四三九〇五*

*去年六七八三月,如無罷工之舉,此數當在三三四,〇〇〇,〇〇〇之譜.

除住戶或商肆外,尚有下列各種工業,全仰或半賴電氣處供給電力焉.

棉紗紡績業	六三六三二匹馬力
麵粉廠	八八四八匹馬力
電車公司	七二六四匹馬力
木工場	三〇四二匹馬力
冷藏及食品	二五八一匹馬力
電梯	二〇七八匹馬力
印刷所及新聞紙業	一八二五匹馬力
油坊	一七五七匹馬力
煙草製造廠	一六四六匹馬力
防火唧水機	一六二〇匹馬力

數年來雖以商務中落,電氣事業未能如五年前預計進步之速,然舍電光電熱等生意之日增外,工廠需用電力,猶方興未艾也.今之尚以電氣處是否爲工部局莫大負担問者,可直捷簡快告之曰,自一九一六年迄一九二五年止,工部局大宗行政費用之取給于電氣處盈餘項下者,已不在五百五十六萬兩下矣.

無綫電交通論

(演辭)

方子衛

鄙人今日得與諸君相聚一堂,研究學術,曷勝榮幸.惟無綫電交通,題目廣而且繁,欲將過去未來之成功及發達纖悉陳之,恐爲時間上所不許,故祗得舉其歷史上原理上及所用機器之重要者述之如次.

略 史

一千八百三十一年, Faraday 發明兩絕對不相連之電路間,有電磁感應作用.

一千八百四十年. Henry 第一次試驗高週率電氣振蕩.且指明積勢器之洩電爲振蕩的情狀.

一千八百四十二年, Morse 用水傳電法而作無綫電試驗.

一千八百四十九年! Dr Pthaughnessy 成功不用金屬而傳信號經過闊四千二百英尺之河.

一千八百七十九年, Hughes 發明一種爲 Coherer 動作所必需之現象而 Coherer 後被 Marconi 引爲實用.

一千八百八十二年, Dr. Bell 用 Trowridge 法在 Potomac 河試驗其結果於半英里之距離,可知信號.

一千八百八十七年. Hertz 證明電磁波浪完全與光及熱之波浪相同並得最近無綫電發信符號之原理.

一千八百九十五年, Marconi 歷經各種觀察後,斷定 Hertzian 波浪能用以傳無綫電.

一千八百九十七年十月一號,第一 Marconi 無綫電台設立於 Needles Alum Bay, Isle of Wight 試驗可以傳電於十四英里半範圍之內.

一千九百零六年,Dr, de Frorest 於一月十八號得眞空燈泡,或稱奧錠燈泡收報機之專利權.

一千九百十五年,美國無綫電話非常進步,在 Arlington, ra.傳出之聲浪可達 Honolulu, Hawaii, 及法之巴黎.

原　　理

以上爲無綫電交通之略史至論其原理,先述電路自由振盪之情狀,吾人皆知電氣能力儲於電綫圈,或積勢器內,其結果則成一電磁,或爲積勢器之洩電,所謂振盪電路,卽此二者連合而成,使一發電機供給電於感應耗阻與積勢器相續之電路,其電流於電綫圈內,爲 $I_L=\frac{E}{\sqrt{R^2+w^2L^2}}$ 於積勢器內爲 $I_C=\frac{E}{{}^1/wc}$, Ic較E.M.F.先行九十度,I_L後行九十度,使φ爲落後之角度.則 $\tan\phi=\frac{WL}{R}$ 假如耗阻小而週率大,則φ近於九十度.而發電機供給二種趨向相反之電流,意卽僅需供給二電流之差,若 $I_L=I_c$ 如耗阻近零,發電機所欲供給之電流亦近零,此種情形,爲 $\frac{E}{\sqrt{R^2+w^2L^2}}=Ewc$ 倘使 R = O（因耗阻甚小可以從略也）, $\frac{E}{wL}=Ewc$ 而 $\frac{1}{wL}=wc$ 因此 $w^2=\frac{1}{Lc}$ 但 $w=\frac{2\pi}{T}$ 故 $T=\frac{1}{n}=2\pi\sqrt{Lc}$, 凡更電流于上述電路內,將連續振盪至能力消失於耗阻上爲止.

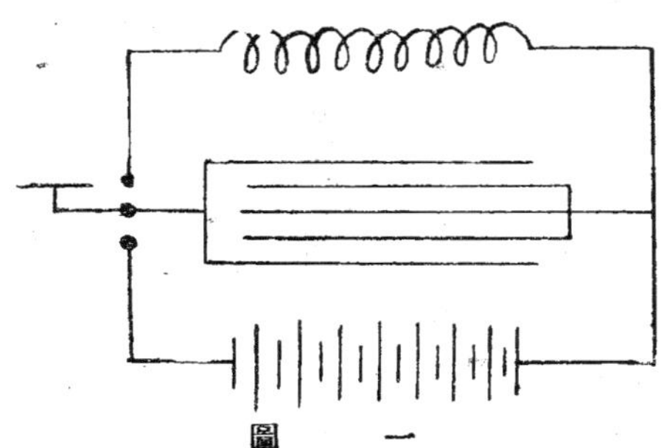

圖　一

如第一圖先充電於積勢器而後洩之,經過感應耗阻,此種洩勢爲振盪的若耗阻強其週時可以上述公式求之.

第二步所欲講者爲傳受綫乃無綫電交通之根本問題,以一直綫下端着地,此法可有一定之週時,但對地之磁感度,及積勢度小,第二圖之虛綫處,表明傳受綫之積勢度可由此求之,欲得較大之積勢度,及較低之自然週率傳受綫當如第三圖之構造,若用一磁感圈或

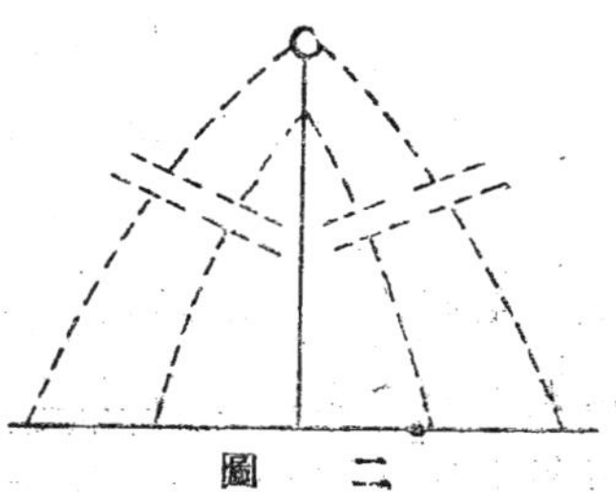

圖　二

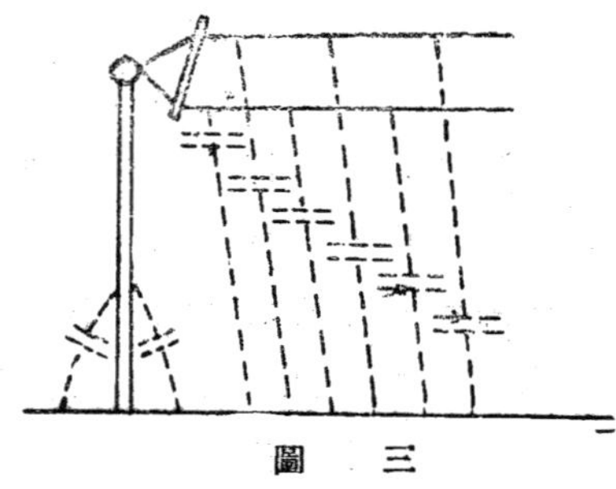

圖　三

變壓器,如第四圖,卽可使之振蕩圖中所示之積勢器C可以自由變動,以便調音與傳受綫之自然週率相彷彿.當電波抵傳受綫時,磁力綫被切E.M.F.因感應而生.故振蕩電流生於傳受綫內,使傳受綫之綫圈與含有感應度之第二綫路作感應上的交通,則第二綫路亦成振蕩如傳受綫及二綫路同傳來之電波調音至諧和狀態,則有若干電流流於第二綫路內,積勢器將變其極,若聽筒繫其兩端,而振蕩係可聽的週率,則聽筒當有

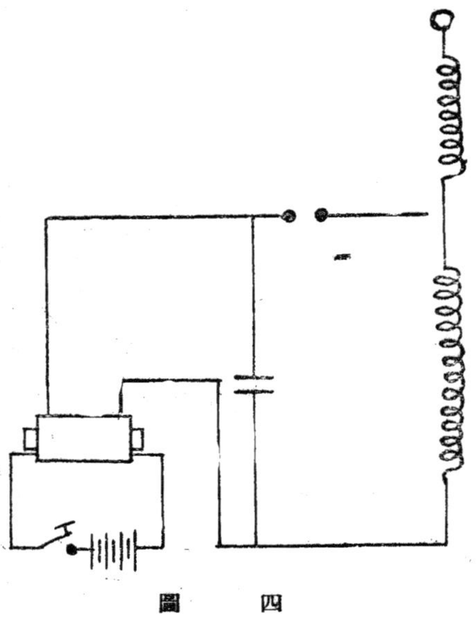

圖　四

相等電壓之差.因此種電波,俱在可聽限程之外,故聽筒中一無所聞,以一檢波器與聽筒連續相接,若電波係成隊而來,且爲可聽之週率,則每隊有一衝擊發現聽筒中.聲音卽可聞得矣.此種聲音視發電站信號之點劃,或播送

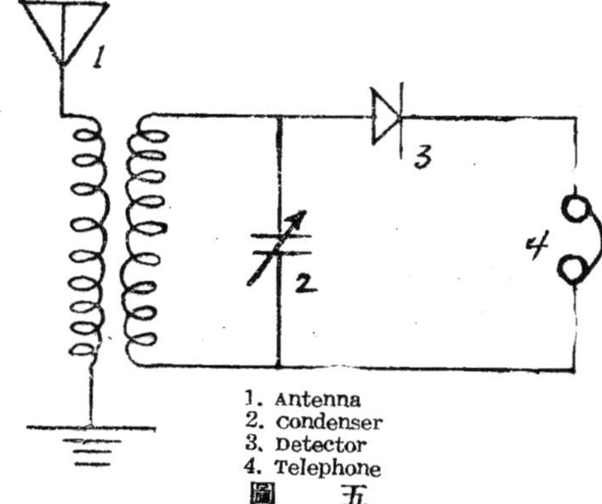

圖 五

站入聲向傳電筒之輕重斷續不定,第五圖示上述之綫路.第六圖示收到之電波,A表明到聽筒及檢波器之電差.B表明經過檢波器後之電差.C表明確爲聽筒綫遞傳之電流,故聽筒內之衝擊,爲可聽之週率,而經過空中傳出之能力爲極高週率,是知檢波器者限制週率之具也,

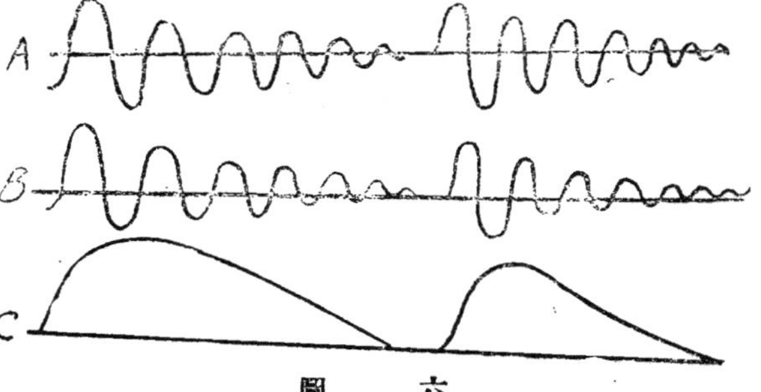

圖 六

檢波器有數種,如礦石.Electrolpic,二電極眞空管,(Fleming valve)及後 Dr. De Forest 再插入一電極(卽電柵)於Fleming valve內構成最新式之三極眞空管.

礦石及三極眞空管檢波器之原理

礦石檢波器之正確定名,應爲礦石更波器.因爲一種礦石,其性實能將傳受綫所收受之振蕩,或更電流變爲觸於聽筒之衝擊直電流也.此衝擊直電流,使聽筒之薄膜更相吸放甚速,發出語聲,至礦石之更波性有四百與一之比較,卽電流經過礦石之一方向,比另一方向有四百倍之便易,是以可得上述之效果,三極管爲一眞空玻管,內中封閉一細金屬絲可用低電壓熱至白熱度,一螺旋狀或交叉式之柵,或隔綫,及一平或曲之鎳片（亦稱電板.）二十二又半弗打之高電池電壓與電板相接,則電板上得陽極之電壓當細金屬絲經過電流發熱時,因電板陽極之吸力,發出陰極電子,至電柵處於電板及細鐵絲之間,外來振蕩電流經過柵路積勢器後卽直達電柵.

外來之振蕩使柵路積勢器荷負極之電,按同性相拒之理,燈絲所發出之負電子,當然被其阻撓,不能前進,故柵路中發生變動,電板路電流亦隨之而變,電板電壓變動,則減少經過聽筒之電流,而生人耳可辨之音聲,可作一簡單之試驗,以明電柵之作用.用第七圖所示之器,使電板綫路內電池之電流徑過 Galvanometer 及燈泡電子在燈泡內爲一種經過電柵之傳導物,倘以一荷電橡皮桿近一與電柵相接之球,則電柵受負極之電量,與電子相拒,電子卽不得流過燈泡,其電流變動之結果,可見於 Galvanometer 或置一 Relay 於綫路內,而使Relay主動電鈴見之若以正極荷電,則增加電壓階級,且與燈絲相近故速電子之流通,而增加電板綫路內之電流,第八圖,天綫吸受外界傳來電力,而使之振蕩於第二綫路內,則柵之電壓升降不定,可以調劑電池所供給燈泡及聽筒之電流.

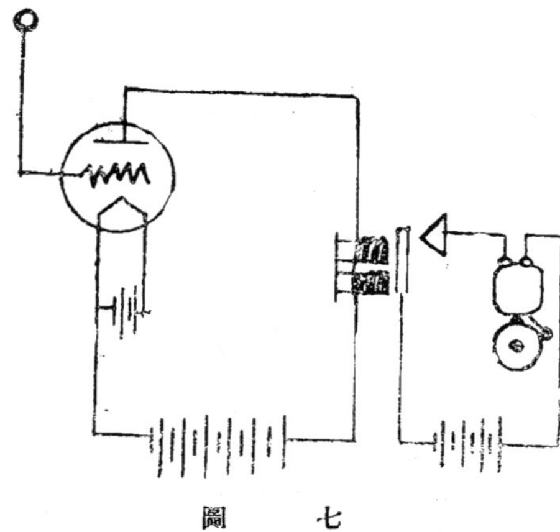

圖 七

收發電路

收發電路已經發明多種茲將目前所常用數種述之.

Regenerative 放音器——於第八圖之簡單收電綫路內插入一綫圈於

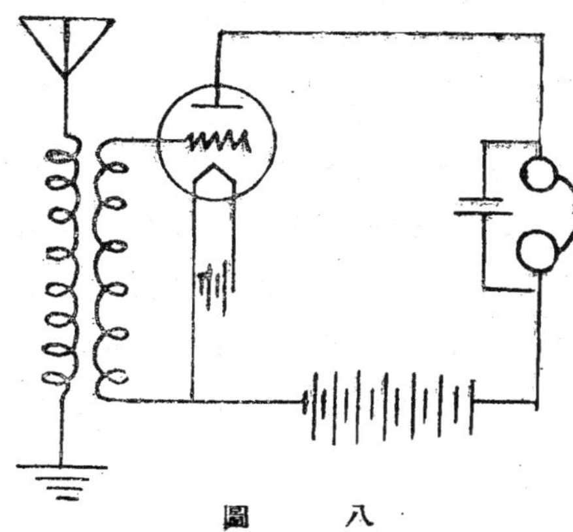
圖 八

電屏綫路,而與振電蕩路之綫圈起磁感作用,則成Regenerative放音器此種設想由於直電流發電機中之Compounding綫圈而起,第九圖表明完全綫路跨聽筒而置之積勢器,係備低Impedance之路,便於電板綫路高週律電流之變動,倘使置於於電板綫路之綫圈轉數比較少,則Impedance低,而電板電流之交電流部分將與柵路電壓同面（Phase）以其因柵路電壓之動作而生也.茲將I代表該電流之一部分,則E.M.F.感應而生於振蕩綫路爲$-M\frac{di}{dt}$ M代表 Mutual Inductance 於a及b之間.此E.M.F.與電板電流及柵路電壓成九十度之角,當積勢器C充足荷電時,柵路電壓最高.卽振蕩綫路內電流爲零,故柵路電壓及振蕩電流成九十度之角.因感應而生之E.M.F. $-M\frac{di}{dt}$及振蕩電流,俱與柵路電壓成九十度之角,則該二者必係同面或相距一百八十度,照第二種情形,Freed Back Coil之兩端必相反,此可見綫圈之情形a及b爲不誤.

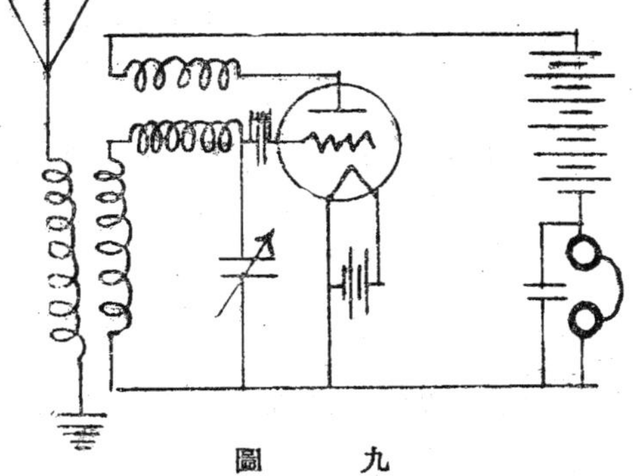
圖 九

問者曰,已生之振蕩何以消滅後,卽不能繼續.當燈泡用以爲Regenerative amplifier而收電信,來自天綫之力消滅時,振蕩亦應停止.設電板綫路與振蕩綫路相Coupling甚疎,卽M小,供給於振蕩綫路之電力,不足以單獨支持振蕩因振蕩綫路內有電阻以消散此電力也.兩綫圈 a 及 b 平常可以自由移動,庶Coup'ing可以隨意變動,以達一種情狀,而得良好之結果.

三極眞空管作爲發電機之用,可證明其重要並不減於檢波器及放音器,其根本原理,與用以爲 Regenerative amplifier 相同.已有許多方法可以用之作爲發電機,但俱不外乎以下三種條件,（a）一振蕩綫路,（b）振蕩綫路及電板綫路間之 Coupling,（c）振蕩綫路及柵路間之 Coupling 有三種方法可使成 Coupling.（1）直接接電法,（2）用二綫圈感應法,（3）用積勢器二極板間之感應作用.

射電(Radio)週律及可聽(Audio)週律放大率

Wave train 週律,卽每秒鐘 Wave train 之數,名 Audio 週律,至每 Wave train 間振蕩之週律爲射電週律,傳來電波之放大率,在到檢波器之前爲射電放大率,在過檢波器之後爲 Audio 放大率,射電或 Audio 放大率,照理想可用至任何次數,但實用上僅三次四次或五次而已.

二級之 Audio 週律放音器

用少量電力於柵路,可調度多量電力于電板綫路.以交電流 E.M.F. 或 Esinwt 接於柵路,卽發生更電流之部分于電板電流,等於 2（Ep－Eg）Esinwt 倘使此電流經變壓器之第一綫路,在第二綫路之更流電壓較原來之更流電壓必甚大,此種新產生之更電流電壓,能用於第二眞空管之柵,而再放大第二眞空管,于是用以成二級放音器,有時再用三級或四級.

際此我國長途電話尙未廣設之前,若代以無綫電話,我國將爲全世界各國始創商用無綫電話之一,豈不懿歟.且我國一千九百縣城間通信種種之困難,如距離過長地勢不平難于植竿等,均可從而解決矣.

眞空燈增幅器之仇敵—長鳴與噪音

The Enemies of Tube Amplifier——Squealing and Noises

黄 耕 生

1. 增幅器概論 Amplifiers in general

增幅器者增加『收入電流或電壓』Incoming currents or voltages 之『振幅』Amplitude, 卽增加『收入信號』Incoming signals 之力量之器具也.其在無綫電及有綫電交通上,實居一極重要之位置,以其能作微弱信號之偵探,藉是得以增進實用上之通信距離也.

現今無綫電用之增幅器必含有一個或多個『三極眞空燈』Three electrade vacuum tube, or triode 及其他適當器具;因在『眞空燈』Vacuum tube 未發明以前,實未有一適用之增幅器也.良好增幅器之優點在乎增加『信號電流』Signal current 之力量而不生任何『歪扭』Distortion;眞空燈實具有適合此兩條件之優點,故能爲實用上惟一適用之增幅器.

三十年來無綫電之所以能由試驗而達於實用;通信距之所以能由咫尺之近而增至數千萬里之遙.在歷史過程上,多項機器之發明,皆各有其相當之價值;而最近遠程通信之成功,廣播電台之林立,質言之.卽最可靠最經濟的通信之成功,要皆眞空燈發明之功也.

近數年來眞空燈進步之速,效用之神,應用之廣,關係之重實已駕各種無綫電機而上之;然其自身在應用上果已臻於完美之地位乎?曰殆猶未也.今試就收信機增幅器論之:吾人每當試驗或使用眞空燈增幅器之際,恆有一種意外擾亂現象發生.其爲害之烈,實足以妨害信號之收受,淆惑收者之聽聞,減低增幅之效率,限制級數之增加,此爲使用無綫電者之所深忌,雖經多數學者之研究與改良,猶未能完全避免也.此現象維何?卽此篇所謂增幅器之仇敵——『長鳴』與『噪音』Squealing and noises是也.此現象果何由而生,將用何法以治醫之, Morecraft 氏論之甚詳.氏爲哥倫比亞大學著名電工教授,其所著『無綫電學原理』Prin ciples of Radio Communication 一書,實爲近今無綫電文藝界僅有之傑作,其立論之新穎,說理之詳明,取材之豐富,遣詞之雅潔,體例之謹嚴,編纂之得體,實屬得未曾有.令人讀之,如據崑崙之巔,觀長江大河向東而瀉,覺諸川百海悉導源於是也;又若置身天際,看汪洋大海,覺諸川百水胥歸納于是也;是書之于無綫電之理論及實用,不啻爲衆水之源,又不啻爲百川之匯;惜我國無一譯本,以供衆覽,殊爲遺憾.

年來我國舊有電台多已改裝眞空燈收信機,新成立者更無論矣.上述現象當爲日常習見之事,其必能引起留心無綫電學者之注意,從可知矣.茲節譯是書中之關于增幅器之長鳴及眞空燈之噪音各節(參看原書870-860 840, 523, 830等頁)惜譯者學力幼稚,文詞譾陋,未能暢達原書之意,讀者諒之.

2. 長鳴 Squealing

增幅器尤其是『感應圈或變壓器交合式增幅器』 Inductance or transformer repeating amplifier,每在『聽筒』Telephone 內產生一種與收入信號全不相關繼續不絕之聲音;此現象曰『長鳴』.極討厭而又甚難避免之障碍也.長鳴之起因,常由于各眞空燈之電路發生『振動』Oscillation之可能一遇相當機會,即起振動『高週波及低週波增幅器』High-frequency and lowfrequency amplifier 皆有此現象.

眞空燈發生振動之原因約有下列數種:

(a) 變壓器『綫圈』Coil 與其『寄生電容』Distributed capacity 成一『振動電路』Oscillating circuit.——如第一圖爲變壓器交合式之低週波增幅器;第二圖爲獨自連接之眞空燈,爲醒目起見,假定第二圖之獨自連接

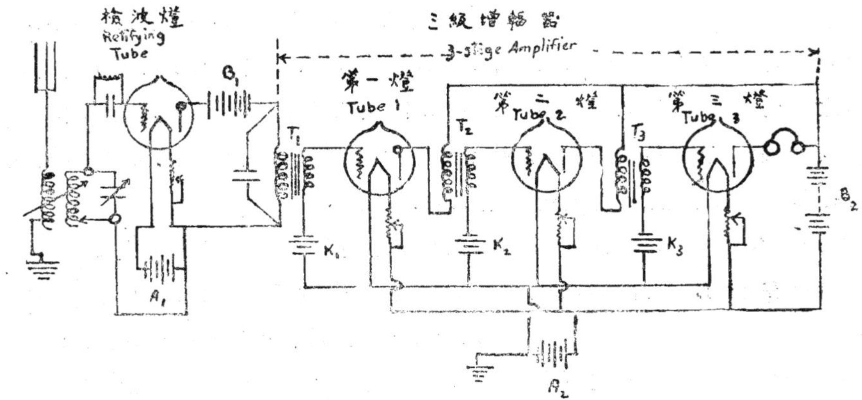

Connection of Tube. Detector Receiving Set to Amplifier.

第一圖——真空燈檢波器收信機與增輻器接綫圖

A_1及A_2爲檢波燈及增輻器之「纖電池」,Filament battery.

B_1及B_2爲檢波燈及增輻器之「屏電池」 Plate battery,

$K_1K_2K_3$爲增輻器各燈之「柵電池」 Gtrid battery.

$T_1T_2T_3$爲變壓器 Transformer.

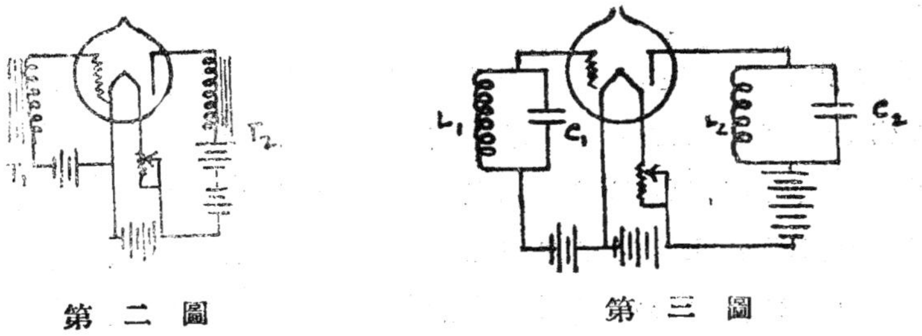

第二圖　　　　第三圖

之真空燈與第一圖之增輻器內之真空燈之一,有同一之作用.因變壓器T_1及T_2綫圈各有多量之寄生電容,今各以C_1及C_2代表之,則第二圈之電路約可以第三圖之相當電路代表之.但須注意（第三圖）L_1-C_1爲振動電路.『柵極』Grid 係跨此電路而連接.且電路L_2-C_2對于電路L_1-C_1之『自然週波電流』Current of natural frequency 可有強大之『複阻』Impedence,發源于電路L_2-C_1之振動,必使『柵電壓』Grid potential 生一變動,柵電壓變則『屏電流』Plate current 變,屏電流變則電壓亦隨之而變.惟 L_2-C_2 之復回係『直接』Connected in series 于『屏電池』Plate battery,故屏電壓之變動可經過屏與『纖』Filament 間及柵與纖間之『電容』Capacity 反應予柵,且可生一較高于第一次所生之電壓于電路 L_1-C_1. 如此自足夠維持 L_1-C_1 之自然週波電流而有餘裕.

此眞空燈振動時亦可爲 L_2-C_2 之自然週波.但其爲 L_1-C_1 抑爲 L_2-C_2 週波,全在乎何種週波能給電壓以『準確之位相』Correct phase, 給全電路以『較小之損失』Smaller losses.設此燈振動時爲『可聽週波』Audible Frequency,則所生之電流,可在增幅器之最末眞空燈之屏電路之聽筒內聽得之,因是卽發生長鳴.設爲『不可聽週波』Inaudible frequency, 則聽筒內無此種電流存在之表示,但對于眞空燈之增幅作用則甚有妨害耳.

若爲感應圈交合式之高週波增幅器,眞空燈之電路亦可振動,但其週波甚高,非吾人聽覺所能覺觸.然增幅之效率,則因擾亂電流之存在,大爲減低也.

(b)因『柵極凝電器』Grid condenser 使柵極變爲甚高之負極.——至若感應圈交合式之高週波增幅器,雖振動週波甚高,有時聽筒內亦有可聽之聲音.因柵極凝電器感受振動後,變爲最高之負極,可使屏電流變而爲零,振動卽因而中止.迨聚于柵極之『電子』Electron 逃逸後,屏電流開始流動,振動又復開始,屏電流又如前狀仍復中止.因屏電流有漲跌,振動遂一發一止,發爲可聽之週波,如是增幅器卽長鳴.

爲便利起見,吾人曾于以上各節討論單獨眞空燈所起之作用.此燈因其屏電路之變動反應于其柵及纖所連接之振動電路,卽起電振.各個眞空燈自皆可以此同一狀態而起振動.其週波雖或有異同.但實際上全部眞空燈與共感受一同樣之週波此週波.爲何?卽使全增幅器振動最易,損失最少,(振動爲已去)之週波也.設此種損失超過屏電池藉屏與柵間之反應作用所輸送之可能的供給則增幅器感受此週波或其他使上述現象（供不應求）占優勢之週波時,卽無振動之可能.

(c)因出入二電路之交合.——增幅器雖就他方言之不致發生振動,若其『出口電路』Output circuit以磁場或電場或磁電兩場,與『入口電路』Irput circuit相交合,則在此情形之下增幅器亦可發生振動.此圖與第一圖爲相似形.設振動電流發源於變壓T之『從綫圈』Secnndary coil,此電流卽由各眞空燈次第響應之,擴大之.如最末眞空燈之屏電路與第一燈之柵電路相交合,最末燈之屏電路之變壓電流能生一變量電壓于第一燈之柵電路;且此電壓有充分之力量及『正確之位相』Right phase能增加且維持發源于變壓器T之電流,則增幅器卽生振動.

如是可知:出口及進口兩電路如有關連,欲使增幅器發生振動,則正源不必起于第一燈之柵電路,因爲振動可發源于任一燈（包括最末燈）之柵電路或屏電路;卽令出入兩電路間之關係甚薄弱,無論發源于何電路之振動,增幅器之『增幅作用』Amplification皆可使之繼續維持.

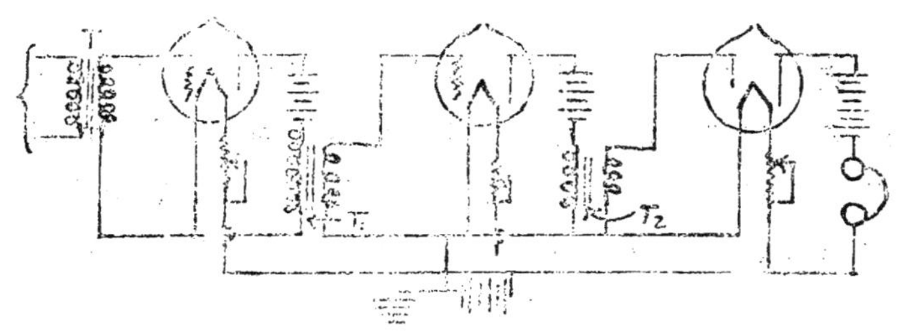

第四圖

上節只假定最末燈之屏電路與第一燈之柵電路相交合.但卽令一中間燈之屏電路與第一燈之柵電路或任一燈之屏電路與前一燈之柵電路相交合,增幅器亦可振動.故發源于任一燈之振動電路之電流,若爲他燈之反應作用所維持,則全增幅器卽可振動.

3. 增幅器長鳴之所醫治法 Remedies. for amplifier squealing.

增幅器增幅愈大,振動愈易.換言之,即欲得一安靜之增幅器,莫如使之無『自振』Self-oseillaton之傾向.欲使一組『縱接眞空燈』Tubes connected in caseade無長鳴之傾向,必須調整之,使其總共增幅作用甚低于其應有數值.

關于各種長鳴預防之方法,雖已注意周到;但當試驗之際,仍不免有此現象發生,下列各點必須注意:

(a) 無任何振動電路之增幅器不易長鳴.『阻耗交合式增幅器』Resistance-repeating amplifier實際上可為一無任何振動電路之增幅器:但須知一雙甚短之道綫所成之電路其自然週波甚高,但仍不失為一振動電路,故即為阻耗交合增幅器亦可依極高之週波振動,設有柵極凝電器從中阻止屏電流,仍有可聽之聲音.現用阻耗交合式增幅器全電壓可放大25,000倍不生長鳴.

(b) 增幅器之出入兩電路必須無互相交合之情形.即甚薄弱之關係亦無之.最好此二電路均用雙紐道綫,此綫愈短愈好,二電路間之距離愈遠愈好.雙紐道綫必須置于連接入地之柔韌金屬箱內以保護之,不使各屏電路之道綫與前燈柵電路之道綫相交合,其在箱內道綫亦須注意此點.

(c) 『每個眞空燈及其住持』Each tube and its holder 必須置於保險箱內.箱之周圍以銅片包之,連接入地,以預防一燈之磁場或電場影響于鄰近之燈.換言之,即預防相鄰眞空燈之交合.因燈之變量磁場或電場之能力為包圍之銅片所生之電流吸收也.若為高週波增幅器,此種預防法尤須特加注意.

(d) 各燈之屏電池及纖電池如可辦到,必須分備,如此則燈與燈間即去一交合之方法.但使用分備電池,即增加增幅器之重量,體積,及價格,除特別試驗室外,此種裝置不適于一般之用,殊為遺憾.但無論如何,屏纖二電池之『阻耗』Resistance總以愈低愈好.

(e)各道綫必須安置于其適當之位置,各接點必須銲接妥善.

上列各點雖已注意周到,然所謂製造精良,使用合法之增幅器,縱將其進口電路『捷徑』Short-circuited(作動字用)之,仍難免有響亮噪音之發生.此或由於增幅器之某一眞空燈之不良,(當于次節討論),或由于A或B電池之故障.『蓄電池』Storage bettery實用上常作爲燃點纖絲之用(卽作爲A電池之用),以其阻耗低小也.良好之增幅器每因A電池將近過量放電(卽電量不足,如鉛電池之電壓低于1.8安者)發生各種亂雜之聲音,如換一電量充足之A電池,則增幅器卽安靜.

上項定則亦甚適用于B電池(卽屏電池.)通常屏電池之各小『乾電瓶』Dry cell,每當枯竭之際,其阻力變動極大.電池之中如有一電瓶,如此則增幅器中卽生一種不良之噪音.今試用阻耗低小之電壓表將各瓶一加檢驗,則此衰弱電瓶不難立卽檢出也.

4. 眞空燈噪音 Tube Noises

其他使增幅器應用時大感困難之點,爲眞空燈所生之噪音.讀者當知眞空燈內之任一燈(尤其是第一燈)之屏或柵電流之一小小變動,一經放大,直可使最末燈之屏電流生一極大之變動,結果卽在聽筒內生一洪亮銳利之聲音.有時此種聲音連綿不絕,噪聒刺耳,高出信號之上,故爲最忌之現象.此種噪音足以限制增幅器級數之增加,爲增幅器前途發展之一大障碍.是因欲使第一燈之電流不生微小之變動,幾不可能,而此微小變動旣經多級之響應放大,直可使正式信號湮沒而無聞.

燈電路內電流之微小變動之成因甚多,其最普通者爲:

(a)各電池之電壓陡起微小之變動(上節已論及.)

(b)燈之各極之機械振動.

(c)少量氣體發生『電解』Ionization;或纖極電子之『發射率』Rate of emission不均勻.此極難醫治之現象,多由於『纖極』Filament外表之不純淨.

燈之各極如發生機械振動則柵與纖纖,與屏.及屏與柵間之距離必變因是屏電流亦隨之而變.故欲避免機械振動,燈之『各極』Elements 必須安置牢固.但安置雖甚穩固,仍不免有振動發生,縱非吾人所能察覺,然若以增幅器探驗之,則甚易知.此安置電極時所應特加注意者也,向者此點之重要尤未大白于天下,昔曾將此種電極安置不牢之眞空燈,用於飛機之上,結果凡含有此種眞空燈之增幅器實際上殆歸無用.支持眞空燈之材料與此種極有關係,亦須特加注意.增幅燈通常以海綿狀橡皮等類彈性物體支持之.其支點必須使燈之全體發生振動時,彼卽依極低之『靜默週波』Inaudible frequeney 而振動,且不將此振動傳達于各電極;又因電極安置甚牢,其自然週波甚高.

欲使多級增幅器之第一燈不生顯著之噪音于聽筒內,其作用必須極爲均匀.例如某增幅器放大『進入電壓』(Input voltage) 10^4 倍,其第一燈之屏電路內之阻耗(或『反動』Reactance)爲50,000『歐』Ohms;設最末燈之柵電壓有.02『佛』Volt 卽可在聽筒內生一可聽之聲音;則第一燈之屏電流之變動僅 10^{-10}『安』Ampere 卽可生一可聽之聲音.然此或僅爲第一燈之屏電流之變動之千萬分之一耳.今試一察放射電子之熱金屬之表面情形,則知欲電子之放射極爲均匀,卽令極小之參差亦無之,似甚難能.是則可知現用眞空燈之屏電流仍有極大之變動繼續發生也.

再則進口電路所感受之任何外界擾亂卽小至僅 10^{-6} 佛亦可在聽筒內生一可聽之聲音.

因此可得一結論:一增幅器之第一級爲靜默燈,若其進口電路所感受之擾亂信號不大于 10^{-6} 佛.則此器之電壓之有效放大可爲 10^{4} 至 10^{5} 倍.現用眞空燈若過此範圍(此或爲極限)卽爲無用;雖可再加一二眞空燈使信號更爲洪亮,但通常信號更難辨識.

同步換流機(Synchronous converter)與同步電動發電機(Synchronous motor-generator Set)在實業應用上之比較

(譯自一九二六年二月份G.E.雜誌.W.B. Snyder原著)

伯 黎

在一發電廠中,兼有此二種設備者甚鮮,故用者於機器之詳情,每知其一而不知其二.此文將此二種直流電力之來源分析比論,使吾人知所選擇,誠有益實業界之作也.

當今中央發電廠所供給之電大抵爲更流電.故實業上須用直流電力者,非用換流機或電動發電機,使更流電力變爲直流電力不可.此二機均屬可靠,且便於節制,而各具短時間之過負量,原無分軒輊.惟就其特性而論,則各有適用之處.爰分別比較之於下:

(一.)價値及效率 (First cost and efficiency)

換流機及其附件之價,較同樣設備之電動發電機約低百分之十,而其效率則較高百分之五至七,就此二點而論則換流機較電動發電機爲優.

(二)電力因數 (Power factor.)

依通常供實業應用之計劃換流機之電力因數在滿荷負與四分三荷負之間,爲百分之一百.若荷負減少,則電力因數減低甚速,二分之一荷負時約爲百分之九十五後(Lagging),四分之一荷負時約爲百分之五十五後,而無荷時僅百分之二十後.故換流機之電力因數在二分一以上之荷負時,雖屬甚高,而欲用以增高全廠荷負之電力因數,則未可恃也.

電動發電機之電力因數,爲百分之一百,百分之八十五先(Leading,)或百分之八十先,視其所用之電動機而定.同步電動發電機之供實業上用者往往配以百分八十五電力因數之同步電動機.此電動機與換流機不同,其電力因數,輕荷時較滿荷時爲優.使磁場不變,一滿荷時百分八十五先電力因數之電動機,在二分一之荷負時,其電力因數爲百分之五十五先;四分之一荷負時,爲百分之三十三先;及無荷時爲百分之十五.故同步電動發電機具增高全廠荷負之電力因數之特長.

換言之,同步換流機無荷時須用其發電量(Rating)百分二十七之蹤後的啓羅安培,滿荷時約爲百分之十二;而百分八十五電力因數之同步電動機,無荷時能供給其發電量百分七十之跨先的啓羅安培,滿荷時減至百分之五十二又二分之一.

(三)電力合同(Power contract.)

電力合同大抵包含需要費(Demand charge)與電能費(Energy charge)兩種,有時再加以電力因數之部分(Power-factor clause,)即遇平均電力因數低於指定數之時用電者須償較高之電費以需要費,與電能費而論,換流機因具較高之效率,自比電動發電機多百分之五至七之利益.使合同包有電力因數部分,則換流機與電動發電機之間,須察其全廠荷負之電力因數,而加以審愼的選擇;因用同步電動發電機以增高電力因數後所省之費,每足抵其較高之需要費與電能費而有餘也,

(四)電力供給(Power supply 此處指更流電)

直流電電壓與更流電電壓之比,在換流機有固定之數,而於電動發電機則否.故欲改變換流機之直流電電壓,以控制更流電電壓之變更,未免有

所限制.例如將換流機之磁場改變.以增高直流電壓百分之十.則電樞 (Armature)銅條之一部,將三四倍熱於尋常.故更流電電壓之調整*(Regulation,)須在直流電方面可許之限制以內,而後換流機可以適用.反是,則寧用價值較昂之電動發電機矣.

(五)直流電荷負 (Direct cur ent load)

若直流電荷負之性質須含有Over-compounding,電壓之時常調節,及與他電動發電機或引擎拖動之直流發電機並行等等,以電動發電機爲宜.換流機,祇能與他換流機,而不易與電動發電機或引擎拖動之直流發電機並行 (Parallel,) 因更流電電壓之變更必影響及於直流電方面,是故換流機宜用於與換流機並行之處電動發電機宜用於已有電動發電機或引擎拖動之直流發電機之地也.

(六)其他比較點.

電動發電機之所佔面積較換流機爲少,此亦一小優點至於機器各部之輕及裝置(Lining up)與調補電樞之便利,則換流機稍勝於電動發電機矣

附換流機與電動發電機之效率,價值,佔地及重量比較表

(一)效率比較表

註——換流機之耗損,包括變壓器之耗損及換流機與變壓器間更流電銅條之耗損.

機之發電量（啓羅瓦特）	百分之效率 同步換流機	同步電動發電機
200	90.8	86.2
400	91.9	87.6
600	92.4	88.3

800	92.7	88.9
1000	92,8	89.2
1200	92,9	89.5
1400	93.0	89,7
1600	93.0	89.8
1800	93.0	89.9

(二)價值比較表

註——電動發電機之價包括電鑰板(Switchboards)之價.

換流機之價包括變壓器,電鑰板,及換流機變壓器間銅條之價.

發電量（啓羅瓦特）	每啓羅瓦特發電量之機器價值（百分數）換流機	電動發電機
200	132	140
400	109	119
600	98	110
800	93	104
1000	88	100
1200	86	98
1400	84	97
1600	83	96
1800	82	95

(三)重量比較表

註——下列二表中,換流機包括變壓器在內.

發電量　　每啓羅瓦特之重量(百分數)

（啓羅瓦特）	換流機	電動發電機
200	147	123
400	124	111
600	113	106
800	107	102
1000	103	100
1200	100	985
1400	985	98
1600	97	97
1800	96.5	96.5

(四)所佔面積比較表

發電量	每啓羅瓦特之所佔面積（百分數）	
（啓羅瓦特）	換流機	電動發電機
200	230	168
400	165	130
600	144	115
800	131	105
1000	120	100
1200	113	96
1400	107	92
1600	101	90
1800	99	88

上列四表原著用曲線表明.（譯者識.）

同期電動機發生困難原因之大概

余昌菊

同期電動機與同期發電機大致相同.磁場亦須用直流電之勵磁機.是故一有困難發生.不獨關於始驅機(Startor)方面應當注意,即供給磁場之電源亦須加以考察.同期電動機發生之困難,與他機同,可分爲二種.一屬之機械方面.一屬之電氣方面.關於機械方面者,即若軸承過熱機器震動.機身不平,負荷太重,起始工作失敗與軸承損移等皆是.關於電氣者,即若起始失敗發聲,發熱,速度不穩與求同期速度失敗等皆是.除所述外未嘗無其他困難之發生.然大抵不外乎是.

軸承普通病源

軸承發生困難爲機器之通病.惟電動機之軸承,若負荷適當,常潤以上好機油,如用皮帶者常維持以適度之引伸力若是則軸承發熱或損壞及各種困難不屢見矣.

軸承普通病源有二(一)引油環(Oilring)之灣曲(二)潤滑油之不潔.引油環灣曲後不能成爲圓形,於是遂不能隨軸同時轉動.若是則阻力以生,軸承即起始爲軸身損移.動樞(Rotor)地位亦因之稍偏.故當電動機新用時,宜將引油環加以詳細視察,以覘潤滑油是否有凝黏之勢.此後每隔一定時期當更詳察之.

潤滑油之雜質每易攙入軸與油環之間,引油環或竟因之阻滯轉動.有時堆積軸室之內(Bearing housing)致油道阻塞,潤滑油不能回入油池.軸承之如第一圖者,油道自軸承兩頭通入油池.其身甚窄.如油有雜質,或電動機四週滿蔽塵灰,此處當屢加視察.若此處被塞潤滑油不能回入油池.勢必溢出軸外,油池時空,即足爲是弊發生之明徵.

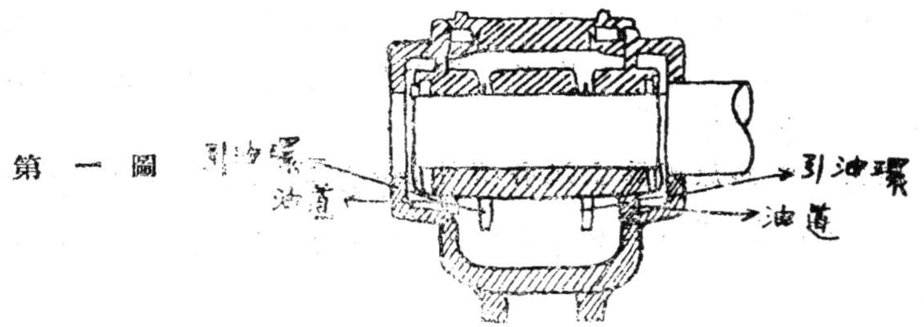

第一圖

此外軸承困難之發生,每因電動機位置之不平,而尤以皮帶拖動者爲甚.蓋動樞重量多偏於一面,其低面負荷太重,軸承於是發熱.且定樞(Stator)與動樞相距之際亦因動樞偏而磁力分佈不均,如此則動樞之重量欲將動樞拖出而磁力則欲將動樞拉入有時軸遂作左右擺動致軸肩與軸承相擊,而困難於是乎發生矣,

軸承發熱除因機位不平外,有時亦因皮帶在引伸力過大軸與軸承之間太緊而致.是故皮帶不可太緊在能使機轉動不致滑去斯可矣.

軸與軸承之間應易兩端擺動,如動樞四面磁力不均則橫壓力發生若是亦足使軸與軸承間發生極度熱量.

電子線及磁場線之受熱

電子線之受熱普通多因磁場電流校正時不甚措意以致電子電流過大而致.同期電動機之電流視磁場爲轉移.變動甚大電能折數(Power factor)亦因之而不同.有時同一負荷因磁場差誤,電流增加有一倍半之多是故電子線電路中,當有一電表使管機者可隨時變動勵磁機電流,俾不太過,以免發生高度熱量.

同期電動機因用途之不同可分爲二大種.一電能整折數之負荷用之,一機械負荷用之,並隨時須能變動負荷之電能折數.前者之磁場線,能容納使電動機受盡量負荷之電流即足.若後者則磁場線之容電量勢必增大不然則當先導電能折數 (Leadingpower faetor) 之輕負荷時,磁場電流增加過大,絕緣體 (Insulation) 將因之破裂,故電動機之作是項用途者,當購買時其磁場電流之容量亟須注意,

電機內線受熱原因除上述各項外;磁場線之斷連或短接,磁場線之顚倒,一相之斷連,電壓不準,或各相之電壓不等,線之通地,接連差誤,俱足爲發熱起因.

當電動機轉動之際,磁場線忽然中斷,則速度即行改變,有時竟停止轉動若負荷不多,則或將變成一感應電動機,繼續轉動.惟電流大增.往往較適量電流 (Normal Current) 大至數倍,於是所生熱亦不少.電動機而有吼聲發生,即爲此種情形之明證.

起始工作之失敗

起始工作之失敗原因甚多,茲將其大略分述於下.

當控御柄在開電動機之際,而電動機不能轉動,往往有三種情形發生.或作微聲,或無聲,或有力發動而無充足扭力 (Torque) 以供負.

無聲爲電源斷絕之唯一表示.管理者當注意接聯是否斷裂.或保護器(Circuit breaker)是否關上有聲則爲一相斷聯之現像.相之斷聯,或因電熔線(Fuse)燒斷,或因開關接點太鬆.或因相內或相外電線之斷聯與鬆動.

斷聯之相可用下法尋出之,

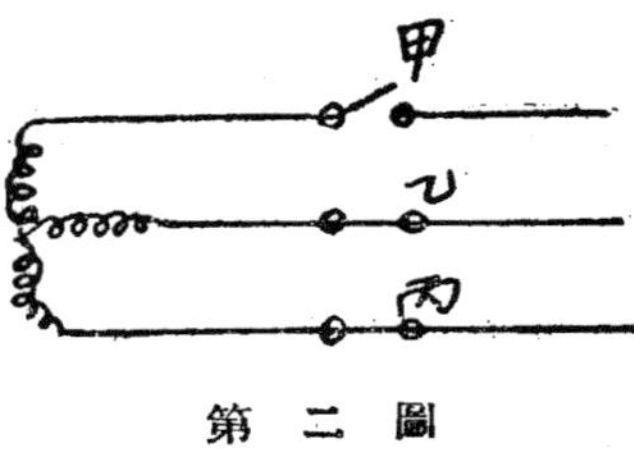

第二圖

先將一相與電源斷絕(如圖二甲.)如甲相非斷聯之相,則微聲即止.蓋電源因是相之斷,亦斷絕矣.若聲不止.則甲相可斷爲斷聯之相斷聯之相既得,則可更用試驗燈(Testing lauip)查察之.若甲相即爲斷聯之相,試驗燈

可接甲乙或甲丙,燈亮則斷聯點在機外不亮則在機內.

電動機之不能發動,有時因電源電壓之太低.起始扭力(Starting torgue)與電源源壓力之方成正比例,電源壓力減少一半,扭力卽減爲原數四分之一.是故電動機之所以不能發動,電源壓力之高低亦當注意.當新機試用時電壓太低或與託變壓器(Auto trausfarner)所接處變壓太低,則校正變壓器之比例卽可.有時亦因來線太細,線路上損失之電壓太多,則惟有將線更換以圖補救,

相內線之短接或接地,亦足以阻電動機之發動.此種困難發生各相電流相間電壓最好加以一度之測量.各相電流及相電壓應各相等,卽相差亦當無幾.若相差太遠,則必有差誤點或損壞點在焉,電流等而電壓不等,困難屬之外來電源,與電動機及驅始器無關.電壓不等甚少,而電流相去甚遠,則爲驅始器或電動機內線之短接或接地若電流表當時並不示數,則爲是相斷聯之明徵.

當電動機發動之際,磁場開關未開與直流電源並未斷接,則起始扭力太小不足使機轉動.故當開機時,當先注意磁場開關之開否以免是弊.

電動機之不發動,有時原因不屬於電氣方面.而屬於機械方面.軸與軸承上之困難,及驅始器之受損,均足使機停止工作.

電動機有時祇能轉動而不能得同期速度,則大多因磁壓太低,或勵磁機方面有所損壞.

有時電動機得同期速度之後,速度屢變,不能持久.且有嘶嘶聲可聞.在試用新機此弊或因飛輪太輕.至於舊機,則多因其他同期電機速度之不穩電源接線長而阻力太多,磁場接線之鬆動,或機內止動線(Dampiugwind-iug)之斷聯而生.

以上所述,均屬電動機困難發生之大概.幷略及補救之法總之,一有困難發生,當細察當時情形,則探本窮源,不難迎辦而解也.

英國電線之新標準

張 延 祥

校中教材均採用美國書籍,故所知電線標準爲Brown & Sharp Gauge.但市上所通用者爲英國之 Standard wire Gauge, or S.W.G. 此二種大小呎时均不難査得.惟近年來英國製造電線廠家,聯合組織Cable Makers' Associati-on, 因覺 S.W.G, 毫無科學統系.重定一新標準,謂之British Standard,係取法德國法國之統系,以電線之斷面積平方时數目稱其線之大小,而廢除號數案德法兩國,不用電線號數,而呼其線之斷面積之平方时數 mm² 如10 mm²之線,卽可知其大小,不必再査表册也.英國用英寸故用平方英时數 sq. in., 如 0.06 sq. in.之類.此法確屬便利,現已各處通行.在校同學不可不備表參考玆介紹二表於后.

第1表 英國新標準紫銅圓電線

在華氏六十度時之直徑(吋)	斷面積(平方吋)	每千碼之重量(磅數)	每千碼之電阻力 (Resistance) (Ohms) 在華氏六十度	每千碼之電阻力 (Resistance) (Ohms) 在百度表二十度
0.0076	0.00004536	0.5246	529.2	538.7
0.0100	0.00007854	0.9083	305.7	311.1
0.0120	0.0001131	1.308	212.3	216.1
0.0180	0.0002545	2.943	94.35	96.03
0.0290	0.0006605	7.639	36.35	37.00
0.0360	0.001018	11.77	23.59	24.01
0.0440	0.001521	17.58	15.79	16.07
0.0520	0.002124	24.56	11.30	11.51
0.0640	0.003217	37.20	7.463	7.596
0.0720	0.004072	47.09	5.897	6.002
0.0830	0.005411	62.57	4.437	4.516
0.0930	0.006793	78.56	3.534	3.597
0.1030	0.008332	96.36	2.881	2.933

第二表 英國新標準紫銅電纜

標準斷面積（平方吋）	實在斷面積（平方吋）	電纜中電線數目及電線之直徑（吋）	每千碼之重量（磅數）	每千碼之電阻力 Resistance 在佛氏六十度（Ohms）
0·0010	0·001018	1/·036	11·77	23·59
0·0015	0·001521	1/·044	17·58	15·79
0·0020	0·001942	3/·029	23·37	12·36
0·0030	0·003217	1/·064	37·20	7·462
0·0030	0·002994	3/·036	36·02	8·019
0 0045	0·004546	7/·029	54·39	5·251
0·0070	0·007005	7/·036	83·81	3·427
0·0100	0·01046	7/·044	125·2	2·294
0·0145	0·01462	7/·052	174·9	1·643
0·0225	0·02214	7/·064	264·9	1·084
0·0300	0·02840	19/·044	340·4	0·8468
0·0400	0 03960	19/·052	475·5	0·6063
0·0600	0·05999	19/·064	720·3	0·4002
0·0750	0·07592	19/·072	911·6	0·3162
0·1000	0·1009	19/·083	1211·0	0·23 0
0·1200	0·1168	37/·064	1403·0	0 2056
0·1500	0·1478	37/·072	1776 0	0·1625
0·20 0	0·1964	37/·083	2360·0	0·1223
0·2500	0·2465	37/·093	2963·0	0·09738
0·3000	0 3024	37/·103	363 · 0	0·07939
0·4000	0·4064	61/·093	4886·0	0·05908
0·5000	0·4985	61/·103	5994·0	0·04816
0·6000	0·6062	91/·093	7290·0	0·03961
0·7500	0·7435	91/·103	8942·0	0·03229
1·0000	1·0376	127/·103	12481·0	0·02314

工程心理調查報告(本校中學部)

南洋大學工程學會調查

工程心理調查一事乃於十三年冬當本校工程學會開全體大會時,經研究部部長顧君穀宜提出而蒙多數會員之贊仝者也.當初目的,乃欲藉調查之結果,得以公開研究各同學對于工程之意趣.俾從事工程教育者不致對于學生方面有隔閡之弊.或亦工程教育上之一大貢獻也.次年春,費君福燾長研究部,卽將此項計劃施諸實行,當時因事務繁多,祇能將大學部工科同學之調查粗告完畢.至于附中同學方面,乃在是年秋蒙中學主任徐先生佩璜竭力贊助方得進行,而于是年冬調查完竣此項中學部工程心理調查表,當初發出者達一百餘份,後來收集時祇得五十餘份,且本校附中同學爲數不下三百餘人,則此五十餘份之調查表似不過示少數人之心理,而未可代表多數同學也.但當時發此項調查表時,因份數不多,祇向三四年級全學散發,而填註此項調查表,亦不過隨各同學之便並非強迫然則填此區區五十餘份之同學,當諒必其對于工程一事確有幾分了解,而逐條答案必係出諸慎重,决非隨意塡寫以爲了事者可比.故此少數之調查表,雖不能代表全體同學之心理,然其結果决不因此而減少其價值可無疑也.(其淵附識)

世界電學名人逝世

張延祥

發明交流電機調裝電壓力之鐵萊耳氏(Allen A. Tirrill) 卽製 Tirrill Regulator 者,於去年十一月中逝世.

題問(一)你爲什麽進南洋

答 案	人 數	百 分 數
因南洋是著名學校	二 三	45.2%
因南洋有設備完善之工程科	二 一	41.2%
因南洋設立管理科	三	5.6%
因便於直接升入大學	一	2,0%
完全屬于旨從者	二	4.0%

問題(二)你對于文理兩科那一科覺得更有興趣

答 案	人 數	百 分 數
理科較有興趣者	三 二	59.3 %
文科較有興趣者	一 六	29.6 %
兩科均有興趣者	三	5.55%
兩科均無興趣者	二	3.7 %
不能辨別者	一	1.85%

(A)對于科學方面是喜歡理論方面還是喜歡演算方面

答 案	人 數	百 分 數
喜理論方面者	二 五	52,1%
喜演算方面者	七	14,6%
均所喜歡者	六	12,5%
均不歡喜者	一 〇	20,8%

(B)關于文學方面是喜歡實用文還是喜歡美術文

答 案	人 數	百 分 數
喜實用文者	三 一	57.5%
喜羣術文者	一 四	26.0%
均所喜歡者	九	16,5%

問題(三)你學畢業後想轉進工科還是鐵路管理科

答案	人數	百分數
進工程科者	三〇	55.5%
進管理科者	一六	29.6%
尙未中奪者	二	2.7%
擬轉學他校者	六	11.2%

問題(四)你課內最喜歡看那種書,課外最歡喜看那種書

(A)課內

答案	人數	百分數
國文	二	4.1%
英文	八	16.3%
社會科學	六	12.2%
自然科學	一一	22.5%
數學	七	14.3%
均所喜看	一〇	20.4%
均不喜看	五	10.2%

(B)課外

答案	人數	百分數
小說筆記	九	18.0%
文集(英文及國文)	九	18.0%
雜誌	七	14.0%
科學	六	12.0%
常識	三	6.0%
各種新文化及其他一切主義之作物	六	12.0%
日報	四	8.0%
其他	六	12.0%

問題(五)你看不看雜誌和報紙.

答　案	人數	百分數
喜看雜誌	〇	0
喜看報紙	三	5.6%
雜誌和報紙都看	五〇	94.4%

(A)什麼雜誌是你最喜看的

答　案	人數	百分數
東方雜誌	一六	
學文雜誌	六	11.3 %
英文週刊	四	75.5 %
英文雜誌	二	3.78%
婦女雜誌	二	3.78%
國聞週報	二	3.78%
其他	一三	24.51%
各雜誌均喜看	五	9.4 %
各雜誌均不看	三	5.6 %

(B)什麼報紙是你最喜看的

答　案	人數	百分數
申報	二二	46.8 %
新聞報	六.五	13.8 %
民國日報	三.五	7.45%
商報	二	4.25%
大陸報	二	4.25%
時報	一	2.1 %
各種小報	二	4.25%
其他	八	17.0 %

問題(六)你同上院同學常常接觸麼同你接觸最多的有什麼關係

係同鄉	一〇	20 %
係親戚	六	12 %
係純粹友誼	八	16 %
係舊同學	一	2 %
與上院同學不接觸者	二五	5o %

問題(七)你對于那一種人物最崇拜

答案	人數	百分數
科學家	一一	23.6 %
工程家	五	10.6 %
資本家	二	4.25%
文學家	五	10.6 %
政治家	九	19.2 %
教育家	九	19.2 %
美術家	四	8.5 %
其他	二	4.25%

問題(八)課外作何消遣

答案	人數	百分數
作室外遊戲運動	二〇	40. %
看雜誌	九	18. %
馬路上散步	六	12. %
弈棋	二	4 %
玩音樂	二	4 %
看小說	三	6 %
看電影	二	4 %
小吃	一	2 %
拍照	一	2 %
閒談	二	4 %
其他	三	6 %

孫中山陵墓所用石頭試驗報告書

楊 德 新 施 孔 範

南洋大學材料試驗室中國工程學會工程材料研究所試驗

材料. 一號二號三號四號四種石頭,由彥記建築事務所送來.

試驗目的 在確定四種中以何者爲最佳,以便建築孫中山陵墓工程處採擇.

觀察 在試驗之先,作詳愼之觀察.一號二號石頭之結構,似屬結晶體,含有石灰石石英及雲母在百分之五十以上.三號石頭之結構,作粒狀,甚脆,石灰石似在百分之五十以上.由石英及銅養膠成.四號石頭之結構甚屬密結,惟非結晶體含有石英.石灰石在百分之五十以上.至於色澤,一號四號白中雜以黑質,一號之黑質一部爲煤炭,指甲刮卽去.三號類似人造石 (Terrazo) 二號色略帶黃,甚老結,

比重試驗

記 錄 及 結 果

石頭號數	重 量	體 積	比 重
一	2291.0克姆	912.0立方生的米突	2.51
二	1528.3克姆	631.5立方生的米突	2.42
三	1356.7克姆	602.8立方生的米突	2.23
四	1041.2克姆	405.0立方生的米突	2.57

備註 求體積之法先用桶盛水繼置石頭於桶內水面之高度,在桶旁作一記號,乃將石頭取出,復加水於桶,至水面與記號平爲止所加入之水量卽爲石頭之體積.以上結果係三次試驗平均之結果.

耐久試驗 法將四種石頭,同置在盛水箱中,燃燒使沸,一兩小時後,取出使冷,置冰水中,日間一小時,夜間則全夜.如此繼續試驗,共十二次,計在沸水中二十四小時半,在冰水中七十四小時又三刻,沸水之溫度,華氏二百十二度.冰水之溫度,自華氏十九度至四十八度不等,試驗結果如下

一號二號石頭,並不因時熱時冷,而發現損壞等現象.

三號石頭發現裂縫,損失數小片,計重三克姆.

四號石頭發現裂縫,損失一小片,計重一克姆.

硬度試驗　法將兩種石頭,安置於刨床,上者固定,下者移動.磨擦之前先秤石頭重量,磨擦之後,再行秤之,兩種之中,失去重量較少者爲硬,然恐因固定與移動位置之不同,影響及於結果,乃將上下位置更易再試.將每種石頭在上下位置時失去之重量相加,再行比較以定孰者爲硬上述試驗治係屬創舉因試驗室未備有硬度試驗機故不能不變通辦理也茲將結果及記錄表列放下:

磨擦試驗記錄及結果

配合	位置	磨擦前之重量	磨擦後之重量	磨去重量	時間	每石磨去重量相加	較硬者
一號二號	一號在下	5磅 23.7克姆	5磅 21.3克姆	2.4克姆	45分	4.2克姆（一號）	二號
	二號在上	3磅167.8克姆	3磅165.4克姆	2.4克姆			
	一號在上	5磅 7.3克姆	5磅 5.5克姆	1.8克姆	45分	3.1克姆（二號）	
	二號在下	3磅163.7克姆	3磅163.0克姆	0.7克姆			
一號三號	一號在下	5磅 21.3克姆	5磅 17.5克姆	3.8克姆	45分	5.2克姆（一號）	一號
	三號在上	2磅447.7克姆	2磅440.3克姆	7.4克姆			
	一號在上	5磅 5.5克姻	5磅 4.1克姆	1.4克姆	40分	9.2克姆（三號）	
	三號在下	2磅432.0克姆	2磅430.2克姆	1.8克姆			
一號四號	一號在下	5磅 17.5克姆	5磅 16.4克姆	1.1克姆	45分	2.7克姆（一號）	一號
	四號在上	2磅131.3克姆	2磅128.4克姆	2.9克姆			
	一號在上	5磅 4.1克姆	5磅 2.5克姆	1,6克姆	30分	5.8克姆（四號）	
	四號在下	2磅109.4克姆	2磅106.5克姆	2.9克姆			
二號三號	二號在下	3磅165.4克姆	3磅165 克姆	0.4克姆	45分	1.9克姆（二號）	二號
	三號在上	2磅433.5克姆	2磅432.3克姆	1.2克姆			
	二號在上	3磅163 0克姆	3磅161.5克姆	1.5克姆	30分	2,9克姆（三號）	
	三號在下	2磅430.2克姆	2磅428.5克姆	1.7克姆			
二號四號	二號在下	3磅165.0克姆	3磅163.8克姆	1.2克姆	45分	1.7克姆（二號）	二號
	四號在上	2磅111.4克姆	2磅109.5克姆	1.9克姆			
	二號在上	3磅161.5克姆	3磅161.0克姆	0.5克姆	30分	5.8克姆（四號）	
	四號在下	2磅106.5克姆	2磅102.6克姆	3.9克姆			
三號四號	三號在下	2磅432.3克姆	2磅432.0克姆	0.3克姆	30分	10.8克姆（三號）	四號
	四號在上	2磅109.5克姆	2磅109.4克姆	0.1克姆			
	三號在上	2磅428.5克姆	2磅418.0克姆	10.5克姆	30分	1.0克姆（四號）	
	四號在下	2磅10.2.6克姆	2磅101.7克姆	0,9克姆			

評　語

觀上列結果悉四種石頭中,三號比重小,不耐久,不堅硬,應列下乘.四號比重雖大,然不耐久,硬度較一號二號亦遜,宜列第三.一號二號均能耐久,比重一號大於二號,硬度則一號不如二號;如以能抵抗風雨之侵入,及不易磨損爲建築要素,則二號其膺選也無疑,惟外觀則一號四號較二號爲美.

討　論

據通常學理,凡石頭之比重愈大則愈屬堅硬耐久,今一號四號之比重,較二號爲大,反脆而易損,不如二號之堅硬.證之於色澤,或係二號開採已久,一號四號新行開採故也.因石頭新從石礦開出,含有礦液(Quarry Sap,)易於磨損.按花岡石之比重當在2.72及2.64之間,所試四之比重均小於限數,是否是花岡石之優良者.一疑問也.

化驗火酒述要

楊耀文

酒之精粹曰醇(Alcohol.)醇有多種,其普通公式爲$C_nH_{2n+1}OH$,爲炭輕基化合物(Hydrocarbons)之一分類,屬有機化學,

醇之主要者有二種.一曰二炭醇(Ethyl alcohol,)亦稱酒精(Spirit of wine,)其公式爲C_2H_5OH.一曰一炭醇(Methyl alcohol,)亦稱木精(Spirit of wood,)其公式爲CH_3OH.因化合之不同,而各自有其性度與作用者也.

酒精之原料,爲穀類,馬鈴薯玉蜀黍等富有澱粉之物,將澱粉施以酒藥(Yeast,)經醱酵(Fermentation)之作用而醞釀成之.木精則由蒸溜木材而得.酒精無毒而木精有毒,皆可供作燃料之用,故世以火酒稱之.

按各國商律,凡醇之供作飲料用者,爲純淨之酒精,目爲奢侈品,取稅重其供作燃料或其他用途者,將酒精雜以木精,揮發油,皮理定(Pyridine,)或別種毒質.因其多寡而損益之,以防制混充飲料,目爲工業品,取稅輕.訂律綦嚴不容稍紊.吾華特畀其名曰火酒,所以別於飲料也.

今以市上發現火酒攙水,混充飲料,幾各種酒類,無一不以火酒爲之.於是有化驗火酒之舉,因述其化驗方法之提要,條舉如下.

一狀態(State) 凡品物之須經化驗者,必先審察其自然狀態,火酒之狀態,爲色澤清濁氣味數端.

二性質(Property) 火酒爲易於化氣之物質(Volatile matter,)其沸度當在攝氏表七十八度.因爲燃料之一,當易於燃燒,而發劇熱藍色之火焰,又火酒當溶解於清水,以太(Ether,)或迷蒙精(Chloroform)諸液質內,可將火酒分別加諸三者而攪和之,其溶解與否,了然可觀.

三比重(Specific grarity) 火酒較水分爲輕.其比重當在溫度攝氏表十五度半時檢定之,實施之步驟,與檢定其他液質之比重相彷彿,特製之儀器有比重秤,比重橹,酒精表等,其用器雖殊,其結果則同歸一致.

四酒精成分(Percentage) 純淨之酒精,頗不易致,其醞釀所得者,中含水分若干,爲勢所必不能免.旣知比重,則酒精之成分卽可檢查酒精量度表而知之,其重量百分數,容量百分數,可以同時檢得者也.

五配置量度(Preparation of exact strength) 火酒旣含有水分,則濃淡不同.有時各種化驗,須依適當之量度者,事前當先爲配置,大概以百分計五十爲適當量度.準檢定成分所得,濃於此者,和以適量之蒸溜水,淡於此者,和以適量之純酒精焉.

六酸量(Acidity) 火酒之中,容有醋酸存焉.惟投以紅藍試紙,當不生變化而爲中性.欲求其酸量,取火酒五十立方公分,用滴管(Pipette)注入蒸發皿內,以十分之一標準苛性鉀試液滴定之.應用之儀器爲量管(Burette,)

指示物爲石油精酸酐化輕養輪質(Phenolphthalein.)酸量若干,準下列公式而求得之.

每百立方公分之火酒含有醋酸量＝6×2N＝12N公絲(mg)

每百立方公分之純酒精含有醋酸量＝$\frac{100\times 12N}{容量百分數}$公絲

N指滴定之苛性鉀立方公分數.

七醋酸炭矯量(Esters) 將中性之火酒(即上滴定酸量之火酒)灌入返流儀器(Reflux apparatus)內加以二十立方公分十分之一標準苛性鉀試液.熱之使沸約一小時許,須令不至化氣有失.待涼定後.加二十立方公分十分之一標準硫酸.其覺硫酸過量者,爲苛性鉀與醋酸炭矯起感化之證.過量之硫酸.可將同標準苛性鉀試液滴定之.準此則醋酸炭矯量可依下列公式而求得其確數.

每百立方公分之火酒含有醋酸炭矯量＝8.81×2×N＝17,12.N公絲

每百立方公分之純酒精含有醋酸炭矯量＝$\frac{100\times 17.62N}{容量百分數}$公絲

N指滴定之苛性鉀立方公分數.

八總殘餘物(Total residue) 量注一百立方公分火酒於蒸發皿內.安置熱水鍋上.蒸發使乾.再放入電氣乾燥箱內約一小時.使其溫度常在攝氏表一百零五度.其乾燥剩餘之質,卽爲總殘餘物.待涼定而秤之.較空皿溢出之重量,卽其重量也.

九有機殘餘物(Organic residue) 將原盛總殘餘物之蒸發皿烈火灼之,則有機物質悉被燒去涼後再秤之其所喪之重量卽有機殘餘物之重量也.

十糠醛(Furfural) 注十立方公分火酒於試驗管內.試以新製之生色精(Aniline)十滴.並濃醋酸一立方公分.乃搖振試驗管,使之完全混合.於是安置於架上.其變成紅色者,爲含有糠醛之證.

十一醛類(Aldehyde) 以十立方公分火酒注入於蒸發皿內.滴入百分計

十之輕綠化間亞輪基二淡輕基質（Meta plenylenediamine Hydrochloride）試液,約一立方公分爲度.爾時宜注意,務使兩液不至混合,三四分鐘後其相接面發現濃密之黃色或橙黃色熱之則變成綠色而發光者,卽醛類之表顯也.或將火酒和以百分計二十之苛性鉀試液,因而溫熱之至沸乃止.如有醛類.則其結果變成黃色或紅棕色之液.因所含多寡不同,而色有濃淡之異點焉.

十二醋酮（Acetone）　取火酒半試管,加以苛性鈉液少許,滴入新配之百分計二之淡養基二鐵青化鈉（Sodium nitroprusside）試液七八滴.再加醋酸少許,其立變玫瑰紅色者爲含有醋酮之證.

十三酒油(Fusel oil)　將火酒五十立方公分,傾注於蒸發皿內,加以苛性鉀液三四立方公分,乃安置於水鍋上蒸發之.待其大部化氣而去,皿內僅存二三立方公分時,加稀硫酸少許,因聞其氣味與原有之酒油兩相比擬,卽可以辨別之.其加五六立方公分之甘油(Glycerin,)或一百立方公分之以太於同量火酒內,則蒸發將乾之際,不必再加硫酸,亦可以聞酒油之氣味.

十四木精（Methyl Alcohol）　取二十五立方公分火酒,和以同量之蒸溜水,加稀硫酸二十滴,並百分計一之鉻酸三四立方公分,乃灌注於蒸溜器內而蒸溜之.其結果則經養化之作用,而蒸溜所得之液,已變爲一炭間質（Formaldehyde,）因木精爲一炭輕基質故.火酒內不含木精,不有此變化也於是將十五立方公分之蒸溜液,試以一立方公分百分計四之輕綠化輪基代雙淡輕基質（Phenelhydlrazine hydrochloride）試液,與半立方公分百分計四之三綠化鐵液,再加二三立方公分濃鹽酸.其混和液若呈絳紅色者,是卽一炭間質之作用,爲火酒含有木精之現象,其他若嗎啡精（Morphine salts,）牛乳,均可作檢驗一炭間質之用品.間亦有以過錳酸鉀爲養化品者,其檢驗之手續,微有不同,其試液與現象,則不免互相懸絕矣.

十五皮理定(Pyridine bases)　將經過蒸溜之火酒約五六立方公分,試以百分計五之綠化鎘試液二三立方公分,因卽搖振之.如火酒含有皮理定者,則立呈白色之沉澱物焉.又法將同樣之火酒二十至三十立方公分,加稀硫酸而蒸發之.待其將乾之際,則加苛性鈉而重行蒸溜.如火酒含有皮理定者,其開始滴出之蒸溜液,卽當發難聞之氣味.因卽取以注之試驗管中,加濃鹽酸數滴.試以百分計一之綠化金試液,淡黃色之透明沉澱物生焉.將此沉澱洗而乾之.和以數滴之苛性鈉.加熱之後,當發皮理定之氣味.

以上諸端,爲化驗火酒必經之手續.雖火酒未必盡含諸質.要亦不必純淨.若飲料之酒精,苟其品物爲純粹之二炭醒,不過稍含微量之雜質而無毒者,是酒精而非火酒也.故酒精須絕對無毒,而火酒則不妨有毒,明乎此而知二者名稱之不同,有由來矣.

四庫全書述略(二)

杜定友

部次第七

四庫全書號稱十六萬八千卷,洋洋大觀.文瀾閣以厨貯藏.文津閣以架庋藏.玆並列其函數册數頁數以示盛况.(一)

四庫全書廚數架數函數册數頁數表

部次	廚數	架數	函數	册數	頁數
經	14	30	960	5482	263,604
史	24	33	1584	9476	697,287
子	14	22	1584	9055	524,160
集	32	28	2016	12262	665,865
	114	113	6,144	36,275	2,290,916

四庫全書部數卷數表

部	類	目	著錄				存目			
					附錄				附錄	
			部數	卷數	部數	卷數	部數	卷數	部數	卷數
經										
	易		159	1748	8	12	317	2400	1	1
	書		55	650	2	11	78	430	1	4
	詩		62	941	1	10	84	911		
	禮	周禮	22	453			37	277	2	44
		儀禮	22	343	2	127	12	111	4	22
		禮記	20	595	2	17	41	571	4	7
		三禮	6	35			20	310		
		通禮	4	563			6	247		
		雜禮	5	35			17	87		
	春秋		114	1801	1	17	118	1521		
	孝經		11	17			18	53		
	五經		31	681	1	36	43	351		
	四書		63	732			101	1396		
	樂		22	482			42	290		
	小學	訓詁	13	122			8	64		
		字書	36	478			68	602		
		韻書	33	313	1	2	61	537		
			678	9989	18	232	1071	10158	12	78
史	正史		38	3681			7	85		
	編年		38	2066			37	847		
	紀事		22	1205			4	26		
	別史		20	1485			36	1304		
	雜史		22	273			179	757		
	詔令		29	652			90	818		
	傳記	聖賢	2	7			32	231		
		名人	13	113			105	514		
		總錄	36	808			209	2337		
		雜錄	9	21			6	8		

	史鈔		3	48			40	1619		
	載記		21	380	2	9	21	106		
	時令		2	29			11	120		
	地理	宮殿					3	3		
		總志	7	941			17	437		
		都會	47	2752			108	2467		
		河渠	23	507			52	246		
		邊防	2	42			21	83		
		山川	7	113			97	900		
		古蹟	14	125			37	372		
		雜記	28	213			42	176		
		遊記	3	15			21	123		
		外記	17	98			34	83		
	職官	官制	15	375			42	354		
		官箴	6	17			8	107		
	政書	通制	19	2298			7	331		
		典禮	24	1051			48	357		
		邦計	6	53			45	249		
		軍政	4	271			2	5		
		法令	2	77			5	117		
		營建	2	35			6	18		
	目錄	經籍	11	424			14	41		
		金石	36	276			22	60		
	史評		22	382			100	868		
			550	20833	2	9	1508	16169		
子	儒		112	1694			307	2369		
	兵		20	153			47	388		
	法		8	94			19	105		
	農		10	195			9	68		
	醫		96	1813			94	681	6	25
	天文	推步	31	435			23	127		
		算書	25	208			4	23		
	術數	數學	16	147			29	166		

		占候	2	135			26	380		
		相宅	8	17			18	132	1	
		占卜	5	25			24	53		
		命書	15	53			18	29		
		陰陽	5	55			27	163		
		雜技					6	52		
	藝術	書畫	71	1066			52	223		
		琴譜	4	29			12	49		
		篆刻	2	9			5	24		
		雜技	4	4			11	48		
	譜錄	器用	24	199	1	3	31	219		
		食譜	10	19			23	60		
		草木	21	145			35	302		
	雜家	什學	22	177			185	740		
		什考	57	707			46	434		
		什說	86	632			168	1116		
		什品	11	83			26	172		
		什纂	11	536			198	2737		
		什編	3	92			45	1396		
	類書		64	6973			217	27500		
	小說	什事	86	580			101	475		
		異詞	32	724			60	352		
		瑣語	5	54			35	227		
	釋		13	312			12	117		
	道		44	442			100	463		
			922	17807	1	3	2012	41290	7	31
集	楚辭		6	65			17	75		
	別集		1075	18072			1267	17614		
	總集		164	9720			401	7216		
	詩文		64	730			85	524		
	詞典	詞集	59	103			25	43		
		詞選	12	262			14	99		
		詞話	5	19			5	13		

南北曲	3	17			8	35
	1388	28988			2122	25619

四庫全書部數卷數總計

部次	著錄		附錄		存目		附錄	
經	678	9989	18	232	1071,	10158,	12,	78
史	550	20833	2	9	1508,	16169		
子	922	17807	1	3	2012,	41290,	7,	31
集	1388	28988			2122,	25619,		
	3538	77617	21	244	6713	93236.	19,	109

合共　10,291 部　171,206 卷㊁

㊀民國九年十二月十二日時報

㊁各類數目係根據武英殿聚珍版四庫全書總目逐類摘出計算

沿革第八

乾隆三十八年,嵗次癸巳(1773),開四庫全書館.以紀昀爲總纂官.編修三百餘人.繕寫千五百人.全書二百二十九萬九百十六頁.均用手寫.字字整齊一筆不苟.起癸巳(1773,)迄甲辰(1783.)前後凡十二年.成書四部.仿浙江范氏天一閣式建四閣以貯之.一文淵閣.二文源閣.三文津閣.四文溯閣.是爲內廷四閣.若「曰淵曰源曰津曰溯.長源萬古之江河.紀世紀運紀金紀元.恢耀九霄之日月.」㊀繼因江浙爲文人淵藪.特命一如內廷所藏.繕寫全書三部.於揚州鎮江杭州三郡建閣以貯之.曰文滙閣.曰文宗閣.曰文瀾閣.

全書分四部.各以色別.經部青色絹面.史部赤色絹面.工部月白色絹面集部灰黑色絹面.

文淵閣.書第一部.成於辛丑(1781.)閣在北京文華殿後.現由內務部清室善後委員會保管.不日將移至北京京師圖書館陳列云.

文溯閣.書第二部.成於壬寅(1782.)閣在奉天行宮.無闕.民國〇年移存北京.去秋由奉天省要求取回仍存奉天文溯閣.(1783.)文源閣.書第三部.成

於癸卯閣在圓明園一八六〇年,美法聯軍之役,全部被燬.

文津閣,書第四部.成於甲辰.閣在熱河避暑山莊.無闕.現存北京圖書館

文匯閣,在揚州大觀堂.毀於洪揚之亂.全部散失.

文宗閣在鎮江金山寺;亦毀於洪揚之亂.

文瀾閣在杭州聖因寺行宮.洪揚之亂,泰半散失.後經杭紳丁松氏及錢恂搜集補鈔,得三分之二.世稱三部半大書.半部指此.

四庫全書佳本極多.當時已鐫刻作傳著,僅什之一.其後歷年雖由各叢書陸續刊刻.似仍多鈔錄儲藏,外間無由窺覩者也.

㊀見表文

印行第九

四庫全書爲世界空前鉅製.百餘年來,無與比倫.初存七部.現僅及半.如不設法印行,自有散失之虞.徐世昌時遂有印行四庫之議.時朱桂莘有歐洲之遊.遂印有樣本,圖謀銷售預約.後忽中止.民國十三年商務書館擬將奉天之存書.運滬印行.後爲曹琨左右所阻.戰後由奉張帶回.今年九月經閣議通過議決付印.

茲錄關於印行四庫全書文體之則,以見其經過情形及將來計劃.

教育部呈　大總統議立四庫全書印行處並派大員督理文.㊀

呈爲照議設立四庫全書印行處,擬請派員督理仰祈鑒核事.竊查本部前呈遵核顧問葉恭綽條陳振興文紀八事,業經奉　令交辦在案.現經國務會議議決.印行四庫全書一項辦法,由政府提倡獎助.設立機關,妥定章程並推舉聲望卓著人員辦理各等.因卷帙浩繁,刊行匪易.應卽設立四庫全書印行處,以爲提絜推行之總匯.所有該處行訂章籌款一切事宜,擬請明令特派前內務總長朱啓鈐爲督理會同本部籌議進行.如蒙俞允,實行增進文紀,闡揚國光,大有裨益.是否有當,理合具呈敬請鑒核施行.謹呈.

九年十月九日　大總統令

四庫全書爲我國最鉅典籍.名播海外.今百載前之分存七部,僅餘其三,旣有日即淪散之虞,而承學之儔,亦末由得資沾溉.中外人士多有以印行爲請者自應設法仿印,以廣流傳而垂久遠.玆據教育部呈請付印,並特派朱啓鈐督理印行四庫全書事宜,印行會商主管各部,擬定辦法,迅速從事,以副本大總統闡揚文化之至意.此令

紀二十四日之國務會議㊁

影印四庫全書,教育部先後籌備,已屆兩載.遲至上星期,始將一切手續,如檢查全部內容,接給影印工程等辦理完竣.昨日國務會議席上,教長章士釗就全案經過,提出報告.並將與商務書館所訂合同,交衆傳觀.討論結果決定照案通過.由教育部遴選專員,押運全籍至滬,就地監督商務印書館進行影印裝訂工事.所印卷帙,預定分甲乙兩種.甲種,三十部.係非賣品.準備將來作爲贈送世界各大國及國內圖書館陳設之用.每部印資一萬元,總共三十萬元.此款由各國退還庚子賠款中,發展文化事業項下提撥.乙種八十部,每部預約特價三千元,由商務書館按照商業性質,承印而銷售之.至關係移運事宜,則由交通部令飭京奉,津浦,滬甯,三路,特備車輛,妥爲裝載於沿途經過,愼加保護.同時並頒發明令一道,昭示國人.謂

四庫全書爲吾國學術總匯.清初曾抄就七部,庋藏內府.現據教育部呈請多加影印,以廣流傳.事關文化,自屬可行.着將全書運滬,由部派員就地監督工事.藉以宏富珍秘典藉,公諸天下.補益文化,導揚國光,本執政有厚望焉此令

㊀九年十一月教育公報

㊁十四年九月二十七日時報

雜議第十

印行四庫全書,甚盛事也而全書卷帙繁博,印行亟宜審愼.竊有議者.印行紙張格式,以及裝釘函架,宜一仍其舊,以存其眞.此其一.每書宜依次編號

然後可以案號陳列,而便於取閱.此其二.各書號次,宜另印簡明目錄,附註於后,以便即目求號.棄號求書.此其三.宜編書名及著者姓名索引,亦將號次附注於每書之後,則雖不知某書入某類者,亦可尋閱.分類出入之弊,亦可免去此其四.宜編讀四庫全書法,按類臚列,摘要指示,以免學者望洋興嘆.此其五宜擇要印行草行本,以備學者採購.此其六.宜搜取四庫未收書及禁燬之書以窺全豹,此其七.宜編續四庫全書搜集乾嘉以來之名著此其八.(各節辦法從略)

民國十年,逆京訪葉恭綽陳圓庵氏,據云;正派員點查四庫全書釐訂卷册字數,結果未得其詳.前月教育部報告點查經過,當係指此.

民國十四年四月,偕美國鮑士偉博士赴杭演講,遇浙江公立圖書館館長章仲銘氏,據云.文瀾閣四庫全書已於二月間完全補鈔完竣.則向謂三部半者,現已成四部矣.亦一好消息也.

七月在甯遇教育廳長沈彭年氏,謂教育部因印行四庫全書至少需三百萬元.現經費支絀,擬先行鈔繕一份.然亦需六十萬元.今又經閣議,交商務書館承印.則所議又變更矣.

九月,聞商務印書館編輯所長王雲五氏言,承印四庫全書雖合同已定但尚有種種阻碍,去事實實現,尚遠云云.

附錄

兹將關於四庫全書之著述,凡傳聞眼見者,略舉如下.疏漏知所不免,幸閱者指正.

一,四庫全書提要考證二卷　見通志卷一百十一至十二

二,四庫全書敍一卷　慎始基齋叢書

三,四庫全書表文箋釋四卷　林樸山箋釋　求恕齋叢書

四,四庫全書考證一百卷　武美殿聚珍版發書

五,批注四庫全書簡明目二十卷　邵懿辰

六部亭知見書目四卷　莫友芝

七,書目答問　張文襄之洞

八,四庫全書的北宋八別集　西諦　見時事新報十四年十月十日

九,印行四庫全書之經過　見申報十四年九月八日

十西報述四庫全書之歷史　見時報九年十二月十二日

十一,對于四庫全書印行之意見　濟滄　見申報九年十一月十五日

十二,四庫全書樣本及印行計劃(?)　葉恭綽等

十三,四庫書目考異　陳援庵

十四,四庫全書述略　王伯祥（見小說月報十六卷十二期第一至廿頁民國十四年十二月十日報務）

十五,四庫全書消息,　陳存仁,　申報十四年十月六日

十六,宛委別藏　阮元

是篇經葉恭綽先生多所指正附此致謝

四庫全述略（一）正誤表

頁數	行數	字數	誤	正
77	12	16	焚	焚
78	9	28	係	繫
78	11	25	板	版
78	13	13	莊	藏
78	22	2	東	樂
80	6	19	面	而
80	8	13	石	右
80	9	3	問	間
80	10	8	經	徑

80	10	22	朋	明
80	18	12	綠	錄
81	14	12	又	文
82	12	18	報	館
82	18	8	遣	遺
82	18	16	驛	繹
82	25	5	爲	初
82	25	9	韶	韻
83	1	1	入	人
83	2	8	績	續
83	6	23	客	家
83	8	23	間	聞
83	13	23	己	已
83	20	18	問	聞
84	8	13	己	巳
84	9	4	韶	韻
84	9	8	己	已
84	18	24	曰	日
85	3	20	作	流
85	6	5	未	本
85	10	17	難	雖
85	12	14	爲	然
85	12	22	緝	楫
85	18	1	調	詞
86	15	5	韶	韻
87	9	8	樂	縣
90	1	11	囘	四
90	4	12		應加㊃
90	5	4	㊁	㊀
90	6	4	㊂	㊁
90	7	4	㊃	㊂
90	8	4		應加㊃章學誠校讎通義敍

工程學會大事紀(中華民國十四年)

余昌菊

本校以五卅事變致上學期大考延至下半年舉行.本會會務上學期亦未及結束.故本會工作之始,已在十月下旬矣.

十月二十七日　晚七時在十二號教室開全體大會,結束上學期會務及選舉本屆新職員.

十月二十四日　下午四時在學生會集室開第一次職員會議,討論進行方針.結果除參觀演說外,决分研究部爲工程常識工廠調查,及數理三股.凡本會會員至少須加入其中之一股.

十一月八日　參觀雙輪牙刷廠及中華琺瑯廠.加入者計有五十人,

雙輪牙刷廠成立已有五年.資本約十萬元,出貨有五十餘種.目下銷路甚廣.往往供不應求.原料出自四川及美國.聞不日即將擴充云.

中華琺瑯廠資本計三萬元.本屬於中華職業學校之琺瑯科.現因該科取消,故於三年前改作商辦.出品有五十餘種,日用品佔其大半貨色甚精美,與舶來品不相上下.原料多來自外國.製法甚簡.先以洋鐵做成之模型,鍍以琺瑯粉.入窰烘後,即成.爲時不過十餘分鐘耳.

十一月十一日　晚七時請本東教授王爾綱先生演講,聽衆有七八十.人.王先生爲本校舊同學.對於鐵路上之經驗頗多.裨益同學,實屬匪淺.講題爲機械救國.其演辭分爲三部.(一)吾國與他國天然富源之比較.(二)人力發展之比較.(三)救國之方.

十一月十八日　請本校教授范藹春先生演講水泥製造法.先生演辭,除製造法之大概外,幷及上海水泥廠採用之水泥濕造法之詳細步驟.

十一月二十一日,　參觀徐家匯固本製皂廠.加入者有三十餘人.該廠原爲德人創辦.歐戰沒讓與華商張雲江,再讓與五洲藥房.該廠除製皂外,幷設製藥部木塞部.凡五州家用各藥.皆在此配製.防疫藥水亦在此製濾.五卅以來銷路日廣.將來發展未可限量.

十二月二日　參觀愛迪生電燈泡廠.該廠爲美國愛迪生之分廠.設玻璃及製燈二部.除我國所銷之「奇異」燈泡外,卽各藥房所用之藥瓶,亦屬該廠承辦.

十二月十二日　由范謁春先生介紹至龍華水泥廠參觀.加入者有四十餘人.由該廠工程師張其學先生領導.張先生爲本校舊同學.招待周到,解釋詳明,裨益參觀諸同學實匪淺鮮.該廠創自民國三年.資本有二百萬.工作日夜不息.每日可出水泥一千二百桶.內有1800K.V.A.透平發電機一只,以供給全廠原動力.更有提士引擎一只,以備透平修理時或損壞時之用.該廠之設備及管理,均甚精密,頗足爲他廠法.現在該廠在水泥事業中已佔一重要位置矣.

十二月十九日　由吳玉麟先生領至上海華商電車公司參觀.加入者有三十餘人.招待者爲該廠工程師徐恩第先生.徐先生爲吳先生之同級友亦吾校之舊同學也.該公司設有8000 K.V.A.及4000 K.V.A.之透平機各一座并有750 K.W.之變流機一座.供南市電車之用.現又新添BLW.鍋鑪兩座.以備發展.該廠并設有修理間,凡馬達之有損壞者,均可由該廠自行修理,不須外求.營業可分爲電力.電車.電燈三項.惟因附近工廠不多.電力之需要尙少至於電車.則因養路及修理費甚鉅,欲期獲利,亦非易事.故最發達者厥惟電燈一項云.

二月二十四日　晚七時假大禮堂開全體大會.到會者有百八十餘人教職員之莅會者.有凌校長及王爾絅吳玉麟.周明誠.李振吾.徐君陶諸先生首由主席余昌菊報告半年會務.次由研究部部長成其淵報告該部進行大概.校長及各教授亦均致訓辭.其後卽選舉下屆職員.散會時已鐘鳴十下矣

本屆	職員
會長	余昌菊
副會長	梁興貴
參觀部部長	陳蔚觀
研究部部長	成其淵
編輯部部長	費福纛
出版部部長	王信吾
通訊書記	歐陽藻
記錄書記	宗之發
會計	蔣大恩

下屆	新職員
會長	梁興貴
副會長	陳蔚觀
參觀部部長	余昌菊
研究部部長	夏清棋
編輯部部長	成其淵
通訊書記	宗之發
記錄書記	歐陽藻
會計	顧毓瑔

南洋一覽稿

（一 續）

柴福沅 芷湘甫擬

建築

主要校舍三座. 上院. 中院. 小學.
學生宿舍三所. 西宿舍. 新中院. 校外宿舍.
職教員宿舍七所.

特殊建築四所. {圖書館. 體育館. 附游泳池. 雨操場. 調養室.

工廠九處. {翻砂廠,電機試驗室木工廠,鍛鐵廠,相聯作一排. 金工廠,機械試驗室,材料試驗室,合一所. 鍋爐室. 無線電試驗室.

本校建築之主要部分爲上中院,居全校之北部,東西並峙樓各三層,中院建築,以外觀平整勝,上院則美術意味較多,且有鐘樓,更爲宏鉅.上中院下層均辦公室,中層教室,上層宿舍,其前爲大操場,綠草如茵地廣三四十畝,操場東爲圖書館,亦三層樓,雄偉壯麗,與上院埒圖書館之北,有屋三排,共七所皆職教員宿舍,操場之西與圖書館相望者,爲新建之體育館,其南亦職教員宿舍,其西南爲新建之調養室其北爲雨操場再北爲西宿舍,大學四年級生寓此,中院之後爲新中院,中學三年級生居之其後小屋成行,爲各工廠,再後爲機械工廠及金工廠,作曲尺形,建以鋼骨凝土,其一旁則與圓柱形之水塔相連,廠後小樓巍然,立於全校之西北隅者,爲無綫電試驗室,其前有天線桿二,能與各國通報,此本校建築之最特色者,操場之南爲校園,中有本校創始人盛杏蓀先生銅像,旁爲同學白雅餘先生之紀念碑,花園之南,附屬小學在焉,有二層樓之屋,作凹字形,禮堂膳廳在其西南,另有職教員宿舍,背臨校門內甬道,出校門,隔路正對者,爲校外宿舍,有二層樓三排,大學新生居之,其後爲本校學生會所辦之義務學校,今校門外馬路有放闊之議,校外宿舍不久當拆卸改建也.

民國十年秋,主任張劍心先生發起籌建三大建築,全校師生,無不歡然贊成,諸校董先生亦皆樂爲提倡,當時預計,體育館約八萬五千圓,學生會集室約五萬五千圓,調養室約二萬圓,計共需十六萬圓,於是開會集議,印發捐册,本校職教員學生認捐之外,復分伍勸募,至十三年夏,鳩工庀材,開始興建時以願大難償,款不易集,乃併會集室於體育館之內,一屋兩用,未始非計之得也,今二大建築已先後落成,美輪美奐,洵足與上中院圖書館相比美,用款約共十二萬六千圓,而募捐至今,將及四載,實收之款,僅九萬四千圓,收支相抵不敷尚鉅.

設　備

1 物理試驗室……………………五間
儀器一千五百餘件

2 化學試驗室……………………五間
標本三百件…………器具萬件
藥劑六百瓶

3 木工廠…………………………四間
機器十九具………手工器具千餘

4 金工廠………………………二大間
機器二十四具………零件二百餘

5 翻砂廠………………………一大間
大鑪二座……………零件具備

6 鍛鐵廠………………………一大間
大鑪九座…………大小器具百件

7 鍋鑪室………………………一大間
鍋鑪三具

8 電機試驗室……………………三間
電機四座………小機及零件三百

9 機械試驗室………………分二部
機器九具……………零件具備

10 無線電試驗室…………小樓一座
機器二十三具……零件二百八十

11 材料試驗室……………………一間
機器三具……………零件數十

12 圖書館………………三層樓一座
中文書三萬九千餘册…外國文書八千六百册……雜誌一百三十種……………………日報十七種

13 體育館………………三層樓一座
附游泳池

14 調養室………………二層樓一座

15 校園……………………………二區

本校設備,除辦公室,教室,宿舍,禮堂,膳廳,及一切附屬部分外,有各試驗室,各工廠,圖書館,體育館等.玆一一分別述之

物理試驗室在上院二層樓東南隅,計力學及熱學試驗室一間,電學試驗室二間,光學暗室一間,儀器及預備室一間.又教室一間.有儀器大小一千五百餘件,除教授講演應用外,可供大學初二年級及中學四年級學生各八組(每組二人)同時試驗之用.大學試驗計度量衡等基本量法物性試驗以及力學熱學,磁學,電學聲學光學等試驗共六十種適合二年之需.每種儀器,同時可供二組之用.課本由本校教授自編.其程度以歐美著名大學所用者爲準,對於工程上之應用,尤爲注重.

化學試驗室設中院樓下西端,內置學生試驗桌九座.煤氣管,自來水管通風管,水槽,汽水,蒸溜器等,設備俱全.同時可容學生四十人試驗.桌下共設學生置物櫃一百零八,二人共用一櫃,計可供大學初二年級學生二百十六人之用.室旁設天平室,藥品室,預備室及儲物室各一間.天平室有分析化學天平三具,普通化學天平八具.藥品室儲無機化學標本約三百件,各項試驗用品及分析化學用各項器具大小約萬具.藥劑大小約六百瓶.足供普通化學,無機定性分析,初級定量分析,及工業化學試驗之用.尤以檢驗煤,水,烟突洩氣,及機器滑油等應用器具爲完備.又教室一間.在試驗室對面.

翻砂廠在上院後.備有鎔鐵鑪,型心鑪,風箱,搖浮桶,盛鎔鐵桶,及各種造型器具.爲學生實習之用.

電機試驗室在翻砂廠西,共分三室.東爲本校電燈總開關處.中爲直流電室,西爲交流電室.直流電室置備發電機兩座.分別與五十馬力及二十馬力感應發動機相接.其他大小發動機,發電機計十五座.專供試驗之用.交流電室備有大號交流發電機兩座.(一與煤氣機相接)感應調整機,感應發動機,轉換電流機,三萬弗脫標準試驗變壓機,水銀更正電流器,以及其他感應式拒力式發動機等.電機儀器室並備電流表,安培表,電力表,電流調節器

交流電變向表,感應電圈蓄電器,以及防電等器,足供試驗之用,與歐美近代電機實驗室相埒,並可試驗單行或多行之電圈,及用電圈所製之發電機電動機等,俾學生得充分之經驗.

木工廠在電機試驗室之西.分二部,西部二室,外間分置木桌十餘,各附以虎鉗,爲學生實習手工之地.內間則木工工作處,東部大小各一室,大室置木車床十一,鋸床三,刨床軋床鑽床各一.又電動機二具,所以運動上述各機器者也.小室儲手工器具千餘件,學生實習,先習手工,次用機器.

木工廠之西爲鍛鐵廠,有鎔鐵爐九具,大小器具約百件,專爲學生練習鎔鐵打鐵之用.

與電機試驗室通連者爲鍋鑪室,可容鍋鑪四.現備有三具.(一)白壳維壳橫式水管鍋鑪.(二)安梅火管式鍋鑪.(三)發漢火車頭式鍋鑪.其白壳維壳及安梅兩鍋鑪與機械試驗室各汽機相接.此外更備有抽水機及鋼製水池等.以備量鍋水之用.再進爲機械試驗室.

機械試驗室及金工廠同在一建築物內.外觀作曲尺形.金工廠居左,其右翼二層樓房,乃機械試驗室之主要部分.內分蒸汽機試驗室.內燃機試驗室,材料試驗室.上樓爲製圖室教室及工廠辦公室.蒸汽機試驗室備有克的蒸汽透便發電機.華新頓蓄電機.華新頓壓氣機.單式高速度蒸汽機,各式唧筒,以及水溝水塔等.內燃機試驗室備有葛羅司雷煤氣機,附置換水乾煤氣機.電流平衡機,諾武石油機.佛林特華林揮發油機,葛羅倍福伯揮發油機等.而葛羅倍福伯揮發油機則與發電機相接,餘地備試驗汽車及貨車之用.

材料試驗室置雷耳普通材料試驗機,水力壓機,磚形水泥試驗機等.儀器室備有氣壓表,氣壓眞空計,標準量試驗器,量熱表,高熱計,燃料及油類之分析器,量水流口閘,片導管,測伸展性表,變撓器,氣壓表,標準篩,維加及摩磁針,高等引力儀器,蒸汽調温器,去潮鑪,磚形模型等,爲試驗各種機器及建築材料之用.

金工廠連接於機械試驗室.樓上一大室.分置虎鉗二十二具.爲學生實習手工之地.下層有大小車床十一.鑽床四.刨床三.鋸車二.解鐵床鉸床各一其他器具約共二百餘件.又電動機二具.爲起動各機器之用.學生實習.先習手工.次用機器.

無線電試驗室爲二層之小樓.教室及電話實驗室在下.無線電信收發處.機器儲藏室.無線電信實驗室在上.計有天線四具.一爲曲形.長二百尺.高一百五十尺.一爲單線式.一爲籠形.一爲地線式.室內置有旋轉火花隙發報機一具.其最高電能力爲一啓羅華德發報兼發電話機一具.其電能力爲二十華德.收報機二具.真空管兩級放大器三具.本校自製真空管收報機二具法德及美國沿太平洋岸各大電台之報.均可接收.關於學生實驗之設備.則有電長計八具.測波器六具.電話聽筒十付.英美德法各類真空管六十餘件及電流電壓計.磁感圈.聚電器等大小共二百餘件.更有高壓蓄電池一具.其電壓爲四百五十弗脫.爲真空管試驗不可缺之設備.電動變流機一座.五百週率發電機一座.真空管發電器一具.其週率高下.可隨意變更.電橋二座.變流器二具.耗阻標準器二具.高週率電橋一座.關於無線電實驗應用機件.均略具焉.

圖書館樓下爲辦公室.成績室.日報室.售書處.及博物陳列室.中層爲借書處.閱書室.雜誌室.備有中西報紙十七種.中西雜誌百三十種.其中以關於工程及管理者爲多.上層爲藏書室.計有中文書約三萬九千餘册.中以史部爲最多.西文書約八千六百册.中以工程爲最多.又有原版古今圖書集成一部.爲珍異之品.該館逐日開放.除供給本校師生閱讀參考外.校外人一律招待.

體育館下層爲各辦公室.招待室.操練室.浴室.及更衣室等.後附游泳池樓上爲籃球場.廣五十尺.長九十尺.爲規定尺寸中之最大者.四周空際繞以跑道.備冬季練習跑步之用.南端有講演台.面向籃球場.場中可容聽衆千三

百人.三層樓南端有辦事室三間,其餘二三層上下通連.屋頂開天窗.俾比賽籃球及室內運動時,光線充足.而亦不致耀目.二層樓正面.臨大操場者爲觀賽台.大操場比賽足球或其他運動時,來賓坐此,可望見之.

調養室樓下有內症室,外症室,看護室各一,病室四,藥品室一.應用藥品悉備.樓上有病室九.看護室一.浴室一,儲物室二,東向洋台裝玻窗及紗窗,備病者曝曬日光及呼吸新鮮空氣之用.校章凡學生患病較重得校醫證明者得居病室.便治療.防傳染也.

校園雜植花木,有亭二.與盛杏蓀先生銅像白雅餘先生紀念碑相間.地不甚廣而點綴有致.課餘游散處也.圖書館後有土山,山有花樹,其前立圖書館捐款人榮熙泰先生銅像,布置略同校園.

附屬小學.另有理化儀器室,圖書標本室.操場,花園等等,專備小學生之用.

南洋季刊創刊號正誤表

發刊辭

頁數	行數	正　　　誤
1	22	「舊」下脫「有」
2	1	「撰述」應作「撰述員」
2	2	員字衍
2	9	「國」下脫「內」

編輯者言

頁數	行數	正　　　誤
2	17	「文藝」應作「文苑」

電力事業發達之掌故

頁數	行數	正　　　誤
1	1	，應在「與」字之前
2	16	「一百陸拾萬萬」誤「一百陸百万万」
2	12	誠非偶然，「誠」誤「事」
3	23	第一字「力」删
4	6	起二日「均為…」應與他行並無須排進
2	17	電解之始，「始」誤「治」
2	底行	應為 $df = \frac{m}{r^2}$ I dl Sing
5	11	「莫屬」二字橫畫應删
2	13	外緣「緣」誤「緣」
6	10	七年「距」墨氏，「距」字應增
2	13	發電「廠」及電力…，「廠」字應增

吾國水泥事業之概況

頁數	行數	正　　　誤
8	32	在此項之末漏去「濕」字
9		「濕法製造水泥之程序」上行「在此處加入定量之水」前有「△」記號

頁數	行數	正 誤
2		乾法製造水泥之程序中「煤粉磨」非「粉煤磨」
11	1	「構造」應作「製造」
		英國現行所得稅制度之研究
20	11	2鎊3先令與4鎊6先令當作2先令3辨士與4先令6辨士
		空隙與完全擠縮在蒸汽循環上之利弊論
34	13	Cearance 應作 Clearance
35	6	燕應作之
35	16	Energy Balance Line.
37	8	Ef' 應作 f'e
38	4	C' 應作 c
38	4	『等 C'ckC' 而于』 應作『等于 C'ckc'. 而』
2	5	d'rdd' 應作 d'kdd'
2	20	線應作汽
		Desegn Of A Reinforced Concrete Floating Dock
40	2	"Very" 誤 "Veay
,,	29	"and" 誤 "ank"
42	7	"of" 誤 "ol"
43	12	"Structure" 誤 "Streecture"
44	8	"$9\frac{1}{2}$" 誤 "$9\frac{1}{4}$"
46	8	"either side a for," "a" 應刪
,,	12	"and" 誤 "aed"
,,	13	"On" 誤 "on"
,,	23	"Comportments" 脫去 "S"

頁數	行數	正 誤
,,	28	DESIGN" 誤 "DFSIGN."
47	11	"Imqrovements" 誤 "Imbnovements"
48	21	"Center" 誤 "Conter"
,,	24	"height" 誤 "hight"
51	30	"Per" 誤 "Pes"
52	3	"incidentals" 誤 "incidentels-

原動力學發明家傳略

頁數	行數	正 誤
53	6	Ludevig W 誤 ev
,,	17	揚 誤 楊
54	1	徑 誤 經
55	8	呎 誤 咫
,,	10	行首加而二字之後應空一格
,,	11	行首想字應在13行之首
,,	20	呎 誤 咫
,,	21	呎 誤 咫

上海法商電氣公司參觀記載

頁數	行數	正 誤
56	8	"Compagnie" 誤 "Chmpagnie
,,	16	"Cudic" 誤 "Cnbic"
,,	20	"Winterthnr" 脫去 "t"
58	17	"併車費時" 應另起一行又同行括弧內 "min" 前脫去 "6"
59	7	"Suisse" 誤 "Stisse"

日晷及時差

頁數	行數	正 誤
59	11	「校」誤「洨」

附圖之位置不合Pp線應稍斜Z點應居正中

頁數	行數	正	誤
2	20	「QMa」 誤 「QMA」	
2	22	aZP 誤 AZP	
60	3	bPb' 誤 BPb'	
2	4	Eb' 誤 EB'	
		不兌現紙幣應如何兌現	
66	19		英國綠背劵當作美國綠背劵
		電氣傳影之新發明	
70	20	簡提	簡捷
		哲學與科學之定義	
75	22	斕然	自然
		化工新志	
90	6	「囿」誤宥	
,,	9	「艾」誤爻	
92	3	「木」誤水	
,,	7	「綻」誤椗	
,,	18	「至」字衍	
93	22	「業」誤學	
,,	23	「抽」誤節	
94	8	「斥」誤斤	
95	3	「遇」誤過	
,,	17	「在美」二字衍	
,,	18	「之二十」三字應排十九行	
,,	19	「國」字衍	
96	19	「料」誤科	

頁數	行數	正　誤
97	1	「比」誤法
2	10	「汽」誤氣
,,	15	「廿」字後缺「爲」字所誤之
,,	16	「貿」誤貿

秤 杆 秤 錘 之 小 科 學

頁數	行數	正　誤
97	末行	述誤說
98	9	括號內三一五前應有小數點
99	15	行末是鈎字
100	圖	Wz應在鉄鈎旁
101	12	段 誤 叚
,,	14	括號前應有十（加號）
,,	16	括號內應作 3.05+0.5=3.55兩

六 十 年 來 中 國 交 通 四 政 大 事 年表

頁數	行數	正　誤
105	23年	『蘆漢借款合同』應改蘆漢借款一萬二千五百萬法郎
,,	,,	應加『法使要求築滇越鉄路』一條
,,	24年	應加『與法訂滇越鉄路章程』一條
,,	25年	應加『英人索雲南境內修路利益』一條
,,	26年	應加『盛宣懷與美合興公司訂粤漢鉄路借款美金四千萬元』
106	27年	應加『英使請求准築鎮緬鉄路』一條
,,	28年	『盛宣懷』誤『岑春煊』
	30年	應加『日本擅築安奉輕便鉄道又接修奉天新民屯間鉄道』

頁數	行數	正	誤
107	33年	路政第三條『債額』誤『債頗』	
109	3年	『派端方』應接於上行『以抵制』下	
,,	民國元年	電政第一條『北京無線電局…』應另起一條與『並購設同式無線電台一座…』相接	
111	7年	電政第一條『桑』字衍	
		應加『海軍部與日商三井洋行訂雙橋無線電台合同』一條	
,,	8年	路政第二條第四行『郎』字應在下行末字『法』之後	

遊張家口賜兒山記

頁數	行數	正	誤
113	3	盜底	溘底

秋草

頁數	行數	正	誤
115	末	白傳	白傅
125	26	「南洋學校」下應加「已於」	

南洋大學技擊部十三年來發達史

頁數	行數	正	誤
127	11	行首觸字應在次行之首	
128	3	攝影搏擊應作技擊攝影	
128	14	賑誤	賬
130	5	行末歐字應在次行之末	

同學會紀載

頁數	行數	正	誤
130	14	籌　誤　溥	
132	20	圖書　應作科學	

校友要訊

頁數	行數	正	誤
134	3	星後脫易字，	繫後脫簡字
134	22	成 誤 城	
135	6	順誤泰，泰誤濟	
135	14	學留二字顛倒	
135	18	八後脫日字	
137	1	杭 誤 抗	

南洋一覽稿

頁數	行數	正	誤
144	14	滑 誤 縎	
126	12	賑 誤 賬	
147	13	毓後脫崑字	
150	下截	脫標題校 址二字	

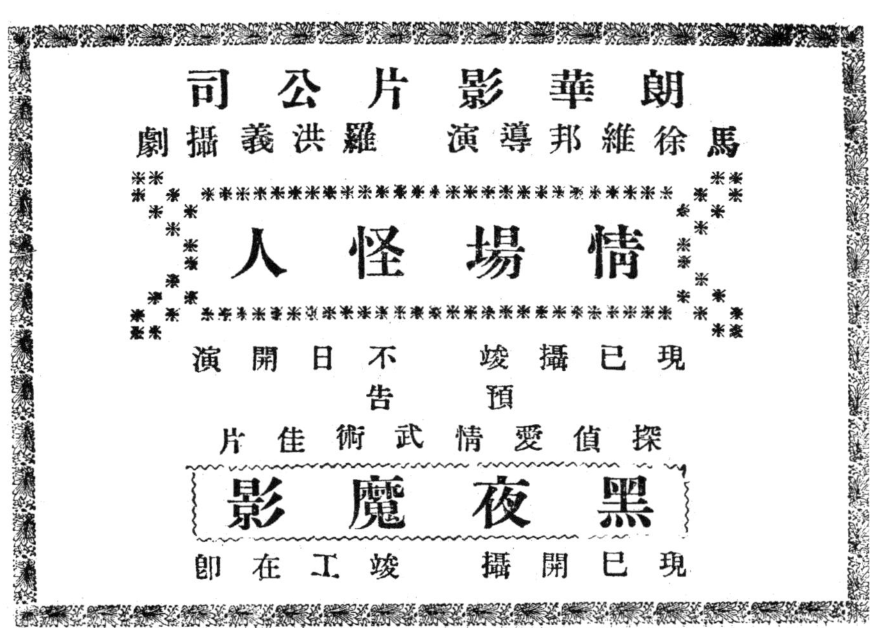
朗華影片公司
馬徐維邦導演 羅洪義攝劇
情場怪人
現已攝竣 不日開演
預告
探偵愛情武術佳片
黑夜魔影
現已開攝 竣工在即

銀行公會會員銀行

新華商業儲蓄銀行廣告

本銀行於民國三年創辦資本總額五百萬元已實收二百萬元公積金九十萬元專辦商業儲蓄銀行一切業務并得受政府委托辦理特種儲蓄事項其營業種類分列於下

定期存款　活期存款　抵押放款　貼現放款

各處匯兌　收解款項　買賣證券　兌換貨幣

各種儲蓄　流通儲券　公共儲金　四季儲金

總辦事處
北京分行　北京廊房頭條　電話南局一八四〇　二二〇四

天津分行　天津法界中街七號路　電話南局三三七　八四一

上海分行　上海天津路五〇八號　電話中央七四六九　四七一四

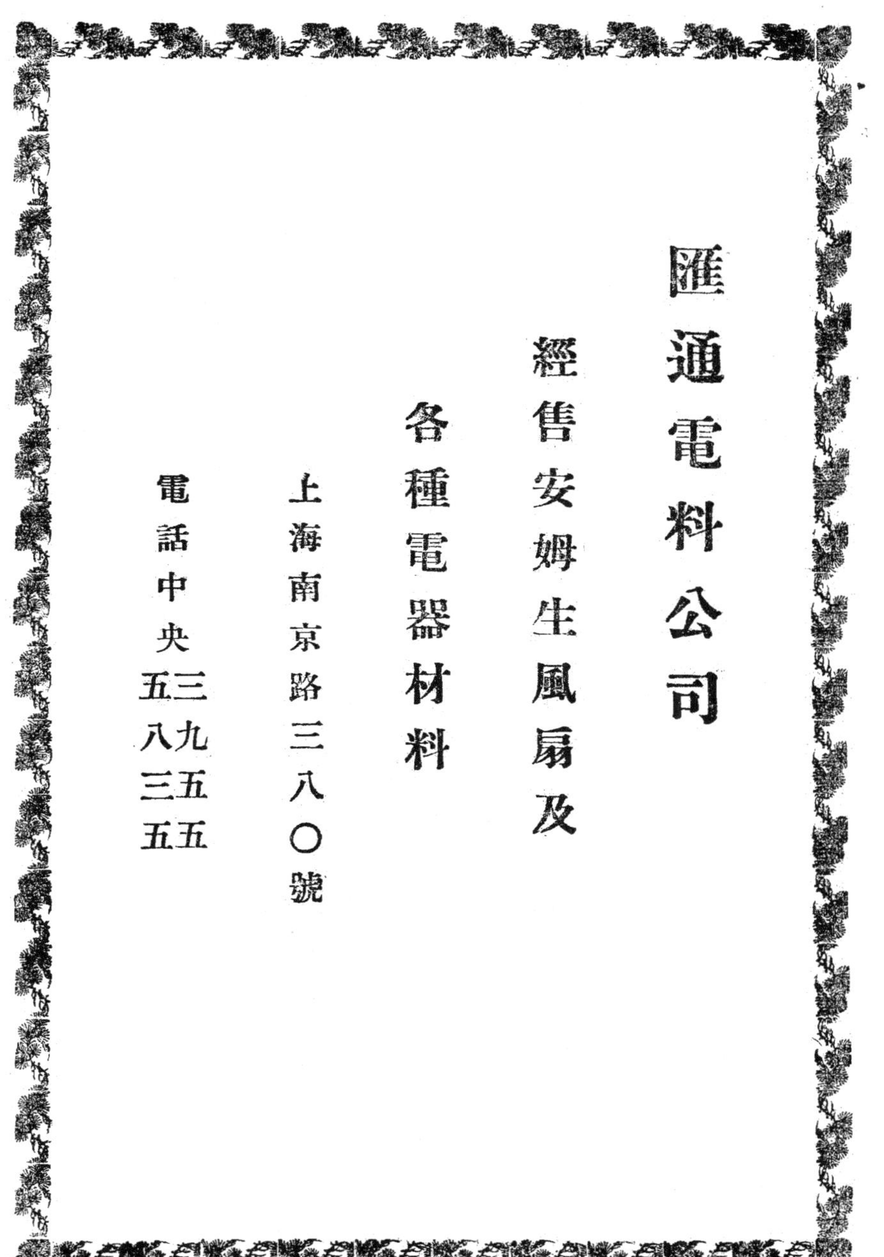
匯通電料公司
經售安姆生風扇及
各種電器材料
上海南京路三八〇號
電話中央三九五五
五八三五

中國路政界唯一之出版品

道路月刊

歡迎投稿

提倡道路建設 紹介治路知識

報告實施狀况 促進交通進步

每月一册一角五分 全年一元五角

道路叢刊

五十餘人編譯

七百九十餘頁 插圖三百餘件

研究路政市政者不可不讀

籌辦長途汽車路者更須參攷

實價四元 外加郵費一角三分

總發行 上海霞飛路中華全國道路建設協會 中華書局商務印書館均代售

中國印刷廠

本廠自開幕迄今營業日益發達玆爲推廣起見特行擴充廠屋添購最新式之美國機械及一切中西文字花紋銅模西字銅模多至四百餘種中字銅模頭號至六號均已齊備無論代數學化學幾何學三角學中西文書籍以及五彩套色傳單清票均可代印無不精美并製三色版銅版鋅版玻璃版凹凸版線劃銅版電鍍銅版鉛版等另有照相製版部精究無比裝璜精緻公署學校醫院銀行商店公司交易所各種簿册表本備有樣張三百餘種任意擇印可省起草手續再本廠宗旨爲振興商業故取價極廉印刷精巧定期不誤非一般祇圖厚利尋常印局可比擬倘蒙光顧請駕臨敝廠或電話通知當派司事前來接洽均竭誠歡迎之至

上海新閘路福康路 電話西二五七九號

上海先施公司

統辦環球貨品　推銷中華國貨

舉凡日用所需無不美備

附設

東亞旅館
東亞酒樓
南貨茶食
銀業儲蓄
屋頂樂園

南洋季刊投稿簡章

一 本刊除聘請特約撰述員担任撰述稿件外校內外無論何人倘有投稿均所歡迎

二 本刊分通論工程經濟科學文藝交通事業工商調査校聞紀要同學會紀聞校友要訊新著述評遊記雜俎等門但投稿者得投寄合於本刊宗旨之任何稿件

三 投寄之稿或自撰或翻譯均可其文體以文言為主但亦得酌用白話或外國文

四 投寄之稿望繕寫清楚並加句讀或新式標點符號能依本刊規定之行格（每面橫行廿五每行三十字）繕寫者尤佳倘有附圖須製版者請另紙用筆墨繪成以便攝製

五 投寄譯稿請附原本如原本不便附寄請將原文題目原著者姓名出版日期及發售書局名稱詳細敍明

六 稿末請註明姓名字住址以便通信至揭載時如何署名聽投稿者自定

七 投寄之稿揭載與否本刊編輯者不能預覆如不揭載得因預先聲明寄還原稿

八 投寄之稿俟揭載後酌酬本刊一期或數期

九 投寄之稿其著作權仍為著作者所有惟於需乘時得由本校其他出版物轉載

十 投寄之稿如已先在他處發布者請預先聲明惟揭載與否由本刊編輯者斟酌

十一 投寄之稿本刊編輯者得酌量增刪之但投稿人不願他人增刪者可於投稿時預先聲明

十二 投稿請寄上海徐家匯南洋大學出版部

南洋季刊第一卷第二期電機工程號

民國十五年四月出版

編輯處　上海南洋大學出版部

發行處　上海南洋大學出版部

印刷者　中國印刷廠

代售處　上海商務印書館　中華書局　世界書局

北京交通部路政司攷工科莫葵卿

青島膠濟鐵路局機務處胡粹士

南京河海大學吳馥初

本刊價目表

定	價	每期郵費	
每期	大洋二角	本埠	一分
		外埠	二分半
每年	大洋八角	國外	十分

本刊廣告刊例

全面	封面裏頁及底面裏外頁	實洋十五元
	尋常地位	實洋十元
半面	封面裏頁及底面裏外頁	實洋八元
	尋常地位	實洋六元

交通部直轄滬寧鐵路廣告

穩安◉迅速

啓者本路每日除按班開行外並加特別快車尋常快車及夜快車每次備有餐車以便乘客取價極廉清潔適口各站經過地點皆爲東南名勝薈華之區風景之佳冠於全國其最著者如蘇州之虎邱天平山無錫之惠山錫山常州之天寧寺鎭江之金焦山甘露寺南京之明陵莫愁湖等處均爲我國特殊勝景如乘車出行作竟日之郊游必能快心悅目於精神上當裨益匪鮮本路夜快車備有臥車牀位清潔舒暢每牀位除加頭等票外售洋三元遠近不計凡旅客欲乘別路通車者可向各大站購買聯運票以免周折倘係團體旅行本路訂有定章以人數多寡核減票價惟須先期函知車務總管核准

車務總管奉命啓

榮昌祥
西裝呢絨號
本號洋服 首屈一指
品質優美 信用久著
今更銳意 研製精良
優待主顧 取價從廉
諸君一試 定能滿意
地址 上海南京路新世界對面
電話中央第六〇五六號
CHONG SHUNG & CO.
HIGH-CLASS TAILOR & GENERAL OUTFITTER
PERFECT FIT GUARANTEED MODERATE PRICES
Give Us a trail and you Will be Convinced
364 NANKING ROAD OPPOSITE NEW WORLD
TELEPHONE NO. C 6056
SHANGHAI

NANYANG QUARTERLY

第一卷　　經濟號　　第三期

本期要目

民國十五年七月

南洋大學出版部南洋公學同學會同發行

中華郵政特准掛號認爲新聞紙類

開洛公司

專門發售**無線電話**收音機並

一切無線電話應用配件

並辦**電話**機及交換機並一切

德律風應用材料

上海南京路十二號

電話中央 六五三四 / 六五三五

開洛三座眞空管收音機 全套二百十五元

開洛四座眞空管收音機 全套二百八十八元

開洛TR五座眞空管收音機 全套三百四十元

開洛八座眞空管收音機 Ultradyne 全套五百元

開洛RFL七座眞空管收音機(連橡座) 全套一千一百元

開洛新式WaveMaster收音機 全套四百四十元

開洛一座眞空管收音機 全套七十元

南洋季刊第四期機械工程號徵稿

季刊第四期收到稿件尚少。甚望本校教員暨校內外同學諸君，於暑假期內，多撰關於機械工程之著作，惠登本期，藉爲季刊生色。倘蒙校外機械工程專家，錫以宏著，尤所歡迎。（集稿期八月廿五日）

卅週紀念學術專刊徵稿展期

八月十五日爲投稿截止期

學術專刊徵稿前後發函數次今已收到名家著作二三十件惟本刊務取博大精深以垂永遠是以敝委員會議定特再展期一月務望校內外校友各就心得撰爲鴻篇於集稿期前投交出版部轉敝委員會收爲荷

南洋大學卅週紀念出版物委員會啓

南洋大學經濟學會全體攝影

本校鐵路管理科統計學教室

本校鐵路管理科會計學教室

南洋大學經濟學會職員攝影

南洋學會書畫展覽會之成績

南洋季刊社職員錄

（民國十四年至十五年）

南洋大學出版部

編輯股　趙祖康（總編輯）　柴福沅（編輯）　王瑞虎（編輯）

事務股　曹毓琮（會計）　王永禮（印銷）　邵禹襄（廣告）　沈元慶（書記）

南洋公學同學會編輯員

柴福沅

南洋大學學生團體選派編輯員

衞杼　戚其淵　薛椿蔭　徐鍾淮　史鵬展　許延暉

※　※　※　※

南洋大學出版委員會及南洋季刊特約撰述員專門校審員名題錄

出版委員會委員

徐名材　李熙謀　范永增

特約撰述員

張景良　張世鎏　李復幾　胡端行　莫衡

薛次莘　周厚坤　鮑國寶　曹麗順　鈕澤全

茅以新　莊前鼎　方子衛　潘世宜　趙曾珏

陳廣沅　楊立惠　王繩善　謝仁　裘維裕

張峻　李聯珪　黃世祚　沈慶鴻　杜定友

唐慶詒　杜光祖　武書常　劉麟生　朱鼎元

施孔懷　沈昌　吳維翰　沈維楨

專門校審員

周仁　吳玉麟　俞希稷　李聯珪　王繩善

周銘　徐佩璜　楊培琫　徐佩琨

編輯者言

一．編者於經濟學術素無研究.本期各篇,但就內容範圍之廣狹為次第.不當之處.幸作者讀者均加原諒.

一．社會科學之研究,數年來風起雲湧.然多震驚於馬克斯經濟史觀之新奇,以專治社會主義的經濟學為急務.銀行也,金融也,賦稅制度也,交易所也.研究之者甚少.此不能不認為一種偏欹之傾向.本期於各問題,皆有論列.讀者對此,當寄同情.

一．共產之說,舉世痛惡.均產之制,古已有之.本期孔孟之經濟思想一文,雖多時賢所已論.實之本刊,或可為古今中外經濟思想調劑融合之一助.讀者其韙我言乎.

一．贖回中東路財政上應有之準備一文,據編者所知,曾譯載四月份商報.題為中東路之現在與將來.原著甚有價值.惟商報所譯,間有錯誤,故錄登邱君所節譯者於本刊.

一．其他各篇,或研究,或批評,或創論,或述作,皆各有其價值.讀者自能鑒別,無俟贅言.

一．機械工程號徵稿數月,已得數篇.惟本刊內容,務求豐富.甚望本校教員同仁及校內外校友多多惠稿,准八月二十五日前寄下.提倡學術,發揚校譽,一舉兩利,幸各努力.

一．本刊現擬於第二卷第二期,出『工程教育研究號.』凡有以國外工程教育之新學說新制度介紹於本刊,或以國內工程教育發展之沿革,現制度之得失.撰文惠登者,均當特別歡迎.

一．本期徵求稿件得沈奏廷君助力不少.至於校勘,因值暑期,什九由編者任之.魯魚亥豕,知所不免,幸讀者指正.　（康）

消費合作概論

華立

(一) 消費合作之眞義

消費合作者.消費者自動之組織.用以避免中間商人之敲剝.直接向生產者以最低價格批購日常用品.以之分售於消費者之購買同盟也.夫合作運動.範圍至廣.如農業合作.信用合作.生產合作.消費合作等.事業雖異.用意則同.本文所論.僅及消費合作一項.蓋消費合作實爲一切合作運動之中堅.歷史最久.成效最著.而又爲我國最需要之一種合作也.

世間一切運動.多半爲學者理想上之產物.惟合作運動.則基於人類之公允觀念而成.故羅虛台爾合作社 Rachdale Coöperative Sociely 成立之時.卽以公平先鋒 Equitable Pioneers 之名詞相標榜也.原此種組織.其動作固不出經濟範圍之外.而其性質則含有平等互助之精神.如會員平權.資本賦利之類.故如認消費合作爲慈善事業或改善勞工之制度者.均不知消費合作之眞諦者也.自亞丹斯密樹自由競爭之旗幟後.輾轉至今.已成爲少數資本家壟斷之護符.而消費者遂成爲犧牲品.故消費合作最後之目的.卽在以合作精神破堅折銳.以消殺資本制度之勢焰.而擁護消費者固有之權利.社會主義者雖亦有此種決心.但其力僅側重於勞動者.而不及於消費者之全部.是爲美中不足耳.

合作主義之定義與效用.吾人人殊.然要之皆不外如歐文氏之所言.『人必自爲商人然後方能得價廉物美之物品.』"You must become yonr own merchants...... to be able to supply yourselves with goods of the best quality and the lowest price" 蓋普通之一般營利商店.其出售物品.專在以高價得厚利.苟有增價之機.無不竭力爲之.小康之家尚無影響.至於胼手胝足之工人.遂受極大之壓迫.於是激烈者遂倡工團主義以相抗.和平者遂倡合作主

義以自救.途徑雖異.其爲反對資本家之壓迫則一.且勞動者購買之物品.通常多於小販之手.輾轉遞嬗.物質損壞無論矣.即物價亦必因之而騰貴.夫物價之騰貴.原因雖極複雜.而中間商人太多.實爲其中主因之一.一物之成.自製造者而至消費者.其間有批發商.有躉賣商.有倌客.有經紀人.依次敲剝.依次自肥.原值一元者.消費者非出一元半或二元不能得.貪婪之商人.又復攙雜劣貨.削減數量.消費者直接間接所受之損失.僕指難數.雖此輩商人亦有構成時間性或地方性之效用.Time and place utility 然遞嬗之次數太多.實於無形之中增高物品之價值.在消費者方面.實感直接之痛苦.而消費合作即爲避免此種損失之一種補救方法.故又可謂最合經濟原則之消費制度也.不但此也.在今日營利競爭劇烈之下.普通商店往往不惜耗費大量之資本於廣告.以鼓動消費者之購買慾.其實此項費用.最後仍復轉嫁于消費者之身.況在今日商業道德墮落之時.賣者往往以廣告欺人.消費者如無精密之鑑別力.無有不墮其術中者.且今日之廣告.大半爲奢侈品.因奢侈品利重.堪負此重費.故消費者又往往被此種奢侈品之廣告.鼓起無意識之購買慾.雖然.余非一概抹殺廣告之功用也.即消費合作亦不能不用廣告以引起買者之注意.然以廣告爲營業競爭之工具.則自不能無損於公衆也.

消費合作除補救上述數種弊端外.尚有一間接改進社會之大功.大功惟何.即無形中消除競爭之慘劇也.蓋在營利主義之下.無不欲攫財逐利.而競爭以起.結果互相排擠.互相仇視.所謂平等.所謂親愛.不過牧師之口頭禪而已.消費合作本互助之精神.用德謨克拉西之手段.爲社會大多數謀幸福.不特合乎經濟原則之消費組織.抑亦改造社會之明證也.茲將其最大之功用.綜述於下.

(一) 免除中間商之層層敲剝.

(二) 節省販賣術中之無謂消費.

(三) 消費者依購買額之大小得分得盈餘之一部分.(下節詳述)

（四）工人得恃合作機關而獨立營生.

（五）消費者所得物品之質地必較通常所得之物品爲佳.且因權度適當.物品數量亦必較普通所得者爲多.

（六）教育事業有發展之機會.因合作社往往以盈餘之一部興辦學校及其他文化機關.

（二）消費合作之實施

賴虛台爾合作社者.消費合作之鼻祖也.今日各國之消費合作社.無一不胚胎於此.故欲明瞭消費合作之經營及組織.非先追溯賴虛台爾之計畫.不足以見其底蘊.

賴虛台爾居英國北國之朗克州. Lancashire 一八四四年有織工二十八人在彼處組織一消費合作社.其計畫可得言者有六.

（一）營業資本由各社員認投

（1）社員卽爲股東.股東卽爲社員.利害切身社務自易發達.

（2）資本均爲社員所出.不另借貸.可免利息之損失.及受人之擘肘.自表面觀之.雖不如尋常公司之易集大資本.然一爲牟利性質.一爲自給性盾.範圍與目的固根本不同也.

（二）社中職員.由全體社員投票選舉.不論認股多少.每人祇限一票. One man one vote（自表面觀之.似失公允.然惟其如此.乃能免少數大股東之把持.）且不准代理選舉. Voting by proxy

（三）社中重要事體.由社員全體公決.（德謨克拉西之精神寄焉）

（四）現錢交易.不准拖欠.

（1）經濟上理由——信用出賣.資金往往不敷.批買時難免拖欠.而進貨條件必多不利.故合作商店如行賒欠制.資金必須加厚.否則周轉不靈.倒閉可立而待.

（2）道德上之理由——賒欠之制.足以養成社員浪費之惡習.有

時積欠過多.無力償還.必致家破人亡.其遺患有不堪設想者.

（五）物品賣價與市價相同

合作出賣物品.按照市價.似與合作之本旨不合.因合作之唯一目的.在於消費之節省.似應按照物品之生產費用出售.惟事實上有下列二弊.

（1）價格低廉.親友之托買.自在意中.即不然安知社員不專事販賣.從中取利耶.

（2）合作之目的.若儲蓄.若保險.若教育.均不能達.

實則或照生產費用出售.或照市價出售.於社員個人之利益均無大異.惟其影響所及.則後法較前法爲大耳.因一含有儲蓄性質.一僅減少費用而已.

（六）盈餘之分配

（1）公積金

（2）股分紅利

（3）除去上述兩項外.如尚有盈餘.則照購買額之大小.分派與購買者.（寓儲蓄於購買）

以上六端.乃賴虛台爾合作社之特點.今日歐美各國之銷費合作社.均以此爲根據焉.今略舉一般合作社經營之方法.俾創設合作社者有所借鏡.

（一）開辦之前.對於將來之營業須有一周密之計畫.如營業範圍甚狹.則可先辦一小規模之購買團. Buying club

（二）銷售物品.是否僅限社員.抑或對外出賣.此種問題.在開辦前必先解決.嚴格而言.對外出賣.出乎合作範圍之外.且與合作本義亦多不合.因合作社專爲供給社員之需要而設也.然賴虛台爾合作社對於公衆.亦仍發賣.惟非社員所享之分紅.祇及社員之半數.而將餘額歸入公積焉.

(三) 初辦時社所不妨從簡.俟營業發達後.再由盈餘中提出一部份作爲建築金.且合作社非一般營利商店可比.不必以華麗之房屋爲廣告.

(四) 社員對於合作主義須有堅決之信仰.

(五) 每股價額.須就地方上各個之經濟能力而定.太大則小資產者無力購認.太小則社員缺少興趣及責任心.

(六) 股銀總額.不必規定.因社員愈多愈妙.

(七) 股銀最好分期交納.以便手中一時無多金者亦得加入.

(八) 股份利率不必太高.在英約長年五厘.在美約六厘.在我國可作八厘.

(九) 設一董事部.總理全社事務.規畫進行方針.規模小者.常以委員會 The committee of management 經理之.

(十) 消費合作初期出售者.多係日用必需之品.(如食物原料之類)然在最後之目的.決不限於食料之供給.凡人生應用之物.不論爲衣爲食爲住.均能適用消費之合作.今美國盛行之住房合作. Building sociely 卽爲明例.

(三) 消費合作之略史

合作運動始於十八世紀之末葉.一七六九年.愛爾州 Agrshire 之芬惠克 Fenwick 村.卽有消費合作社之創設.然其組織與計畫.均無精細之考慮.自洛勃歐文氏 Robert Owen 起.合作主義遂樹鮮明之旗幟.歐氏於一千七百七十一年生於英國蒙德高滿利州之新村.家貧.十歲時嘗布店學徒.十九歲時任某紡織工場之經理.對於勞工待遇之改善.進行不遺餘力.如設立職工娛樂部.廢除雇用童工.施行勞工教育等.均爲不可磨滅之功績.一八二五年.歐氏在 New Harmony 處創設大規模之合作社.但不久卽歸失敗.其後在美國亦曾努力宣傳其主義.雖當時無實效可見.然今日合作運動之所以能

旁礴于新舊兩大陸者.實歐氏宣傳之功也.一八四四年.賴盧台爾之公平先鋒社 The Rachdale Society of Equitable Pioneers 始發現.至此合作運動遂自主義之宣傳一躍而進於實施時代矣.初賴盧台爾之法蘭絨織工爲要求增加工資而罷工.結果工人完全失敗.於是决定組織一消費合作社以爲自全之計.最初之資本.僅一百四十鎊.專售麵粉牛油雀麥之類.是後社務日進.社員日衆.至一八九〇年.會員人數達一萬一千餘人.資本增至三十六萬餘鎊.營業總額計二十七萬鎊.盈餘計四萬七千餘鎊.進步之速.實爲各種事業所未有.雖辦事者富有毅力.然亦足以見此組織之適合潮流也.此後各國踵相效法.遂成今日魄力雄厚之消費合作運動.

(四) 消費合作在各國之現狀

合作運動肇始於英.嬗遞至今.不過六十餘年.德國僅廿年.美國俄國等亦不過二十餘年.然其進行之速.殊出意料之外.英德兩國消費合作社社員各占全國人口三分之一.試觀大戰前後各國合作營業之統計.即知其發展之神速矣.

	1914年	1920年
英國	34,910,000 鎊	105,440,000 鎊
丹麥	3,886,000	11,300,000
法國	700,000	6,640,000
德國	24,649,000	140,073,000
瑞士	5,746,000	13,233,000
荷蘭	365,000	1,199,000

今姑就英美兩國之消費合作運動.略述一二以概其餘.

英國　據 Prof. Frank Parsons 之調查.英國在一八三〇年時.已有合作社二百五十餘處.惟規模粗具.尚無十分功效.自一八四四年賴盧台爾合作社成立後.消費合作運動.始有鞏固之基礎.一八六一至一九〇一之四十年中爲

英國消費合作運動激進之時.據統計所得英國在此四十年中人口之增加為百分之四十三.製造品之增加為百分之五十二.對外貿易之增加為百分之一百三十.而消費合作之營業則遞增至百分之五千三百.社員人數亦自四萬八千一百八十四人增至二百餘萬人.一九一八年.消費合作之營業為一,〇〇〇,〇〇〇,〇〇〇元.社數共有四百萬處.歐戰發生.消費合作社更進而為供給糧食之主要機關.近年以來.更復致力於批發合作社 Coöperative Wholesale Society 之發展.蓋鑑於以前消費合作社向躉賣商批購貨物時.往往因交易額小.不能享折口之利.致賣價較市價反昂.故於一八六三年間.英國各地著名消費合作社.各出巨資.創設批發合作社於孟却斯脫.專事躉買事業.直接向製造者批購大宗貨物.分銷於各地.消費合作社.今日規模日宏.事業日繁.除批購貨物外.復兼營生產事業.如設立工廠.舉辦銀行及保險公司.凡麵粉.糖果.肥皂之類.無不自製.至消費合作遂更進一步而從事於生產合作矣.由此以觀.消費合作實為生產合作之基礎.而生產合作又為合作制度之極峯.無消費合作.則生產合作無由發展.無生產合作.則雖有消費合作.而社會之經濟改造.終無由貫澈.德談克拉西之工業制度亦無從實現也.最近英國合作社社員.竟占人口三分之一.洛斯勃萊 Lord Rosebery 稱合作運動為「國中國」(A state within a state) 者.有由來矣.

美國　美國之合作運動亦甚早.一八三一年時已有合作店 Cöoperative store 之組織.雖南北戰爭時稍受挫折.但不久便復舊觀.Knights of Labor 尤奉合作主義為圭臬.一九〇五年時.全國共有合作店三百四十三處.資本八百五十二萬元.會員七萬六千一百餘人.每年營業計二萬萬元.一九二〇年.全國共有消費合作社三千處.每年營業達二萬萬元.所售物品有菜果.魚肉.麵麥.學校用品之類.其進步之速.固可謂一日千里矣.然與歐洲各國比較.則尚遜一籌.此中原因.據克洛斯 Cross 云.不出下列三點.

(一) 多數合作運動為勞農運動之產物.勞農運動自身陷於失敗地位.

合作運動當然無進展之可能.

(二) 無批發合作社之組織.故合作店向普通批發商進貨時.吃虧甚大.

(三) 百貨商店五分貨十分貨商店 Five and ten-cent store 競爭極烈.使合作店無發展之餘地.

(五) 消費合作在中國之地位

消費合作運動.在歐美各國固已風起雲湧.達於極盛時期.返顧我國.則主義之宣傳.猶在萌芽之時.遑論實施乎.此雖由於我國民衆合作思想之薄弱.然社會經濟狀況.亦有可研究者矣.蓋合作運動之產生.乃資本制度之反動.在各國資本制度之勢焰.固已不可嚮邇.至於我國.資本制度尚甚幼稚.一般消費者當然不知其威力之何.雖然.萬事非必任其自然之消長.如能察知未來之趨勢.而加以預制.則何苦而不思避免之計.況消費合作之功用.不僅消弭資本制度缺陷.且能扶助教育事業.改善勞工生活.實經濟而兼文化之運動也.今我國除少數學者對於合作主義已有眞實見解外.餘多不知合作爲何物.故今日之工作.不在實施而在主義之宣傳.近年以來.上海復旦大學頗盡力提倡.如編輯平民週報.組織合作銀行及合作商店等.此外江灣吳淞等處.亦有職工合作商店.同學合作社.國民合作儲蓄銀行.吳淞合作商店之設.然皆草創伊始.不能稱爲完善之組織.內地各處.則闃然無聞矣.本校學生會雖亦有消費社之設.然規模粗具.尚不見有特殊之效果.甚望當事者擴充資本.推廣範圍.則非特與全校同學更大之利便.卽其盈餘亦必較爲可觀.以之補助教育.出版體育諸部.則將來我校學生事業.殊未可限量也.

本文參攷書——

東方文庫合作制度

新文化辭書

消費合作綱要

Carlton: History and Problems of Organized Labor

工場委員制

周增奎

一 總論

(一) 工場委員制之旨趣　近數年來.世界各國.恆有罷工風潮.勞資爭執.所受損失.不可數計.然吾人須公認勞工與資本非處於勢不兩立之地位.勞工與資本間實有共同利益.相互關係.蓋無勞工則資本成爲無用.無資本則勞工無從發展也.當勞動者與資本家相遇時.雙方恆有階級思想.敵對態度.此種互相反對行爲.實於勞資雙方皆有不利.因世間未有資本家無勞工爲之助.而可以繁昌.勞動者無資本爲之用.而可以隆盛者也.雖然.勞資間時發生齟齬.而互相仇視.成此階級爭鬬狀況者.亦有故焉.蓋雇主與雇員之閱歷與經驗.在工業上各各不同.雇主平日所見所聞.無非關於契約買賣財產權.法律規則.市價漲落.商業財政.管理才能等.種種非專門技藝之事.而雇員日常所接觸者.爲實質物料.手工氣力.及其他可以接觸之貨物.如機器原料.人工物品等.夫雇主與雇員所處之環境.及所受之經歷.既大不相同.無怪其思想.見解習慣.亦因之而各異.由是乎偏見生矣.不特此也.勞工與資本時不被認爲共事伴侶.而常誤認爲買賣關係.雙方遂無情感之可言.蓋時至今日.仍有多數守舊雇主.視勞工爲一種商品.其所付工資之漲落.以工人欲謀事者之多寡而定.若勞工供給多需要少.則工錢隨之而減.若勞工供給少需要多.則工錢隨之而增.雇主之雇用勞工.猶之顧客之購買商品.而雇主付工值之高下.亦猶之顧客之付物價.視該貨在市場之供求情形而定價之大小.況雇主方面.恆思付勞工以最小之工資.而用各種方法.使工人勤力.而獲最優美之結果.因雇主之所希望者.在增加純利.多得花紅.欲求利益增.自非減少工值以輕成本.督促勤工以增產量不可.然工作雖欲其勤.產量雖欲其增.而工資則不肯加.在雇員方面.則適相反.因雇員純恃作工得工資以爲生.故徒

往要求增加工資.且彼等熟知雇主恆得巨利.而彼等朝夕勤勞.日受工頭之斥責.常遭工資之剋減.所得反甚微細.且又見儕輩因工作過度而致疾病死亡者甚夥.事之不平.莫有過於此者.彼等始知雇主之用意.在少付工資而使彼等多工作.與彼等之目的.多得工資而少工作.完全相反.於是勞資雙方.意旨愈趨愈遠.而態度兩歧.偏見各執矣.從此爭執迭起.各趨極端.勞工集合工人.組織工團或職工會.以抵抗雇主之壓迫.資本家聯絡同業.創設雇主協會.以保護其利益.雙方儼成對峙之形.此種工業上階級戰爭.於工業本身.於勞資兩方.皆有害而無利.其結果增長自私自利之心.減少雙方合作精神.互相猜疑.誤會叢生.生產數量.因之減少.

勞資雙方雖時有衝突.然吾人不可忽略其雙方有相互利益之處.其所以互相仇視者.實由於管理者之不良.漠視工人之利益.以致發生反感.工場委員制.即所以袪除勞資雙方隔閡.構通雇主與雇員間之意見.俾雙方不致發生誤會.並可增進功率.助長生產.至其組織法.不過由工廠內工人與管理工廠人員雙方.各舉同等人數之代表.合議關於工人公共利益之事.如工資.工作時間.工人衛生.防禦危險等問題.及其他工作條件.關於工人全體者.此種工場委員制.與職工會雇主協會不同之點有二.職工會雇主協會係單方的.祇代表工人雇主偏面利益.工場委員制.係雙方的.可代表工人與雇主公共利益.此其不同之點一.職工會雇主協會之主旨.在保護本身利益.抵抗對方壓迫.故含攻擊性.破壞性.工場委員制之組織.基於合作精神.公開討論.雙方同意.衆議取決.故含和平性建設性.此其不同之點二.苟各工廠而能採用工場委員制.大可遏抑現代過激潮流.雖不能永息勞資爭執.根本解決工潮.然敢謂為改善雇主與雇員間關係之最妙方法.亦可謂為維持工業和平.減少罷工風潮之惟一捷徑.

(二)雇主雇員間關係今昔之比較　疇昔工業幼稚工場規模狹小時代.投資者即是雇主.雇主即為投資者.雇主與投資者往往為一人.非若現今

工業發達時代.投資者爲公司股東.雇主爲代表公司之董事經理.隱將投資者與雇主劃分爲二.且昔時之雇員.大半爲雇主之親戚朋友.或鄰里熟識之人.故雇員與雇主關係非常親密.而雇主與雇員每日見面.接觸甚多.一方面有不滿意之處.其他一方卽可與之說明或理直.因之雙方感情頗厚.罕有問題發生.迨乎今日.情形大異.一廠雇員往往多至數百人或數千人.雇主與雇員各不相識.接觸時少.雙方人的關係.完全消滅.由是互不信任.互相猜疑.而發生誤會.引起變端.苟雇主能設法常與雇員識面談話.交換意見.消除誤會.博取工人好感.而恢復從前人的關係.則雇主雇員間關係卽將改善.而雙方衝突自免矣.

(三) 勞資雙方近年來之情形　近年來勞工與雇主.往往濫用其權力.各走極端.實於公衆大爲不利.卽雙方亦蒙損害.雇主倚仗資財雄厚.團體結合.以不公平之道待遇勞工.以壓制手段對付勞工.而工人組織工會.藉端滋事.橫肆要求.甚至聚衆要挾.同盟罷工.以破壞工業.雙方皆流於偏激.欲救此弊.惟有使雙方明瞭工業與社會之關係.及其本身對於社會之責任.了解對方爲難之情形.及本人應取之態度.雙方互相諒解.感情自易融洽.

(四) 現代工業需要工場委員制　際此工業發達時代.投資於工業者.一公司多至數百千人.傭工於工業者.一廠多至數千人.勞資雙方.人數既如此之多.斷難互相認識.接觸機會自少.意見隔閡.在所難免.欲溝通雙方意旨.重立人的關係.非採用雙方舉出代表合議制不可.此工場委員制之所以倘也.若用此制.公司方面代表.可常於會議中與工人代表晤面交談.得知工人方面之情形.而工人代表.亦可於會議中討論議題時.略知公司方面情形.轉告全體工人.誤解自無由而生.工潮自因此而少.況今日工人程度日高.往往要求廠主.關於彼等切身利害問題.許彼等以參預之權.不願長此爲被處分者.而受非人之待遇.工場委員制.適合彼等心理.苟能妥訂章程.恰如其分.謹愼辦理.不偏不倚.不但可以減少雙方無謂之爭執.大可增長合作精神.總之

自工業革命以後.企業家資本家工程師科學家所殫精竭慮.朝夕不遑者.在於如何可以積省材料.如何可以增進效率.如何可以改良機器.如如可以多得產量.而對於人工管理適當方法.鮮有研究.素來漠視.以致近年來.工潮迭起.罷工時聞.苟雇主而能稍稍注意工人人格.尊重工人權利.以愛惜物料之心.愛護工人.以重視機械之念.厚待工人.則於解决勞工問題之道.思過半矣.

（未完）

補白一

五大洲鐵路之比較

（一九二三年之統計）

洲別		哩數	均數（總哩數百分之幾）	面積（平方哩）	均數（總面積百分之幾）	比率（哩數均數/面積均數）
亞		71,374	10	17,250.000	33	0·303
美	北美	325,800	50	9,000,000	17	2·941
	南美	11,864	2	7,000,000	13	0·154
歐		210,240	30	3,800,000	8	3·750
非		28,808	4	11,500,000	22	0·181
澳		24,623	4	3,600,000	7	0·571
總數		699,709	100	52,150,000	100	1

交易所對於生產及民生之關係

貢乙青

尙古之世.文化未開.人類穴處巢居.茹毛飲血.生活上之需要.極爲簡單.自鑿自居.自覓自食.初無所謂交易.迨夫智識稍開.慾望增進.自作自食者.漸覺不足以滿其慾望.於是相互之間.交易漸起.以物易物.相通有無.同時各人所業.亦漸異趨.耕種者專心耕種.捕漁者一意捕漁.以粟易魚.耕者可以不漁而食魚.以魚易粟.漁者可以不耕而食粟.然物物交換.供給終難投合需求.況人類慾望.日見增長.而生產則日見專異.耕者所得惟粟.而所用之器具則日新月異.且何人欲易吾之粟.何者爲吾所欲易.繁複不便.即有之.其價值是否與吾之物品相等.面面諮詢.個個相求.不勝其煩.由是物價之尺量.交易之媒介起矣.其始也以貝以石.遞假而至以金屬定爲貨幣 (Money). 轉讓流通.以吾之粟.變爲貨幣.將此貨幣.以換各物.交易之道.至此進步多矣.洎乎晚近.文化猛前.貨幣制度.猶以爲未能盡善.信用制度 (Credit system) 出而代庖.由是交易愈形便利.惟其便利.交易之市場.亦因而擴充.初僅一隅.終達全國.今且合全世界爲一大市場.市場旣廣.同時一物之需求亦隨之加增.各種大規模之生產乘時崛起.經濟制度.幡然一新.各種經濟機關 (Economic institutions). 蔚然並起.交易所即其一也.

交易所之興也.以奧大利爲鼻祖.自一八七五年.首先創立.其後歐美各邦.羣起仿行.東隣日本.相繼學步.我國則至民國七年.日本取引所發現於上海.政府諸公.始如夢醒.准予商民.集資開辦.根本建設.皆法日本.行股份制 (Corporate form). 非若歐美各國之用會員制 (Association form) 也.吾國自採股份制.種種流弊.亦遂於此發生.如買賣本所股票.此種制度.是否相宜.本爲彼邦人士所訾議.乃我國不論長短.羣起效尤.於是創辦者.祇求股票買賣上收得操縱之利益.公司將來之成績如何.本所應行應辦之事業如何.丁

不之顧.故初創時.風起雲湧.不數月竟達百餘家.曾幾何時.情態畢露.倏起倏落.幻若曇花.其中資本雄厚者.尚可以勉強支持.薄弱者.不得不倒閉擱淺.與之有關係者.敗家蕩產者有之.爭訟流離者有之.以致洋厘銀拆.漲落無常.金融紊亂.商民交困.與社會,以極痛之創傷.貽人民以極惡之印像.甚矣哉.交易所之流害地方.遺誤民生也.

雖然.交易所果何如耶.彼歐美各邦.行之則企業日興.民生日裕.試行我國.則成績爾爾.非其于交易所之原理及目的關係.皆未能盡其道乎.夫交易所者.商業上一種保證信託之機關也.彼其任務.在于物品證券以一極有組織之繼續市場(Coutinuous market).生產者可因之以最廉之市價.買得其原料.或最平之市價.售出其物品.企業者可因之以極便之市場.售出其股債.或最公之市場.投放其現款.故吾人可名之爲分配機械.(Distributive mechanism).有此分配機械.生產與消費.得以銜接.企業與投資.因而相連.兩端之間.免生傾軋.機關本身.全賴其所員(如經紀人等).運轉一切.倘所員運轉此機.幸而順乎此機之原理.則生產民生.胥蒙其澤.不幸而背乎此機之原理.則生產民生.反受其殃.吾人今且觀其所員之所爲.即可知其運轉此機之何如矣.

交易所之所以能爲繼續市場也.全賴所內之買賣作用.虛實互行.投資者有時帶有投機之行爲.投機者有時含有投資之性質.虛者未必盡虛.實者未必盡實.至其交易種類.曰現貨曰期貨.經營之物.亦可分爲二種.曰證券.曰物品.現貨期貨.作用不同.證券物品.機能斯異.夷考其實.其各含有投機性質則一.蓋證券物品.價格斷無不變之理.現貨期貨.均有依價格消長之勢.價格變化.則風險(Risk)隨之.投機行動.因而起矣.其變化之程度愈甚者.其風險亦愈甚.是以期貨爲時較長.其間變化較大.因之做期貨交易者.其風險亦較大也.

當交易所之未實現也.一切價格升降風險.均由物主負之.蓋此時無論何物.須由供者覓得求者.或求者來覓供者.生產者欲覓得相當之消費者極

難消費者欲求得相當之生產者亦不易.即偶有少數人在中間融通市面.無如市場組織終欠完備.是以價格一升一降.則生產者風險乘之.生產者一方既負生產之責.又感風險之苦.又何能望其有盡量之發展.是以欲望生產規模之日宏.同時買賣市場分配機械遂覺有改良之必要.此交易所之所以應運而生也.

今設有一農夫.其種者爲棉花.其售棉花之法有二.一直接售與紗廠.一先售與中間人(Middleman)如棉花商者.由棉花商再售與紗廠.當春夏之交.棉花轉少.秋收之候.棉滿市場.際此棉花上場之時.無論間接直接售出.因一時供過於求之故.市價必一落千丈.蓋農人一方急於求售.廠主一方又圖壟斷.如有交易所.則農人可先於五月中賣出期貨.十月交付.或棉花商亦於此時經營期貨.十月買進交付.如此則十月棉花市面.需求加增.五月市面.供給乍長.供求相調.市價自平矣.

假如上述期貨交易.係棉花商委託一號經紀人在交易所賣出.買者爲二號經紀人.言明每担十元.共棉花百担.十月交貨.在此五月之內.棉價無定.忽漲忽落.譬如棉價每担漲至十元一角.二號經紀人即將此棉售與三號經紀人.二號經紀人可賺洋十元.以後棉價忽落至十元.三號經紀人恐價之繼跌.賣給四號經紀人.共損失洋十元.但四號經紀人.乃係做空頭者(Bear).在未買進以前.已以十元二角之價.賣與五號經紀人.由五號復賣與六號七號八號經紀人爲止.列表如下.

1 —十元→ 2 —十元一角→ 3 —十元→ 4　五月五號買進

8 ←— 7 ←— 6 ←— 5 ←十元二角— 4　五月一號賣出

今將其買賣兩方銜接之成爲下圖.

1 ——→ 2 ——→ 3 ↘

8 ←— 7 ←— 6 ←— 5 ←— 4

倘上圖內八號經紀人.是承一紗廠之委託代爲買原料者.於是紗廠與棉花商卽可成交.此五月之內.價格漲落無論至任何程度.棉花商與紗廠.皆可不冒其險.各得於極自由公開之市場.以自願之價格.售出或買進其目的物.毫無風險.各得安於其業.進而言之.紗廠之售紗與織布廠.亦可如是.推而廣之.麥商及麵粉商.亦莫不可如是.在生產方面觀之.可以極平允之市價售出其物品.在消費方面觀之.可以極廉之市價買進其原料.價格升降之風險.於企業前途.毫無關礙.此種便利.非受分配機關交易所之賜乎.

更就證劵交易方面觀之.疇昔各種有限公司之所以不能發達者.其最大原因爲證劵不能流通於市場.近世各種生產.規模極大.欲運用或維持此種大規模之生產.非有極大之資本如有限公司者不爲功.若證劵不能流通.招募股債.定必困難.蓋商人資本.以流通爲第一要義.若以活動之資本.購不流通之股債.曷若購不動產之穩妥.故欲生產規模之擴大.必先有大公司.欲發達大公司.必須有分配機械以造成繼續市場流通證劵.信乎美銀行家兼經濟家Charles A. Conant之言曰.交易所者.乃資本之儲蓄器兼分配機也.其放款及收款以興實業也.一若尼羅河 (Nile) 之蓄水放水以灌溉田畝.尼羅河以閘口定水量之多寡而爲出入.猶交易所以利率量資本之裕否爲收放.世苟無此儲蓄器.則資本缺乏.市面恐慌.金融阻滯.價格紊亂.種種惡現象.必將常常發現矣.

至若現貨期貨交易之區別.乃時間長短問題.現貨交易者.契約定成貨物價錢立卽交付之謂也.此種交易.使生產者隨時可以賣出貨物.或買進原料.簡而言之.生產者於此可得一極公開自由易達之市場也.在證劵方面言之.則凡持有證劵者.隨時可變作現錢應用.卽所謂疏通市面也.微此市面.則價格難以維持.前段固已言之.故其關係於生產.尤爲切要.期貨交易者.謂買賣契約已成立.所有貨物價錢.均待至定期始行交付也.此種交易.前段已有引例.生產者可預計其產量而爲供給.或籌算其銷路先事屯積.以免貨成待

沽.壓積資本.或臨時羅致.成本蝕虧.所謂希繁（Hedging）作用也.期貨證券交易.效用極大.較諸現貨證券交易.效用尤多.投資者可以因之而獲較厚利益之證券.投機者可以預爲希繁以達其賣空或買空之目標.因之措置穩定.損益預知.其競爭愈烈者.則市價愈平衡.供求愈調和.生產者之股債.因而增加流通.資本亦因而易籌焉.

交易所對於生產有保護風險開闢資源調劑供求平準價格之關係.已如上述.然交易所內多頭空頭.虛搆市面.致價格升降.異乎常軌.得毋爲生產前途病乎.曰不然.虛搆市面（Fictitious market）終爲眞正市面所制.蓋價值.（Value）價格（Price）.本屬二物.價值之高低.未必因價格轉移.價格之漲落.則因價值變動.假如某公司之股票.價值百元.因空頭之故.價格落至九十五元.價格雖變.價值未變.於是一般知該股票之眞價值者.定必羣起買進.同時空頭者見需求加增.價格已低至無可再低.亦必買進（Covering）.價格之復漲.可想而知.其或該股票因多頭之故.漲至百零五元.一般知其眞情者.亦必羣起賣出.同時多頭者見供給加增.價格已至無可再漲之勢.亦必賣出（Liquidating）價格之復原狀.亦可想而知.由是觀之.多頭空頭.因一時偏重之故.固於價格有一時之影響.惟其眞正結果.實足以使價格得有緊密之市場（Close market）.多頭空頭競爭愈劇烈.市面愈流通.價格亦最平允.繼續市場.亦因之而維持.其於生產前途.非徒無害.且又益之.

批評交易所者.謂交易所囤積一部份現款.將使供給生產資本（Finance production）.因而減少.此言驟聆之.似亦近理.然考其實際.交易所之現款.大半來自拆銀（Call loans）.拆銀在銀行係屬過量之現錢.此種過量之現錢.或爲指定用途而存積.或爲準備金而保留.如欲用之於商業借款或他種投資.既不穩固.又無大利.故此種過量現錢之唯一用途.祗有作拆銀借出.易放易收.與原定用途.初無防礙.而與生產資本.亦不相干.惟一經交易所.反可以資助市面.使不動之現款.轉而爲生利之資本.由是以觀.交易所非特不

困積生產資本.且能增長生產資本也已.

交易所對於生產有如此之重大責任.故民生前途.實利賴之.政府以之爲理財機械.鐵路以之爲資本來源.以其有流通證劵之能力也.農人以之爲市場.事業因之而促進.以其有負擔風險之效用也.資本家用爲投資之南針.企業家用爲集資之外府.以其有調劑金融之能力也.消費者因可得廉價物品.生產者用爲公開市場.以其能平準價格故也.工人因生產促進.而得職業.因分配改良.而得廉物.社會因供求之調劑.市面得以維護.因虛實之互行.爆裂(Panic)因而減少.總其影響所及.國家社會利之.其或視爲賭局.爲私謀.以個人爲前提.置原理於不顧.行見弊端叢出.累國害家.道德淪亡.市面擾亂.推其所極.必使全社會爲之動搖.經濟界爲之傾覆.是則非吾人所欲言矣.

上段言交易所能減小爆裂.此中理由.似宜申說.時將恐慌(Crisis)也.生產者可於交易所買賣集合各方可恃之消息以知供求之現狀及將來之趨向.因而預爲防備.不致生產過剩.貨物供求不調之弊.或可略減.將來爆裂之害.遂可縮小.蓋價之高者其跌愈重.生產過量越大.一旦爆裂.其禍亦最大也.更有一事堪爲吾人注意者.即爆裂之候.市價日跌.一落千丈.市場上祇見求賣者不見買者.一般投資者又復裹足不前.此時無論何種投資.因市價日跌之故.終歸失敗.其不敢投資也勢所宜然.惟交易所空頭者.所處境地不同他人.市價日跌.正是爲利之良機.其賣空也愈甚.其買進也亦愈甚.蓋此種空頭.無論如何.終必買進以實踐其前約也.顧市場上爲有此輩空頭買進之故.需求之象.始見發生.一落不止之象.始見稍殺.否則盡市場之人.相率賣出不敢買進.則市場物價不將愈跌.爆裂之禍不將更甚乎.

前段又言交易所能負擔風險.以促進事業.所謂風險者即不定之意也.大凡事業.除少數特別者外.鮮有能預測其結果者.其結果者不能預測.即是風險.如開礦者不易預知其礦之產量.農人不能預料其田之收穫.倘能預定一切.則風險可盡除矣.然則風險者.視乎吾人之知與不知.如吾人能預知其

如何.則無風險.是所以風險之量.視乎人類智識之長進而逐漸減少也.昔者航渡海洋.視爲極大風險.今則以航海術發明.視航海若常事而不覺其風險矣.惟是人類智識之增進終覺有限.而未來之事不能預測者甚多.惟有竭吾人之智力.以求減少風險.改良方法.以轉讓(Transfer)風險.是二者.交易所之作用兼而有之.假如某公司之股票.持有之者負有此公司成敗之風險.如此證券在交易所轉讓他人.此風險亦隨之而去.如持有證券者見市價已跌.猶且固持不讓.其負風險必更大.爲有交易所繼續市場之故.隨時可以轉讓.是風險可以隨時減少.晚近生產之所以日宏.實業之所以日進.政府之所以日裕.鐵路之所以日展.公益事業之所以日興.經濟制度之所以日固.凡此種種.皆由買賣證券者因有交易所可以負擔風險之故.坐是膽量日壯.勇往直前發生一種冒險心進取性創造力.爲百業之先鋒.萬事之前導也.

交易所分配功用對於生產及民生之關係.約如上述.竊猶有進者.交易所之分配作用.非特能調劑現在之供求.且又能調劑將來之供求.蓋交易所內有「擔負未定用處之供給」(Carrying of floating supply)之功用也.時至今日.世上物品.漸趨全世界爲一市場之勢.因此生產與消費.難以適相抵消.供求方面.長短之情勢難幸免.譬如棉花現在之生產.過乎消費之量.此種過量之生產.因有交易所內之投機買賣.可以擔負過渡.留待將來之需要.一方可以免此種過量之生產擾亂現今之市面.一方又可以使將來之市場.加增供給.倘將來之供給不足時.正可因此彌補.以免發生供求不調之情.經濟組織.得以穩固.社會治安.不見動搖.此與生產民生之又一關係也.

交易所以其分配作用兼及將來之故.又加以所內設備傳佈消息機器.運轉靈通.故社會上細微變動.交易所作用即隨之轉移.商業情形.又隨此交易所作用之轉移而爲升降.西人嘗謂交易所爲商業氣候表.良有以也.

交易所與吾人有重大關係如此.故其間弊竇如操縱(Manipulation)沖賣(Wash sales)相對委託(Matched orders)及壟斷(Corner)傾軋(Squeeze)

等等.不可不注意及之.此數種弊竇雖名目不同.要其有害於生產民生也則一.虛構市面.紊亂價格.推其所極.徒使眞假倒置.是非莫明.將見其害適與其益相反.故論者目爲交易所之流弊.平心論之.操縱等弊.乃利用交易所者爲謀利起見.坐是利令智昏.異途橫出.或則市場組織未能盡善. Prof. H. C. Emercy有言.證券之所以爲操縱者.以其市場有限 (Limited market) 故也.若市場極大.鮮有能操縱之者.故操縱者.非交易所本身之病也.此言雖近乎理想.然實有至理.況此種惡習.倘政府加以取締.交易所加以嚴禁.並非不可避免者.不觀乎停止買賣.壟斷者因而胆寒.驅逐爲戒.冲賣者因而勢殺耶.所望此後道德增進.法律嚴密.庶幾大好之分配機械.不致引入歧路.則生產民生.俱可利賴.彼西人嘗以一國之交易所.覘其事業之興替.經濟之盛衰.謂爲商業氣候表.市場之市場.豈無故哉.返觀我國.歧途橫出.不加取締.版圖內之上海.任人設置似乎交易所之取引所.外侮內侵.力不能禦.開各國未有之先例.痛哉.實業不興.此非其徵兆也歟.

本文參考書列下

J. E. Meeker: The Work ot Stock Exchange

J. G. Smith: Organized Prodnce Market

Hardy: Risk aud Risk-tak'ng

文明書局: 交易所要覽

文明書局: 證券買賣秘術

文明書局: 交易所一覽

商務印書館: 馬寅初演講集（第一集）

商務印書館: 投資常識

交易所所員暑期養成所: 交易所大全

銀行公會: 銀行週刊六卷八號（恐慌預防號）

銀行之責任及應辦之事業

尤玉照

時至今日.銀行林立.凡可以流通金融發達商業開闢財源者.無不應有盡有.日臻完善.而各國政府.復汲汲焉皇皇焉惟銀行之是務.一若銀行爲邦本.舍此無以立國者.返顧我國.幅員之廣.人民之衆.較之東西巨邦.有過之無不及.獨銀行之創辦.垂二十餘年.非特中央之組織.仍付闕如.抑且濫發紙票.不事準備.因此破產之噩耗.近迫燃眉.危乎殆哉.國運阽危.金融主權外溢.吾人欲挽此狂瀾.使我國金融前途.重見光明者.則于銀行之責任及其應辦之事業.可不一究其底蘊乎.

夫欲知銀行之責任.及應辦之事業.則銀行之緣起及其分類不可不知矣.嘗考往昔之銀行.所經營者.僅爲貨幣之兌換.或兼任放款而已.其主要之目的.僅使貨幣流通.未有以一方受入之信用.復授與他人或包銷證劵及信託爲業務者也.夫所謂信用者.現今經濟組織之要素也.蓋信用能增加資金之效用而利生產.非獨有利生產.且能扶助消費.故信用可依其用度.分爲（一）投資信用(Investment Credit).（二）商業信用(Commercial Credit)（三）消費信用(Comsumptive Credit)三種.投資信用.專以發達工業.興築鐵路.擴充農場.以及採辦礦物.簡言之.則此種信用.用以造成固定資本者也.商業信用.用以供給製造銷貨資本.此種信用.強半爲短時期之借款.所謂流動資本是也.消費信用.大抵指借與消費者之借款.此種信用.不能立刻生利.故往往有到期不付之危險也.

上自政府.下至個人.以及一切公司機關.凡能利用信用之際.無不轉求于銀行.銀行制度.因社會之需求.與時之變更.責任既殊.性質頓異.而根本建設.因之而不同.顧名思義.爰有下列之派別.

（一）投資銀行(Investment Bank)

（二）信託公司（Trust Co.）

（三）儲蓄銀行（Savings Bank）

（四）商業銀行（Commercial Bank）

（五）中國之錢莊（Chinese Native Bank）

（六）馬立司式銀行（Morris Plan Bank）

銀行制度之分類.在現今時代.已如上述.然則吾人欲知各種銀行之責任.各種銀行之業務及其能辦之事業.不可不先加說明.玆攷投資銀行業務有三（一）考查（Investigation）及分析（Analysis）.（二）承包（Underwriting）（三）分銷（Distribution）例如某公司請求銀行代銷股票或債票.於是銀行須先決定此所要求代銷之證券.究竟有代銷之價值與否.是否合於投資性質.分析既明.然後承包.此其利點.可分爲兩層.對于發行公司（Issuing Co.）.可使之於預定期內募足預定資本以振興企業.對于投資者.可使其得確實之保障.穩固之南針.若所發債票甚大.難以單獨包銷.則可組織銀行團承包之.以減輕風險.至于分銷之法.或由銀行親自售去.或託經紀人等出外推銷.投資銀行.以有上述諸作用.故各種經濟機關之設立.實有賴于此也.蛛網鐵道之建築.縱橫河道之開濬.以及水火保險事業之發達.皆由此種銀行之資助.他若普通工業.得以開辦.邊疆拓墾.得以實現.礦產森林.農工畜牧.無不因之而發展.以免一國之間.民衆麕集一隅.此投資銀行之所以盛行於美國也.

信託公司者.以經營信託業務爲主.信託云者.信任之意也.吾人對于信託公司.必先信任而後始願以財產委託公司.代爲保管及整理.例如意欲出遊之前.可將各種資產委託公司.代爲保管或整頓.如其財產爲債票與股票則抽籤還本付息買賣等一切.均可付託之.又如其資產爲不動產.則修理等事.亦可請其代勞.又如捐助鉅資于慈善事業以爲基金.爲免流弊計.可委信託公司掌理之.是皆信託公司承個人委託代辦之事也.他若各種實業公司亦有委託信託公司代理事務者.例如鐵路公司.以全路作抵.發行債票.其抵

押契據.以債權者人數甚多.勢不能直接交債權者.故不得不請信託公司.代爲保管.如鐵路公司倒閉.信託公司代表債權者沒收其抵押品.此實業公司委託信託公司之一例也.

至於儲蓄銀行.乃經理儲蓄存款之特別機關.即保管平民儲蓄金而爲之生利.所謂舉無用之財.轉而爲生利之資本也.嘗觀平民智識膚淺.終日孜孜.朝之所得.暮必罄之.鮮有儲蓄之習慣.即或有擔石之儲.又不免有盜賊之虞.若是而欲期儲蓄心之發達.誠戛戛乎其難矣.惟設有儲蓄銀行.爲之保管.爲之利殖.日積月累.爲數甚鉅.且勤儉之風日益長.儲蓄之心日益熾.而平民養生送死盡其道.疾病顚連得其養.其結果使自治獨立者.日益增加.是儲蓄銀行之所以爲社會公共必要之設備.營利之中寓有慈善目的者也.是以儲蓄銀行與其他銀行性質不同.蓋蒙其澤者.泰半在普通平民.

其能便利商人.通融資金.爲各種銀行之中心點者.當首推商業銀行.商業銀行者.貼現及存款之機關也.蓋普通商人需要之固定資本.爲數極少.而以迅速運動流動資本爲第一要義.譬如買入之商品.一時銷滯.或憑信用而賣出之商品.一時不能收回貨價.資本勢不能轉而運用.因此縮小其營業範圍者有之.陷于極困難之地位者有之.甚或因此迫而倒閉.夷爲清算.現今商人.爲避免上述種種困難計.於是將顧客之期票.持往銀行.請爲貼現.或則自書匯票.使顧客承受 (Accept) .承受之後.與銀行貼現.名雖貼現.實則借款.蓋因此期票或匯票.即可轉爲存款(Deposit credit).據此存款.以簽支票.藉以補助一時阻滯.由是市面得以流通.金融於此運轉矣.貼現交易.在商人方面.可以運轉難關.在銀行方面.可以獲得厚利.顧銀行並無一文借出.所借出者.信用而已.惟賴此信用.商人易于運轉.銀行因此獲得厚利.市面因此流通.商業因此繁盛.是則商業銀行之所以爲現今銀行之中心點.信用制度之樞紐也.其省卻現金之機能.則在票據交換所.銀行因支票之欠人與人欠兩項.可兩相抵冲.故現洋之引用可簡省.此外如發行鈔票.予商人以便利穩妥之交易

媒介.並補助貨幣之不足.以及匯兌現款.金銀買賣.皆足予商人以極大之便利.更有所謂拆銀（Call loan）者.可以使經紀人買賣.而交易所亦得以運轉.

錢莊者.吾國原有之金融機關也.此種名稱.雖與銀行相異.攷其實在事業.乃與銀行大致相同.其在中國.銀行史上之最初機關也.究其大宗贏利.皆由洋厘之漲落而來.惟其放款大多無須擔保品.故吾國商人.均喜與錢莊往來.而今日之莊票.反較銀行支票易于流通.雖銀行盛行.舊風猶未能改.推厥原因.無非吾國商人.除少數新式商人外.皆不欲與銀行有何往來.因其放款手續煩冗也.

以上所述之信用.皆爲用于生產方面者.對于消費信用.猶未提及.試觀以供給消費信用爲業者.在各國有當舖.在美國有借款造屋會（Building & Loan Association）最近美國又有馬立司式銀行.是三種組織.以馬立司式銀行爲尤要.是行之放款.與其他不同.其放法以對人信用爲要義.並不以物品作抵押也.

綜觀上列各種組織及其業務.似處置各有不同.然吏攷其實.各項業務.並不如是之分歧.如商業銀行.現亦兼營儲蓄.甚或兼行投資.至于信託公司.則一切信用事業.無不可兼營.並御.蓋各種組織.皆所以予社會以信用便利.有時投資信用而兼商業信用.或商業信用而轉兼消費信用.其各種業務之不同.要皆所供信用之不同耳.吏考投資信用.分內所應經營者.在募集資本使各種資本.大宗小數.併入生產一門.由是精益求精.使生產資本.轉而爲更生產.由是分析承包及分銷等.皆爲分內所兼營.使小本平民.得一儲蓄之機會.投資之方針.簡而言之.即可使小數之現金.不致流爲阻滯.廢爲無利.流入于生產資本.而各種生產機關.若鐵路採礦等.遂得開辦.是則投資信用之流爲銀行務者也.

消費一事.爲人生所必需.在經濟學方面.爲經濟組織之一則.故消費信

用.爲吾人不可或缺者.且大多信用借款.雖名爲用于消費之途.然入後終歸于生產.例如借款就學.目前觀之.有如消費.然學而有成.服務社會.予人類以文明之進步.予國家以幹柱之傑才.推原其故.全賴此種借款.有以促成之.故曰消費信用.名爲消費.實則間接爲將來之生產信用也.經營消費信用者.當以供給一時無力.而所消費者爲人生及社會所必需者爲限.以免濫用信用.流入歧途.若無產階級.予以造就.或窮苦無告.予以扶助.俾得救急一時.利用終身.國家社會.皆蒙其澤焉.

信用之在今日.其重要如上述.然考信用制度之中心點.則在商業信用.據普通人之心理.商業愈發達.則商業信用亦愈膨脹.蓋商業之繁盛.實有賴于商業信用.徵諸學理及事實.皆足取信.譬之商業銀行.將利率放低.則製造者.將羣向銀行籌借.通融資金.買入原料.加工製造.以待物價騰貴.至平準以上.收莫大之利.他若批發所與小販商人.亦以便宜之信用.買入商品而儲藏之.以待善價而沽之.其時百業繁興.民生日隆.生產卽有重量亦不之顧.投資信用及消費信用.見民生日進.世運愈隆.亦盡量發展.由是而恐慌 (Crisis) 而爆亂 (Panic).可不愼哉.

爆亂者.乃由於生產與消費不能調和.供給與需要不能適合.致債務者不能履行其償還債務之義務.而信用交易之作用.遂發生一種紊亂之狀態也.考其由來.非發生于工商業之變動.乃基于金融上之變動.而爲一時發生之變態.故其原委.約分二種.(一)信用之充分膨脹.引起投機與生產過剩.(二)因不測之事變.而信用交易驟呈破裂.茲分述之.

據上述第一原因.乃由于經濟社會之變動.如商業交易之膨脹.紅利與工銀之激增.商工業關係者收益之增加.投資之過分踴躍.證券市價之騰貴.新證券之發行.企業之勃興.馴至投機狂盛.銀行營業.充分膨脹.紙幣濫發.準備金處理失當.因此紙幣不能照票面使用.卽使使用.未必能兌現.甚至市場往來不願接收紙幣者.同時存款信用 (Deposit credit) 難以付現.物價水平線

日益漲高.於是人心皇皇.遂成恐慌之象.恐慌至于極點.所謂爆亂者生焉.

第二原因.乃由于不測之事故.而信用交易突然破裂也.例如戰事之發生.政治上之革命.大公司大銀行之突呈破綻.一時經濟社會驟生恐怖.債權者以急欲自謀安全起見.爭先收回其債權.於是信用交易頓告停滯.而惹起恐慌發生爆亂矣.

爆亂之發生.有一定之時期.依規則之期間相循環.周而復始.無或相差.其普通期限.大都以十年爲率.觀于英國自十八世紀以來.殆於每十年之間.恆發生一次.卽可以徵之矣.恐慌定期之發生.從來學者承認此說者頗多.然其總歸宿大致相類.如 John Mill 氏之信用輪環說 (Thery of Credit Cycle) 及 Jevon 氏之太陽黑點說 (Sunspot Theory) 是也.

爆亂狀態.旣如上述.而以信用往來之紊亂關係爲主.然在今日.銀行實處于信用制度之中心地位.是以爆亂之豫防銀行實當其衝.然爆亂之來必經恐慌.前已言之.則是欲防爆亂.必先救濟恐慌矣.夫恐慌之象.乃由于資金需給之不調.如就銀行營業實際上言之.若因準備金之減少而生者.則其救治之根本方策.除力謀準備金之增加外.無他道也.又有因生產過量.而危及信用者.於是往往有增加資金之供給.以鎮壓恐慌.其實不增加準備金.而用其他方法.不足以救濟恐慌.加以信用已過度膨脹.若更加膨脹.則其制度之基礎.愈加薄弱.實非救濟恐慌.反有以激成爆亂.是以恐慌之際.必先謀準備金增加.對于信用之膨脹.加以適宜之限制.以鞏固其基礎.並提高利率.以制止信用有不正當之膨脹.恐慌之際.并需矯正市場.從外國吸收現金.是爲至要.千八百六十六年來.據英蘭銀行數回恐慌之實驗言之.依此方針處置.有謂其爲激成恐慌者.然而比之恐慌之際.仍不顧前途之危險.膨脹信用.任令其制度崩壞者.其利害不可同日語矣.

馬克拉得氏所謂收縮政策 (Restrictive Policy) 者.非謂銀行對於顧客.不加區別.一概採用收縮政策.而不與通融.如此則全體社會.將發生恐怖之

心.非獨使確實有信用之人.受恐慌之累.並足以促進一般人提取存款.所以一方面行收縮政策.一方又實行膨脹政策 (Extensive Policy). 對于確實有担保者.又持有信用票據者.不論其爲商人爲銀行爲票據經紀人.均與之以融通.以鎮壓市場之恐慌.則提取存款.追迫債務.可以免矣.千八百二十五年之恐慌.英蘭銀行果如何鎮壓之乎.當時之銀行當局者.採取膨脹政策.對於以確實有價證劵爲擔保者.則與以資金上之融通.苟其資力之所能及者.無不與以融通之道.恐慌鎮壓.與有力焉.千八百九十三年.紐約市場之融通.亦用膨脹政策以鎮壓之者也.

徵之實例.紐約之銀行.平時貸出金額.在存款以內者爲常.超過之者甚少.千八百九十三年一月之第一週間.紐約會員銀行之貸出金.爲四億四千十八萬美金元.其存款爲四億五千五百三十六萬美金元.又是年十二月之末.貸出金爲四億千六百六十萬美金元.其存款爲五億六百四十三萬美金元.在七月四日恐慌之初.至八月五日.其存款僅五千八百四十六萬六千美金元.而其貸出額達四億八百七十六萬美金元之多.一方則存款減少.一方則貸出增加.蓋以在恐慌之際.破裂之前.則收回放款.及爆裂之後.利用交換所貸款證劵 (Clearing-house loan certificates) 之發行.力求通融.是以前後相對觀察之.收縮膨脹兩政策.最爲適用.且有併用之必要.學者實際家.幾於一致承認之矣.基阿特氏有曰.

鎮靜恐慌.是爲必要.假使利率雖高.銀行尙可以融通資金.則信用制度.不致全體破壞.又何必呈一種狂態.而爭相取現乎.

膨脹收縮兩策之併用者.爲巴氏之宿論.以爲在恐慌之際.對于社會表示尙有資金融通之餘力.又在必要實行之時.中央銀行不着眼於自己之利益.而在社會上打算.故最後之責任.歸之於中央銀行.至爲確當.然就資金融通言.銀行亦不無非常應付法也.巴氏之論.以下舉二策爲必要.

(第一) 放款非高利率不可.

（第二）提高利率總以對於有善良担保者爲要.

雖然恐慌之來.若急取非常手段.非策之上也.要在於恐慌之前.適當改正其營業方針.而有以準備之耳.今舉其方法之重要者於下.

（一）到期之債權.從速收回.若尙不能用以應付自己之債務.則賣却所有之證劵.

（二）或以所有之貼現票據（discounted bills）向中央銀行重行貼現.

（三）對于信用不確實之票據.拒絕貼現.實行收縮政策.如此則銀行最爲安全.且可遏抑投機之風.一時雖于銀行無大利益.然可不致膨脹信用.而遭反動之不幸也.

恐慌之際.銀行互相協同.以謀鎭壓.近年來在經濟上.已呈一顯著之現象.美國聯合準備金制度.其適例也.歐洲諸國各銀行之準備金.集中於中央銀行.恐慌之際.雖無聯合之必要.尙有以別種方法.在國際間取營業上共同之方針.例如千八百二十五年之恐慌.英蘭銀行三日間.發行五百萬鎊之紙幣.又從法蘭西銀行借入二百萬鎊之資金.其後恐慌遂不致擴大.則是爆亂之來.銀行之負任.豈不重且大哉.

返觀我國.中央銀行.組織闕如.票據交換所.依然虛渺.而社會之積習.復牢不可破.素重現幣及莊票之慣例.難以改良.坐是銀行開辦二十餘年.強半金融勢力.仍操諸不適世變之錢業.可慨也夫.

欲超勝錢業幷使支票流通.則上海必須先行設立票據交換所.蓋上海爲吾國商業之中心.金融之樞紐.雖不能與英之倫敦.美之紐約相媲美.然其經濟上地位之重.適相等也.使交換非現洋不辦.則非特攜帶不便.亦且檢點費時.此外如銀質之磨損.保管之責任.利息之損失.以及鼓鑄之煩瑣.均爲極不經濟者.長此以往.社會愈進步.此項損失必愈大.幾何其不陷于十八世紀黑暗之境地也.今日上海銀行林立.類皆資本充足.信用素孚.而勢力不及錢莊遠甚.即平日之收支各款.非委託錢莊代理不可.蓋錢莊有匯劃總會.以爲

交換票據之所.而銀行不得加入也.於是銀行之款.存放于錢莊者.爲數多則千餘萬.少則五六百萬.此卽以己之予.攻己之盾也.何其傎耶.雖然.銀行之委託錢莊代爲收付者.原因頗多.卽自設據票交換所.以爲相互間收支之清理.恐亦不能遽與錢莊斷絕關係.顧大勢所趨.優者必勝.經濟社會之發達.由簡單而複雜.由小規模而大規模.小資本之營業.其退也速.大資本之企業.其進也驟.日本自維新迄今.不過四五十年.吾國實業因受政局之影響.不克兼程進行.然其進步.不可謂不速.將來各種大規模之企業.相繼而起者.必不可勝數.其需要之程度.決非小規模之錢莊所能計及.據此以觀.上海之銀行.今日雖不能與錢莊相抗.然最後之勝利必歸銀行.可斷言也.欲得此勝利.非先爲種種籌備不可.票據交換所爲籌備中之最要者.斷不能待時機已過.方始着手籌備也.

況票據交換所者.係銀行抵抗外敵之一種武器.蓋交換所成立之後.銀行相互間之欠人與人欠兩項.可以倣錢業軋公單之方法.兩相抵消.現金之用途減少.搬運之麻煩可去.旣省手續.又免風險.銀行從此可以致全力于營業矣.況在市面恐慌.或金融緊急之際.現金之需要驟增.銀拆飛漲.借貸停頓.苟有交換所以爲調劑.各行間可以不用現洋.清理其存欠.如是可以騰出若干現金.以應市面之需.非特銀行可以減卻擠兌之風險.卽商家亦易得資金之援助.豈不一舉兩得耶.進而言之.上海一埠旣設立交換所.循此推廣.通行各埠.爲策亦不難矣.

支票流通後.則期匯票相繼出現.可在意料之中.期匯票旣多.銀行貼現事業.亦因而增加.然于金融奇緊之際.若普通銀行不能持.已貼現而未到期之票據 (discounted bills).向中央銀行重行貼現 (rediscount).以謀存款信用 (deposit credit) 之伸縮.則其勢甚虞.況中央銀行有伸縮 currency 之能力乎.是故中央銀行之有伸縮 currency 及 deposit credit 等權力.吾國當代銀行界實不可不注意及之.如猶一意孤行.不顧利害.則銀行事業之發展進

步，不僅遙遙無期，根本破產之禍，旦夕可見，此余之所以大聲疾呼，願吾國銀行界闢一線曙光也。

補白二

各國每十萬人所得之鐵路綫

國別	哩數
奧大利亞	404
坎拿大	308
合衆國	261
荷蘭	254
瑞士	78
法國	64
德國	57
英國	52
西班牙	48
意大利	31
俄國	26
日本	12
印度	11
暹羅	9
中國	2

工業儲蓄之銀行功用

(Industrial Savings Banking)

Leo Dav Woodworth 原著

貢乙青譯意

時至今日.生活程度日高.勞工者與儲蓄銀行之關係遂日益親密.蓋資本需求.日益增進.勞工者薪金雖小.較諸曩昔已加高多多.倘得集腋成裘.未始不無小補.在工人方面.若無一極便利之儲蓄機關.一旦工資到手.幾何其不揮霍無餘.儲蓄銀行者.以養成儲蓄性節儉心爲職務者也.視此無數工人將血汗所積之金錢.隨意濫用.不將失其儲蓄銀行之天職乎.

以經濟制度家庭爲單位而論.銀行可以鼓勵工人節儉之道有三.(一)工人以工業儲蓄制度而節儉.(二)孩童以學校儲蓄制度 (School Savings System) 而節儉.主婦以銀行家庭經濟部 (Home Economics Dept, in Banks) 而節儉.本論所及.僅爲第一項.

I

照一九二十年 The Gommittee on Profit Sharing and Allied Thrift Plans of the National Ass'n of Corp. School 之報告,現今儲蓄之法若儲蓄銀行人壽保險郵政儲蓄等等.皆非足以使凡有餘資者儘量儲蓄.蓋不便利也.不能接近也.缺少鼓勵也.皆足以阻儲蓄之普及.至若付托失人.以保護投資爲名.行其投機之實.遂使工人血汗金錢.坐受損失.因此工人之間.不願儲者爲數亦多.惟極多工廠.設有數種儲蓄之法.任工人自由選擇.毫無父母管理態度 (Paternalism) 之可言.是乃今日行之最爲有效者也.

現在所行工業儲蓄制度.並非另設新異制度.不過就原有儲蓄銀行之功用.加以改良.俾各工人皆可利用而已.

II

工業儲業制度.爲儲蓄銀行推其效用於工廠之內.與此制度有極要關係者凡三.一工人.二僱主.三銀行.故欲此制度施諸實行.必將此三方利益.統籌兼顧.不使觝觸.

（一）工人方面　所有此制度之宗旨.務必使工人個個明瞭.免生誤會及猜疑.否則.必有謂爲徒受他人利用者.此乃銀行家所應注意及之者也.

（二）僱主方面　僱主之欲其工人有節儉之風也.人各具有同心.惟因實行此種制度如「扣薪儲蓄制」時.僱主方面.不免多一手續.然此不足爲僱主害.如僱主誠不欲舉此煩勞.吾人猶有他法以補救之也.所謂他法.請於下段論之.

（三）銀行方面　此項存款.雖其存戶極多.然其爲數極小.故爲銀行營業計.務必設法減少開支.更有一事應注意者.卽此種制度.雖於銀行極有利益.由其業務方面觀之.實屬創舉.

III.

工業儲蓄制度.考其與銀行合作情形.殊不盡同.分類觀之.約有四種.（一）於僱主事務所設立分行.（二）遣派職員至工廠招徠存款.（三）僱主扣留工資.送至銀行代工人儲蓄.（四）售出印花或證書.工人可持之向銀行存款.此四種制度.美國各工廠行之者甚多.著成效者亦不少.玆將其各種辦法詳情.略述于下.

（一）設立分行制　於工廠發薪員事務所內或另建房屋於廠內.設一分行.專收工人存款.美國 New Orlean Bank 行之.又有幾家銀行.於發薪日期.遣員至廠內收此項存款.此種制度.固屬便利.然工人猶謂無選擇投資之可能,一旦工人與銀行發生意見.卽有不再存款者.此其弊也.

（二）遣員招徠制　美國 New England Bank 實行之.此制之長處.在行使銀行職務.無須僱主之援助.且人工招徠.最易推廣營業.至其短處.則在太

糜費.因工人儲蓄.爲數極小.所得利益祇能與一銀行職員之開支勉強抵消.故爲銀行計.人工招徠.最爲糜費.務必設法推廣營業.或減少開支.以資抵補.

更有一事.爲前述二制之病者.卽銀行營業時間.往往與工廠工作時間.互相衝突.極多數工人.遂有因此不儲蓄於銀行者.由是「扣薪儲蓄制」及「儲蓄證書制.」出而補其不足焉.

(三) 扣薪儲蓄制　此種制度除予工人以時間便利外.工人之意志游移托故不能盡量儲蓄者.將于此制度之下.因預定扣薪之數.不得不儘量儲蓄.惟其短處亦有二.一爲工人之私業易爲僱主所知.一爲僱主方面易含有父母式的作用(Paternalistic activities)因此工業方面.時有不滿之論調.謂在此制度之下.工人竟無處置私人財產.發展個人判決力投資力之自由.但此種論調.其根本誤點.在僱主信用未著.工人遂不願其私業被理於僱主.果僱主信用已著.工人且將羣向僱主請願.代爲保存或儲蓄.何况扣其工資代爲儲蓄.且已得其心所許乎.惟僱主方面.則反因此加增手續矣.

此種扣薪儲蓄制.因工廠之大小.手續有繁簡之不同.由簡至繁.約有下列三種.

(甲) 美國 Nerm:nt Marble Co.所行之「扣薪儲蓄制.」其法由僱主貼出宣告(Announciation)凡工人之願儲蓄者.可寫一委托書(Authorization)至僱主方面.於發工資之日.將認定存數.按次扣留代存指定銀行.故此委托書實含有合全性質.至爲重要.僱主旣將款項扣下.遂書一通知(Notice)與工人.亦有僱主買銀行所發儲蓄證書交與工人以代通知者.工人遂可持此證書向銀行付款或存蓄.但此項證書.不可轉讓他人.以爲流通契據

(乙) 第二種扣薪儲蓄制.乃於前法略加改良而已.美國現在行此法者甚多.其法乃由僱主發出宣告書於各工人.內載種種儲蓄說明.蓋

僱主不過爲代理工人儲蓄而已.但僱主於此項手續.並不取經手費.凡工人自願儲蓄者.可於此宣告書附帶之委托書.將所認儲蓄數目寫下.並書一簽名于銀行簽名單.持至發薪員處.發薪員即可於發工資時,照數扣留.發薪員須爲工人作一事務所記錄.每次存款至銀行.作存款單 (Deposit Slip) 兩張.一正一副.將各工人存款.載於其上.使銀行將各工人存款登載各人來往簿.此正張存款單留於銀行.至副張存款單.退回工廠作爲工廠記錄.工廠每次存款之後.作一通知書與各工人.使各工人知其現存銀行總數.及新近所扣數目.至於來往簿.放在銀行或放在僱主或交與工人.皆無不可.惟就大概而論.則留諸僱主方面爲多.蓋銀行方面.大半不願代藏此項簿子.而此項簿子.又須時時持向銀行登記存款.故置諸僱主處較爲便利.然而工人如欲此項簿子.則可事先知照發薪處.發薪處自可定期歸還.

(丙) 美國 Goodyear Tire and Rubber Co. 工廠所行之扣薪儲蓄制.其大概情形.均載於該公司工廠組織規程之內.吾人觀其規程.或可知其崖略.規程如下.

「工人凡欲儲蓄者.須填一聲明書（此聲明書由工廠印就備用.）交與工廠事務所.聲明本人自願按次扣下工資若干.向某銀行儲蓄事務所接到此書後.用書面函復工人.工人即可持此回信至銀行開戶.銀行方面.接到此信後.隨即將存戶號碼.通知工廠事務所.由是工廠發薪處.實行扣留工資代爲存蓄.將所扣工資.按次書一收條夾在薪水封筒之內.交與工人.工人持此收條按月或隨時向銀行記載于來往簿上.倘工人意欲支付時.必須持來往簿同行.所支數目.以積存爲限.」

(四) 儲蓄證書制　是種制度.最利於凡工人之不欲其僱主知其私人狀況者.且較扣薪儲蓄制之必須依約定數目而爲儲蓄.爲有伸縮餘地.故工

人多喜之.其法有三.

(甲) 售賣節儉證書.以鼓勵儉德.此法不若扣薪儲蓄制之必須與僱主相輔而行也.現在此法.是否有實行之必要.己否有工廠曾經試行.尙未有正式之調查.今玆所言.不過理想中之一法耳.

(乙) 自動收納員節儉制(“Automatic Receiving Teller Thrift System.”)其法爲設置一縱削機器(Slot Machine)于工廠.售賣印花.五分十分不等.印花上刊有銀行牌號及號碼.發行銀行見此印花.卽認爲存款.銀行備有紙摺以貼印花.摺上載明儲蓄之名姓地址及號碼.贊成此制者.謂爲旣極便利工人.工人私人狀況又不易爲僱主所曉.美國Stewart-warner Speedometer工廠行之.

(丙) 工業銀行功用制(“Industrial Banking System”)美國雅魯工廠所行之印花儲蓄制也.其手續大致如下.由工人塡就銀行簽名單.將單及第一次存款交與僱主.由僱主轉交銀行.銀行依之頒發來往簿.此來往簿與尋常通行者式樣不同.前面印有空格.編有號碼.以便日後依次將印花貼上.此簿由僱主轉交工人.工人日後如欲存款.卽向僱主購買印花.此印花有一正一副.上面刊有銀行牌號及號碼.正張貼在來往簿上前面空格.副張貼在來往簿後面坿紙上.將坿紙裁下寄至銀行.所有來往簿.仍交與工人(照實在情形.來往簿大半保存僱主處.)銀行審查此項印花正副相對.將存款登載簿上.所有印花.以後作爲無效云云.總觀此制.可以使僱主免爲工人作何種記錄.而工人方面.因此制售賣印花.含有招徠性質.且隨意存儲.數額不定.都願採行此制.

結論

工業儲蓄之銀行功用.研究者殊不多覯.作者此篇.又屬初創.不到之處諒難幸免.所望此後實業家銀行家.以經驗之報告.作爲學者之討論.俾此制

度.推廣施行.儲蓄前途.實利賴之.

譯者附言　吾國今日.各種實業都在幼稚時代.他日欲施行各種建設.以脫此經濟侵略下之現狀.斷非空言救國所可彌補.必也未雨綢繆先事準備.如鉄路外債.抵押無餘.安有新建之望.而舊債末日.轉瞬即屆.倘一旦不能清償.是又必重求外債.去歲五卅案出.舉國若狂.抵制風聲.驚天動地.而今如何.據海關報告.輸入祇見增加.此無他.實業未發達耳.假若此後全國奮起.於儲蓄之道各謀改良.大家小戶.視力實行.以儲蓄之財興辦實業.安見十年之後.不全國工廠林立鉄路縱橫乎.本文所譯.乃美國銀行公會秘書華氏所著.原文以家庭節儉分爲三章.其中學校儲蓄及家庭經濟兩章容後續譯.不敢謂他國之制定可施於我邦.不過他山攻石云爾.

補　白　三

十四年度各路之收入

據交通部路政司統計十四年度各路收入狀況如下（單位國幣一元）

1. 盈餘各路

路	收入	路	收入	路	收入
京漢	11,950,000	京奉	618,684	津浦	2,746,687
滬甯	2,419,734（軍運在內）	滬杭甬	204,538	正太	2,143,938
膠濟	1,940,676	吉長	399,490	道清	790,860
汴洛	965,000	隴海	2,000,000	湘鄂	1,872,054
株萍	6,000	四洮	35,680		

（附註）隴海路尚未竣工上列二百萬僅爲營業盈餘債項支出尚未扣除

2. 虧折各路

路	金額	路	金額
京綏	1,056,000	廣九	671,500

3. 路政收入總計

項目	金額	項目	金額	項目	金額
營業收入	118,288,944	營業支出	68,359,440	營業盈餘	49,929,554
債項支出	29,622,548	債項收入	2,334,637	債項淨支	27,287,911
純　利	22,641,643				

記賬單位整理法

兪希稷講　沈奏廷記

我國銀兩習慣,迄未改除,授受雖用銀元,而記賬仍有用銀兩者,因洋釐之升降,賬目與實數即發生差異,如今日收洋百圓,洋釐爲七錢二分五厘二毫半,則賬上即記收入七十二兩五錢二分五厘,隔日以原洋百元付出因洋厘已跌至七二二二五,則賬上當記付出七十二兩二錢二分五厘,收付相抵,賬上尙餘銀三錢,但事實上收入之款,已全數付出,並無分文餘留,是賬目不與實況相符,記賬有何用處,倘收付款項增多,則不符之數愈大,苟不設法整理,則準確之營業報告,無從產出,玆姑以上海規元爲例,擬具整理方法,凡記賬與授受單位不同者,皆可引用此原理,並不限於銀兩也.

整理方法用於西式簿記者,其格式與用於中式簿者不同,爰分西式中式二種分論之.

(一)　西式簿記

(甲) 假定賬簿所屬機關以七錢三分爲標準洋釐.

(乙) 銀錢流水簿內另闢申水虧水二欄,以記市上洋釐與標準洋釐之差數.

(丙) 凡收款時洋釐較標準洋釐大,則將差數記入虧水欄,小則記入申水欄.凡付款時洋釐較標準洋釐大,則將差數記入申水欄,小則記入虧水欄.

(丁) 結賬時應將虧水各數相加,俾知其總數幾何.申水亦然.倘虧水總數大於申水總數時,則將相差之數與付出各款相加.（即記入貸方）否則將相差之數與收入各款相加.（即記入借方）然後計算現存銀錢之數目.

上列四種手續.可表明如下.

(1)　未整理時之賬

收項			付項		
日期	摘要	兩	日期	摘要	兩
二月初二	協和 貨洋	72.50(100元)	二月初三	裕大 貨洋	36.187(50元)
初五	裕豐 仝上	72.00(100元)	初七	泰安莊	71.25(100元)
初九	中國銀行	71.50(100元)	拾六	元泰莊	36.76(50元)
			拾八	生財	73.25(100元)
		216.00			217.447

上列之銀錢流水,收入爲三百元,付出亦爲三百元,收付應相抵銷.但以用規銀記賬並因洋釐上落之故,結果付款多於收款,相差至一兩四錢四分七厘,結賬時卽難符合.但此一兩四錢四分七厘又非損失,將何以處之.此整理之所以必要也.

(2) 整理後之賬（標準七錢三分）

收項				付項			
日期	摘要	兩	申水	日期	摘要	兩	虧水
二月初二	協和 貨洋	72.50(100元)	50	二月初三	裕大 貨洋	36.187(100元)	313
初五	裕豐 貨洋	72.00(100元)	100	初七	泰安莊	71.25(100元)	175
初九	中國銀行	71.50(100元)	150	十六	元泰莊	36.76(100元)	
十六			26	十八	生財	73.25(100元)	
十八			25			1.44	1447
	申水	1.447	3510				3510
		217.447				217.447	

將申水虧水之差數加入收項,收付卽能相抵,蓋表示收入之款,已全數付去也.此與事實正相吻合,整理之功用可知矣.上列之賬,收付適相抵銷.若倘有眞正餘款.則又如何.曰餘款之數.以七三(標準洋釐)除之.卽得現存洋元實數.例如二月初十又收洋百元.記賬爲七十一兩五錢.此款並未付出.則結賬後之結果.應如下式.

收項				付項			
日期	摘要	兩	申水	日期	摘要	兩	虧水
二月初二	協和 貨洋	72.50(100元)	50	二月初三	裕大 貨洋	36.187(50元)	313
初五	裕豐 貨洋	72.50(100元)	100	初七	泰安莊	71.25(100元)	
初九	中國銀行	71.50(100元)	150	十六	元泰莊	36.76(50元)	
初十	元康莊	71.50(100元)	150	十八	生財	73.25(100元)	
十六			26	十八	現存	73	
十八			25				2.947
	申水	2.947	5.01				5.01
		290.447				290.447	

現存既爲七十三兩,則以七錢三分除之,適得壹百元,此又與事實相符者也.爲明瞭起見,上例所用之數,皆爲五十元,一百元,若代以他數,亦無不可.

(二) 中式簿記

(甲) 假定標準洋釐爲七三.

(乙) 遇申水則收之,遇虧水則付之.

(丙) 結賬時申水與收款相加,虧水與付款相加,然後相銷,卽得現存.

補白四

敦慶法

泰西諸國。夙有年金。Annuities 凡人民納一定金額與政府。則政府分期付還之。此分期付還之本利。卽爲年金。此法之普通者也。敦慶法者。爲一意大利人所發明。亦年金法之一種。其法卽由人民付一定金額與政府。政府每年付還若干本利。此付還之數。分給與捐款者。若捐款者有死亡。則分給其餘生存者。故死亡者愈多。則生存者每年所得之金額亦愈多。例如捐款者一萬人。每人出百元。共爲百萬元。政府每年付還五萬元。分給捐款者。則每人年得五元。倘萬人中死亡數人。則其餘生存者卽可年得五元以上。若生存者僅五人。則每人年得一萬元。若僅一人。則獨得五萬元矣。苟他人不死。則一年穩獲五元之進款。苟死者甚多。則有一躍而暴富之希望。人心皆視己爲必享上壽者。故皆願醵資以冀富也。聞用是法集資。西國曾頗著成效。蓋亦巧矣。惟集資者必爲不死之政府。而政府又必須有強固之信用。不然。必莫之應也。

例如下式

二月初二日

收協和洋一百元規元七十二兩五錢

收申水　規元五錢

應存元七十三兩正

二月初三日　付裕大洋五十元規元三十六兩一

錢八分七

付虧水　規元三錢一分三

應存元三十六兩五錢

二月初五日

收裕豐洋一百元規元七十二兩正

收申水　規元一兩正

應存洋一百零九兩五錢

二月初七日　付泰安洋一百元規元七十兩二錢

五

應存元三十六兩五錢　付虧水　規元一兩七錢五

二月初九日

收中國銀行洋一百元規元七十兩五錢

收申水　規元一兩五錢

應存元一百零九兩五錢

二月十六日

收申水　規元二錢六　付元泰洋五十元規元三十六兩七

應存元七十三兩正　錢六

二月十八日

收申水　規元二錢五　付生財洋一百元規元七十三兩二

應存元〇兩　錢五

在總清簿內當再立一兌換賬.逐日將申水過入收方,虧水過入付方,俾結賬時可明知申虧總數及其差額,於核對錢總時頗有用處.

中式銀錢.流水逐日結算,其結果尤爲易見,手續亦甚簡捷,或較西式簿記更形便利.今市上有收銀後,再付兌換,然後再收標準銀數者.(如收洋百元銀錢流水內記收元七十二兩五錢,付兌換元七十二兩五錢,再收元七十三兩)法煩而不明.不若記申水虧水之較醒眉目而省手續也.若未採整理方法之商家亟宜採用.庶幾賬目精確並免結賬時之困難.事半功倍.奈何忽之.

要之整理之基礎.卽爲標準洋價.無標準卽無整理之可言.但標準之大小,可隨各機關自擇,毫無根本關係.不過就普通情形而言,七錢二分爲適中數耳.又若用大洋記賬,而受授時有小洋,有銅元,亦可按此原理,以若干小洋會若干大洋,定爲標準計算,差數或申或虧,爲之收付,理法相同,不贅.

基本金及儲備金問題

楊培琫

基本金與儲備金.在工商業上最爲重要.忍每見學者對於深奥不切實用之數學.研究之惟恐不力.而於經濟有用之算術.反少注意.因作問題數則.藉以引起學者之觀念.且以明此種算術與經濟之關係.

基本金定義: 以款存放生利機關.(如銀行之類)所得利息.以作建築或設備某事某物之用.倘經過若干時期.物事損壞,不堪應用,又將所得利息,爲之重新建設,使事物永久存在,應用無窮者,謂之基本金.

總基本金定義: 總基本金者.卽事物初次之價值.與基本金相加是也.

基本金公式: 推求基金公式之法有三.一由年金公式推求.一由無限比級數推求.一由複利公式推求.由年金公式推求.各理財算術書言之綦詳.惟用複利公式推求.尙少人道及.予以其淺顯易明用之.今假定A爲本利之和.(簡稱曰總數).P爲本金,i爲利率,n爲年數,I爲利息.則由任何算術書中,得複利公式如下.

$$A=P(1+i)^n \quad \text{……公式(1)}$$

但利息等於總數減去本金

故 $I=A-P$

$$=P(1+i)^n-P$$

$$I=P\left[(1+i)^n-1\right]$$

依基本金定義.所得利息作爲建設事物之用.今假定物事之價值爲C_2.則C_2須與利息相等卽$I=C_2$.

故 $C_2=P\left[(1+i)^n-1\right]$

變換之.則得

$$P = \frac{C_2}{\left[(1+i)^n - 1\right]}$$

又假定用 i 乘分子分母.方程式關係不變.即

$$P = \frac{C_2}{\left[(1+i)^n - 1\right]} \times \frac{i}{i}$$

$$P = \frac{C_2}{i}\left[\frac{i}{(1+i)^n - 1}\right] \text{……公式(2)}$$

此基本金公式也.P字係代表基本金.今又假定 C_1 爲事物之初次價値.則

$$\text{總基本金} = C_1 + P$$

$$= C_1 + \frac{C_2}{i}\left[\frac{i}{(1+i)^n - 1}\right] \text{……公式(3)}$$

如初次之價値與事物後期之價値相等.即 $C_2 = C_1$ 而以C字代表之.則

$$\text{總基本金} = C + \frac{C}{i}\left[\frac{i}{(1+i)^n - 1}\right]$$

又以 $\frac{i}{i}$ 乘C.則得

$$\text{總基本金} = \frac{Ci}{i} + \frac{C}{i}\left[\frac{i}{(1+i)^n - 1}\right] = \frac{C}{i}\left[\frac{i}{(1+i)^n - 1}\right] \text{……公式(4)}$$

今設問題數則以明各公式之運用.

例題一

吾校體育館預料可用三十五年.三十五年後.則破舊不堪.須宜再造.如其時造價爲十四萬元.問今須存款若干於生利機關.使吾校永久有體育館一座.銀市利率八厘.

答　依公式(2) C_2 爲事物之價値即 = 140000元. $i = 0{\cdot}08$. $n = 35$年.

$$故基本金 = P = \frac{140000}{0\cdot08}\left[\frac{0\cdot08}{(1+0\ 08)^{35}-1}\right]$$

$$= 1750000 \times 0\cdot00580326$$

$$= 10,155.70元$$

答曰.如今放存一萬零一百五十五元七角於銀行.又如銀行給予年息八.厘.滿三十五年則得利息十四萬元.以爲重建體育館之用.又再過三十五年卽吾校百年紀念.又得利息十四萬元.爲新體育館之造價如是體育館永久存在矣.

例題二

(a) 吾校近來籌備三十週年紀念.擬建築工業館一座.假定其造價爲六萬元.問須籌款若干.使吾校永遠有工業館一座.假定該館可用三十五年而銀市利率八厘.

答.此題未有說明三十五年後之造價若干.吾人祇可當爲六萬元.如是.依公式(4). C=60000. i=0·08. n=35.

$$故總基本金 = \frac{60000}{0\cdot08}\left[0\cdot08+\frac{0\cdot08}{(1+\cdot08)^{35}-1}\right]$$

$$= 750000 \times 0\cdot08580326$$

$$= 64,352\cdot45元$$

答曰.共須籌六萬四千三百五十二元四角五分.內六萬元可作建築工業館之用.餘四千三百五十二元四角五分可作爲基本金.存放銀行生利.則吾校當永遠有工業館以作紀念也.

(b) 或問曰方今生活程度日高.三十五年後之造價.非六萬元可能辦到.今假定日後造價爲十萬元.則如何計算.

答曰.可用公式(3)以求之.卽

總基本金 $= C_1 + \dfrac{C_2}{i}\left[\dfrac{i}{(1+i)^n-1}\right]$ 此式內 $C_1=60000$元. $C_2=100000$元. $i=\cdot08$. $n=35$.

$$\text{是以總基本金} = 60000 + \frac{100000}{0\cdot08}\left[\frac{0\cdot08}{(1+0\cdot8)^{35}-1}\right]$$

$$= 60000 + 1250000\times0\cdot00580326$$

$$= 60000 + 7254\cdot$$

$$= 67254$$

答曰.須共籌六萬七千二百五十四元.

例題三

或又問曰.如能籌得此款.使該館與天同壽.甚善.顧今日籌款匪易.倘籌不到此數.作退一步計畫.使本校六十五週年紀念時.又得款十萬元.建一新工業館則又當如何計算.

答曰.可用現値法以求之.倘將公式(1)變之.則得

$$P = \frac{A}{(1+i)^n} \quad\text{……公式(5)}$$

此現值公式也.其意卽三十五年後.欲得A元.今須有款P元是矣.故若以十萬元代A., ·08代i., 35代n, 則得

$$P = \frac{100,000}{(1+0\cdot08)^{35}}$$

$$= 100,000\times0\cdot06763454$$

$$= 6763\cdot45\text{元}$$

卽以此款放存銀行.則三十五年期滿本利共得十萬元也.

答曰.一共須籌(60000+6763·45)六萬六千七百六十三元四角五分.例題二(b)所得結果.與例題三所得者相差不過(67254－66763·45)490·55元.爲久遠計.基本金之籌籌尙矣.

例題四

或再問曰.假如籌款祗得六萬元.建築之費倘虞不足.則有何易舉之法.使三十五年後.卽吾校六十五週年紀念時.有款十萬爲重建工業館之用.

答.可用儲備金之法.如將公式(2)中之$\frac{i}{(1+i)^n-1}$倒置.則得一元年金之總數平常以$S_{\overline{n|}}$代之.卽

$$S_{\overline{n|}} = \frac{(i+i)^n - 1}{i}$$

此公式之意義.卽每年年終存銀一元於銀行.倘銀行利率爲i.則到n年期滿.本利一共得$S_{\overline{n|}}$是矣.倘每年存放銀行之數不止一元.而爲R元.而又以$A_{\overline{n|}}$代表總數.則得式如下.

$$A_{\overline{n|}} = R\left[\frac{(1+i)^n - 1}{i}\right]$$

變換之.則得

$$R = A_{\overline{n|}}\left[\frac{i}{(1+i)^n - 1}\right] \cdots\cdots\cdots\text{公式(6)}$$

此儲備金公式也.今若以100000元代$A_{\overline{n|}}$, i及n如前.則

$$R = 100000\times\left[\frac{0\cdot08}{(1+0\cdot08)^{35}-1}\right]$$

$$= 100000\times 0\cdot00\ 580326$$

$$= 580\cdot33$$

答曰.無論籌款多寡.盡數撥爲建築費.然後每年年終由校於收入項下提出五百八十元三角三分放存銀行.則三十五年期滿.可共得本利十萬元爲重建該館之用也.

（未完）

對於淞滬試辦宅地稅之管見

直夫

淞滬宅地稅局自奉省令頒布設立後.已於五月十六日正式通告成立自此稅議起.淞滬各界之贊成者固不乏人.反對者尤屬多數.贊成者之言曰淞滬自開商埠以來.外人於華界毗連之地.往往越界築路.供給水電.征收房捐實與國土稅權有關.是以宅地稅之舉辦刻不容緩.而反對者之理由則約爲二.一謂華界既納糧稅.又納他種稅捐.如捲烟稅印花稅等.名目繁多.不克再加負擔.一謂宅地稅雖云加諸富戶.將來宅地勢必增高租價.負擔仍在平民.且年來上海迭遭戰事.商業凋零.兼以米價奇昂.民間生活力已薄.故上年上海市公所因擴充公益事宜.欲增加公益稅.旋復停止.今宅地稅值千抽五較公益稅尤鉅.如果舉行.深恐羣起反抗.

按上所述.贊否兩方.各具理由.然贊成者係在外交上立論.與宅地稅之創辦.似無直接關係.夫越界築路.違反條約.卽無宅地稅.亦應取締.至於反對者之第一項理由.謂舊稅已多.不能復加新稅.是殆不然.查淞滬施行宅地稅條例第六條.試行宅地稅區域內之原有通常課稅.除丁銀另一性質外.其已完漕蕩等非宅地稅者.得驗明串據.按數在應納宅地稅內減除之.若夫捲烟稅印花稅等.目的既與宅地稅異.稅源亦與宅地稅殊.分道揚鑣.自可平行不悖.其第二項理由雖較第一項爲充分.然地主將所納稅轉嫁於人.實爲宅地稅根本上所不許.蓋此稅之負擔者明明爲有宅地之人.若得任意轉嫁其負擔於租地人.毋甯直接增加房捐之爲愈.又何必征收宅地稅乎.此由於一般人民不明是稅之眞相也.

考宅地之稅.自古有之.禹貢著降邱宅土之文.周禮立載師任土之法.成周九賦.首及邦中.孟子亦曰國中什一使自賦此卽爲一般土地徵稅之明證.前清戶部則例.田賦名目有田地山蕩之別.所謂地者.卽兼種植與非種植而

言，實包宅地在內.而揆諸實際.各處城內地畝無稅者多.以都會論.則京師無稅.以江浙論.則江蘇江甯省城皆無稅.而浙江有之.以北部論.奉天吉黑省城均有稅.而其餘各省無之.至府縣城內市鎮等.有有稅者.有無稅者.究其無稅之原因.或起自唐宋食邑之制.或兆自前代復賦之例.因循既久.影射益多.漏稅之地.遂日漸增加耳.民國四年春.財政部以鄉鄙之地.農民胼手胝足.終歲勤苦.尚須竭力輸將.而都會市鎮.商賈輻輳.有尋丈之地.價值千金者.對於國家並無絲毫之擔荷.殊失賦稅公平之道.遂籌議舉辦宅地稅.討論數月.意見各歧.未能定案.茲事體大.于此亦可概見.非常之原.黎民惧焉.殆無足怪矣.

竊以爲施行宅地稅.非特可增國庫之收入.且足使民間負擔平均.夫稅本無利弊.當征之則利.不當征之則弊.政府固不可恃大權而開強征暴斂之端.納稅者亦何得因有取乎己而遽行反對.今日吾人所急欲研究者.當爲宅地稅之用途.財廳頒布淞滬施行宅地稅條例.而於此稅征收後作何用途並未有明文規定.第云國庫空虛而已.若錙銖取之.泥沙用之.僅增有宅地者之負擔.而不使之享有納稅後之權利.則無論羣情有所不願.且宅地將難有增高價格之望.而宅地稅亦不能隨之而增加其收額.非計之得也.竊者省當局對於淞滬商埠有積極開發之决心.正在籌備鉅款.卽以此款供開展商埠之用歟.果爾.則取乎斯.用乎斯.淞滬人民雖有一時之反對.終必樂爲輸將.蓋商業或將賴此稅而發達.華界之興盛不難與租界媲美.或竟駕而上之.則淞滬地價亦必因此而增高.查租界宅地每畝價值.動以萬兩計.以彼例此.則納宅地稅者所盡之義務小.所獲之酬報大也.

抑又有進者.案宅地稅條例第三條.謂宅地之所有權者.應直接負納稅之義務.而對於地主將其所納稅轉嫁于租地人時.該條例中並未言明以何種方法限制之.淞滬係商業繁盛之區.宅地既多.租者自衆.地主不難以宅地稅轉嫁于人.是則有宅地稅者之義務未盡.而租地者已首蒙其害.夫宅地稅爲平均有宅地與無宅地者之負擔而設.今受此負擔者.乃爲一般無宅地之

人.是以不平均而設此稅以平均之.而其結果乃更不平均矣.故欲使有宅地者直接負納稅之義務.於淸丈地畝.估計價格時.應使租宅地之人塡明其租金非俟地價變動.租金不得增加.蓋地價未漲.則地主應納之稅額亦未增.加若遽增租金.卽爲地主轉嫁宅地稅之特徵.稅局若不出而阻止之.則地主與租地者之間.勢必日滋紛擾.其時不明內容者.又將藉口宅地稅爲害地方.而請求撤銷矣.今宅地稅局調查表.僅列戶名畝分坐落土名等九項.租金竟不列入.未免疏漏.此亟宜增訂者也.夫淞滬襟江懷海.民物殷阜.爲中外觀聽所集.宅地稅一項.果能辦理合宜.卓著成效.將來各處仿辦.推行盡利.創興事業調劑貧富.國計民生.兩有裨益.當局者幸善自圖之.

補白五

英國失業保險

凡職業之常有淡旺季節者。其工人每有一時失業之虞。使平時無蓄貯。則失業者之痛苦可知。於是有失業保險之法。以爲補救。失業保險之立意良。而施行難。非有良好之組織。與政府之扶助。則斷難持久而收救濟之效。考英國失業保險制度。頗多優異之點。足爲他國圭臬。爰略述其特點如下

（一）被保險者之範圍。限於建築業。營造業。造船業。機器業。煅冶業。造車業。鋸木業七種。蓋此七種業務。最多失業之季節也

（二）保險費由雇主與勞動者各出其半。幷由國庫補助之。

（三）以職業介紹所爲保險機關。保險金卽由介紹所收付。凡欲得失業保險金者。須每日親至職業介紹所登錄失業。介紹所與以相當職業時。勞動者不得拒絕。然一面仍爲其籌盡利益。不使其充任因勞動爭議而生之空席。且勞動者無以惡條件就職之義務。

（四）凡雇主用一雇人至四十五星期以上者。得請求豁免對于此人每年應負擔之保險費三分之一。

（五）雇人達六十歲後。已付過五百星期以上之保險費者。將其所付之保險費。依複利週年二厘半算還之。惟須扣除其從前失業時已受之保險金。

觀上述第二點。保險費分配法。至爲公允。有國庫補助。則無不足之虞。由勞資並出。則無偏重之弊。意至善也。第三點所以防勞動者之欺詐。故爲之覓相當職業。若非眞失業者。則必拒絕就職也。且介紹所熟悉各業狀況。眞僞一查卽破。法莫妙於是矣。第四點所以獎勵雇主繼續使用同一雇人者也。雇主不常斥退工人。則失業較少。亦根本補濟也。第五點則爲鼓勵雇人加入保險之法。蓋加入保險者愈多。則受失業痛苦者愈少。然工人往往不自爲計。不識失業保險之重要。故設此規定以勉之。

我國民衆應如何節制生活上之消費而維護生產之能力論

沈奏廷

一國之消費.與生產有直接之關係.消費得其道.生產乃能發展.個人社會.交受其益.是以三代尚樸實.其民豐.其物阜.降至兩晉六朝.奢靡相尚.君民交困.羅馬以節儉興邦.而以奢侈亡國.德意志人民節約.嗇己奉公.故能勝法蘭西而稱雄於歐陸.法於敗後.負賠款五十億佛郎.而轉瞬間卽淸償無餘.非人民平時節約.投資海外.曷克臻此.然則一國人民之消費.直接影響生產間接影響國計.可不三致意哉.我國今日之消費.果何若乎.察其實況.失道者居多.原因複雜.節制不容或緩.請分別論之.

(一) 消費之現狀

國窮民困.我今日經濟上之病態也.然一觀其消費.則似又無窮困之可言者.蓋惟其消費過濫.斯其生產減色.消費之不足爲富力之表示.由來久矣.第於我國爲尤易見耳.玆就我國民之消費.分類述之.

(甲) 有害之消費　有害之消費.烟酒賭博其著者也.試一察我社會.城市之中.幾無家不有賭.無人不嗜賭.金錢之耗於是者.每年何止千萬之數.常人不識經濟原理.以爲賭博之錢.來往無定.有害於個人經濟極鮮.不知金錢用於賭博.則流入不生產之途.影響社會經濟至深且巨.何以知之.彼賭博者每次出入.自數元以至數千元.故其錢囊內.必儲現金以爲準備.苟其人一旦捐除賭癖.則此種現金可不儲於身旁.而存於錢莊或銀行或各種工商事業.錢莊銀行卽可轉貸於從事生產之人.一元存款.卽可有數元放款之產生.工商事業得此存款.卽可直接用於生產之途.是一轉移間.非特存款者得利息之報酬.而金融生產機關.咸蒙其惠.推而至於生產機關所用之工人職員.亦

因以得衣食之資.而國家視生產之狀況.亦得酌課營業稅.以裕國庫.一舉而數善俱備.全社會咸沾其澤.然則賭博卽直接無害於個人經濟.（此亦不盡然.以賭博而傾家者.國內不乏其人.）而間接影響於社會國家.使金融枯竭.生產衰頽.爲害不更烈乎.國內類似賭博者.又有流行之獎券.其阻礙金融.妨害生產.與賭博無異.亦我國民消費項下亟宜剷除者也.次及於烟.烟之爲害最烈者莫如鴉片.而害之最普及者.莫如紙烟.考我國紙烟消費額.年達二萬萬元.其中一萬四千餘萬元.純由英美烟公司輸入外人之囊橐.大利外溢.洵可驚人.至鴉片則近時吸者.又多.有由海外輸入者.有在國內自種者.自海外輸入.則利盡外溢.與紙烟同.在國內栽植.則稻麥減收.糧食價昂.遂致以農立國.而食料品轉求諸海外.據每年海關統計.食料品之輸入.自二億至二億五千萬兩之巨此又間接之漏巵也.又次及於酒.國內嗜酒者雖不若吸烟者之多.然亦不在少數.惟無統計可考耳.酒亦爲有害消費之一.故各國皆課重稅.美國且禁飲之.獨我國對於酒之取締特寬.以致衣食不周者.亦多沉緬於酒.生活程度.愈趨愈下.殊可懼也.玆試以數額估計烟酒賭博之經濟影響如次.

（1）每年消費於賭博者　約計　215,000,000元

說明:假定百人中一人嗜賭.每年每人須消費於賭博中者五十元.則四萬三千萬人共達二億一千五百萬元.

（2）每年消費於購買獎券者　約計　12,900,000元

說明:假定每千人有一人購買獎券.每年每人須耗三十元.則得上列之數.

（3）每年消費於紙烟者　200,000,000元

（4）每年消費於酒者　約計　64,500,000元

說明:假定每千人有五人飲酒.每年每人須耗三十元.則得上列之數.

(5) 每年消費於鴉片者　約計　12,900,000元

說明:假定每萬人中有二人有烟癖.每人每年須耗一百五十元.則得上數

以上五項有害消費.每年當不下五萬萬元.此數純爲不生產的.若舉而儲蓄

之.令三分之一存入普通銀行,三分之二存入儲蓄銀行.前者得一萬六千六百餘萬之現金.以百分之六十作準備.則生產者卽可得二萬八千萬之借款.以爲運用.其餘三萬三千萬.則由儲蓄銀行用以購入實業債券.以助生產.易言之.市場上將多六萬萬元之流通資本.以年利一分計.全社會亦可多六千萬元之進益.若專用以興築鐵路.則五萬萬元之資本.（純以現金計算）可築壹萬里之路線而或尙有餘.卽使有害消費不能盡除.然苟各減其半.則亦有五千里鐵路可以興築.數十年後.交通卽可與西國媲美.況因交通之便利.他種生產事業亦必緣以發展.國富之增.更難以數字計矣.

(乙) 無益之消費　此類消費.對於個人爲無益.而對於社會則仍爲有害如用不必需之洋貨是也.夫洋貨之爲必需者誠夥.若書籍若文具.以及工藝上必用之品皆是.然不必需之洋貨.國內消費亦多.考乙種奢侈品之輸入.年達二萬七千一百九十四萬六千兩.約合國幣三萬八千餘萬圓.雖不能全數視爲不必要之消費.然姑計其半.每年亦達二萬萬圓.加以棉貨之輸入.年約二萬萬兩.合國幣二萬八千萬圓.其中大部分雖已爲日用所需.然至少百分之二十.未必不可以國貨代之.是則無故之漏巵.又增五千六百餘萬圓.綜計無益之消費.年可二萬五千萬.卽此數不用以儲蓄.而仍用以消費.惟以國貨代洋貨.使利益不流出海外.則國內工商業.每年必多二億五千萬之交易.國中可多養二十餘萬之工人.資本家所獲之剩餘.又可投入他途.以爲輾轉之生產.而工人之消費.又足助衣食供給事業之發展.交相爲用.年復一年.又豈僅二三億之交易而已哉.考生產原則.一物之價.一部分爲成本.一部分爲剩餘價値.剩餘價値之大部分.爲資本家之利益故購用外貨.卽我輸外人以剩餘價値.以雄厚其勢力而已.苟我改用國貨.則所輸之剩餘常在本國人之手.今旣不能盡用國貨以代洋貨.則此無益之消費.必先改除.以補救於萬一.査我國每年入超.約二萬萬兩.苟能節制此類消費.或代以國貨.或竟屛除之.則適能補救貿易之損失.使債台不再高築.此又消極的利益也.

（丙）過度之消費 嘗觀中國家庭中消費往往過度.一物可供數日之用者.一日內或已告罄.此於大家庭中尤習見之.消費過度.損及個人經濟.似甚易見.而對於社會之損害.則非人人盡知.或謂我之消費多.則生產者可多銷其出品.工商業必受利益.何害及社會之可言.此大謬也.蓋過分消費所耗之金錢.本可用以儲蓄而存入銀行者.銀行貸與生產之人.助其發展.其惠及工商也同.而儲蓄者又得利息之報酬.非一舉兩得乎.此過分消費之不利一也.一物因消費過度.則價必漲.獲利者僅產此一物之人.而他人需用此物者.咸蒙其害.例如煤之消費過甚.則業煤者固利市百倍.然冶鐵業製造業.必致無利可圖.利彼而害此.得不償失.又若貧戶小民.以物貴而生計愈艱.生計艱則生產力減.社會必呈不安之象.此過分消費之不利二也.又或過分消費之物.以需求隨價昂而減縮.亦必無利可獲.然過度消費之人.已蒙個人之損失不消費之人.已受無謂之不便.此過分消費之不利三也.是以過度之消費.在個人爲損害經濟.在社會爲妨害生產.而觀察我國家庭.中人以上.消費過度者居其半.亦我生產前途之危機也.

（丁）無形之消費 儲蓄非消費.人所共知也.乃在我國.儲蓄中亦有消費在焉.何以言之.我國儲蓄銀行.尚未遍設.外人越俎代謀.乃設有獎儲蓄.以誘我.我民衆何知.羣爲所誘而趨之.於是汗血之資.爲人運用.問其利息.則未嘗有也.若欲中止儲蓄.則折扣達二分之一以上.未嘗能全數收回.是豈儲蓄銀行所宜有哉.或謂吾既有得獎之機會.則吾利已厚矣.不知儲蓄十餘年.利息可逾其本金.區區獎金.何足比數.試設列以明之.

存款之收入	100,000 圓
本期獎金之支出	20,000 圓
本期投資額	80,000 圓
十五年後之本利和(年利六厘)	191,724.66 圓
應還存款人之本金	100,000.00 圓
儲蓄銀行之利益	91,724.66 圓

若半年存款一次.每次收款十萬元.支出獎銀二萬圓則十五年後.本利和當爲六百三十二萬四千六百五十四元八角九分.($6,324,654•89)蓋以年息六釐計也.而十五年終應還之本金.僅二百四十萬元.故儲蓄機關之盈利.當爲3,924,654•89元.儲戶莫能染指.若存款加多.則盈利更大.今我四萬三千萬人中.設有四萬叁千人從事此種儲蓄.每人每半年存銀二十元.則每期存款.當爲八十六萬圓.按上列算得之結果.十五年後.我國應損失33,752,032•05元.平均每年應輸出二百二十萬圓.雖然.利率豈僅六釐.儲戶豈僅四萬餘人.每人存款豈僅二十圓行見其日與月盛.漏巵正未有底止也.是以擲資金於此然類投機之投機.與消費同爲不生產之支出.所不同者.尚有收回本金之望耳.其助金融之枯竭.阻生產之發達.較諸消費於本國奢侈品時爲尤甚.吾無以名之.因名之曰無形之消費.(按外國人壽保險公司.用我資金以牟利.其爲吾民無形消費之促進者.正與儲蓄機關同.)

(二) 消費失當之原因

既知我國民消費之概況矣.乃更進而研究其失當之原因.以爲補救之豫備.愚謂有主因.有輔因.主因者.釀成消費之失當者也.輔因者促成消費之失當者也.二者缺一.消費即不致大失其道.蓋相互爲用之惡因也.請分論之.

(甲) 主因

(子) 經濟常識之未普及　有經濟常識者.方能節制其消費.使無害於個人及社會.有害與無益之消費.固在屏除節約之列.卽過度與無形之消費.亦能知所避免.乃我國人無經濟常識者多.故嗜賭者不知賭之害.而輒以無礙個人經濟爲辭.嗜煙者不知烟之害并不悉利權外溢之幾何.消費過度.則猶以爲助工商業之發達.儲蓄失當.亦不知個人社會損失之有無.長此普營損耗日亘.要皆缺乏經經常識之咎也.

(丑) 社會觀念之缺乏　有經濟常識而消費亦有不知節制者.則社會

觀念缺乏故也.無社會觀念.則雖知利害關係.亦以冷淡處之.知賭博有害於社會經濟.而以其無大害於個人經濟.則亦爲之.他如無益之消費.過度之消費.無形之消費.亦以僅與社會有礙.未嘗思所以節制之.故有經濟常識而無社會觀念以輔之.所裨益於消費之道亦鮮.今國內無社會觀念者.較無經濟常識者尤多.消費之不得其道.此亦一大主因也.

(乙) 輔因

(子) 遺產制度　遺產足使受繼者墮落放蕩.國內已屢見不鮮.嘗察消費之最失當者.當推富家之子.一以其缺乏教育.不知消費之利害.一以其財產過剩.自知有恃而無恐.約計此輩之消費項下.除正當支出外.有害之消費當佔百分之五十至六十.無益之消費.當佔百分之二十至三十.過度之消費當佔百分之十至二十.無形之消費.尚在少數.非有遺產以助之.則彼之消費未能出軌至於此極也.

(丑) 大家庭制度　我國崇尚大家庭制度.而惟恃禮教以爲維持.遂致實際上損耗橫生.莫能挽救.兄弟伯叔同居.爭以揮霍爲能事.消費過度.無人節制能之.嘗見一物足供半月之用者.在大家庭內.二三日告罄矣.使早各分居.自理其家務.則消費之節省何止數倍.此於個人.於社會.皆有重大之影響不可不亟謀補救者也.

(寅) 儲蓄機會之缺乏　無儲蓄之機會.則雖有心儲蓄者.亦難如願.此於實際上常見之.普通商店銀行.不收受零星之存款.日儲數十或數百文.亦無由存放.必日積月累.集成數十金.方可出貨生息.常人之情.未有能若是堅忍者.卒至意欲儲蓄之錢.亦以不便故而遂用於消費矣.每日每人.爲數固少.然以四萬萬人計之.每人日儲十文.則每日存款一百十一萬餘元.每年達三萬九千九百餘萬元.效果之大.不言可喻.今儲蓄機會國內既形缺乏.即使無謂消費.鏟除淨盡.然亦埋金地下.所有遊資.仍難盡入生產之途.每年坐受數百兆之損耗.仍與前同.故儲蓄之不普及.乃無謂消費之促進者.而節制消費

之善後尤在普及儲蓄之機會.

(卯) 職業之不普及 無職業者消費每多於有職業之人.故不惫能生利則往往惫能分利.工人於輟業時.每多沉湎於酒.轉事揮霍.此於西國常見之大學云生之者衆.食之者寡.則財恆足.今我現狀適反是.計分利者有如下述.(1) 一般之女子.(2) 富家之子弟.(3) 遊民.(4) 過剩之兵士.除兵士外.皆有以無職業故而消費特多者.若輩苟有所事.則亦無暇於烟酒賭博矣.故謂職業不普及爲消費失當之重因.非無故也.

(辰) 地方之不靖 政治混亂.盜賊徧野.人多以爲朝不謀夕.尙何所用其儲蓄.不若及時行樂.頃己所有.以塡一時之慾壑.若談節約.則轉笑其迂.此種心理.雖云事實爲之.然與其消費而有害.莫若節儲之無弊.吾人當放大眼光.爲後日處慮.若一意放任.則眞萬刼不復矣.

(三) 節制我國民消費之方法

旣知我國民消費之槪况及其原因矣.則當進而求補救之方.以節制之.果能人人猛省.各自爲謀.則事莫善於此.不然.則必鼓勵之.強迫之.規勸之.合國家社會個人之力.以爲消費節制之敦促.使人人有節制消費之知識.有節制消費之機會.幷有不得不節制消費之環境.而後可以言生產.言富國.爰不揣譾陋.略擬補救之具體計畫.如下.願識者敎之.

(甲) 教育上之補救

(1) 學校 各高級小學及初級中學.此後皆添設經濟常識一課.用淺顯之理論.詳釋經濟社會之種種關係.教科書內目次之重要者.爲(一) 個人經濟之意義(二) 國民經濟之意義(三) 個人與社會經濟上之關係(四) 消費之界說(五) 正當消費與不正當消費之區別(六) 中國消費之現狀(七) 消費與生產(八) 中國生產之現狀(九) 中國消費及於生產之影響(十) 中國消費應有之節制(十一) 消費節制後預計之利益(十二) 各國消費與中

國消費之比較.專使中小學校學生.入社會後.對於個人消費.確有經濟知識.社會觀念.蓋改造中國消費前途.舍此無更善之計畫也.

(2) 出版物　出版物以新聞紙爲最普及.雜誌次之.故第一各種新聞紙此後當以灌輸經濟常識爲己任.用淺顯之文字.宣傳國民經濟之觀念.而以節制消費爲旨歸.并介紹各國消費狀況.社會經濟情形.國內外生產之發展或衰頹.儲蓄之增進或減少.俾不受教育者.亦知消費之重要.已受教育者.亦當知所警惕.雜誌亦然.其目的在灌輸學識者.尤應注意及此.務求文字淺易而有趣.使粗通國文者.亦能讀之.或用敘述.或用理論.或用問答.或用寓言小說.或用寓意畫圖.爲中國生產前途計.務期出版界起而圖之.

(3) 智識階級　有智識者於事餘之暇宜集合同志向平民講演節制消費之必要與方法.俾不識文字者.亦有機會領略消費之意義.是在智識階級之努力.不必多贅.

(4) 領袖人物　君子之德風.小人之德草.草上之風必偃.古今未嘗異也.故欲節制消費.領袖人物當先以身作則.何謂領袖人物.在社會則爲紳董.在家庭則爲尊長.在各機關則爲各該機關之主持者.皆當以移風易俗自任.不爲無謂之消費.如其下屬不知感化.則當以職權告誡或禁阻之.以輔政府權力之不及.嘗考無謂之消費.輒由摹倣而來.若領袖者亦耽於是.則羣視消費之失當者爲尊榮爲可貴矣.又智識界爲全國之領袖者.其行爲之影響.不僅限於一家一處.尤應自加檢束.節制消費.吾願爲學生者聽之.

(乙) 國家職權上之補救

(A) 現時可實行者

(1) 嚴禁賭博及類似賭博之投機　賭博之懸禁久矣.或以實行不力或以胥吏爲奸.法令弁髦.與不禁等.此後應更厲行禁止.加重罰款.毋稍通融.廣事布告.以塞賭徒之膽.并禁止賭具業.賭具進口.各地.嚴爲檢查.查出入官.又流行之獎劵.同在嚴禁之列.較賭博尤易搜查.自亦不容漏網.吾願官廳努

力行之.

（2）推行烟稅酒稅　茲姑舍本國菸葉不論.而論捲烟.捲菸特稅.浙省首創行之.愚謂寓禁於征.此稅極可推行考各國國產稅內大都以菸列入.美國規定捲烟每千枝納稅自一元八分至三元六角.蓋視重量而定.法國且以烟業爲國有.年入六萬餘萬佛郎.他如英德諸國.亦莫不徵烟稅.今察國內國民生活程度.遠不如泰西各國.彼且以烟之消費爲戒.而征稅以制之.以我之貧更當如何阻遏其蔓延耶.故我主張捲烟特稅.宜速推行.並重其率.蓋率不重.則稅者自稅.吸者仍吸.徒苦平民耳.必使稅率極高.中人以下.無力購吸.而後節制消費之目的乃達.至論酒稅.則政府於酒特寬.查江浙兩省.紹酒稅率.爲每石四角二分與三角六分.公賣費不計.較諸日本酒之每石徵銀八元五角者.相去奚啻天壤.然日人未嘗覺其苛.良以酒非必要品耳.故我國酒稅.若加重十倍.亦僅及日稅之半.於民生决無妨礙.今設每斤征銀四分.則飲者自減.倘仍不減.則再加之.國家爲全體利益計.不能姑息釀酒之家也.（洋酒可徵內地稅以取締之.稅率至少與土酒等.）

（3）實行遺產稅　遺產制度.不能改除.補救之方.惟稅遺產.遺產稅之目的有二.（一）減少受繼者揮霍之資.使知有所警惕.因不得不節其揮霍.（二）所納之稅.本或用於消費.一入政府之手.即利用之以生產.或助與公益之事.此遺產稅之所以能補救消費也民國四年.財政討論會議.嘗訂有遺產稅條例.後經參議院修正.辦法頗詳.嗣以政局傾擾.致未果行.愚謂此稅儘可由省政府施征.以免中央權力之莫及.庶幾實行之期.指日可待.願當局注意及之.

（4）獎勵儲蓄　在儲蓄銀行未推廣以前.政府可將郵局作儲蓄機關.令人民向之儲蓄.并爲引起信用起見.儲蓄時可給以特種之郵票.他日取款.除簿摺外.憑原發之郵票.照數付還.此類郵票.可作投寄信件之用.或轉讓他人作郵寄之用.惟受讓者不能向郵局取款.郵局於付息時.則查儲戶現存郵

票之數以便核算.凡付息還款.均可利用信差遞送.以圖儲戶之便利.倘該地已有儲蓄銀行.則可弗與之逐利.幷應預爲宣示.凡將來儲蓄銀行.其營業區域與郵局儲蓄機關相同者.郵局應減其儲款之利息.俟大部分儲蓄皆棄郵局.而趨銀行時.郵局卽宜告停止儲蓄.以免與銀行競爭.又儲戶存款.徵稅機關應向郵局詢查.凡存款至某數者.納稅時獎以若干之免除.無稅者與以他種之獎勵.他日郵局停止儲蓄.由銀行經營時.亦如之.

(B)將來宜實行者

(1)重徵相當之外貨 此於關稅未自主前.不能實行.惟欲節制無益之消費.應重徵何種之外貨.則此時有研究之必要.夫甲種(酒與烟)乙種(化裝品精製棉織物首飾之類)奢侈品.固在重征之列.不必贅言.吾謂外國輸入之棉貨.尤應擇要加徵.不可爲互惠二字所欺.而與人以便宜.庶幾上述之無益消費.可免去不少.使國人服御之費.多流入本國布商之手.卽此一端.已足塞貿易上之漏巵矣.

(2)禁鴉片之販賣 禁吸鴉片.首在禁止販賣.禁止販賣.現有兩種困難.(一)他國無禁烟誠意我以領判權未撤無力阻其進口.(二)軍閥橫行.強令人民種烟.政府無力顧問.故欲禁烟風.在目前爲不可能.然亦爲節制消費之一要點.用述及之.

(3)取締外國在華之儲蓄機關 此非國家權力充分時.不能有爲.亦不能因目下不能爲而忽之.將來外國在華之儲蓄機關.雖不必禁設.但必須取締.凡關於紅利之分配.存款之投資.有獎之是否合法.年限之長短.停儲之應付方法.皆可於銀行律內規定之.務使國內儲蓄者.不受外人之盤剝.全國年省數百萬之無形損失.惠及生產前途.未始非淺.今國人談經濟侵略.目光遠大.忽於此種無形消費.未嘗道及.將來卽能撤除領事裁判權.此中盤剝.亦將漏網.爰揭而出之.期他日政府有力時.不忘以職權取締之也.

(丙)實業與金融界應有之補救

（1）普及營業投資　各國有或新興之實業.發行債票時.應特備若干份數額極小者.俾少有儲蓄者.亦可投資.一面并使公司易於籌款.愚謂鐵路債票最宜此法.以其資產可靠.小資本家可無慮危險也.如是則不向儲蓄機關儲蓄者.可直接投其所蓄於實業.亦吸收遊資節制消費之善法也.惟小資本家於投資之前.應就教於他人.確知其擔保之可靠.然後投資.以免被欺.此又國人應有之常識也.

（2）推廣儲蓄銀行事業　此爲輔助消費節制之唯一善法無極便利之儲蓄機會.則消費節制.與生產仍無大利.且恐不能維持不敝.我國所謂儲蓄銀行.姑不問其內容如何.然皆在通都大邑.安能收消費之實效.蓋存一二元之款者.烏能不遠百里而來耶.故儲蓄機關.應分佈徧設.窮鄉小鎮.最不可忽.且支行費用不大.一切投資業務.終須由總行擔任.支行之所事者.收款匯款付息還款及供問訊而已.今欲辦儲蓄業務.以助消費之節制.必推廣之而後可.倘擔保確實.利息相宜.則樂於儲蓄者必多.厥業前途正遠.况據愚見.始其事者.乃國有之郵局儲蓄機關.儲蓄銀行躡其後.必能推行盡利也.

（3）自辦保險事業　此爲減少無形消費之一法.我國保險事業外人經營者多.自辦者雖有.然較不多觀.此後宜漸將保險事業權收回.自爲經營.所幸者.（一）國內熟悉保險專才.已不乏人.（二）國人已漸知保險之意義及功用.（三）外人之經濟侵略.國人已悉其害.有此三利.保險事業不難舉辦.辦後不難與外人競爭.尚望學者圖之.以補救我之無形消費.

上述各種補救方略.不能謂爲完全.如大家庭制度之改革.以及職業之普及.目前皆不能有具體計畫.惟前者可於灌輸經濟常識之間.微寓勸導之意.使聽者讀者.猛然於過分消費之害.後者非生產進步.不能見諸事實.他日消費漸事節約.生產漸事發達.則無業者亦能漸事減少.故普及職業.祇能與節制消費並進.不能先之而實現也.除此兩點及國家職權上尚難推行之數事外.所陳節制消費之方略.均可及早施行.事實上無大障礙.坐言起行.尤貴

合作.望各界協力圖之.

結論

由此以觀國內消費之失當.爲害已深.一也.原因繁多.補救時宜兼籌並顧.二也.補救之方.目下可實行者多.三也.綜計四項消費.爲數極巨.所估計者.尚與事實難符.若確實調查.數必倍之.則失當之消費.縱不盡除.每年節省.至少亦可六七萬萬元.於此吾人欲研究者.卽何以利用此資耳.愚謂利用之方.在前十數年.莫如振興交通.而振興交通.莫如興築鐵路.查現今交通上債務已達五萬九千餘萬元.其無確實担保者.且佔百分之七十五而強.若再專恃外債.則負擔益重.蓋外債糜費.遠甚於內債也.且借外款以築路須視他國之金融狀況.以爲進退.如隴海粤漢川諸幹路.皆以歐戰影響.款難募集.陷於停頓狀態.使能利用內資.則可自由進行.須知交通一日停頓.國家卽受一日損失.提倡進行.豈容緩哉.況鐵路爲各種實業之命脈.未有鐵路不興.而工商業能發展者.鐵路猶血脈.工商猶臟腑.血脈通而後臟腑健.故吾謂在前數年中消費節制後之餘資.宜專用以築路也.年多七萬萬之遊資.卽年多一萬五千里之鐵路.十五年後.卽logs二十二萬五千里.若以餘利築新路.則假以二十餘年交通不幾與北美抗衡乎.大利所在.吾人未嘗深察.孰知一啄一飲之節約一絲一縷之省儉.卽能產生數十萬里之鐵路.而臻四萬萬人於富強之域乎.然則節制消費.又豈僅維持生產力而已哉.

田賦在我國稅制上之地位及其應興應革之要點

沈奏廷

近世稅制學說.日臻進步.學者莫不以產業稅爲一國稅制之詬病.言之有理.持之有故.稍知租稅原則者.類能言之.第農業國之財產.與工業國之財產異.以工業立國而專行產業稅.則所入有限.而漏稅無窮.以農業立國而廢除產業稅.則將無物可征.減稅亦必多.所入亦必減.苟農業國能採用所得稅制.以輔產業稅之不足.則固有利而無弊.若欲鏟除產業稅而以所得稅代之.則必窒礙難行也.我國農業國也.我之田賦產業稅之一也.田賦之與我稅制之關係.迄今最爲密切.良以農業國家所恃直接稅源.惟田地而已.田賦之爲我最重要之稅課.至今尚難否認.其在我稅制上之地位.應駕各他稅而上之.在我未工業化之前.所得稅既難推行.整稅制.開稅源.自當自田賦着手.蓋田賦雖爲產業稅之一.不能免學者所持產業稅之缺陷.然能加以整頓.亦未始不能略採所得稅之長.而除產業稅之短.況在農業國家.產業稅之弊竇.尚較不易發生乎.考田賦收入.民五以後.中央既無預算.各省亦少報告.惟據五年度預算.則有如下表.（單位國幣一元）

京兆	434,032	直隸	6,070,951	奉天	3,331,110
吉林	1,084,442	黑龍江	1,263,701	山東	9,502,355
河南	7,700,750	江蘇	11,092,580	安徽	4,035,619
江西	5,397,626	湖南	3,335,606	湖北	3,233,782
福建	3,263,809	浙江	7712,259	廣東	4,403,985
廣西	1,248,000	山西	5,949,516	陝西	5,793,967
四川	6,866,911	雲南	1,094,449	貴州	745,044
甘肅	1,457,453	新疆	1,818,224	熱河	93,660

察哈爾 283,741 歸綏 86,599 川邊 253,369

綜計各省賦銀.共爲九千七百五十五萬三千五百十三元.以我國疆域之大.而收入僅達此數.則欲以供國家地方行政之需.亦難濟事.無怪雜稅苛斂.雜捐叠出.以彌縫省庫.而國庫尙不容染指焉.此眞蘇軾所謂苟且衰世之法.不終月之計也.試問我國田賦收入.果僅九千餘萬而無可增乎.苟有可增之望.則病民之稅.概可鏟除.而無損于庫帑.法莫善於是焉.然欲知其是否有增收之可能.則有待乎統計的研究.請先觀下表.而後分敍各要點焉.

省名	田畝數	預算賦銀	每畝平均稅銀	各省面積
	以頃(百畝)計	以銀元計	角分厘毫	平方哩
直隸	693,048·23	6,070,951	876	115,830
山東	1,259,314·05	9,502,355	754	55,984
河南	716,751·85	7,700,750	1074	67,954
山西	564,766·83	5,949.516	1053	81 853
江蘇	1,108,253·70	11,092,580	1000	38,610
安徽	411,130·28	4,035,619	981	54,826
江西	473,415·80	5,397,626	1140	69.495
福建	134 000·56	3,263,809	2435	46,332
浙江	467,705·15	7,712,259	1648	36.680
湖北	1,173,229·55	3,233,782	276	71,428
湖南	348,742·55	3.335,606	956	83,398
陝西	305,913·30	5,793,967	1893	75 290
甘肅	167,751·60	1,457,4[illegible]3	868	125,483
四川	464,158·95	6,866,911	1479	218,533
廣東	347,318·25	4,403,985	1268	100,000
廣西	89,637·83	1,248,000	1392	77,220
雲南	93,193·60	1,094,449	1174	146,714
貴州	27,842·06	745,044	2675	67,182
共計	8,846,175·14	88,904,662		1,532,795

上表中之田畝數.乃前清統計.光復後未有確數可稽.大約計之.當無十分出入.各省除福建湖北貴州外.每畝稅銀.均在一角左右.而無超過二角者.故平均全國田地.每畝總可課稅一角.是可無疑者也.十八省總面積計爲一,五三二,七九五方哩.一方哩約合四千一百八十四畝.則各省地畝總數.當爲六十四萬一千三百二十一萬四千二百八十畝.就中因磽瘠低窪.有不可耕種或樹藝者.有係江河沼澤.非田地或山蕩者.有位於省會都市.不抽地稅者.此三項面積.究佔全面積幾成.則不易探考.玆姑以百分之四十計之.則其餘百分之六十.卽三十八萬四千七百九十二萬八千五百六十八畝.(6,413,214,280畝×0•6=3 847,928,568畝）當必爲可以課稅之地.今每畝課銀一角.則每年賦銀收入.當爲三萬八千四百七十九萬二千八百餘元.但民五預算.十八省總計.僅列八千八百九十萬四千六百六十二元.而田畝統計.亦僅八萬八千四百六十一萬七千五百十四畝.畝數稅數.與估計者相差甚遠.此何故耶.蓋有數因在焉.各地田畝大小不同.彼倍於此者有之.或以大畝與小畝同計.而征同量之稅銀.一也.未經淸丈.漏稅殊多.二也.可耕之地.尚未墾植.三也.徵稅弊竇難免.中飽難除四也.苟此四弊盡去.則田賦增收.可立而待.且非特田賦增收已也.經界旣分.田畝大小皆同.而漏稅盡除.則負擔平衡矣.此稅制上之最要點也.墾可耕之地.以裕民生.則社會經濟蒙其利矣.剔除中飽.嚴査隱稅.則上下道德可免淪喪矣.固非僅增加稅收而已也.今弊深矣.將若何.請分論之.

一.　籌辦淸丈

民初亦曾籌議淸丈.後卒未果.苟大局底定.淸丈自爲第一步辦法.可由中央政府.通令各省.轉飭各縣遵辦.各縣分區進行.每區由縣派淸丈委員二人.會同該區公正士紳.一一丈量.丈量之先.可令各田主自行呈報.報不實者處罰.其從實報告而曩時係隱稅者.准免追究.淸丈之際.士紳代表人民.淸丈委員代表政府.士紳司指導.淸丈委員司監督.此區丈畢.復至他區覆勘.他區

亦如之.庶幾此區或有之情弊.可由彼區士紳與清丈委員察出也.清丈委員隨帶書記.將丈量時所得各項要點.一一記錄.然後各區會齊.縣署編訂圖册.田地分等.可仍沿用上中下三則.則分三等.惟須以三年平均每畝收入爲標準而定等則.如每畝收穀三石以下二石以上（三年平均荒年除外）者.爲上則.二石以下一石以上者.爲中則.一石以下者.爲下則.每則復以收入之多寡而分等級.則庶幾按收入徵稅.去所得稅之道亦不遠矣.等則既分.則可着手編製清册.以及各戶方單.清册應載之主要款項.不外戶名,畝數,坐落,四至,等.稅額可於册首註明.如某等每畝應納若干字樣.財產可分數類.如田爲一類.地又爲一類.山又爲一類.每類備製清册一種.每一種清册分爲三部第一部爲上則.第二部爲中則.第三部爲下則.茲將擬擬清册格式.縮小錄於下.

（清册中葉）

戶名	各戶住址	畝數			坐落	地號	四至	稅額
		上等	中等	下等				

此爲一種土地（如山或田）清册三部中之一部.故祇分等而不分則.稅額在製册時可以塡入.以便檢查.倘日後土地易主.再照册首所註某則某等每畝稅銀.比例計征.至於買賣過戶.應由賣者於賣契成立後十日內呈報徵收官署.如不呈報.則稅仍向賣者征收.徵收官吏得呈報後.卽記入過戶册.過戶册載賣者姓名,住址,所賣畝數,買者姓名,呈報年月日,以及土地坐落各項.此册係流水性質.每屆開征前一月或半月.將過戶册登載各款.轉入清册.斯時買者姓名.卽載清册內固有各戶戶名之下.與製册時登載原主戶名相同.並將其所買畝數坐落諸項.逐款塡入.如是清册內又多一戶矣.若買主爲清

冊原有之戶.則於清冊中葉之左填註下列款項.格式如下.

(左葉清冊)

買入或獲得日期	買入或獲得畝數	坐落	地號	四至	賣戶或讓戶	民國某年上忙應征新畝數	稅額
	上 中 下						

至於賣戶則清冊中葉之右登記下列各項.

(右葉清冊)

呈報過戶日期	賣出或轉讓畝數	買戶或獲得戶	民國某年上忙應征畝數	稅額	總稅額
	上 中 下		上 中 下		

(註) 總稅額為新得田畝應征之稅與舊有田畝減去賣出或轉讓田畝應征之稅相加而成之數.又賣出或轉讓田畝.不必再記坐落地號等項.因中葉內相同之款.可借用也.

清冊大都寬大.上列各款.可備十個同樣格式.並列而摺之.共二十期.可供十年之用.所載過戶畝數.即賣出之畝數.民國某年上忙應征畝數.即截至該期止.該戶所有或未賣去之畝數.稅額一項.可由冊首所註每畝稅銀分別乘各等應征畝數得之.須於轉冊時載入.以便發通知單（由單）時之稽查也.至於方單.則係填給各戶者.所列款項.與清冊內左葉所載相同.若遇過戶.則須於呈報時呈繳方單.俟買戶登記稅契.或用他種方法呈報後.填給新方單二紙.一單載賣戶未賣出之地.授與賣戶.一單載買戶所買之地.授與買戶.與公司換給股票之法相同.此籌辦田畝統計之大略方法也.愚意苟按此法辦理.則非特土地現狀.洞若觀火.而契稅收入.亦可增加.將來如欲試辦遺產稅制.比較亦易着手.蓋賣戶懼稅之加及己身.必能呈報也.即不呈報.他日於收稅時.亦必水落石出.前述負擔不平漏稅隱稅之弊.至此盡剔除矣.質言之.始之以清丈.繼之以製冊.復輔之以平日之轉載登記而已.循法而行.務求精

確是在人爲.

二. 提倡移墾

有可耕之地.而無可徵之稅.蓋半由於地利未盡闢耳.嗣後政府宜注重移民.以啓墾荒土.田賦增收.半宜於此中求之.前朝亦常有招民射田.三年起科之舉.今日當更視爲急務矣.然民之樂其鄉土.天性使然.而以我國人爲尤甚.欲其移墾他鄉非有種種鼓勵之法不可.其法維何.愚以爲有下列數端.

(一) 減除川資　通鐵路之地.可由政府與鐵路合作.凡移民乘車.免收運價.不通鐵路而通輪船之處.則可由政府與輪船公司訂定合同.凡移民乘船.免收船資.由政府補償之.凡不通輪船之地.則可由政府雇備船隻.以供輸送移民之用.故無論如何.應由政府設法.減輕移民個人之費用.以資鼓勵.此爲第一步辦法.

(二) 創設農工銀行　田地雖由國家供給.而耕植在在需款.苟利息過重.農民借款難艱.雖移之於其地.亦無力從事耕墾也.故必在各開墾之地.創設農工銀行.籌集資金.轉借農人.使就地資本階級.無從盤剝.惟所辦銀行.勢力宜厚.令農人皆向銀行借款.期限長.利率低.使重利者無投資餘地.於是就地資金.必皆向銀行存儲矣.如是銀行之根基愈堅.農民之負擔愈輕.鼓勵移墾.舍此莫由.是爲第二步辦法.

(三) 移民回籍津貼　移墾後或遇天災歉收.連年無利.移民生計難支.有不得不回籍時.政府應准其徙歸.授以來時同樣之免除.惟他處如有田土可墾.政府可於得移民本人同意時徙之該處.再事墾植.此二種優遇條件.當於舉辦移墾時公佈之.

(四) 定升科寬大期限　新墾之地.必不能卽課賦稅.應規定每畝收入平均至若干限度時.始行升科.古時定三年起科之法.愚謂不若定收入額之限度較爲平均.惟查察稍費事耳.無論如何.於佈告舉辦移墾時.終以以收入額作升科之標準較爲妥善.苟後日酌量情形.人民確能

負擔課稅時.政府亦得立時宣告開徵.於公於私.兩有裨益也.

以上四端目的皆在鼓勵移墾荒士既墾.稅收自加.此清丈而外.整理田賦之最要者也.

三．改良徵收辦法

一稅之經濟與否.泰半視其徵收法之優劣而定.有良徵收法.而後徵稅之費以省.而弊以除.我國田賦徵收辦法.尚欠完善.其應改良之點.有如下列.

(一) 設立金庫直接征收　現時徵收機關.暫爲縣署.此法殊陋.宜各縣設一金庫.或其分支機關.專理稅收事宜.催徵之責.仍在縣署.人民於納稅之前.應向縣署領取納稅憑單.持向金庫繳納.取得收據.復向縣署報驗.如是徵收機關.彷彿會計.僅司記賬催繳事宜.金庫彷彿銀錢總管.司稅銀收入并記賬之責.二者可相參照.情弊盡除.此法除英國外.(英國稅收與徵收銀行之資金混合)各大國皆用之.然又豈待宜於征收田賦已哉.

(二) 改良徵稅單位　民國以來.各省錢糧.皆已折合銀元征收.較諸前清.自屬簡單.惟由單執照上所記單位.尚係銀兩.仍須折算.而漕米一項.所用單位.尚係石斗升合.再由一石折銀一元五角征收.似此轉折計算.即使無弊.亦屬多事.倘能概以銀元表示.使納稅者一望而知其數之多寡.當不較善.蓋普通人能知一兩一石合銀若干元者甚鮮.納稅時難免被蒙.且與租稅便利原則有背.洵不可不圖改良者也.

(三) 化簡稅項　目今田賦.已非中央所有.而地方仍有附征雜稅甚多.任意添征.殊非善制.將來田稅劃歸中央.雜項宜悉蠲除.惟得帶征省附稅及地方附稅兩種.此外不得巧立名目.如蘇省漕米浙省抵補金等.亦可歸入正稅併收無庸另列.庶幾一方面國家地方兩稅劃清.又一方面稅項簡單.人民易於記憶.遇有他項發生.即欲疑問其原由.杜來日之弊者在此.化簡稅項.洵急務也.

田賦興革要點已略具其梗概矣.一曰籌辦清丈.二曰提倡移墾.三曰改良徵收辦法.目的皆在直接增加稅收.間接改進民生.一三兩法.爲消極的.第二一法.乃積極的.爲便利計.可先由消極方法着手.然後向積極一方進行.固不妨循序籌畫.從容從事也.預料按此整理之後.可得下列美滿之結果.

(一) 國庫可年增二萬餘萬元.建設事業.不患無款籌辦.

(二) 釐金雜稅.概可免除.年需抵補八千萬元足矣.利商利國.計莫善於此

(三) 墾荒以後.糧食自足.目下我國輸入米糧.年達九千八百二十萬兩.合銀元一萬五千三百餘萬以農業國而輸入若此巨額之糧食.洵可駭人.倘能民歸於農.非特足以自給.抑可分供他人.塞漏卮.挽利權.固不宜僅於製造品着想也.

其他間接影響於國民經濟者.一時尚難縷舉.屆期自能一一表現.吾人拭目俟之可耳.然則整理田賦.關係有若是之大.奈何坐而忽之哉.吾願舉國財政家經濟家.共起倡辦.成此大業.而當局迷夢.尤望從茲速醒.大利在前.不較勝於爭攘剝奪.搾取垂盡之民人膏血乎.願當局者思之.

補白六

國庫券

國庫券爲政府最短期之負債。每於收支一時不能相抵時發行之。迨收入的款。即行贖回。蓋爲一時通融之策。非國家眞正負債也。其特點有六。

(一)國庫券無抵押品。(二)國庫券期限。不超過會計年度。(三)國庫券可視同票據。用貼現法發行。(四)國庫券應視需要之狀況。而異其期限之長短。例如三月後能收入的款。則即發三月期之庫券。(五)國庫券爲無記名證券。故面額不應過低。過低則有流爲紙幣影響金融之虞。(六)每一會計年度內所發行之庫券額。不得超過該年度之預算額

考我國國庫券規則。曾有下列之規定。

(一)歲計必要時。得發行國庫券。(二)發行額不得超過歲入豫算額。(三)發行價格。不得與票面價格相差。(四)利息不得過年利七釐半。(五)發行期限不得逾一年。(六)庫券期滿。得用以完納各種租稅。(七)庫券得充銀行發行紙幣之準備。

觀上述國庫券之特質及規定。則知有抵押品者必非國庫券。期限逾一年者必非國庫券。利息奇昂者必非國庫券。他如發行至歲入豫算額以上。以及不用貼現法。而發行價與面價相差者。皆有損國庫。而與國庫券之原則及規定相牴觸者也。

考中央政府稅源都爲直接稅者。則每有發行國庫券之必要。蓋直接稅徵收有定期。國家收入。因常有青黃不接之時。若間接稅則源源而來。無季節之分。國家恃間接之稅爲收入者較少發行券之必要。近世文明諸國。中央稅源。直接間接並重。故庫券一物。爲中央財政之必要工具。不能廢棄也。

孔孟之經濟思想

華 立

近世經濟學說.可謂磅礴煒爍.如日中天矣.而其說之始發.亦不過一百六十餘年.中世以降.重農重商.名哲代興.洎英儒亞丹斯密集前賢大成.斯學遂勃然以興.返觀我國自唐虞迄今.已四千餘年.所守者唯一重農政策.所重者唯一節用主義.濡滯遲迴.數千年如一日.毋亦學說不倡之咎歟.雖然.我國經濟思想之濫觴固甚早.如大學言生財分財.史漢貨殖平準食貨諸傳志.大都與近世經濟學說相符合.片羽吉光.終古不能磨滅.惜後人未能整理推演以光大之.是則後世學者.不能無罪於先哲矣.

我國經濟思想之勃興.實始於春秋戰國時代.因彼時政治棼亂已極.殺伐兼併.干戈擾攘.民生之憔悴.實不輸於今日.於是民食理財諸問題.應時而起.聖人治國平天下之王道.遂時有經濟思想羼雜其中.孔孟倡王道最力.故其思想之及於經濟者亦甚多.今稍事條析.以見我國古代經濟思想之一斑.惟薄學如予欲以管窺蠡測之見.作仰高鑽堅之舉.乖謬傅會.自知不免.尚望海內學者有以正之.

孔子之經濟思想

(一)承認『慾望』『慾望』爲人類一切活動之動機.而爲經濟學直接研究之對象.社會上一切事業.一切組織.不外人類慾望發達之結果.所謂世界文明史者.亦不過一部慾望發達史耳.禮運曰『飲食男女.人之大慾存焉.』是孔子已承認人類之慾望矣.但孔子深恐後人不明利義之分.妄逞私慾.故又曰『聖人耐以天下爲一家.以中國爲一人者.非意之也.必知其情.辟於其義.明於其利.達於其患.然後能爲之.』至於老子之思想則不同.其言曰『小國寡民.使有什百人之器而不用.使民重死而不遠徙.雖有舟輿.無所乘之.雖有甲兵.無所陳之.使民復結繩而用之.甘其食.美其服.安其居.樂其俗.隣

國相望.雞犬之聲相聞.民至老死不相往來.』孔子老子之經濟觀念.其根本不同之點.卽在此處.孔子以爲人之慾望.乃與生俱來.祇能善導之.而不能強制之.故但主『因人之情而爲之節文以民坊.』而不主去慾.其慾望之正當者.更應擴充之滿足之.使人類幸福日益增進.故繫易有言『備物致用.立成器以爲天下利.莫大乎聖人.』是孔子因承認人類之慾望.遂進而承認物質文明之功用矣.

（二）薄斂節用　薄斂節用.實爲我國四千年來唯一之理財方策.順之者王天下.逆之者滅其國.其對我國經濟思想上之影響.蓋可想見.

『道千乘之國.敬事而信.節用而愛人.使民以時.』

『禮與其奢也寧儉』,『奢則不孫.儉則固.與其不孫也寧固.』

『節以制度.不傷財不害民.』

孔子對於聚斂之臣.更肆力掊擊.其意以爲國家而務財用.則國民生計必受壓迫.故其言曰.

『財聚則民散.財散則民聚.』

『季氏富於周公.而求也爲之聚斂而附益之.子曰.「非吾徒也.小子鳴鼓而攻之可也.」』

『畜馬乘.不察於雞豚.伐冰之家.不畜牛羊.百乘之家.不畜聚斂之臣.與其有聚斂之臣.寧有盜臣.』

『長國家而務財用者.必自小人矣.……此謂國不以利爲利.以義爲利也.』

孔子之所以大唱此節用薄斂主義者.蓋見於當時暴君貪吏.橫征暴斂不顧百姓之疾苦.惟求一己之享樂.故不禁大聲疾呼.以拯人民於水火之中於是我國數千年來之理財方針.遂以此爲圭臬.雖然.『量入爲出.』在個人經濟固爲得計.然以之施於國政.其流弊足使百政廢缺不舉.國家及社會事業俯俯無發展之可能.循是不變.是亦坐困也已矣.故在今日國家經濟發達

之時,『節用薄歛.』『量入爲出.』已成歷史上過去之陳迹.惟當軸對於徵稅之方法.不能不有嚴密之考慮.是則亞丹斯密之四大原則尙矣.(按四大原則爲(一)公平 Eguality (二)明確 Certainty (三)便利 Convenience (四)經濟 Economy 嚴復譯爲(一)平(二)信(三)便(四)嗇.讀者請參看 The Wealth of Nations, Book V, Chapter II, Part II. 或嚴譯原富戊部下第二篇)

(三)先富後教 『子適衞冉有僕.子曰「庶矣哉.」冉有曰.「旣庶矣.又何加焉.」曰「富之.」曰旣富矣.又何加焉.」曰「敎之.」』

『足食足兵.民信之矣.』此與管子之『倉廩實而知禮義.衣食足而知榮辱.』同一思想.洵千古不易之通論.蓋人性本善.其所以敢作奸犯科冒死爲盜寇者.初非天性較人凶惡.實衣食問題迫之使然也.故國民生計富裕.敎化如能順利無滯.否則終見其紙上談兵.徒唱高調而已.

(四)消費生產平衡論 『生財有大道.生之者衆.食之者寡.爲之者疾.用之者舒.則財恆足矣.』此誠今日經濟學者所持消費生產平衡論之極好注解.寥寥數語.概括經濟學半部.中國人得此遺產.亦足自豪矣.

(五)均富主義 孔子於消費生產間之關係.旣已洞如觀火.故對於分配論亦有精意.

『丘也聞有國有家者.不患貧而患不均.……蓋均無貧.……』

今日中國所患者卽爲『不均.』坐臯比者不勞而擁巨貲胼手胝足者.粟六終日.猶恐不得一飽.在國民經濟方面.固爲極壞之病象.卽以倫理言.亦非平準之道.故生產消費旣欲其平準.財富之分配.更不能不力求均衡.否則擁貲千萬者愈多.飢民餓莩亦將隨之日多.貧富不均.敎養無法.雖欲言治.皆苟而已.

(六)大同主義 禮運『大道之行也.天下爲公.選賢與能.講信修睦.故人不獨親其親.子其子.使老有所終.壯有所長.矜寡孤獨廢皆有所養.男有分.女有歸.貨惡其棄於地也.不必藏於己.力惡其不出於身也.不必爲己.是故謀

閉而不興.盜竊亂賊而不作.故外戶而不閉.是爲大同.』此爲孔子政治經濟思想之最高義.誠如所言.則私有財產制度不破自廢.共產主義不求自至.惜人類道德程度相差太遠.恐終不免爲烏託邦而已.

孟子之經濟思想

(一)樂利主義　孟子闢墨最力.而其政治經濟思想之受墨子之影響者亦最多.孟子非惟尊重民權.且欲使百姓享受樂利.所謂『仁政』『王道.』大部分爲樂利主義.其對齊宣王言樂及好貨好色數節.最爲明顯.故胡適之稱孔子之政策爲『爸爸政策』Paternalism 孟子之政策爲『媽媽政策』Maternalism 『爸爸政策.』要人正經規矩.『媽媽政策.』要人快活安樂.享受幸福.如『五畝之宅.樹之以桑.五十者可以衣帛矣.雞豚狗彘之畜.無失其時.七十者可以食肉矣.』此類『衣帛食肉』之政策.非『媽媽政策』而何.(見胡著中國哲學史大綱)

孟子之樂利思想.固已灼然可見.但對於『利』字.則攻擊不遺餘力.其初見梁惠王時.開口便痛詆『利』字.由此以觀.孟子一方面既贊成『樂利主義.』一方面又極端抨擊『利』字.豈非自相矛盾乎.其實前後兩『利』字根本不同.前者爲『自利主義』之『利.』乃『上下交征利』『懷利以相接』之『利.』後者爲『利民主義』之『利.』乃最多數人之最大『樂利』孟子所攻擊者.乃暴君汙吏之『自利主義.』其所主張者.乃聖人賢君之『利民主義.』是不可不明辨也.

孟子之經濟思想.所以趨向於『樂利主義』者.實見於當時民不聊生之景象.有感而發.今試略舉當時民衆生活情形.以覘孟子經濟思想之背景.

『狗彘食人食而不知檢.塗有餓莩而不知發.』

『庖有肥肉.廐有肥馬.民有飢色.野有餓莩.』

『奪其民時.使不得耕耨以養其父母.父母凍餓.兄弟妻子離散.』

『仰不足以事父母.俯不足以畜妻子.樂歲終身苦.凶年不免於死亡.』

觀此可以想見戰國時人民顛沛流離之苦況.其所以然者.實暴君汙吏之『自利主義』爲之厲階.孟子之大倡『樂利主義.』有由來矣.

（二）富而後敎　孟子時代之國民生計.較孔子時更壞.人民之道德觀念亦更薄.故孟子先富後敎之思想.亦較孔子爲盛.且對於富民之方法.提出具體之主張.

（甲）鼓勵生產

『不違農時.穀不可勝食也.數罟不入洿池.魚鼈不可勝食也.斧斤以時入山林.材木不可勝用也.穀與魚鼈不可勝食.材木不可勝用.是使民養生送死無憾也.養生送死無憾.王道之始也.』

『不違農時』者.謂凡有興作不違春耕夏耘秋收之時.此國家行政上維護生產之方法.與干涉保護主義相同.

『數罟不入洿池.斧斤以時入山林.』此節制消費以維護生產之方法也.

『五畝之宅.樹之以桑.五十者可以衣帛矣.雞豚狗彘之畜.無失其時.七十者可以食肉矣.百畝之田.勿奪其時.數口之家.可以無飢矣.……七十者衣帛食肉.黎民不飢不寒.然而不王者未之有也.』

『五畝之宅.樹牆下以桑.匹婦蠶之.則老者足以衣帛矣.五母雞二母彘.無失其時.老者足以食肉矣.百畝之田.匹夫耕之.八口之家.可以無飢矣.所謂西伯善養老者.制其田里.教之樹畜.導其妻子.使養其老.五十非帛不煖.七十非肉不飽.謂之凍餒.文王之民無凍餒之老者.此之謂也.』

此與管子之『一農不耕.民或爲之飢.一女不織.民或爲之寒』同爲獎勵生產事業.使百姓自食其力.無凍餒之虞.孟子對於生產制度.更側重社會主義.其言曰『民非水火不生活.昏暮叩人之門戶求水火.無弗與者.至足矣.聖人治天下.使有菽粟如水火.菽粟如水火.而民焉有不仁者乎.』今日生產

之制度.不外資本制度與社會制度兩種.前者以價値爲標準.故專生產價値高獲利豐之物品.而對於全人類效用之如何.則完全置之度外.後者以效用爲標準.故其生產乃爲全人類而生產.譬如何項物品.人類需要最廣最亟.卽生產此項物品.吾人處於今日資本制度淫威之下.日見富人侈品之增多.生活需要品之日昂.讀孟子『菽粟如水火』句.不禁有同慨焉.

（乙）制民恆產

『無恆產而有恆心者.惟士爲能.若民則無恆產.因無恆心.苟無恆心.放辟邪侈.無不爲已.及陷於罪.然後從而刑之.是罔民也.焉有仁人在位.罔民而可爲也.是故明君制民之產.必使仰足以事父母.俯足以畜妻子.樂歲終身飽.凶年免於死亡.然後驅而之善.故民之從之也輕.今也制民之產.仰不足以事父母.俯不足以畜妻子.樂歲終身苦.凶年不免於死亡.此惟救死而恐不贍.奚暇治禮義哉.』此言富民民自仁卽富而後教之義.

（丙）節用主義．鼓勵生產.制民恆產.固足富民.然苟浪費無度.民生仍不能富裕.故孟子對於消費.又重節儉.其言曰『食之以時.用之以禮.財不可勝用也.』『無政事.則財用不足.』所謂政事者.卽生之有道.取之有度.用之有節也.質言之.物質生活豐富.然後始能進於精神生活.天下未有衣食不足而治禮義者.

（三）薄稅斂 孟子承孔子之教.故對於國家理財.亦主薄斂節用.惟孟子之言.較孔子更詳.

『今之事君者曰「我能爲君辟土地.充府庫.」今之所謂良臣.古之所謂民賊也.君不鄉道.不志於仁.而求富之.是富桀也.』

『易其田疇.薄其稅斂.民可使富也.』

『施仁政於民.省刑罰.薄稅斂.深耕易耨.壯者以暇日.』

『關市譏而不征.澤梁無禁.』『古之爲關也.將以禦暴.今之爲關將以

爲暴.』按關爲道路之關.市爲都邑之市.關市之吏.察異服異言之人.而不征商賈之稅也.

『市廛而不征.法而不廛.則天下之商.皆悅而願藏於其市矣.關譏而不征.則天下之旅.皆悅而願出於其路矣.耕者助而不稅.則天下之農.皆悅而願耕於其野矣.廛無夫里之布.則天下之民.皆悅而願爲之氓矣.按廛市宅也.或賦其市地之廛.而不征其貨.或治之以市官之法.而不賦其廛.助而不稅者.但使出力以助耕公田.而不稅其私田.廛無夫里之布者.鄭氏謂宅不種桑麻者.罰之使出一里二十五家之布.民無常業者.罰之使出一夫百畝之稅.一家力役之征也.蓋當時治市既治法.又有廛稅.又有貨征.稅斂極繁.故孔子日以薄稅斂爲言也.

『治地莫善於助.莫不善於貢.貢者.校數歲之中以爲常.樂歲粒米狼戾.多取之而不爲虐.則寡取之.凶年糞其田而不足.則必取盈焉.爲民父母.使民盻盻然.將終歲勤動不得以養其父母.又稱貸而益之.使老稚轉乎溝壑.惡在其爲民父母也.』

『有布縷之征.粟米之征.君子用其一.緩其二.用其二而民有殍.用其三而父子離.』朱子註曰『征賦之法.歲有常數.如布縷取之於夏.粟米取之於秋.力役取之於冬.當各以其時.若並取之.則民力有所不堪矣.唐世之『租』卽粟米之征.『庸』卽力役之征.『調』卽布縷之征.蓋循戰國時舊制也.其後王安石改雇役.遂去力役之租.庸調改爲兩稅.兩稅改爲一條鞭.卽本孟子『用其一緩其二』之意也.上古國家事業簡單.故賦稅主輕.時至今日.國家經濟日臻發達.人民被利日多.義務自亦日增.時勢不同.非猶可泥於古制也.康有爲嘗言『中國稅於民極薄.然不足以立國.養兵興學勸業修道衞生恤貧皆不能舉.國體薾然.是亦不遵孔法而爲貉法矣.』

(四) 提倡井田制　井田制者.中國最古之均產制度也.『方里而井.井

九百畝.其中爲公田.八家皆私百畝.同養公田.公事畢.然後敢治私事.』方一里爲一井.其田九百畝.中畫井字.界爲九區.每區百畝.中百畝爲公田.外八百畝爲私田.八家各受私田百畝.而同耕公田.是九分而稅其一也.

『夏后氏五十而貢.殷人七十而助.周人百畝而徹.其實皆什一也.』夏時.一夫受田五十畝.而每夫計其五畝之入以爲貢.此爲我國田賦之起源.商時以六百三十畝之地畫爲九區.每區七十畝.中爲公田.其外八家各授一區.但借其力以助耕公田.而不復稅其私田.故曰助.是井田制在商時已有矣.周時一夫受田百畝.八家同井.耕則通力而作.收則計畝而分.又徹者通也.周制夏商兩法通則.鄉遂用貢法.都鄙用助法.故謂之徹.

『夫仁政必自經界始.經界不正.井地不均.穀祿不平.是故暴君汙吏.必慢其經界.經界改正.分田制祿.坐而定也.』經界者.置溝洫畎澮經遂道路以區畫井地(即井田)也.此法不行.則田無定分.強暴者遂得兼併.暴君汙吏得以多取.故欲行仁政.必自經界始.蓋經界旣定.分田制祿.自能平準也.

當時助法井田之制已廢.而孟子獨竭力提倡.且列爲仁政之端者.蓋此制一行.可得三利.

(甲)無貧富階級 土地國有.由國家分配.依人授田.則人民之產業均等.自無貧富階級發生.

(乙)民有恆產 一夫授田百畝.二十受田.六十還田.使人民各有恆產自食其力.仰足以事父母.俯足以畜妻子.樂歲終生飽.凶年免於死亡.安居樂業.共享太平.

(丙)賦稅得平準 八家同耕公田.助而不稅.是力役之征也.君暴汙吏不能多取.人民不致受苛稅之苦.

(五)不贊成專利及操縱市面

『古之爲市者.以其所有易其所無者.有司者治之耳.有賤丈夫焉.必求

龍斷而登之以左右望而罔市利.人皆以爲賤.故從而征之.征商自此賤丈夫始矣.』

今之龍斷市面.操縱行市者.祇圖一己之私利.而不顧大衆之利害者.由孟子觀之.皆賤丈夫而已.

(六) 獎勵儲蓄　『周於利者.凶年不能殺.周於德者.邪世不能亂.』此孟子獎勵儲蓄.使人民未雨綢繆之微意也.蓋周者.足也.平時能儲蓄.則患難時自不致窘迫而陷於飢饉矣.

(七) 分功交易論　孟子對於分功交易之理論.亦甚透徹.觀其駁許行之言.何一非與近世經濟學說.若合符節.

『陳相見孟子.道許行之言曰.「滕君則誠賢君也.雖然.未聞道也.賢者與民並耕而食饔飧而治.今也滕有倉廩府庫.則是厲民而以自養也.」孟子曰「許子必種粟而後食乎.」曰「然.」「許子必織布而後衣乎.」曰「否.」「許子衣褐.許子冠乎.」曰「冠.」曰「奚冠.」曰「冠素.」曰「自織之歟.」曰「否.以粟易之.」曰「許子奚爲不自織.」曰「害於耕.」曰「許子以釜甑爨以鐵耕乎.」曰「然.」「自爲之歟」.曰「否.以粟易之.」「以粟易械器者.不爲厲陶冶.陶冶亦以其械器易粟者.豈爲厲農夫哉.且許子何不爲陶冶.舍皆取諸其宮中而用之.何爲紛紛然與百工交易.何許子之不憚煩.」曰「百工之事.固不可耕且爲也.」「然則治天下獨可耕且爲歟.有大人之事.有小人之事.且一人之身而百工之所爲備.如必自爲而後用之.是率天下而路也.故曰或勞心.或勞力.勞心者治人.勞力者治於人.治於人者食人.治人者食於人.天下之通義也.」』

『子不通功易事.以羨補不足.則農有餘粟.女有餘布.子如通之.則梓匠輪輿.皆得食於子.』

許行並耕同賈.親爲捆屨織席.蓋主平等苦行之說者.以督勞民縱慾自

飧者.固自爲勝.然以之施於國政則不可.蓋文明愈甚.分業愈多.故機器旣昌.一針一綫之微.分功至細.一人所成之物無數.其精亦無藝.况一衣乎.又况治國施政乎.惟所謂大人之事小人之事.則不免存有幾分階級觀念也.

（八）價值論　孟子對於物品價格.亦有正當之觀念.其駁許行之言.尤爲允當.陳相言許行之道曰『從許子之道.則市賈不貳.國中無僞.雖使五尺之童適市.莫之或欺.布帛長短同.則賈相若.麻縷絲絮輕重同.則賈相若.五穀多寡同.則賈相若.屨大小同則賈相若』孟子駁之曰『夫物之不齊物之情也.或相倍蓰.或相什伯.或相千萬.子比而同之.是亂天下也.巨屨小屨同.賈人豈爲之哉.從許子之道相率而爲僞者也.惡能治國家.』

孟子以爲交易上之物品價格.不能僅以數量定.當更以品質作標準也許行陳相及陳仲子均傾向個人主義.與托爾斯泰之汎勞動主義頗相似.孟子則主互助及分功.蓋有近世國家社會主義之氣息焉.

中國鐵路管理問題

孫詠沂

我國鐵路.自創始迄今.不過五十餘年其間阻礙迭生.幾經頓挫.方有此少許之成績.而年來內亂頻仍.各路機件之毀損.收入之減少.爲數實屬不小.所望今後或能入承平之境.則各路皆有整頓之機會.而我國鐵路事業庶幾隨之而發達乎.本篇所述.謂之作者之希望可.謂之一得之貢獻亦無不可.

(一) 關於財政者

鐵路財政實爲最難解決之問題.非一二語所能解釋明瞭者.以下所述.不過其淺而易見者耳.

(甲) 整理　我國築路借款之總數.據財政部之調查爲三萬三千四百八十萬二千六百三十一元（至民國十一年止）又依據交通部之統計.全國鐵路之盈餘爲三千六百萬（民國八年）由此以觀.路債之償清.實非絕難之事.如粵漢川漢之付息誤期.並非鐵路之不發達.實別有故焉.茲略述之.當宣統三年（即一九一一年）清廷向四國銀行團（德英法美）借款六百萬鎊.以建粵漢川鐵路.將湖南湖北之釐金販糶捐等作抵.合同訂定後即行開工.時適辛亥革命起.工作隨之而中止.至一九一三年繼續進行.不幸一九一四年歐戰起.而是路之建築又中止.後交通部更改計劃.決定先築粵漢線之湘鄂段.至一九一九年告竣.計長二百五十九英里.而同時六百萬鎊之借款亦已無所存矣.是年二月實行通車.由各方面之情形推測.是路之發達可以預卜.孰知其結果乃有大謬不然者.蓋自開車後.內亂不已.全路爲軍人占據者五年有餘.如此而望其有盈餘也難矣.故付息之誤期實非鐵路本身之不善.其餘各路亦何獨不然.

前交通總長葉恭綽氏施行特別會計制.將鉄路收入與政府賬目分清.能如是.復何愁債之不能清償.以每年三百六十萬元之進款.償三千餘萬元

之債款.不出十年.本利盡償矣.惜於民國十一年時特別會計制又遭取消.殊屬可嘆.今後欲望鉄路財政之整頓.非恢復特別會計制不爲功.

（乙）鼓勵人民之投資 我國鉄路.類皆以外款建築.此實昔日政府與人民不明鉄路重要之果.今者德意俄法等國.類皆自顧不暇.無餘力以投資於遠東.而我國商界銀行界近年進步之神速.皆能使人引起以內債築路之觀念.民國十年交通部向銀行團借六百萬元以添置四幹綫（京漢.京奉.京綏.津浦.）之機頭與車輛.實銀行界進步之明證也.故計劃中之幹綫.可在國內集資建築.支綫則由商民自行建築.而同時政府與以各種權利以資鼓勵.所謂權利云者.即如築路開墾荒地時.由政府給與路基.或由政府給與建築時期資本之利息等.凡此種種.皆歐美各國之用以提倡築路者.其成績之卓著.盡人皆知.故欲商民築路非由政府資助不可.

（二）關於營業者

（甲）運價之訂定 運價之關係於鉄路營業甚巨.故於施行之前.非加以切實之考察不可.我國現在之運價.悉依路之遠近（Distance Principal）然我國地大物博.情形複雜.僅用此種最簡單之定價法.而欲求其適合於各方.勢所不能.茲將中國各部之情形略述之.以作定價之參攷.

1. 滿州 東三省農產木材鑛產之豐富.實爲全國之冠.南部之煤.幾遍地皆有.曾估計至少在八百萬噸以上.此部南接高麗.北鄰西伯利亞.於訂定運價時國際聯運方面.須加以注意.

2. 平原諸省 中國地勢東北低而西南高.今試劃出一平原.自山海關起沿長城至山西.向南經河南湖北而至洞庭湖.順長江東下至南京.再沿江蘇省界而北至山東.復沿海面北回至山海關.此平原內農產豐富.居民稠密.直隸山東河南湖北之煤礦亦甚可觀.其間鉄路之運價.可以路程爲標準.而以京漢路之價目作爲參攷.

3 河流密佈區域 此區包括江蘇浙江江西三省.其間河流甚多.故定

價決不可過高.以致減少營業.江浙絲業發達.江西磁器之出產.皆須藉鉄路輸送.且我國進口貨中.有百之五十在上海起貨.故鉄路之運價雖較低.而貨物之待運者甚多.必不至使路局有所虧負也.

4. 沿海諸省 福建廣西廣東諸省南瀕大海.北障羣山.與中部諸省相隔.故運輸至爲不便.福建之菓品.出產甚豐.然因交通不便.未能銷及遠方.將來粵漢路如能接通.則此種出產.亦必爲營業中之一大部份.再此路如能接通.則由廣東登岸之貨物可直接運至中部與西部諸省.不必繞道上海矣.故其營業之發達.可操左劵.然水道之競爭甚烈.定價須較低.或竟將直達海口之運價.低於較近之內地各地.以資抵抗.亦無不可.

5. 山脈連綿諸省 四川雲南貴州諸省.萬山重疊.最低之處.亦高出海面五千尺以上.居民雖較少.然礦產甚多.金銀銅鉄鉛煤等.幾無所不有.但因建築上之困難.除外人所辦之滇越鐵路外.我國並未有所建築.然而大好富源終須開闢.鐵路之建築.遲早間事耳.此段因建築上之困難.可照營業支出(Cost of Service)之多少.以定運價之高低.

6. 內地諸省 山西煤產之豐富.甲於全球.每年產額.曾估計爲二百五十萬頓.陝西甘肅.亦以煤著.此種富源.須得正太與隴海路之沿長爲之開發.山西爲大平原與蒙古高原之接連處.平均斜度每英里約三尺.甘肅省內亦有山嶺.故鐵路之建築費較巨.將來運價之訂定.或將以營業支出爲標準.但對於日用必需之品.最好較低.亦推銷貨物以增加鐵路收入之一法也.

7. 高原諸省 此高原區域包括西藏新疆及蒙古等省.此區至今尚未有鐵路之建築.以其費用大而酬報小也.然欲工業之發達.西北之開闢.非築路不可.更有進者.是路費用雖大.而其運價必須低廉.以鼓勵人民之移殖.能如是.則不出十年.路局之盈餘必較開辦時之虧損爲大.

(乙) 營業部之重要 路局之欲求營業發達者.不可不注重營業部.路局各部之中.亦以營業部與公衆之接觸爲最多.是部之職務.乃推廣鐵路之

營業.以增進路局之盈餘也.美國鐵路近有工業部之組織.專門研究營業之狀況.及增加營業之方法.且不僅注意於營業之推廣.而兼及研究各地工業之缺乏而提倡之.如沿路皆爲工業發達之區.則其路收入之巨無疑矣.

此種組織.於我國需要尤亟.我國人民類皆喜靜不喜動.是以商人則多僅於本地經營不思推廣.農民則泥守成法.不思改良.各路局應設專部.調查各地之需要以報告於各工廠.工廠之銷路增加.路局之進益.亦隨之而增矣.對於農民宜教以改良種植之法.并宜施送種子等等.以增加其出產.此法津浦路曾實行.惜爲時不久.故收效不著.凡此種種.如能切實施行.路局固能增進利益.而社會上工商業之發達亦必可觀.誠兩得之舉也.

(三) 關於行車者

(甲) 標準時 標準時之規定.實爲行車之最大問題.美國面積不及我國而有四標準時.我國西起經度七十八又十分之四度.東迄一百三十四又十分之三度.自西至東.共五十五又十分之九度.以如此大國.而僅有一標準時.實屬不敷.故標準時之增加.實爲今日鐵路行車之一大問題.

(乙) 車輛之添置 依據民國八年之統計.我國車輛效率 (Car Efficiency) 爲百分之七十七.較各國爲巨 (美國之報告爲百分之五十六) 實我國鐵路之好現象也.我國車輛之調用.其所以能較他國爲佳者.其故有二.(一) 貨物之裝卸較他國爲速.故貨物不致堆積於車中.致阻車輛之運用.(二) 延期費 (Demurrage) 較他國爲高.故貨主類皆於貨到後即提取.他國因延期費之低廉.竟有以車輛爲堆貨之所.願出延期費而節堆棧費者.故其車輛之運用.至爲不便.然我國車輛效率雖較高.終不能完全免除車輛缺少問題.(Car shortage) 故車輛之添置.亦屬不容再緩.

(丙) 車場調車 工商業愈進步.則鐵路之營業愈發達.營業愈發達.則車輛之調遣愈重要.蓋車輛調遣不善.乃車輛缺乏之一大原因也.我國車輛之調遣.皆受制於站長.而無一定之規則.因調遣之不善.致將車場閉塞至數

小時之久者.數見不鮮.故路局須有車輛調遣法之規定.以資查考而減無謂之損失.

(四) 關於其他管理者

(甲) 僱用部(Emp'oyment Deqartment)之設立. 我國鐵路向無所謂僱用部者.故國人知之者鮮.然在美國幾各路皆有之矣.良以其關係於鐵路者至大.而於鐵路人員.又皆能使之忠於厥職無慮無故被撤也.是部專任路員之選擇.僱用.訓練等等.凡路員之升降.皆由是部定之.局長無權過問.我國路局人員之任用.皆由局長一人主之.故每逢局長調動.勢必牽及大部路員.且賞罰之不公.私人之任用.皆爲意想中事.凡此種種.皆足使路員時時慮及無故被撤.以致不能忠於厥職.而貽害於路局.此皆局長集權之弊也.若能將任用路員之權.劃歸一部.則諸弊悉除.局長之調動不致牽動全部.賞罰不致不公.私人無從任用.而路員亦能忠於其職.無所顧慮矣.故此部之設立.實屬有利無弊而急須實行者也.

(乙) 材料之供給 我國各路材料及一切用品之供給.皆由各該路之債權國任之.(於合同中訂定)貨物之昂貴.固無論矣.即因材料之不適用.而視作廢料者.亦不爲少.此中損失.爲數甚鉅.欲求補救.則各路之於材料及用品等.必須有一定之標準.標準既定錯誤自減.而路局亦不致受此暗中之損失.

上述各項.雖皆顯而易見者.然其關係於鐵路之發展與營業之增進至爲重要.故略述所見如此. (終)

贖回中東鐵路財政上應有之準備

邱褚聯 譯

緒言

根據華府會議而產生之關稅會議,修改中國稅率,已引起世界各國之注意,因其於財政及政治上之關係,重且大也.然余意尙有更重要之問題在焉.此問題旣較關稅自主爲重要,較之增加稅率更爲重要,非特於中國之政治經濟社會有密切之關係,對於遠東之和平,亦有極大之影響,此卽中東鐵路之贖回問題是也.吾人固應以關稅會議爭得之權利,以達贖回中東鐵路之目的,然吾國人士對於此點,論者極罕.玆篇所述,乃中東鐵路之狀況,贖回之重要,估價之根據,及應有財政上之準備也.

中東鐵路之狀況

一八九六年九月八日,中國與華俄道勝銀行原訂之『東省鐵路公司合同』中（註一）關於東省鐵路之建築及行車,雙方簽定如下;

> 『……從開車之日起,三十六年後,中國政府有權可給價收回,按計所用本銀,并因此路所欠債項並利息,照數償還,……』

根據舊有之紀載,中東全線,（自西伯利亞鐵道經滿州里,至海參威,以及自哈爾濱達旅順之一段,於一九〇一年秋完全竣工.（註二）倘依此推算,則於一九三七年,中國卽可備款贖回,吾人對於贖回中東鐵路,應如何預先籌劃,使外人築於吾國彊土之鐵道,收回自備,以爭主權於萬一耶.然該合同又謂中東鐵路全線築成後八十年,俄國應無報酬將中東全線交與中國收管,（註三）則吾國將待至一九八一年後收回中東路乎,抑至一九三七年行使吾國所有之取舍權乎.吾人於此,應知此「三十年後備款贖還」之取舍權,實爲全約中吾國惟有之主權,况八十年後,吾國能否無價收回,爲一極大疑問.故吾人應毅然决然,而準備贖回中東鐵路也.

蘇俄政府對華之政策,表面盛唱親善,而一究其實,固未嘗稍異於以前二百五十年間之侵略政策也.據紐約晚報（一九二五年十月七日）之報告,蘇俄正與外蒙政府簽訂條約,自赤塔城至庫倫,築一鐵道,此線一成,蘇俄得自此線而達北京,可不受南滿支線之束縛.（按南滿線本爲中東鐵路之一部,爲一九〇四——五年日俄戰後,割讓於日本者）至俄蒙契約,除訂定建築鐵路權外,並許以沿路一百俄里以內之土地買賣權,造屋權,礦權,開墾權等,與昔日俄皇政府時代所訂之東省鐵路合同,無以異也.由此觀之,可知現今蘇俄政府之對華政策,無稍異於昔日之侵略政策,所異者口頭之親善而已,故吾人對於蘇俄所謂親華政策,宜明其詐僞,不爲所欺,否則將無以自拔.慨自一八九五年,我敗於日,我國應付日本大宗賠款,俄國借與我國幾及半數,彼固何爲出此友誼之援助乎,滿洲鐵路與經濟勢力之擴張,卽爲其酬報之一,然日俄戰爭之惡根,亦種於是矣.

贖回中東鐵路之重要

今欲論中東鐵路之贖回,請先述該路於國際間及遠東和平之關係,當俄國之攫取中東鐵路之建築權也,本挾有極大之詭謀,以行施其政治侵略政策於遠東,吾人須知俄皇政府之建路計畫,蓄有在太平洋得一立足地之預謀.西伯利亞鐵道之建築,實爲進行此項計畫之初步,其先後租得旅順大連,卽其野心之暴露.及中東鐵路之建築權攫得,而俄國遠東侵略政策乃大告成功矣.然俄國在遠東之地位,與日本有勢不兩立之傾向,兩雄相遇,必有一傷,日本地狹人衆,爲國家生存計,不得不極力擴張其勢力於國外,倘俄國仍霸佔遠東.日本必不甘心,第二次之日俄戰爭,行將重演於遠東,我國土地將再爲二國之戰場,徒供犧牲而已.故今日如欲免除此種不幸之戰爭,須求一根本之解決.俄國旣以中東路爲其施行遠東政策之利器,該路卽無異於俄國之命脈,倘命脈一斷,則俄國將不復能張牙伸爪於遠東.此從政治方面而論中東鐵道贖回之重要也.請再從經濟方面言之.

中東鐵路爲帝國主義極盛時代之產物,俄國卽以中東鐵路爲武器,實行其經濟侵略政策.托詞建築鐵道須用各種材料,沿路土地之開墾權,落於俄人之手,其他如礦山經營權,林權,電權,航權等,無一不爲俄人所攫.尤可痛者,卽俄國有該鐵路附近之行政權也.俄人之所以野心勃勃者,蓋滿州實爲遠東唯一之富原,(註四)因其地勢氣候之適當,有極大之生產力.卽以今日而論,已有三大實業之發展,卽畜牧農產及森林也.農品出產之中心爲哈爾濱.約有二十萬方哩之地從事耕種.五百英畝之大黃豆爲哈爾濱大宗之出產.其他農產,爲麥,黍,蕎麥,亞麻等等,加之生產力之增進甚速,據一九〇三年之統計,穀類之運於中東路者,僅一二五,〇〇〇噸,迄一九二二年,驟增至一,九〇〇,〇〇〇噸,其前途之發展,正未可限量.以森林論,尤爲豐富.北滿有大森林三:興安林,松花江林及沿中東路之森林是也.據中國官廳之報告,以吉林省中東鐵路而論,已有材木一,五〇〇,〇〇〇,〇〇〇立方呎.錦安一帶.有一二二,〇〇〇,〇〇〇,〇〇〇立方呎之多.其木料之豐富,可想見矣.滿洲非特富於農產森林,卽畜牧一項,亦爲其大宗出產之一,據最近之估算,該地約有羊一千萬頭,大角牛五百萬頭,豬三百萬頭,馬三百萬頭.

滿洲地廣人稀,宜於殖民.據最近調查,共佔地四十萬方哩,而人口僅二千萬.中國其他各省,人口稠密者,大可移民於此,開闢東省之富源,故贖回中東鐵道,非特於政治上及經濟上有重要之關係.社會上亦有莫大之影響也.

中東鐵路之估值

贖還中東鐵路之重要,已如上述.然於贖還之前有先決之問題二,一曰鐵路之估值,卽我國贖回該路應付之贖價.二曰財政上之準備.卽如何能集款以贖路也.請先論其估值.按中東全路自西比利亞鐵道東達海參威,南至旅順,約一千六百哩,自日俄戰爭後,南滿支線自寬城子達旅順,割讓於日,故現在之中東鐵道,僅一千〇七十英哩.按理於一九三七年,中國亦可向日本或俄國贖回.倘旣付款於日,可不須付款於俄,惟中國直接向俄贖回,事較簡易，至日俄間之問題，中國可不問也。

贖回中東鐵道估値之根據有二：其一，即東省鐵路公司合同弟十二條：

『……從開車之日起，三十六年後，中國政府有權可給價收回，按計所用本銀，并因此數所欠債項並利息，照數償還。其公司所賺之利，除分給各股人外，如有盈餘應作爲已歸之本，在收回路價內扣除。……』

由此觀之，贖回該路之款，約等未歸還之債票，及現有之資本。此一根據也。

其二即華俄道勝銀行總辦羅啓泰（Rothstein）之公函也。（註五）其譯文如下：

『……本公司賬目，按年結算刊布。其中載明各項賬目，及一歲出入款項，并所欠之債，所借之款，還本付息等情，將來中國給價收回此路，應以每年結算刊布之帳爲憑，其收回緣由，詳載公司章程之內……』

倘此種文件及帳目尙完全存在，則中東鐵道之估値，匪難事也。

嘗聞中東鐵路之建設費，約爲四二二，二九二，〇〇〇盧布，約合華幣四〇〇，〇〇〇，〇〇〇元。現信一部份債票已分期償還，故現在之實値，遠不滿四萬萬元，然今旣無完全可靠之依據，則試與中國其他各路每哩之建設費一相比較，雖不能知中東路實在建設費，亦可窺其一斑矣。一九二三年中國國有各路每哩之建設費如下：（註六）

路　　名	哩數	建設費總數	每哩之建設費
京漢鐵路	825	$120,968.000	$146,600
京奉鐵路	605	94 263,000	155,800
津浦鐵路	687	118,999,000	173,200
滬寧鐵路	203	32,960 000	123,000
道清鐵路	110	8.351,000	75,900
湘鄂鐵路	260	59,396,[illegible]00	228,400
京綏鐵路	550	56.17[illegible].000	102,100
國有鐵路共計	4267	629,074,000	147,400

自上表觀之,湘鄂鐵路每哩之建設費爲最高,達二二八,四〇〇元,道清鐵路每哩之建設費爲最低,僅七五,九〇〇元.而國有鐵道,平均每哩之建設費爲一四七,四〇〇元也.以地位及運輸事業性質而論,則中東路每哩之建設費,當與京奉鐵路每哩建設費相近.故以每哩一五五,八〇〇元作根據.則一千六百哩之中東鐵路,僅須二四九,二八〇,〇〇〇元而已,倘以建設費最低之道清鐵路爲根據,祇須一二一,四四〇,〇〇〇元.即以建設費最高之湘鄂鐵道爲根據,亦僅須三六五,四四〇,〇〇〇元.然余信中東鐵路每哩之建設費,當遠在湘鄂之下也.

財政上應有之準備

今吾人雖不能確實推算中東路之所值,然若決意贖回,其需千百萬之大宗的款也無疑.此實爲中國財政上之重大問題.故欲達贖回之目的,必須有相當之準備,庶可免「臨渴掘井」之譏.然中國今日財政之紊亂,幾蹈於不能自拔之地位,入不敷出,幾將破產,各部需款日甚一日.處此「家徒四壁」之環境中,其財政之前途,實少光明.然細析之,中國財政之整理,倘有專門理財家出任其難,以全國民衆爲後盾,尙非絕望.蓋中國有四萬萬之人民無窮之富源,加之中國內外債之總數,除鐵路借款外,僅二十萬萬,每人平均僅負債五元,較之美國平均每人負債一四〇〇元,法國一三〇〇元,美國四〇〇元,比利時三〇〇元,意大利一九〇元,日本五〇元,有天壤之別也.故今日整理財政之急務,爲恢復歷年吾國所失之信用,則將來贖回中東鐵路之舉,或有成功之望,否則亦徒喚奈何而已.

今中國未償還之無担保內外債款,達六萬萬元.大部分皆到期不付本息.倘長此以往,則中國政府之信用,將一落千丈,故解決無担保之內外債,實爲目前整理財政最重要之關鍵也.億梁士詒於「整理財政會議」席上曾提出下列五條(一)中央政府與省政府之權力,須完全劃清,使中央與各省之收入,得以分清.(二)中央及各省政府之財政,須受預算表之約束.(三)實行各種改革,如裁厘及修改稅率等,以改進人民之生活狀況.(四)解決現在一切無担保之借款.(五)改革現行軍隊之組織,以減少國家之支出.余信此數項者,確爲整理財政之方法也.

今北京舉行之關稅會議,已辦到稅率增至七五,並已原則上承認中國關稅自主,此正吾國整理財政,恢復國家信用之好機會也.據民國十三年海關報告,共收入海關銀七千萬兩,約合銀元一〇五,〇〇〇,〇〇〇元.則增加二.五,所增收入,可有五二,五〇〇,〇〇〇元.依此計算,則每年海關之收入,可得一六〇,五〇〇,〇〇〇元.除九〇,五〇〇,〇〇〇元,須償還內外債外,尙可餘七〇,五〇〇,〇〇〇元.每年貿易之發展及舊債之漸次償淸,此數當可逐年增加.設每年有此巨額之餘款,儘可發行新債票七萬萬元,以償還無担保之借款,國家信用,亦可漸次恢復,故關稅之用途,莫善於此.俟將來關稅自主後,得多發公債,以用於各種建設之事業也.

國家信用旣復,則贖路之事方能有所進行,第一步須組織委員會,專司其事.此委員會須由精於理財工程及法律者組織之,則各事有專門之人才庶可事半而功倍,如能得出版界有經驗者從事宣傳,喚醒民衆.則中東路之贖回,誠易易也.委員會之主要工作有二:曰鐵路之估值及贖回鐵路財政上之準備.對於鐵路之估值,前已詳述,至財政上應有之準備,須具二條件（一）將來之財政計劃,須視力之所及,使此項投資,萬分穩當,以得投資者之信仰.（二）此項財政計劃須與事實不相抵觸,有充分實現之可能.此二條爲任何財政計畫所必有之原則,非特贖路爲然.有其一,不有其二,將來之失敗,可立而待.惟此偉大之工作,非一二人之力所能成.民衆之贊助,及監視,實爲至要之後盾.

贖還中東路財政上之準備,可分二部論之.(一)贖還以前財政上應有之準備.(二)贖還以後財政上應有之整理.財政上之準備爲發行債票惟須包括下列諸點:

(一) 票額總數,爲四萬萬元,可分四期,其債票名稱,可謂之『中國政府中東鐵路贖路公債第一期,』『中國政府中東鐵路贖路公債第二期,』餘類推.債票銷售於國外市場者,票面可以該國貨幣計數惟此種債票票面之總數,折成國幣後,仍不得超過或低於原定之數目.至債票之期限,利率之高低,還本及到期之時間等,均須參照當時之市情定之.

(二) 發行公債所得之款項,須用於下列各項:

一、贖回中東鐵路.

二、關於贖回中東鐵路之其他一切用費.

三、除以上二項用途外,倘再有餘款,得用於穩當之投資,但無論如何,不得再有其他用途.

(三) 持有該路原有之債票者,得照換時之匯價,以舊債票調換新債票

(四) 此種債票得於將來轉換中東鐵路公司發行之他種債票.倘於某時期內,持票人不向公司轉換新債票,得由公司依照一定之價格收還全部或一部.

(五) 此種債票爲中國政府直接之負債,遇必要時,應指定確實資產以爲担保,

(六) 新債票票面,須大小均有,以便銷售.照現下之經濟情形,可發行五元,十元,五十元,一百元,五百元,及一千元六種,最爲適宜.

贖還後須從事於財政上之整理,該路可發行整理抵押公債,其用途應歸定如下:

(一) 償還「中國政府中東鐵路贖路公債」全數 發行整理公債以償還前次所出之公債實爲要圖,蓋一方可減少政府之担負,一方可使中東鐵路之債務,集中於少數種類之債票.

(二) 改善鐵路上之設備組織及管理.

(三) 改換鐵路軌距,使與中國標準鐵路軌距相同. 據原訂之東省鐵路合同第三條,(註七)鐵軌之寬窄,應與俄國鐵軌一律,即五俄尺,約合中國四尺二寸半.以政治及經濟上之利害而論,此種鐵軌應一律改爲英尺四尺八寸半,以合中國之標準.

至此項整理公債,應以全路之資產爲担保,利息應以盈餘爲担保,遇必須時,中國政府應另外指定資產,担保將來本息之償還.至於其他瑣事,如利率,還本,及票面等,得於將來參照當時市情,及投資市場,再行定奪.惟最要者投資者之利益,須有鞏固之保障,則不難得全國人士之贊助也.

結 論

贖還中東鐵路既關於遠東之和平,又關於中日俄三國間之利益,加之於經濟上,及政治上,有重大之影響,吾人當決然準備贖囘.雖有極大之犧牲,亦當忍痛一時,以爲一勞永逸之計.不觀夫俄國野心之表露乎,於一九二四年九月二十日之奉俄會議契約中,將一八九六年之『東省鐵路公司合同』第十二條『……八十年限滿之日,所有鐵路一切產業,全歸中國政府,毋庸給價……』一段中之八十年,改爲六十年.此實無異以餌誘我,以預防吾國贖路之舉動也.然中國昧於利害,毅然簽字,以爲強國之以平等對待中國者,其惟俄國,而不知中國已受愚矣.蓋六十年後,亦俄已將張其牙,舞其爪於遠東,不可以理論喩之矣.據某鐵路專家之報告,中東路五年之收入,已足贖囘該路而有餘.則即六十年改至五十年,亦與中國無益也.然此偉大之工作,須得世界人士之贊助,欲得全世界人士之贊助,非從恢復國家信用不爲功.

節譯 The Chinese Eastern Railway
Its Redemption by the Chinese Government
The Financial Involvements

(註一) 見『中國鐵路借款合同,』及 Mac Murray 著作之 Treaties and Agreements With and Concerning China.

(註二)　見徐著『中國鉄路問題』(Hsu M. H.- Railway Problems in China.)

(註三)　一九二四年奉俄條約改爲六十年,

(註四)　滿州經濟狀況之詳細討論可參閱中國經濟月刊一九二三年十一月份中之"The Chinese Eastern Railway and the Development of North Manchuria"

(註五)　東省鉄路公司合同十二條内載給價收回一節,因恐將來解釋有異,復商華俄道勝銀行總辦於光緒二十二年七月二十五日,即西歷一八九六年九月二日,另繕憑函,附於合同之後,以期相信.

(註六)　見一九二五年之China Year Book第三四五頁

(註七)　見『中國鉄路借款合同』

補白七

英意法三國對美債務償還法

英意法三國爲大戰時協約國中之強有力者。但其對美債務爲數均達數十億。計英債爲四十六萬萬美金元。意債爲二十萬零四千二百萬美金元。法債爲二十九萬萬美金元。茲英債意債已議訂償還辦法。經美國參院批准。法債償還法亦已有成議。爰將其三種辦法披露於下。

(一)　英債

分六十二年攤償。利息前十年爲年利三厘。第十一年後年利三厘半。

(二)　意債

分六十二年攤償。除前五年不計外。分爲六期。每期十年（末一期祇得七年）。利息按期遞增如次(年利率)。

第一期(第六年起)八分之一厘　第二期(第十六年起)四分之一厘　第三期(第二十六年起)二分之一厘　第四期（第三十六年起）四分之三厘　第五期(第四十六年起)一厘　第六期(第五十六年起至六十二年止)二厘

(三)　法債

分六十二年攤償。第一兩年每年付還三千萬元美金。第二兩年每年付還三千二百五十萬元美金。嗣後逐漸加增。至每年付一萬二千五百萬元爲止。利息前五年不計。嗣後第一十年年利一厘。十年後增至三厘半云。觀三種清償方法。以對意者爲最寬洪。蓋意國經濟狀況較遜也。法國財政紊亂。能否任此艱巨。尚待觀其後耳。

從利權得失觀劃分中國近世交通史之時期

（收回交通權芻議之四）

趙祖康

吾國交通史之編著，至今蓋甚寥寥，據余所知，武進王倬氏曾輯交通史一書，然而古今中外，兼容並包，分別觀之，乃甚簡陋，且祇敷陳往事，毫無創見。王作而外，惟聞北京某氏有中國交通史之著，惜未得讀爲憾。亦不稔確有是書否也，交通史既不多覯，鉄路郵政航政等史亦罕見。此或因余於交通掌故，素無研究，故益覺其少。然而一考本校圖書館所藏有關交通史料諸書，誠屈指可數也。茲以拙作六十年來中國交通四政大事年表爲根據，而論中國近世交通史劃分之法，謬誤之處，幸讀者正之。

考吾國之有新式交通事業。（就路電郵航四政論）當以郵政爲最早。蓋海關郵政部之創設，事在清咸豐十一年（西歷一八六一年。）然而吾國交通事權之喪失，則遠在吾交通事業發生之前。是誠可怪而亦可痛之事。世界各國所僅見者也。清道光二十二年（西歷一八四二年）吾國以鴉片戰敗，與英訂立南京和約。是爲吾喪權辱國。外人實行侵略之始。而我交通權之喪失，亦卽始於是時。案和約第二條明許英國以五口（廣州福州廈門甯波上海）通商貿易。所謂通商貿易者。卽含有英國船隻得自由航行於五口間之意，是實吾國沿海航行權失敗之第一步，而亦吾交通權喪失史之第一頁也。嗣後咸豐八年（西一八五八年）中英續約又許英船得由海口駛入長江，至於漢口。於是吾內河航行權亦與人以共有。外國航業得在吾國橫行者是。而吾則至同治十一年（西一八七二年）方有李鴻章奏請創設招商局之議也。咸豐十一年，郵政矪辦。然甚簡陋，附設於海關，權在外人之手。則與其謂爲吾國交通事業之濫觴，毋甯視爲外人侵奪吾交通權之又闢一徑也。

是以溯吾國交通權之喪失。當與不平等條約同歸於一八四二年。論吾國交通事業路電郵航四政發生與受創之歷史,則斷自同治初元,未爲不可.自道光二十二年至今,爲時八十餘載,自同治元年至今,則祇六十餘年.交通大事年表之所以始於同治元年者以此.

然則此六十餘年之交通史,果如何而劃分乎.玆爲先示各期之年代與名稱於下.

第一期 利權萌芽時期 自一八六二年（同治元年）至一八九四年（光緒二十年）

第二期 利權外喪時期 自一八九五年（光緒二十一年）至一九〇三年（光緒二十九年）

第三期 利權收回時期 自一九〇四年（光緒三十年）至一九一一年（宣統三年）

第四期 利權重創時期 自一九一二年（民國元年）至一九二一年（民國十年）（十年以後暫置不論.說見芻議之三.）

此四時期之分,實以路政爲主,電政次之,郵政又次之.航政幼稚已極,獨在外人勢力之下,無所謂利權之喪失與收回也.示漆樹芬氏,關賡麟氏,曾鯤化氏三人中國鐵路史期劃分法以資比較.

時期＼分法	漆氏分期法		關氏分期法		曾氏分期法	
第一期	鉄路建設妨害時代	同治二年至光緒二十年	閉關時期	同治五年至光緒二十年		
第二期	利權獲得競爭時代	光緒二十一年至三十一年	借債造路時期	光緒二十一年至二十九年	外國承辦及借款官辦時期	光緒二十二年至三十年
第三期	利權收回時代	光緒三十二年至宣統二年	拒款自辦時期	光緒三十年至宣統二年	官商合辦及官督商辦時期	光緒三十一年至宣統二年

第四期	利權獲得競爭復活時代	宣統三年至現在	國有時期	宣統三年	國有釀變時期	宣統三年
			項城當國時代	民國元年至四年	國有完成時期	民國元年至三年
			洪憲時代	民國五年	籌路舉債時期	民國三年至七年
			段內閣時代	民國五年至六年		
			安福當國時代	民國六年至八年		
			靳內閣時代	民國八年至九年		

附註　上表曾氏分期法,係依據曾氏中國鉄路史而分.書中並無明白之分期.惟就其編著大意分之耳.

就上表各分期法與余交通史分期法比較觀之,即見其互有異同,而以漆氏分法爲最相近.蓋皆從利權得失一點上觀察者也.玆論漆氏等分法與余分法之差別,以見余劃分之根據.

漆氏以鉄路建設妨害時期始於同治二年.蓋因是年上海英美商人向蘇撫李鴻章請築上海蘇州間鉄路不獲批准之故.余之所以以同治元年爲始者,即取漆氏之意,惟因年號關係,多推一年,所以便劃分,記憶,討論也.且合交通四政論,是時路政雖在妨害時期,郵政則早叛設,而轉輾醞釀於外人之手,倘認爲妨害,其妨害固已久矣.

自同治初至光緒二十年,漆氏稱爲妨害時期,關氏稱爲閉關時期,曾氏且置而不論,余則名之曰利權萌芽時期.蓋此三十年間.言路政則雖曰妨害,而卒有唐胥鉄路津(沽)闆(莊)鉄路之告成.言電政則津沽津滬京津等陸線,除口海線先後設置.言郵政則逐漸擴充,光緒四年且發行郵票.言航政則吾之江南造船廠福州船政局輪船招商局皆創設於此期.而英商太古怡和兩大公司亦於是時成立以攫我航權.是蓋不特萌芽之時,而實已啓侵略之機矣.

光緒二十年,吾國敗於日.老大衰弱之徵象畢露.於是東西列強爭先恐後,急進侵佔,開第二期利權外喪之局面.

就交通四政論,首先圖謀奪我交通利權者當推二十一年法人索辦隴州鐵路之要求.是年,日本大阪商船公司侵入我長江航路.故利權外喪之期卽以是年爲始.

自光緒二十一年至二十九年,此九年間,吾如鼎鬻俎肉,各國競思染指交通利權,喪失至多.大概言之,則如下列.

路權　外人直接投資經營者四線.長凡七千餘里,資本額七千餘萬鎊.
借款興築者十線,凡一萬三千餘里,借款額以訂立正式合同者論,凡二千萬鎊.

電權　丹商設滬烟沾正線.
丹人濮爾生設天津北塘塘沽北京等處電話.

郵權　大清郵政局成立.總稅務使赫德兼領總郵政使.外人之操郵政大權,於以確定.

航權　公布內地水路航行章程.我國內河航權於是爲各國所共有.
先後與英美日締結通商行船條約.明許外人以我國全國航路內航行之自由.

上舉各種利權,均因列強侵略而被迫被騙以喪失之者,故本期稱之爲利權外喪時期.非若第四期之半由我國自殺政策所致也.

光緒三十年至宣統三年,余稱之爲利權收回時期.蓋其命名與漆氏同.其年代與關氏拒款自辦及國有兩時期相當.本期之特色,卽爲因中日日俄兩戰役之激刺.國人漸知愛國禦外.而前期所失之交通權利,或由我收回,或由我糾正是已.

光緒三十年國人力爭收回粵漢鉄路自辦.美合興公司不得已停止工程.是爲路權收回運動之濫觴.至今此路雖牽涉各國,糾葛滋多,然有粵漢之奏凱,而後各省人士乃皆急起直追,或爭廢舊約,或力圖自辦,得以造成收回交通權之一時代.又丹人濮氏乘筝亂所設之北京電話,亦於是年收回,余是以定光緒三十年爲交通權收回時期之開始.

宣統三年,關氏特標之爲國有時期.曾氏則稱爲國有醞釀時期.而以民國元年至四年爲國有完成時期.鐵路收歸國有之政策,至民國四年始克完成.關氏祇以宣統三年屬之,自屬欠當.至漆氏以之歸入第四時期,或因其年有盛宣懷向四國銀行團簽訂粤漢川鐵路借款之事.惟余以爲納於收回時代,亦無不可,且滬杭甬路借英款約之廢除,可謂爲路權收回之餘波.而外交部始將郵政局移交郵傳部直轄,亦可視爲部分的收回交通權之差強人意之事.

如是光緒三十年至宣統三年,此八年間,收回交通權及積極整頓之事件,其重要者可略舉於下.

一，光緒三十一年向美贖回粤漢鐵路.

二，光緒三十四年向比贖回京漢鐵路.

三，同年蘇杭甬路之改正苛約.

四，光緒三十二年設郵傳部.

五，光緒三十三年廣澳鐵路之廢約.

六，各省官紳自辦鐵路者紛然並起.

七，矯正歷來鐵路借款條約之失敗,外國承辦之路,永遠絕迹.

八，收回丹人濮氏之京津兩處電話,德人之津沽電話,上海英商私設之無線電台,九，電報收歸國有.

十，郵政局由郵傳部直轄.

然而本期中亦未嘗無損失者,惟大多種因於前期,本期其結果而已.如就鐵路言,則外人建築之鐵路,有日本之安奉新奉爲其例.京漢雖得向比贖回,然因債務轉而與日英法發生關係.粵漢雖得向美收回,然而開國際資本家協以謀我（銀行團）之局,此實侵略史上之一大關鍵.至於南滿鐵路之淪陷於日人之手,其關係於吾國二十餘年來之國運,亦至重大.是皆本期中大不幸之事件,而實皆胚胎於前期者也.

民國元年至十年,余稱之爲利權重創時期.以其不特外受列強之侵略,抑且內壞於軍閥官僚之蹂躪與斷送.曾氏所謂「藉路舉債,」蓋盡之矣.茲摘錄曾氏鐵路史一節,以見本時期中內外交迫下之交通利權之一斑.

「……若中東之由我代管,若膠濟之完全贖回,皆我路史上極光榮之事實.然藉路自殺之政策,亦適於此時發生.是則不能不歸咎於袁氏稱帝,與直皖之一役也.當商辦空氣風靡全國之後,所謂借款官辦者,僅僅收買已成之道清.洎清廷主張國有,始訂漢粵川大借款.而清卽因以召亡,民國成立.袁世凱……帝制自爲.於是藉築路美名,大舉借款以供軍費政費之挪撥.而隴海,浦信,同成,寧湘,欽渝,沙興,濱黑,株欽各借款合同,遂陸續簽訂矣.計路線幾一萬八千里,債額逾八萬萬元.其時歐戰方興,各國原無餘勇可賈.然彼利我之僅交墊款,卽永據路權,我利彼之饒有現金,能立躋寶座.故一拍卽合,彼此樂從.至路成無期,六千萬元之墊款,化歸烏有.……嗣後政府因歐戰綿長,加入協商國與德奧宣戰.籌餉購械,羅掘無門.於是空名借債之聲,又大爲轟動.七年九月二十八日,與日本興業朝鮮台灣三銀行訂濟順高徐借款豫備合同,先交墊款二千萬元.又同日與該三銀行訂滿蒙四路借款豫備合同,亦先交墊款二千萬元.所謂四路者,卽一熱洮.二長洮.三吉開.四自熱洮之一路達某海港,均由駐日公使章宗祥簽字.本利八厘,期限四十年.旋又與訂吉會借款,(祖康按,吉會訂約期爲七年六月十八日,在濟順高徐及滿蒙四路之前,此處似有誤.)亦交墊款一千萬元,類皆悉供西北邊防軍之用.而京漢京綏等路收入,亦大半被挪.然其最後結果則並非對外參戰,而從事於直皖之內爭.致路未修而款已罄……」

茲更將本期內所訂各路借款列表於下:(一)

路名	距離(二)	訂約年月	借款總額(三)	已發行額或墊款數	債權國	訂約人	時代
津浦墊款		元年七八月	900,424鎊	仝左	德	朱啓鈐	袁政府
隴海	1,296	九月	10,000,000鎊	4,000,000鎊	比	周學熙 朱啓鈐	仝
同成	960(3,925)	二年七月	10,000,000鎊	999,862鎊	法比	梁士詒 朱啓鈐	仝
滬寧購地		十月	150,000鎊	仝左	英	周自齊	仝
浦信	350(1,050)	十一月	3,000,000鎊	198,792鎊	英	熊希齡 周自齊 沈雲沛	仝
欽渝	1,430(3,000)	三年一月	600,000佛	32,115,500佛	法	熊希齡 周自齊	仝
滬楓抵欠		二月	375,000鎊	仝左	英	朱啓鈐 周自齊	仝
甯湘	714(2,000)	三月	8,000,000鎊	2,468,000兩	英	周自齊 朱啓鈐	仝
沙興	760(2,315)	七月	10,000,000鎊	50,000鎊	英	周自齊 梁敦彥	仝
四鄭	(見下四洮)	四年十二月	5,000,000日金	仝左	日	周學熙 梁敦彥	仝
濱黑	(1,650)	五年三月	50,000,000羅布	500,000兩	俄	仝上	仝
株欽 周襄	800 300	五月	無定數	1,150,000美金	美	曹汝霖	仝
吉長二次		六年十月	4,350,000日金(四)	仝左	日	仝上	段內閣
四鄭短期		七年二月	260,000日金	仝左	日	仝上	安福當國
道清贖車		三月	300,000美金	仝左	英	仝上	仝
吉會	275(830)	六月	未定	10,000,000日金	日	仝上	仝

濟順 高徐	169 240 (600)	九月	仝上	20,000,000日金	日	章宗祥	仝
滿蒙四路	(1)111(2)120 (3)230(4) ?	仝上	仝上	仝上	日	仝上	仝
道淸二次		八年三月	無定數	126,839鎊	英	曹汝霖	仝
隴海二次短期		五月	20,000,000佛	仝左	比	施肇曾	仝
四洮	(690)	九月	45,000,000日金	5 000,000日金	日	曾毓雋 李思浩	仝
漢粵川湘鄂短期		十一月	2,000,000元	仝左	英	曾毓雋	靳內閣
四洮短期	——	九年三月	13,700,000日金	仝左	日	曾毓雋李思浩等	仝
隴海比荷借款		五月	150,000,000佛 50,000,000荷幣	75,000,000佛 16,667,000荷幣	比荷	施肇曾	仝
淸孟	(110)	十二月	350,000鎊	7,619鎊 300,000元	英	葉恭綽 周自齊	仝
京奉唐瀋雙軌		十年五月	500,000鎊 2,000,000元	仝左	英	張志潭	仝

附註

(一) 本表係參攷(1)漆樹芬氏之『經濟侵略下之中國』(2)曾鯤化氏之中國鐵路史,(3)張恩鍠氏之鐵路借款提要,(4)關赓麟氏之中國鐵路史講義,(5)商務書館出版中國年鑑等製成.民國十年所訂之滄石路借款,因各書均無詳細記載,未列入.

(二) 所示距離無括弧者英里數,有括弧者華里數.間有不和,恐有錯誤.

(三) 債額單位如下:『鎊』爲英金鎊數,『佛』爲法佛郎數,『日金』爲日金元數,『羅布』爲俄幣,『美金』爲美金元數,『荷幣』爲荷幣弗羅令數,『元』爲國幣銀元數.

(四) 與第一次光緒三十三年所訂借款日金2,500,000元合計共6,500,000元.

從上表可得數種特點 (一) 本期簽訂借款之鐵路,其距離之長,就上表中所列已知之數計,凡 8,272 哩,約合 13,200 公里,或 24,800 華里,據最近統計,我國已成國有鐵路,計共9,260公里.今乃過之,豈非可驚.至其借款數額之大,墊款之多,亦均較前數期有超過之勢.(二)本期內新借款之路純屬外人間接投資之路,而無一爲直接投資者.(三)本期內除隴海之一部爲已築.及『購車』『購地』『抵欠』等各借款與築路無關外,其他皆屬未成路綫,僅由承辦國交若干墊金,作爲永佔路權之保證.(四)本期各借款,可說與各時代政潮如帝制,參戰,直皖之役等皆有關係.由此數點,我人可進而得一結論,如曾鯤化氏之所言,『其時歐戰方興,各國原無餘勇可賈,然彼利我之僅交墊款,即永據路權,我利彼之饒有現金,能立躋寶座.』云云.蓋本時期之利權重創.實國中野心之軍閥造成之.漆樹芬氏謂爲列國侵略主義愈呈露骨者,就日本言,誠哉其如是,就其他各國言,猶未其見眞確也.何也.無餘勇可賈也.惟此局面,至歐戰停止.民國十年冬華盛頓會議開始後.乃又一變.是則非本文之範圍.茲從略.

上述本時期路政,在列強侵略軍閥蹂躪下之情形,可推論電政航政之同一命運.此余之所以深致慨於軍閥之罪.應與帝國主義者同科.而定本期爲重創時期,不采漆氏『利權獲得競爭復活時代』之名稱也.至於本期電政航政在二重侵略下之情形,究屬如何,當俟芻議之五『我國交通權喪失及被侵略之內容』中詳論之.

倫敦金融

諫初

倫敦之爲金融中心.已百餘年.雖大戰以後.世界金融重心.轉向北美.然美之金融市場.究尙幼稚.倫敦之地位.曾未遜於前.一九二五年.英國恢復金本位.准金貨之出口.倫敦金融.漸復原狀.目下英蘭銀行之存底.雖遠不及戰前之豐厚.然他日發展.未可豫測.旦夕之間.北美决難取而代之.蓋其組織之完密.實英之特殊地位有以造成.苟英之特殊地位一日不消滅.卽倫敦必一日爲金融之中心.其基礎之固有如此.欲知其基礎何以能固.則請先講其原理.

考世界金融中心之要件有四.(一)金貨出入須自由.(二)須有極大貼現市場.(三)須有強有力之中央銀行.任調劑之責.(四)須有巨額之流通資金存留海外.此四要件倫敦咸備之.玆所欲研究者.卽金貨行動.何以必須自由.一也.貼現市場.究有何種作用.二也.中央銀行.何以能調劑金融.三也.海外流通資金.有何效用.四也.請一一詳論之.金貨自由云者.卽銀行存款或紙幣.可隨時兌現.供輸出之用之謂也.今國際貿易.多用票據.設德國輸出商向英國輸入商收款.則出一匯票.向其本地甲銀行貼現.或僅請其墊款.甲銀行送匯票至其倫敦代理銀行.(乙銀行)請其轉囑英輸入商承受.或轉囑輸入商所指定之倫敦某銀行承受.承受後該票卽可流通.以承受人之信用.必甚高也.於是輒由乙銀行代德國甲銀行在倫敦丙銀行貼現.將貼現所得款額暫存丙銀行.供隨時支取之用.此卽所謂銀行存款也.支取銀存款時.乙行可出一支票.囑丙行付款.丙行苟不付以現金.而付以紙幣.而紙幣苟又不能兌換現金.或可換現.而此項現金(如銀貨是)苟又不能供輸出之用時.則乙銀行永不能將其存款輸回德國.蓋德銀行必不收受英國不換紙幣或銀貨也.易言之.卽德國甲銀行永不能將票據之價值收回.以抵償其貸款.此在匯

兌平衡時.固屬無礙.蓋甲銀行又可賣出倫敦票據.囑乙行付款.或乙行亦可買進德國票據.令甲行收款也.然苟德國之甲銀行買進之倫敦票據.多於其賣出時.或倫敦之乙銀行賣出多於買進時.則輸出商之銀行付款太多.而收款太少.債務皆在本地.而債權（即貼現之票據）皆在海外.勢非向其倫敦代理銀行輸回現金不能應付.苟代理銀行不能將貼現款額換現金以輸回.則輸出商銀行海外之債權.即不能利用.有與無等.此無他.銀行存款或紙幣不能兌現輸出故也.故銀行在借款與輸出商之前.必審察票據之承受在何處.付款在何處.苟明知該處現金不能自由輸出.則銀行可拒絕借款.或請輸出商與輸入商接洽.另易一承受及付款處所.務須該處之存款或紙幣.可隨時換現金輸出.然後該銀行始可借款與輸出商.而收受其票據.是可知現金輸出不自由.即其他承受之票據不受歡迎.苟承受之票據皆趨他途.則其地尙得爲金融中心乎.故法國中央銀行兌現時.可付金亦可付銀.其地永難成爲金融之中心.蓋銀貨非世界通用之貨幣.輸出亦無用也.由此可知倫敦匯票.何以世界皆歡迎之.銀行歡迎倫敦票據.於是商人亦歡迎倫敦票據.以其易於向銀行貼現也.苟倫敦非金貨自由市場.則斷不能居今日金融中心之地位.是以存款紙幣之能隨時換現以供輸出.實爲金融中心之先决條件.此第一問題之解答也.貼現市場爲流通票據之要素.苟倫敦所有票據.不能向市場貼現.而必須俟期滿收款.則亦奚用此金融中心耶.譬有一法人運貨至英.請法國某銀行墊款.而授以票據.法國某銀行卽囑其倫敦代理銀行攜該票向英某銀行承受.法銀行卽可囑其代理銀行.將承受之票據.在倫敦貼現.一面卽可在法國賣出倫敦票據.以補償其墊款.兩相冲銷.匯兌適得其平.然苟倫敦並無貼現市場.則該票據不能卽時換現.惟有俟期滿收款.同時法國銀行亦不能賣出倫敦票據.以其倫敦代理銀行尙無款可爲代付也.此賣出票據時之不便也.若法國銀行繼續買進在倫敦付款之票據.則其在法之債務日增.在英之債權亦日增.非債權可隨時換現.卽不能隨時應付債務.吾人

已知債權卽爲票據矣.已知票據貼現後不能換現以輸出之不利矣.今苟票據無從貼現.則在期滿前.與存款或紙幣不能換現輸出.厥弊正同.當法銀行正欲現款以應付在法之債務時.而遇在英之票據尙未到.雖倫敦爲金貨自由市場.而一時亦無由獲得金貨.以輸入法國.此時法銀行之困難.可以想見.此又買進票據時之不利也.故倫敦苟無貼現市場.則法銀行惟有俟一票據滿期.然後再買賣他票據.若欲在滿期前匯款至英.則匯兌率將與金輸出點相齊.不利於匯款者可知.英銀行繼續買進倫敦票據.則有不能應付國內債務之虞.不利於銀行又可知.足見一地苟無貼現市場.則各國銀行斷不願收受該地承受或付款之票據.是卽該地永不能成爲金融中心也.雖然.無貼現市場.固不能成金融之中心.然苟貼現之市場不大.亦不能成金融之中心.蓋無大市場以供貼現.則票據在平時固有貼現之機會.然貼現率必高.貼現率高.則貼現者之損失大.若遇金融緊急.因供貼現之資金不多.必致無由貼現.此其危險處也.故爲全世界所最歡迎之票據.必由有大貼現市場之地承受或付款者.苟其票據爲世界所最歡迎.則其地必爲金融之中心.此第二問題之解答也.至中央銀行何以爲金融中心之要件.則復加詳釋以明之.吾人已知金貨自由與貼現市場之重要矣.然金貨之自由.非僅爲輸出之自由.而亦爲輸入之自由.專注意於輸出之自由.則外人固欣然載現金而去.然國內之現金匱矣.國內現金旣匱.則無復有金貨可供輸出矣.無金貨可供輸出.則其地尙得爲金融中心乎.故必有中央銀行以節制之.遇金貨輸出過度時.則高其重貼現率.不足則告貸於市場.以促利率之升漲.而後可阻金貨之輸出.引金貨之輸入.國內現金.常得保留.足見金貨自由.非金貨節制.不能維持.節制之責.非中央銀行莫屬.此第一條件之有賴於第三條件也.吾人又知貼現應無限度矣.貼現率僅可提高.然貼現之機會不可一日或缺.此所謂大貼現市場也.但遇金融奇緊之時.銀行皆祇收不放.貼現商之借款.盡欲收回.此時苟有人持票貼現.則貼現商必無以應之.是向之所謂大貼現市場.今爲無貼現

市場矣.無貼現市場.即無金融中心.維持之責.又非中央銀行莫屬.各銀行迫貼現商時.中央銀行能救貼現商.收其票據.貸以現款.於是貼現商又有資金可以周轉矣.貼現率雖漲,欲貼現者不致向隅矣.貼現市場既得維持.則金融自漸寬緩而還復原狀.此第二條件之有賴於第三條件也.故無中央銀行.第一第二兩要件.皆不能維持.金融中心.必有分崩之一日.此第三問題之解答也.一國在海外之債權多.則應付匯兌之需求易.今出入貿易之票據多在倫敦貼現.即他國相互間之貿易.亦多由倫敦墊款.(此層詳述於後)是一旦國外金貨之需求陡增.大部份已貼現之票據.皆欲變金貨輸出.中央銀行雖可提高利率.然亦有不見功效之時.惟一善策.即平日在海外握有債權.必要時供可供利用是已.譬如英國貨物之輸出與輸入相等.匯兌上不生問題.但意國向法國輸入大宗貨物.票據係由英國某承受店承受.在倫敦貼現.假設意國急需現款.令其倫敦代理銀行.將貼現款額兌金輸回.則此時倫敦執票者尚不能向法商收款.現金無從輸入.而意銀行之債權.必須立時用金輸出.雖中央銀行提高利率.亦屬無用.然則倫敦市場.當不有現金匱乏之虞乎.詎料英國向為世界之債權國.雖其貨物貿易.一時出入相等.以常例言之.無由向海外調度現金.但或意國適欠英國大宗之利息.法國適欠英國大宗到期之債務.日本適欠英國大宗之運費.於是英國即可利用留存海外之債權.以應付意銀行之需求.現金即可不致流出.即或流出.亦可由他方輸回以補之.此非債權國必不能語此.非債權國惟恃貨物之出超.以製成其海外之資財.第貨物出超.不能確定.不得視為有恃無恐之債權.若遇現金流出.而無貨物出超.則國內金融.仍不免影響.此海外可恃之流通資金.所以為調劑金融之要件也.中央銀行重貼現率.有時而窮.得海外債權.以補救之.適得匯兌平衡之利.故第三條件尚有賴乎第四條件之接濟.以共維金融中心之基礎.此第四問題之解答也.

既知金融中心之要件及其關係矣.乃可進而觀倫敦金融之實況.其主

動機關有幾.各機關之作用若何.關係若何.爲吾人所當研究者.第在討論其主要機關以前.吾人應知倫敦之銀錢往來.大半皆用支票.而不用鈔劵.故雖一八四四年皮爾律限制英國鈔劵之發行.而對於金融流通.毫無影響.貨幣之漲縮.隨銀行存款之增減.存款增.支票亦增.減則支票亦減.鈔劵之功用.僅與現金等耳.德法等國.貨幣之增減.隨鈔劵之漲縮而定.英國以用支票故.其鈔劵猶德法之現金而已.但以支票代鈔劵影響於金融何在.則更不可不知者.(一)英國鈔票不根據商業票據.而根據現金存儲.若商人支取存款時.皆欲鈔票而拒用支票.則市上鈔票.必不敷用.且存款銀行.非常向中央銀行重貼現不可.其金融必難活動.今旣皆用支票.在平時各銀行互相冲銷.準備不必甚巨.而放款貼現.可以充分膨脹.工商業因得需用之款項.皆能自由發展.(二)在用鈔票之國.各銀行在放款急增之際.終須向中央銀行重貼現.蓋非重貼現不能得多量之鈔票以爲應付.中央銀行以鈔票發行過多.現金準備低落.則大都由政府課以鈔票稅.一面增高重貼現率.以示限制.若在用支票之國.放款膨脹時.各行不必向中央銀行重貼現.除存款被外國用金輸出外.各行往往可互相冲銷.在此時政府無由課鈔劵稅.中央銀行無由提高貼現率.則似毫無限制矣.但各行旣不重貼現.則必無金貨流出之虞.中央銀行或政府.自無干涉之必要.苟干涉之.適足阻國內工商之發展.此與用鈔票之國.貼現雖增而鈔票稅尙未課徵時相似.此時苟中央銀行.果欲干涉.亦可向他行借貸.促利率之提高.故用支票與用鈔票之原理相同.未嘗因用支票.故金融即可無限膨脹也.(三)支票旣爲人所樂用.中央銀行準備.卽不受影響.何以言之.例如某貼現商向甲銀行借款.甲銀行給以上英蘭銀行之支票.貼現商卽以支票存入英蘭銀行.以便隨時支取.是英蘭銀行之負債.甲由銀行之賬移至貼現商之賬而已.迨貼現者向貼現商取款.貼現商亦給以上英蘭銀行之支票.貼現者以支票存入乙銀行.乙銀行復爲存入英蘭銀行.是英蘭銀行之負債.復由貼現商之賬.移入乙銀行之賬.對於準備.仍無影響.足見資金

如何移動.不必顧問.除非流出海外.皆僅中央銀行一轉賬而已.此無他.用支票故也.若貼現者不樂用支票.而堅欲鈔券.則貼現商卽不能以一紙支票與之.必向英蘭銀行取出鈔券.轉給貼現之人.但鈔券卽現金.鈔券流出.卽中央銀行存底減少.此在昔時英國國內金融恐慌之際常見之.此無他.支票不流通故也.由此數點觀之.在現今英國鈔券制度之下.苟無暢行之支票.倫敦金融.斷難發展.其能爲金融中心.未始非受支票之賜也.

倫敦金融主要機關.共有五種.請爲略述之.

(一) 外國分銀行

外國在倫敦分銀行.包括印度分行英殖民地分行及眞正外國分行而言.諸分行之唯一任務.爲代其各地總分行收賣票據.主持匯劃.其任務性質可分兩種.(一)關於英國與外國之貿易.(二)關於外國相互間之貿易.(其票據係在倫敦承受者.)凡英商向外商買貨.其票據輒由外國送達倫敦外國分行.由倫敦分行轉送英商承受.承受後仍還倫敦分行.倫敦分行或保持至期滿.或在倫敦貼現.均視金融狀況而定.苟貼現率甚高.卽不以之貼現.或外國需款甚殷.則貼現率雖高.亦有不得不貼現者.貼現之後該分行卽可隨時取得現金.輸至其本國.故外國分行在倫敦.實有左右金融之勢力.倫敦市場唯一金融問題.卽在於斯.此指英國輸入貿易而言也.輸出貿易亦有同等之影響.蓋英商輸出貨物.並不囑外商承受票據.乃由外商向英國某行或某承受店接洽.請其代爲承受.俾票據易於在倫敦貼現.故在票據期滿以前.輸出貿易.亦須運用倫敦之資金.迨票據期滿.始由外國轉倫敦分行輸入的款.交付承受之人.轉付執票者.此英國與他國貿易之關係於外國分行者也.若他國相互間之貿易.票據亦多在倫敦承受.例如意商輸貨入法.意商不欲法商承受之票據.而欲倫敦可恃之行家承受者.於是由法商與倫敦某行接洽.請其代爲承受.其票據卽由意國送至其倫敦某分行.分行卽照例持向承受.承受後在市上貼現.與英國輸入貨物時相同.他日法商輸貨入意時亦如之.

足見倫敦資金.非特用於英國輸入貿易.且用於其輸出貿易.及他國相互間之貿易.而主其事者.則外國在倫敦之分行是也.於此兩大任務之外.倫敦外國分行.間或承受票據.倫敦稱之曰 Foreign Agency Bills. 此種票據.不受貼現市場之歡迎.英蘭銀行未嘗願貼現之.又或外國間之貿易.其票據不在英國承受.而在倫敦付款.例如德商運貨至法.囑法商承受票據.但付款須在倫敦.於是即由德商將票據送達德國倫敦某分行.由分行轉送法國.承受後復還倫敦德分行保管.此類票據.名曰 Foreign Domicile Bills. 亦不受倫敦貼現市場之歡迎.蓋較外國分行承受之票據尤難取信也.外國分行於經營票據之外.尙有一重要業務.即貸款與貼現商也.當貼現商資金迫促之時.外國銀行常有餘力貸以現款.惟爲期頗短.普通越宿而已.抵押品概爲公債.及他種流通可恃證券.因商業票據大半由外國銀行而來.不能向之作抵押也.

(二)貼現商

貼現商經營票據之買賣.處金融市場極重要之地位.能知票據之優劣承受人之信用.其經驗遠勝銀行.故銀行在倫敦不皆直接購買票據.而以貼現商爲中間人.但貼現商之購買票據.並非作銀行之掮客.盈虧由己負責.與商人自設店鋪.買賣貨物同.惟貼現業需款莫定.非如商人買賣之有定額.若遇市上票據多時.貼現商僅以個人之資本經營.必難應付.故必向銀行貸款.以票據作抵.期限往往爲一星期.利率輒較貼現率爲低.銀行視此貸款.爲其第二重之準備金.有時需款浩繁.貼現商亦可借入一日期之貸款.可見貼現商非借款不能營業也.若遇銀行需款孔殷.如國內金融恐慌.及國外需求金貨之時.則貼現商之借款.必一一收回.銀行對於星期借款.滿期即不續借.一面對於貼現商之票據.亦必停止購買.於是貼現商即難繼續其營業.外來票據.不能再爲貼現商業活動.勢必中止.此時出而維持者.舍英蘭銀行莫屬.英蘭銀行收其票據.貸以現款.若平日普通銀行然.貼現商得英蘭銀行之貸款.即可繼續貼現.付款時可以英蘭銀行支票與之.於是商業票據.仍可流通市

上.庶無錢荒之患.至英蘭銀行何以獨能貸款.當詳於後焉.

由此可見倫敦貼現商之特質有四.(一)作供款者與需款者之中間人.其作用與他國之商業銀行相埒.(二)代銀行識辨票據.並自任盈虧之責(三)平時須各銀行之援助.自有資本.不足應付其營業.(四)金融緊急時.必須求助於英蘭銀行.以維其業務.其地位之重要可知.其處境之奇異亦可知.使倫敦無此貼現商.則偌大交易.孰能主持.倫敦之票據數量.遠過別地.若欲各家銀行一一收買之.恐必無此應付之力.銀行不能應付.則交易必形停滯.謂他國商人尚能歡迎倫敦票據.吾不信也.故貼現商之在倫敦.實爲維持金融市場之一大勢力.紐約苟欲取倫敦而代之.亦必先有如倫敦之貼現商而後可.不然.大貼現市場.莫由產生.現今美國正在提倡票據之承受.以圖貼現之擴充.將來貼現或亦成專門業務.而與倫敦抗衡乎.

(三)五大銀行

倫敦有五大銀行.爲普通商業銀行中之巨擘.一爲密德蘭銀行.Midland Bank二爲國省銀貸, National Provincial Bank 三爲巴格來銀行. Barclays Bank四爲勞合氏銀行. Lloyds Bank 五爲西明斯透銀行. Westminster Bank 倫敦總稱之曰五大"The Big Five"其業務最與倫敦金融有關者.爲貸款與貼現商一事.蓋貼現資金.純由此普通銀行得來.銀行對於此種放款.競爭殊烈.一因爲期短促.普通都一星期.足爲存款第二重之準備.一因銀行存款.在倫敦雖活期亦須付息.故放款於貼現商.利息雖低.終較存款庫內爲愈.有此二因.遂致市上利率.愈趨愈下.貼現商以借款利輕.貼現率亦可隨之而低.信用膨脹之虞.即在於斯.各銀貼現金資產.或存本行.或存中央銀行.毫無異點.平時各行在英蘭銀行總有若干存款.惟不如美國之受法律規定耳.故銀行貸款與貼現商時.或與以本行支票.任其隨時支取.或與以英蘭銀行之支票.令其向英蘭銀行取款.均無不可.此平時各行之與貼現商之關係也.若至金融奇緊之時.如遇銀行或貼現商所買票據.其代價因國外之需求.皆須用金輸出.或遇海外大批借款.在倫敦發行.致貿易有入超之虞.或遇外國債券.在倫敦脫售金貨.不得不令流出.又或遇國內生產事業.須用大批現金或鈔券.供支出之用.銀行支票.不能代庖.凡此種種情形.皆足使銀行需求現款.以實準備.而供應付.銀行欲增其現金準備.厥有二法.一為將買進票據向英蘭銀行重貼現.一為收回貼現商借款.并暫時停止放出.但重貼現率為市上最高之利率.銀行視為畏途.非必要必不願攖其鋒.故銀行第一步辦法.必為收回貼現商借款.收回貼現商借款維何.即（一）索還一日期之借款.不令續展.（二.）收進到期之星期借款.不再即行借出.一面將抵押票據.歸還貼現商.此時無論貼現商有款無款.皆感困難.苟票據多未到期.復又無從賣出.則無款可還.處境固是不易.願即使現款充足.有償還之力.但以還後不再續放.此復票據之貼現.將何以應付耶.故在平時.各銀行為貼現商之泰山.一至金融緊急.即崩頹而壓之.使無英蘭銀行為之居間.則困難不堪設想矣.各銀行其他之業務.與倫敦金融有直接關係者.則為承受票據.直接貼現二種.倫敦除公司式之銀行外.尚有私人銀行業務亦同.倫敦所用之支票.全由銀行及中央銀行發行.貼現商不發行支票.故向貼現商取款.不嘗向銀行出支票也.但各銀行可發支票.而不能發鈔票.故鈔票純為中央銀行所發.足為各行之現金準備.各行需用鈔票時.除現存外.非重貼現或出現金不能得也.各行準備.無法律上之限制.故信用之漲縮.全在銀行之手.其左右倫敦金融之勢力.不言而喻矣.

（四）承受商

承受商專以承受票據為業務.倫敦之票據買賣.固在貼現商之手.然無承受商.貼現商亦將無現可貼.猶甍賣商無製造出貨之人.亦必無貨可甍也.承受商所承受之票據.大別為四.（一）國內貿易上之票據.（二）英國輸出貿易上之票據.（三）英國輸入貿易上之票據.（四）各國相互間貿易上之票據.承受商承受票據後.即負到期付現之責.雖出票人無款匯來.承受商亦必應

付.第一類票據.出票者必爲英人.第二類票據.出票者或爲英輸出商.或爲外國輸入商.第三類票據.出票者常爲外國輸出商.第四類票據.出票者必非英人.而常爲外商.故到期應付之款.在第一與第三兩類票據.不過國內一轉移而已.至第二第四兩類票據應付之款.則須由他國運至倫敦.蓋付款者皆非英人也.此票據承受之大略也.第承受商之與倫敦金融關係果何如耶.第一第三兩類票據.爲各地所皆有.即無承受商之處.亦皆由銀行或私人承受.第二第四兩類票據.則爲倫敦所獨有.倫敦有信用卓著之承受商.故英國輸出貿易之票據.與各國相互間貿易上之票據.亦皆送至倫敦承受.俾得在倫敦貼現（非倫敦承受.倫敦貼現市場即不歡迎.）遂致倫敦資金.於助國內貿易及輸入貿易外.復須用於輸出貿易與他國貿易之大部分.宜其處境之難也.或謂第二第四兩類票據.在倫敦承受貼現.固也.然倫敦亦因而在海外獲得同量之資金.未嘗須補墊分文也.曰然.但時間之參差.不可忽耳.凡票據貼現.拒到期約三閱月.一經貼現.我（指倫敦貼現商或銀行.）即有立時付現之責任.此責任即我之債務也.但我之債權.非三月後.不能收回.是倫敦貼現商.以將來之債權.易目前之債務而已.倘貼現者爲英輸出商（第二類票據）則似無索現輸出之虞.但彼或偶買一外國證券或股票.向貼現商取款.貼現商與以銀行支票.該支票.即入經理外國證券或股票之倫敦外國分行.分行即送支票至銀行.易以外國匯票.但此時因此種匯票之需求過巨.而海外債權.(即已貼現之票據)須三月後始可到期.無款抵銷.匯率必漲.於是外國分行即不買匯票.而直接索現輸出可矣.若爲第四類票據.則貼現者爲外國在倫敦之分行.周折更少.若外國欲將貼現所得之款輸回.則匯率必漲.金貨即有流出之虞.影響尤較常見.是以因承受第二第四兩類票據之故.倫敦金貨.遂較普通易於流出.若承受之數過多.即倫敦之目前債務與將來債權.俱形急增.在短時間內.將來之債權.不能用以抵目前之債務.於是匯兌漲.現金不可留矣.使倫敦向不承受此種票據.則英商輸出貨物時.或出票囑輸入商

承受.在輸入國貼現.一面可在倫敦某銀行.先將該票出賣.取得信用.此時即使輸出商買進外國股票.欲將其信用匯至外國.銀行亦能應付.不必提高匯率.蓋票據已在輸入國貼現.將來債權.已變現金矣.至第四類票據.旣不承受.則他國自不能向倫敦索款.更無影響之可言.由此兩方觀察.足見承受第二第四兩類票據之影響於倫敦金融之大矣.是皆承受商有以爲之也.然承受商未嘗以承受此種票據.破壞倫敦金融.使之入於困難之境.其實正所以促進倫敦之地位.使爲唯一之地位中心耳.蓋不承受此類票據.即非金融中心.金融中心之責任無他.助國內貿易與國際貿易之發展而已.其助力愈大.其處境愈艱.此事勢所必然也.至承受商自身之地位在金融出軌時.亦頗危險.所承受之票據.到期必付.若應付款者不將款匯來.則必爲之墊付.苟款額甚巨.承受商必無力應付.但若不應付.執票者皆將向隅.且執票之人.大都爲銀行及貼現商.彼等賴票據以周轉資金.票據到期不付.彼即無以應付其存款之人.(貼現商無以還銀行之貸款.即銀行無以應付其存款者.)存款人無款可支.即有破產或擱淺之虞.於是星火燎原.殃及全體.一棟折而全屋傾矣.此種變態.戰時輒有之.承受商之救星.又非中央銀行莫屬.爰次述英蘭銀行以覘其奇偉之功用與勢力焉.

(五) 英蘭銀行

英蘭銀行爲近世各國中央銀行之範本.其最有關係金融之任務.即保管各銀行之現金準備是也.故在各銀行不能放款之時.英蘭銀行獨能放款.全市場之資金無論如何移轉.或由政府付人民.或由人民付政府.或由此銀行付彼銀行.或由銀行付貼現商.或由貼現商還付銀行.倘用支票收付.普通皆僅英蘭銀行一轉賬而已.銀行向貼現商進款之時.在市場上觀之.金融緊急非常.但自英蘭銀行視之.則或並無變動.不過市上資金.欲從貼現商之手.還至銀行而已.倘貼現商無力償還.英蘭銀行儘可貸與現款.收其票據作抵.蓋所貸之款.即入銀行之手.輾轉付用.亦僅由此賬轉彼賬.英蘭銀行.不必支

出分文.他日票據到期.押品自變現款.足與貸款相抵銷而毫無差訛.此在金融奇緊之時.英蘭銀行所以獨有巨款可放也.於此必有人懷疑焉.曰銀行倘果索現金.則英蘭銀行又將何如.且事實上金融緊急之時.現金之需求必巨.僅一轉賬.恐不足以了事.曰是誠然也.但不足爲英蘭銀行病耳.(一)英蘭銀行戰前存底.常在百分之五十以上.現金之需求.儘足以應付之.(二)一遇現金流出.英蘭銀行卽可提高貼現率.貼現商旣向英蘭銀行借款.亦不得不提高其貼現率.貼現率高.則貼現少.而現金之需求自斂.有此二因.英蘭銀行遂能控制市場.而不爲市場所困.其勢力之偉大如此.若承受商受困.則英蘭銀行將又何以拯救之.大戰之初.英國承受商卽遭此厄.國際貿易.中途停止.各國皆不能匯款至英.以償其債務.欲運金貨.已遭禁阻.卽不禁阻.而海上危險滋巨.故倫敦承受票據.到期無款可付.英蘭銀行.遂出而救濟.凡一九一四年八月四日以前承受之票據.確係良好者.執票者皆可持向重貼現.票據到期.不令承受者付款.但令款未匯到之前.按日計息（利率爲中央貼現率加二釐）而已.如是執票者有款可用.承受者不須付現.但以須付重息.亦必設法催前途匯款.人心於是大定.蓋此時市場上所需求者乃支付之媒介物.而並非現金.英蘭銀行儘可貼現而無庸顧忌.卽使人心恐慌.需求鈔券.亦可請求國會將一八四四年鈔券律暫行廢止.并發行五鎊以下之鈔票.以爲過渡.至匯兌方面.此時各國商人正欲匯款入英而不得.更無金貨流出之可虞矣.（倫敦金貨之流出約在戰事將發以前.及貿易恢復以後.）綜上以觀.英蘭銀行實爲貼現商承受商與各銀行之救世主.其所以能應付裕如者.非偶然已.英蘭銀行爲信用節制機關.然欲節制信用.必先有人向之借款.而後中央貼現率.可影響於市上貼現率.今若銀行信用膨脹過甚.但以用支票授受.收付在交換所抵銷.各銀行不必請求英蘭銀行買其票據.以易鈔券或易存款.則中央銀行之貼現率.與市場完全脫離關係矣.雖信用膨脹.此時尚無大礙.然工資之急增.現款之需求.假以時日.必急起直追而來.至是而驟加制止.則害

於工商必大.故必先爲防範.使信用之增加程度.緩而不急.英蘭銀行因不得不向各銀行借款使其存底減少.存底減放款利率必增.借款者稍稍減退.而英蘭銀行節制信用之目的達矣.此其於用貼現率外所設之巧計也.關於英蘭銀行可述之點甚多.惟直接影響倫敦金融者.不外節制信用.救濟市面而已.

倫敦金融之大要.已略如上述.欲求一可與倫敦比擬之金融市場.目下尙屬難能.良以其所有特殊條件.舉非他國所易致也.雖然.北美合衆國.戰後崛起.其鋒不可當.其有意攫取世界金融之霸權.在在可得而見之.玆舉數點.即足知其意而有餘矣.(一)仿歐洲制度.於一九一三年創設十二準備銀行此雖爲整頓國內金融之辦法.然亦爲控制世界金融之初步.(二)準備銀行收入金貨.即可用以發鈔.此項金貨.可充他鈔（即由貼現發出者）之準備此爲吸收現金之辦法.與英國中央銀行.收金一兩.必須還以七十七先令九辨士之國幣（鈔券或貨幣）用意相同.誠以中央銀行不設法吸收現金.即難維持金本位制度.金本位制度不能維持.即無居金融中心地位之希望.（三）獎勵銀行承受之票據.圖貼現市場之推廣.(四)發展生產事業.擴張國外貿易.以便將來由生產國而變爲投資國.握海外巨額之債權.與今日之英吉利相埒.或遠勝之.舉此數點.即可按金融市場之原理.而懸想其關係矣.

總之倫敦金融之基礎.爲金本位制度一物.此制一破.倫敦地位.即無足重輕.凡世界各國能維持金本位制度.而與倫敦並駕齊驅者.皆有崛起而成金融中心之望.所謂維持金本位制度者.則須先具上述之必具條件而善爲主持之.凡金本位一日不改.則金融現象.必一如疇昔.無論金融中心在倫敦在紐約.原理必無不同.是以研究倫敦金融原理.爲研究現時之金融.亦所以研究將來之金融.成敗與廢.事難易測.因姑揭其原理.而拭目以觀其後.

十五年.五月.十二日.脫稿於上院.

美國經濟前途之預測

奏　廷

處茲國際貿易時代.一國之經濟狀況.可於其對外之債務債權測之.其債權逾於債務者.則其經濟地位.必已甚高.否則必尙在發展時代.未握經濟之霸權者也.凡一國之發展.必經四大時期.第一期爲貿易入超.蓋方借資金於海外.以助興國內實業.所借之款泰半以貨物代現金而輸入也.第二期爲貿易出超.蓋至此海外借款.多告結束.國內實業.已臻發達.而借款本息須對外支付者.爲額已巨.自不得不以貨物代現金輸出以償之.是以貿易遂告出超也.第三期爲貿易繼續出超.時也借款大都償還.實業更形發達.所出產之貨物.源源輸出.出超所造成之債權.純爲其國之進益.不必用以抵付債務.從生產立論.其國蓋在全盛時代也.第四期爲貿易入超.一國至此始握經濟霸權矣.第三期出超所生之債權.泰半投於海外之實業.而國內工商.競爭日烈.故有資金者.皆紛紛向海外投資.是以國內實業如舊.而對外債權日增.每年應輸入之本息日多.外來之貨物.遂多於輸出之國產.此所以有入超之現象也以目今世界各大國例之.則在第一期者爲我國.在第二期者坎坎拿大.在第三期者爲美國.在第四期者爲英國.惟以大戰影響.美國一躍而執世界金融之牛耳.其經濟前途.豁然開朗.將來是否能取英吉利而代之.頗爲有興趣之問題.然欲得確切之答覆.實爲事實上所難能.吾人惟能就美國經濟現狀.以爲一二言之預測.言之中否.請拭目以觀其後可耳.

吾人先就美國實業方面觀察.凡一國之實業.最要者爲煤爲鐵.次爲紡織.爲煤油.考美國所產之煤.佔全球產額百分之四十四.每年出六億噸.鐵占全球產額百分之六十強.全年可產三千數百萬噸.鋼鐵占全球產額百分之五九.八年出四千三百萬噸.棉花產額極巨.足覘其紡織之盛.去年產額爲一五,六〇三,〇〇〇包.（每包五百磅）佔全球產額百分之五十一.煤油爲美國之特產.出產額占全世界所出百分之七十二.達四萬六千九百六十餘桶.（六大桶等於一噸）他如銅產佔全世界產額五分之三.木材占二分之一.商船噸數.已視戰前加增三倍.製造品自一九〇〇年至今.增加百分之一八五.在在足見其經濟力之日厚.經濟力厚.則對外之債權日增.故從實業方面觀察.美國實足為金融之主人翁.苟無意外之阻力.則其將來之借出資本.必超過其國內生產資本.由第三期而入第四期.可斷言也

既知其實業之盛况.則其對外貿易如何.為吾人所急欲知者.美國在一八七四年以前.歷年入超.蓋方在利用外資時期也.是年以後.則頻年出超.惟在戰前.出超之一部.尚充償還外資本息之用.至戰後則純為應收之債權.其出超之歷史.可於下表覘之,

一八七四年至一八九四年	每年平均出超	113,000,000金元
一八九四年至一九一四年	每年平均出超	485,000,000金元
一九一四年至一九一八年	每年平均出超	2,624,000,000金元
一九一九年	出超	4,136,000,000金元

一九一九年後出超漸減.去年(1925)出超為684,511,000金元.蓋戰後由美輸歐之貨急增.如食料.如戰用品.需求均巨.一九一九年後.始漸復原態.綜觀其歷年出超.為數均大.而戰後之大出超.更為美國由債務國躍為債權國之明證.此後逐年出超.將純用以增高美國海外投資之基礎.他日輸入.必如今日輸出之遞增.可無疑也.按常理言之.美國現金輸入.必繼續超過輸出.然觀一九二五年之統計.現金輸入為128,000,000金元.輸出為263,000,000金元輸出超過達135,000,000金元.可見美國貨物之出超.非特不輸入現金以償其代價.且并已輸入之現金.亦從事輸出以貨他國.易言之.美國近來之出超.皆為債權而非現款也.蓋美國已患金多.戰後吸收全世界金貨百分之四十五.若再加增.無論各國無力支付.而美國亦將有通貨膨脹之可虞.是以輸出現金.為美之急務.從可知其此後之貿易出超.必不取金貨以為代價.而必令

資金留存海外.以發展他國之實業.而已則惟盼他日本息之源源輸入.以享其厚利耳.

試再觀察美國之對外債權.其最令人奇異者卽變遷之速耳.考戰前美之債務達五十五萬萬元.每年應付利息約二萬七千五百萬元.對外債權.僅十五萬萬元.每年應收利息.僅七千五百萬元.不圖戰後債權.一躍而達百萬萬元以上.每年應收利息.當不下六七萬萬元.此六七萬萬元.當仍出貸於人.利上生利.數可驚人.且每年尚遞加未已.而戰時之債.尙不在內.計英國對美債務.爲四十六萬萬美金.現定分六十二年攤還.前十年年息三厘.後乃五厘半.則每年收入.當爲二萬一千二百萬元.又意國債務.不下二十萬萬美金.現亦定六十二年分還.惟利息較低.目前亦可收入五千餘萬元.後當漸增.蓋利率遞加故也.法國亦欠美國七百五十萬萬紙佛郎.約合美金二十九萬萬元.現尙在議訂清償辦法.將來收入爲數必有可觀.他如比國捷國波蘭以及其他小國.皆對美負有債務者.美眞投資之巨擘耶.觀於上陳之各種債權.卽知美國貿易.縱不再事出超.海外本息之輸入.已足駭人.此後數量.當更膨脹.所可斷言者.美國債權.必將居其經濟生活首要條件之地位.而生產與貿易.將退而爲次要耳.

復査美國儲蓄之程度.則又可知其富力之雄厚.與年俱進.據一九二二年之調査.則貯蓄數量如次.

存於儲蓄銀行者 $7,181,248,000 存於郵局儲蓄銀行者 $137,000,000

存於國家銀行者 $3,046,000,000 共計 $10,364,248,000

又據一九二五年之調査.則有如下列.

存於儲蓄銀行者 $9,070,033,000 存於郵局儲蓄銀行者 $132,173,000

存於國家銀行者 $4,558,889,000 共計 $13,761,095,000

三年之間.全國儲蓄增加三十四億.蓋每人增蓄三十四元也.一國之儲蓄增卽其投資力增.投資力增.卽其國已由生產時期.而入借貸時期.卽由第三期

之發展而至第四期也.觀美人之儲蓄亦可知其爲將來唯一之金融主人翁.

方今美國內部.尙未完全發展.故欲其入第四期.如英國之專恃投資爲生活.必尙有待.第其生產愈盛.貿易愈旺.卽其債、權愈增.將來之入超愈大.有善因必有善果.美人其智矣哉.夫一國之發展.與個人無異.譬有農夫.其始也無資本以爲耕作.乃告貸於人.以貸款購肥料.備器具.付工資.以經營其田畝.是猶國家之在第一期也.迨墾田已熟.年有收穫.則以一部分進益購衣食.一部分付償借款之本息.是猶國家之在第二期也.厥後收穫大增.債已清償.乃以收穫之一部分.供生活之費.一部分出售.以其代價存入銀行生利.是猶國家之在第三期也.洎乎連年大有.貯款日豐.乃視田中收獲爲次要.以其全部及貯款利息之一部分.充生活之費.於是農夫之門楣頓換.而面悶團作富家翁矣.是猶國家之在第四期也.今美國尙爲力田之農夫.而英國早已爲豐衣足食之田舍翁.行見數十年後.美國將由畎畝之中而登廟堂之上.彼田舍翁者.所處地位.將瞠乎後矣.

顧返觀我國.力田人耶.田舍翁耶.曰否否.窶人耳.遊民耳.我國經濟地位雖號稱在第一時期.然名不符實.無發展之可言.所借外資.供消費者多.猶農人無力經營其田畝.乃告貸於人.而又浪費之於賭博烟酒.卽有一部分用以購肥料.買器具.而又不善自經營.任其田畝之荒蕪.謂其能穫大有.其誰信之.謂其能作富家翁.更其誰信之.故我國今日之經濟地位.眞與一貧且惰之遊手無異.債臺高築.尙事荒淫.卒至任人宰割而已.國人乎.一農夫而欲爲富翁幾何困難.不謂我堂堂華夏.幷農夫之資格而未有乎.欲圖富強.與英美抗衡.謂非夢想.吾不知信.觀乎美國之經濟前途.吾爲美人喜.吾爲白人賀.而吾更不勝爲我國民悲.爲我國家前途懼.

十五年四月廿五日脫稿于上院

英美現行之遺產稅率

諫　初

英美二國之遺產稅皆從遺產全體徵收.而不計及受繼者每人所得之數.惟英國有兩種特稅一曰動產遺傳稅 Legacy duty. 一曰不動產遺傳稅 Suecession duty. 凡遺產與非親生子者皆須於遺產稅外納此二種特稅.蓋按受繼人之親疎以爲累進也.美國各州遺產稅.皆從受繼人所得之產額徵收.且按親疎累進.惟中央遺產稅則僅按產之大小累進.不計受繼者之親疎耳.玆覓得英美兩國現行遺產稅率.特錄之以資研究.

(一) 英國遺產稅率

產額	稅率
一百鎊至五百鎊	百分之一
五百鎊至一千鎊	百分之二
一千鎊至五千鎊	百分之三
五千鎊至一萬鎊	百分之四
一萬鎊至二萬鎊	百分之五
二萬鎊至四萬鎊	百分之六
四萬鎊至七萬鎊	百分之七
七萬鎊至十萬鎊	百分之八
十萬鎊至十五萬鎊	百分之九
十五萬鎊至二十萬鎊	百分之十
二十萬鎊至四十萬鎊	百分之十一
四十萬鎊至六十萬鎊	百分之十二
六十萬鎊至八十萬鎊	百分之十三
八十萬鎊至一百萬鎊	百分之十四

一百萬鎊至以上……………………百分之十五

(二) 英國動產及不動產遺傳稅率

受繼人	稅率
兄弟姊妹或姪或姪女……………………	百分之三
伯叔父母……………………	百分之五
伯叔祖父母……………………	百分之六
其他……………………	百分之十

(附註) 遺產額百磅以上三百磅以下者.一律納三十先令.三百磅以上五百磅以下者.一律納五十先令.又遺產與非親生子而產額不逾一千磅者.免納動產遺傳稅.

美國中央遺產稅率（一九二六年新制）

（產額100,000元以下者免稅）

應稅產額	稅率
五萬元以下……………………	百分之一
五萬元至十萬元……………………	百分之二
十萬元至二十萬元……………………	百分之三
二十萬元至四十萬元……………………	百分之四
四十萬元至六十萬元……………………	百分之五
六十萬元至八十萬元……………………	百分之六
八十萬元至百萬元……………………	百分之七
一百萬元至百五十萬元……………………	百分之八
百五十萬元至二百萬元……………………	百分之九
二百萬元至二百五十萬元……………………	百分之十
二百五十萬元至三百萬元……………………	百分之十一
三百萬元至三百五十萬元……………………	百分之十二

三百五十萬元至四百萬元……………………………百分之十三

四百萬元至五百萬元………………………………百分之十四

五百萬元至六百萬元………………………………百分之十五

六百萬元至七百萬元………………………………百分之十六

七百萬元至八百萬元………………………………百分之十七

八百萬元至九百萬元………………………………百分之十八

九百萬至一千萬元…………………………………百分之十九

一千萬元以上………………………………………百分之二十

(附註)各州遺產稅可從中央遺產稅扣除.惟以百分之八十爲限.如中央遺產稅計應納一萬元.但省政府業已徵收九千元.則中央遺產稅得減爲二千元.又產業在死前二年贈與他人者.亦作遺產算.應納中央遺產稅.

按美國遺產免稅額僅一百磅.約合美金四百八十餘元.而美國免稅產額竟達十萬元.相差至巨.但其原因頗多.其易見者.(一)美國各州大多皆有遺產稅.中央自不能再加重稅(二)美人財富較英人爲豐厚.而在目下爲尤甚.(三)美政體與英不同.人民對於中央政府較對省政府感情稍遜.倘徵重稅.必起反抗.舊制千萬元以上須納百分之四十.今年已減至百分之二十.其亦職是故歟.(四)美稅對于產額較小者固寬.而對于產額極大者則較英稅爲重.蓋一至百分之十五爲止.而一則達百分之二十也.

民國四年.我國總統府財政討論會議亦議有遺產稅率.其制與美國各州遺產稅制相似.按產之大小及人之親疎而累進.特錄於下以資比較.

(一)遺產三千元以上一萬五千元以下者

親生子　百分之一　兄弟之子　百分之二　從兄弟之子　百分之三　再從兄弟之子　百分之四　同高祖兄弟之子　百分之五　其他　百分之六

（二）遺產一萬五千元以上三萬元以下者

親生子　百分之一•五　餘爲百分之三，四，五，六，七

（三）遺產三萬元以上五萬元以下者

親生子　百分之二　餘爲百分之四，五，六，七，八

（四）遺產五萬元以上十萬元以下者

親生子　百分之三　餘爲百分之五，六，七，八，九

（五）遺產十萬元以上十五萬元以下者

親生子　百分之四　餘爲百分之六，七，八，九，十

以上每加五萬元各加稅百分之一.（至百分之幾爲限尙待考查.）

然則遺產五萬元者親生子應納之稅爲七百四十五元.按諸國中經濟及生活狀況尙不爲過.惟恐貧困如今日.縱能推行.收入亦不多耳.

補白八

中國最近小統計數種

（譯自經濟討論處經濟月刊）

一	人口（民國十三年）	
	郵政局佔計，蒙古西藏及滿州少數縣分不在內	四三六，〇九四，九五三
	海關估計	四四四，六五三，〇〇〇
	外僑留滬人數	三二〇，八二九
二	面積	四，二七八，三四七方哩（約數）
三	國有鐵道長度	九，二六〇千米
四	其他鐵道	六，〇〇〇千米（約數）
五	國有路綫投資總額（民國十二年）	六三五，二七九，四八六元
六	國有路綫營業收入總額（十三年）	一一八，二八八，九九四元
七	電綫長度（民國十二年）	二三五，六五九華里
八	郵件寄數（民國十三年）	五二二，三五二，〇九五
九	包裹寄費總額（民國十三年）	一四〇，六八九•九二元
十	郵政局數（民國十三年）	一一，七九〇

參觀日本大阪合同紗廠記

偉　仁

合同紗廠.創自大正三年二月.（卽中華民國三年）地居大阪西隅.離城約五十餘里.火車電車均可直達.玆先述該廠之沿革.該廠於日本明治三十三年一月八日.以日金七十三萬圓.買進朝日紡績株式會社（卽現在能美今宮兩處分廠）爲創始.同年六月.歸併天滿紡績株式會社.（卽現在天滿分廠）明治三十五年八月.歸併中國紡績株式會社（卽現在廣島分廠）三十六年二月.歸併明治紡績株式會社.（卽現在住吉分廠）三十九年十一月.增設天滿第三工場.大正二年六月.新設神崎分廠.四年十二月.再添第二工場.六年五月.並設織布工場.十一月.更設第三工場.十一年六月.新添小松島分廠.十二年十月.收買今治紡織廠.（卽現在今治分廠）該廠資本金一千八百七十五萬圓.股本繳過一千四百零六萬二千五百圓.公積金一千九百八十七萬七千五百六十四圓.最近股利約二分.出品商標.綿沙爲雙鹿,地球.綿布爲指輪,福壽草,二仙圖,二軍人,福美人,裹地,鍾馗.總董谷口房藏.副縣董秋山廣太.董事隅田光藏,飯尾一二,能松太郎,坂田幹太,瀨川虎吉,河野義一郎.監査三谷軌秀,山本條太郎,秋田久.事務員總數.男六百七十八.女一百零二人.工人總數.男三千七百六十四人.女一萬二千七百十五人.錠子數.紗錠三十三萬二千四百八十只.綿錠五萬七千一百七十六只.織布機三千一百九十八部.該總廠及分廠共十四處.此合同紗廠沿革之大略也.

四月六日.先由日本東棉洋行介紹.得行員一人引導.至該廠參觀.是晨十時進廠.該公司董事多人.趨門招待.先進來賓室.寒暄片刻.漸談及上海近來滋生罷工風潮.並以後之趨向將來之處置工會接濟之能力極詳.將參觀時.由該董事贈送工場圖樣三紙.然後引導.至（一）工人寄宿各寮所.統計寮所約有十餘幢.每幢有中國四十餘間之長.惟均係平屋.細觀內容.整潔異常,

紙戶席地.古雅可風.初望之.覺不類工人苦力所居之處也.按其屋椽如是之簡單.木料若是其薄弱.其成本之輕.可想而知.日人經營事業.於設施方面.往往不尙外觀.而求實用.不好奢華.而喜樸素.此爲今日華人辦實業所最宜注意者.於出品方面.則恰成一反比例.例如機械一道.所謂日新月異.無不力求改良.雖多費財力.亦所不惜.惟能得一較適當較靈巧之器械.則公司無不樂從之.就寮宿附近設備而論.則有用品供給所.健身場.公園.寄兒所.醫室.閱報處.講習處.以上各種設備.雖非華人目光中之要務.然不能不歎日人設施之完善體恤之周到.而使工人能安心樂業也.

（二）自運動場折入發動機間.內有德國西門子式透平一隻.計五千K.W.又美國奇異透平三隻.計每座二千K.W.今所用者.僅西門子一座.取其簡便而省煤故也.紗廠部份.共分三處.每一範圍之內.揀花清花粗紗細紗搖紗打包等部均全.惟其機械新舊.則依其年限組織之早晚.各有不同.故其式樣亦各殊.總計錠數共十五萬四千五百枚.內供給織布紗錠五萬三千三百枚.工作時間.日班自早晨六時起.至下午五時止.正午用膳.休息一時.夜班自七時至晨六時.內休息一時.全廠工人.男一千四百十一人.女五千三百五十三人.資金男工最高五圓五角一分.最低九角四分.平均一圓五角七分.（日幣）女工最高一圓九角六分.最低六角.平均一元一角四分.

（三）就細紗內容而言.其最足動目之事.即紗頭絕無鬆斷之患.蓋因其用花得宜.揀花適合.溫度確當.女工藝高.有以致之.聞其所用之花.大率爲印度花.如平格兒.孟買花等等.然亦並非最上等之花.（甲）室內之溫度.平時常在八十五度.冬日則放熱氣以禦寒.夏日則送冷氣以却暑.所用器械.不過一普通12寸經口之鉛管.利用其管內空氣流通之動力.同時可使吸去棉絮灰絲.使空氣淨潔.紗色成分加白.誠一得兩便也.（乙）工人方面.服裝上具大衆一色之精神.男女工人.無有不服白色制服.或白色白套者.夫制服之用意.蓋可使工人時時不忘一己之責任.一己之本能.藉以刻刻振作精神.以盡其職

守.則工作自收競進之功.非徒事形式也.(丙)由大衆工人年齡而言.男子大率爲年富力強之壯夫.女子則大半在成丁以上.或中年左右.最堪注重一點.即工人中無幼童弱女之任事者.想幼年之流.大抵強迫進校.不論貧賤.均不得工作.致失其求學之機會.(丁)管理方面.該廠對於工人處置職守待遇賞罰.自有定章.工人照章而行.依法辦理.絕不勉強.故管理員寥寥數人.已足監視全部治安.決不若今日華廠管理員之諸般棘手也.觀於日人之堪稱得力者.即在富有自治力.服從性.及公德心.按此數端.不惟華人望塵莫及.即歐美工人.亦容有未逮.觀其全國極少罷工之事.可以信矣.但此等效果.均非一朝一夕所能收.其得力之處.正在平時政府嚴格之教育.愷悌之訓練.仁愛之引導.主其事者又能用平等之待遇.公平之賞罰.有以潛移默化之也.

(四)粗紗間之形式及設施.與華廠不相上下.其特殊之處.即對於粗細車馬達熱汽之設施.頗足效法.例如用伏地汽管.吸收每座馬達之熱力.而使常保溫和及安全之狀況.至地面光滑.機件整潔.廢物有所.飛花絕跡.均足爲該廠生色.而華廠所不及者也.

(五)清花間所用機件.都係潑拉脫牌子.惟於鋼刷之上.設有吸灰管一具.按此機華廠大都不備.蓋是機試用以來.不及三載.審其功用.有吸收屑子.提出灰絲.以及不純之物.經此一番手續.則花色純粹.紗色能加白也無疑.

(六)拚花間該廠立有配合份數表.以作按日拚和各方花衣之準.按拚花一部.乃全廠最要機關.故亦不常公開.走馬看花.竟不得窮其底蘊.至以爲憾.

(七)搖紗間.搖機由馬達引動.華廠大半有之.查各種機件.多係日本自製.職工工資.憑出貨而給價.其章程與華廠無異.

(八)打包間機件大多自製.打包用料.多數廢除鋼皮包紮.因鋼皮性易破裂.價格高昂.故不若全用麻繩捆紮之爲美.此中利弊.當在實驗後.方知究竟.吾國行之.不知適合否.按打包一部.乃紗廠出品結束之所.故觀畢之後.於

紗廠方面.可告一段落矣.統計每日出貨.約棉紗五•五〇〇捆.合四〇•〇〇〇紋.(合中國四百五六十件)推銷之處.以印度南洋各地.中國各部爲中心點.至日本國內推銷.比較反少.由此可見日本國外貿易之盛矣.

次參觀織布廠.(一)織布間.入廠時.既十一時半.故參觀時間.較爲局促.布廠布機.不過見其三廠之一.惟統計當在一千四百四十臺.職工司事.每人管兩機.例與華廠相同.惟司事者之學藝程度.較紗廠工人更高一層.所用布機.乃日本豐田廠自製.聞出數能力.不弱於歐美出品云.(二)筒子紗廠.與申新三廠所用者無異.惟於紗線經過之處.別設圓滑鋼珠球一排.以拭去紗頭之參差結核,及脫毛等弊.華廠苟能仿行.必見效也.(三)漿缸間及經紗間等處.除潔淨整齊溫度適合之外.別無優點.(四)布疋接頭機.係該廠新添者.意在連接碎布.以成正疋.但聞設備此機.成本頗重.故極不適用.此等器具.用之於歐美人工較貴之地則宜.於遠東人工衆多工資較廉之國則不宜.即欲連接布疋.儘可顧工以敏捷之手工代之也.按參觀合同紗廠.時間甚促.未及精密詳察.僅就所見者約記之.以資吾華紗廠之參考耳.惟查日本全國紡績公司.共有五十餘家.其所開携之錠子數.約共四百八十九萬五千八百五十錠.每月出紗數.約二十一萬四千五百三十包.每月銷售於該國國內數.約十三萬七千包.每月出口紗數約二萬包.足徵日本紗業發達.組織完備.工作勤敏.出品精良.是以能執東亞紡織界之牛耳.吾華有志紗業者.急宜遠師歐美.近法日本.悉心研究.竭力提倡.改良工作.擴充營業.庶可挽回利權.振興國勢也.

補白八（續）

十一	郵政儲金存款（民國十二年）	五,〇五三,九七三元
	廣東毫銀	一,〇八四,二一二元
十二	輸入貨物（民國十三年）	一,〇一八,二一〇,六七七海關兩
十三	輸出貨物（民國十三年）	七七一,七八四,四六八海關兩
十四	本國新式銀行資本金總額（民國十三年）	
	額定資本金	三〇〇,七七〇,〇〇〇元（約數）
	已募資本金	一三一,一一七,七〇〇元（約數）
	公積金	一九,三二八,九〇〇元（約數）
十五	公債總額（民國十二年）	二,二四八,一〇七,八四八元（約數）
十六	每人担負公債（民國十二年）	五•〇四元（約數）
十七	公債利息總額（民國十二年）	一〇〇,〇一九,二九五元（約數）

參觀日本大阪造幣局記要

偉 仁

日本造幣事業.約可分作二期.維新時幣制不統一之一時期.維新後幣制統一之一時期.在不統一時期.該國金融狀況.完全屬于幼稚時代.與中國今日幣制現象一較.可稱不相上下.當時日本以國外貿易之不利.幣制之紊亂.逐有採取金本位之議.先自統一銀本位而及鞏固附幣.于西歷一千八百九十七年十月（即明治二十七年）實行金本位.本位既定.該國幣制亦漸次按班就序.金融狀況.亦漸趨澄清地位.國家財政信用.因之益堅.

國幣之所以能統一金融之所以能穩固.其勢非有極充裕之資本.設極宏大之造幣局不可.幣局鎔化雜色之貨幣而成一標準之幣制.或化鍊各項之金屬.使成一公認之貨幣.無論于財政.于金融.均具有相當之利便及進益.故吾人不可不詳加注意也.

日本國有造幣局.共設二所.一設東京.一在大阪.除此而外.任何人任何團體均不准設立.意在謀出品之一致.權限之集中也.四月五日.東遊道經大阪.承東棉總董之介紹.得以一覩大阪造幣局.入廠之後.蒙該局局長款以茶點.並作短時間之談話.略謂「本局自明治四年開設以來.迄今已達五十六載.廠內原有機件.均極陳舊.所幸逐年革新之處.尚堪娛目.倘蒙不棄.敝局當盡地主之誼」

該局創立資計九十五萬五千二百兩.佔地共一五,八三〇坪（約合中國二百餘畝之譜）每年盈餘.計三千萬元.平日合計鑄五十錢銀貨五十五萬個.男女職工計五百十二人.參觀所得.可分三段申述.（一）庫房及貯存所（二）工場方面（三）從工之施設.至於出品之種類.分課之組織.鑄幣之順序.動力之統計.當于後表內詳載之.

（一）庫房及貯存所. 庫房之內.滿貯淨金大條.該項大條已由局中

經一度之鎔化.故成淨金.鑄幣之時.再酌加一成銅類金屬.以成九成之比例.該項大條.合計日金四千萬元有奇.又淨銀條核計八百九十三萬七千餘圓.鑄幣時則配成八成之比列.庫內所以有此充份之原料.實以現時無金洋及銀圓之陶鑄.因人民對于國家準備金之信用.極爲鞏固.對于附幣之供給流通.極爲充足.平日市上所見.除銀角五十錢.十錢.五錢.一錢.之外.其餘都係紙幣.日常通用.數自五元至十元不等.（每圓值華幣約九角）至較高用款.則以票據代現.金幣一層.市上絕少應用.由此可見紙幣之代價.實駕乎金幣之上也.金銀原料之供給.大都仰給于英美各國及高麗等處.本國產額.極爲少數云. 貯存所一.大半堆積銅條鎳貨及其他應用物料.除此而外.兼藏不純粹之金銀原料.及已成之貨幣等等.

（二）工場方面可分兩組.一組係鑄錢部.一組係製像部.前者陶製金銀銅鎳諸貨幣.後者代塑銅像獎章紀念章等等. 鑄錢部除銅鑄廠正在作工外.其餘金銀鑄錢諸部.均無工作.即銅鑄廠方面.亦係代暹羅國所鑄者.（代辦人爲三井洋行）一俟銅幣交貨.若無他項額外承辦.則該部亦將停歇.于此可知日本貨幣之富足.應付裕如.近時苟無承鑄國外營業.則决無趕鑄本國貨幣之恐慌也 製像部當時正在刻鑄大阪電氣博覽會出品紀念獎章.工作順序先自圖案而塑模型.由模型而印入金屬版.于是經縮小印像機而成一正式模型.更用壓花機印上銅片.略加燒煉.待冷着色.經一度之檢查.手續可稱完備矣（附貨幣鑄造順序表見下頁）

（三）從工之施設 該廠從業人員約可分爲三項.（一）職員統計一百四十八人（一）職工統計男三百二十七人.女六十一人（專使計算錢數）（一）傭工三十六人.工價男工每日二元.女工每日一元二十錢.工人年齡.最高五十歲.最低十五歲.平均每日工作八小時.夜工時間短促.工資較優.

（甲）住宿及飲食 工職人員住宿寮房.均由局中供給.職員臥室.計有

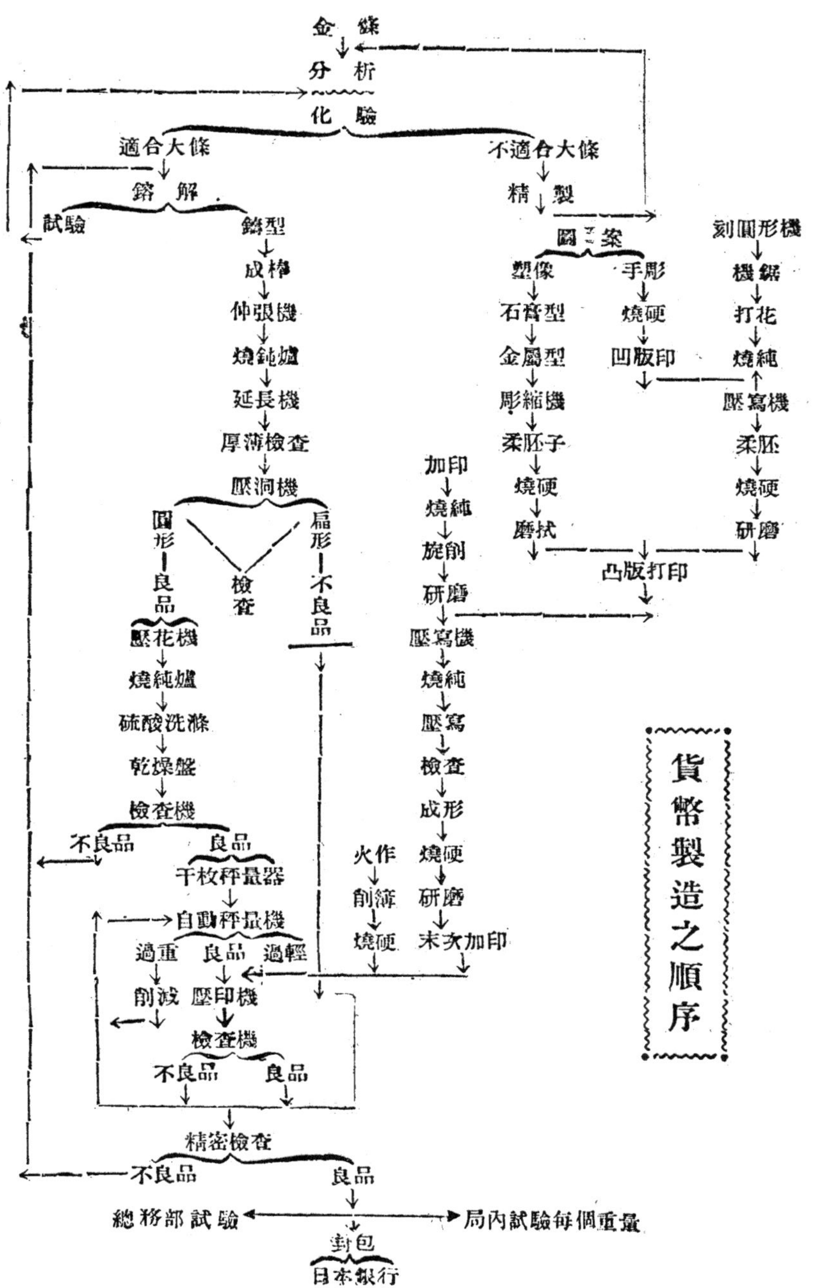
貨幣製造之順序
金條
分析
化驗
適合大條
不適合大條
鎔解
精製
試驗
鑄型
圖案
刻圓形機
成條
塑像
手彫
機鋸
伸張機
石膏型
燒硬
打花
燒鈍爐
金屬型
凹版印
燒純
延長機
彫縮機
壓寫機
厚薄檢查
柔胚子
柔胚
加印
燒硬
燒硬
壓洞機
燒純
磨拭
研磨
圓形
扁形
旋削
凸版打印
良品
檢查
不良品
研磨
壓花機
壓寫機
燒純爐
燒純
硫酸洗滌
壓寫
乾燥盤
檢查
檢查機
成形
不良品
良品
火作
燒硬
千枚秤量器
削薄
研磨
自動秤量機
燒硬
末次加印
過重
良品
過輕
削減
壓印機
檢查機
不良品
良品
精密檢查
不良品
良品
總務部試驗
局內試驗每個重量
封包
日本銀行

一百〇八戶.工人宿所二百間.又公宿所一處.足供五十九人之用.飯食方面.大都簡便衛生.上自經理總監.下及傭工苦力.均用膳于一處.所謂濟濟一堂.樂也融融.勞資之間.一視同仁.當局並容納任何工人之建議.苟能有利全局.則多數無不贊同云.

(乙)診調　局內別設醫院.從工及其家族.均得調治.工人如爲公而病則免費.否則略取低廉之藥資.以助經常費用.局中每逢春秋二季.例有大規模之衛生檢查.以定職工身體之健全與否.而促進公共衛生之改進.

(丙)救濟會　由當局與職工一同組合.內分（一）撫卹部.例如工人爲公罹災身死.或致殘廢.得由該會負責償恤生活費.及撫養家族費等等.（一）儲蓄部例如積金貯存.藉得重利而免浪費.局中成例.職工每月至少須儲薪金百分之三.工人每月百分之一.多則更佳.

(丁)教育　內分補習教育（一）普通科爲義務教育性質.二年爲限.（二）專門科包括機械化學彫刻諸門.以一年修業爲限.

(戊)娛樂及體育　娛樂有俱樂部.圖書館.雜誌室等之施設.體育有各項運動.例如遠足會.野球足球等.

(巳)獎勵　職工之勤勉者.有功績者.有發明者.均得由廠內給予自製獎章.及政府獎狀.他如局役子弟.學資統由局中代出.俾使工人各能安心樂業云.

（附造幣局事業一覽表見下頁）

補白八（二續）

十八	每人担負利息	〇·二二元(約數)
十九	政府預算收入額(民國十二年)	五二八,〇三六,五一七元
二十	政府預算支出額（民國十二年根據八年度預算）	五四八,六七八,八四〇元
二十一	每人收入額	一·一九元(約數)
二十二	每人支出額	一·二三元(約數)
二十三	海關收入（民國十三年）	六九,五九五,一三一海關兩
二十四	鹽稅收入（民國十三年）	九四,六五四,〇〇〇元
二十五	煙酒稅收入（民國十一年）	一五,〇六九,六八六元

日本大阪造幣局事業一覽

(一)(創業) 明治四年四月四日(迄今五十六年)

(二)(創立費) 九拾五萬五千貳百兩

(三)營業收入支出
- 大正十三年度收入 四千八百萬九千七拾六元
- 大正十三年度支出 千七百六拾九萬五千九百五十七圓

(四)(A)貨幣出數表(大正十三年)
- 五圓金幣 叁拾八萬〇一百八十五圓
- 五十錢銀幣 四千五百萬八千九百貳拾七圓
- 十錢白銅元 貳百萬九十八圓
- 一錢青銅元 七拾七萬叁十七圓
- 記章及奬牌 拾五萬叁千五百六十八圓

(B)貨幣種類
- 金幣 成色十份之九 (9/10 fine)
  - 二十元
  - 十　元
  - 五　元
- 銀幣 成色十份之八 (8/10 fine)
  - 五十錢
  - 二十錢
  - 十　錢
- 鎳幣 中央鑿有圓孔
  - 拾　錢
  - 五　錢
- 銅幣
  - 一　錢 合每圓百份之一
  - 一　零 合每錢十份之一

(C)中日匯兌之比例
- 日金百圓＝申規銀六十六兩三七五(五月廿六日市價)
- 日金百圓＝中國通用銀幣九十元

(五)分課組織
- 總務部
  - 人事課(秘書系—文牘系—施設系—醫務系)
  - 經理課(會計系—金銀物料系—用度系—營業系)
- 作業部
  - 計畫課(事務系—工務系—研究系)
  - 工程課(鎔解場—伸延場—壓印場—彫刻場—試金務—精製場)

(六)原動力
- 鍋　爐
  - 水管式(Water tube) 四座
  - 煖氣施用 一座
- 發電機
  - 座數 四
  - 容量 九四〇 K. W.
- 他廠供給電力 九五〇 K. W.
- 電動機
  - 座數 二二六
  - 容量 三四〇四匹馬力
- 蒸汽引擎
  - 座數 一
  - 容量 二二〇馬力

利農磚瓦廠磚頭試驗紀錄及結果

楊德新　施孔範

利農磚瓦廠始創於民國九年.由無錫紳士唐保謙發起.廠址在錫之東南隅嚴家橋.資本二十萬元.占地百餘畝該處地勢奇高.農民苦於灌溉.自該廠設立後.即在附近沿河高地掘取原料.而農民亦得灌溉之便.誠得孔氏因民所利而利之之義也.該廠出品以紅磚爲大宗.銷路以錫地爲最廣.蘇常上海各處用戶亦不少.民國十三年.添製青磚火磚洋瓦等出品.製造法係天津式.其內部之布置及管理甚有條理.經理係留美工科碩士唐君炳源云.

試驗紀錄

(一) 試驗所　南洋大學材料試驗室與中國工程學會合作

(二) 製品由何處送來　無錫利農磚瓦廠

(三) 取品樣者施君孔懷

(四) 品樣外觀　輕紅色

(五) 試驗日期　(一)　橫撓力一元月十一號及十五號，(二) 吸水量一元月十四號，(三) 擠壓力一元月十三號

吸水量試驗紀錄

品樣重量	重量			吸水量（以百分計算）$\frac{B-A}{A}\times100$	備註
	乾的 A	濕的 B	乾濕的比較 A—B		
1	$4\frac{13}{16}$ 1bs.	$5\frac{8}{16}$ 1bs.	$\frac{11}{16}$ 1bs.	14.3%	
2	$4\frac{15.5}{16}$ "	$5\frac{11.5}{16}$ "	$\frac{12}{16}$ "	15.1%	
3	$4\frac{11.5}{16}$ "	$5\frac{6.5}{16}$ "	$\frac{11}{16}$ "	14.6%	
4	$4\frac{11}{16}$ "	$5\frac{16}{16}$ "	$\frac{11}{16}$ "	14.7%	
5	$4\frac{12}{16}$ "	$5\frac{6}{16}$ "	$\frac{10}{16}$ "	13.2%	
總數	…………	…………	…………		
平均	…………	…………	…………	14.4%	

擠壓力試驗

（磚頭放法一半個側放）

品樣號數	磚頭大小 闊(d)以英吋計	長(l)以英吋計	面積(a)，a=dl	擠壓力（以英磅計）初次發見裂縫	破壞(L)	擠壓力 $\left(\frac{1}{a}\right)$ 以每方吋磅數計
1	$1\frac{3}{4}$吋	$4\frac{19}{16}$吋	7.96方吋	6600	8215	1035
2	$1\frac{3}{4}$ "	$4\frac{9}{16}$ "	7.96 "	19320	21755	2725
3	$1\frac{3}{4}$ "	$4\frac{9}{16}$ "	7.96 "	8850	18160	2280
4	$1\frac{5}{8}$ "	$4\frac{9}{16}$ "	7.40 "	20780	21155	2860
5	$1\frac{3}{4}$ "	$4\frac{9}{16}$ "	7.96 "	6640	14210	1785
平均						2137

橫撓力試驗

品樣號數	磚頭大小 闊(d)以英吋計	高(d)以英吋計	跨度(l)以英吋計	橫撓力(W)以磅數計	撓力繫數 $R=\frac{3wl}{2bd^2}$ 以每方吋磅數計
1	$4\frac{1}{2}$吋	$1\frac{3}{4}$吋	7吋	565	430
2	$4\frac{1}{2}$ "	$1\frac{3}{4}$ "	7 "	490	373
3	$4\frac{1}{2}$ "	$1\frac{3}{4}$ "	7 "	930	709
4	$4\frac{1}{2}$ "	$1\frac{3}{4}$ "	7 "	755	575
5	$4\frac{1}{2}$ "	$1\frac{3}{4}$ "	7 "	1000	762
平均					570

平均結果

吸水量以百分計算	擠壓力以每方吋磅數計	橫撓力繫數以每方吋磅數計
14.4	2137	570
試驗結果認爲及格已由工程學會給予證書矣		

一年來經濟學會大事記

邱褚聯

自吾校開辦鐵路管理科以後,即有鐵路管理協會之組織.然而成立不久,舊會長畢業離校,新職員無由產生,以致負責乏人,會務廢弛,章程文件,散佚殆盡,精神既失,於是無形解散矣,然關心管理科之發展者終以此爲憾.乃於十二年九月,陳君文松,曹君麗順等,發起另行組織經濟學會.此議既起,各級先後贊同,各舉委員四人籌備組織,是年十月十八日,會章告成後,籌備委員會卽行宣布解職,由正式職員負責進行.當時會初成立,事務甚繁,如呈請校長立案,徵收會費,徵求準會員,聘請顧問,籌備成立大會等等.十三年六月經濟學報第一期出版,深得各界之贊助.其他各種進行,已詳載於經濟學報第一期.茲將十四年十一月起之大事及議決案,紀錄如下:

十一月六日　舉行全體大會,議決各案如下:

(一) 邱君褚聯辭會長職.經全體竭力挽留.

(二) 經濟學報加入校中出版部,由編輯部長薛椿蔭代表出席.

(三) 經濟學報旣已併入校中出版部,議決將原有本會之出版科及廣告科取消.

十日　由正副會長發起將會中餘存之濟學報第一期,分發管一及管二諸會員,經全體職員贊成施行.

十六日　請潘序倫博士演講,題爲「關稅管理問題」

十二月五日　請李權時博士演講,題爲「消費論.」

卅日　呈請淩校長轉請交部加派出洋留學額.

十五年三月八日　舉行職員會議議,決事項如下:

(一) 舉行經濟論文比賽.

(二) 聘定俞行修徐叔劉張直夫三顧問為評判員.

(三) 論文比賽題目由評判員擬定公佈.

(四) 管四論文擇優登入南洋季刊.

(五) 演講科及參觀科應竭力進行.

(六) 在下星期內須舉行全體大會.

廿二日　本日應舉行全體大會,惟以北京慘殺案發生,不能進行.

四月十日　舉行全體大會議決各案如下:

(一) 恢復原有之經濟學報.

(二) 本學期籌備稿件,以便下學期開學時,即可出版.

(三) 每月出學報一期,頁數多寡以稿件及經費為準.

(四) 出版學報之詳細辦法,由職員會議討論之.

廿二日　公佈論文比賽題目.

五月七日　請姚公鶴先生演講,題目為『今猶昔也之外交途徑.』

十三日　攝全體會員及職員照片.

廿七日　公佈經濟論文比賽結果:第一賈乙青得金質奬章.第二尤玉照,得銀質奬章.第三沈奏廷,得銅質奬章.

廿八日　舉行職員會議,議决事項如下:

(一) 自下學期始,經濟學報每月逢十五日出版一次.

(二) 會費擬增至一元惟須經大會通過方得實行.

(三) 印調查紙若干,分發會員,以便於假期內調查各地經濟及社會各種情形.

(四) 請本會顧問,本科教授,及畢業同學為特約編輯.

(五) 指定邱褚聯及華立二人參與五卅烈士奠祭禮.

(六) 本學期須再開大會一次,日期由會長决定之.

附本屆職員名單:

（會長）邱褚聯　（副會長）華立　（經理部長）郁仁充　（研究部長）費振東　（會計）徐昭誠　（文牘）章煥昌孫孝鈞　（參觀科長）應餘度　（編輯科長）薛椿蔭　（演講科長）關鐸　（調查股長）徐開宗　（編輯股長）沈奏廷　（校對員）王素　（管四幹事）蔡光績　（管三幹事）朱溥仁　（管二幹事）林宗哲　（管一幹事）吳祿增

南洋一覽稿

（二續）

柴福沅芷湘甫擬

編制

現狀

大學設電機.機械.及鐵路管理三科.均四年畢業.現計有三科.四門.四級.十七班.

附屬中學係舊制中學.四年畢業.現計有四級八班.

附屬小學係舊制高等小學.三年畢業.現計有三級五班.又補習科一班.一年畢業.

本校有沿用最久之名詞二.曰上院.曰中院.始則僅爲建築物之名.繼乃漸有程度區分之意.上院程度爲專門.爲大學.中院爲中學.又附屬小學之程度.初甚淺近.後乃定爲高等小學程度.

上院科門之因革.班次之增減分合.至爲繁複.南洋公學成立之初.感師資之缺乏.乃首先設立師範院.學生國學.均有根柢.兩次招考之外.有聞名羅致而來者.無定班.亦無定課.其次爲日文班.附屬於譯書院.以肄習日文迻譯新書爲目的.開辦未及半年.因事解散.其次爲蔡孑民先生主任之特班.備應經濟特科而設.歷時僅二年.政治科光緒二十七年設立.商務科一稱商業科.

由政治科改辦.有畢業生一班.

鐵路科光緒三十二年設.有頭二三三班.三年畢業.宣統二年.因第二班人少裁併.故次年無學生畢業.民國元年.擴充範圍.改稱土木科.十年秋移併於唐山學校.

電氣機械科原名電機科.光緒三十四年設.有頭二三三班.亦三年畢業.是科及土木科.自民國六年夏專門預科裁後.均改四年畢業.十年.改大學.分立電力工程門.有線電信門及無線電信門.十三年.併後二門爲一門.曰電信門.

光緒三十一年.本校隸屬商部時.與電機科同時規畫者.尙有機輪船政二科.船政科宣統元年開辦.四年畢業.三年受課.一年在船實習.其後移至校外.宣統三年.建商船學堂於吳淞.至民國元年.乃脫離本校而獨立.機械科範圍.較機輪科爲大.民國十年.改組大學時始設.分立鐵路機械門.機廠工務門及工業管理門.十三年.後二門亦合併爲一.名工業機械門.

本校現行編制.電機機械兩科.一二年級功課從同.通稱工科.僅依人數多寡.分班授課.三年級始分電機及機械.至四年級又各認定專門.其詳如附表.

大學工科現行編制表

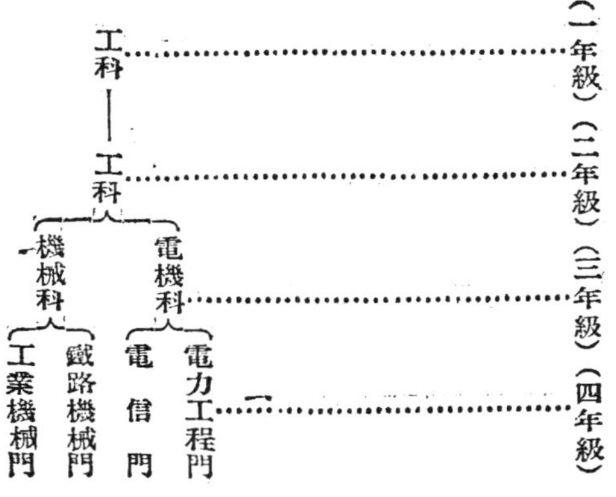

鐵路管理科民國七年春設立.卽由土木電機二科之有志管理者改組爲頭班.三年畢業.其後各班皆秋季始業.四年畢業.十年秋.改大學.移併於北京學校者一年.現仍由本校繼續開辦.

中學初名中院.繼改高等預科.四年畢業.宣統元年.始正中學之名.改五年畢業.每級設兩班.計共十班.民國元年.復改四年畢業.畢業後入專門預科又一年.乃升專科.六年夏.改專門預科爲專科一年級.外院者.對師範院而言之也.南洋公學初辦時.程度至不齊一有大中小三班.每班又分三級.其後學生遞升中院.外院遂裁撤.

附屬小學光緒二十七年設.有高等科及補習科各一班.翌年.改爲六級每級半年.二十九年夏.改一年爲一級.計三級.三十一年秋.添設四年級.規定四年畢業.民國二年.復改三年畢業.另設補習科.實卽前之一年級也.

宣統二年.曾一度招收通學生.補充上中院各班餘額.住徐家匯鎮上之指定宿舍.俟住校生出缺.擇尤拔補.翌年.校外宿舍落成.通學生一律遷入.其制遂廢.

新學制頒行已久.本校迄未更改者.實緣本校中學之程度.已與高級中學相當.附屬小學之程度.亦與初級中學相彷佛.所不同者.名稱及年限耳.(編者按.從十五年度起.已添設新制初中.以便將來逐漸改成高初中兩部.各三年.並附高級小學二年.)

（本篇未完）

南洋季刊第一卷第二期正誤表

編輯者言

頁數	行數	正	誤
1	2	屬於記載	屬於載記
1	4	讀者能因此	讀者因此

震華製造電機廠實習記

頁數	行數	正	誤
172	倒算第三行	汽鍋用水進水機	汽輪用水進水機
,,	,,	feed-water	fled-water
173	6	Exhaust steam	Exhousteam
,,	倒算第四行	Measurement instruments	Measuremeut instrumeuts
174	倒算第六行	勵磁機	礪磁機
,,	倒算第四行	抽汽鍋用水用	抽汽水水用
,,	倒算第二行	8·0烟突	1·0烟突
175	倒算第六行	空氣中之氧	空氣中之氣
176	9	Induction	Inducton
,,	11	plate	blate
,,	12	媒介	煤介
177	13	Single	Siugle
180	3	type	井 type
,,	6	經過程序	徑過程序
,,	倒算第二行	Rheostat	Rhostat
181	15	Shell	Shll
182	17	Watthour meter	井 Watthour meter
184	倒算第三行	競智與良	競智對與良

孫中山陵墓所用石頭試驗報告書

頁數	行數	正	誤
261	9	「指甲刮」之下脫去「之」字	
262	6	「試驗」兩字下多「治」字	

化驗火酒述要

頁數	行數	正	誤
264	13	Specific gravity	Specific grarity
265	3	12N公絲	1N公絲
265	12	17·62N公絲	17·12N公絲
266	1	Phenylenediamine	Plenylenediamine
266	20	Phenylhydrazine	Phenelhydlrazine

四庫全書述略

頁數	行數	正	誤
267	2	函數	函数
271	17	不苟	不苟
,,	,,	甲辰(1784)	甲辰(1783)
,,	19	長流萬古	長源万古
,,	22	子部	工部
,,	27	(1783)衍	（應加）
272	1	癸亥(1783)	（應加）
,,	2	甲辰(1784)	
,,	11	無與比倫	比偏
,,	15	議決以文津閣所藏者付印	（加）
274	2	案號求書	桒號求書
,,	6	印行單行本	草行本
,,	19	傳聞眼見	傳問眼見
275	10	商務	報務

南洋一覽

頁數	行數	正	誤
283	6	鋸	踞
283	16	樓上	上樓
292	12	址	扯

南洋季刊定報單

茲寄上報費　角郵費　角　分
定閱南洋季刊　期年自第　卷
第　期起請按期寄交下列地
點爲荷

定報人簽名

中華民國　年　月　日

南洋季刊投稿簡章

一　本刊除聘請特約撰述員担任撰述稿件外校內外無論何人倘有投稿均所歡迎

二　本刊分通論工程經濟科學文藝交通事業工商調查校聞紀要同學會紀聞校友要訊新著述評遊記雜俎等門但投稿者得投寄合於本刊宗旨之任何稿件

三　投寄之稿或自撰或翻譯均可其文體以文言爲主但得酌用白話或外國文

四　投寄之稿望繕寫清楚並加句讀或新式標點符號能依本刊規定之行格（每面橫行廿五每行三十字）繕寫者尤佳倘有附圖須製版者請另紙用筆墨繪成以便攝製

五　投寄譯稿請附原本如原本不便附寄請將原文題目原著者姓名出版日期及發售書局名稱詳細敍明

六　稿末請註明姓名字住址以便通信至揭載時如何署名聽投稿者自定

七　投寄之稿揭載與否本刊編輯者不能預覆如不揭載得因預先聲明寄還原稿

八　投寄稿件俟揭載後酌酬本刊一期或數期

九　投寄之稿其著作權仍爲著作者所有惟於需要時得由本校其他出版物轉載

十　投寄之稿如已在他處發布者請預先聲明惟揭載與否由本刊編輯者斟酌

十一　投寄之稿本刊編輯者得酌量增刪之但投稿人不願他人增刪者可於投稿時預先聲明

十二　投稿請寄上海徐家匯南洋大學出版部

南洋季刊創刊號要目

巳於本年一月出版

南洋季刊電機工程號目錄

巳於本年四月出版

南洋季刊第一卷第三期經濟號

民國十五年七月出版

編輯處 上海南洋大學出版部

發行處及訂購處 上海南洋大學出版部

印刷者 中國印刷廠

代售處 上海商務印書館 中華書局 世界書局
北京交通部路政司攷工科莫葵卿
青島膠濟鐵路局機務處胡梓士
南京河海大學吳馥初

本刊價目表

定價		每期郵費	
每期	大洋二角	本埠	一分
		外埠	二分半
每年	大洋八角	國外	十分

本刊廣告刊例

全面	封面裏頁及底面裏外頁	實洋十五元
	尋常地位	實洋十元
半面	封面裏頁及底面裏外頁	實洋八元
	尋常地位	實洋六元

交通部直轄滬寧鐵路廣告

穩妥 ● 迅速

啓者本路每日除按班開行外並加特別快車尋常快車及夜快車每次備有餐車以便乘客取價極廉清潔適口各站經過地點皆爲東南名勝薈華之區風景之佳冠於全國其最著者如蘇州之虎邱天平山無錫之惠山錫山常州之天寧寺鎮江之金焦山甘露寺南京之明陵莫愁湖等處均爲我國特殊勝景如乘車出行作竟日之郊游必能快心悅目於精神上當裨益匪鮮

本路夜快車備有臥車牀位清潔舒暢每牀位除加頭等票外售洋三元遠近不計凡旅客欲乘別路通車者可向各大站購買聯運票以免周折倘係團體旅行本路訂有定章以人數多寡核減票價惟須先期函知車務總管核准

車務總管奉命啓

榮昌祥
西裝呢絨號
本號洋服 首屈一指
品質優美 信用久著
今更銳意 研製精良
優待主顧 取價從廉
諸君一試 定能滿意
地址 上海南京路新世界對面
電話中央第六〇五六號
CHONG SHUNG & CO.
HIGH-CLASS TAILOR & GENERAL OUTFITTER
PERFECT FIT GUARANTEED MODERATE PRICES
Give Us a trail and you Will be Convinced
364 NANKING ROAD OPPOSITE NEW WORLD
TELEPHONE NO. C 6056
SHANGHAI

南洋季刊

NANYANG QUARTERLY

第一卷　　機械工程號　　第四期

本期要目

民國十五年十二月

南洋大學出版股南洋公學同學會同發行

中華郵政特准掛號認爲新聞紙類

南洋季刊創刊號要目

已於本年一月出版

南洋季刊電機工程號目錄

已於本年四月出版

南洋季刊經濟號目錄

已於本年七月出版

南洋季刊投稿簡章

一　本刊除聘請特約撰述員擔任撰述稿件外校內外無論何人倘有投稿均所歡迎

二　本刊分通論工程經濟科學文藝交通事業工商調查校聞紀要同學會紀聞校友要訊新著述評遊記雜俎等門但投稿者得投寄合於本刊宗旨之任何稿件

三　投寄之稿或自撰或翻譯均可其文體以文言為主但得酌用語體文或外國文

四　投寄之稿望繕寫清楚並加句讀或新式標點符號能依本刊規定之行格（每面橫行廿五每行三十字）繕寫者尤佳

倘有附圖須製版者請另紙用黑墨水繪成以便攝製其有用藍墨水繪成或用藍照相圖者恕從割愛

五　投寄譯稿請附原本如原本不便附寄請將原文題目原著者姓名出版日期及發售書局名稱詳細敍明

六　稿末請註明姓名住址以便通信至揭載時如何署名聽投稿者自定

七　投寄之稿揭載與否本刊編輯者不能預覆如不揭載得因預先聲明寄還原稿

八　投寄稿件俟揭載後酌酬本刊一期或數期

九　投寄之稿其著作權仍為著作者所有惟於需要時得由本校其他出版物轉載

十　投寄之稿如已在他處發布者請預先聲明惟揭載與否由本刊編輯者斟酌

十一　投寄之稿本刊編輯者得酌量增刪之但投稿人不願他人增刪者可於投稿時預先聲明

十二　投稿請寄上海徐家匯南洋大學出版股

本刊特別啓事

本刊自第二卷起，增設問答一欄。凡本刊讀者，如有關於下列規定範圍以內之問題，均得向本刊詢問。規則如下。

（一）問題範圍限於下列三種：（甲）工程，（乙）經濟，（丙）數理化。

（二）問題程度限於中學以上。過於淺近者，恕難一一作答。

（三）詢問函件，須敍述明白，繕寫清楚。

（四）所有問題，均請本刊特約撰述員或專門校審員（均爲本校教授或校友）担任解答。隨時於本刊各期披露。如願先行函覆答案者，每一問函應附郵票五分。

（五）函詢時，須將右示印花剪下，粘於詢問紙上，方爲有效。

南洋季刊社職員錄

（民國十五年秋學期）

總編輯	趙祖康
編輯	柴福沅
本期特約編輯員	顧毓琇
發行	沈元慶

南洋大學出版委員會及南洋季刊專門校審員特約撰述員題名錄

◉出版委員會委員◉

徐名材　李熙謀　范永增　俞行修
張貽志　王永禮　張孝安

◉專門校審員◉

周仁　吳玉麟　俞希稷　李聯珪　王繩善
周銘　徐佩璜　楊培琫　徐佩琨

◉特約撰述員◉

張景良　張世鎏　李復幾　胡端行　莫衡
薛次莘　周厚坤　鮑國寶　曹麗順　鈕澤全
茅以新　莊前鼎　方子衛　潘世宜　趙曾珏
陳廣沅　楊立惠　王繩善　謝仁　裘維裕
張峻　李聯珪　黃世祚　沈慶鴻　杜定友
唐慶詒　杜光祖　武書常　劉麟生　朱鼎元
施孔懷　沈昌　吳維翰　沈維楨

本校卅週紀念工業展覽會

中國行家陳列之一斑（一）

本校卅週紀念工業展覽會

中國行家陳列之一斑（二）

本校卅週紀念工業展覽會

中國行家陳列之一斑（三）

本校卅週紀念工業展覽會

第二會場前之小火車

圖一　奇異公司總廠全景（工作面積六百三十七萬方呎工人二萬）

圖二　奇異公司所造最大蒸汽透平發電機（該機爲六萬基羅瓦特）

圖三 試驗科學生工程師試驗大號發電電動聯接機

圖四 試驗科學生工程師試驗大號蒸汽透平發電

編輯者言

本刊創始,距今一年,時值本校學生團體所出之工程,經濟兩學報停止刊行,本校出版事業中落之候.本刊既出,謬以內容豐富,得各地校友及讀者之贊許,銷售因之日廣,而校內同學著述創作之興趣,亦復不期爲之鼓起.此屆雙十節,本校舉行卅週紀念,經濟學會於是又以經濟學報第二卷第一號問世,而工程學報近亦有繼續出版之議.是則民國十六年之本校出版物,將一變中落而爲中興時代,本刊竊忻然以爲與有力焉.

惟一校之出版物不嫌其多,而各刊物之分野,則務求其劃然淸晰,庶獲分工並進之效,而免疊牀架屋之病.今者工程,經濟兩學報既重行出版,本校同學作品發表之機會倍增,本刊當仍本提倡專門學術之旨,自第二卷起,進而謀專門教育者之聯絡,通俗學識之普遍,及校友之智識的結合,而於校內同學之著述,一如昔日之歡迎,俾本刊不失爲校內外師生校友與夫有意於工程,經濟科學之研究者之共同刊物.此則本刊同人所黙望者也.

本刊第二卷第二期擬出『工程教育研究專號』.此事編者早於本刊上期言之.徵文條例及現在已得稿件,俱詳本期廣告欄內.甚望國內外工程教育專家咸能錫以宏論,互相發明,庶爲專門教育者聯絡之先聲也.

第二卷起本刊當增設問答一欄.凡本刊讀者均得享詢問一切疑難問題之權.其範圍以屬於工程,經濟,自然科學爲限.其答覆由本刊特約撰述員或專門校審員（均爲本校教授或校友）任之.詳細辦法見本刊啓事欄內.此乃本刊企圖通俗學識普遍之微意.外此當時請經驗宏富專家撰述通俗著作以餉讀者.甚望惠稿諸君亦能常以通俗工程及經濟稿件見賜也.

下卷起並擬增設讀者論壇一欄,凡本校校友或讀者對於某種學術研究,有所心得,有所討論,而無暇撰爲精密冗長之論著者,可著之短篇提出研究各點,以爲公開之討論.如此則本校校友將因本刊而得與國內其他專門學者有所聯絡,倘幷能由是而造成一種學術研究之風氣,則所謂校友與讀者之智識的結合,意在斯乎.

本校近得留美同學會捐贈銀杯一具.凡在校同學在本刊及工程學徵一年內發表工程著作文字最佳者,鐫其姓名於杯上,如此繼續三年.現校中已請出版委員會主持此事.第一年比賽期自今年春起至明年夏止,即自本刊一卷三期起至二卷二期止.一卷三期適爲經濟號,二卷二期擬出工程教育研究號,均於專門工程著作無甚關係.本期季刊又已出版.是以凡欲參預此榮譽之比賽者,在本年度將惟有二卷一期一次努力之機會.此二卷一期之本刊,所以特別希望在校同學之能踴躍投稿也.

本期所載各篇,大多爲機械工程之專門著作.編輯時幸承周子競,王叔培,王爾綱,周明誠諸先生之審閱,顧毓瑔君之襄助徵稿,合應聲明誌謝.

本刊篇幅有限,稿件頗多.上期所載『工場委員制』與『基本金及儲備金問題』兩作,以及本期所載各篇之未完者,均容後續登請讀者注意.

本期季刊機械工程號本應於十月中出版,惟以本校卅週紀念適於雙十節舉行,同時並出版紀念刊物若干種,(徵文集,校業册,校友錄等.)編輯者撰稿者均以籌備紀念苦無餘暑,本刊於是不得不延至今日出版,尤希愛讀諸君鑒諒是幸.（康）

本刊第二卷第二期,近應本校經濟工程兩學會之請,改『工程教育研究號』爲『鐵路問題號』,附此聲明,並向讀者徵稿.（編者）

氣渦輪效率之研究

黃叔培

引言

近日工程界人常謂氣渦輪（Gas Turbine）將來必爲主要原動機關之一種.此言之能否成爲事實,頗具研究之價值.就近來試驗之結果觀之,氣渦輪之困難雖多,而其成功實爲可期.況各種發明之成功,往往經歷無數困難.活塞氣機（Piston Gas Engine）如是,蒸汽渦輪（Steam Turbine）如是.而氣渦輪欲由理想成爲事實,由試驗品成爲工業品,又何能獨有捷徑.故今日氣渦輪之困難雖多,若具決心以研究之改良之,未始不可將其所有障礙一一解除,而使氣渦輪得在動機界上佔一重要之地位也.

活塞氣機之熱力効率高,而扭力不均,且構造極爲繁複.蒸汽渦輪之扭力均,而熱力効率低,且必恃鍋爐（Boiler）爲之蒸發水汽.氣渦輪之目的,卽欲兼活塞氣機及蒸汽渦輪二者之所長,而擯其所短.卽効率高,結構簡,而扭力均也.

似此之熱力機關,可謂盡善盡美矣.然欲達此目的,頗非易事.(1)氣渦輪所用之溫度甚高,而渦輪之旋轉部分,每易爲其所傷.(2)氣渦輪所需之空氣,必取給於旋轉壓氣機（Rotary Compressor）.旋轉壓氣機之効率低,故氣渦輪之効率亦受其影響而下降.然則欲氣渦輪之成功,非將以上兩端困難解除,或將其影響減輕不可.

氣渦輪之種類頗多.其結構及佈置,大概如第一圖.此種氣渦輪乃由三要部合成,卽旋轉壓氣機,火箱（Combustion Chamber）,及氣渦輪之本部是也.空氣由壓氣機入火箱,而燃料亦於同時射入.二者自外源源以來,而在火箱內燃燒不斷,故火箱內之壓力不變.由燃燒所得之熱氣,經過伸漲氣管

(Diverging Nozzle)後,即衝入氣渦輪,而使其旋輪轉動矣.

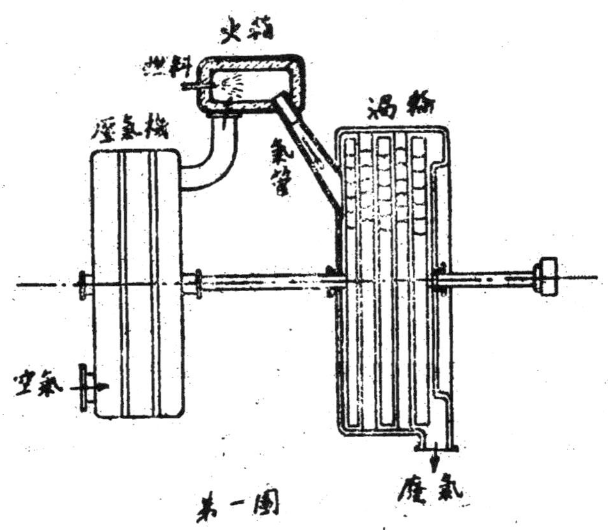

第一圖

循環効率

當未比較氣渦輪各種循環(Thermodynamic Cycles)之前,姑先將其極端溫度,及其壓縮空氣所需之工作,略加討論.因前者與循環本身之効率有大關係,而後者則有大影響於氣渦輪之機械効率也.茲分論之.

極端溫度　極端溫度,即氣渦輪所用之最高溫度,及最低溫度也.最高溫度,即火箱內燃燒之溫度.最低溫度,即氣體經過氣管後在旋輪內之溫度.極端溫度雖不能爲循環効率之絕對標準,然其影響於循環効率之高下者則甚大.凡氣渦輪効率高者,其極端溫度相去恆遠.然二者之高低,相關甚切,而不能使之絕對向高低兩端各自進行.故効率高之氣渦輪,其最高溫度往往甚高,而其最低溫度亦甚高.且在事實上,氣體在氣管內之伸漲不能完全,故氣體入旋輪時之溫度恆高,而渦輪每易因之以受損壞.此實爲氣渦輪之一大病.欲除此患,不得不使氣渦輪之最高溫度降低,而同時犧牲循環之効率.其結果務使氣體在旋輪內之溫度不能爲害.據經驗所得,旋輪能受700°C絕對溫度而無傷.故在討論循環効率之時,若假定700°C絕對溫度,爲旋輪所能受之溫度,其結果當不致與事實相遠也.氣渦輪所用之最高溫度,爲火箱及氣管之抗熱性所限定.然若在火箱及氣管之內層,裹以矽化炭（Carborundum）,則循環中所發生之溫度,不論若何,皆可無患.依最高溫度,可謂不成問題.但兩端溫度互有關係,故最低溫度已有限制,而最高溫度亦不能不有限制矣.其限制之程度,卽使氣體在氣管內伸漲之後,其溫度不致超過700°C絕對溫度也.

氣渦輪之機械効率　氣渦輪之機械効率甚低,因其所產生之機械工作大部分爲旋轉壓氣機所消耗,而供其壓縮空氣之用.高壓空氣已爲氣渦輪所必需之物,故壓氣機所需之工作與氣渦輪所發生之工作,二者之比例成爲一重大問題.此項比例愈低則愈妙.若其比例高,則循環之効率雖高,而氣渦輪之効率仍必甚低.故近于一之比例,不適於用.欲求此項比例低小(1)在改良壓氣機,（2）在減少壓氣當用之工作.改良壓氣機一事,已有多人進行.壓氣機需用工作之大小,則爲各種循環之特性.而在比較各種循環時不可不特別注意者也.玆將壓氣機與氣渦輪機械効率之關係演述如下.今以

Q = 每兙氣體在火箱內所發生之熱量

q = 每兙廢氣所帶出之熱量

f = 循環之効率

E_c = 旋轉壓氣機之機械効率

E_t = 氣渦輪本部之機械効率

E = 壓氣機及氣渦輪之總機械効率

J = 熱能之機械當

Wc = 理論上壓氣機應需之工作

W'c = 事實上壓氣機應需之工作

Wt = 循環之指示工作

W = 理論上氣渦輪發生之總工作

W' = 氣渦輪軸上之實在工作

W'' = 可以供給外用之工作

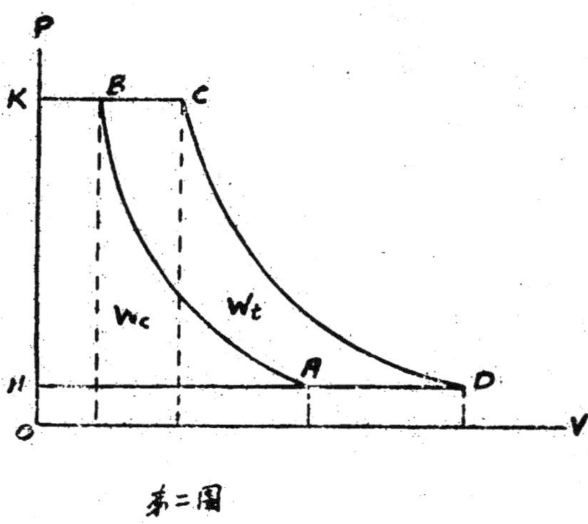

第二圖

見第二圖.循環之指示工作等於ABCD.理論上壓氣機應需之工作等於ABKH.氣渦輪之總指示工作則等於HKCD.因事實上機械效率恆小於一,故氣渦輪軸上之實在工作必小於HKCD.而壓氣機應需之工作必大於HKBA.此二者之差即爲供給外用之工作.而必小於ABCD.

按熱力學,循環之効率爲 $f = \frac{Q-q}{Q}$

循環之指示工作爲 $Wt = fJQ$

理論上壓氣機應需之工作,即其指示工作,等於壓氣機實用之工作乘

其機械効率.卽

$$W_c = E_c W'_c$$

$$W'_c = \frac{W_c}{E_c}$$

在理論上.來自壓氣機之空氣,所給於氣渦輪之工作,其量適等于壓氣機應需之工作.故氣渦輪所發生之總指示工作爲,

$$W = W_t + W_c$$

在氣渦輪軸上實在有用之工作爲,

$$W' = E_t W = E_t (W_t + W_c)$$

可以供給外用之工作,爲氣渦輪軸上之工作,與壓氣機實用之工作,二者之差.卽

$$W'' = W' - W'_c$$

$$= E_t (W_t + W_c) - \frac{W_c}{E_c}$$

氣渦輪及壓氣機之總機械効率,爲供給外用之工作,與循環之指示工作二者之比例.卽

$$E = \frac{W''}{W_t} = E_t + \left[E_t - \frac{1}{E_c} \right] \frac{W_c}{W_t} \cdots\cdots\cdots\cdots (1)$$

據經驗所得氣渦輪本部之機械効率,與壓氣機之機械効率約70%.代入第(1)公式,得

$$E = .700 - .729 \frac{W_c}{W_t} \cdots\cdots\cdots\cdots\cdots\cdots\cdots\cdots (2)$$

由此可知壓縮空氣所需之工作,與渦輪所發生之工作,二者之比例,有大影響於渦輪之總機械効率也.

（A）等溫循環（Constant Temperature Cycle）談熱力原動機者,必及卡諾循環（Carnot Cycle）,卽等溫循環,以其効率高也.但此循環之効率雖高,而不適用於蒸氣原動機,及活塞氣機.熱學家每以爲憾.茲在研究各種循環之始,特先將此循環加以討論,而覘其是否適合氣渦輪之用.

第三圖指示卡諾循環之特性.因求簡便起見,暫設工作之媒介物爲一瓩空氣.此氣在A時之溫度爲T_0壓力爲P_0.自A至B空氣受等溫度壓縮(Isothermal Compression),壓力自P_0增至P_1而溫度不變.自A至B所需之工作爲

$$Wi = RT_0 \log e \left(\frac{P_1}{P_0}\right)$$

自B至C氣體再受等能壓縮(Adiabatic Compression).壓力自P_1增至P_2而溫度由T_0增至T_2.在此運動所需之工作爲

$$Wa = JCp(T_2 - T_0)$$

自C至D氣體受Q熱量而澎漲.經此變動氣壓自P_2至P_3而溫度仍爲T_2.此項變動可稱爲等溫受熱(Isothermal Introduction of Heat).熱量Q與壓力變更之關係爲

$$Q = \frac{RT_2}{J}\log e\left(\frac{P_2}{P_3}\right)$$

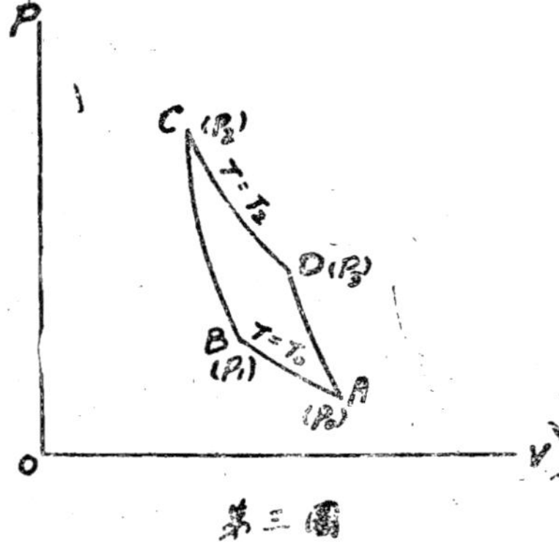

第三圖

按熱力學,卡諾循環之効率爲

$$f = 1 - \frac{T_0}{T_2}$$

如是循環之指示工作爲

$$Wt = JQ\left(1 - \frac{T_0}{T_2}\right)$$

壓縮空氣所需之工作爲

$$Wc = Wi + Wa$$

$$= RT_0 \log e\left(\frac{P_1}{P_0}\right) + JCp(T_2 - T_0)$$

壓縮空氣所需之工作,與循環之指示工作,二者之比例爲

$$\frac{Wc}{Wt} = \frac{RT_0 \log_e\left(\frac{P_1}{P_0}\right) + JCp(T_2 - T_0)}{JQ\left(1 - \frac{T_0}{T_2}\right)} \quad \cdots\cdots(3)$$

按熱力學
$$\frac{P_1}{P_0}=\frac{P_2}{P_3}=e^{\left(\frac{JQ}{RT_2}\right)}$$

故
$$\frac{Wc}{Wt}=\frac{T_0}{T_2-T_0}+\frac{JCp_o}{R\ log_e\frac{P_2}{P_3}}\cdots\cdots\cdots\cdots(4)$$

由第（4）公式,可見壓縮空氣所用之工作,及循環之指示工作,二者之比例,全賴循環上最高最低兩端之溫度,及其等溫度澎漲之壓力比例.兩端溫度相去愈遠,及壓力之比例愈大,則Wc與Wt之比例愈小.循環上最低之溫度可與尋常空氣之溫度相等,即 300°C 絕對溫度.其最高之溫度,則不能超過 700°C 絕對溫度.因在此種循環氣體在壓氣機內已達循環上最高溫度.今使循環上之最高溫度超過 700°C 絕對溫度.是使壓氣機受 700°C 絕對溫度以上之熱也.如此則壓氣機將受損傷矣.P_2及P_3二者之比例,則爲氣渦輪之體力所限.最高亦不可過五十.今設T_0等於 300°C 絕對溫度; T_2 等於 700°C絕對溫度;P_2及 P_3之比例等於五十.〔按米突制機械熱量 J=426.5, 空氣之等壓比熱 Cp=.2375, 而空氣之恆數 R=29,4〕代入第（4）公式

$$\frac{Wc}{Wt}=\frac{300}{400}+\frac{426.5\times.2375}{29.4\times3.912}=1.63$$

將所得數代入第（2）公式,其結果竟使氣渦輪之總機械效率在零之下.換言之,渦輪軸上之工作乃未足供給壓氣機之需要.卡諾循環之不適於實用,從可知矣.

B.　等壓循環（Constant Pressure Cycle）等壓循環之種類甚多,如不勒頓（Bravton）,提士爾（Diesel）,伊力孫（Ericsson）,等是也.姑就不勒頓循環而討論之.見第四圖.空氣自A至B受等能壓縮而壓力自P_0升至P_1.同時溫度則由T_0升至T_1.自A至B所需之壓縮工作爲

$$Wc=JCp(T_1-T_0)$$

自B至C,燃料在火箱內與空氣化合,而發生Q量之熱力.同時氣體之溫度自T_1升至T_2.溫度與熱量之關係爲

$$Q=Cp(T_2-T_1)$$

自C至D氣體發生等能伸漲(Adiabatic Expanssion),并使其溫度自T_2降至T_3.自D至A廢氣(Exhaust Gas)由渦輪排出而其所帶之熱量爲

$$q=Cp(T_3-T_0)$$

循環之効率爲

$$f=\frac{Q-q}{Q}=1-\frac{T_0}{T_1}$$

循環之指示工作爲

$$Wt=JQ\left(1-\frac{T_0}{T_1}\right)$$

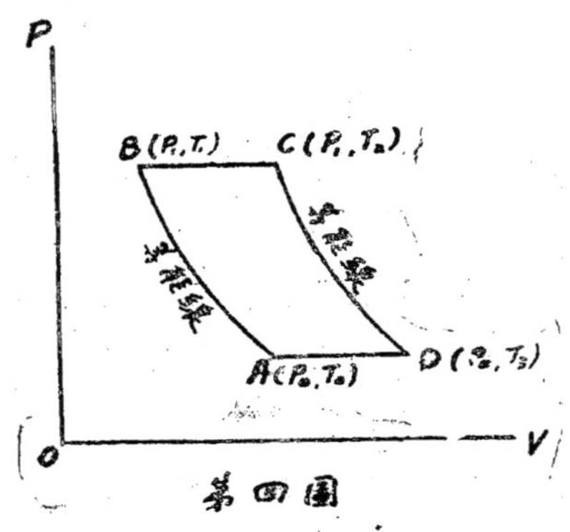

第四圖

壓縮空氣所需之工作,與循環所生之工作.二者之比例,爲

$$\frac{Wc}{Wt}=\frac{JCp(T_1-T_0)}{JQ\left(1-\frac{T_0}{T_1}\right)}$$

$$=\frac{CpT_1}{Q}=\frac{1}{\frac{T_2}{T_1}-1}=\frac{1}{\frac{T_3}{T_0}-1}\cdots\cdots\cdots\cdots(5)$$

由第(5)公式觀之,可知T_3與T_0二者之比例若高,則Wc與Wt之比例小.但T_0爲尋常空氣溫度所限,最低約爲300°C絕對溫度;而T_3則爲旋輪之抗熱性所限;最高不能超過700°C絕對溫度.茲以二數爲限,代入第(5)公式得

$$\frac{Wc}{Wt}=\frac{1}{\frac{700}{300}-1}=.75$$

將所得數代入第(2)公式得　　$E=.700-.729\times.75=.15$

可見不勒頓循環之効率亦甚低而不適於實用.

C.等壓循環而用等溫壓縮方法　不勒頓循環之大病為其施用等能壓縮方法.用等能壓縮之害有二:—(1)壓縮比例有一定之限制.過此則壓氣機內之溫度過高,而壓氣機易受損害.(2)壓氣機所消耗之工作過大,而使渦輪之總効率甚低.欲除二病莫善於利用等溫壓縮一途.等溫壓縮方法,不易在活塞壓氣機內施行,然在旋轉壓氣機則較易着手.因在旋轉壓氣機,空氣受多層級之壓縮始至其適當之壓力.在各層級之間,欲使空氣冷却,固甚易也.

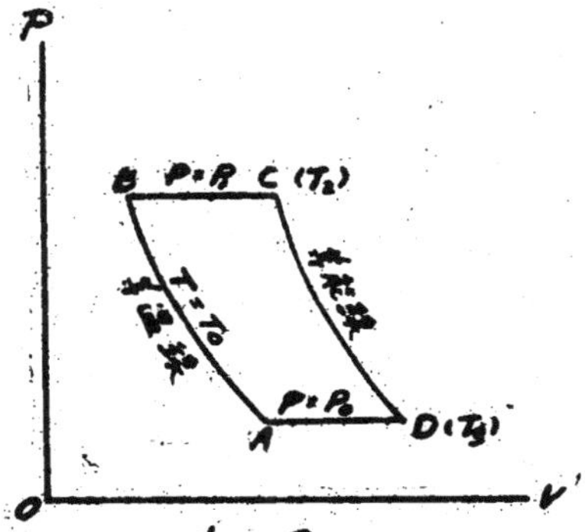

第五圖

見第五圖.空氣自A至B受等溫壓縮.其壓力自P_0增高至P_1,而溫度不變.壓縮所需之工作若化為熱量,等於

$$Q'=\frac{RT_0}{J}\log_e\left(\frac{P_1}{P_0}\right)$$

自B至C所受之熱量為

$$Q=Cp\left(T_2-T_0\right)$$

自C至D氣體發生等能伸漲.其產生之工作若化為熱量,等於

$$Q''=JCp\left(T_2-T_3\right)$$

自D至A所失之熱量為

$$q=Cp\left(T_3-T_0\right)$$

循環之効率為

$$f=\frac{Cp\left(T_2-T_0\right)-Cp\left(T_3-T_0\right)-\frac{RT_0}{J}\log_e\left(\frac{P_1}{P_0}\right)}{Cp\left(T_2-T_0\right)}\cdots\cdots\cdots\cdots(6)$$

按節(6)公式壓縮之比例愈高,則溫度T_2亦愈高,而同時循環之効率亦愈高.今設循環之壓縮比例爲80而T_2爲600°C絕對溫度,則T_3將爲2150°C.用以上數目代入節(6)公式,得循循之効率爲.635.壓氣機所需之工作,與渦輪所產生之工作二者之比例爲.325.而渦輪之總効率爲.29.似此結果雖不能與提士爾引擎之効率相較,然與其他活塞氣機相比,固不劣矣.

D.等壓循環而用等溫壓縮及重熱器方法　此種循環與C節所論者大概相同.其不同處,卽在此循環,空氣受壓後,須從重熱器(Heat Regenerator)經過而收回廢氣中大部分之熱力,然後始入火箱.空氣已受等溫度之壓縮,故其溫度在進入重熱器時爲300°C絕對溫度.使重熱器之面積極大,則廢氣中所有之熱力皆可爲空氣吸收.但事實上重熱器之面積不能大至無窮.故廢氣中之熱力祇有一部分可再供循環之用而已.

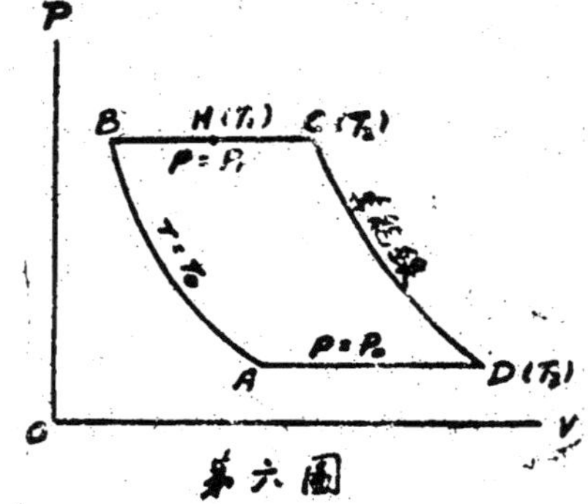

第六圖

第六圖指示此種循環之變化.空氣受等溫壓縮自A至B所用之熱力爲

$$Q' = \frac{RT_0}{J} \log_e \left(\frac{P_1}{P_0} \right)$$

自B至H,空氣在重熱器內吸收K量之熱力,而其溫度則自T_0升至T_1.

$$K = Cp\,(T_1 - T_0)$$

自H至C,空氣在火箱內與燃料化合,發生Q量之熱力,而其溫度再自T_1升至T_2

$$Q = Cp\,(T_2 - T_1)$$

自C至D氣體再經等能伸漲,其溫度自T_2降至T_3,而其壓力則自P_1降至P_0.

氣體經此伸漲所生之工作,若化爲熱量卽等於

$$Q'' = JCp(T_3 - T_2)$$

自D至A,氣體經過重熱器而向外排出

若重熱器能如理想之完善,則廢氣經過此器後其溫度當降至T_0而其在器內所放棄之熱量爲$Cp(T_2 - T_0)$.但在實際上重熱器之面積不能過大,故氣體之溫度不能降至T_0.且重熱器由發射及傳遞失熱甚多,故所收囘之熱力不外廢氣中之一部分而已.設重熱器之効率爲U,則

$$K = Cp(T_1 - T_0) = UCp(T_2 - T_0)$$

循環所受之熱量共爲Q＋K,而用以壓縮空氣者爲Q.'其隨氣體而排出者爲$Cp(T_2 - T_0)$.於是則熱力之變爲有用之工作者爲 $Q + K - Q' - Cp(T_2 - T_0)$.但其由燃料所供給之熱量爲Q.故循環之効率爲

$$f = \frac{(K+Q) - Q' - Cp(T_2 - T_0)}{Q} \quad \cdots\cdots\cdots\cdots(7)$$

設T_0爲 300°C 而T_2爲 700°C 絕對溫度,則此種循環所生之効果如第一表.

應用重熱器之利益,卽使等壓循環不用高壓比例,而能發生等量有用之工作.如使重熱器之効率爲0.75,壓力比例爲25,則渦輪之總効率爲0.30.若不用重熱器,則欲得此効率,非用60之壓縮比例不可.

由第一表可知循環之効率,與機械之効率,皆隨壓縮比例而增加.使60氣壓爲渦輪最高壓力之限制,而重熱器之効率爲0.75,則渦輪之總効率爲.363矣.有此好結果,可知氣渦輪之前程誠不可限量也.

第 一 表

壓縮比例 $\frac{P_1}{P_2}$		5	10	15	20	30	40	60	80	100
燃燒溫度 T_3		1120	1365	1533	1680	1880	2050	2300	2500	2670
受熱總量 Q+K		197	256	292	328	375	415	480	522	563
壓縮空氣所需之熱能 AWc		33	48	56	62	71	76	85	91	95
循環所發生之有用熱能 AWt		70	114	144	174	212	247	303	339	377
Wc/Wt 比例		0.47	0.42	0.39	0.36	0.34	0.31	0.28	0.26	0.25
機械總効率 E		0.36	0.39	0.42	0.44	0.45	0.47	0.49	0.51	0.52
燃料所供之熱量 Q	u=0.50 K=46	151	210	246	282	329	369	434	476	517
	u=0.75 K=69	128	187	223	259	306	346	411	453	494
	u=1.00 K=92	105	164	200	236	283	323	388	430	471
循環之熱力効率 f	u=0.00 K=0	0.36	0.45	0.49	0.53	0.57	0.60	0.63	0.65	0.67
	u=0.50 K=46	0.46	0.54	0.58	0.62	0.65	0.67	0.70	0.71	0.73
	u=0.75 K=69	0.55	0.61	0.64	0.67	0.70	0.71	0.74	0.75	0.76
	u=1.00 K=92	0.66	0.70	0.74	0.72	0.75	0.77	0.78	0.79	0.80
渦輪之總効率 fE	u=0.00 K=0	0.130	0.180	0.205	0.233	0.255	0.280	0.310	0.330	0.348
	u=0.50 K=46	0.167	0.210	0.245	0.270	0.290	0.315	0.342	0.360	0.380
	u=0.75 K=69	0.198	0.238	0.270	0.235	0.315	0.335	0.363	0.380	0.390
	u=1.00 K=92	0.239	0.273	0.300	0.323	0.337	0.360	0.382	0.402	0.415
每瓩氣體所供之熱量,加羅利		25	45	60	77	96	116	148	173	195
每馬力小時所需之氣體,瓩		25.5	14.3	10.3	8.2	6.7	5.5	4.3	3.7	3.3

E.等容循環.（Constant Volume Cycle）. 等容循環亦有應用等能壓縮及等溫壓縮二種.其用等能壓縮者,效率甚低,茲不具論.其用等溫壓縮之循環,則表示於第七圖.

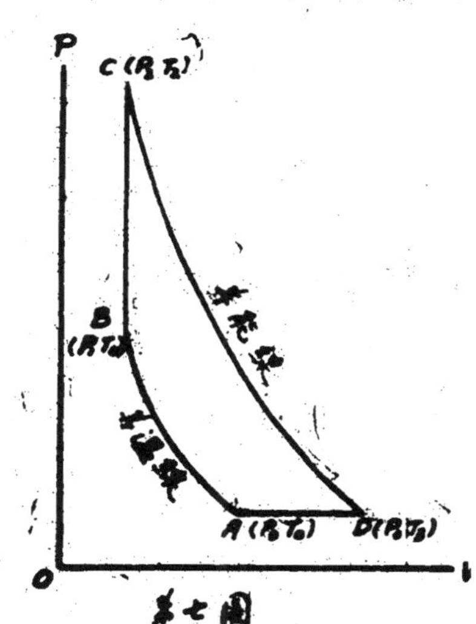

第七圖

按第七圖,空氣受等溫之壓縮自A至B,其壓力自P_0升至P_1而溫度不變.其所需之壓縮工作,變爲熱量,等於

$$Q'=ART_0\log_e\left(\frac{P_1}{P_0}\right)$$

自B至C所受之熱則爲

$$Q=Cv\,(T_3-T_0)$$

自C至D所生之工作,變爲熱量等於

$$Q''=Cp\,(T_3-T_b)$$

自D至A所失之熱爲

$$q=Cp\,(T_3-T_0)$$

循環之效率爲

$$f=\frac{Cv\,(T_3-T_0)-Cp\,(T_3-T_0)-ART_0\log_e\left(\frac{P_1}{P_0}\right)}{Cv\,(T_3-T_0)}\quad\cdots\cdots(8)$$

茲再設T_0爲300°C,T_3爲700°C絕對溫度,而以此種循環所生之效果列於第二表.

由第二表可知等容循環之機械效率頗高.因其壓氣機所消耗之工作在比較上爲甚小也.但此循環之弱點亦多.（1）等容循環不能應用高壓比例.如使壓縮比例爲10,則循環內之極高壓力已在80氣壓之上.但此壓力管理已感困難,若欲應用較高之壓縮比例,勢有不可.今使80氣壓可用於氣渦輪,然其總效率仍不外0.33而已.以之與D節所討論之循環相比,爲較低矣.

（2）等容循環之壓力不齊,故渦輪不能平穩旋轉.但用等容循環之渦輪,結構較簡,故小渦輪多採用此循環者.

第二表

壓縮比例 $\frac{P_1}{P_0}$	1	5	10	15	20
燃燒溫度 T_3	980	1820	2120	2850	3210
受熱量 Q	115	255	355	430	490
廢氣所失之熱量 q	92	92	92	92	92
壓縮空氣所需之熱能 AWc	0	33	48	56	62
循環所發生之有用熱能 AWt	23	130	215	282	336
Wc/Wt 比例	0	0.25	0.22	0.20	0.19
循環之効率	0.19	0.51	0.61	0.66	0.68
機械總効率	0.70	0.52	0.54	0.55	0.56
渦輪之總効率	0.13	0.27	0.33	0.37	0.38
P_3 與 P_1 之比例	3.27	6.1	8.1	9.5	10.7
P_3 與 P_0 之比例	3.27	30.4	80.7	143	214
每小時每馬力所用之空氣瓩	39.5	9.4	5.5	4.1	3.4
可供外用之熱能	16	64	116	156	188

以上不過擇其較要之循環加以討論.其由以上各種循環略加更改而生之循環甚多.最著爲噴水入火箱而使其溫度低落,及利用重熱器以蒸發水汽各循環.此等循環効率不能超過D節所論之循環.然其所用之溫度較低.動作較爲可靠.

實驗

亞孟高（Armengaud）與利馬兒（Lemale）二氏在聖丁尼斯(St. Denis)工程實驗室,製成氣渦輪一座,如第八圖.其結構之大概與克提斯（Curtis）蒸氣渦輪相似.依壓氣機之大小,可發生四百至八百馬力.渦輪之速率爲每分鐘四千轉.其制速器則爲哈同式(Hartung Governor).此機可隨渦輪負荷之輕重,限制渦輪所用之空氣及燃料.渦輪之附機有壓氣機抽水機及抽油機.

第八圖

火箱爲鐵製.其形如梨,內裹以矽化炭,如第九圖.渦輪發動時,液質燃料受壓經噴油器(Atomizer),由E射入火箱同時空氣受壓由D流入而與之混合.此種混合氣經過G處時與發熱之白金絲相遇而燃燒.燃料與空氣自外源源以來,而火箱內之燃燒繼續不絕,故火箱內之壓力及溫度不變.由燃燒所生之熱氣則自H氣管射入渦輪而使之旋轉.H氣管之結構與得拉禾(De Laval)蒸汽渦輪所用之伸漲汽管相似.熱氣經過此管後其壓力與溫度俱下降,而渦輪可免過熱之病.

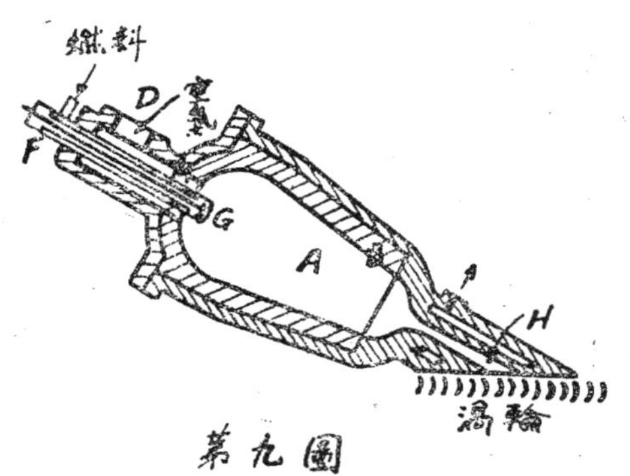

第九圖

旋輪之構造如第十圖.此輪之特點卽其內部有A,B,E等水洞.冷水自輪軸內之小洞流入經E而A與B.再由A,B二洞而入輪葉(Bucket).其目的卽欲旋輪冷卻.已熱之水則由輪葉及旋輪上與E相當之洞流回輪軸而外排.

第十圖

空氣之供給全賴雷陀壓氣機(Rateau Compressor).此機旋輪上之輪葉構造適與渦輪之輪葉相反.全機爲多數之旋輪集合而成.旋輪轉時卽將空氣步步壓縮以至適當之壓力.雷陀機所用之速率極大.故可與渦輪同軸.今日雷陀機之効率尙未甚高,普通爲百分之六十五而已.

此氣渦輪在聖丁尼斯工程試驗場已有數載,動作極爲靈便.可見氣渦輪已爲事實而非紙上之空談也.渦輪軸上有六百馬力.但半數爲壓氣機所消耗.故可供外用者,不過三百馬力而已.其所用之油則每小時約三百磅.但該工程學會至今未有正式之宣佈.

因氣渦輪之輕便,法國海軍近來多利用此機,以放射魚雷.一百二十馬力之機,其重量不過六百二十七磅,卽每馬力爲五磅左右而已.

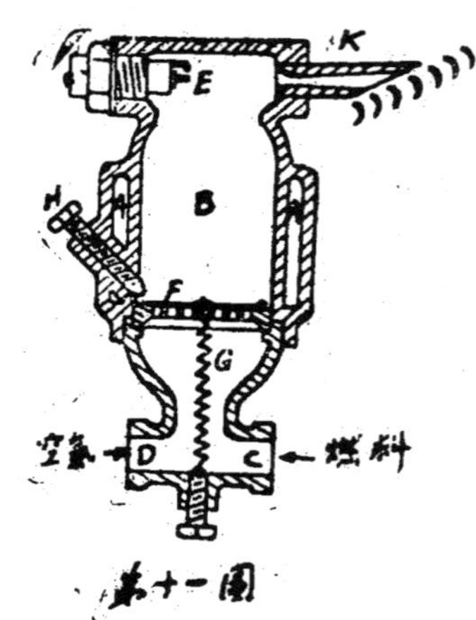

第十一圖

加拉滑丁(Karavodine)在巴黎(Paris)造有二馬力之氣渦輪一座.此機極爲簡單,而饒趣味.其火箱之結構如第十一圖.箱爲鐵製,外有水套.在火箱之下端有入口C,爲氣體燃料入箱之路,對面有亦口D,爲空氣入箱之路.二口皆有開閉機關（圖不示明）,爲調劑燃料成分之用.旋輪轉動時箱內之壓力較箱外之壓力爲低.在G之混合氣卽推開開關F而入火箱.至相當之時E卽發火.其火星能使混氣燃燒而增其壓力.箱內之壓力旣高,開關卽自閉,而熱氣由氣管K冲入渦輪.氣體已由K管射出,故箱內之壓力漸低.再借旋輪抽氣之作用,及熱氣外動之恆性,而火箱內之壓力竟能較低於箱外之氣壓.在此時間,空氣與燃料,借外面氣壓之力,再入火箱.機器之動作遂循環不絕.

欲知火箱內壓力之變遷,可閱第十二圖.自A至E,火箱內之壓力較低於箱外.混氣卽在該時流入火箱.自E至D火箱內之氣壓較高而熱氣由氣管衝入渦輪.在B時燃料卽開始燃燒.至C而壓力達其最高之點.由第十二圖更可知每循環所需之時間不外0.026秒鐘而已.換言之,每分鐘混氣在箱內爆發約二千二百次.

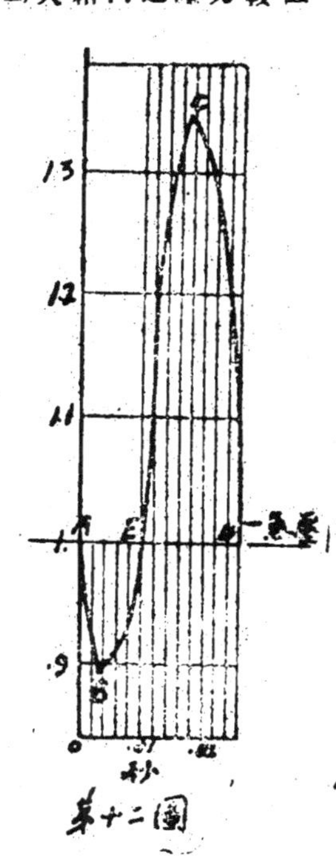

第十二圖

此機共用火箱四個.每箱之容積爲 200 c. c.(14立方吋)旋輪之直徑爲150c.（5.9吋）.其速率爲每分鐘一萬轉.每小時用油約4.5Kg（9磅）而發生2.1馬力.

由效率一方面觀之.此機似乎欠佳.然其效率低小爲意中事.（1）機小則效率自低.（2）所用之空氣未曾先受壓縮.（3）熱氣衝入渦輪時其速率時變,因之損失動力甚多.若使渦輪較大而應用較佳之循環,則其効果必遠勝以上所得.

結論

由以上之討論觀之.可知今日氣渦輪之効率,未能超出提士爾引擎之効率.因氣渦輪之循環効率雖高,而其機械効率則甚低也.其機械効率之所以不高,則因壓氣機之効率太低.但壓氣之効率有改良之可能,故氣渦輪之効率尚有增進之望.

効率固爲動機主要條件之一,而不能爲其絕對標準.機體之輕重也.扭力之均否也,結構之繁簡也,燃料之貴賤也,往往於動機之取捨有莫大之關係.例如提士爾引擎之效率雖高,而不用於飛艇.蒸汽渦輪之效率雖低,而多用於發電所.氣渦輪之効率.現雖未能超出提士爾引擎之上,然其結構簡而機體輕.故在陸上雖不能與提士爾引擎爭雄,而在潛艇及商船則有代興之勢.其在汽車及飛艇上之應用雖有機體稍重之嫌,然其扭力均而燃料賤,故氣渦輪不日成爲汽車及飛艇之原動機關,亦意中事耳.

氣渦輪今日尙在試驗時期.其重要問題,如壓氣機所需工作之大小,燃料及空氣之成分,燃燒之溫度,燃燒所需之時間,火箱之容積,水汽在火箱內之影響.及氣體在伸縮氣管內之動作等,皆有待於學者之硏究.若能在試驗室內將此數端完全解決,則氣渦輪之成功爲事實矣.

提士引擎在今日工業界中之地位

單炳慶

溯自德人羅杜甫提士（Rudolf Desiel）於一千八百九十四年發明提士引擎迄今三十餘年.迭經改良.日臻完善.故用之爲原動力者亦漸多.而我國工業界之先進.亦知提士引擎較其他原動機爲優.用之者已不乏其人.故提士引擎之所以優勝於其他原動機者.約有四端.略述於下.

（一）提士引擎之效率爲各種原動機之冠.普通四程式之提士引擎其效率常可在百分之三十以上.而最新式最完備極大之蒸汽凝結透平機亦不過百分之二十.至若普通蒸汽機.則僅在百分之十左右.由下列之約略計算.即可明瞭提士引擎因效率較高而省燃料之理.

設一四程式之提士引擎.其效率爲36%.

每小時每匹馬力＝2,545 B.T.U.

則每小時每匹馬力應用去之熱力爲 $\frac{2,545}{0.36}=7,060$ B.T.U.

設提士引擎所用之黑油每磅有18,000 B.T.U.

則每小時每匹馬力應用之油爲 $\frac{7,060}{18,000}=0.392$磅.

設每噸黑油售洋四十六元.

則每小時每匹馬力應用之燃料費爲 $\frac{0.392}{2,000}\times 46=0.009$元.

又設一普通完備之凝汽透平機其效率爲10%.

則每小時每匹馬力應用去之熱力爲 $\frac{2,545}{.10}=25,450$ B.T.U.

設每磅煤有12,000 Btu.

則每小時每匹馬力應用之煤爲

$\frac{25450}{12000}=2.12$磅.（生火時應用之煤尚除外.）

設每噸售洋十二元.

則每小時每匹馬力應用之燃料費爲$\frac{2.12}{2000}\times12=0.0127$元.

兩相比較,則蒸汽機每小時每匹馬力須多用熱力18,390 B.T.U.或多用燃料費洋三厘七毫.驟視之似爲值極微.然此僅爲每小時每匹馬力多用之熱力或費用.設一原動機有數千匹馬力須用數十年之久,則用提士引擎所省之費用,當不知凡幾矣.

由是觀之,提士引擎之省燃料,可以明矣.雖然,或有謂用水力原動機,可利用天然瀑布以爲動力,無需燃料.其費用將更減省.然而建造非易,價值昂貴,且瀑布非各地皆有.不若提士引擎之隨處可以設置也.又有以爲水銀透平機與蒸汽透平機相連而成動力機.(水銀沸點極高,自水銀鍋爐蒸發成水銀氣,入水銀透平機工作後,洩至水銀凝結器,以水爲冷却物.而在水銀凝結器中之水銀,因其溫度極高,在凝結時,水遇之卽爲其蒸發而成蒸汽.故水銀凝結器卽可作爲蒸汽鍋爐.此蒸汽卽用於蒸汽透平機,)其效率之高,可與提士引擎不相上下者,然水銀產額有限,價值昂貴,用之者極少.更有以爲高效率之內燃機與簡單之透平機合併而成內燃透平機.可得甚高之效率.然而內燃溫度極高,機件每易損壞.迄今猶未見成功.是則今日工業界中自當以提士引擎之效率爲最高矣.

（二）提士引擎可用高壓力空氣開動.蒸汽機則先須燃煤於爐,使鍋中之水蒸發而成蒸汽,至一定壓力時,方可應用.其間須費數小時.與數十秒鐘卽可開動之提士引擎相較,便不便之相去,何啻倍蓰.

（三）提士引擎汽缸中之空氣經壓縮後,常在每方英寸五百磅左右,熱度在華氏表一千度左右.故燃料射入後,卽化氣燃燒.非如其他內燃機之尙須用化氣機及火星塞熱球等.故管理簡易,修理亦便.

（四）提士引擎較之同一馬力之蒸汽機所占地位略小.因蒸汽機除

引擎外,尙須有鍋爐等設備也.

以上所述僅舉其最顯著者.其他如缺乏水源之地,用提士引擎爲最宜.如上海法租界盧家灣發電廠,即因缺少水量,不適於建築蒸汽發電廠而用提士引擎,其一例也.

凡原動機效率愈高,則燃料及費用愈省,此爲原動機之主要條件.今提士引擎之效率既爲各原動機之冠,則其在今日工業界中地位之重要,可以概見.故現今千四馬力以下之發力廠,用提士引擎者日多,惟現在所製之引擎每部最大不過四千馬力,過大之發力廠,因所需部數必多,價值既昂,占位亦大,尙難適用.吾國今日工業方在萌芽,大規模之原動機尙非所需,而灌溉,碾米,織造以及鄉村小規模之發電,其有賴於提士引擎者至殷.外商之競相輸入,廠家之努力倣造,良有以也.且提士引擎以其燃料輕便易貯,用於船舶者亦甚多.俄國近且有用之於機車者.是則提士引擎非特在工業界中占重要之地位,而在航業農業交通界中亦爲發達之要具矣.

南洋季刊第一卷第二期電機工程號目錄（已於本年四月出版）

熱力工程界之新趨勢

殷文友

現今歐美各國,工業日益發達,其所賴以發達之原動力(Power)自日以增加,而中央原動力廠(Central Power Station)亦應運而生.中央原動力廠者,即中央發電力廠也.分布動力,必有藉乎電,故電實輸送動力之媒介.大抵事業愈發達,則分工之原理愈顯,電力廠之流行,可使諸小工業放棄其獨具之原動力創造機關,而惟以購進電力爲動力之源.此等現象,固爲諸小工業日益發達,有以助成之,而同時原動力廠,亦足以促進諸小工業之振興者也.

默察我中國之現象爲何如乎?工業方在萌芽,固不足與歐美抗,然而諸小工業之漸興正有賴乎原動力廠之供給,則在在足以見之.試以吾蘇省爲例,近則有振華電力廠之創設,此即其徵兆也.

工業界之現象,就原動力之供給一端而論,旣有日趨於分工之一途.換言之,原動力之爲物,在乎『躉造而批用』.是故所謂熱力工程界之任務,大都亦傾向於此.熱力工程(Heat Power Engineering)云者,亦可名之爲原動力製造工程.惟此原動力製造工程,有藉乎熱之一能力耳.如由煤炭造作蒸汽,由蒸汽產生動力,即熱力工程界或原動力製造工程界之任務也.

熱力工程界現方日進不已,研究其所用工具之效率(Efficiency).在初工程界以爲已至無可發展之境者,今則發展之方向繁多,而試驗實行,未嘗或輟.茲舉其犖犖大者,以見工程界趨勢之一斑.

(一)利用高壓及高溫　普通熱力工程界所採用之汽壓及汽溫,大都不出乎二百五十磅(250Lb.)及六百度(600°F)以內.今則因工程界發展之力已窮,乃思利用高壓及高溫以破之.夫普通引擎(Engine),效率甚低,以引擎中效率較高之透平(Turbine,爲引擎之一種)論,其熱效率且常不到百分之二十五（25%）其故由於透平中之蒸汽祇一部分能變爲有用工作（Useful Work）餘則分成爲種種損失（Loss）。而損失中之最大者莫如冷結器損失（Condenser Loss）。試以替菲表（T, ф diagram）表之如第一圖。蒸汽在透平間P之一點情形變至Q點若除去透平間種種較小之損失不計單記冷結器（Condenser）之損失則知A與B二面積之和之所示者爲蒸汽入透平時所含之熱量而B之一面積爲蒸汽出透平時所含之熱量此後者之熱量即入冷結器而成爲一種損失者也冷結器內有流動水（Circulating water），此熱即爲流動水吸去而失其效用又A面

第一圖

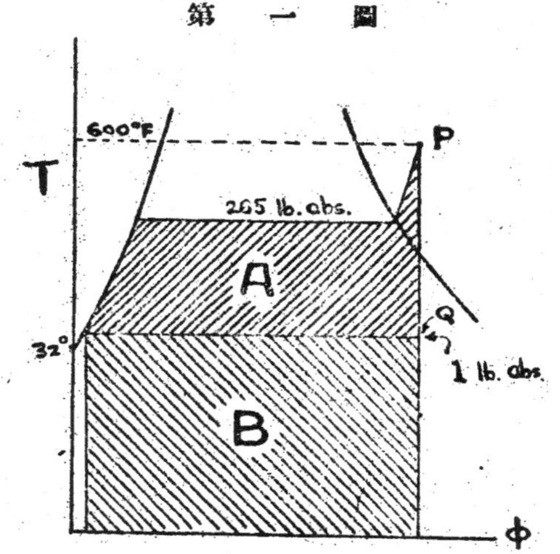

積之所示者爲理想中之有用工作此面積與A加B全面積之比$\left(\frac{A}{A+B}\right)$稱之爲理想熱效率（Ideal Thermal Efficiency）若實際上之有用工作不過爲理想上之什之七八此實際有用工作之相當面積與A加B全面積之比$\left(\frac{KA}{A+B}\right.$，其中K爲一係數約可爲十分之七或八），稱之爲實際熱效率（Actual Thermal Efficiency），即余所述爲百分之二十五以下之效率也此實際熱效率與理想熱效率之比又稱爲引擎效率（Engine Efficiency）總之工程師之目的在乎三效率之皆能增加而已。

若須理想熱效率增加則既知冷結器內之一大損失爲無可免者於是惟有增加汽壓及汽溫之法。

設令蒸汽之汽壓及汽溫增高則蒸汽入透平時之狀況在替菲表間以

一點P表之者成爲第二圖所示.試以第一圖及第二圖比較之,則知有用工作A面積與損失B面積之比

第二圖

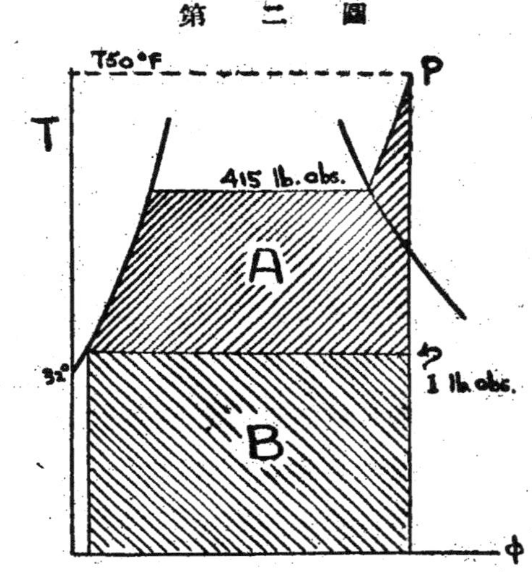

$\left(\frac{A}{B}\right)$，在第二圖者大於第一圖.於此可知直接去冷結器損失之不可能,而設法減少之者卽增加效率之一法也.吾人知歐美各國,今日起用五百五十磅(550 lb.)汽壓,與七百五十度（750°F）汽溫者,實繁有徒.甚焉者,有起用高壓,直逼至千二百磅（1200 lb.）,以爲嘗試.英國現正設計一試驗所,擬造三千四百磅（3400 lb.）之蒸汽,壯哉工程界之所爲.夫理想爲事實之母,進步必有待乎嘗試也.

（二）汲出半伸漲汽以熱飼水　工程界誠所謂無隙不入,苟有其道必竟其功者.飼水（Feed water）未入鍋爐（Boiler）之前,利用諸附小引擎（Auxiliaries）內之廢汽（Exhaust）,以溫熱之.而其溫度最高不過可二百十度（210°F）.今則利用透平中腰汲出之汽以溫熱之,其溫度乃大增.例如汲出之汽其汽壓若爲五磅（5 lb.）則理想的飼水溫度,約可至二百三十度（230°F）若爲十磅,則可至二百四十度（240°F）………等等.飼水之溫度增.則所需送入鍋爐間之煤炭減,因飼水有增得熱故也.而增得之熱,卽爲自冷結器所節得之損失.蓋吾人方病蒸汽一入冷結器,無形間卽成大損失.今則蒸汽之一部分在透平間半伸漲（Partially Expanded）後,卽汲出之以與飼水攙合.故應入冷結器之損失.乃爲飼水所利用矣.此法今歐美中央電力廠類皆採用之.惟汲汽熱水之方法,卽級數問題（No. of Stages）殊費研

究.蓋級數愈多,則飼水之溫度愈得盡量增加,而同時因所用器皿之數亦增,成一經濟的問題.工程師之目的,在就各廠之情形,求其至當之解決耳.

（三）汲出蒸汽復行加熱　熱力工程界中既知蘭根循環（Rankine Cycle，第一第二圖所示者）之不能滿意,而又不克直接取得卡諾循環,以爲替代.於是思得種種近於後者之循環,以爲彌補.若前述『汲出蒸汽以熱飼水』之一法,即其例也.試以此一法之循環,表之如左,則成第三圖.此時之理想熱效率亦即A面積與A加B面積之比.然較第一圖第二圖均大勝.不獨此法爲然也.今如汲出透平間之汽加熱之,復送入透平作二度之伸張,則可得循環如第四圖.此時之汽壓不期然而增高,然須知惟利用此一循環而後可.吾人知汽溫宜有一定之限度.如云七百五十度（750°F）,過此則通常之透平材料不能耐.（固知工程界人,方在試驗良材,而吾人不妨假定以此爲止境.）若蒸汽之汽溫一定,則知汽壓至四百餘磅,亦已爲止境.過此則蒸汽在透平間伸張,將不須臾而成濕汽.由

第三圖

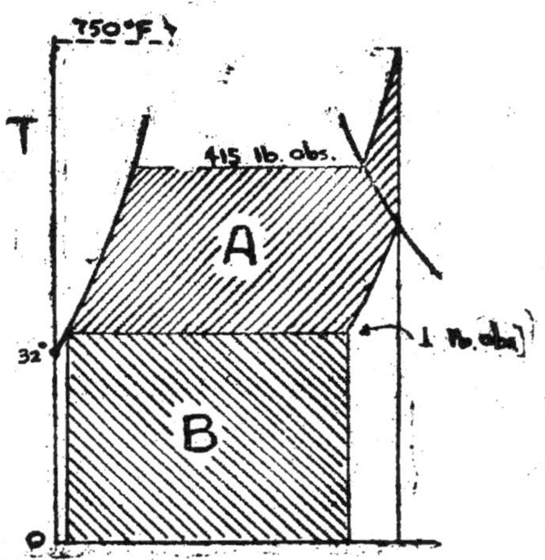

第四圖

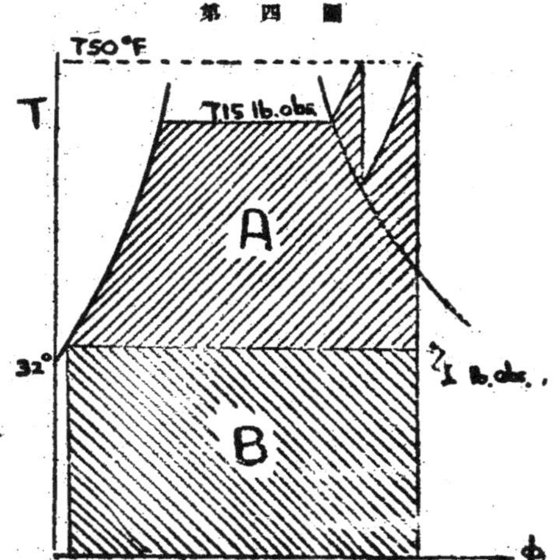

實驗知濕蒸汽之伸張,實較乾蒸汽之伸張,損失爲大.故就冷結器之損失言,增高汽壓,無往而不收效（至千二百磅爲止）.然以視濕蒸汽伸張之損失即所謂液動損失（Hydaulic Loss）之巨,則不若不增.今若汲出此將成濕之汽加熱之,使成過熱（Superheated）,乃復導入作二度之伸張,則其困難轉消.故應用此法,亦可如其餘二法增加透平之效率.觀圖知此一循環既自別於蘭根氏之循環,復非即卡諾氏之循環.其效能實介於二者之間.今美國有數廠採用是法,其汽壓爲五百五十磅（550 lb.）,汽溫爲七百五十度（750°F）先使入複式透平之高壓方伸張之,繼復汲出導入鍋爐內之熱管,使成過熱.終乃引入其低壓方作二度之伸張.又有一二廠應用是法於單式透平者,其最初壓力爲一千磅或千二百磅（1000 lb. or 1200 lb.）在高壓透平伸張至約三百五十磅,（350 lb.）然後加熱,復送入低壓透平,使伸張至冷結器內而後止.

上述三法,皆熱力工程界對於透平作困苦研究之成績也.凡新興之廠莫不思所以一試之.卽偶不能得實際上之酬報（往往爲設備費用所限）,亦所不計.而就現狀觀之,則可斷其爲好現象也.

熱力工程界所恃以產生動力之工具,透平固其中佼佼者.而鍋爐亦居重要位置之一.鍋爐通常之效率約在百分之七十以內（70％）,其百分之三十,則分成種種損失.其走失於烟囱外者,居其大半,其他若爐壁傳失之熱,若煤之未完全燃燒,而漏入火格子下者,亦佔其一部分,工程界甯願坐聽損失,不別求消減之方？若今之試驗不倦,而爲中央電力廠所特別注意者,則有下之二法焉.

（一）起用粉煤　用粉煤（Powdered Coal）之利益,在使煤能在鍋爐間充分燃燒其初塊煤（Bulk Coal）之漏入於火格子（Grate）下,未經完全燃燒之損失,今則可以減免.且炭養化合,調劑未得其宜之不完全燃燒亦免.此之不完全燃燒,卽廢氣之走失自烟囱者,含有一養化炭（Co）氣之由來也.若是應用粉煤,旣可增進鍋爐之效率.且供應鍋爐之負荷,有大小咸宜之便.卽如所用煤炭之等級,亦宜優宜劣.其初劣等之塊煤,有不宜於某種煤床(Stoker)者,今以之加工舂爲粉形,則無有不相宜者矣.工業界所未敢遽行採用是法者,以在備此粉煤之種種設備耳.美國如 Lakeside Station of Milwaukee Railway & Light Co. 及 Cahokia Station of The Union Plant Electric Light and Power Co. 等,皆著名用粉煤之廠也.

(二)應用預熱氣箱　前已言之鍋爐間最大之損失,莫若走失於烟囱間者.故歷來有置節熱器(Economizer)於烟囱下部,中貫飼水,使廢氣中所含熱之一部分,經節熱器爲飼水吸收.不幸廢氣所含熱之全部旣不能完全利用.且凡廠之充分用『汲出汽以熱飼水者』,則用節熱器轉屬多事.要之,無論如何,廢氣內之熱,尙有充分利用之道,此卽歐洲早經嘗試,頗見有效之設備預熱氣箱(Air Preheater)法是也.其法卽利用烟囱間之熱,經預熱氣箱,以熱將送鍋爐間燃燒之『空氣』.此法旣可節得廢熱,抑且煤爲空氣預熱,其燃燒亦增完全,(Perfect)故近今美國各大廠間,莫不注意及此.雖有病其空氣溫度過高,有害於某種之煤床(Stoker)者.然據美國(The Underfeed Stoker Co.公司之計算,每增加氣溫二三十度(20° or 30°F),至少可省煤百分之一.

上述關於熱力工程界對於鍋爐及透平之種種努力,惟建造大動力之廠,方足以語此.換言之,惟動力建造,乃可以享此優越權利.吾國實業界中人,其急起直追,庶無爲歐美各國專美於前乎!

揮發油引擎熱力效率之研究

黃　潔

揮發油引擎爲內燃引擎之一種.其用途至大最著者應用於汽車.飛機飛艇.及坦克 (Tank) 砲車等.此種引擎都係四行程週期 (Four Stroke Cycle) 而二行程週期(Two Stroke Cycle)爲較少.

最初計算引擎理論之熱力效率（Theoretical thermal efficiency）.乃假設氣缸（Cylinder）內燃燒過之氣體.與純空氣有同樣之性質及變化.此效率之高低.在乎引擎之壓縮比（Compression ratio）之增減.其關係已明示於下列公式. $\text{Efficiency} = 1 - \left(\frac{1}{R}\right)^{r-1}$、R卽引擎之壓縮比.由製造引擎時定之.

後知氣缸中燃燒過之氣體.與空氣大不相同.由是照空氣性質所算之效率太高.不能定實在氣缸中之熱力損失.遂名前者爲空氣標準之熱力效率 (Air standard thermal efficiency).用以作引擎熱力效率最高之標準而已.

第二種算法.先分析氣缸內燃燒過氣體之化學成分.再依其各分子比熱（Specific heat）之變化而定.此各分子之比熱隨熱度而高.不若空氣比熱之不變也.由此所得之效率.較爲準確.是名理論之渥拖週期熱力效率（Theoretical "Otto"cycle thermal efficiency）.其所示之數.卽能力 (Energy) 之有化成工作之可能者.其餘均係損失.不能致用.上述效率祇包括燃燒時之損失.自此數再行減去在汽缸中之損失與消耗.卽係引擎之指示效率（Indicated thermal efficiency). 卽百分之熱能(Heat energy)加入引擎後.由引擎換成若干機能（Mechanical energy）之數也.由此再除去所有機械上之損失.卽係淨得工作（Net work）之效率（Efficieney based upon brake horsepower）.又名引擎之總效力（Overall efficiency）.既明效率之分別.茲將其在設計或運用時所應注意各點略述於後.

(1)壓縮比（Compression ratio）

如壓縮比增高.則效率增加.

（A）就理論言.因公式爲 Eff. = 1 − $\left(\frac{1}{R-1}\right)^{r-1}$.其中R爲壓縮比.r爲燃燒過氣體之比熱（Specific heat）於壓力不變（Constant pressure）與容積不變（Constant volume）之比.若壓縮比加高.則效率亦大.

（B）就事實言.高壓縮能加高效率.其理有三.（1）減少內部露於燃燒室（Combustion chamber）之面積.因壓縮率增高.即空隙（Clearance volume）減少.即面積之暴露於高熱度者減少.熱力之爲氣缸壁所傳散者當然亦少.是則壓力增高.而工作（work）與效率均增也.（2）減少熱力損失之時間.或縮短燃燒之時間.而熱力之損失者可稍減.（3）加重所吸入之燃燒劑（Combustible charge）因空隙減少.所遺留燒過之氣（Residual gas）亦少.即吸入之新燃燒劑加多.而其熱度則減低.（因燃燒過之氣.熱度甚高.）若是則工作加多.損失又減矣.

但如壓縮比增加太高.亦有流弊.蓋以其熱度（Temperature）隨壓縮比而亦高也.壓縮比過高.其爆發時之壓力與全週期（Whole cycle）之熱度均高.則非特熱力損失于周圍冷卻水（Cooling water）中者增多.且因氣門與活塞之太熱.引起先期爆發（Pre-ignition）及 detonation.則其效率反而大減矣.

(2)油類之本性

用酒精之引擎效率最高.用本茶爾（Benzole）者次之.用揮發油者又次之.因酒精.火焰之傳佈（Flame propagation）較遲.成分較純.並因須多量之熱力以助其汽化（Vaporization）.吸入之燃燒劑溫度甚低.而全週期之熱度因之皆低.是以損失可減少.而高壓縮比可用.不致生上述之弊.惟酒精

有一弊.即汽化與傳佈之困難(Troubles of carburetion and distribution).且其價貴於揮發油.此其應用上之大障礙也.

(3)空氣與油相互之比

凡空氣之成數少於理論所需之數(Theoretical air value),(此數由油之化學成分所定.使油質燃燒完全毫無廢棄時之數)則養氣不足使油質燃燒完全.所藏熱能(Heat energy)半由排洩放出.不能應用.其效率自然低下.

若油過少.則效率亦低.因(a)多加之空氣於排洩時多帶出熱力.(b)燃燒太遲.非特所發之能力不足.引擎不克平穩轉動.且當排洩廢氣時.尚在燃燒.及新入之燃燒劑遇之.即於未入氣缸之前.或在化油器(Carbureter)中.先已燃燒.此現象名曰『退火』(Back fire).

若油與空氣之比.略少於理論之數.則其效率較爲最高.因其所含之總熱量較少.熱度低.熱力之經氣缸壁上傳出者亦少.且熱度既低.其燃燒過氣體之比熱(此種比熱隨熱度而增)亦低.在同量熱能(Constant heat energy)中.能得較高之爆發壓力(Ignition pressure.)而熱力之由排洩而出者亦減.(因其比熱減低).此所以能得較高之效率也.此種結果.於引擎試驗中極易得之.

(4)燃燒室(Combustion chamber)之式樣

若引擎燃燒室成圓球形.則效率最高.因就同容積論.圓球形之面積.比任何體之面積爲小.引擎之熱力損失因此亦少.故燃燒室之面積愈少愈佳.

(5)氣缸壁

壁之構造亦有關係.凡壁面粗糙而不整齊者.比光滑面易於吸收熱力.以傳諸周圍之冷卻水中.故燃燒室擦光之引擎.其效率較高.

(6)氣缸之大小

凡引擎內部面積與體積之比愈小.則效率愈高.其理已言之矣.但各物

之容積.隨物之單直線之三次方（Cubic of linear dimension）而變.而面積則隨物之單直線之二次方而變.若是則氣缸之容積愈大.（如其他之情形不變）.則熱力之損失愈少矣.於此可知引擎大.則效率高.但亦有限止.過限則所吸燃燒劑太多.引擎之各部易起過熱.（Over heated），並不克担當其過大之壓力.若將各部加重.則他種損失如機械損失亦增矣.

(7)引擎之行程 (Stroke)

設有二引擎.其活塞之排積（Piston displacement）與壓縮比均相等.當活塞在上死點（Upper dead center）時.長行程之引擎.其內部面積與體積之比.比短行程之引擎為小.專就此點而論.則長行程能得高效率.但在活塞速度（Piston speed）相同時.在長行程氣缸中所燃過之氣體.須較長之時間方得膨脹完全.若是則正在膨脹之氣體接觸於氣缸壁者較久.熱力之被傳出者較多.故就此點論.則短行程之引擎為有利.其實在低速度時.長行程（Long stroke）之引擎弊過於利.故短行程之引擎為適用.在高速度時.長行程之引擎利過於弊.故其效率為高.且在壓縮時.熱力損失多.壓縮熱度（Compression temperature）較低.而較高之壓縮比可用.不致有先期爆發及"detonation"之現象.

(8)速 度

速度低則吸入之燃燒劑易熱至與引擎同度.而重量減少.且爆發之時間長.在膨脹時之熱力損失更多.其壓力亦低.故效率弱.若過高則機械損失（Mechanical loss）太大.因此種損失隨速度之二次方而變.且速度過高.其限數易到.則易起先期爆發等之弊.而燃燒時因時間太短.所起化學作用更不能完全.〔在高熱時.氣體有分解（dissociation）之現象.故化學作用，（Chemical action）本不能真正完全.〕

(9)氣缸之斜放(Off-set cylinder)

在熱力方面此種斜放有利有弊.如熱力損失增多是其弊.體積不變之

時（Constant volume）較長是其利.二者大致相等.故未能斷定有無關著之益.惟在機械方面其利甚大.

（10）火焰之傳佈（Flame propagation）

火燄之傳佈速.則能於體積不變時燃燒完全,故效率增高.惟過速則易起"detonation".此種性質爲燃燒劑所固有.改變其相互之成分.可改變其遲速.

（11）發火塞（Spark plug）

爆發速.損失少.而爆發之遲速.系於發火塞.故與效率亦有關係.發火塞之地位最爲重要.以能置於中心.使四周之距離愈短爲愈妙.

（12）爆發之時間與活塞之地位（Ignition timing）

爆發之時間.與燃燒完全（Complete combustion）有密切之關係.因燃燒劑之燃燒速度過遲.不能在體積不變時完全燃燒.惟有改早於活塞未至上死點時卽行發火.是故當活塞方過體積不變時.燃燒卽已完全.則所得工力最大.而效率亦高.在高速度之引擎尤爲重要.惟發火太早.活塞所受之壓力在未至上死點時.與其行動之方向相反.此爲流弊.若能使發火不提早.而燃燒則於短時間中完全.則其效率當更高矣.

（13）活門開放之時間（Valve timing）

吸入門（Inlet valve）開放與閉合之遲早.支配燃燒劑吸入之多少.排洩門（Exhaust valve）關閉之遲早.定熱力損失於排洩時之多寡.排洩殘氣之完全與否,以及膨脹之度數.蓋欲殘氣完全放出.惟有使排洩門於膨脹未完全時卽行開放而減低効率.

（14）吸入管之熱點（Hot spot in induction manifold）

此熱點（Hot spot）能提高效率.因在驟改引擎速度與工力時.油與空氣之成分大變.加以氣化與傳佈之困難.每使已化氣之油.重行凝結於管中.若將此管完全加熱.或將入內之空氣加熱.使油再行氣化.則易有其他之流

弊.今將油類易凝聚之處加熱.使已凝之油遇之卽再化氣.有助於效率者甚大而無流弊.

(15) "Detonation"

高壓縮比旣得收效於重油引擎.學者乃幷思加高揮發油引擎之壓縮比.蓋 Otto 週期之效率比 Diesel 週期之效率.在同壓縮比時爲高.故若能將揮發油引擎之壓縮比亦加至十三左右.其效率比重油引擎爲更高.(若壓縮比超過十四.則其他損失太大.不合應用矣.)按此種引擎之空氣標準效率.在壓縮比五時爲百分之四十九.在壓縮比十時爲百分之六十一.其所增之多少可以想像.惟 Detonation 爲唯一之阻力.若能免此困難.則可成揮發油引擎未有之奇功.而燃料亦可減省矣.故歐州學者(德未知其詳.英國有多人正在研究解決之方法.)三數年前卽已研究.惟尙未能竟其全功.而用 "Ricardo head" 之引擎能得稍高之壓比.卽 Mr. Ricardo 之一部分成功也.其原理與方法甚繁.當俟另篇述之.

此外引擎各種之損失.以及吸入管(Inlet manifold)與損失之關係等.亦不贅述.

總之.此種引擎之原理與應用極繁.卽先進各國尙未能研究精深.對於氣體之變化.尙無準確之定斷.非比水蒸汽之性質已大明於世也.

汽車發動機中之機械損耗

(Mechanical Losses in An Automobile Engine)

胡嵩嵒

弁言　吾人試就一切機械工程歷史觀察之,則見各種發動機之進步程序,大都可別爲三時期.在最初第一時期中,世人之視發動機,不過爲一種新奇之玩具.是以其時發明者與製造者之惟一目的,在使其機械能應實用.在第二時期中,則專趨於局部改良之研究.然而天下事無不受經濟原則之支配,因之乃入第三時期.在此時期中,發動機之製造與設計者,不但使其機械完美可靠,而尤必注意於其施用之經濟.即須求確知以若干價值材料造成,及用若干燃料之發動機,能發生若干有效工作是已.

汽車機械工程之在今日,適由第二時期演進至第三時期.年來世界燃料將近短缺之警告,與夫施用者之求實用,促進汽車關於經濟方面之改良至多.然而英國汽車工程專家李卡多氏(R. H. Ricardo)有言,今日習用四行程週期汽車發動機之理想熱效率(Theoretical Thermal Efficiency)與實際熱效率之比,大概在百分八十六至八十八之間,而此種發動機之機械效率亦約在此數.故熱的與機械的之損耗實際相同.自經濟方面言之,設法減少此等損耗,均屬重要.李氏並於其所著『內燃發動機』一書中論及云,近代內燃發動機無論其爲何式,苟非能另發現一種新式週期,或設法利用損耗於廢氣或水套中之熱能,其實際熱效率恐無改良增進之可能之望.是以近日改良發動機之關鍵,不在於熱損耗,而在於解決如何能使機械損耗減少之一問題,耳.茲請略述之.

釋名　工程名詞各國均尚未能有統一標準,而吾國譯名,歧異尤多.爰以此文中所引用之重要名詞,先爲略加詮釋如下.

(一)機械損耗(Mechanical Losses)此乃指發動機之指示馬工率

(Indicated Horsepower)與其實際馬工率(Brake Horsepower)之差而言.

（二）磨阻馬工率(Friction Horsepower)爲『機械損耗』之又一名稱.此『磨阻』兩字,非謂機械損耗均屬磨阻之損耗.

（三）機械效率（Mechanical Efficiency）爲實際馬工率與指示馬工率之比.以式示之如下

$$\text{機械效率}=\frac{\text{實際馬工率（B.H.P.）}}{\text{指示馬工率（I.H.P.）}}$$

$$\text{或}=\frac{\text{指示馬工率(I.H.P.)}-\text{機械損耗（F.H.P.）}}{\text{指示馬工率(I.H.P.)}}$$

（四）平均有效壓力(Mean Effective Pressure)在尋常四行程週期內燃發動機中,於進氣行程時,有一負向之壓力,即吸力,使燃料與空氣混合劑可以吸入機內.至壓迫行程時,則有一正向壓力.在此兩行程中,燃料與空氣混合劑皆處於被動地位,受活塞之工作.及至爆發行程時,則燃料混合劑起始燃燒而生工作,若干倍於其在壓迫行程時所受者.最後則又係活塞工作,生一正向壓力,排除氣缸內已經燃燒之廢氣.此種種施於活塞面上壓力之平均數即稱爲『平均有效壓力.』其單位爲『平方吋磅』平方吋指活塞之面積而言.尋常指示馬工率即由此平均有效壓力求出.

（五）磨阻平均有效壓力,英文縮寫爲（F.M.E.P.）上節已述平均有效壓力與指示馬工率之關係.可知機械損耗（或稱爲磨阻馬工率）亦可以在活塞面積每平方吋上之平均有效壓力表示之.以此表示機械損耗,可使各種大小不同之發動機互相比較.蓋可免去氣缸之大小與多寡及其他不同諸事所發生之比較困難點也.

機械損耗之原因　汽車內燃發動機中之機械損耗,可就其來源分爲三大類.

（一）吸唧損耗(Pumping Losses)

（二）磨阻損耗（Frictional Losses）

（三）附屬損耗（Auxiliary Losses）

發動機在其以自身吸進燃料而轉動時,合此三部損耗即爲全部機械損耗.此三部損耗之多寡及相互成分,視各種機式與施用情形而異.試爲分析研究之.

吸唧損耗　在汽車發動機中,所謂「吸唧損耗」者,即汽機指示馬工率之耗失於吸入燃料空氣混合劑以及排出廢氣者.設此種發動機爲其他電氣發動機所拖動,則有熱能耗失於氣缸壁.而此損耗亦歸此類,統名爲吸唧損耗.

尋常在進氣行程時,氣缸內之壓力恆較大氣之壓力略低.而廢氣之壓力,因所有已經燃燒之混合劑氣體不能立被排除,故其壓力較大氣稍高.此項用於進氣與排氣時之工作,即爲吸唧損耗.在尋常工作指示圖中,下半吸進與排除曲線所成之環形,即表示此負向之工作.

氣缸內溫度能影響於每行程吸進汽油與空氣混合劑之多寡.溫度高時,氣體運動所生之磨阻每較冷氣爲小.故吸進與排除氣體時所需之工作,大部份隨氣缸內溫度高低而有不同.

容積效率（Volumetric Efficiency）對於吸唧損耗亦有若干關係.設使每週期吸進之氣劑多寡,不受經過氣門時速率變易之影響,則其所需之工作將等於速率之二次方程.因之吸唧損耗亦將隨速率二次方程而增減.但實際上,經一大小不變之氣門,容積效率將因速率之增加而減小.蓋氣缸內外壓力相差較小故也.由是可知吸唧損耗並非完全隨速率二次方程而增減,乃爲較複雜之關係.惟吾人尚未能確切知之耳.

除上述之種種主要吸唧損耗外,在壓迫行程時氣門裝置不良者,活塞環與氣缸壁間每發生漏隙損耗,亦可歸入此吸唧損耗類中.惟在製造精良之汽車發動機中,此種洩漏損耗其量固甚微小也.

磨阻損耗　汽車發動機中之磨阻損耗,爲機中各種運動部份所生之阻力.依磨阻力之性質別之,可分爲兩種.（一）『動的磨阻,』發生於運動部份動作時.（二）『靜的磨阻,』發生於運動部份始動及其運動方向轉換時.

若以磨阻力發生之所在而言,亦可分爲兩種.（一）『活塞磨阻,』即活塞與氣缸壁磨擦所生之磨阻.（二）『軸承磨阻,』發生於曲柄軸偏心輪軸等等之軸承間.

活塞與氣門機件之動作,皆非永向一方向進行者.故每一行程中必有一始一止.靜的磨阻因之而生.但此種磨阻之多寡迄今尚未有人能研究確定之.

磨阻損耗中,尚可包括若干微細損耗.例如曲柄室中因運動部份於高速率時所生之空氣磨擦阻力.機身震盪及不均衡所生之影響等等皆是.

上述種種磨阻損耗中,活塞磨阻爲最大最重要之一項.活塞磨阻之所以發生,大概係活塞與氣缸壁間潤滑油膜受『切』（Shear）之結果.故耗於此項之工作當視油膜之厚薄,其面積之大小,油料黏性之強弱,及速率之高低而異.

活塞與氣缸壁間之磨阻系數（Coefficient of Friction）較尋常軸承間之系數爲大.此或因（一）此處潤滑油料不若軸承間之多,（二）此處之潤滑料易於炭化,而使抗『切』之阻力增加.

惟活塞上潤滑料亦不能太多.太多則有一部份將流入燃燒室中,直接間接均足使內燃機發生『早燃』（Pre-ignition）之現象.直接方面,因潤滑料遇極熱部份,例如排氣門等處,則將解化爲較輕與化學的不固定之物體,而在較低之溫度發生燃燒,故當先燃料而『早燃.』間接方面,因潤滑料受高熱而化爲純粹炭質,滯於燃燒室之壁上及活塞面上.此種炭質爲一種不良之導熱體而能蓄熱.苟蓄熱高至某種程度,則將使燃料未至其應燃之時而早燃矣.爲避免炭化作用,須用一種油料能受高熱度而不起分解作用者爲佳.惟此種油料,其黏性勢必甚強.因之,其所生之抗切阻力亦大.

使油膜之厚薄不變,則抗切阻力之大小將與活塞之速率成正比例.至於活塞之速率是否因由旋轉速度增減或由活塞行程距離之增減而變易,可以不計也.惟油膜之厚薄乃隨活塞與氣缸壁間壓力之大小而變易.而在一種接連桿與曲柄之比之情形下,活塞施於氣缸壁上之壓力將視氣缸內之氣壓及惰性壓力(Inertia pressure)而增減.

惰性壓力乃運動部份因動作而生者,其大小隨運動部份之重量及動作之速率而異.重量愈大,速率愈高,則此種惰性壓力亦愈大.今日通行之汽車發動機速率甚高,故惰性壓力輒超過氣缸內之氣壓.設以一全週期平均計之,可謂活塞磨阻大部份係於惰性壓力.故在速率相同情形之下,發動機中之活塞磨阻將因運動部份重量之大小而異.

活塞環施其壓力於氣缸壁上,產生一種恆數之磨阻.活塞環之堅性不同,此種磨阻乃因之而異.使此環能自由在其槽內,則此種磨阻可與速率及其他情形(環之堅性除外)均不生關係.

此種磨阻與氣缸壁上因壓迫時壓力所生磨阻之和在尋常發動機中,大約爲每方吋二磅.依李卡多氏之試驗報告謂單活塞環一項所生之磨阻,最多不過每方吋十分之三磅.若發動機工作已開始後,活塞環已安於其槽,且面上已經磨光,則此項磨阻之數甚小.

活塞之負荷面積(Bearing Area)與活塞磨阻極有關係.惟各專家對於此點,意見紛歧,有謂面積愈大,每方吋之荷重愈小.故活塞與氣缸壁之損壞均少.此論不甚可信.吾人前已述及除在極低速率之發動機中,平均高大壓力均爲返復運動部份發生之惰性壓力所致.活塞之負荷面積若大,其重量自增.雖可以僅僅放長活塞外壳之長度以求負荷面積之加大.但實際上面積一增,其重量不能不隨之俱增.是以負荷面積加大之結果,不過使總壓力增加,而每方吋之壓力將仍如前不變,因是活塞上之損壞程度不見減輕,而氣油壁上之損壞反將加厲.蓋氣缸壁上之損壞視總壓力之大小而增減也.

換一方面言之,負荷面積亦不可太小.設小過一種界限,則重量之減輕甚少,而每方吋之壓力增大,活塞之損壞更速,活塞磨阻所減有限,所得將不償所失.

速率對於磨阻損耗之關係,亦爲正比例.蓋油膜抗切之阻力與速率成正比例,故速率愈高,則阻力愈強而磨阻損耗亦愈大.

一切潤滑油料之黏性,皆隨溫度之高下而變易.溫度高則黏性弱.故發動機水套(Water Jacket)中水之溫度愈高,則磨阻損耗愈小.

附屬損耗　汽車中之麥尼多(Megneto),配電器(Distributer),水唧器,風扇等等皆爲附屬機械,其所需之工作自是一種損耗.故統稱之爲「附屬損耗.」此種損耗視發動機之構造裝置而異.但就一發動機言,在一切轉動情形之下,其值恆不變,不過水唧與風扇所耗之工作隨速率而俱增.附屬損耗之總值遠較前述二類爲小.故速率之影響,可不必注意.此種損耗在各種荷載情形之下,其值亦無甚出入.故發動機在全荷時,其比值尤小.

三類損耗之成分　三類損耗已如上述.惟其各類所佔之成分,每因發動機構造設計之不同與速率之變更而異.故在一種發動機中,假設其返復運動部份甚重,其磨擦部份計劃不良,其活塞環太緊或其潤滑裝置不佳等等,則其磨阻損耗必將爲三類損耗之首.換言之,設有一種發動機,其氣門狹小,其氣門提高程度與對時均不精確,進氣導管設計式樣不良,則其吸唧損耗必大.

依英國工程家久治氏(Gudge)之試驗結果,一種舊式泰爾白特(Talbot)四氣缸發動機中之磨阻損耗佔四分之三,吸唧損耗佔四分之一.久治氏以爲若在新式發動機中,容積效率較高,吸唧損耗大約至多不過百分之十五云.

美國采司氏(Herbert Chase)曾試驗六氣缸之皮亞司亞羅(Pierce-Arrow)汽車發動機,得結果如下:

活塞磨阻	4.7	馬工率
吸唧損耗	3.4	馬工率
其他磨阻	1.4	馬工率
總計	9.5	馬工率

在其試驗時,活塞之速率約爲每分鐘一千二百呎,計合旋轉率每分鐘一千二百轉.此處之吸唧損耗佔百分之三十五點七(35.7%),磨阻損耗佔百分之六十四點三(64.3%).所可注意者,活塞磨阻幾佔總損耗之半.

結語 此篇僅爲研究機械損耗之來源與其性質而作.限於篇幅,未能詳論.關於測驗損耗方法,俱未述及.蓋目下方法雖多,尙無一盡善盡美者,各有缺點困難,不能備述.容俟將來另文論之.

十五年八月脫稿於美國波士登.

南洋季刊創刊號要目（本年一月出版）

空氣預熱機

(Air Preheater)

張錫蕃

尋常在管理完備之原動力廠內熱力被烟突出氣（Flue gas）帶出因而廢耗者,佔燃料原有熱量（Heating value）百分之二十至百分之三十.蓋烟突出氣普通在華氏表四百五十五度至五百五十度,故含有一大部分顯熱力（Sensible heat）出氣從烟突出,此一部分顯熱亦隨之而出.此乃原動力廠內各項熱力廢耗中之最大者.此種熱力廢耗可用下列公式表明之:

$$h = w(t_c - t)C$$

公式內之 h 乃每磅燃料此種廢耗之熱量,

w 乃每磅燃料烟突出氣之重量.

t_c 乃烟突出氣之熱度,

t 乃進爐空氣之熱度,

C 乃烟突出氣之比熱.

觀上式,欲令此種熱力廢耗減少自非降低烟突出氣重量或減少烟突出氣與進爐空氣之相差熱度不可.欲降低烟突出氣重量必先降低進爐空氣之過限量（Air excess）但在一定之鍋爐及燃料,進爐之過限空氣亦有一定,俾得最高之總效率（Overall efficiency）.縮短烟突出氣及進爐空氣熱度之相差,可減低烟突出氣熱度或加高進爐空氣熱度行之.平常用省煤機（Economizer）置於烟突內,則烟突出氣可以減低而進爐水（Feed water）亦可吸得一部分熱量.倘代以空氣預熱機,則非但減低烟突出氣熱度,且可加高進爐空氣熱度.因烟突出氣經過空氣預熱機.一部分熱力即被空氣吸去,故熱度減低.而進爐之空氣先通過預熱機然後入爐,則熱度自加高.

歐美各國四十餘年來雖間有用空氣預熱機者,但不甚注意之,以爲無甚關係.近年來工程專家始確實指出空氣預熱機除保留廢耗熱力外,對於現代鍋爐燃燒發展方面尚有絕大貢獻.於一千九百二十二年間美國動力雜誌(Power Magazine)曾發表工程師好特萊氏(J.C. Hoadley)空氣預熱機試驗之結果.其結論云鍋爐裝置空氣預熱機後可增高鍋爐效率百分之十至百分之十五.彼於新式之好特萊氏空氣預熱機作幾度精密之試驗,其結果則稱可增加總效率百分之十八.好特萊氏空氣預熱機爲二百四十根二十呎長二吋直徑之鐵管組織所成,每管之外更套以三吋直徑之薄鐵管.烟突出氣從二吋管通過,空氣在兩管之中隙通過,故空氣與烟突出氣隔離至爲接近,而熱力得以傳導焉.

空氣預熱機除保留廢耗熱力增加鍋爐效率外,并能使燃料燃燒完全.進爐預熱之空氣能使灰燼中未燃著之灰質減少,故炭養二物之化合亦得加多.鍋爐傳導效率(Efficiency of heat transfer)之加高及吸熱力之加強.亦歸功於進爐空氣預熱後所得之鍋爐高熱度.通預熱空氣於鍋爐火牀上,可使含多量化氣物(Volatile Matter)之煤,在較小之燃燒空間(Combustion space)內得較善之燃燒.煤中含高成分之水氣,亦易得適合之燃燒.

空氣預熱機之優點既如上述,其缺點亦分述於下.欲預熱空氣必先增長氣筒或烟突.有時吸收空氣處需用風扇,是以工作動力加大.預熱空氣不適用於煤之灰燼烊解度較低(Low ash fusion point)者,因預熱空氣之熱度足令灰燼結成硬塊(Clinker),此種硬塊對於爐底有損,且不易除去.總之,空氣預熱機實爲近代省熱機械上之新進步.現雖採用之者寥寥,而將來之趨勢或可以奪省煤機之位置而代之也.

重油機車

Heavy Oil Engined Locomotive

鈕因梁

（一）緒言

（二）重油機之發達

（三）機車製造之進步

（四）重油機車之歷史

（五）重油機車之種類

（六）各國應用狀況

（七）重油機車之優點

（八）重油機車對于鐵道事業之討論

（九）重油機車之于中國

（十）參考書目錄

著者于機車學一知半解.未嘗深究.近來瀏覽關于重油機之應用諸書.頗饒興趣.拉雜作是篇.深希　讀者指教.

（一）緒言

實業之振興.端賴交通之便利.而交通之發達.由於實業之進步.是則實業與交通相因而生相輔而行者也.傳遞與運輸均爲交通事業.而運輸尤爲實業上一大問題.各國于海陸空運輸事業之發展.均有一日千里之勢.溯自一八一五年喬治史蒂芬孫George Stephenson發明機車.一八七九年賽兒登Selden發明汽油自働車.及一九〇〇年美國自働車展覽會後.經營之發明之.改良之.于是有現今陸地運輸之迅速與便利.考蒸汽機車之發源.由于一八〇七年富爾丹Fulton之以蒸汽機航船應用于陸行.而一八七〇年自働車之大發達.引起一八九七年汽油機發動機車之提倡.一九一四年歐戰時

汽油機發動機應用尤巨.近今工程家以汽油機不及重油機之經濟.於是重油機之製造日益完備而合用.預料將來當有大發達之可能.列國鐵道界亦必為之鞏起注意焉.

（二） 重油機之發達

重油機乃內燃機之一種.一八九三年.德國提士 Diesel 首以其學理倡于世.厥後逐漸發達.于是有所謂半提士機 Semi-Diesel 全提士機 Full Diesel 冷引重油機 Cold Starting Oil Engine 等等（閱下表）

- 重油機 Heavy Oil Engine
  - 無空氣注射 Airless Injection
    - （一） 高壓 High Comp. / 冷引 Cold Starting / 固射 Solid Injection
      - 直接 Direct
        - 自動噴放 Auto Spray
        - 機械噴放 Mech. Control Spray
      - 間接 Indirect
        - 噴放 Sprayer
        - 黑維式 Hvid Type
    - （二） 低壓 Low Compression / 面燃 Surface Ignition / 半提士 Semi-Diesel
      - 熱泡 Hot Bulb
      - 半冷 Partially Cooled.
  - 空氣注射 Air Injection
    - Open
    - Closed

以熱力學理而論.在同等比壓(Compression Ratio)情形之下.重油機之效率.不及汽油機.然重油可得較高壓度及較高熱度.故實際上之效率.較汽油機〔或稱烏托式(Otto)〕為高.

煤油之出產.自揮發油（汽油）.石油.重油.以至柏油.均有極大之應用.除柏油尚不能應用于發動機外.其他可用之種類不下數十.然以近年來自働車(Automobile)之發達.輕油價格之昂貴.擣之用於蒸汽鍋下燃燒之重油皆應用於重油機.于是重油機日益發達.而美國燃油蒸汽鍋將漸次淘汰去

年且有禁燃重油于鍋爐之說云.

重油機之始創.祇有四週單行式(Four Cycle Single Acting.)其後逐年進步.乃有二週雙行或對行諸式(Two Cycle Double Acting, or Opposite Pistons). 重油機之功用.以應用於海船爲最大.歐洲各國提倡尤甚.瑞典新造一艘名葛利卜化林(Grepoholin)(見Oil Engine Power, Jan. 1926).乃世界第一重油機船.計可載重一萬七千噸.發動力爲三座七百五十馬力之重油機.美國近年來努力提倡.預計數年中將所有國家船政局(United States Shipping Board)之航船.盡改爲重油機發動.可見重油機在海上發達之一斑矣.

陸上動力廠之可否應用油機.觀上海法租界電燈電車公司可知.該公司廠中之機.卽世界最著名之瑞士蘇氏兄弟公司(Sulzer Bros.)所造.目下世界第一重油機發電廠.乃在英國倫敦.其次則在德國之物利門(Breman.)他若法國邦答蓮生(Pont-a'-Mousson)及意多瀾斯(Etupes)及意國那不勒斯(Naples.)均較上海法界者爲大.美國往年所有重油機發電廠均爲小規模.不及一二千基羅華特(K.W.)以去年成績言.美國製造重油機最大不過四五千匹馬力.而歐洲各國則不然.近今德國物斯公司(Blohm & Voss)由Augsburg. & Nursburg Machenwork 計劃所造之世界最大重油機.乃有一萬五千馬力.此機有九缸(Cylinder.)均三十三吋半直徑.占地長七十七呎.闊十四呎.高度爲三十九呎.

重油機動力之總效率可過百分之三十.而蒸汽機動力雖用最新高壓高熱諸方法.不易過百分之廿.然以油與煤之出產量及機廠原價(Initial Cost.)之比較.互有出入.此二種動力機之優劣.乃引起工程界之研究與討論.

（三） 機車製造之進步

近年蒸汽機車之進步.雖稱迅速.然似已達效率最高之點.故近今多課

改良製造與完全變更之計劃.如電機機車汽輪機車油機機車之相繼應用.惟後者究以價值太貴.往往尚未十分發達.以蒸汽機車論.新式計劃大都注意于下列諸端.

(甲) 通風(Draft)用汽射法.則汽缸內洩路之壓力(Exhaust Pressure)加高.故機械通風有定度之伸縮.

(乙) 機廠汽鍋(Boiler)用煤粉(Powdered Coal)以增加效率.機車亦可用之.故將來機車上.可燃劣煤而得較高效率.

(丙) 欲得高壓及高熱之蒸汽.非用水管汽鍋不可.

(丁) 熱力學理上一流汽缸(Uniflow Cylinder)及圓軸汽瓣.爲經濟故應用于機車.其結果必佳.

(戊) 加高汽壓後.可用複式汽缸(Compound Cylinder)以增高其熱力效率.

(巳) 應用三汽缸之簡單機車(Three Cylinder, Simple Locomotive)則增進來復機件之平衡(Balance of Reciprocating Parts.)得平均之轉角力(Torque)不必增加軸負(Axle Load)而可增進拖力(Tractive Power.)且得一平匀之洩汽動作.

(庚) 自動截汽(Automatic Cut-off Control).完全機廠汽機實用之.但機車用之.則可得一不變之洩路壓力(Exhaust Pressure)及平匀之通風(Draft).尤爲經濟.

其餘改進如添水加熱具及機車推助器(Booster).均已于近幾年得成效矣.

汽輪機車乃意大利之班羅查(Belluzo)于一九〇七年所首造.瑞典Ljunstron新造一座.今已實用於瑞典省鐵道矣.

該機車對於改速齒輪.添水加熱器.凝水箱(Condenser).以及抽空與打水機.均有最新法裝置.而熱量分配表上Heat Balance計得百分之十四之總效率.幾兩倍于最近蒸汽機車.李特曼利(Reed Macleod)機車爲北英機

車公司及瑞士査來 (North British Loco. Co & Zoelly) 所合造.爲齒汽輪機車 (Geared Turbine Locomotive.) 又蘭珊 (Ramsay) 汽輪電機車(Turbo-Electric Loco.) 有二萬二千磅之拖力 (T.F.) 則已于倫敦蘇格蘭鐵道試驗有成績矣.

電機機車自一八八七年范得爾 (Van Depoele & Spragne) 發明後.各國均大有成績.近五年前與蒸汽機車之爭勝尤甚.然以蒸汽機車之日益進步.蒸汽鐵道電化之未易速進.未能爲最上上品.蓋此亦鐵道事業上一大經濟問題也.其發達略史殺不具述.

以上略述近今蒸汽機車及汽輪機車之發達.其他如內燃機車.當在下章略爲記述.電池機車等則以限于輕便應用.故從略.

(四) 重油機車之歷史

重油機車之製造.由於一八七〇年時之自働車之發達.可無疑也.自働車發明後.歐美工程師卽應用于鐵道.謂之鐵路自働車(Ralway Self-Propell Car).鐵道自働車者機械與客貨合佔一輛.或另拖一輛.負重甚輕.不能如機車之能拖數十車輛也.

一八九七年支加哥城所造畢登 (Patton) 鐵道摩托車 (Railway Motor Car). 乃內燃機車之原始.此車可拖三十噸重之車輛一座.其原動力爲二十五馬力之來蒙 (Raymond) 汽油機及一發電機.一八九七年之後.法國西屋公司爲匈牙利亞利散 (Arad Csand) 鐵道造輕便汽油機電機車 (Light Gas Electric Car).爲歐洲創舉.一九〇四年英國東北鐵道工程師韋司敦 (Wilson Worsdell) 首先製造英國之內燃機機車.其原動力爲何斯來 (Wolsley) 之八十馬力汽油機及英國西屋公司之五十基羅華特之直流發電機.車長五十二呎.可容五十二人.其速率爲每小時三十六哩云.一九〇五年美國奇異公司造六十五呎長足容四十人之木身汽油機車.此乃美國完

全容積(Full Size)之鐵路車也.一九〇六年司屈萊 (Strang) 車造于美國費城之畢利爾 (G. J. Brill) 公司.利用電池爲助力器(Booster.) 而一九一一年則奇異公司又改良其木身爲鋼身.一九二四年美國鮑爾温機車廠爲墨西哥國家鐵道製造之汽油電機車頗似奇異所造.惟動力爲百十基羅華特.車身長六十呎.容五十四人.且速率可達每小時五十哩.則爲汽油機車之較完美者矣.

以上所述.盡係汽油電機車.非直接推動 (Direct Propell).之汽油機車即用電機而尙未有變速齒輪及離合子(Change Speed Gear And Clutch.)者也.

一八九〇年支加哥氫炭公司 (Hydro-Carbon Co.) 所用之念一噸重四十五馬力之汽油機車.及一九〇五年美國狄克公司試造之三十六馬力汽油機車.均爲直接推動機之一種.當一九〇一年美國梅金氏 (Wm. R. Mc Keen)爲太平洋聯合鐵道 (Union Pacific R. R.) 之機務總管時.極主利用汽油機車.該項機車于一九〇五年造成.計長卅一呎.用一百馬力之汽油發動機.其傳達即用帶鍊 (Link Belt or Chain) 及離合子.其後此項機車益多.車身長至七十餘呎.動力增至二百馬力.一九〇五年至一九一〇年.該路造車最年年增加.一九一〇年竟造三十七輛.惟至一九一八年即停造.現計尙有二十五輛應用于該路.

歐洲各國自大戰之後.普法瑞著名之輕便汽油機自動車.均以汽油價貴而退步.于是航用之重油機.應用于鐵道事業.此重油機鐵道自動車之由來.亦即近來重油機車之發源也.

重油機用於鐵道車上首見成效者.爲瑞典著名之波勒特爾 (Polar Dera) 油機.據一九二二年之調查報告.該機平均費油率(Oil Consumption Rate,) 在每哩一•三磅左右.

今日歐洲之最新式鐵道重油自動車則爲瑞士之蘇氏 (Sulzer)重油車.考瑞士國之幹路鐵道已完全電化 (Electrified). 而其支路運輸卽用油機自

動車.此項機車乃用二百馬力之雙週重油機(Two Cycle Heavy Oil Engine).其軸連於一百四十基羅華特之發電機.油機全身置于前輪座 (Leading Truck).機車開動時.油機之速率不變.後輪 (Rear Truck) 之曲軸 (Jack Shaft.) 即為兩馬達機所推動.從挺桿(Connecting Rod)而達于發動輪(Driving Wheel).車重六十六法噸(Metric Ton=1000 K.G.=1·102 Short Ton).而速率可達每小時四十七哩.費油率每噸每哩約計〇·七英兩(0·7 Ounce/Ton-Mile).一九二四年該廠新式之車.用二百五十馬力之固射(Solid Injection)重油機.車長六十五呎.重五十八噸.可容五十乘客.且備行李間.頗似通用之客車(Passenger Coach).其費油率則減至每噸每哩只耗三分之一英兩.可謂歐洲最著名最滿意之油機自動車矣.

加拿大國家鐵道亦于近時製造二種重油自動車于蒙特利爾機車廠(Montreal Loco Works).其一為單車式.車長六十呎.裝置于二具四輪座(4 Wheel Truck.).可容五十七人.車重五十五噸.動力則為百八十五馬力之比特麻(Beadmore)重油機.接連一百〇五基羅華特之發電機.其另外一種乃雙車式 (Articulated Type) 裝置于三具四輪座.其中間輪座跨接兩車.全車長一〇二呎.重九十四噸.可容百二十八人.其動力則為三百四十馬力之比特麻重油機.連接二百基羅華特之發電機.以上二種.均為雙向式 (Double End Control.)且均可達每小時六十英里之速率.經幾番試驗.屢次往返于溫哥武及蒙特利爾間.得極高之效率云.

美國雖無此項重油機自動車之發達.然白利爾公司 (Brill Co) 最近製造一輕油機自動車頗類似之.計車長六十呎.重四十五噸.可容五十人.其餘行李間九十方呎.動力則為二百五十馬力之汽油機.直接一百八十基羅華特之發電機.近來此種車輛已有二十餘座.且有七十噸之五百馬力機車式者.都應用于美國東部各路.燃油極省.且極安全.惟年來輕油價貴.此項車輛未必再能發達也.

重油機之由來與進化大致如此.

(五) 重油機車之種類

重油機車之製造.已十餘年于茲.構造之種類.計劃之方法.頗多不同.今先將種類順序說明於下.

重油機車之分類.非以油機之種類而別.蓋以油機燃着法(Ignition System)而分.已不下十餘種.本篇分類.乃從其動力傳遞法 (Transmission System.)而言.

(甲) 直接傳遞

(乙) 直接傳遞而變化重油機動力

(丙) 固體傳遞

(丁) 液體傳遞

(戊) 電機傳遞

(已) 氣體傳遞

其他種傳兩式併合諸法

(甲) 直接傳遞者.即以重油機直接聯于動輪軸 (Driving Axle) 或先經一反軸也.此項傳遞發動機所生轉力率(Turning Moment).全賴注射油量之多寡.而不在發動機之旋轉次數.故用定量注射之油.則拖力必相同.與車之遲速無關.即此一點.爲機車事業所不許.蓋機車需極大之拖力而遲行於高斜之山道.拖力與速率須成一反比例乃佳.若用此項傳遞.則平常速率所用油量.將爲較高速率所用之半.此乃完全不適於實際.研究此事者.或主放大氣缸.則徒增機身重量.而氣缸(Cylinder)內「均壓」(Mean Effective Pressure)之加高有限.或主多加空氣.(Supercharging)則氣缸傳熱不易而或致破裂.均困難不能實行者也.

(乙) 直接傳遞而變化重油機動力者.即所以免除甲項之困難.而應用著名

之司的爾 (Still) 機也.司的爾機爲單行油機(Single Acting Oil Engine).而構轄之另一面則以蒸汽爲動力者.雖蒸汽由油機方面之洩氣(Exhaust)之熱而成.然汽鍋裝置.頗占地位.且製汽需油(以油爲燃料.)開動需時(因用汽鍋.)較勝於蒸汽機車能有幾許.英國克珍史及李特公司(Kitsons & Leed)從事製造此式有年.將來試驗結果.或能得工程界之注意也.

(丙) 固體傳達者指齒輪聯合子變速齒輪等而言.此種計劃.已見成效.詳見下章.

(丁) 液體傳達者.以水或油爲傳達媒介物也.此種計劃在歐洲亦已告成功.詳見下章.著名之約梅及華德堡式(Wm. Jamer Pump & Waterbury Gear)與萊士式(Lentz System)二種.即爲液體傳達.德國 M. A. N. 廠從前亦曾試驗數年.後以無效而中止矣.

(戊) 電機傳達乃用油機運發電機.而車軸上裝置齒輪及電動機.此式已爲工程界認爲重油機車傳遞動力法中之最上乘者.十餘年來.此項製造最多.成效亦特著.(詳下章)

(己) 氣體傳達者以氣體作媒介物 (Medium) 也.完全蒸汽傳達用于挪威之 Christiani System. 蓋以蒸汽作一循環流動 (Continous Girculation) 也.其法以油機洩氣爲汽鍋熱源.而所有高壓蒸汽則流入汽缸而發生工作.油機則專司運動壓氣機 (Compressor) 及吸收凝結器 (Condenser) 之水.打回汽鍋.據云此項傳達可得百之七三效率云.審萊底 (Zarlatti) 制亦用壓氣機而以蒸汽爲介物.其熱亦由油機導冷套缸之水及洩氣 (Cooling Jacket Water and Exhaust Gas) 而來.高壓空氣與蒸汽同時應用于汽缸而生効力.蓋空氣與蒸汽合併傳達者.聞此項効率可達百之九十.以上二式均已在意大利開始製造矣.

德國哥立氏(Goeritz)新近製造一種乃用洩氣爲傳遞動力品.聞其特殊

優點在于無油量燃響時之危險.此項小機車已在新近德國塞庭(Seddin)機車展覽會出世.

德爾奇干(Geiger)氏在一九一九年輒介紹用油機推動壓氣機.使空氣於高壓之下.熱以油機之洩氣.于是用之於機車上氣缸.而運動其機輪.奇干氏頗以此法爲盡善.且以爲熱力效率最高.故德國之M. A. N. 及 Augburg二大名廠已將該項試造一座一千二百馬力(B. H. P.)之幹路機車矣.

以作者個人意見而言.以爲傳達動力可以齒輪及液體二式合用.蓋在發動時用液體傳達.及車已行動.則用機件撥改齒輪.運用其傳達.如是發動時之困難可免.而機械之價值或不高.但此種見解歐美或早已有所實行.且或以爲不可能之議說.則研究機車之讀者想必能瞭然也.

(全篇未完)

FUNDAMENTAL CONCEPTION OF THERMODYNAMICS

陳廣沅

Extract from the Writer's Letter to the Editor

I am sending you under the same cover the following four papers, which I hope will reach you in good condtition:

1. An Application of the General Formulas.
2. Relation of Freight Train Resistance to Axle Loads.
3. Friction of Railroad Car Journals.
4. The Study of Air Resistance to the Movement of a Train.

The first paper is a continuation of the paper I sent you last year, the title of which if I am correct is "Fundamental Conceptions of Thermodynamics". So far, I have contributed something about one of the foundations of Mechanical Engineering, and that is the Thermodynamics. About the other one, Mechanics, I am going to write some of the most important topics in Chinese, because the treatment of the Science of Mechanics is more or less standardized, and it is senseless to re-treat them in English for Chinese Magazines.

The reasons why I have been writing these articles in English are these: 1. all these papers with the exception of Thermodynamics are the products of my own investigation, and before put into printing, I want to be sure that the authorities in this country have not found serious mistake in it; 2. Prof. Goodenough's way of treating the subject of Thermodynamics is unigue in itself and the method of calculating his Steam Tables is not very well known, so I think most of the students in this country want to know it too; 3. I often find authors of this country refer to magazines of the Imperial University of Japan and it is always a shame to me that not a single technical magazine in the whole territory of China is referable, except the official reports by the Board of Communications, the Geological Survey and the like, so let us get busy to put up something which has an universal value in English and give them a chance to refer to for at least once in a while.

All of these papers have been read by Mr. W. E. Mao, and he encourages me for several times that I should send them to the American magazines to be published, but I think that if they have any value at all, I would rather send them to our Nanyang Quarterly, and let Nanyang Quarterly show to the world that there is a little spot in China whcih is cultivating the real engineers, and not to be neglected.

The topics which I have in mind to write on in Chinese are the following:

1. Moment of Inertia and Product of Inertia.
2. A Study of Unsymmetrically Loaded Beams.
3. An Investigation of Curved Beams.

Most of the engineering students excuse themselves for not writing something for the benefit of the fellow students, either by saying that there is no proper Chinese translation for engineering terms especially such as moment of inertia and product of inertia, or by saying that we do not want to write what has been written and we want to initiate something which has not come to us yet. The former statement shows that they do not try, and the latter one that they not only refrain themselves from doing but also discourage those who are doing. Well, then, let us show them that we can if we will, and that there are lots to be done and every little bit helps.

Well, if you will excuse me, I have to dwell upon this subject for another paragraph. I have a notion that if I keep on writing like what I have outlined and already sent, the whole book of the Mechanical Number of Nanyang Quarterly will be monopolized by a single writer - that is not fair. May I suggest what to do? Give me as much space as it is justified and print them in the sequence as I have listed above, because there is a little reference to the former of the series by the latter.

Another thing which I want to beg your attention to is my work here in the University. My personal news has been given as "serving the University of Illinois". I think I owe the reader a word of explanation. Once we had a caller and on his calling card there was a phrase "Union Station, Chicago", one of my friends remarks, "what, a janitor?" The same joke can be applied to several names reported in our news columns. My service here is in connection with the Engineering Experiment Station, as a Research Graduate Assistant, of which an explanation appears in page 10 of the enclosed book" The Functions of the Engineering Experiment Station of the U. of I.", you will please refer to the topic "The Training of Men for Research Work"

I First Law of Thermodynamics

In thermodynamics, we have a fundamental equation like this:

$$\triangle Q = \triangle U + \triangle W$$

Where Q denotes heat, U the energy and W the work. Each of the three members may be positive or negative. Positive Q means increase of heat, positive U means increase of energy, and positive W means work by the body under consideration; while negative Q and U mean their decrease, and nagative W means the work done on the body under consideration.

Suppose a body of enclosed gas is being heated from outside as shown in the figure. Evidently the kinetic energy on the gas is increased and we denote that by K. At the same time, the volume of the gas is increasing, that is, energy is being spent to separate the molecules apart against their mutual attraction we call this potential energy. But we have two kinds of potential energy, one is to separate the molecules which are alreaby at a distance to each other, and the other is to break the molecules which are aggregated togather; let us call the the former P' and the latter P". P" is the energy to increase the volume and P" is the energy to change the state, such as from ice to water. Therefore U in the general equation has these 3 items.

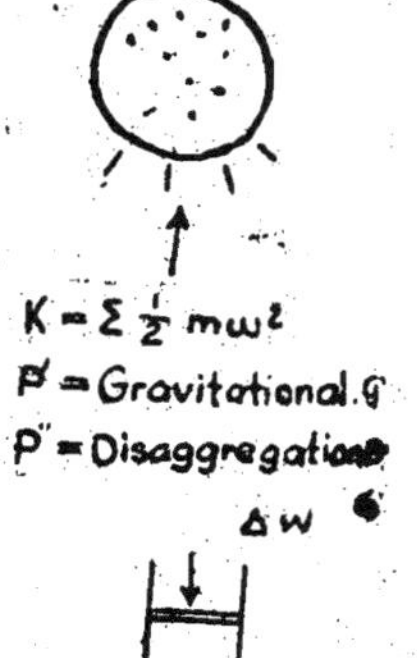

ΔQ

If the vessel containing the gas tends to expand as the gas is receiving heat then a certain amount of energy has to be spent in doing this work. This explains the term W in our equation. Suppose we have another vessel as shown containing gas which is not only heated but also compressed by an external work, then the work is negative and our equation becomes:

$$\Delta Q = \Delta U - \Delta W. \qquad \Delta U = \Delta Q + \Delta W.$$

Now let us examine Joule's experiment. Suppose we have air under 22 Atm. pressure in the left branch of the vessel and a vaccum in the right one; then we open the cock at the centre of the connecting tube. First, suppose the vessel was covered with asbestos and examine the equation, what ought to happen.

$$\Delta Q = \Delta K + \Delta P' + \Delta P'' + \Delta W$$

Q is 0, for no heat is received from outside. P" is 0, for there is no change of state. W is 0, for there is no work done by or on the gas. Therefore the equation becomes this:

22 At. 0
water
∴ P' = 0

$$0 = \Delta K + \Delta P'$$

Since volume is bigger so P' must be positive; then, in order to satisfy the equation, K must be negative, i.e., the temperature of the gas after expansion must be lower.

But, when Joule took this experiment, he did not have any asbestos around the vessel and the temperature of the water did not show any change after the gas expanded. Then, K must be zero and P'' must be zero too.

So the conclusion is that for a perfect gas the potential energy P' is zero.

Now question arises, "Does friction have any to do with the First Law?"

Before we answer this question, let us first examine what kind of friction is it. Suppose a body of gas is heated and some outside work done on it too then the equation which expresses this fact is this:

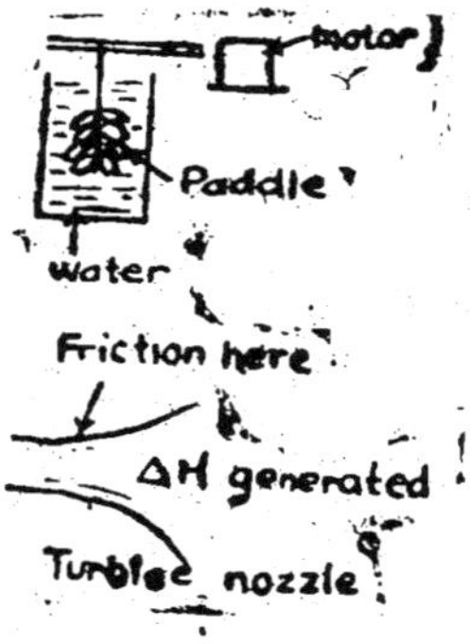

$$\triangle Q = \triangle U + \triangle H. \ (\triangle W)$$

Suppose a body of wat r is being heated and a peddle is driven in the water by an outside motor, the heat generated by the friction of the peddle in the water is added to the water and the equation ought to be the same thing:

$$\triangle Q = \triangle U - \triangle W$$

But we have another case which is entirely different from the above: in steam turbine nozzles steam rubbing on the wall generates heat by virtue of friction. Are we going to use the same equation to express this fact? No, this generated heat which is generally denoted by H, is not added from outside but generated at the expense of the capacity to do work. That is, a certain amount of energy is taken away from the W term to be added to the U term.

There needs some remark on the term W. This is gerally expressed by F.dv in thermodynamics. But its use is not limited to it. It may be E. de where E is the electromotive force and e the quantity of electricity. It may be X.dx in mechanics where X denotes torque and x the angle. It may be in chemistry X.dx, where X denotes the chemical affinity and x the quantity of chemicals.

So far we have talked about the fundamental equation, now let us examine the different terms in connection with the variables on which they depend.

Let us talk about U first. U depends upon the three variables p, v, and T. In a body of gas we have three kinds of energy: K which is indicated by T, P' which is indicated by v, and P'' which is indicated by aggregation, such as 10% of water mixed with 90% of steam. Suppose this body of gas originally at a state of p, v, T, after a series of changes, came back to the original state; then the gas has the same energy as before, that is, U has the same value as before. We say that U is fixed by the state only. This can be seen on the T-v diagram.

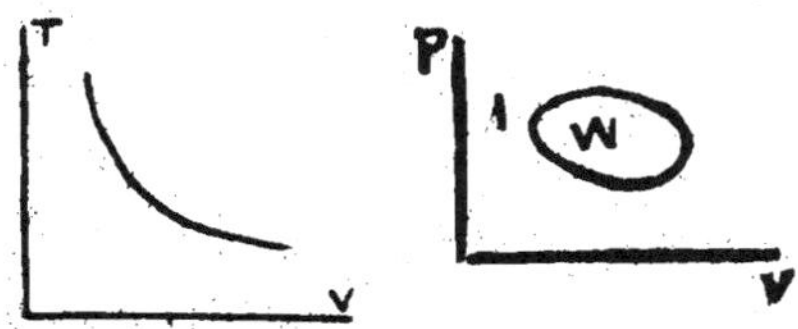

Now, how about W? Let's see how it behaves on the p-v diagram. Suppose a body starts from the state I, goes around the closed curve and comes back to the original state. Then, we have an amount of work done represented by the area enclosed by the curve. So, we don't have any work done unless the point moves, that is the value of W is not a point function, and we can not say work done at a certain point.

$$\therefore \triangle Q = \triangle U + \triangle W$$

$$_1Q_2 = U]_1^2 + {}_1W_2$$

Since the increment of Q is the sum of increment of U and that of W, and since W is not a function of state only or is not a point function, Q is not a functin of state only nor is a point function.

What does it mean by point function mathematically? Now, see the two functions:

$$dZ = ydx + xdy \quad \ldots\ldots\ldots\ldots 1 \text{ (point funetion)}$$

$$dZ = ydx + 2\,xdy \quad \ldots\ldots\ldots\ldots 2 \text{ (not point function.)}$$

ydx is the vertical strip on the Y-X diagram, and xdy is the horizontal strip. The integral of the sum of xdy and ydx is the area ab2cdl Now, suppose we change the curve between 1 and 2 we still get same area. And the integral of the function is xy-xy

For the second tunction, we can interpret it in the same way, only that we have to extend the horizontal strip to the left so that the whole length will represent 2xdy. The integral of the function will be the area represented by 01'b2"2cd1. Now suppose we change the curve 1a2 to the form 1a'2

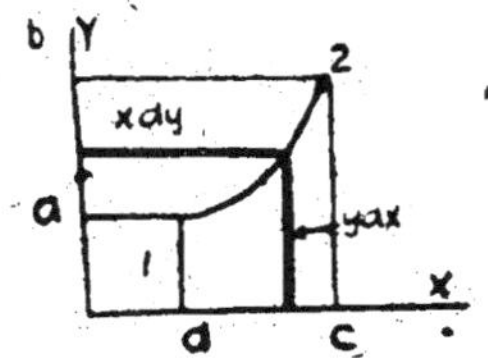

the area thus generated is not the same as before. And, we can't get an exact answer for this integral.

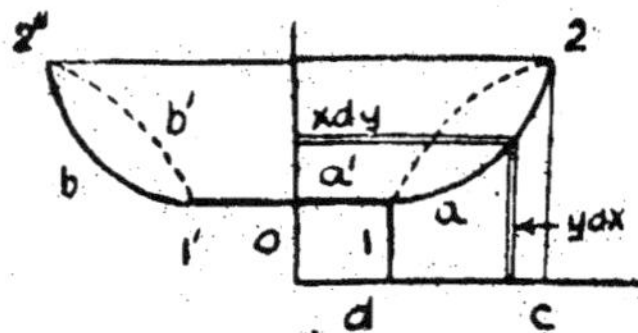

So, we call the function 1 exact and 2 inexact.

Therefore we call W and Q inexact function, and U an exact function:

U = A point function.

dU is exact.

$u = f(v, T)$

$du = M\,dv + N\,dT.$

$\frac{\partial M}{\partial T} = \frac{\partial N}{\partial v}$, They are rates and Partial Derivatives

$Q \neq$ a point function.

dQ is inexact.

Q is not a function of (v, T.)

But $dQ = A\,dv + B\,dT.$

$\frac{\partial A}{\partial T} \neq \frac{\partial B}{\partial v}$, They are rates only and not Partial Derivatives.

Now, we know something about the first law. Before we start on the Second Law of Thermodynamics, let us see what we can do without the knowledge of the Second Law.

Let us first play with the laws of Perfect gas in connection with the first law. Remember that before the year of 1835, people did not know anything about the second law and all they could do was to play with the first law.

for perfect gas, $pv = BT$,

$$\frac{du}{dv} = 0, \text{ or } u = f(T) \text{ only.}$$

In general, $dq = du + p.dv$

$$dq = c.d\,T. \qquad c = \text{sp. heat.}$$

In the case where V is kept constant, then,

$$dq = du, \qquad (p\,.dv = o)$$

$$dq = c_v.dT.$$

$$\therefore du = c_v.dT.$$

Graphically,

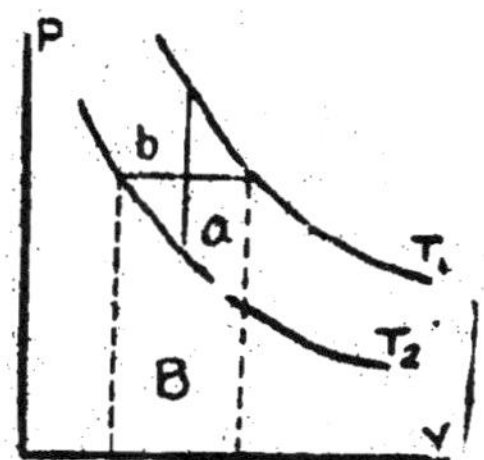

$${}_1q_2 = u_2 - u_1 \text{ (any path whatever)}$$

$${}_1q_2 = c_v\,dT \text{ (a)}$$

$${}_1q_2 = c_p\,dT \text{ (b)}$$

The undergraduate students have lots of questions about the expression thus arrived. First of all, they forget what has been said of the U which is a point function, whose value is determined by state only, irrespective to its previous history, that is, the difference between the value of U which is represented by a point on the curve T and that represented by another point on the curve T is the same, no matter where these points are situated. Then the change of U represented by a ought to be the same as that by b, but they are obviously different from the two expressions (a) and (b), how do we account for that? Equation (b) does not represent the change of U only, it implies the work done which is represented by the area under the line b and that is B.

Now, suppose you know the following laws of perfect gas and see what we can do with them:-

1. $pv = BT$
2. $du = c_v.dT$
3. $dq = c_v.dT + p\,.\,d\,v$

For constant pressure,

from (1) $p.dv + 0 = B.dT.$

from (3) $dq = c_v dT + B.dT$

$= (c_v + B)\ dT.$

But $dq = c_p\ dT.$

$\therefore\ c_v + B = c_p$

or $c_p - c_v = B.$

From the lst. law equation, $dq = c_v\ dT + p.dv.$

$\therefore\ dq = (c_p - B)\ dT + p.dv$

$= c_p\ dT + (p.dv - BdT)$

But, from (1) $p.dv + v.dp = B.dT.$

$\therefore\ dq = c_p\ dT - v.dp$ ....(4)

This is an expression analogous to,

$dq = c_v\ dT + p.dv.$

Now, get an expression with p and v only, by eliminating T from (3) and (4). Suppose an adiabatic change, then,

$o = c_v\ dT + p.\ dv$

$o = c_p\ dT - v.\ dp$

i. e. $c_v\ dT = -\ p.dv$

$c_p\ dT = v.dp.$

$$\therefore\ \frac{c_p}{c_v} = -\frac{v.\ dp}{p.\ dv}$$

$$\therefore\ k = -\frac{v}{dv}.\frac{dp}{p}$$

$$k.\frac{dv}{v} = -\frac{dp}{p}.$$

$$\therefore \log {}_vk = \log p^{-1} + \log c$$

$$\therefore {}_vk = \frac{c_1}{p}$$

$$\therefore p_vk = c_1$$

Next, we want an expression between p and T only — get rid of v.

from (4) $o = c_p.dT - v.dp.$

from (1) $v = \frac{BT}{p}$

$$\therefore o = c_p.dT - \frac{BT}{p}.dp.$$

$$\frac{c_p.dT}{T} = B.\frac{dp}{p}$$

$$c_p.\log T - B\log p = \log c'.$$

$$\therefore T^{c_p} = p^B.c'_1$$

$$\text{or } \frac{T^{c_p}}{p^B} = c_1'$$

$$\therefore {}^* \frac{T^{c_p}}{p^{\frac{k-1}{k}.c_p}} = c_1' \quad \text{i. e.} \quad \frac{p^{\frac{k-1}{k}}}{T} = c_2$$

$$* \quad c_p - c_v = B$$

$$\frac{c_p}{c_v} = k$$

$$\therefore c_p - \frac{c_p}{k} = B$$

$$\therefore B = \frac{k-1}{k}.c_p$$

Again, we want an expression between v and T, eliminate p.

from (3) $o = c_v.dT + p.dv$

from (1) $p = \frac{BT}{v}$

$$\therefore o = c_v.dT + \frac{BT}{v}.dv$$

$$-c_v \, . \, \frac{dT}{T} = B \, . \, \frac{dv}{v} \, .$$

$$c_v \log T + B \log v = \log c_2'$$

$$T^{c_v} = \frac{c_2'}{v^B}$$

$$T^{c_v} . \, v^B = c_2'$$

$$\because \; c_p - c_v = B,$$

$$\frac{c_p}{c_v} = k$$

$$\therefore \; k\,c_v - c_v = B$$

i. e. $B = c_v\,(k-1)$

$$\because \; T^{c_v} . \, v^{c_v(k-1)} = c_2'$$

$$\therefore \; T v^{k-1} = c_2$$

So, without knowing the second law, we have

$$pv^k = c_1$$

$$Tv^{k-1} = c_2$$

$$\frac{p^{\frac{k-1}{k}}}{T} = c_3$$

$$\therefore \left(\frac{p}{p_1}\right)^{\frac{k-1}{k}} = \left(\frac{v_1}{v}\right)^{k-1} = \frac{T}{T_1}$$

That is, we have the three projects of a line in space.

Really, the first law or the energy equation has many applications in Mechanics as well as in hydraulics and some other branches of science such as Chemistry. Take the case of fluid flow in a pipe.

For any thing other than the perfect gas, U is a function of both volume and temperature. Before we are going to discuss the flow, let us introduce another term in thermodymics, i.

$u = f\,(v,\ T.)$

pv ft—lb.
u ft—lb.

$i = u + pv$ (general)

$d\,i = du + p.dv + v.dp$ (general)

$\therefore\ d\,i = dq + v.\ dp$ ....(A)

This expression is analogovs to,

$d\,u = dq - p.dv.$ ......(B)

for perfect gas (special.)

$dq = c_p.\ dT - v.\ dp.$ (special)

$\therefore\ di = c_p.\ dT$ (special.)

make v const., from (B).

$dq = du = {}_1q_2 = u_2 - u_1$

make p const., from (A)

$dq = di = {}_1q_2 = i_2 - i_1$

Fluid Flow

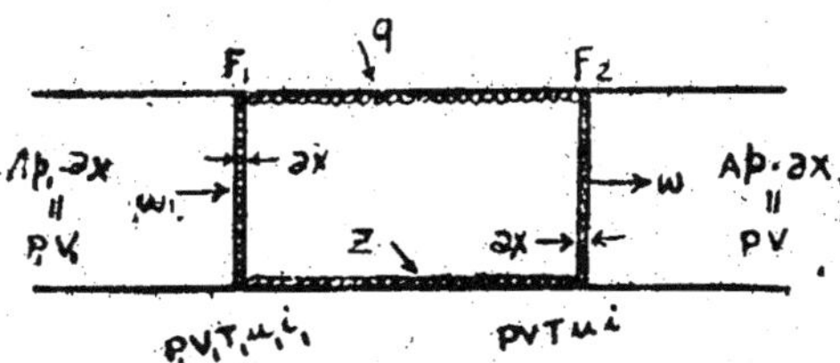

$\because$ A is area

$\therefore$ A. δ x is v.

On lamina F_1 we have a stripe of water of conditions $p_1\ v_1\ T_1\ u_1\ i_1$

On lamina F_2 we have a stripe of water of conditions $p\ v\ T\ u\ i,$

q is the heat received from outside.

Z is the heat gained at the expense of equivalent work due to friction.

w and w_1 designate velocities.

Now, let us record them by using accounting method:

Received	Lost
$\frac{w_1^2}{2q}$	Z (work)
u_1	pv
q	
(heat) Z	
$p_1 v_1$	
	Left
	$\frac{w^2}{2q}$
	u

$$\therefore \frac{w_1^2}{2q} + u_1 + q + z + p_1 v_1$$

$$= z + p v + \frac{w^2}{2q} + u$$

Suppose it is adiabatic, $q = o$,

and $u + p v = i$

$$\therefore \frac{w_1^2}{2q} + i_1 = \frac{w^2}{2q} + i$$

This is true provided all the particles are going along in one plane, such as F_1, F_2.

Corollary

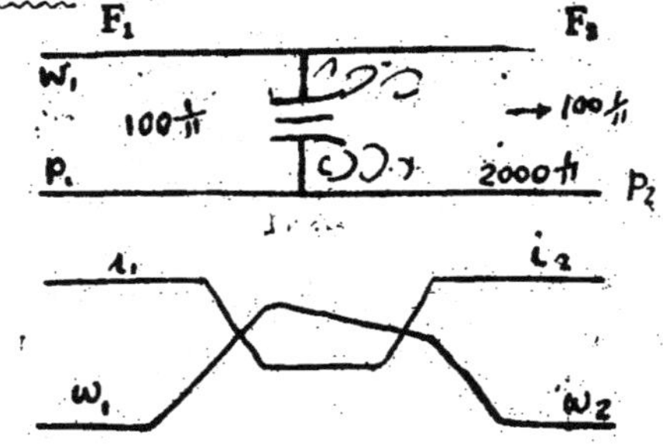

The above formula is not applicable to this case, but $i_1 = i_2$, or $u_1 + p_1 v_1 = u_2 + p_2 v_2$, if F_2 is taken far enough from the orifice.

II Second Law of Thermodynamics

Now we are going to discuss the second law, the law of degradation of energy, or the law of dissipation of energy. In connection with this we have to pay special attention on Carnot's Cycle and the meaning or conception of Entropy.

In starting, it is very important to recognize the famous Cycle. Which one of these two figures is Carnot Cycle? Well, both of them are! The left one is for the perfect gas, while the right one is for steam.

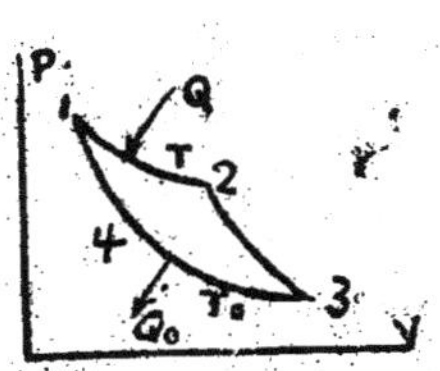

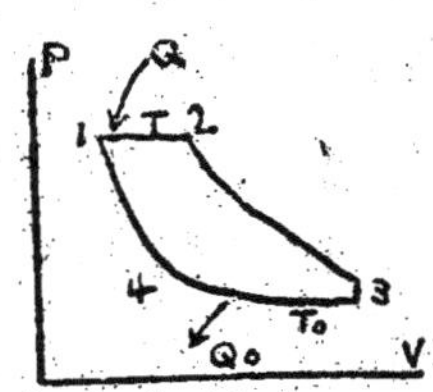

$Q \gtreqless Q_0$?

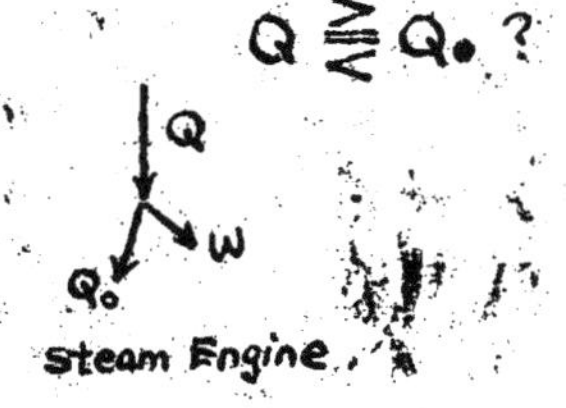

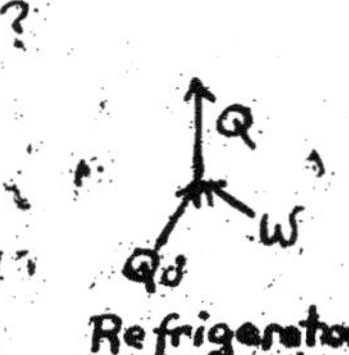

Next, it is important to know the relation between the two Q's. Is Q equal to, bigger than, or less than Q_0? Well, let's see. In the case of steam engine, Q is split into Q_0 and the work done as shown in the left figure. In the case of refrigerator, energy process is reversed, that is, work has to be added to the Q_0, so Q_0 is still to be bigger.

Remember that these two questions always bother the undergraduate students, so we have to be careful in these things.

$\therefore\ Q > Q_0$

$T > T_0$ no matter which direction it goes.

$$(\oint) dQ = (\oint) dU + (\oint) dW.$$

in a close cycle, u has the same state.

$$(\oint) dU = o.$$

$$\therefore (\oint) dQ = (\oint) dW \qquad {}_1Q_2 = Q$$

$$(Q) = (W) \qquad {}_2Q_3 = o \text{ (adiabatic)}$$

$${}_3Q_4 = -Q_0$$

$$\eta = \frac{(W)}{Q} = \frac{Q-Q_0}{Q} \qquad {}_4Q_1 = o \text{ (adiabatic)}$$

$$(Q) = Q - Q_0 = (W)$$

Carnot's Cycle is claimed to be the most efficient reversible engine, irrespective of the material of the medium. First, we have to prove this statement that it is the most efficient. Next, we prove that it is the most effi.ient irrespective of the material.

There are two ways of proving this first part. Really, the two methods are using the same principle, only different in application. They both start in saying that suppose another reversible engine which is more efficient than Carnot's engine, then they can be connected togather running the Carnot's engine reversed, they both lead to a conclusion which is contradictory to the very foundatien of thermodyuamics, the experience.

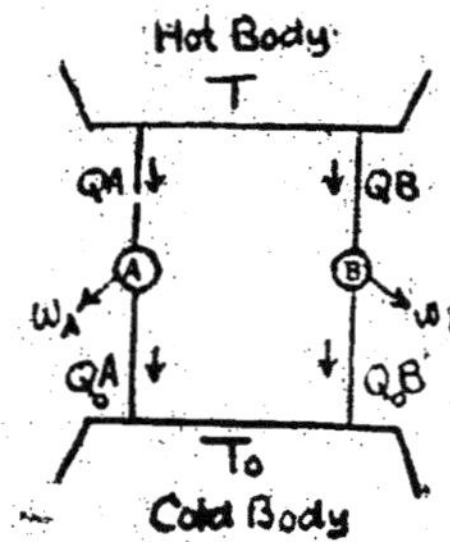

(A) and (B) are

Two Reversible Eng.

Suppose,

$\eta_A > \eta_B$,

if $Q^A = Q^B$

then, $W_A > W_B$

$\therefore Q_0^A > Q_0^B$

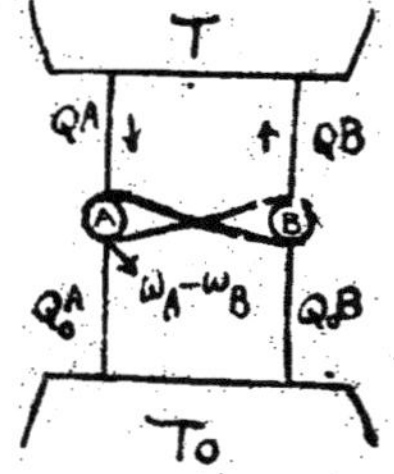

Now, if run (B) reversed, and connect (A) and (B).

$Q^A = Q^B$

$Q_0^B > Q_0^A$

and more work is done, the amount being

$w_A - w_B$.

i. e. we come to a conclusion that we have a device which can convert unavailable energy to useful work which will lead to the possibility of the perpetual motion of the 2nd kind.

Suppose, $\eta_A > \eta_B$
if,
$w_A = w_B$,
Then,
$Q^A < Q^B$
$Q_0^A < Q_0^B$

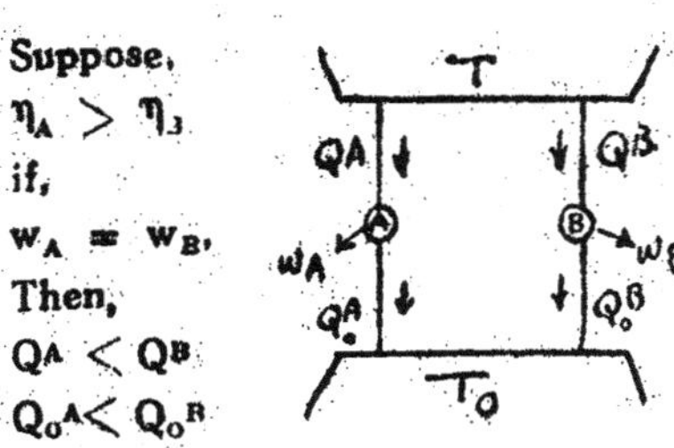

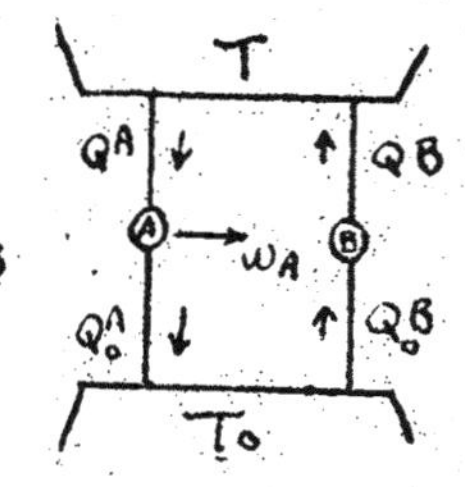

Reverse (B).
(A) Supply (B) with w_A. Then
$\because Q^B > Q^A$
$\therefore Q_0^B > Q_0^A$
i. e. heat can be transferred from lower temperature to higher without external expenditure of wovk, impossible.

It remains to be proved that the Carnot's Cycle efficiency is independent of the medium. If there is any thing which is proportional to the heat absorbed and the heat rejected, then the efficiency expression can be expressed in terms of that thing, and the resulting equation will be independent of the material, such as temperature which is not independent of the material and therefore not proportional to the heat absorbed or rejected. Any thing in the universe can be used as a thermometer to measure the heat, but none exists whose indication of temperature is proportional to the heat absorbed or rejected. The elongation of mercury stem, the volume change or the pressure change of a gas, the melting of a wax, etc., but none of them serves our purpose.

From the investigation of the Carnot's cycle Lord Kelvin in 1848 proposed a scale known as the Absolute Scale because it is independent of any substance. The scale is simply such that any two temperatures on it are proportional to the heat absorbed and that rejected by a reversible Carnot's engine working between these temperatures. If this scale is adopted, then the Carnot's efficiency formula is a function of absolute temperature which is independent of the medinm.

$q_1 > q_2 > q_3 > q_4$ Heat.
$l_1 > l_2 > l_3 > l_4$ Mercury stem.
$v_1 > v_2 > v_3 > v_4$ Gas vol.
$p_1 > p_2 > p_3 > p_4$ Gas pres.
$w_1 > w_2 > w_3 > W_4$ wax.

$Q_1 > Q_2 > Q_3 > Q_4 \rightarrow$ indicates temperature (Abs.) here.

$$\eta = 1 - \frac{Q_1}{Q_3}$$

$$\therefore \quad \eta = f\,(T_1, T_2)$$

(Since Carnot's cycle eff. is fixed, hence the temperatures indicated by Q's must be unigue.)

In another way, $$\eta = \frac{BT.\log_e \frac{v_2}{v_1} - B\,T_o \log_e \frac{v_3}{v_4}}{B\,T \log_e \frac{v_2}{v_1}} = 1 - \frac{T_o}{T} \left[\begin{matrix}\text{independent of} \\ \text{medium}\end{matrix}\right]$$

Now we will discuss ENTROPY which is to be derived from the conception of the Carnot's cycle. Particular attention should be directed to the way the term ENTROPY is introdnced .. there are only two books in existence which deal with entropy in this way, one is Bryan's book (German), the other is Goodenough's book (American.)

By Carnot's cycle, we know that a certain amount of heat can be changed into useful work and all the rest is discarded. We call the part which is changeable to useful work, the Available energy; and the other part wnich is discarded, the Unavailable energy. In the left picture, we have a Carnot's engine working between the two temperature levels, T and T_o. Then the efficency of the engine is $1\text{-}T_o/T$.

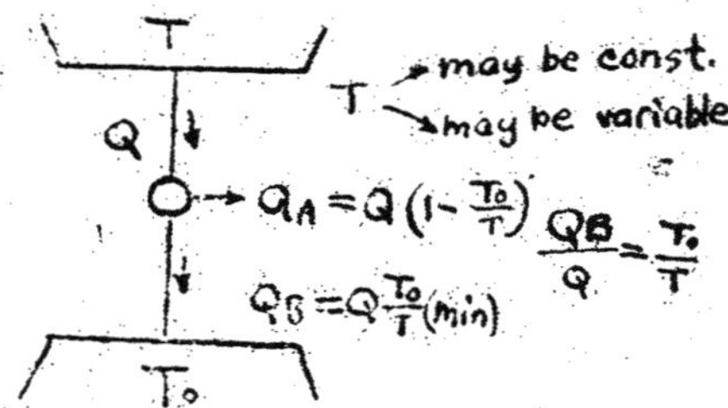

Hence the available energy Q_a must be $Q\,(1\text{-}T_o/T)$, and the unavailable energy Q_b must be $Q\,(T_o/T)$. Since the Carnot's Eff. is the highest obtainable, so the expression for Q_a is the maximum, and the expression for Q_b is the minimum. The temperature of the source T may be constant or variable. If it is constant it is easy; if variable, it needs differentials.

In dealing with any kind of engine or any kind of energy transformation, we have the four conditions involved, not necessarily all of them but a combination of some of them; the heat received from outside, the heat from friction, the phenomina of mixture and the work. All the four factors to be considered are diagramatically shown in the following figure. (The first term may be positive or negative; positive means heat received, and negative means heat rejected. The second is positive only, no matter whether the friction is overcomed by the expense of the internal heat or of the external heat supplied. The third term is always positive. The fourth term is zero.) No matter how the energy changes, there must be a part rendered unavailable, the minimum of which is Q (T_0/T) or as shown in the figure by means of dQ. Then it is easy to see that the first term may be positive or negative, that the second must be positive for there is always a part of available energy rendered unavailable through friction that the third is always a positive quantity for it can be easily proved or demonstrated that there is always an increase of unavailable energy through mixture, and that the last term is zero because it is reversible and nothing is rendered unavailble.

Q W H W

$$\Delta u_3 = T_0\int\frac{dQ}{T} + T_0\int\frac{dH}{T} + T_0\sum\frac{Q}{T} + 0$$

External Internal or External Internal

In the last expression, we have T_0 in every term in the right hand side. If we divide through by T_0, we get an expression below. And this, according to Clousius, is given a name, the Entropy. We designate this term in thermodynamics by s.

$$\frac{\Delta u_B}{T_0} = \int\frac{dQ}{T} + \int\frac{dH}{T} + \Sigma\,\frac{Q}{T}$$

$$S = \frac{u_B}{T_0} \text{ ---- Entropy.}$$

Now, let us see how should T_0 behave itself. We always say and have proved that U is a point function, that is, if it is plotted with a certain point on the plan and passes through a complete cycle to return to its original position, it has the same value as before no matter what has been done on this before it came to the original position. That means that the co-ordinates of the plan are not changed in the mean time; if they are changed, the same position means different values then. That means what? That means the value of T_0 ought not to be changed, or must be kept constant.

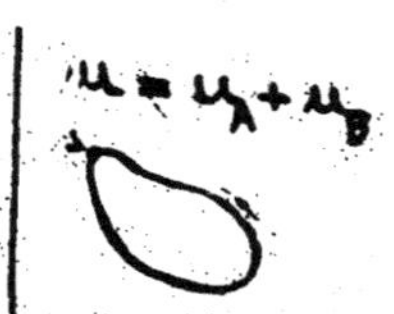

(T_0 must be unchanged.)

Well, some thing more about ENTROPY. In the last expression for entropy, we have three terms. In steam engine practice, we always talk about the medium of Uniform Temperature, so the last term may be cut out. And the resulting equation becomes,

$$S_2 - S_1 = \int_1^2 \frac{dQ}{T} + \int_1^2 \frac{dH}{T} \; ; \; ds = \frac{dQ}{T} + \frac{dH}{T}$$

$$Tds = dQ + dH$$

This is the expression generally applied to steam turbine where lots of energy are rendered unavailable through friction of the nozzles and blades.

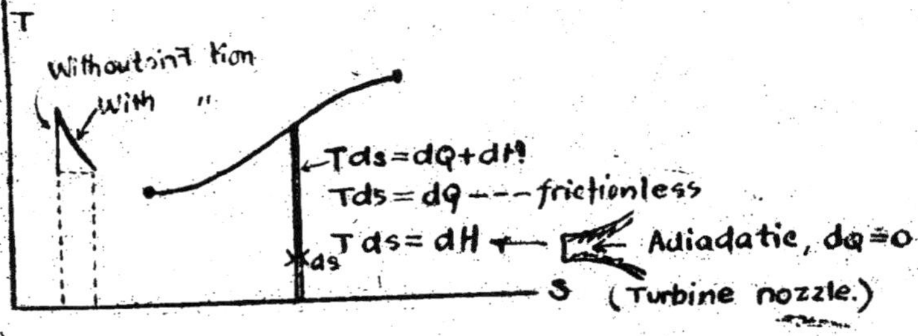

Graphically, s can be used as one of the coordinates, in T-s diagram we have the advantage of having the area under a curve represent amount of heat. But, caution! Ordinarily, the area represents Q and H togather. For

frictionless engine, the area represents Q only. For adiabatic change, it represents H only. There is something about which we ought to be very careful: Adiabadic change is generally represented on the T-s plane as a vertical line, that is not always true! With friction, the adiabatic line falls to the right of the vertical, because we have shown that the unavailable energy and therefore the entropy always increases when there is friction involved.
For reciprocating engine, H may be drop out and the general equation becomes,

$$ds = \frac{dQ}{T}, \quad \text{or} \quad Tds = dQ.$$

This is the formula with which most of authors introduce the term entropy to the students. we see now how absuad it is to use a special case to introduce the general term. And some of the authors even define this term by means of tne graph, saying one axis is temperature and the area under the curve is heat and we call the other axis entropy. If the students wonder about the friction, the mixture, no body knows what they will do.

Well, question arises, in the expression for the entropy we have in every term an inexact quantity Q, how it became that the entropy itself is an exact quantity or a point function? Very good, we will introduce the classical proof of its being exact regardless of the Q.

In the following process, we can prove that in a close cycle the change of entropy is zero no matter what has become of Q, that is, entropy is a point function regardless of Q. First, we use a single Carnot's cycle; then, we use several and lastly we extend the process to any cycle, because any cycle can be splitted into infinite number of Carnot's cycles.

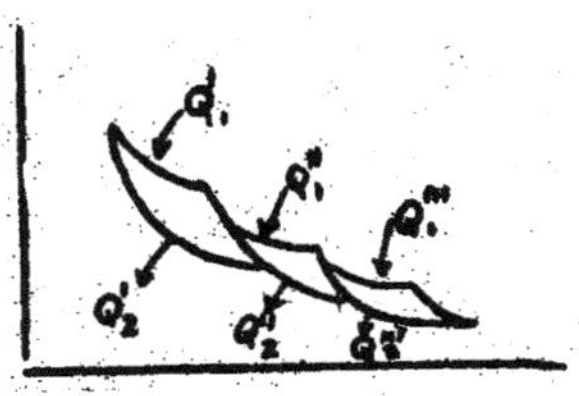

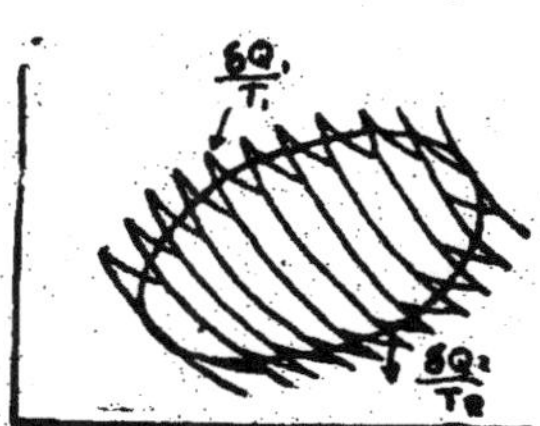

$$\frac{Q_1}{Q_2} = \frac{T_1}{T_2} \qquad \frac{Q_1'}{T_1'} + \frac{Q_2'}{T_2'} = o \qquad \text{In each element, we have,}$$

$$\frac{Q_1}{T_1} = -\frac{Q_2}{T_2} \qquad \frac{Q_1''}{T_1''} + \frac{Q_2''}{T_2''} = o \qquad \frac{\delta Q_1}{T_1} + \frac{\delta Q_2}{T_2} = o,$$

$$\cdots\cdots\cdots\cdots \qquad \therefore \int \frac{\delta Q}{T} = o.$$

$$\frac{Q_1}{T_1} + \frac{Q_2}{T_2} = o \qquad \therefore \Sigma \frac{Q}{T} = o \qquad \therefore (\int) \frac{\delta Q}{T} = o = (\int) ds = s.$$

Now, let's see how does it apply to the case of perfect gas. We know very well that in a close cycle in this case the increment of heat is not zero, but after transformed into an expression for entropy, the expression is at once seen to be an exact function.

$$\Sigma Q \neq o.$$

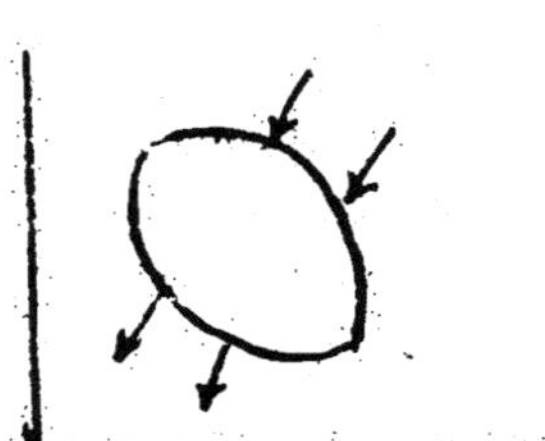

$$dq = c_v . dT + Ap. dv \quad \left[\begin{array}{c} pv = BT \\ \frac{p}{T} = \frac{B}{v} \end{array} \right]$$

$$\frac{dq}{T} = c_v . \frac{dT}{T} + A.B \frac{dv}{v} = ds.$$

$$\left. \frac{d.c_v}{dv} \right|_T = o, \quad \frac{d}{dT} .A.B \Big|_v = o, \quad \therefore ds = o$$

(the end)

RELATION OF FREIGHT TRAIN RESISTANCE TO AXLE LOADS.

陳廣沅

(K. Y. Chen)

The purpose of this paper is two-fold:

1. To find the relation between freight train resistance and axle loads, for 4-wheel truck cars;
2. To find the same relation for 6-wheel truck cars.

The results of the tests made by Prof. E. C. Schmidt and presented in Bull. 43 of the Engineering Experiment Station, University of Illinois are the most exhaustive for freight cars having 4-wheel trucks. The results are expressed in terms of "pounds per ton" for different car weights. In order to express the resistance in pounds per ton for different axle loads, it is necessary either to find the standard axle capacity, or to assume different axle loads. We will do both in the following, so that the results found may be conveniently applied to find the freight train resistance of different axle loads, or to find the resistance offered by a locomotive truck or a tender truck.

There are six standard car axles which have the following designations and capacities:

Designations	Axle Capacity
A	15,000 lbs.
B	24,000 "
C	32,000 "
D	40,000 "
E	50,000 "
F	60,000 "

If we find the corresponding car weights for the different axle capacities, and perpendiculars are erected in Fig. 10, Bull. 43 (This figure is reproduced in Fig. IV for reference,) at the different points on the abscissa representing the corresponding car weights, we can find the resistance for different speeds.

Table I gives the values thus found. The curves in Fig. Ia are plotted from the values of this table.

Table I

Axle capacity (lbs)	4-axle Car Wt. (tons)	Freight Train Resistance						
		Speeds: in miles per hour						
		5	10	15	20	25	30	35
15,00	30	5.45	5.75	6.25	6.75	7.45	8.00	8.75
24,000	48	4.50	4.70	5.05	5.50	6.00	6.50	7.20
32,000	64	3.15	3.40	3.60	3.85	4.25	4.65	5.15
40,000	80	3.00	3.15	3.45	3.65	4.00	4.50	4.80
50,000	100	"	"	"	"	"	"	"
60 000	120	"	"	"	"	"	"	"

It is to be remarked here that the results given in Bull. 43 (See Fig. IV) are for cars having a weight not more than 76 tons each. The values in the above table for cars of 80 tons and upwards are obtained by extrapolation. A glance over Fig. 10 of Bull. 43 will make it evident that the resistance at a certain speed is constant for any weight above 80 tons.

To make the results thus obtained more applicable, another table of values and another set of curves are constructed for several assumed axle loads at regular intervals, and they are respectively Table II and Fig. Ib.

Table II.

Axle loads (lbs)	4-axle Car Wt. (tons)	Freight Train Resistance						
		Speeds: in miles per hour.						
		5	10	15	20	25	30	35
10,000	20	6.75	7.30	7.80	8.50	9.25	10.00	10.85
15,000	30	5.45	5.75	6.25	6.75	7.45	8.00	8.75
20,000	40	4.40	4.70	5.05	5.50	6.00	6.55	7.20
25 000	50	3.75	3 90	4.25	4.50	5.00	5.50	6.05
30,000	60	3.30	3.50	3.70	4.00	4.40	4.80	5.40
35,000	70	3.10	3.25	3.50	3.75	4.10	4.50	5.00
40,000	80	3.00	3.15	3.40	3.65	4.00	4.40	4.80
up	up	"	"	"	"	"	"	"

(The same remark for Table I is applied here.)

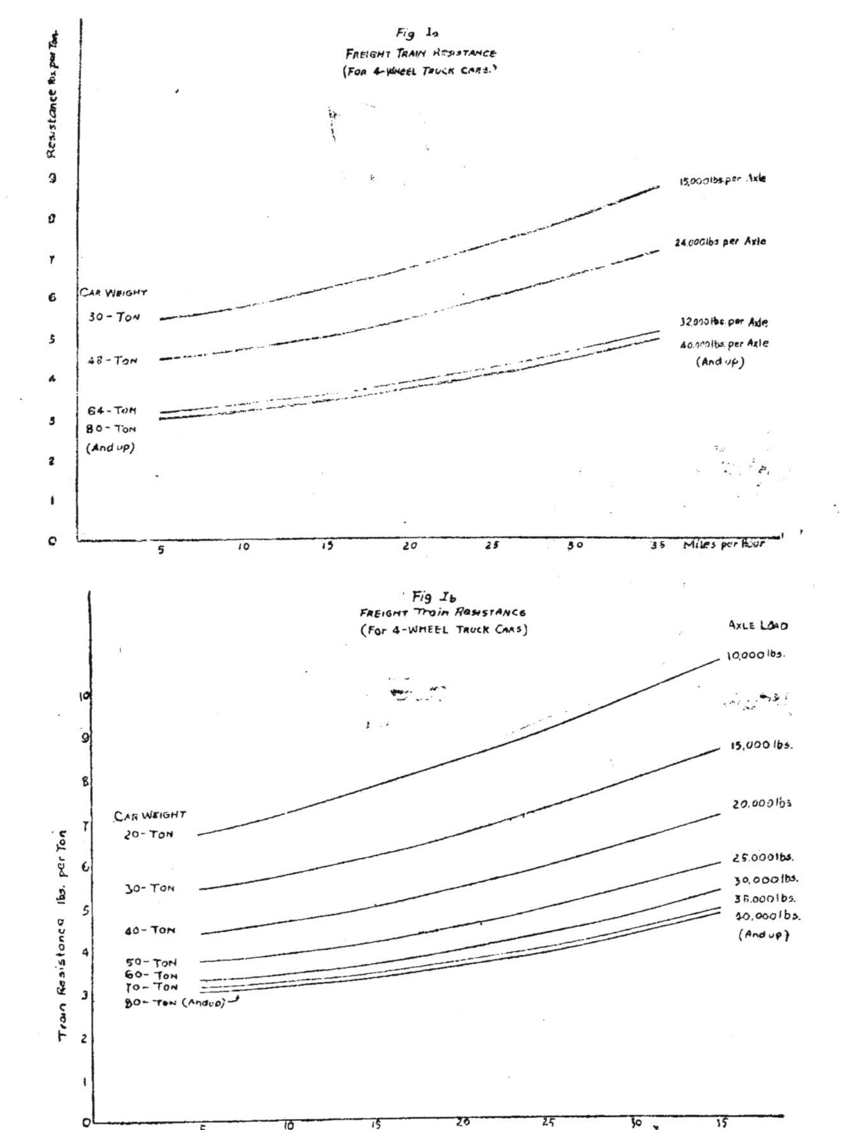

Fig 1a
Freight Train Resistance
(For 4-Wheel Truck Cars.)
Resistance lbs. per Ton.
Car Weight
30-Ton
48-Ton
64-Ton
80-Ton
(And up)
15,000 lbs. per Axle
24,000 lbs. per Axle
32,000 lbs. per Axle
40,000 lbs. per Axle
(And up)
Miles per Hour
Fig Ib
Freight Train Resistance
(For 4-Wheel Truck Cars)
Axle Load
10,000 lbs.
15,000 lbs.
20,000 lbs.
25,000 lbs.
30,000 lbs.
35,000 lbs.
40,000 lbs.
(And up)
Car Weight
20-Ton
30-Ton
40-Ton
50-Ton
60-Ton
70-Ton
80-Ton (And up)
Train Resistance lbs. per Ton
Miles per Hour

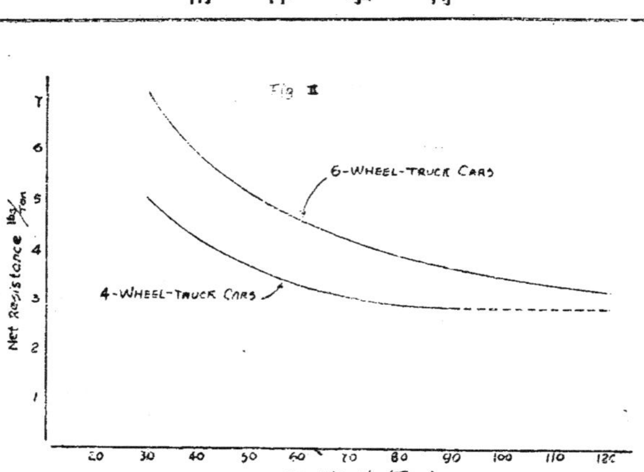

It is to be noted that so far we have only considered the resistance offered by freight cars having 4-wheel trucks, and the two tables and figures are only applicable to 4-axle cars or cars having 4-wheel trucks. Next, we will take up the 6-wheel truck cars.

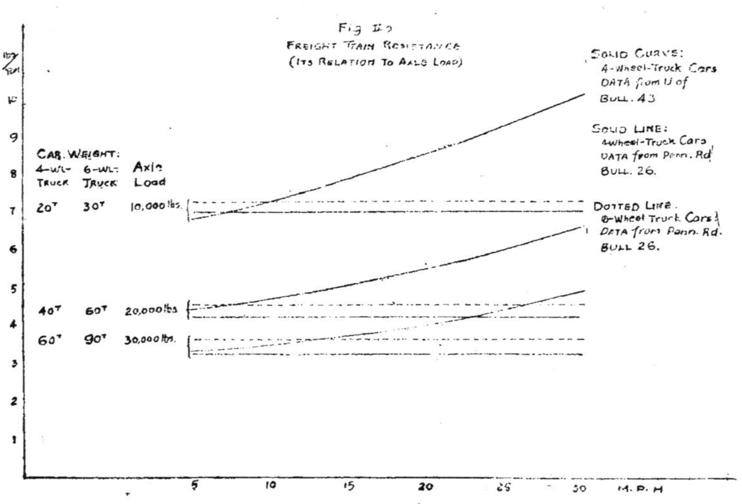

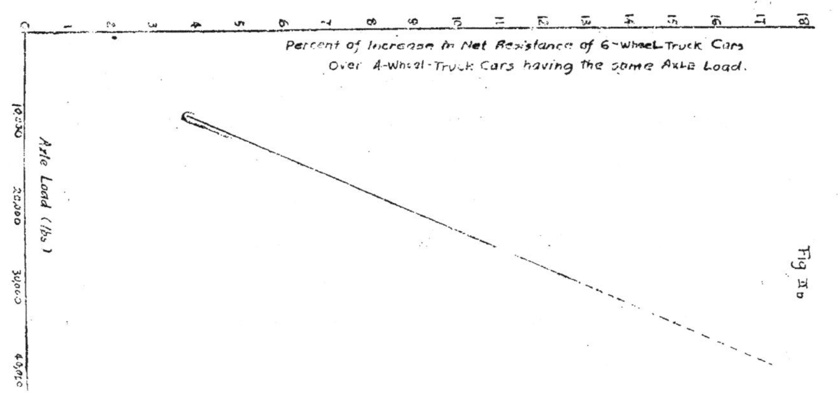

Now, we will consider the 6-wheel-truck cars. Since the Bull. 43 of the U. of I. was out there have been in practice some cars and tenders having 6-wheel trucks. The Norfolk add Western Railway Co. made some tests of such cars, and the results can be found in both the proceedings of American Railway Master Mechanics Association, Vol. 49, page 418, and Bulletin 26 of Pennsylvania Railroad Co., page 15. For convenience, it is reproduced in Fig. II wherein is also shown the resistance of Pennsylvania Railroad H21a cars which have 4-wheel trucks.

Fig. II shows the fact that for the same car weight, the one with 6-wheel-trucks offers more resistance than that with 4. The difference runs from 1.1 lbs. per ton for a car weight of 70 tons, to more than two pounds for a car wesght of 30 tons.

In fig. IIa, the relation of freight train resistance with axle loads are represented by graphs. There are three sets of lines. The curved lines are plotted from the data of Bull. 43 of the U. of I. The straight solid lines are from Pennsylvania Railroad Co. Bull. 26. Both of these two are for 4-wheel truck cars. The straight dotted lines are plotted also from Bull. 26 of Pa. Rd. Co., and they are for 6-wheel truck cars. The resistance given by the Pa. Rd. Co. is constant for all speeds and much lower than that given by the U. of I. test.

The assumption that the resistance of freight trains is constant for all the speeds of freight service is not justified either from theory or from practice, so it can not be universally accepted. The conditions which prevailed in these two tests will account for the higher and lower values. The Pennsylvania Rd. as a whole has heavier rails, more solid roadbed, and better epuipments than the Illinois Central Railroad where the U. of I. tests were carried. As the latter railroad is more representative of the average conditions of all the railroad operation of U. S. A., it is justified to accept the results of this test to find the freight train resistance.

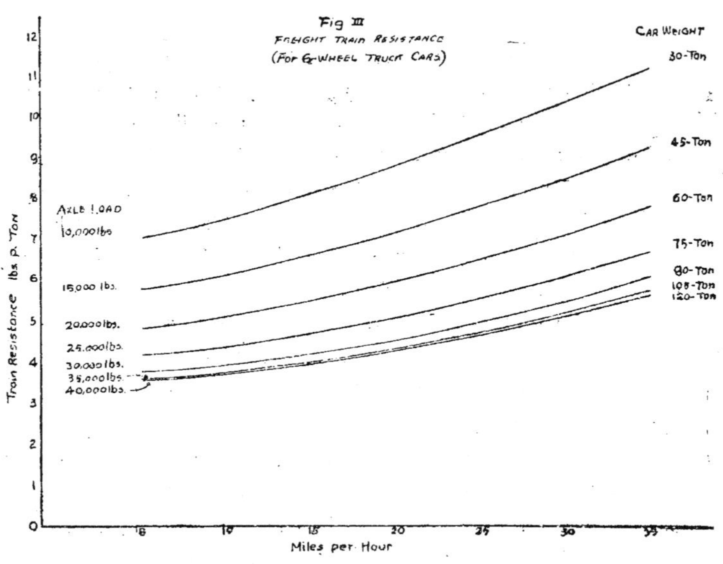

However, we are attempting to find the resistance offered by 6-wheel truck cars, the only information we have is the test result made by the Norfolk and Western Ry. Co., referred to adove, and this result is expressed in the same way as the Pa. Rd. Co.'s result, that is, assumed to be constant for all speeds. Now, if we make this assumption, and that is probably true, that the Norfolk test result bears the same ratio to Pa. test result as the true resistance of 6-wheel truck cars bears to tho test results of the U. of Ilinois, we can use the same results of the U. of I. to 6-wheel truck cars by the introduction of a correction factor.

Let us see how much higher resistances are the 6-whesl truck cars offering to the movement of a train. In Fig. IIa, the dotted straight lines are higher than the corresponding solid straight lines, but they are not at the same distance apart from the corresponding solid straight lines. If we express the difference of the resistances offered by the two kinds of cars in percentage of the resistance of the 4-wheel truck cars, we have the following table III.

Table III

Axle Load in lbs.	Higher resistance offered by 6-wheel truck cars	
	in lbs./Ton	in percentage of 4-wheel truck cars
10,000	0.25	3.6
20,000	0.35	8.3
30,000	0.40	12.5

The percentage of increase in resistance is plotted against the axle loads in Fig. IIb; and this is evidently a straight line.

Now, we will apply the same ratio to the resistances given in Fig. Ib., and Table IV and Fig. III are constructed to show the relation between the freight train resistance and axle loads for 6-wheel truck cars just as those are for 4-wheel truck cars, always ready and easy to apply.

Tadle IV

Axle loads (lbs)	6-wheel Car-Wt. (ton)	Freight Train Resistance. Speeds: miles per hour. 5	10	15	20	25	30	35
10,000	30	7.00	7.56	8.08	8.80	9.58	10.36	11.23
15,000	45	5.78	6.10	6.63	7.15	7.90	8.48	9.28
20,000	60	4.77	5.10	5.47	5.96	6.50	7.10	7.80
25,000	75	4.14	4.31	4.70	4.97	5.52	6.08	6.68
30,000	90	3.72	3.94	4.16	4.50	4.95	5.40	6.08
35,000	105	3.56	3.73	4.03	4.30	4.71	5.17	5.74
40,000	120	3.51	3.68	3.98	4.26	4.67	5.15	5.61

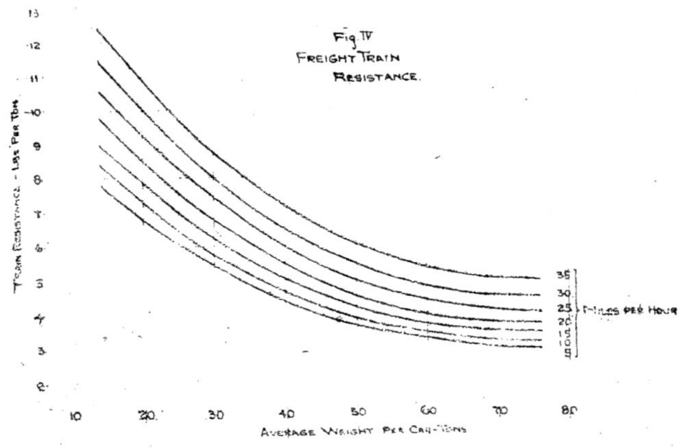

the end

坎拿大之鐵路問題

茅以新

1.坎拿大概述　坎拿大位於美洲北部,與美國爲近鄰.佔地3,729,665英畝,幾與中國相同.氣候寒冷,然在南部與美國鄰近一帶,一至四月即甚溫和.地質肥沃,物產豐富.西部平原,綿延數千里,素稱世界糧穀出產大宗之地.極西沿太平洋一帶則森林叢密,每林有佔地數千畝或竟萬畝者.中部東部近北一帶,樹木亦甚繁茂,坎人多伐以製紙.至於礦產則除金銅鎳鉛並煤外.石綿之出產,幾足供給全世界之用.大西洋沿岸一帶,大湖(Great Lakes)地域,漁業亦稱重要.

然以坎拿大地域之廣,物產之富,人口則僅九百萬.不及美國十分之一,不及中國四十分之一.此乃坎拿大之最顯著而最難解決之問題也.考坎拿大實乃一極新之國.一百年前除沿大西洋岸,聖老倫河兩旁略有白人之蹤跡外,全坎拿大一片荒野,不見人跡.間有土人居于穴中.亦寥若晨星.五十年前此溫大列阿(Ontario)省,全爲樹木森林.人跡所絕不到者.今則稱坎拿大人口最密之省.一百年內人口自極少數增至九百萬,亦不可謂非速矣.蓋多自英,法,德等處移民而來者.記者居坎將一年,所遇坎人,詢以家世,皆來自歐洲.故歷年人口之增加,其原因完全爲移民,而不得謂爲自身之增加.晚近數年,移民趨勢,又有轉向.其影響於坎拿大之前途者甚大.此即移民入美國之日見增多也.坎人喜赴美國,原因不一.其大要不外美國生活較易,工資較高,而美國大城之繁華亦有關係焉.每年轉赴美國之坎人數約四五萬.而此四五萬人,皆少壯有爲青年.國家正賴以發展種種事業者.易言之,坎拿大每年費巨款教養此四五萬之青年.而至成人時竟不得其服務,反以供給美國.此坎拿大人口問題之焦點也.

2.坎拿大之鐵路　坎拿大全境有鐵路39,062哩,雖不及美國六分之一，而以人口比例計算，則坎拿大人民每人享用鐵路哩程爲世界冠。可于下表見之：

國別	人口	鐵路哩數	每千人享用鐵路哩數
中國	400,000,000	8,000	.02
英國	45,000,000	23,700	.52
德國	60,000,000	39,000	.65
法國	41,000,000	32,000	.75
美國	112,000,000	252,000	2.25
坎拿大	8,800,000	39,000	4.43

觀上表可知坎拿大之鐵路，發達甚于世界各國。而坎拿大之鐵路問題，亦集中于此發達過甚之一點。地積遼闊，人民稀少，鐵路橫跨大陸，路線冗長，耗費亦大。營業數最常與人民數爲正比例，今人民稀少，故營業亦不發達。加之鐵路費用，百分之七十爲定數。無論營業衰旺，此百分七十之費用，必須支付，不能節省。易言之，坎拿大之鐵路，實人民之重負。此節當於下文詳述之。

坎拿大鐵路之歷史前後不過八十年。1852年祗有159哩，多在滿地可（Montreal）附近1854年始達都朗度（Toronto）。時軌間爲五呎六吋，較標準軌間爲廣。與美國鐵路接軌至多不便。越數年即改爲標準軌間四呎八吋半。今則坎拿大全境鐵路皆爲標準軌間。通達無阻，此彼時鐵路人員眼光遠大之福也。

1870坎拿大東境沿大西洋殖民地一帶鐵路勃興。1871年坎拿大西境版圖達太平洋，乃有建造坎拿大太平洋鐵路（Canadian Pacific又譯名昌興公司）之議。全路分三段建築，至1885年全路方告成功。1896年西方營業發達，鐵路需要增廣，於是有坎北鐵路之興造。1910年，坎拿大太平洋鐵路營業大爲發達。乃有其他資本家建議興築另一線橫跨大陸直達太平洋以與坎太鐵路分利。中經幾多困難，迄1914年方告工竣。然自此競爭在所不免。甚方嘗受重大損失坎太公司卒以資本雄厚,營業得法未受重創.其他小公司之與競爭者,不能支持,幾頻破產.坎政府數次助款助地,卒無效果至1922年乃合併所有各小鐵路成坎拿大國家鐵路(Canadian National Railways),規模宏大,辦事較易.至今日則營業狀況日見進步.雖尙不足以與坎太鐵路相比衡,已非昔日紛亂之可同日語矣.

坎拿大全境之39,062哩鐵路,除4,300哩為美國鐵路道經坎境者外,餘34,700哩中,20,900哩屬坎拿大國家鐵路公司,13,800哩屬坎拿大太平洋鐵路公司.其1925年營業狀況如下:

	坎拿大國家鐵路公司 Canadian National	坎拿大太平洋鐵路公司 Canadian Pacific.
營業進款		
貨物	$ 180,482,543 54	$ 128,410,055.84
旅客	36,618,481 66	33,126,445 42
郵件	3,554,200 23	3,552,416.06
其他	24,315,977.18	18,267,088 20
共計	$ 244,971,202 61	$ 183,356,005 52
營業出款		
養路	$ 43,006,813 70	$ 25,473,903.69
修理機車與車輛	47,902,092 16	33,108,544 89
廣告等	6,726,472 90	8,477,102.58
運輸	106,477,437.08	65,009,476 79
其他	10,359,676 84	11,132,201 71
共計	$ 212,706,787 82	$ 143,201,229 66
營業淨收	$ 32,264,414 79	$ 40,154,775.86
營業百分率	86.83%	78.20%

觀上表可知坎拿大鐵路規模之大矣.細察坎拿大國家鐵路公司之營業狀況,收入支出皆較坎拿大太平洋鐵路公司為多,但結果淨收反較少.此爲宜注意之一點也.然1925年實坎拿大國家鐵路公司成立以來成績最佳

之一年.1924淨收僅$15,020,163 31,營業百分率爲92.68%.未合併以前歷年皆有虧蝕.今年（1926）三月份營業更有猛進.此皆足顯合併之利者也.

3.所謂坎拿大之鐵路問題 然則何謂坎拿大之鐵路問題？欲明此點,不可不述二鐵路之資金資產支配.

坎拿大太平洋鐵路公司乃完全私有鐵路公司.當建造之初,本爲坎拿大國家企業.後因工程浩大,坎拿大政府恐人民負担太重,建議招募私有公司承辦,而坎政府當竭全力以助其成.於是有坎拿大太平洋鐵路公司之組織.坎政府除將已成路線及測量圖案無價交與公司,實値$38,000,000,外,又准用國家土地25,000,000畝,又助國庫$35,000,000.加之適在1880年時工價物價皆賤,故坎太公司能以$1,113,872,692.54之資金成全路.坎拿大國家鐵路公司則不然,除小部分在東方與中部之鐵路,營業素旺,不成問題外,大部分乃橫跨大陸之長距離路線.多於1910年間建造者.物價工價騰貴,政府亦未能多助.以故坎拿大國家鐵路公司之資金竟達$2,119,811,644.22路線雖較坎太路長,而設備之精良與完美,遠不及坎太.每年所需修理與養路費用亦遠過坎大.

尙有一點,其關係亦甚重大,非可忽視者,卽資金之如何徵收是也.按鐵路資本可以細分二種,一爲股票,一爲債票.股票有選舉與被選舉權,但無擔保之利息.債票則無選舉或被選舉權,但其利息爲擔保的.若債票利息到期不付,則鐵路公司卽將宣告破產.坎拿大太平洋鐵路公司之資金大半爲股票,極少數爲債票.蓋當時股票信用與債票不相上下,發股票已能集資.坎拿大國家鐵路公司之資金大半爲債票,極少數爲股票.當歐戰初起時各處金錢緊張,股票難以集資,故必發債票方能集資.易言之,坎拿大太平洋鐵路公司無重大之定期擔保利息.除每年$14,000,000爲債票利息外,其餘可付可不付.公司信用毫不受影響.坎拿大國家鐵路公司則不然.每年定期債票利息必須照付者達$77,000,000.苟不能照付或稍延期,公司卽將宣告破產.其困難可知矣.

但坎拿大國家鐵路公司每年淨收,從未有達此數者.即以 1925年最旺年論,亦不過 $32,000 000 較 $77,000,000 相差甚遠.何以至今尚未宣告破產?無他,坎拿大政府每年以國庫之款補此不足耳.蓋公司各債票利息皆注明由坎拿大政府擔保.不然連債票亦無人顧問.易言之坎拿大人民每年所納稅中,一部分乃用以經營此國家鐵路.

於是所謂坎拿大之鐵路問題在此矣.

(1)坎拿大國家鐵路公司每年耗國庫不下四千萬.人民負稅已重,鐵路原為生利之事業,今不能生利,反增加人民重負.此爲問題一.

(2)坎拿大太平洋鐵路公司之不平鳴.謂兩鐵路同在境內營業,有同樣競爭機會.今一則每年接受國家大宗款項,一則置諸不聞不問,未免太不平允.

(3)政府之欲罷不能.苟政府一旦中止補助,鐵路宣告破產,全國運輸將受莫大影響.其損失遠超所補助之數.且鐵路費用,改良,修理等皆萬不可少.若修理費養路費被裁省,將來苟欲整理,將不啻新置.費用更爲不貲.

4.鐵路國有與私有之爭論 坎拿大太平洋鐵路乃私有企業,坎拿大國家鐵路乃國有企業.今二鐵路既有此顯著成敗之分,乃有多數坎人謂國有最不經濟,苟皆由私有公司管理,則成績必可較佳,坎人亦不致受重負.此浮面之言也.然亦須細察雙方細情.大凡鐵路企業最能表現其營業實況者爲營業百分率(Operatiug Ratio)營業百分率小于65%者皆得稱爲興旺.大于65%者則鐵路管理與經營必尚有可以改良者.觀坎拿大兩大鐵路之營業百分率,坎太公司爲78.20%.坎國爲96.83%.二者皆高于65%,是二者皆尚有發展之餘地.然坎國之情形爲尤失望.細察兩路出入款項,則知兩路之異同,全在養路與運輸費用中.此次國無可如何者也.蓋坎國于建築之初路基設備既非完美,其養路與運輸費用自然超過他路.國有私有無與也.使『

坎大」人員經營「坎國」亦無可如何.境不同勢不同,不能混而論之也.

吾人苟再細察坎拿大國家鐵路之組織則可知國有與否與管理經營毫無影響.坎拿大國家鐵路之已發股票大多數爲坎拿大政府所有,則選擇鐵路董事與經理之權自亦操于政府.但舍此以外,政府絲毫不干預鐵路行政用人或任何事務.當政府任明香氏爲坎拿大國家鐵路總董事並總理時,曾鄭重聲明凡關于鐵路行政用人一切完全聽其主持,政府决不干預.故明香氏得展其偉才整頓路政.數年來日見進步未始非其功績.設明香氏每任用一機務長,或段長,或廠長,必先請命于政府,或政府所薦人員必須安插,則事務紛亂,百業難舉,其情況將與中國鐵路之糾紛相同矣.謂之國有不若私有之佳,誰曰不宜？今坎拿大國家鐵路能除此惡例,努力于管理與經營之改良,雖私有不能過之.

且以晚近趨勢而論,公衆事業如鐵路等應歸國有,已成定論.良以鐵路關係全國人民,爲國家命脈,其性質不僅營業而已.若歸私有,則經營者純以營利爲主,忘其對于國家與人民之責任矣.德國鐵路國有也,其成績爲任何私有鐵路企業所望塵莫及,則國有私有何與焉？

然著者于此不得不向讀者鄭重申說,即鐵路國有,其行政管理必須獨立是也.若以中國爲例,則交通部除規劃新路線,制定規劃與條例並審查轉運價格外,舉凡關于行車管理用人等一切應交與鐵路董事會.董事若干人由人民投票選舉,董事長即掌執全國鐵路事務,董事會每年應將經過與出納報告國會.如有疑問,國會得查究之.鐵路與政府之關係止於此.此外關於鐵路範圍以內之事,政府不得干預.如此則鐵路之發展乃有把握.然以今日之軍人霸佔路綫,戰事頻仍,求按日轉運之便尙不可得,奚云效率,更不必言改良發展矣!

3.國際投資之研究 設吾人以坎拿大全局而觀察兩鐵路之情形,則知其範圍實不止坎拿大已也.按坎拿大太平洋鐵路之債劵除少數操于坎拿大人民外,大多數操于英美資本家與銀行之手.坎拿大國家鐵路之債券亦然.故每年利息若干多數流至外國.易言之坎人血汗經營期年之盈餘,其結果乃不能留爲自用,反以肥其他各國.此情況萬難久持.其結果實與外貨充斥市場利益外溢者相同.以兩鐵路統盤計算每年債券利金不下$90,000,000,其中至少$50,000,000流至英美各國.則十年卽達$500,000,000二十年已逾坎拿大太平洋鐵路公司之全數資本額,豈不驚人？故以著者觀之,坎拿大鐵路之大問題不在國有私有,而實爲此國際投資之現象也.

然則補救之道惟何？曰坎拿大人民應努力收回所有債券也.兩鐵路現有人員十五萬人,以每人購債券一張卽達$15,000,000之數,再加人民之投資,不數年卽可收回.然坎人是否有此實力,尙屬一疑問耳.

6. 移民與鐵路之關係　以坎拿大鐵路發達過甚之現象,人民之稀少,欲其集實力以購回所有債券,實不易易.目前惟一希望,在人口之增加,則每人負担較輕,百業易舉.人口增加本分二途,一爲本身之繁殖,一爲移民之增加.本身繁殖較緩,移民之希望則甚大.吾人皆知英國失業工人常數逾百萬,若以此百萬移居坎拿大,則二者皆受其益,一舉兩得之道也.

然移民亦有困難.其一則坎拿大氣候之寒冷也.普通工人每年夏季所積存儲金,至冬季皆化爲煤煙以禦寒.人以畏寒而裹足者爲數不少.其二則工資較少,難以招致.其三則鄰國美國之競爭,移民自多喜居于美國,而坎拿大患人稀矣.

7. 預測　著者居坎雖不滿一年,但從各方面之觀察與研究,可預測坎拿大鐵路問題之將來,不外下列兩途.兩者可行其一,能全實現,自爲更佳.

(1)兩鐵路之合併　坎拿大太平洋鐵路與坎拿大國家鐵路規模皆至宏大,競爭在所不免.競爭固足以使雙方管理人員,努力改良路政,增加效率,然競爭至無限制,則危險叢生,爲害甚大.卽以兩路而言,橫跨大陸之按日列車,雙雙開行,各皆乘客稀少.若能合併之,則乘客安適,公司亦可節省大宗費用矣.再以電報營業論,無論大小城市,兩鐵路之電局,雙雙並立.甚一局之不能應付,競爭之現象耳.類此者甚多.以著者估計,合併之後,所省費用至少可達百分之二十,爲數已足驚人矣.

（2）坎拿大與美合衆國之合併　坎拿大名屬英國,實則自設總理自設內閣.一切由坎人選舉美國名爲異國,實則交通往來,異常密切,以民性論坎人與美人最相似,與英人則有顯著不同.再按實際而言,二國之分離,實非其福.坎人購美貨須納重稅歷年辛苦經營之鐵路贏餘反無價歸諸美國.合併則納稅可以平允,政費可以節省,鐵路問題亦可從此解決.蓋鐵路之虧蝕由兩國人民共同担負,無所謂利權外溢,苦負重稅矣.質之讀者,以爲何如?

燃料概論

周　熙

機械工程大都以熱爲原動力.熱之來源不止一端.而能施諸實用者,厥惟燃燒所生之熱也.

燃燒　燃燒者,燃料與養素化合之謂也.此種作用,須在適宜狀況中,始能發生.第一,燃料必須與空氣觸接,以便化合.第二,溫度必須提高,使燃料着火.普通燃料着火,在紅熱時,約600°c.第三,燃料須成碎分子.分子愈碎,則觸接空氣之處愈多,燃燒愈速.惟過於微細,集合成堆,以致空氣不能透入,亦不易燃燒.須用空氣鼓動之,使成霧狀,乃有氣體之性質.其燃燒極其猛烈.

焰　燃料有有焰與無焰之別.焰乃氣體燃燒之現象.故實體燃料,常屬無焰.氣體燃料,莫不有焰.木與煤燃燒時亦有焰,係因其中氣體物,蒸溜而出,着火成焰.焰或有光或無光.凡空氣充足,燃燒完全者無光.否則有光.

烟　燃料焚燒之際,往往有烟.是爲燃燒不盡之表示.其故由於空氣不足溫度降低.以致炭素分子.自然涼冷.不能與養素化合.遂與廢氣并行散去.故烟者.即未經燃燒之炭素分子也.烟愈多則燃料之損失愈大.應設種種方法.以防止之.

空氣 燃燒之廢氣隨時自烟囪散去.空氣亦以時引入.爐中廢氣之重量本大於氣.惟當散去時.溫度增高.其重量減少.故能自烟囪上昇.將空氣引入.蓋空氣之流通.全恃烟囪內之熱氣與其外之冷氣重量參差.故廢氣愈熱.烟囪愈高.則與冷氣之重量相差愈遠.空氣之流通愈便.於是燃燒之事.始進行無礙.

發熱量 一磅燃料所生之熱量.謂之發熱量.此係燃料各分子燃燒之熱.集合而成.故發熱量應依燃料之成分計算.燃料皆有炭輕養三素.炭素燃燒之熱等於8080單位.輕素燃燒之熱等於34000單位.養素常與輕素化合.化合量爲一與八之比.是項與養化合之輕素.不能燃燒.應行減去.發熱量之算式如下.

$$C.P. = C \times 8080 + \left(H - \frac{1}{8}o\right) \times 34000$$

式中C.P.爲發熱量.C,H,O爲炭輕養三素之成分.$\left(H - \frac{1}{8}o\right)$謂之可燃輕.

蒸汽量 一磅燃料蒸水成汽（水與汽均在100°C.）之重量.謂之蒸汽量.阮根教授(Prof. Rankine)定此標準.用於機械工事.若以蒸汽潛熱(537C.單位.)除發熱量.即得蒸汽量.但燃料內本有水分.又其中輕素於燃燒時成水九倍之多.皆須用熱蒸發成汽.故應減去一部分發熱量.是爲燃料自0°升至100°C.之熱量也.蒸汽量之算式如下.

$$E.P. = \frac{C \times 8080 + \left(H - \frac{1}{8}o\right) \times 34000 - (9H + W) \times 637}{537}$$

式中E.P.為蒸汽量.W為燃料內原有水分.餘與前式同.

體熱計　發熱量亦可用體熱計測定之.其種類至多.而以陶卜生體熱計（Thompson Calorimetre）運用爲最便.茲述之於下.

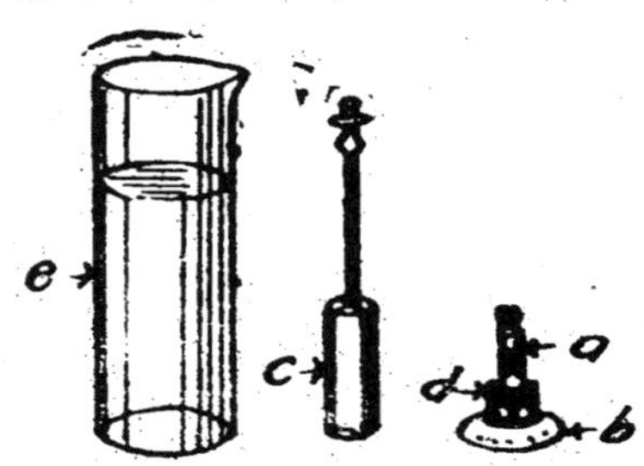

（a）銅筒.（b）底座.（c）銅帽.其下周圍有孔.上有活塞.（d）彈簧.（e）水杯.以燃料和綠酸鉀與硝酸鉀置筒內.上加引信.先測水之溫度.次燃引信.急以帽加於筒上.用彈簧夾緊.閉活塞.置水中.俟燃燒完畢.開活塞.再測水之溫度.乃可推算之.茲設一例於下.

水	2000 克
燃料	2 克
第一次溫度	15° C.
第二次溫度	23°.5 C.
升高溫度	8°.5 C.
加熱量損失10%	.85
	9.35

發熱量等於 9.35×1000=9350 加洛里.設用水537×2克.燃料2克.升高溫度即等於蒸汽量.

燃料分類　燃料可依物體三態.大別爲三類.

（一）實體燃料——木.泥煤.煤.木炭.焦.煤磚.

（二）液體燃料——石油.酒精.

（三）氣體燃料——天然氣.煤氣.製焦氣.西門士氣.冶爐氣.

茲錄其中用於機械者.分别論之.惟木炭.焦.煤磚.絕少用於機械.故不及焉.

(一) 實體燃料

木　森林廣闊之區.即以木爲燃料.其焰甚長.宜於輪船火車之用.二者之鍋爐.受熱面積甚大.易於吸收.此種燃料之優點有三.一易於着火.二焰長.三灰少.且無損害爐柵之物.缺點亦有三.一水分多.吸收一部分熱量.二養素多.可燃輕減少.發熱量亦減少.三體積過大.不易收藏.幷須闊大之爐灶.

木分軟硬二種.凡比重在0.55以上者.謂之硬木.橡.楓.核桃.等樹屬之.比重較低者.謂之軟木.柏.榆.楊.柳.等樹屬之.完全乾燥之木.比重可至1.5.着火之難易.亦視堅度之高低爲斷.

木之主要分子曰纖維素.$C_6H_{10}O_5$.中有炭素44.44.輕素6.17.養素49.29.故無可燃輕.

木內常有若干無機物.不能燃燒.是爲灰分.內含炭酸鈣.炭酸鹼性物.硫酸.綠化鹼性物.硅酸.無水燐酸.苦土.養化鐵.養化錳.礬土等物.

木中之水分.多寡不一.凡性質堅實.生長年久之樹.在冬季時.含水最少.但甫經斵伐.仍含水分百之五〇.以此去皮置露天中.使風吹拂.自能日就乾燥.

木之平均成分如下.

	全乾	吹乾
炭素, C	50	40
輕素, H	6	4.8
養素, O	41	32.8
淡素, N	1	.8
灰分,	2	1.6
水分,		20.0
	100	100.0

木之發熱量等於4346加洛里.蒸汽量等於7.4磅.

泥煤　泥煤產於緯度高處.與空曠高原.以及温帶無樹之地.慢流河川之濱.其原始爲各種水蘚.(Sphagnum).自生自滅.日就腐爛.積久而成厚層.泥煤有高地低地之別.與新成舊成之分.又因探取之法不同.而有割取掘取之殊焉.

亞歐美三洲北部.均產泥煤.英法德俄美諸國.出產甚富.巴威利亞鐵路.以爲火車燃料.惟體積過大.不便容載.故用寬大煤車.或加以壓縮.以減其容量.

泥煤中無硫磺與砒化物.水分居其大半.濕者居百分之七〇.乾者亦百分之二五.其他各分子之成分如下.

	(1)	(2)
C	61.04	54.02
H	6.67	5.21
O及Z	30.46	30.38
灰分	1.83	9.73

灰之成分.計有石灰.養化鐵.硅酸.燐酸.硫酸.炭酸.鹽基物.礬土.苦土.磺化鐵種種.

發熱量視水分灰分之多寡而異.無水而灰分少者.發熱量可至5237加洛里.低者僅3000加洛里.蒸汽量約抵煤之百分之五〇.

比重自0.25至0.9.乾燥疏鬆者.最易着火.約在200°c時.潮濕堅密者.着火較難.

煤　煤爲植物原始.本無疑問.其構成狀況.說者不一.或云煤層之下.恆爲黏土層.中多化石樹根.足見植物叢林.曾生於其上.有如熱帶海濱之紅樹,(Mangroves).後其地陸沈.植物分解.乃成今日之煤層.此就地構成之說也.或云煤層中植物根幹.橫臥倒立.似非本地所生.或由上游漂流至此.而且煤層之厚薄不等.性質不同.尤非甯靜沈積之現象.故又有漂流構成之說也.二者曾言之成理.惟地內煤層.爲數無限.其構成狀況.當非一致.應視煤田之個性爲斷.大抵煤層中植物純一者.屬於第一例.植物混雜者.屬於第二例.

植物變煤常以細菌爲媒介.故煤中時有微生物.以千倍顯微鏡察之可見.當植物叢林陷落水底.有所謂避養菌者,(Anaerobic bacteria).使之腐爛.繼有地內強熱重壓諸力.使之分解.木質遂變化爲煤.此種變化.可分三次.第一.炭素與炭化輕溢出.第二.灰酸纖維溢出.同時輕養二素化合成水.第三.炭酸炭化輕與水并行溢出.其化學方程式如下.

$$4(C_6H_{10}O_5)=C_9H_6O+7CH_4+8CO_2+3H_2O$$

纖維素　煤　冶氣　炭酸　水

美國有一煤礦,(Dorashra mine).其中水石充塞.近於其中發現四百年前之撑木.其外色黃有纖維狀.斷口黑色有光澤.已完全化爲褐煤.此木質變煤之實例也.大抵年代愈久.經過之變化愈多.則揮發分愈形減少.炭分愈形增加.是以褐煤可變爲黑煤.黑煤可變爲無焰煤.例如比國孟司,(Mons)煤田.上層爲黑煤.下層爲無焰煤.因下層曾受重壓.其中揮發分已經排除.又如美國賓夕,(Penn.)煤田.自西之東.黑煤漸變爲無焰煤.是則因東部曾經地震.當時溫度增高.故將揮發分溜出.木質變煤.各分子之增減表列於下.

	C	H	O	可燃輕
木	100	12.18	83.07	1.80
泥煤	100	9.85	55.67	2.89
褐煤	100	8.37	42.42	3.07
黑煤	100	6.12	21.23	3.47
汽煤	100	5.91	18.32	3.62
無焰煤	100	2.84	1.74	2.63

煤礦在地質各時紀中.自志留紀以至第三紀.均經發現.而以石炭紀所產爲最豐富.中國東三省煤田.沿長城而西.均屬於石炭紀.而最大煤.則在西北疆域.北出蒙古.南入內地.其大可知.濱海及沿江諸省之煤田.則屬於其他時紀.世界各地之煤田與地質時紀.表列於下.

地質時代			煤之出產地
新生代	多新生層		意大利
	稀新生層		德國
	始新生層		美國
中生代	白堊紀		德國英屬哥倫比亞
	侏羅紀		英國匈牙利安南東京
	三疊紀		印度澳洲
古生代	兩疊紀與三疊紀之間		好望角
	兩疊紀與石炭紀之間		澳洲
	石炭紀	煤層	英比法德美
		磨石	英國
		石灰	英國
		砂石	英國

煤之種類至多.用途各有所宜.皆能用於機械工程.尋常分爲五類.以其炭素與養素之比例爲標準.

（甲）褐煤　此爲第三紀之特產.復分爲四種.一纖維顯著者.二斷口多泥者.三斷口狀如介殼者.四色黑有光澤.含有油質者.前三種用爲燃料.焰

長多烟.第四種用以製造煤餅.

(乙)黑煤 此皆由石炭紀各種植物構成 (Sigillaroicl tree, Ferns, etc.) 若以顯微鏡察之.猶能見其胞子.質堅密而易碎.條痕黑色.燃燒時有烟焰.亦分爲四種.一製氣煤.用以製氣.每噸能製氣10500方呎者.始爲優良.(60°F,30吋)硫分不得過百分之一.二製焦煤.受熱則膨脹.火焰甚短.惟成焦之理殊不易解.例如(a)與(b)二種煤.成分相同.但(a)能成焦.(b)不能成焦.

	C	H	O	灰分	水分
(a)	75.2	4	16	3	6.3
(b)	76	4.3	16	3.3	5.4

三家常用煤.火力不宜過烈.亦不宜成焦.硫分與炭分均宜少.四鍊鐵煤.固定炭分宜多.硫與灰宜少.

(丙)蒸汽煤 此煤專用於蒸汽.光澤顯明.燃燒時焰短烟少.硫分灰分均少.蓋硫分多則損害爐柵.灰分多則減少熱量也.

(丁)燭煤 色黑有光澤.斷口爲層狀或爲介殼狀.有植物痕跡.確係漂流構成.燃燒時光焰明亮.兼有濃烟.

(戊)無焰烟 此乃黑煤變成.其中揮發分悉爲熱力與壓力排除.色深黑.觸之不致污染.燃燒時無烟無焰.紐約.包.斯頓.芝加高.各城皆用此煤.故各地空氣異常清潔.發熱量極高.而不猛烈.

各種煤之成分.有詳計與約計之別.求其炭.輕.養.淡.硫.各分者.謂之詳計.求其水分.揮發分.炭分.灰分.者.謂之約計.茲舉三表爲例.灰之成分以及發熱量蒸汽量.亦各爲一表.

詳計分析

號數	種　類	比重	成分百分							焦
			C	H	O	N	S	灰	水	
* 1	褐　煤	1.129	66.31	5.63	22.86	0.57	2.36	2.27	34.66	30.79
2	仝		55.57	4.13	15.67	1.15	0.36	9.00	14.12	
* 3	黑　煤	1.278	78.57	5.29	12.88	1.84	0.39	1.03	11.29	57.2
4	仝		85.74	4.54	3.57		0.81	4.64	0.70	76.10
5	汽　煤	1.310	86.80	4.25	3.06		0.83	4.40	0.66	84.42
* 6	仝		91.45	4.18	2.12			2.25		89.40
* 7	燭　煤	1.276	80.07	5.53	8.03	2.12	1.50	2.70	0.91	
* 8	仝		63.10	8.91	7.25		0.96	19.78		19.78
* 9	無焰煤	1.392	93.39	3.28	2.98	0.83	0.91	1.61	2.00	
* 10	仝	1.462	90.45	2.43	2.45			4.67		

* 水分不在百分之內

約計分析（一）

	水　分	揮發分	焦	固定炭分	灰　分	硫　分
褐　煤	4945		50.55	36.30	14.15	2.61
黑　煤	1.35	31.95	66.7	64.63	2.07	.74
汽　煤	2.32	15.01	82.67	78.77	3.90	.59
無焰煤	10.06		89.94	85.48	3.46	.83
燭　煤	50.8		49.2	47.75	1.45	1.76

約計分析（二）

	水分	揮發分	炭素	灰分	硫分	比重
撫順煤	6.64	33.21	60.15	4.92	0.74	
宣城煤	0.80	16.50	62.70	20.00		
萍鄉煤	1.70	30.33	53.34	4.63	0.48	
開灤煤	0.62	29.49	65.10	4.78	0.68	
本溪煤	0.65	23.38	68.99	7.07	0.48	
臨城煤	1.97	28.80	69.115	17.085	0.65	1.84
井陘煤	5.9	27.97	71.44	7.68	0.69	1.3
清化煤	2.36	2.88	94.76	14.94	0.35	1.85

灰之成分

	(1)	(2)	(3)	(4)
硅酸	40	28.81	34.21	53.00
礬土 養化鐵	44.78	86.95	52.00	35.01
石灰	12.00	5.10	6.19	3.96
苦土		1.19	0.66	2.26
硫酸	2.22	7.23	4.12	4.86
燐酸	0.75	0.74	6.63	0.88

發熱量與蒸汽量

	發熱量	蒸汽量
褐煤	6500 加洛里	3.9 磅
黑煤	9000 ,,	7.8 ,,
汽煤	9300 ,,	8.4 ,,
燭煤	8500 ,,	7.0 ,,
無焰煤	9500 ,,	9.05 ,,

0,252 Kilogram calories = 1 B. T. U.

（二）液體燃料

石油　石油之原始.有兩種學說.一曰有機.二曰無機.較其理由.自以第一說爲可信.有機原始之說.有種種事實.足以證明.凡頁岩.煤.以及一切動植物化石.施以毀滅汽溜.可得若干產物.中有油狀炭化輕.與美國之石油成分無異.此其一.他處所產石油.雖與此成分不同.自其狀態視之.似屬動物遺體.曾經地熱強壓.分解而成.加拿大志留紀石灰岩中.有珊瑚化石.其空隙間常有石油.此其二.石油層之下.必爲頁岩.中有無量數生物化石.可爲石油之原料.此其三.無機原始之說.法國化學家多主之.以實驗爲根據.設用白熱之鐵加於蒸汽及炭酸.則二者之養素與鐵化合.其輕素與炭素於初生時.化合而成油狀液體物.與石油性質相同.若以此爲無機原始之證.須認定是種學說爲確實.但此種學說尙屬懸擬.據以爲說之事.更覺無稽也.

產生石油之處.其地勢必爲背斜峯與對斜澗.互相起伏.礦內兼有水與氣.三者之輕重不等.故氣居上.油居中.水居最下.出產之多寡.與地形極有關係.大凡地層整齊而斜度較低者.則出產較富.含油之岩石.必爲砂岩.礫岩.石灰岩.其性質鬆疏.是以儲藏.更有堅實頁岩居其上.以防蒸發.養化.及水冲盪

作用.

世界各地.皆有石油礦產.惟出產最多者.始有經營之價值.產油之區.均在赤道以北.而與各大山脈尤爲接近.其故由於山谷變遷.地層摺皺.石油得以匯合其間.在地質各時紀中.應以志留,石灰,第三,各紀出產爲最富.美國東部之油田.屬於志留紀.俄國南部與美國中部之油田.屬於石炭紀.日本.緬甸.爪哇.蘇門達拉.婆羅島.羅馬尼亞.奧國.之油田.屬於第三紀.吾國陝西延安府延長縣之油田.屬於石炭紀或三疊紀.其他石油流露於延水巖岸間.色黯質稠.二十年前試行開採.掘井二十四丈.已及油層.足見出產豐富.惟未能積極進行.故未臻發達耳.

採取石油.以鑽孔法爲最便.初取出者.謂之原油, Crude oil. 須加以蒸溜.始合各種之用.第一次溜出部分.謂之揮發油, Gasoline. 加高温度.續行溜出部分.謂之燈油, Kerosene. 再加高温度.最後溜出部分.謂之重油, Heavy oil. 此數者皆可爲內燃機之燃料.其發熱量如下.

	每磅之發熱量	
原油	18400	B. T. U.
揮發油	19000	,,
燈用油	18500	,,
重油	19210	,,

用於外燃機者.係用爲蒸汽燃料.取原油加以蒸溜.去其揮發分.增高着火點, (Flash point). 便爲適用.其適當成分如下.

C	88.00	%
H	10.75	,,
O	1.25	,,
	100.00	,,

此種燃料之安全標準.以引火點爲依據.引火點愈高.則愈安全.茲將各種規定分列於下.

英國海軍部	270°F.
德國海軍部	187°F.
英國商船註册公司 (Llyod's)	150°F.
英國商部	185°F.

英國海軍部之標準.似覺過高.故燃燒不便.其餘各標準.皆無危險.此皆指輪船而言.至於火車之標準.則不若是重要.緣火車之油箱與鍋爐.皆得空氣流通也.

油中之水分足以減少熱量.硫分足以損害爐柵.均須排除.

以石油爲燃料.始於俄國.其初提煉燃油.所餘之物.皆視爲無用.後有煉油家欲利用此種廢物.取此濃厚液體.引入氣管.另以小管相連.以高壓蒸汽入之.二者皆噴入鍋爐.成爲霧狀.再加充分空氣.卽能燃燒不息.自此法行之有效.嗣後用之者日多.近年中國.日本.緬甸.皆盛行液體燃料.英國本以產煤著名.近亦以油爲燃料.其大東鐵路.(The Great Eastern Railway).有燃油車頭百餘具之多.太晤士河沿岸工廠.特向美國定購大宗石油.以爲燃料.

油與煤之比較.油之發熱量較大.工事較簡.油因噴霧作用.與空氣混合.能盡量發展.故蒸汽可至一六磅之多.用油一噸可抵用煤二噸.至少亦有二與三之比.據英國鐵路之比較.同樣馬力之車頭.用油祇須七磅.用煤須三五磅.至於工事之勞逸.尤爲顯然.用煤必須車馬取重機以資轉運.又有添煤除灰之煩.用油祇須引導管抽吸器等簡單之物.再加有限人工.斯爲足矣.

火車用油.須用特別燃燒器.以此伸入鍋爐爐柵上.覆碎煤一層.以便引火.此種燃燒器.以 Holden 式爲最便.其圖如下.

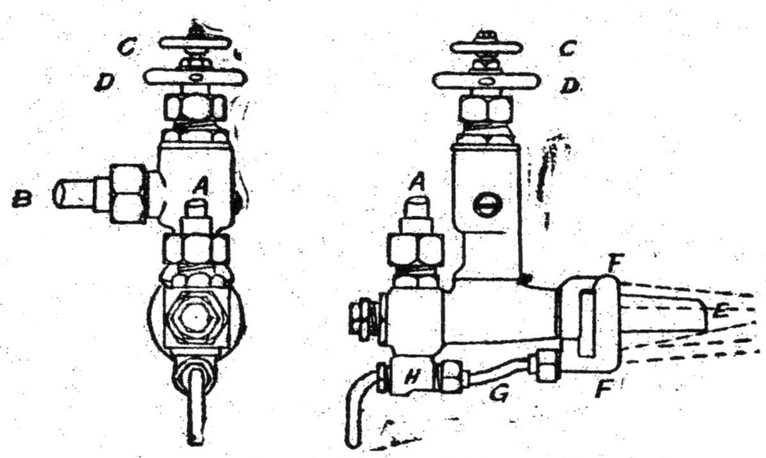

A爲汽管.B爲油管.C與D爲手輪.調度內部之孔口.E爲短管.伸入鍋爐.FF爲外圈.另有小管G與傍弁H供給蒸汽.由外圈噴出.引導空氣.以助燃燒.

現今水陸交通,用油亟廣.故世界各大海口.均設油站.各國航海公司.如 The Shell & Transport Trading Co., The Hamburg American Steam Navigation Co., American Trans-Atlantic Lines 以及德法荷蘭之商船.多用燃油鍋爐.以

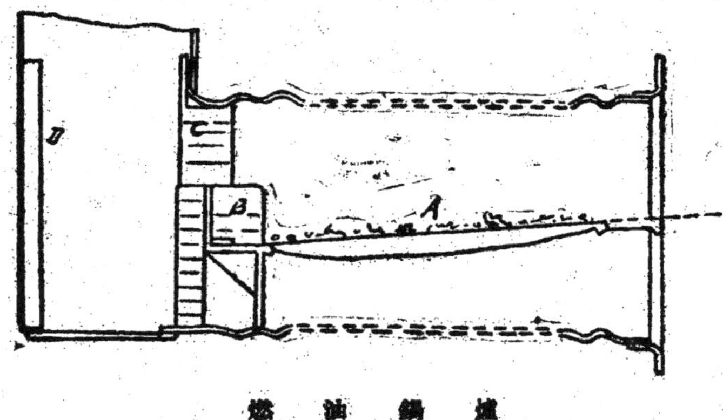

燃油鍋爐

油存於雙底之空間.不用壓艙水.而以煤艙爲貨艙.則噸量與容量均形增加.太平洋大汽船用油者可增噸量1000噸.容量100,000立呎.

燃油鍋爐圖見上頁.圖中A爲碎火泥磚.鋪於爐柵上.B爲磚橋.C爲磚頂.保護鐵板聯縫.D爲磚壁.以防火焰損害鐵板.

酒精 酒精之性質.與石油相似.而能受較高壓縮.其發熱量不及石油之高.而每磅所致能率.并不稍遜.以其能受高壓縮而得較大比效也.純粹酒精之發熱量.每磅11,664 B.T.U.含水百分之十者10,080 B.T.U.此種燃料.在歐洲用於機械.已數見不鮮.用時須加熱使之化氣.其中水分不得過百之十.市售酒精.水分僅百之五.

（三）氣體燃料

天然氣 發明天然氣之功用.始於中國.今美國於各種工業.用之尤廣.其原始與石油相同.皆由動植物分解而成.存於古生代稀疏砂岩與石炭岩間.氣壓甚高.每方吋四五〇磅.其上更有堅實頁岩爲蓋.以防散失.其地形爲背斜峯.氣體積於其巔.成分爲沼氣.輕氣.含水耶取連.假立芬氣.養氣.養化炭.炭酸.淡氣等物.發熱量15000加洛里.

煤氣 煤氣用於家常及工業各事.而於化學試驗室尤爲適宜.製造煤氣.概以黑煤爲原料.施用蒸溜.凝冷.清潔.諸手續.然後儲藏之.以備應用.蒸溜器爲圓形長筒.長十餘呎.徑呎許.用鐵鑄.泥塑.或磚砌.等法造成.鐵鑄者.用於小工廠.泥塑者.有破裂之虞.磚砌者.價廉而耐久.故爲最佳.以此長筒平列爐內.加煤取焦之事.均甚便.製成之氣.由升管引入水槽.去其煤脂.復由此引入凝冷管.去其重炭化輕.并減其溫度.氣在水槽時溫度140°F.減至空氣溫度爲止.氣內仍有安摩尼亞.硫化輕.炭酸等物.須用清潔器除之.先使安摩尼亞在水中溶化.再用石灰去其硫化輕炭酸等物.經此一番洗滌.乃可適用.以之收入蓄氣缸.以備不時之需.此種燃料之發熱量.等於煤之百分之二一.并須人工機械等費.惟分佈簡易.運用便利.種種優點.亦足以償其費用.茲將煤氣

之性質列表於下.

	體積	重量	每立积之發熱量	每立积各分子之發熱量	總發熱量
輕素, H_2	47	7.4	2582	1213	22.8
沼氣, CH_4	34	42.8	8524	7898	54.5
一養化炭, CO	9	19.9	3043	273	5.1
偏陳, C_6H_6	1.2	7.4	33815	405	7.7
耶取迎, C_2H_4	3.8	8.4	13960	530	9.9
二養化炭, CO_2	2.5	8.6			
淡, N_2	2.5	5.5			
	100.0	100.0		5319	100.0

0.1123 Calories per cubic metre = 1 B. T. U. per cu. ft.

製焦氣　舊式製焦爐爲蜂房式.不能收集附產物.近年歐美各國改用新式.均能收集製焦之氣.去其烟脂.安摩尼亞等物.可爲種種之用.其成分與煤氣相似.惟重炭化輕較少.發熱量較低.

西門士氣　維廉西門士 (Sir William Siemenes) 創造氣爐.用無焰煤製氣.其中不含煤脂.適於內燃機之用.爐或爲圓柱形.以鐵板爲函.以火泥磚爲裏.上有納口.下有底柵.用排空法吸收助燃空氣.亦有用風扇或藉蒸汽灌入者.若不用蒸汽則養素與炭素化合成爲二養化炭.及其上升與熱煤觸接.又化爲一養化炭.其反應式如下.

$$C + O_2 = CO_2,$$

$$CO_2 + C = 2CO.$$

爐內溫度在 1000°C 以上時.一養化炭絕少.氣質自佳.若用蒸汽.即自行分解.成爲輕素.一養化炭.二養化炭.等氣.其反應式如下.

$$H_2O + C = H_2 + CO,$$

$$2H_2O + C = 2H_2 + CO_2.$$

以此用於內燃機.應有輕素百分之一五.始易着火.發熱量每立呎(0°C., 760 mm.)須有1500加洛里.

道生（F.E. Dowson）改良氣爐.所製之氣.用於內燃機, Crossley Gas Engine 最為便利.此種氣爐足以供給6000馬力以上之氣機.其圖說如下.

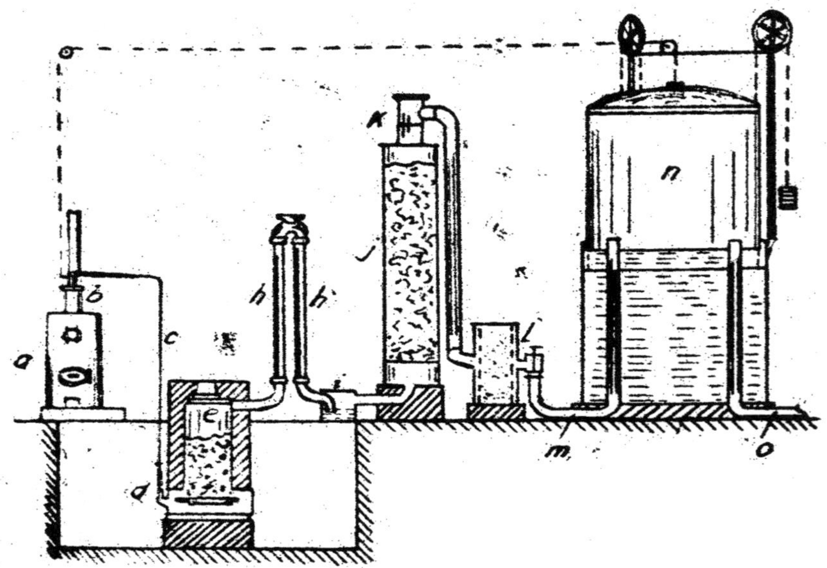

(a)蒸汽鍋.(b)高熱管.(d)空氣注射器.(e)氣爐.(f)爐柵.(g)納口(h)涼冷管.(i)水箱.(j)焦屑.(k)接管.(l)鋸屑.(m)收氣管.(n)蓄氣缸.(o)出氣管.

高熱管供給乾蒸汽以此注入氣爐.有兩種作用.一使之自行分解.乃從輕素.二引入空氣.以助燃燒.

造生氣爐試驗表

號數	每啓羅無焰煤及焦煤製成之氣 0°C,760m/m.	氣之體積百分							燃料之發熱量	氣之發熱量 0°C 760mm.	比效	每立尺氣之發熱量 0°C 760mm.
		H	CH_4	C_2H_4	Co	Co_2	O	N				
	立 呎								加洛里	加洛里		加洛里
1	5.00	18.73	.31	.31	25.07	6.57	.03	48.98	9350	7100	75.9	1420
2												1350
3	5.02	17.00	2.00		23.00	6.00		52.00	8790	7130	81.1	1420
4	4.74	16.67			27.50	8.40	.90	46.73	8740	6450	73.8	1360
5		24.00			22.50	7.50		46.00				1430
6												1487
7	5.34	16.50	1.00		25.40	4.80	1.20	51.10	9160	7390	80.7	1384
8	5.04	19.80	1.30		23.80	6.30		48.80	9500	7370	77.6	1463
9	5.07	15.30	1.40		27.60	3.90		51.80	9120	7350	80.6	1451
10	4.88	17.50	2.10		26.50	4.40		49.50	9200	7570	82.3	1552
	平 均	18.18			25.17	5.98		49.36	9123	7194	78.9	1432

據上表每啓羅無焰煤能製氣五立方呎.即每磅80方呎.以此運動氣機.每小時每馬力需煤454克即一磅.合爐內之煤與蒸汽鍋內之焦均在內.

表內發熱量係根據以下各數

	每立呎之發熱量	
H	3070	加洛里
CH_4	9550	"
C_2H_4	14970	"
CO	3070	"

冶爐氣 此氣自冶鐵爐溢出.爲量至大.成分與西門士氣相似.惟二養化炭較多.一養化炭較少.輕素尤少.發熱量每立方呎800至1000加洛里.用以蒸汽或直接供給氣機.均無不可.1000馬力之氣機.能以此氣驅動之.昔時此氣含有微塵.殊不適用.今已有法去之矣.冶爐內選用各種燃料.所出之氣成分不同.表列於下.

	N	CO	CO_2	CH_4	H	C_2H_4
木炭	63.4	29.6	14.9	1.0	0.4	
焦	64.4	34.6	0.9		0.1	
煤	56.3	21.5	15.2	4.2	1.0	1.8

（完）

交通部直轄京奉鐵路唐山製造廠概況

繆錫康　徐名植

京奉鐵路西起京都,東達瀋陽,幹路長八百四十三公里,爲今日吾國東北交通之要道.沿途物產富庶,貨運極繁,開灤之烟煤,關外之糧食,尤爲該路主要之運輸品,營業發達,爲國內鐵路之冠,其唐山製造廠,專事該路機車,車輛之製造及修理,規模之大,尤爲他路所不及.此中情形,想必爲諸君之所樂聞.作者去夏離校後旋奉部派來此實習.一年以來,略知梗概,爰不揣譾陋,將該廠概況,草述成篇,以供諸君之參攷.惟自慚學識有限,觀察未遍,而文詞不工,辭不達意.謬誤之處,尚望閱者諸君有以教之.

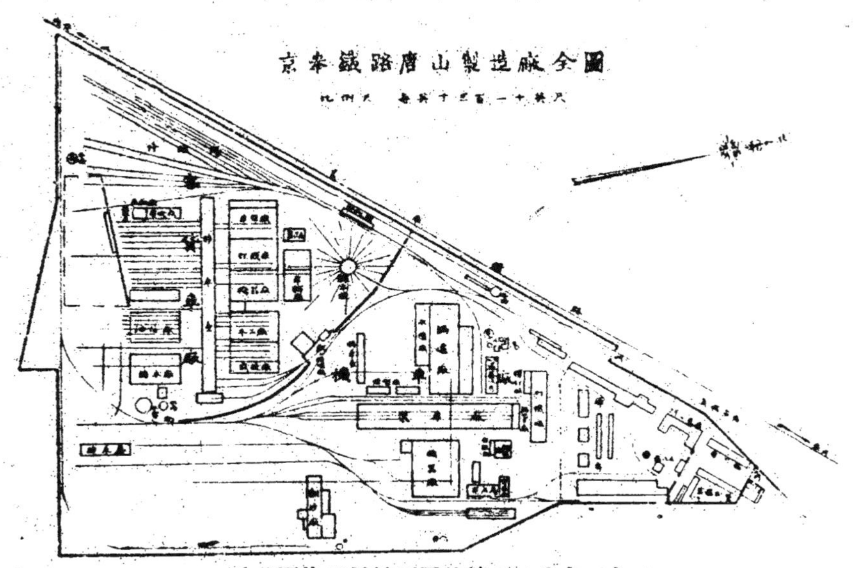

（此圖比例尺較原圖約縮小二分之一）

歷史　初,前清光緒二十三年間.關內鐵道已自唐山修至塘沽,總辦伍廷芳氏暨總工程司金達氏于胥各莊河岸塢工庀材,修理車輛.越二年遷于唐山,與開平煤礦聯合,就其礦井之西設製造廠焉.廠之初設,聘英人邱瓦德氏專管廠務,規模粗具,又三年,中國自製之機車第一百號出現,形質極爲堅美,是時鐵道亦已西至京師,東達營口,乃議擇地于路線之南,建築大廠,以應需求.庚子以後,歷經擴充,乃有今日之成績.今全廠佔地約五百畝,職員二百餘人,工人約三千餘.

組織 該廠隸路局機務處處長駐此統轄全廠.下分三部:一曰管理部,主持廠中總務,凡文案,會計,廠監,查工,繪圖,存圖,醫藥等處皆屬焉,二曰材料部,亦名庫房,存儲各項材料,及各廠工作品,備待沿路各機車房修理之需,三曰工作部,復分機車,客貨車二部,而輔以原動力部,茲列表于後.

工作部

(甲)機車部

(一)模型廠 Pattern Shop

(二)鑄冶廠 Foundry Shop

(三)打鐵廠 Smith Shop

(四)機器廠 Machine Shop

(五)鍋爐廠 Boiler Shop

(六)螺釘廠 Bolt and Nut Shop

(七)鋼管廠 Tube Shop

(八)裝車廠 Erecting Shop

(九)水櫃廠 Tender Shop

(十)氣軔廠 Air Brake Shop

(十一)銅器廠 Copper-Smith Shop

(十二)白鐵廠 Tin-Smith Shop

(乙)客貨車部

(一)鋸木廠 Saw Mill

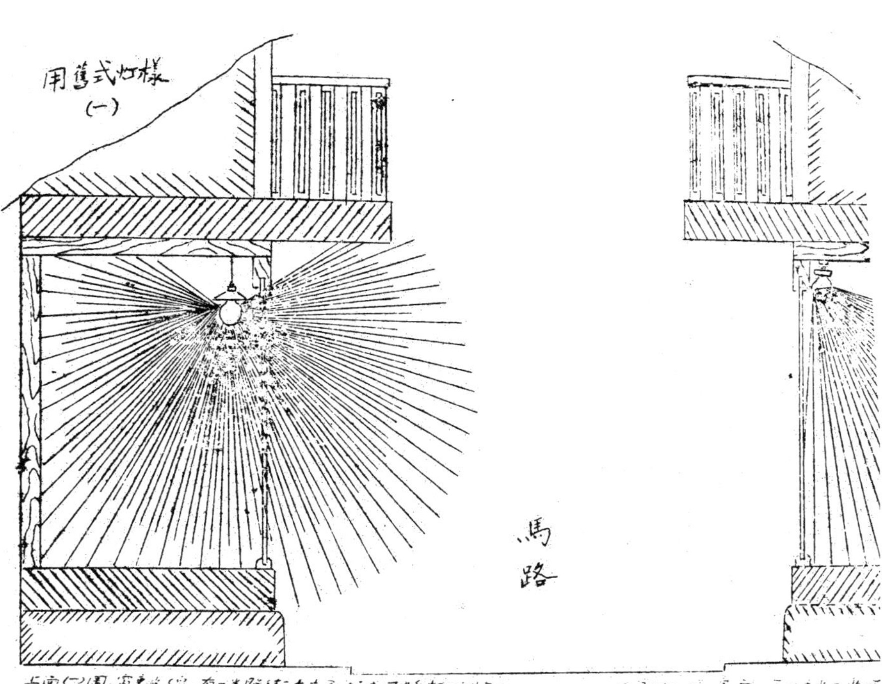

上面(一)圖，窗裏光線，有一半照街上去了，简直同路灯一般無二。然而没有人給你這一筆路灯費，並且裏面光線很少，外面的光線，射到主顧的眼光裏，反覺得有些討厭，裏面有牛毛的東西，也就不肯多看，就此去過了，豈不是對于營業上面就受了影響？

上面(二)圖[illegible]完全照在裏面，可使主顧看清[illegible]東西在[illegible]一定要買[illegible]故[illegible]

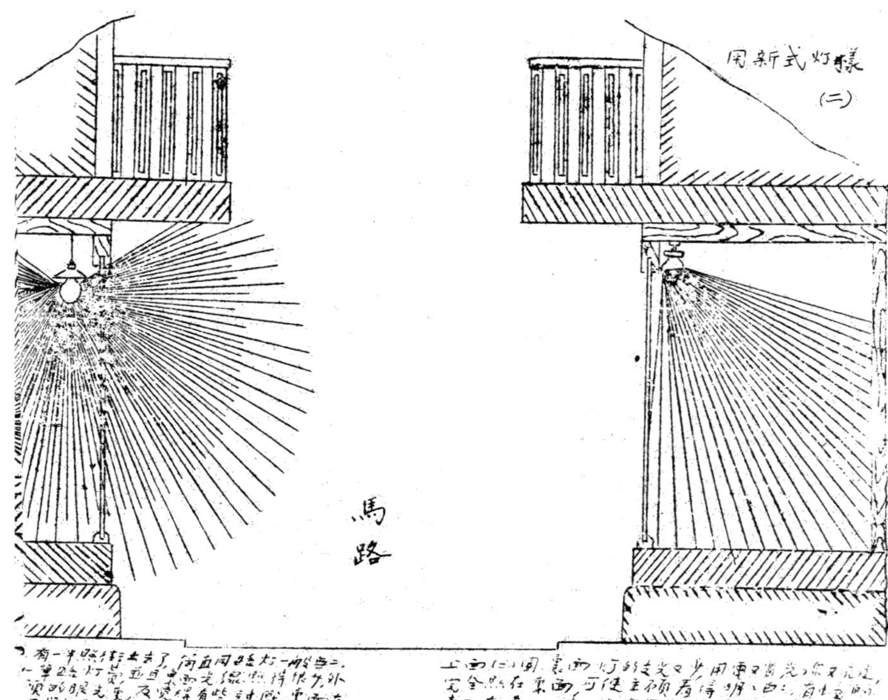
用新式灯樣
(二)
馬
路

(二) 木工廠 Carpenter Shop

(三) 裁縫廠 Upholstering Shop

(四) 打鐵廠 Smith Shop

(五) 機器廠 Machine Shop

(六) 車架廠 Frame Shop

(七) 轉向架廠 Bogie Shop

(八) 輪軸廠 Wheel and Axle Shop

(九) 電燈廠 Electrical Department

(十) 油漆廠 Paint Shop

(十一) 修理場 Repairing Yard

(四) 原動力部

(一) 總蒸汽房 Main Boiler House

(二) 機器廠蒸汽房 Machine Shop Boilar House

(三) 客車廠蒸汽房 Car Works Boiler House

(四) 氣制廠蒸汽房 Air Brake Boiler House

(五) 新蒸汽房 New Boiler House

(六) 電氣房 Power House

(七) 氣力房 Pneumatic Power House

(八) 水力房 Hydraulic Power House

(九) 唧水間 Pump House

管理　全廠最高管理當局爲廠長,即由機務處長兼任,承命于路局局長,而主持全廠公務者也,與廠長同級而隸屬于處長者,爲路上機務總段長,其下爲各段段長,管理各段機車房,及查驗機車之狀况.廠長華洋各一人,一正一副,廠長之下,即爲前述三部之主任職員,及下級職員.茲舉其重要者,列表以明之.

處長兼廠長

文牘課長

會計主任

材料管理

繪圖師

廠工總理

各廠廠監

工目

工匠

匠副

小工

學徒

全廠平面圖（見篇首插圖）

各廠概况　工作部爲製造廠之本部,範圍甚大,且關係工程技術頗多足供吾人研究之處,故特將各廠大概情形分別述之.

（甲）機車部

（一）模型廠　此廠長九十一呎,闊二十四呎,佔地二一八四方呎.另有木樓間一所,儲藏已成備用之模型.廠屋以磚砌成,光綫充足,空氣亦佳.廠內工作,均賴手工,故祇有鏇機一,鋸木機二,係用電動機推動.所製模型,如汽筩爐座等,費工極大,此外零星小件,以塞門Cock 閥 Valve 軸襯Bush等爲多,大半係機車客貨車上應用之物.即全廠各機器損壞部份之修理,所需模型,亦莫不出於是廠.廠中工人計十餘人,有工目一人統率之.

（二）鑄冶廠　此廠佔地一九一二一方呎,較模型廠約大九倍.內分鑄鐵鑄銅二部.其鑄件Casting均爲粗形,須經機器廠鏇刨,方可應用.廠內有鎔鐵爐 Cupola二座,爐身直徑三呎六吋,高十三呎,爐底有門,以便用後清理之需,爐旁有風扇間,置電動機一,吸風扇二,專供燃爐鎔鐵時之風.鑄銅部有鎔銅爐七爐分二種,一係 Morgan 廠製造,計兩座爐與電動打風機成爲一體,其餘五爐橫置地下,旁有打風機,亦以電動機轉動之,此外尙有磨沙機一,和沙機一,篩沙機一,壓氣製型機三,外項軸箱製型機四.電移起重機一,舉運廠中重件,在鎔鐵爐旁,亦有起重機,專爲運鐵塊及焦炭之需.此廠工人共一百數十人.

廠中工作,以翻製沙型爲初步,鎔金澆鑄次之,而以刷淨鑄件終.

翻製沙型,分爲二類,一爲濕型 Green-sand moulding,一爲乾型 Dry-sand moulding.前者用細沙成型,澆鑄時沙中含有水份,惟型面之沙,因空氣之吸收,較裏面稍乾.凡小件銅鐵之鑄件,概用此種濕型鑄之.乾型則用於燒鑄大件,沙粒較粗,而性亦較黏,沙型翻成,塗以黑鉛 Graphite,送入大烘爐內烘之,歷一夜之久取出,將煤灰吹淨,始可澆鑄.蓋此時沙型中之水份,蒸發殆盡,成一乾燥堅固之型矣.此外尙有製型心一種,用以按入沙型,以成鑄件之空洞.型心製就,亦須焙乾,方可應用.

鎔鐵之先,將鎔鐵爐底閉以火磚,並塗火泥,嗣用木料燃燒約三小時,待爐內乾燥,而熱度均勻,然後焦炭及鐵,始可投入.爐底全放焦炭,約佔爐身十分之三,其上則鐵與焦炭,分層互投,每層高約一呎.然後開吸風扇,將風打入.歷十餘分鐘鐵卽鎔化,鎔化之鐵,卽流入爐前之藏鐵室,下開小洞,直徑約二呎,以火泥塞堵之,用鐵時鑿去泥塞,鐵卽流出,注入鑄桶 Ladle 內,澆鐵用人工者爲少,通常均用起重機提桶澆之,容量既大,費工尤少.

鑄件凝固後,將其取出,面上所附之沙塊,用鐵錘打毀之,再以鋼絲刷刷淨.其型心之沙,亦一併除去,重大之鑄件,則用壓氣鑿 Pneumatic Chisel 移去之.

鎔鐵之原料爲生鐵 Pig Iron,分英國貨本國貨二種.鎔化之鐵液,品質

(附注) 科學術語,我國尙無標準譯名.本篇所用,係根據交通部所編之鐵路詞典,與普通譯名,間有不同.附以英名,以備參攷.

稍有高下.凡澆鑄汽箭等件,係用英國生鐵鎔化.其餘普通機件,則以本國生鐵或與廢鐵攙和鎔鑄之.每四日鎔鐵一次.鑄件重量,自一萬磅至二萬六千磅不等.鑄銅則每日行之,用爐四五具,鎔銅平均約一千餘磅.所鎔之銅分爲四種,因應用之不同,而成分亦隨之而異.茲將各種成分及其用途,列表于下.

銅	錫	鋅	鉛	銻	用途
86.6%	8.1%	5.3%	——	——	軸承襯
68.0%	——	30.0%	2.0%	——	爐面機件
5.2%	82.4%	3.6%	——	8.8%	軸承襯上之白色金屬
0.5%	——	——	80.0%	19.5%	金類填料

（三）打鐵廠　凡機件之用鋼及熟鐵者,其粗形先在此廠打成之.廠長三百呎,闊五十四呎,內有鍛鐵爐 Eorge 三十三只,鳥嘴砧 Anvil 數如之.汽鎚五圓鋸 Circular hot saw 一.旋樞起重機四.返射爐 Reverberatory Furnace 一.各爐通風由毗連之螺釘廠內吸風扇供給之.經地下總管,導入打鐵廠,從分管而通至爐底.至其工作步驟,則先以鋼或鐵置于爐中,待燒至固定之熱度（視其色而定）,小者於砧上以人工打成之,大者則置于汽鎚下爲之.使用汽鎚時,以一人司鎚之上下,一人持鐵鉗夾所打之鋼或鐵,擱于鎚鐙之上.於汽鎚上下時,以靈活之動作,左之右之前之後之,使之成形,大小合度,如圖所示而後已.打鐵之動作凡六;一曰引伸 Drawing,將燒紅之鐵塊,擊之壓之,使之向各方引伸之謂也.二曰彎曲 Bending,直者使之彎曲,成弓形或爲角形.三曰絞繞 Twisting,將直條絞繞成螺旋形.四曰縮短 Upsetting,將鐵豎直擊壓,使其長度縮短,因之直徑得以增大,細薄可成粗厚.五曰縮緊 Shrinking,將鐵圈燒熱使漲,套於他物之上,冷卽縮緊.六曰煅接 Welding,以燒紅之二鐵塊或鋼塊,將兩端擊壓,使之接合爲一.鋼與鐵亦可鍛接,惟燒紅之熱度各異耳.此廠工人共計一百餘人.

（四）機器廠　此廠長二百四十呎,闊一百八十二呎,佔面積四三六八〇方呎.尚有裝輪箍廠,長五十二呎,闊五十呎,毗連於廠之西南角.另有儲藏所一,貯存備用之銅件,及一切應用器具之類.廠屋均爲磚砌,上設天窗,室內空氣流通,甚爲暢達.冬日取暖,用暖氣法 Hot-air or Fan System.備有暖氣爐兩座,分設於廠之南北部,爐旁置吸風扇,以直立小汽機轉動之.當吸風扇旋轉時,吸收爐外之冷空氣經過蒸汽管,及吸風扇,而打入送氣總管,輸送至各處分管中,管口成八形,距地約六呎,煖氣卽由此口分兩途而出.(夏日此爐不開蒸汽,卽打送空氣以成風冬夏兩用.)除此項暖氣爐外,尚有溫暖器 Radiator 數具,置於機器之旁,如水力壓輪機等,所以防水之凍結也.

此廠工作,劃分爲二大部:一爲裝配部Fitting Work,一爲機器部Machine Work,各有正副工目統率之.

裝配部位於廠之中部,有工作檯 Bench 三,成一直線,橫貫全廠,檯上共置虎鉗 Vice 一百餘只.其工作均用手工,不外截削 Ch'pping,磋磨 Filing,及刮削 Scraping 三種.將各項機車上之零星小件,或截或銼,使之尺寸合度,試裝密接,然後將零件聚集裝配,成爲完全之機件,以備裝車廠之裝置,此部計有工人一百三四十人,照機車機件之種類,分爲八組如下.

1. 連桿及搖捍組 Coupling and Connecting Rod gang
2. 閥動機關組 Motion gang
3. 韛韛及十字頭組 Piston and Crosshead gang
4. 汽鍋配件組 Boiler Mounting gang
5. 軸箱組 Axlebox gang
6. 彈簧組 Spring gang
7. 轉向架組 Bogie gang
8. 軔機組 Brake Gear gang

機器部據南北二部,有各式鏇機 Lathe 六十一具,刨機 Planer 七,成形機 Shaper 十,鑽機 Drilling Machine 十九,鏇孔機 Boring machine 十,豎刨機

Slotting machine 九,豎鏇孔機 Vertical Boring mill 四,鑽刨聯合機 Drilling and Slotting machine 一,車輪鏇機 Wheel lathe 七,齒刮機 Milling machine 二,圓鋸機 Circular Saw 二,磨光機 Grinding mahine 二,工具磨機 Tool Grinder 八,水力壓輪機 Hydraulic Wheel Press 一,曲拐銷鏇機 Crank-pin Turning machine 一.此外並有電移起重機一架,手移起重機二架,及靠牆起重機七架.全廠有五統軸 Line Shaft, 由五電動機引動之,統軸引動副軸 Counter-shaft, 間接引動各機器之轉軸.惟大機器.則自有電動機直接轉動之.凡各項機件無論爲鑄冶廠製成之鑄件,或爲打鐵廠打就之粗形,大之如汽筒,爐座,車軸,車輪之類,小至零星小件,莫不經此部製成,由裝配部裝配之.此部工人計有一百八九十人,

裝輪箍廠 Tyre Fitting Plant 附屬於機器廠.內置輪箍爐 Tyre Heater 一,電動吸風扇一,油唧機Oil Pump一,水池一,堅煉爐 Case-hardening Furnace 一,電力旋樞起重機 Electric Pillar Crane 一.凡鏇就之輪箍,均在此處裝之.其法先以輪箍置於輪箍爐中心,燃爐燒之,約歷二十分鐘,乃取在移置台上,乘其熱漲之際,將輪體 Wheel Center 放入,繫而浸於水池內,則箍冷而緊縮於輪體之上.然後取出,加扣環 Retaining Ring 於其間,以防分離,而裝輪之手續遂完.舊輪換箍時,亦先置爐中燒熱使漲,將舊箍擊下,然後易以新輪箍.

燒銲 Welding 部亦附屬於機器廠.燒銲之法有二:一用電力 Electric Arc Welding,一用養氣與阿西台體之參合物 Oxy-Acetylene Welding, 電力燒銲,將電流通至待銲之機件爲一電極,一端通至金屬銲條 Metallic Electrode 爲一電極,以銲條接近燒銲之處,乃發爲極強之弧光,其熱度約在華氏表六七千度間,此時兩極之金屬,均被鎔化,銲條之鎔化物,流滴於機件之上.如是則破裂之處,因以銲補,或兩塊金屬,因而銲接矣.此項銲條,亦分鋼鐵數種,隨所銲機件質料而定,惟鑄鐵燒銲時,多用銅條以代之.其第二法,則將儲存筒中之養氣及阿西台體,用橡皮氣管分接於火把 Torch 後端,因而混合,

由火把口而出,燃燒時之熱度,約至六千度左右,以火焰向待釬之處燒之至紅熱,另以銅條鎔化釬補之.燒釬之用,能使損壞之件,回復可用,且能切斷厚鈑等件,故修理機車,賴此極多.

（五）鍋爐廠 佔地六八〇四〇方呎,計有剪機 Shearing machine 一,衝孔機 Punching machine 二,剪衝合機二,旋臂鑽機十三,刨邊機 Edge planing machine 一,撓輥機 Plate bending machine 豎橫各一,水力帽釘機 Hydraulic riveting machine 三,壓氣帽釘機 Pneumatic rivetting machine 一,螺紋鏇機 Screw cutting machine 三,鏇機四,水力壓機 Hydraulic press 二,大反射爐一,及小爐十餘只,廠內工作,分為三部,曰新鍋製造,曰舊鍋修理,曰試驗.新鍋之製造法,首以鋼板按圖上之尺寸,或依樣規 Templet, 用白粉畫於其上,何處須鑽孔,何處須剪去,一一標明.然後經過剪機,衝孔機,刨邊機,而置撓輥機中滾之,使成圓形,或∩形（火箱之形）,各節互相套上,以帽釘釘之,外形既成,乃裝內火箱,內火箱與外火箱之間,用螺撐Stay緊密繫之,因鍋中之水,燒至每方吋為一百八十磅之壓力時,內外火箱,同時受此極大壓力,故以螺撐持之使不致有浮凸爆裂之虞.其次則裝置火管,及鍋上零件,而新鍋乃成.舊鍋修理,則視各鍋損壞情形,而為局部之處置,通常以更換火管及內火箱為最多.無論新鍋造成,或舊鍋修竣後,均須經過試驗是否勝任.其法儲鍋以水,加以壓力,至每方吋二百五十磅,是為 Hydrostatic test, 後再燃鍋,至蒸汽壓力每方吋一百八十磅為度,是為 Steam test,經此二種試驗,如堅固無漏,始可應用.若稍有罅漏,亟須以擠縫器 Caulking tool 擠塡之.

本路所有機車汽鍋,半由英美購來,半係本廠自造.汽鍋大小,因機車之種類而分別之,各類式樣大小,均不盡同,故製造新鍋一座,費工自一千至一千五百不等（一人作工一日為一工即 Manday 也）,廠中工人約二百餘,有工目四人率領之.

（六）螺釘廠 此廠位置在打鐵廠之旁,長九十呎,寬四十三呎,有電動機一座,螺紋鏇機七部,螺栓帽釘製頭機 Bolts and rivets forging machine 五部,製螺帽機 Nut making machine 一,螺帽紋鏇機 Nut tapping machine 一,吸風扇三,鍛鐵爐五,吸風扇經皮帶拖動後,供給本廠及打鐵各爐之風.螺紋鏇機專做螺釘及螺撑之螺紋.帽釘及螺帽製造,先以鐵條燒紅,插入機內,經脚一踏,機內機關卽自動作,帽釘及螺帽,遂各形成.故工作極速.工人約三十人.

（七）鍋管廠　此廠在裝車廠盡頭,有洗管機 Tube cleaner 二,伸管機 Tube stretching machine 一,試管機 Tube tester 三,切管機 Tube cutter 二,接管機 Tube welding machine 二,電動機一,吸風扇一,水唧機 Water pump 一,爐三,鳥嘴砧三,虎鉗六.工人約二十餘人.鍋管可分三種.一爲火管 Tube,一爲焰管 Flue,一爲過熱汽管 Superheater element. 凡新管裝用前,必先經水力試驗,以求安全.過熱汽管用後,遇有漏洞,則以燒釬法補之.焰管,火管,時有水垢 Scale 聚積,厚則傳熱効用較遜,故必須將管取出,至此廠洗管機洗淨,惟各管自鍋中取出,兩端已切去少許,火管卽改用於較小汽鍋中,而焰管則可在切管機中將頭上不齊處切去,另以六吋長之新管一段,同時置爐中燒紅,然後取出,在接管機上鍛接之,如試驗固妥,仍可應用.

（八）裝車廠　爲全廠主要部份,新車之裝成,舊車之拆修,胥在于此.廠介於鍋爐,機器兩廠之間,蓋所以便汽鍋及機件之輸送也.廠屋寬一〇二呎,長六〇〇呎.爲縱式車廠 Longitudinal type, 中部敷有軌道三條,軌下有坑 Pit, 以便修理車底,此部可容機車二十餘座.兩旁爲工作場所,有工作檯 Fitting bench 數處,其東北一段爲驗看機件之所,有鹼水槽 Lye bath 一,又有房屋二間,存貯各種器具,及舊車修理時拆下之銅器機件.廠中備有機車搆架台 Locomotive erecting frame 一,電動機一,軸箱頰板鏇面機 Hornblock facing machine 一,汽筩鏇孔機 Cylinder boring machine 一,閥襯筒鏇孔機 Piston valve bush boring machine 一,鐘形汽室鏇面機 Dome facing machine

一,衡車機 Weighing machine 十二,並有電移起重機二架,起重量各四十五噸,用以起運機車,及一切笨重機件.此外則尚有暖氣爐四座,用吸風扇輸送室各處,裝製與機器廠同,冬日用之.工人約百餘人,分爲六組.

凡路上駛行之車,經二年之時期,或十萬英里之行程,爲規定大修General repair 之期,大修者,即全部修理之謂.其通常局部之修理,輕者即在機車房行之.其損壞較重者,則送入廠中修理.機車送廠大修,用起重機舉起,移置於適當地位,然後將各部依次拆下,並在各件上,標明機車號數,及左右前後之位置,以免與他車互混.拆卸次序,視各車構造而定,尋常先拆車底之連桿及搖桿,制機機關,彈簧機關,閥動機關,轉向架等,同時拆卸車頂之烟囱,氣唧機 Air pump, 及一切汽鍋配件銅管等.各件拆盡,然後及於車輪.其法以起重機鈎於機車前後二端,將車身高舉,車輪因已與車架分離,仍在軌上,遂可向前或後滾出,或竟將車身舉運他處,放置於大木,或螺旋支重機 Screw Jack 之上.最後將汽鍋舉起,送鍋爐廠修理.有時並將汽箭拆下,僅留車架及氣制儲氣主箭Air brake main reservoir 等而已.

機車拆下各件,除汽鍋,氣制,銅管,有專廠修理外,其餘概歸機器廠負責修理.其車底機件,則於送至機器廠前,先在本廠鹼水槽內洗淨,以去油塵,然後加以驗看,若者當修,若者當另換新件,若者完好,可無庸修理,一一加以標明.機器廠接收此車機件後,即分發各部修理,或轉翻沙打鐵諸廠另製新件.以在本廠範圍之外,茲不贅述.至規定期限,各廠修理完畢後,即將該車機件全數送回.裝車廠即可逐件裝配,成一完全之機車.

機車出廠之前,先經試車,加水熱爐汽蒸以待,此時僅留汽箭上各件,尚未裝置,用一百八十磅之蒸汽,將導汽管及汽缸內之汚穢雜物吹淨,然後將滑閥Slide Valve, 鞲鞴 Piston, 及汽箭蓋 Cylinder cover 裝就,再校準保安閥 Safety valve 內之彈簧,並試用氣制,一切裝妥,即在廠內開車試行,如無阻礙,便可出廠,至路上行駛矣.

本路機車有購自英美者,有本廠自造者,式樣種類,至爲不一.就水櫃煤倉之位置而論,可大別爲二類.一爲煤水櫃機車 Tank engine, 卽水櫃煤倉均裝在機車之上,因容量不多,不能長途駛行,祇供廠內及各站拖車調軌之用,故名調車機車 Shunting or switching locomotive. 二爲煤水車之機車 Tender engine, 卽機車之後,另有煤水車一輛,可容水四五千加倫,裝煤六七噸,此類機車,用以拖行路上客貨車,其車輪排列,則爲 2—6—0 Mogul 2—6—2 Prairie, 2—8—0 Consolidation, 2—8—2 Mikado, 4—6—0 Pacific 等式.後二式均裝過熱蒸汽管,改用構輪閥,汽筩亦較大,故力量極爲強大. 2—8—0 式機車亦間有用此者.

（九）水櫃廠　是廠連接鍋爐廠,長二百六十呎,寬五十二呎,橫列軌道十三條,軌下有坑,以備修理水櫃車底之用,有電移起重機一,以便運輸.廠中工作,新造修理均有,水櫃本身之工作,歸鍋爐廠管理,車底車輪則歸裝車廠負責,蓋工作相似,如此分配,一切較爲便利.工人約二三十人.

（十）氣韌廠　此廠在全廠之西南角,長五十呎,寬四十二呎,與電燈廠連接,另有裝韌間,長一百四十呎,闊二十五呎,專事裝置氣管及氣韌機件.氣韌廠則專修一切機件,廠內計有帶副氣筩之韌筩 Brake cylinder with auxiliary air reservoir 一,（供試三通閥 Triple valve 之用）,及虎鉗三十只而已.此廠光線甚爲充足,因所修各機件,均甚纖小精細也.工人約六十人,其所修機件,爲氣喞機 Air pump, 司韌機 Driver's brake valve 三通閥,氣喞調整器 Air pump governor, 韌筩餵氣閥 Feed valve., 及各種塞門 Cock 等.茲將各件之應用,作一有統系之說明如下:

蒸汽由鍋爐經氣喞調整器,而入氣喞機之汽筩 Steam Cylinder. 氣喞機卽上下起動,空氣因是而入氣筩,被壓至儲氣主箱.箱內壓力,至每方吋九十磅時,氣喞機因調整器之作用,卽停止動作.如將司韌機柄移至全鬆位 Full release position 時,高壓氣卽由儲氣主箱,經司韌機及所附屬之餵氣閥,而入主要管 Brain pipe,復由主要管經三通閥,至儲氣副箱.當高壓氣經餓氣閥至主要管,儲氣副箱,及三通閥時,其壓力已減至每方吋七十磅,因餓氣閥有彈簧控制之也.此壓力經常不變.若將司軔機柄移至緩止位 Position for moderate application 時,主要管中之高壓氣,經司軔機,而至外界空氣中,氣壓卽因以降低.此時三通閥卽行動作,使儲氣副箱內之高壓氣,流入軔箱,推動箱內隔板 Diaphragm 使之向外,軔履 Brake block 卽與輪箍相抵,列車遂因此項阻力而停止.當開車時,司軔機柄移至行車位 Running position,高壓氣由儲氣主箱經司軔機而入三通閥,三通閥因是項壓力而又動作,使高壓氣一方入儲氣副箱,一方則由軔箱經三通閥,而與外界空氣相通.軔履卽放鬆,不復妨礙車輪之轉動矣.

（十一）銅器廠　佔地三九九〇方呎,有爐四,吸風扇一,水槽一.該廠工作,為專配機車上之水管,油管,氣管等.凡原件銅管,在此處切斷,然後依車上位置,彎曲就形.管上之摺緣 Flange,及結合 Coupling,均臨時加上,用銅屑釬合.鐵管亦有在此廠如法彎曲釬接者.廠內有工人二十餘人.

（十二）白鐵廠　與銅器廠毗連,專製車上油燈,及一切洋鉛器具.工人計十餘人.（未完）

直隸臨城縣臨城煤鑛實習記要

張陰煊

歲乙丑夏,煊實習于臨城煤鑛.為時一月.其間在鑛面實習二旬,鑛井實習一旬.今將經歷大概,擇要記述如下,以求讀者諸君指正焉.

I.臨城煤鑛沿革及其現狀

II,機械工程

III.電機工程

IV.鑛井工程

I. 臨城煤鑛沿革及其現狀

凡乘京漢車經北段鸚鴿營站.向西遙望.見荆棘中豎立二大烟囱黑煙繚繞不息者.乃臨城縣所在地也.昔年當地有鈕姓者.出巨貲.在臨城開闢土窰.以中國土法採煤.其所掘之井大小與現時新法開掘者相仿.而不砌井牆.見煤即取.見水即棄.今日臨城一地此種見棄之井已不下數百.當時交通不便.屯積煤量數萬噸.未能暢銷外埠.嗣京漢路築成.計劃全路工程者.多屬比法人.比工程師以調查沿線煤源抵臨城.於是鈕姓積煤盡于此時出運.此臨煤顯頭角于京漢路之始也.

自後比人頗覬覦此鑛.亟亟侵謀不遺餘力.卒於光緒二十八年鈕姓將鑛權盜賣.成立中比合辦之羅漢公司.光緒三十一年經我政府追認.乃更名臨城鑛務局.資本三百萬佛郎.盡力經營.剷嶺塡谷.成爲平原.開築新井.建立機廠.用科學方法採煤.數年間高峯起伏荆棘滿地之臨城.竟成爲大廈林立機聲軋軋之實業區域.主其事而擘劃一切者.比人馬眉也.惟煤質不甚佳.加以國中實業尙在萌芽.推銷煤量頗費手續.此臨城煤鑛經辦于比人時代之經過也.

民國八年.北洋巨商李公等以利權外溢.殊屬非是.乃募集商人資本.經一番爭議.始在比國正式簽約.將比款部份完全收回.李公等仍處比款部份地位.繼續原有比約權利.惟直隸省署加派大員.襄助辦理.即成立今日官商合辦之臨城鑛務局.至工程設施.仍請比人主持.此臨城煤鑛官商合辦之經過也.

京漢路以取用石子設支路五十英里.自鴨鴿營站直達臨鑛左近之石子山.運採石子.此路于臨鑛之發展至有關係.加以今日臨煤需求者衆.以地位及時遇論.臨鑛實今日國中致富事業之一也.

現共有煤井三.二大一小.大者深計七百英尺.小者五百尺.距臨城者公

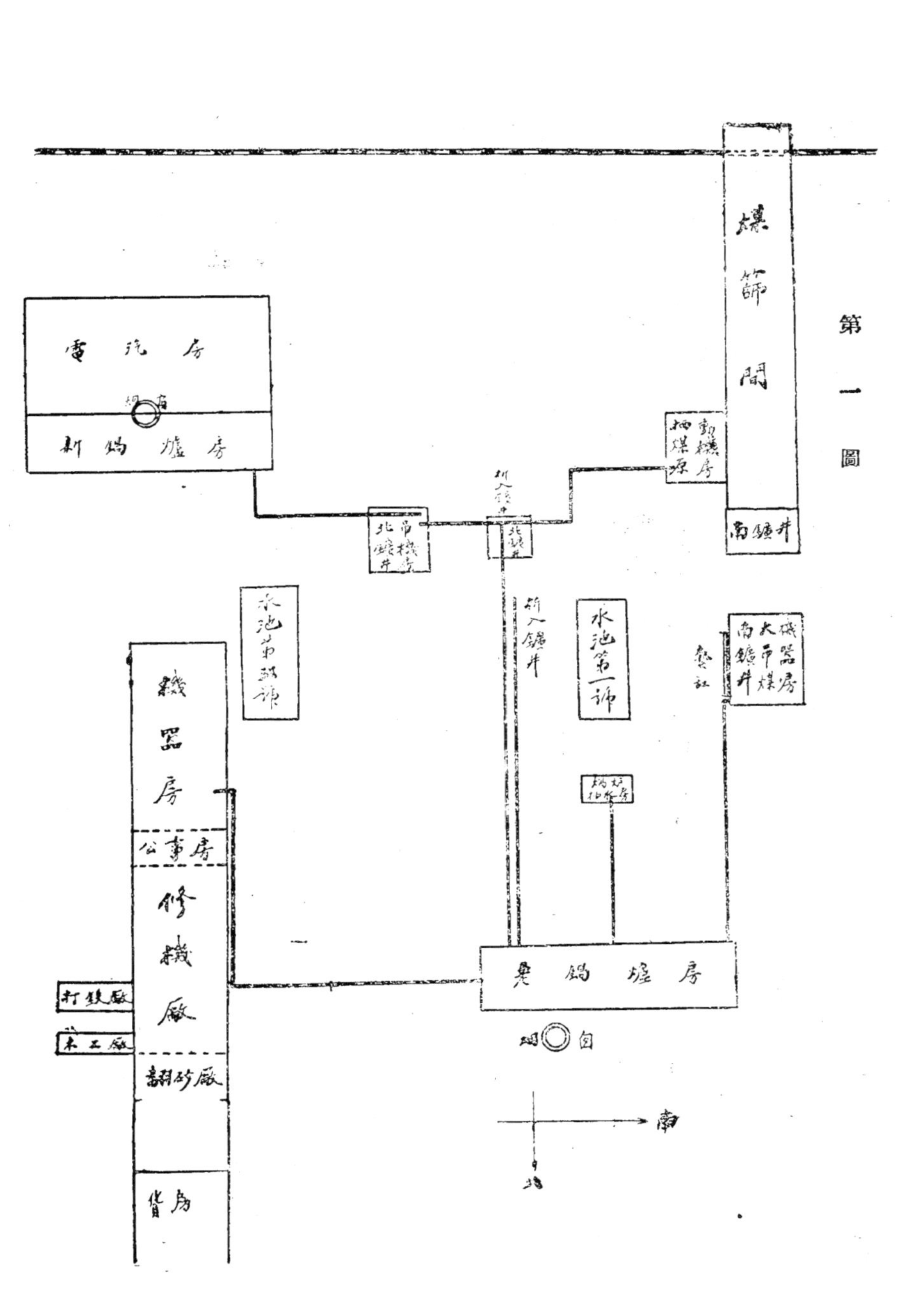

第一圖

一大一小.餘一則在臨城左近里許之石固.每日總共出煤量可八百噸云.

近年來鑛局聘請國內專家從事計劃新井.對于各項工程均大加革新.是則此鑛前途.正方興未艾也.

鑛廠現分鍋爐房,修機廠,原動機房,翻沙廠,木廠,木模廠,打鐵廠,發電廠,貨房,煤篩間等.其佈置略如上頁第一圖.

II. 機械工程概況

1. 機械力需要及荷載量:

鑛廠需要機力屬之鑛面者（一）鑛面吊煤捲繩機.（二）井內用高壓空氣擠氣機.（三）井內通風機.（四）修機廠原動機.（五）翻沙廠風機（六）汽錘.（七）電機等.

是鑛開辦遠在二十年前.上述機力完全利用來往行動式蒸汽機之機械力.今日統計之共一千馬力(1,000B.H.P).

2. 重要機器述略:

A. 南鑛井捲繩機.

第二圖

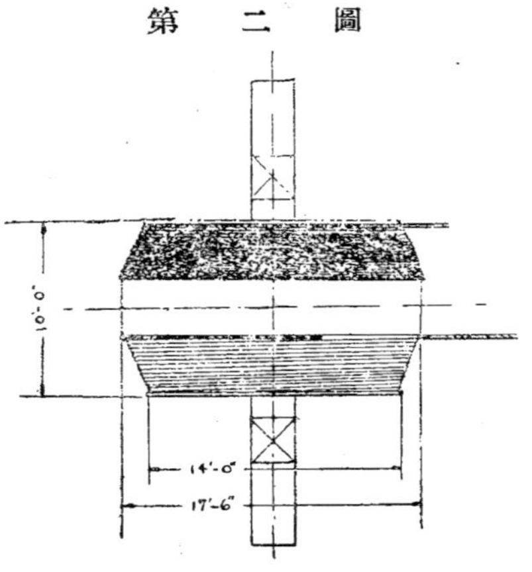

此機係 Corliss Valve, reciprocating, single expansion, double acting, non-condensing and duplex tybe,造自比國拉米斯公司.全機動作等于兩汽機合力轉一鐵繩盤.盤分兩部.動作適反.一部收繩.一部放繩.使鑛中升降得時間上之經濟.而捲機自身亦得一種能力上之節省.盤之本身作圓錐形.吊籠在鑛底時.鐵繩在圓錐之小端.吊籠在鑛面時.鐵繩在圓錐之大端.蓋鐵繩直經爲一又四分之三英寸.吊籠在井底時.鐵繩長爲八百餘英尺.其重量當亦不

輕.吊籠自井底吊出時.捲機須負吊籠之重量及鐵繩之重量.迨吊籠至鑛面.捲機祇須負吊籠之重量.但機力與磅尺乘數成正比例.爲求捲機常出始終如一之機力.必使其受始終如一之磅尺乘數.大重量乘小圓半徑.等于小重量乘大圓半徑.此理甚明.吊籠自鑛井底吊出.鐵繩逐漸減短.空懸重量如之.故爲劃一機力計.捲盤圓徑自不得不逐漸加大.此捲盤之所以成圓錐也.平均計算圓盤一轉可吊出五十尺.自鑛井底吊至鑛口需時不過四十五秒.(通常自四十至四十五秒).鐵繩盤大略形狀如第二圖.

捲繩機附帶機械.至爲複雜.捲盤而外如制動器(Brake)等.至關重要.今附草圖以示其動作功用如下:

第　三　圖

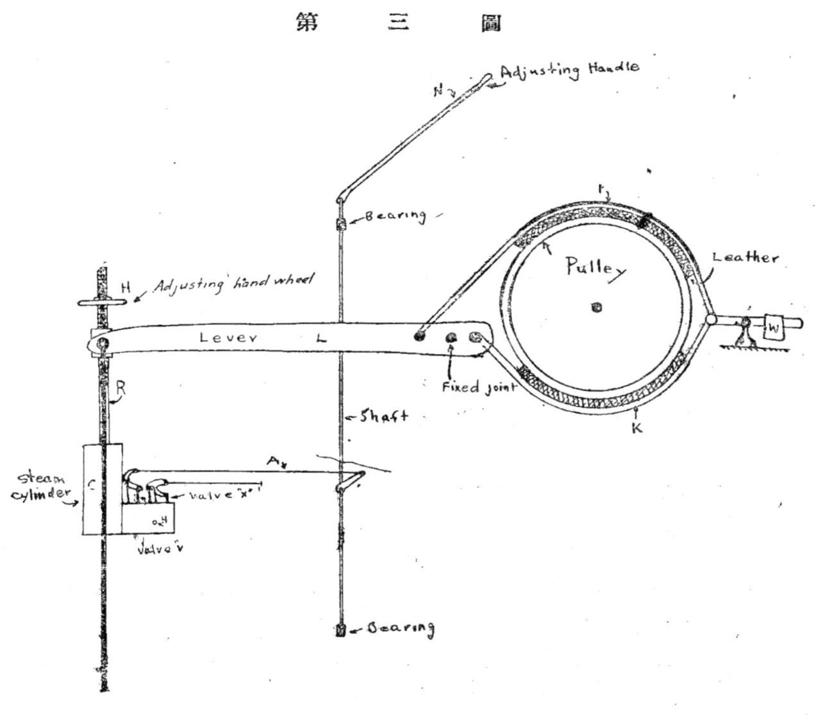

上圖KK.卽制動器之主要部分.開機時先將N移動向左.A隨之而亦左.進汽門V卽開.蒸汽卽衝入汽筒C.將圓筒塞柱R推動向上.槓竿L亦如之.于是鐵片KK向外放開.繩盤卽能自由轉動.關機時將N移動向右.進汽門V卽關閉.同時出汽門卽開.圓筒內之蒸汽外出.于是槓竿L被重物W重拖下垂.同時KK向內夾緊.繩盤乃不能行動.

吊籠升降均有一定限度.偶過限度.則危險叢生.例如吊起時過限.則吊架等物將被擊毀.故捲繩機對于升降限度之保險機械至爲重要.今略示此保險機如第四圖.

第四圖

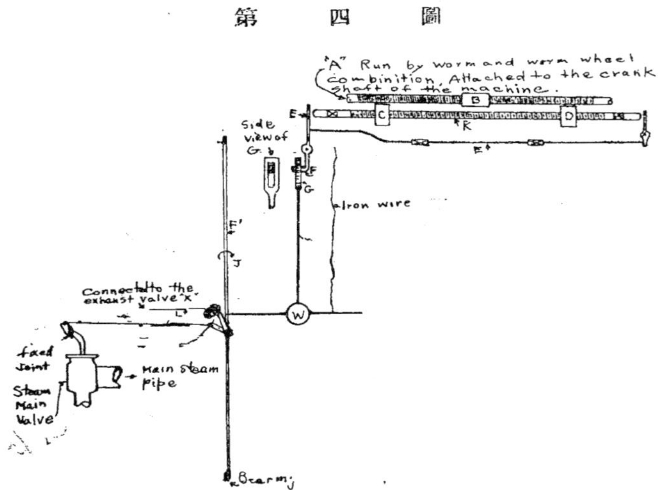

鐵魂B,C,D緊着于圓鐵柱A及K.在校正時.B,C,D多可由螺紋移動.一經校正.B,C,D卽緊着于圓柱不能移動.圓柱A在捲繩盤轉動時.以Worm及Worm Wheel之互連.亦被轉動.B亦沿螺紋向左或向右移動.當吊籠至限度時.B必與C或D相碰.若過限E必左移而將G脫落.于是W下垂.同時H及L右行.H右行.總汽門卽被關.L右行.第三圖之X汽門放開.汽筒內之

汽向小孔H（見第三圖）逃出.制動器卽緊夾繩盤.使不能動.故H及L右行均能使繩盤卽時停動.以免危險.G既落下.仍可以鐵線提起接上F如前.以復原狀.此外緊要之機件.尚不一而足.因限于篇幅姑不贅.

此機圓筒直徑爲三呎.長五呎六吋.荷載量爲六百馬力.（I. H. P.）

B. 空氣擠縮機.

空氣擠縮機于鑛井中最關重要.井底斜槽煤開掘既深.欲吊出之全恃機械之功能.若用汽機.鑛中既增水復增熱.或致白霧滿佈.妨害井底交通及工作至大.若用燃燒機則更不宜.故以用電機爲最宜.若發電廠無有設備.當以高壓空氣機爲最佳.此鑛以最初無電力廠之設.故井底吊煤全用高壓空氣機.此項機器與蒸汽機完全相同.進機之高壓空氣.纔膨脹發出一部份內藏功能.變成低壓空氣逃放機外.復供鑛中工人吸養之用.一舉兩便不可謂非善策也.惜井底佈置空氣管費用甚大.亦缺憾也.

此機原動係一並列複式汽機.蒸汽入高壓汽筒.經膨脹出高壓汽筒.入接受器而進低壓汽筒.再經膨脹.出低壓汽筒.放逃空間.此蒸汽之行動也.外間空氣由低壓蒸汽筒接連之空氣塞來往運行.先被抽入.再被壓迫至三個空氣壓力時卽放入空氣積受器內.受冷環境之吸收熱量.再進高壓汽筒接連之空氣筒.再被壓迫至六個空氣壓力時.始放入另一空氣積受器.由鐵管之排佈.引入鑛井應用.

此機蒸汽筒尺寸爲: 15"×24"×20", 又空氣筒尺寸爲: 14"×23"×20". 原動荷載量二百馬力（B.H.P.）. 速度每分鐘一百三十五轉.空氣抽送量（壓力爲六個空氣壓）每分鐘二十八立方咪.

此機附帶機械足資記述者如下:蒸汽筒及空氣筒潤滑機械.

下圖乃此機之潤滑機械有小圓筒C,筒塞P,滑油箱O,各四.故全具成一立方形.在四個圓筒之底出小油管四.連接於擠空氣機之二個蒸汽筒及二個空氣筒內部.在擠空氣機開始應用時.先將F放鬆.轉動搖手H.此時因

第五圖

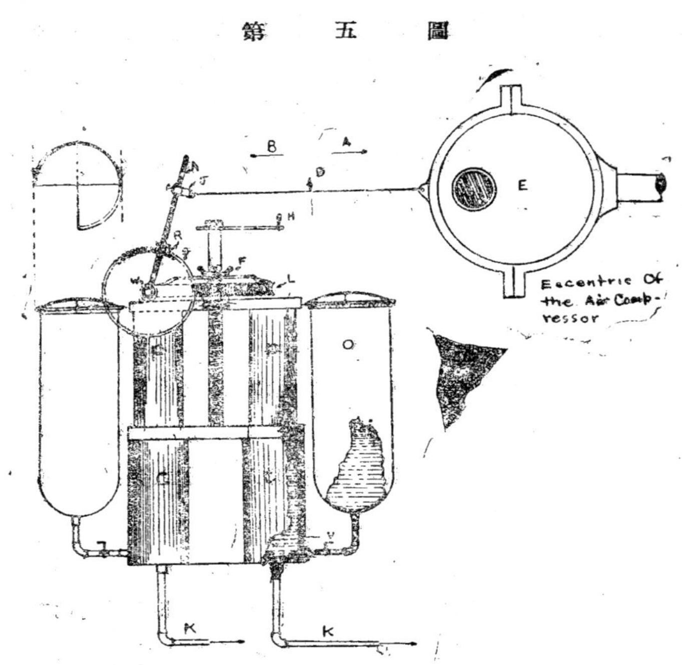

F已鬆故. Worm Wheel L與H之轉動全無關係.但四個筒塞則隨螺紋而上舉.同時因油箱之開關V已開.滑油即填塞圓筒之空容積.當P舉起至一定限度時.即停止轉動H.轉緊F.關閉油箱開關V.此時H轉動.L亦必轉動無疑.擠空氣機既開始行動小鐵竿D因附着於偏心盤E之故.即作左右運動.齒輪G賴彈簧R之忽離忽附.即徐徐轉動. Worm W亦動.L亦動.P乃徐徐下行.而滑油即被逼出小油管K.入目的地以爲潤滑.此種滑油之多少.可將J上下配置以節制之.

C. 鑛井通風機:

夫鑛中毒氣及輕硫混合物其量甚多.若不設法抽去使工人日常呼吸

惡劣空氣.勢必有絕大危險.故鑛面設通風機一具.另置風道.使全鑛得有佳良之空氣成分.通風機全部不過一蒸汽機.與一大風扇而已.

風扇抽風量爲每分鐘十五萬立方英尺.抽吸力$\frac{1}{2}$"H_2O. 扇面直徑三十英尺.

D. 煤篩機:

鑛井吊出之煤.塊末間雜.推銷時難於分別定價.故有煤篩之設.將鑛井出煤分成大小類別.今該鑛暫分大塊(Lump, diam. 6'' 以上).中塊(Small Egg, 3" diam.).小塊(Chestnut, $1\frac{1}{4}$" diam.).煤末(Coal dust $\frac{1}{2}$" diam.)四類.廠中備煤篩一具.略述於下.

第六圖

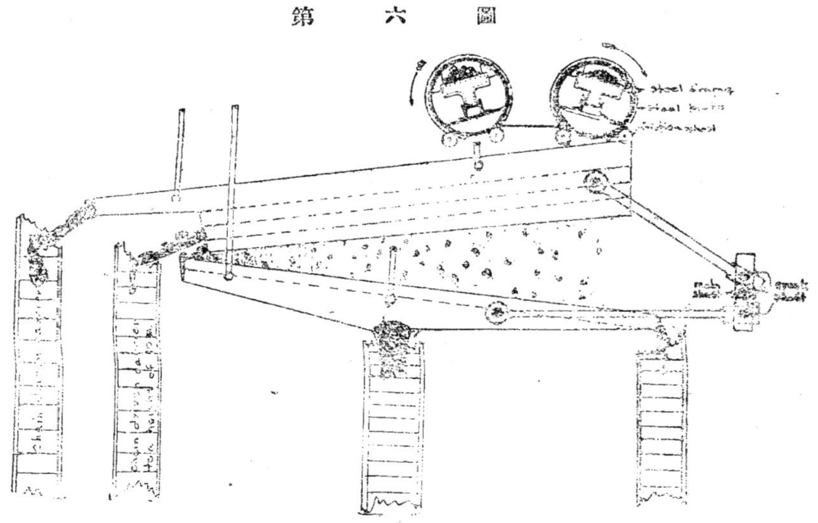

如圖篩分二部.一向左斜.一向右斜.篩盤藉偏心機械作用.得各自左右搖動.鑛中出煤推入搖筒W.搖筒轉動.煤即倒入上層篩盤.篩盤搖動.大塊煤即傾入大塊煤溝中.其餘則篩入上層篩盤之二層篩.再經搖動.中塊又傾入

中塊煤溝中.餘則入下層篩盤.又經搖動.小塊煤傾入小塊煤溝中.煤末則入煤末溝中.計每小時可篩煤百噸左右.

各類煤溝均向上斜約三十度.高出地平五十尺.由小方鐵板連成.經齒輪之轉動.每板各自帶煤上行.至中途即有童工提筐拾取煤中石塊.故運至頂上之煤.已絕無石片.卽墜入各類漏斗.漏斗口高出火車軌道約四十尺.裝煤時煤車停息其下.煤得自行裝入車中.法至善也.近年鑛中出煤各類成分如下.

大塊	16.11%
中塊	10.68 „
小塊	25.00 „
煤末	48.21 „
總共	100.00 „

3. 修機廠內容:

此廠內分機器作,打鐵作,木作,木模作,翻沙作等.機器作內有大車床五.小車床一,刨鐵車(Shaping Machine)一,磨刀機一,大老虎鉗八,剪鐵打洞機一,齒輪機一.打鐵作有打鐵爐七,汽錘一.木作有飛輪鋸一,刨機一.翻沙作有二熔鉄爐(Cupola).小者內圓直徑三十英寸,每小時熔鐵三噸.大者內圓直徑四十八英寸.每小時熔鐵七噸.

此廠能修理各種鑛上已置備之機器.且能製造 4-Stage Turbine Pump 抽水機.以供本鑛及隣鑛抽水之用.

E. 井底蒸汽抽水機:

井底抽水機甚多.大部爲比國製造.美國 Worthington 公司所製者亦有之.而國貨亦佔一部.今足爲記述者.如噴水式凝水器之利用.蓋井底不若鑛面.任何少量之出汽散放.終爲不宜.故各抽水機原動出汽.多進一連帶之噴水式凝水器.蒸汽遇噴水卽凝爲水點.同時縮小其體積.成一息時之真空.以其壓力較外面空氣壓爲低.空氣卽驅鑛水上升.繼續其噴水本職.如是鑛

水連續抽上.此項上噴之水與出汽凝成之水被凝器附帶之抽水塞抽送入一圓水箱.高可十尺.箱內積水自行流入各抽水機抽塞下.抽送至鑛面.如此既略省機力.又免去井中出汽之患.亦一舉兩得之道也.

井內蒸汽抽水機之現有總共抽水量.爲每分鐘水頭八百五十尺之水.四千咖崘.

4.　鍋爐及鍋爐荷載量:

廠中機力凡關乎機械一方面.如上述各汽機.均仰給於老鍋爐房之蒸汽.今爲述其鍋爐設備.及其總荷載量於下:

老鍋爐房共有比國象式(Elephant Type)鍋爐八具.又斜水管式鍋爐一具.象式者每具一百二十鍋爐馬力.斜水管式者每具三百七十七鍋爐馬力.上年毀象式鍋爐一.合計現有一千二百十七鍋爐馬力.蒸汽壓力(汽表壓)一百磅.鍋爐用水溫度因鑛面各汽機全無凝冷設備.故隨氣候而變動.

鍋爐加煤全係人工.運煤之術.先裝煤車約盛半噸.藉蒸汽吊煤機(Coal Elevator)吊至離地面十英尺之處.由煤工推行鐵軌上.運至各鍋爐火門前

第七圖

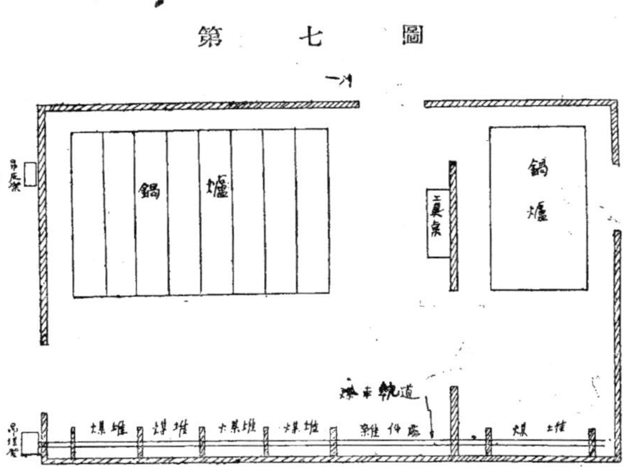

倒下.以便火夫用煤鏟送入爐內.

鍋爐出灰均在爐底.另設地道以為運送.再用吊灰籠附於吊煤機上吊上地面棄於灰堆.

鍋爐用煤出自本鑛.含硫質甚多.火力為每磅十一千B.T.U.

鍋爐統括效率照目前情形.為百分之五十以下.

煙囱一.係各鍋爐公用磚砌構造.計內直徑六英尺.高一百十五英尺.外底圓直徑十英尺.斜度一比三十.計劃時以風力三十五磅作算云.

今示鍋爐房內部佈置草圖如第七圖.

（II節完,全文未完）

美國太康車輛公司實習記

茅以新

美國太康車輛公司（General American Car Co.）在美國芝加哥.專造鐵路運貨車輛規模很不小.是美國有名的造車工廠民國十三年我和鄭泗君來美在這廠實習.前後共歷七月.極有興趣實習時間雖然很短對于造車程序略有些大意.這篇實習記本來久要寫的.也因言之不詳,不如不寫的好.略寫得瑣細些便要費很多時間.現在趕南洋季刊出版,特匆匆將這篇草成.不妥的地方一定很多.希望讀者諸君糾正和指教.

——第一章——

美國太康車輛公司這名字,我們在學校中從未聽見過後來.我們竟和他做了七個月的朋友,說起來也是一件巧事.我們在民國十二年七月間離了南洋母校,便往青島膠濟鐵路管理局實習.十二月三日,便是葛叚長被匪架去的第二天,我們離青島往北京呈報準備來美臨行時特于四方機廠廠長楊毅先生處得一介紹信給美國太康車輛公司北京分經理的.這便是我們到這廠實習的起原.我們到了北京,見了那經理,談了幾句話.說也奇怪,那經理便一口應允了.叫我們第二天去取信.我們也料不到這事這樣容易第二天信取到手,事情便也成功了.但是我們自己反猶疑起來了.後來上船,在船上又將這事盤算了幾次.不實習便去讀書,但是讀書後總還要實習的.究竟先讀書或先實習着實不容易決定.先實習固然很好.但是這太康車輛公[illegible]知是好是壞.安知不是一個規模很小,待中國人很苛,無從得什麼實習經驗的小公司?先讀書又怕錯了這個機會,學校到底無論何時可以進去的.心中盤算不定.船到了西雅圖,我們才決定先實習.但是從西雅圖到芝加哥的途中,又時時揣測將來實習的情况,人生地疏,又覺得心虛.幸好我們兩人在一起,也互相壯壯膽.火車到了芝加哥,只見人聲嚣雜,確是一個大城.我們那時只知覓旅館安息,尋這太康車輛公司接洽實習事務.那許多揣測猶疑和恐懼,一切都丟到九霄雲外,一心一意先實習一年半年再說.

我們十三年二月八日到芝加哥,恰是星期五.住在青年會頂層樓上.二月九日清晨便去尋太康車輛公司.問了路徑,尋到一所高大房屋.這房屋共有二十多層,內中足有幾十家公司,各賃幾間房間辦事.太康車輛公司便在第十七層上賃了十來間作爲總公司辦事處.我們上了樓,問了確實.原來這美國太康車輛公司規模確是不小.是一個新起的造車公司.美國做遠東營業的車輛公司要算太康爲最大了.除在北京設立分公司外,總公司並有一遠東部.我們先見這部部長,說明來意,遞了北京帶來的信.那部長很和善,說總公司久已知道我們要來,已經等候一個月了.隨即去見公司經理.那天恰逢總經理往紐約.便見副經理.那副經理事務極忙,我們候了一小時多才能見到.一見面也着實使我吃驚不小.原來這副經理是一個英秀少年,年紀不過二十多歲.在太康公司做的年數並不多,便升到副經理的位置.雙眸銳利,使人不敢逼視.而說話聲音很和善.見了我們,早已知道情形.略爲應付幾句,便讀了兩封信,由書記速記打成,差我們帶到工廠交給廠長.一件事從頭至尾不過十分鐘便辦成.這十分鐘裏又不時有電話來請教他.只見他應付自如,腦中變化神快.一件事應如何辦理,略轉思慮,便有見地看那神氣又好似記憶力極好,並且很能識人的.那時間我雖然是初到美國,第一次和這班商界巨子接觸,心中却起了無窮的感想.覺得這種人辦事,效率最好.一個人可抵許多人.而那種應付才,果決才,實在是一個公司發達的關鍵.常聽人說美國商界巨子每小時薪金百元.照這樣看來,百元還嫌太少呢.當時我們不敢多留,卽便退出.那遠東部部長和我們說明天是星期日,後天我們再去,由他領我們到工廠去.我們便回到青年會休息.這實習的事可算十分成功了.

這天下午有一位芝加哥大學中國學生陪我們逛大街.芝加哥是美國第二大城,居民有三百萬.街市繁鬧,實有可觀.有高架電車,吵鬧異常,晚間安息,未免可厭.次日是星期日,街市全休息.除戲館飯館電車汽車等外,其餘幾盡休業.亦可見七日中休息一日的習慣,奉行惟謹.下午特往芝加哥大學參觀.芝加哥大學創立于1890年到現在方三十四年.學生人數已增至一萬二千七百人.建築之華麗,風景之秀美,無以復加.大學產業共値一千四百萬元.大半是煤油大王洛克菲勒捐助的.此外還有基金三千二百萬.每年利金連捐數可有二百六十萬,便是學校的經常費.我們讚賞了一番,心中未嘗不驚訝美國大學之大.回想到中國最大的北京大學,學生也只是他那一萬以下的零頭兒.南洋大學算有三十年的歷史稱爲東南學府的,只有他那一萬二千以下的零頭兒,談到經費更足令人傷心了.北京八校一年到頭經費欠不清楚.其他各省學校也只聽見經費不足,教員枵腹從公.似此不知那一年才得好呢!從芝加哥大學回到青年會,便休息了.

——第二章——

二月十一日星期一清晨,又到太康車輛公司晤遠東部部長.十時半上火車往工廠.原來太康車輛公司共有工廠三處.一處在沃海沃省瓦倫地方,一處在美國南部沙泉地方.二處都是很小的修理廠.還有一處在東芝加哥,在芝加哥東南二十五哩.是公司的總廠,規模極大的.我們坐上火車,行約四十分鐘,下車.換電車,又行約十分鐘便到了太康車輛公司的總廠了.遠望只見廠屋綿延不絕,煙突高出雲霄,着實可觀.不覺心中又忐忑不定,想到實習便要開始了,不知究竟如何.我們進了廠先到公事房,見了廠長,說了來意,繳了副經理的信.那廠長看了信又看了我們二人的上上下下,很猶疑不決的樣子,想了一想,叫請工程師來.不到一會工程師到了.他們商量了一會,然後開口問我們打算怎樣實習.我們那時早已胸有成竹,知道他們從來沒有過中國人來實習,這例要我們去開的,便回答道我們遠道從中國來對于這公司還不大明白.我們的意思是先在繪圖間實習些時日,藉此對于工廠各部先有個大意.然後按部分行實習.至于各部程序,我們做定了自可和工程師商量妥定的.那廠長也以爲然,便吩咐那工程師領我們到繪圖室看了地方,見了大衆,準定次日正式上工.這可算萬事如意都安定了.那遠東部部長交代清楚便回芝加哥總公司去了.我們且暫先覓定旅館住了,再慢慢託那副廠長代覓房屋.

這天下午廠長派一人陪我們參觀工廠全部.共歷三小時,草草的看了一遍.現在且先說個大概.這廠分爲東西二大部分,當中是公事房有電車經過.東部純是鋼製廠.西部是木製廠.一輛貨車,車樑是鋼質製成的,而車身則有鋼有木,有的全鋼,有的全木,都看情形而定.鋼製廠所需機器和木製廠所需機器完全不同.所以分爲二部便于管理.鋼製廠中計有裝置廠,壓孔剪鋼廠,翻砂廠,鍛煉廠,帽釘廠,輪軸廠,和存儲場等.木製廠中計有裝置廠,木工廠,木型廠,存儲場等.另有油漆廠,原動力廠,露天修理廠,接收原料場,車輛完成出發場等.井井有條,各有次序.全廠共有大小建築約百所,佔地約二百畝.廠內交通除汽車,電池引重車等外,尚有火車頭五輛,來往不息,輸送貨物.後來和那引導人談起來,才知道這美國太康車輛公司是個新起的公司.從創起到現在才二十五年.起初進步極慢.在 1917—1918 幾年裏,公司驟然發達,成今日的規模.據年老的工人相傳,二十五年前,現在的西部木製廠完全是水草,和米希根湖相通的.現在米希根湖岸已經移出二哩外了.那片水草也完全是工廠房屋了.最初創辦時,只有一個工頭,十來個工匠,每天工頭也不管事,整天的睡覺.到放工時候他早預備好一個鬧鐘,叫醒他回家.現在的工人不止三千,工頭也有百來個,前後實在無從比較了.

東芝加哥是一個工業地段除太康車輛公司外,還有三四個翻砂廠,一個鋼鐵製造廠,機車過熱氣管廠,化學工藝廠,養氣廠,煉油廠等都是規模很大的.居民約三萬五千人.有銀行四家,旅館五六家,熱鬧街市五六條但是經過東芝加哥的火車線足有七條.這並不因東芝加哥是什麼重要城市,是因爲東芝加哥離芝加哥近,許多到芝加哥的路線都要經過東芝加哥的市上所有的中國人便是幾位開洗衣店和雜碎館的,也從沒有中國學生來過我們初到這地方,街市上人很注意我們大驚小怪不知把我們當作什麼而最可惡的是尋房屋了.我們看了報知道某處有招租,尋到那兒裏是黃種人,便回說『很對不起房子已經租出去了』.竟有一次回說『我們不要中國人!請你們別處去尋罷!』如此的艱難鬬尋了一個星期,方才尋到二間小房子.還要五元一星期的租金,二人便是十元但是這也沒法,只得便住定了.幸好這住處到工廠並不遠,十分鐘可以走到房間設備也還安適,所以也就安心下來了.地址一定,這才能寫信給朋友們,報告平安.

二月十二日是我們第一天上工,那時我們還住在旅館中清晨起來坐電車到廠門口.見了繪圖間的工程師,略談些我們來美情形他便向別的繪圖員分些工給我們做那些繪圖的人看見我們二個黃人也來繪圖,都有輕鄙的意思所幸我們在校中都學過儀器繪圖.也曾計劃過機車,用過滑尺的.第一張圖來了並不見難.不一會功夫便畫好了.接連又畫第二張.漸漸的那些繪圖的人不輕視我們了.後來同他們談起,我們都是工科學士.那些人都驚奇得了不得,未敢深信.原來這繪圖房裏上上下下連工程師在內,沒一個是大學畢業的.最好的是中學畢業,然後學習繪圖,做了幾年,有了資格,便可漸漸升做工程師了.那總繪圖連中學教育都沒有受過.只是一個小學畢業生便了.從這一點上我們也很可看到美國社會的心理並不迷信學位頭銜.儘管是一個小學畢業生,只要學問經驗實是超衆.辦事司職勤懇可靠,便可以做工程師或廠長.學位是不成問題的.在中國就不同了.留學生得了頭銜回國的都可以任大事.多走幾國地方,雖然看得多些,但並不一定便是學問經驗,任職勤懇更是另一件事.結果現在許多留學生在國外鬼混了幾年,那文憑和學位,本來容易拿的.拿了文憑回國便可自欺欺人,掛起留學生招牌,貿然受聘任職了.這是多麼危險的事呵!將來留學生的數目漸漸增加,或爲一特殊階級,可和農工商學兵五種合爲農工商學兵留六種了.我這話並不是籠統指一切留學生都是這樣的,當然也有優秀分子在內.但是優秀分子究竟佔極少數呢.現在暫且不提,再說我們在太康車輛公司工廠繪圖的狀況.

——第三章——

我們這繪圖間是太康車輛公司惟一的繪圖間.那沃海沃省的分廠和南部沙泉的分廠,如要什麼圖樣,都要從這總廠來取.所以繪圖間也粗粗的分爲兩大部.一部完全管總廠的圖樣,一部管分廠的圖樣.而總廠的出貨在近幾年來都是平常式樣的貨車,分廠除南部沙泉廠純爲修理外,沃海沃廠的出品大半是運油貨車.車的形式如桶,又名桶車.所以這兩部又可分爲一部專管平常貨車的圖樣,一部專管桶車的圖樣.兩部各有一工程師,各有繪圖員若干人.各人的責任雖然明白分定,有時一部的人員忙了,也可請別部的人幫忙.總計兩部繪圖人員有二十四人.分爲五小團,每團五六人不等.各有一領班.圖樣由工程師分交領班,由領班負責繪成.五小團的責任分列如下:

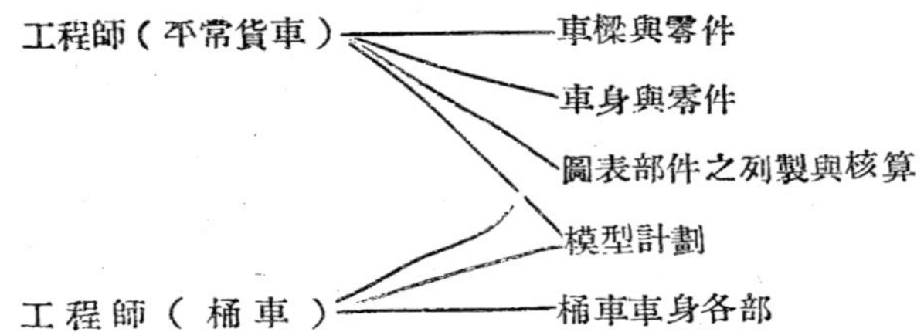

車樑是一車的骨架,其他的附枝零件都生根于骨架上.是一車的最要緊的部分.平常貨車有運煤,運汽車,運牲畜,敞口,高身,和凝冷等種種不同的式樣.但是車樑大都相同,不同的只在車身的構造而已.桶車車樑也和平常貨車之車樑大同小異.車身爲圓桶式,製造方法和蒸汽鍋鑪相同.形式也很相像,只是沒有火箱火管,比較的簡單得多.模型計劃是造車的重要關鍵.車輛各部件中.有許多是必須用特種方法,計劃特種模型來製造的.如將鐵板一塊,用高壓力壓成各種形式,以爲應用,這壓鐵的模型種類繁多,每次不同,便是我們繪圖間計劃的.圖表部件之列製與核算也是一件大事.一批車輛未造之先,必先預計須用幾何材料,何種材料廠內備有的,何種材料要購買的,價值幾何.這些都應有圖表說明,列製清楚,還要核算準確才行.這又是我們繪圖間的事務.模型計劃和圖表列製二小團,因爲事務比較清閒,每團同時做平常貨車與桶車兩部的事,每部不另分團,以省經費.

認眞說來,一輛貨車各種不同的零件何止二三千.每種多也百來件,少也二三件.單是帽釘一項,最少也有三千個.計劃起來,如果每零件都要計算那大小尺寸厚薄,不繁得可怕？我們繪圖人員再加十倍也未必能做得下去.幸好美國鐵路車輛各部除少數特件外幾都有標準計劃.車輪大小早已一律,車軸尺寸也有一定.我們計劃繪圖只要抄抄老文章,並不費心思的.有時鐵路購車早將圖樣送來.各件計劃都已齊備.我們只另抄一份,藍印許多份,交廠應用.又可留一底稿備將來參考之用.所以事務雖然很多,我們二十四人也就安然忙過來了.

圖樣分大小五種.頭四種大小都有標準尺寸.第五種是大圖樣,大小不一,圖有幾何,紙也幾何大.每圖都有一號碼,按號保存.另有查圖簿,如要翻閱舊圖,一查便知.有一人專管此事.

我們在繪圖間練習從二月十二日到三月三十一日,恰好七個星期.每天早八點一刻上工,十二點休息午飯.下午一點又上工,五點散工回家.一天做八小時弱.早出晚歸很有規律.三餐也很自適.有時自已煮中國飯食,有時到飯館去吃.有談有笑.此間樂不思蜀.同事中有一德國人,兩俄國人,其餘都是美國人.比較起來俄國人德國人待我們中國人好些.我們向他們問什麼,他們都很情願告訴我們.美國人大半眼眶小,平時見的中國人都是洗衣作的.早存了輕視的心.所以我們要和他們接近,是很不容易的.我們在繪圖間的末了一個星期,很注意各種圖樣的計劃,和車輛構造原理.有一次見一本車輛定規,內容很好.我們竟取回家趕夜的抄成一份.至今還留存呢.我們每天午飯不用一小時.餘下時間,同事們都頑紙牌.我們總到廠中各處參觀.漸漸的廠內各部分性質關係知道些大概了.又細看造車程序和方法,再與所繪圖樣相映照.每天必多懂些.非常有興趣.在這時期裏我們和工程師商量入廠實習次序及時間,粗定了一個表作爲準繩,後來雖然不能完全依照也相差不遠.入廠第一部定在木工廠,因木工廠最清潔,最適宜我們初步實習.四月一日便是我們入廠的第一天.

——第四章——

這時候我們已在廠幾將兩月.對于廠內組織情形約略有點大意.現在不妨寫些.原來這廠的創辦初衷只是修理些運油桶車.美國在二三十年前汽車用途漸廣,汽油的需要也漸大.美國的產油區域都在西部和南部.運轉很是一件大事.所以那時運油桶車的需要也很緊急.各地製造桶車的工廠都紛紛創立.那時太康公司才只是修理桶車的小廠.後來也漸漸自已製造桶車.但是運油用桶車是最笨不過的事.油運到了,空車回去.雙程行數千哩,只運了一桶油,最不經濟.所以各產油公司想法改良裝埋鐵管于地下.從產油區域直到需用區域.也不管幾千里路長短,都裝了這鐵管.用以運油,捷速而省費.所以桶車的用途便驟然減少了.太康車輛公司經理有鑒于斯,見不是勢頭,連忙改轉方向兼造平常貨車近五年來桶車的營業幾等于零,只不過修理工作.幸平常貨車生意大好.公司反因此大發展.新造許多廠屋,成現在的規模全廠工人時有多少.最多約四千人,最少約一千八百人.平均以三千五百人爲準.每日造車約五十輛.也時有多少.1924年四月裏有一天竟造了一百輛,是從來沒有的成績.1923年共造車10019輛.1924年迄八月底止約造成6501輛.大約每年一萬輛是現在的產額.查1923年全美國新添車輛共爲四十五萬輛.太康公司約造其四十五分之一,成績已經很好了.全廠分五十三部.各部名稱如下:

1. 機工廠
2. 鍛煉廠
3. 鋼製裝配廠一
4. 鋼製裝配廠二
5. 穿孔廠
6. 鋼製裝配廠三
7. 雜件訂貨部
8. 帽釘廠
9. 鐵管與風閘廠
10. 動力廠一
11. 油漆廠
12. 露天修理場一
13. 露天修理場二
14. 電機修理場
15. 車輪車軸廠
16. 儲貨房
17. 銅與灰鐵翻砂廠
18. 機車與起重機車房
19. 壓剪廠
20. 木製裝配廠
21. 木料存儲房
22. 廠內道路與軌道修理房
23. 器具間
24. 木工廠
25. 木匠廠
26. 桶車修理場

27. 動力廠二
28. 廠內車輛部
29. 警察部
30. 煉鋼廠
31. 樣板廠
32. 廠內安全部
33. 保管機器部
34. 廠長室
35. 繪圖間
36. 會計部
37. 出貨部
38. 匠工部
39. 採買部
40. 交通部
41. 雇工部
42. 工作安全宣傳部
43. 工人餐館
44. 養氣廠
45. 查察出品部
46. 工人消費合作社
47. 總辦事處
48. 汽車房
49 醫院
50. 總工程師室
51. 傢俱房
52 經理駐廠辦事處
53. 材料供給室

各部的權限都明白訂定.現在再將全廠組織列表如下:

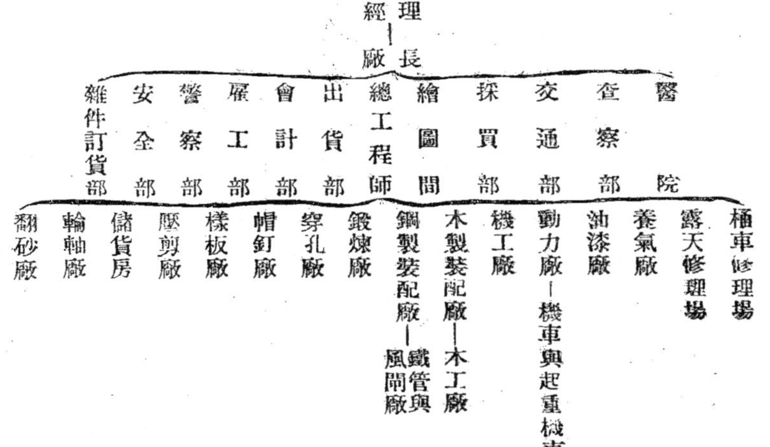

各廠直接受轄於總工程師.但是有許多事也直接與廠長接頭.不經總工程師的.各部的責任,都可從名稱上看出,不用細述.出貨部是管廠內出車多少,而設法增進工作效率,改良工作方法,務使省費而出貨多.交通部管廠內貨物運輸,造就車輛的運出,和修理車輛的進廠.雜件訂貨部管外界來信訂購雜件廠內各工廠出品,除供給本廠造車之用外,尙有餘額可以應外界之需.所以有這部專管此事.（未完）

道馳式提士引擎觀察記

孫尊衡

溯自提士引擎發明以來,因其運用靈便,熱力效率高大,幾超蒸汽引擎而進佔原動力首位.故雖僅有極短時間之歷史,然已引起全球工業界之注意,認爲機械工程上,最有價值發明之一.上月校中三十周紀念盛典,舉行工業展覽會.上海德商,以道馳式提士引擎全部來加陳列.著者因得考察一切,玆將所得擇要誌之.

引擎爲立式,有氣缸二,（two cylinders, vertical type）共一百馬力.速率每分鐘三百轉.每小時耗油量爲三十七磅半（柴油）.熱力效率在百分之三十五以上.全身佔平面積一百二十英方尺,高十尺.共重十噸左右,飛輪佔其百分之四十.全部除總軸（Shaft）,搖捍（Connecting rod）,及摩擦部分用純鋼及合金製成外,餘均爲生鐵澆成.各部搆造及運用分門述之於下.

一,裝置　氣缸蓋（Cylinder head）位於引擎最高部.進氣（Admission）洩氣（Exhaust）高壓空氣進氣(Compressed air inlet)諸氣塞（Valve）,及注油器（Nozzle）附焉.進氣及洩氣管亦連接於旁.氣缸緊連氣缸蓋,長計二尺,四周附水夾（Water jacket）外圜直徑約二尺,內心估計一尺四寸,活塞(Piston)於此上下活動.活塞頭平,內附軸心(Piston pin).搖桿(Connecting rod)

繫此而傳達動力至總軸.總軸直徑七英寸半,作兩彎,與飛輪軸用攷潑靈（Coupling）連接.總軸旁有副軸,用齒輪嚙接,上置偏心輪（Cam）.氣缸蓋上各氣塞及打油機,仰此動作.壓氣機（Air compressor）打水機(Water pump),及潤油機（Lubricating oil pump）,連接總軸左端,由齒輪及偏心盤(Eccentric）傳達動作.飛輪直徑七英尺,外邊厚一尺三寸半,生鐵澆成,分作兩瓣,用螺絲（Bolt）鐵板鐵針箍緊於總軸上.

二,熱力循環　引擎爲提士循環無空氣注射式（Diesel cycle, airless Injection).其循環由活塞來去四次成之.謂之四行程式（Four stroke cycle）.其循環上壓力與容積之變遷,如圖一所示.圖二爲活塞之連帶地位.

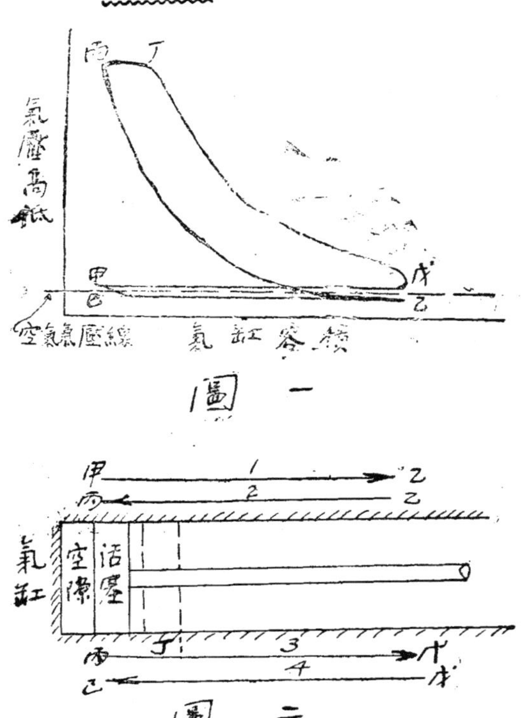

圖一

圖二

第一行程—吸氣　活塞起自左端甲點,漸向右移動,氣缸容積隨之而大,氣壓變低（低於空氣氣壓）,同時進氣氣塞洞開,空氣遂乘隙而入,至乙點而氣缸完全裝滿空氣.

第二行程—擠壓　活塞向左回至丙點,氣塞緊閉,氣缸內空氣遂被擠壓至極高氣壓,如圖一乙丙曲線.熱度亦增高至華氏千度以上,或攝氏六百度左右.乙丙曲線,或稱等能擠壓線

(Adiabatic compression)因活塞極快之擠壓,熱氣不及發散也

第三行程—動力　動力行程中,包含兩步變遷例.(一)油料燃燒,發生熱力.(二)熱力膨脹變成動力第一步在圖一上爲丙丁線,第二步爲丁戊線丙丁線約佔全行程百分之十左右,當第二行程告終時,氣缸內有華氏千度以上熱度.故第三行程起始,油料注入,立即燃燒(無需另用發火機關,亦無需高壓空氣輔助注射,故名無空氣注射.)油料注入,至丁點而停止.氣缸內所得熱力,遂依丁戊等能膨脹線(Adiabatic expansion)發展,推動活塞,而成動力.

第四行程—洩氣　活塞由戊點囘至己點時,洩氣氣塞開,活塞將氣缸內餘氣排洩,以待第二次循環引吸新氣.

三,氣塞運動　進氣,洩氣諸氣塞,均爲"T"字式(Poppet valve).每氣缸各自齊備.其動力傳自總軸,如圖三,經齒輪而至副軸,再由偏心輪擊接捍,經槓捍而至氣塞頂.平時氣塞有彈簧彈緊.當第一行程起始時,偏心輪依副軸之轉旋將接軸抬高.進氣氣塞遂受槓桿作用而壓開.第四行程時,洩氣氣塞亦同樣被槓桿推開.排洩餘氣氣塞各有偏心輪主之,不相連絡.其啓閉之時刻,及時間之長短,各由偏心輪之地位式樣定之.

四,燃料注射　燃料爲柴油.煤油及汽油亦可應用.惟不若柴油經濟.柴油注射,由打油機司之.機爲塞針式(Plunger type),有凡爾(Valve)量進油多少.打油機動力,與氣塞相同,亦由副軸偏心軸而來備用之油,經濾濾後,即由手搖抽油機,打至較高鐵筒內貯之.用時,由鐵管導至打油機當第三行程時,塞針得偏心輪之抬力,將燃油擠至相當壓力.燃油經凡爾之釐正後,(如太多則由支管流囘)假此壓力,遂由注油器噴入氣缸而燃燒.注油器上有極小細空三四,油注射時作細點如霧.故燃燒得以非常完全.注油器上亦備支管,以便餘油流囘油箱.

五,開車　開車,先用高壓空氣衝動活塞而使飛輪旋轉氣壓爲每方英

寸四百廿磅高壓空氣先由壓氣機製成（壓氣法詳後）貯於堅固鐵筒內,制以凡爾,導以鐵管,以待需用.開車之前,先視察活塞,校正至適宜有力地位.（卽離氣缸而蓋冋頭之時）.如活塞與壓氣

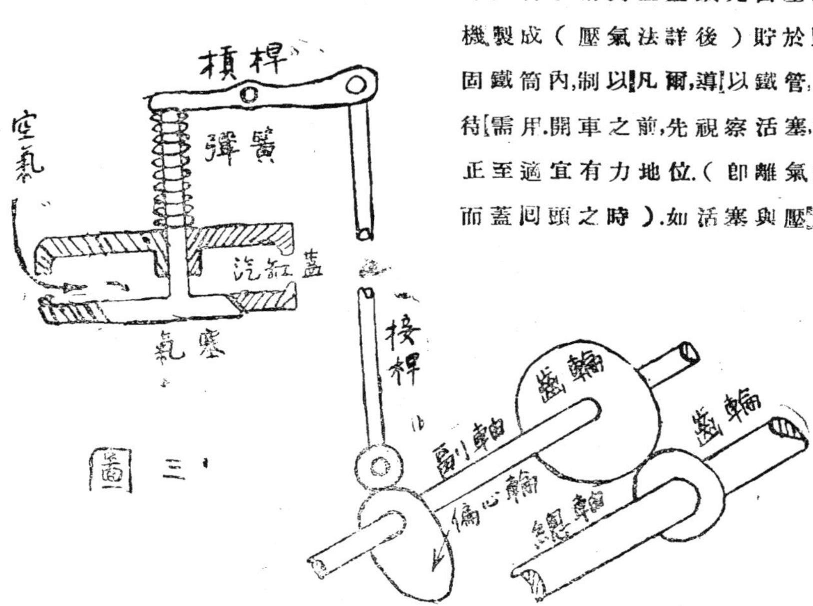

圖三

不處相順地位而適相反,則不能運動此機爲雙氣缸,兩活塞處相反地位,故祇可擇一主之,兩者不可兼顧.校正後,將手制機柄劃動,使高壓空氣氣塞上之槓桿,接桿等,與副軸上偏心輪連接,以備運動.於是啓高壓空氣管凡爾,導高壓氣至氣缸蓋,經氣塞而至氣缸,衝動活塞,旋轉飛輪.此時高壓空氣之注射,由高壓空氣氣塞主之.當飛輪至一二轉時,引擎自動擠壓力已得,急將高壓空氣凡爾關去.同時將氣塞脫離運動.一面卽將進油機接桿.及進氣,洩氣諸氣塞,接連副軸,開始運動,按時動作.引擎遂處自動地位.開車手續乃畢.

六,速度節制　引擎每因負重之變更,速度隨之不同.此機速度快慢,由注油量之多寡制之.惟打油機所打油量,爲一定數目,不能變更.故另用凡爾規定之.因凡爾啓口之大小,制定餘油流入支管之多少,而氣缸注油量得以

多寡不同.凡爾運動,與塞針同得自副軸.惟因有橫桿之節制,啓口因之變更,其機械連絡如圖四.

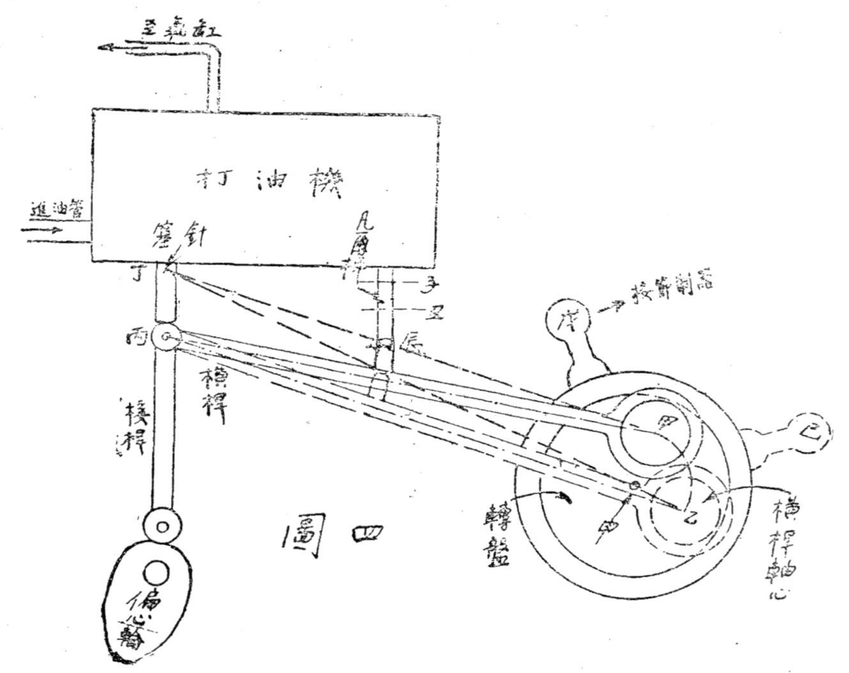

圖四

橫桿動作,間接由節制器(Governor)管轄之.節制器爲飛球式,由齒輪與副軸相連接,故隨總軸旋轉.總軸速度變更,飛球之離心力亦隨之不同,而節制器上之游標,因離心力之不同,遂忽上忽下.其動作乃由數橫桿之連接(節制器及橫桿連接,圖四中未詳)達至轉盤戊點.轉盤因之依申點轉移.同時橫桿因軸心之隨轉盤移動.地位變遷.而凡爾桿之移動,亦隨之變更.其原理可閱圖四.

當轉盤在戊點,其所連橫桿,處甲丙地位.後丙點因偏心輪之抬動,移至丁點,橫桿乃作甲丁式,同時凡爾桿支點辰遂上至子點,設轉盤隨節制器之運動,而至已點,橫桿軸心,依甲乙曲線,下降至乙點,橫桿變爲乙丙式,當丙點至丁點時,凡爾桿支點僅升至丑點,故轉盤轉移於戊已間,凡爾啓口卽有子丑之伸縮,支管流油量因之不同,氣缸注油量隨之多寡,而速度亦依之變更.故於引擎速度太快時,轉盤自向已點移動,多分油量至支管,以減殺速率.反之則向戊點.及至適當地位,卽適宜速度而止.

七潤油法　引擎摩擦部分,每易生熱,必用潤機油潤之.此機潤油之法,其於凡爾,接桿,副軸,汽缸等負重較輕,摩擦力不大之處,潤油卽從潤油箱用細銅管分導各處.惟於總承牀（Bearing）及軸心承牀等處,負重極大,有頑強之抵抗力,潤油不易注入.故用潤油機,將潤油擠壓至相當壓力.輔助注入之.潤油機之構造與打油機相彷彿.由偏心盤接至總軸而運動.軸心承牀之潤油,由潤油機經軸心油道而注入.承牀中均有油漕,以利潤油之分佈.潤油用過後,經濾瀝器之瀝淸而再用.

八散熱法　氣缸用冷水傳熱.此機氣缸熱度,規定不得過攝氏七十度,合華氏一百五十八度.冷水用打水機,從氣缸下部水夾打入,由氣缸上部流出.他如壓氣機之氣缸及洩氣管等,亦用冷水傳熱而凝冷之.回出之水,常在攝氏六十度左右.

九壓氣法　高壓氣用壓氣機製成.壓力每方寸爲四百二十磅.壓氣機爲單級式（Single stage）,構造與空氣引擎同.氣缸,活塞,及吸氣,排氣等氣塞齊備.氣缸容量爲八十立方英寸.動力由總軸用偏心盤帶至接桿,運動活塞.空氣先由進氣氣塞吸進,裝滿氣缸,繼由活塞之擠壓至規定壓力,於是衝開排氣氣塞而入貯氣筒.筒上及氣缸上,均置安全凡爾,以防壓力過量.筒內所容高壓氣,可供四五十次開車之用.

十停車　停車時,將手制機柄移動,使打油機脫離運動,油料斷絕,引擎自停.

總觀全部引擎優點有三,缺點有二.優點甲:熱力效率較高同樣沃脫式(Otto)內燃引擎熱力效率,僅有百分之二十左右.蒸汽引擎,多在百分之十以下.效率旣高,燃料自省.此引擎每十小時,耗柴油三百七十五磅.合銀七元八角.如同樣馬力蒸汽引擎,每十小時須耗煤一•九噸合銀二十元九角.故燃料消耗不過蒸汽引擎百分之四十.卽低壓內燃引擎,消耗費亦須倍之.乙:不需多量冷水.此機僅用極少水量以傳熱.故水源不充足之處,用之更宜.丙:熱力發自內燃.無需置備輔助器.(如鍋鑪汽櫃等物)故地位經濟重量減少.管理便利,人工可省.缺點甲:開車須藉外力.扭力不均,須用重大飛輪.乙:速度不高.普通發電機不能直接.

吾國工業.素稱幼稚於原動力上,尤少建樹.近年以來,經工程界盡力提倡,漸有起色如煤油,柴油,等低壓內燃引擎,均能自造.雖精巧不如舶來品,然其進步不過時間問題.惟於靈便,經濟,合用之提士引擎,則國人對之,尙未有相當注意.故成績極少.實爲一大缺憾.深望此次展覽會能引起國人興趣,研究提倡而製造之.斯則作者之微意也.

參觀南通大生紗廠記

王樹芳

丙寅之夏.余乘校中暑假之期往遊南通.並在大生諸紗廠中一度實習.以補平日課讀之不逮.祇以余習機械.原動之部.尤所關切.故記之較詳.其他紡織等項未加注意.幸讀者諒之.

大生紗廠爲南通最大之廠.成立最早.現分四區.第一廠設立已三十年.位于距通城十五里之唐家閘.第二廠設在崇明.第三廠設在海門.第八廠亦名副廠,設在通城之西南.余所蒞者爲一.三.八廠第一廠因建立時早.原動部設備較舊.故所記甚略.而於組織及會計情形.較多採錄.以便有心實業者之參攷茲就各廠調查所得.分述於下.

第一廠 第一廠創立於光緒二十三年.距今已三十載.初祗紗廠一所後以營業發達.增立新廠.迄今亦十二年.年來復添織布廠一所.資本先後共四百五十萬元.佔地約三百餘畝.職員共計三百餘人.機匠三百.工人一萬.其警務則由實業鹽墾警務團司其事.該團乃各實業機關合資所組者也.廠中組織.計分會計.攷工.營業及庶務四科.由總經理統轄之.廠中屋宇甚多.宿舍約十餘區.鍋爐間兩所.引擎間兩所.紡紗廠兩所.織布廠一所.金工廠一所.發電廠兩所.並附設醫院及公園.又設紡織學校於廠左.費由諸紗廠供給.廠按月撥洋一千元.其中常年開支.以機工紡工爲最大.合計每年約三十六萬兩.職員薪水約六萬兩.教育慈善費約三萬二千兩.警衛等費約一萬六千兩.全廠紗機計七萬七千錠.布機七百二十只.產紗約分六支.八支.十二支.最細至四十八支.每日可出紗二百箱.（每箱四百四十磅）出布八百疋.每日工作時間爲二十四小時.耗煤約七十噸.煤係購自直隸撫順煤礦公司（由上海謝蘅牕裕昌棧經理）

廠中鍋爐爲內燃式（Lnternally fired Scotch Marine type. Yates and Thom. Ltd, Blackburn.）.其安全活門爲撲伯式（Pop safety valve,）.其氣流則爲自然式（Natural draft.）

茲將新舊兩廠鍋爐不同之點列下:

	舊廠	新廠
爐鍋數目	七只	四只
磚建烟突高度	一百四十英尺	一百二十六英尺
蒸汽壓度 Steam Pres,	一百二十磅	一百六十磅
高熱器 Superheater	有	無
省熱器 Economizers	有	有
爐柵 Stoker	手工加煤	鍊式（Chain grate）

新舊二廠之引擎均爲考立司式(Cross compound Corliss Engine).舊者爲一千五百匹馬力.新者爲一千匹馬力.皆具有眞空凝汽器(Jet Condenser),並各有一飛球式調準器(Fly-ball governor).

第三廠 三廠地在海門之東十八里距南通城約九十里.佔地可二百七十畝資本爲五百萬元.成立於民國十年.全廠職員計二百人工人三千.紗機計三萬錠布機四百二十只.每日出紗約九十八箱布五百匹紗類普通分十二支及十六支最細可紡三十二支.所產之紗都銷售於本邑.紗之市價（如以上月論）每箱爲一百九十六元其中紗之成本爲一百五十餘元.（淨花三百五十斤可紡紗三百斤.淨花價每百斤約四十四元故三百五十斤價一百五十餘元紗三百斤即四百磅.成一箱.）工料約十六元除淨每箱計可餘七八元倘平均每日以九十箱計算.則月可進洋一萬八千元.廠中屋宇.整齊宏敞爲各廠之冠.其紗布廠.鐵筋水泥房.引擎.汽爐水塔.皮棍房.飛花洞.升降梯.繩子衖.送紗室.計一千零三十二間.軋花.揀花廠.脚花機.翻砂間.機匠房等.計九十一間.辦事室.營業處等.計三百九十餘間.工作場所.夫役室等.計一百二十一間.工人寄宿舍計三百九十五間.另設港賬房於長江岸畔青龍港上.爲程十里.特築輕便鐵道往來其間以便運輸焉.

茲將該廠原動部機器圖於下.各機亦購自英國.裝置之法與第一廠大致皆同.

說明 內燃式鍋爐共四只.皆具一省熱器（Economizer）.並各具一高熱器（Superheater,）爐柵爲動鍊式.由一附設之小蒸汽引擎所逐駛煤及灰燼均用人工輸送.烟突高一百二十英尺.爐中空氣用自然氣流法(Naturol draft.）尋常壓度爲一百六十磅.進水之途有二.其一由一抽水機直運自河.其一則由另一抽水機運自眞空凝汽器.原動機爲一千匹馬力之英國交復臥式考立司引擎（Horizontal Cross compound corliss Engine.）高壓汽爲一百六十磅.每分鐘行七十轉.其飛輪（Fly-wheel）之直徑爲二十二英尺半,

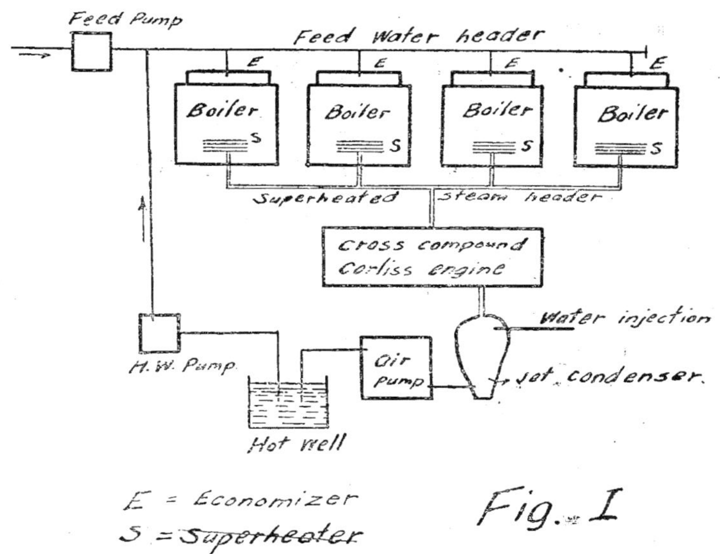

Fig. I

皮帶爲二十條皮索.各長一百五十英尺.蒸汽自引擎低壓筒(Low pres. engine Cylinder)入眞空凝汽器.遇冷而凝爲水.經過熱水池(Hot well)復入於鍋.其熱度常在華氏八十度以上.引擎佔地面約一千四百五十英尺.眞空凝汽器(Jet Condenser)及空氣帮浦均係置於引擎地下.每日耗煤約二十餘噸.耗車油約十三磅.

第八廠　八廠又名副廠.亦名永豐.(近已正式改稱副廠)去通城約四里.成立於民國十三年冬.創立較晚.故其原動部設備較新.建置費約三十八萬元.紗機概用馬達轉動.不若一.三廠之用皮帶也.全廠職員約一百人.工人一千.共有紗錠一萬五千.而無布機.每日出紗約五十箱.其紗之佳.爲各廠冠.廠中有鍋爐間一所.引擎間一所.所發電力每基羅瓦特小時(Kw-ht)耗蒸汽約十八磅.每小時進水量爲一千二百加侖.即一萬磅.每日耗煤約十七

噸.煤購自開灤公司每噸約價銀七兩半.尋常統計電流每度（即基羅瓦特小時）約費洋三分.

第二圖爲該蒸汽力廠之管子圖樣. (Piping diagram.)

The Piping Diagram of the

Dah Sun Spinning and Weaving Co. No. 8, Nantungchow.

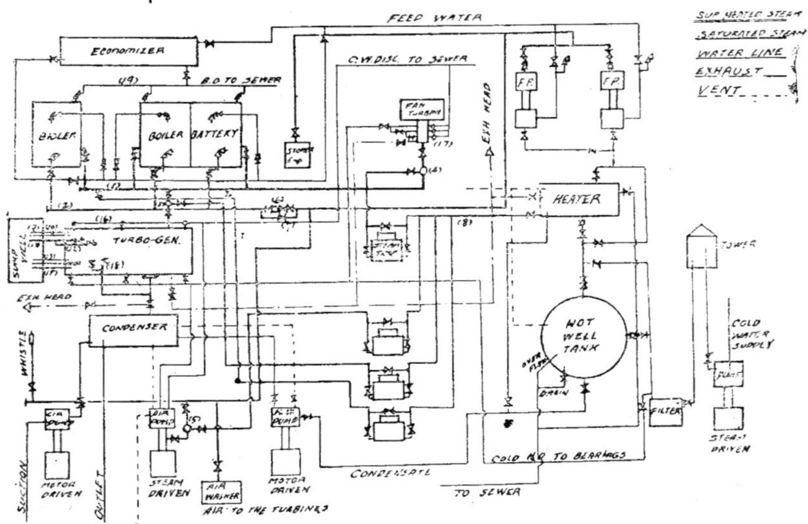

The steam from the boiler is distributed into two headers, one carries the superheated steam while the other carries the saturated steam.

(1)Superheated steam header. (2)Saturated steam header. (3)Steam separator for the turbo-generator. (4)Steam separator for the fan turbine. (5)Steam separator for the air pump. (6) Strainer. (7) Reducing Valve. (8) Trap discharge to heater. (9) and (10) Drain from packing. (11) and (12) Drain from steam chest. (13) Drain from packing. (14) Drain from pilot volve. (15) Drain from operating cylinder. (16) Three funnels for turbo-generator (17) Three funnels for fan turbine (18) Drain from wheel casing. (19) Blowoff heater.

Fig. 2

煤由人力曳至高煤籮中（Overehad bins.）然後自籮底管口（Spouts）垂入自慟爐柵（Mechanical stoker.）其灰燼則沉於爐底而用人力撤去.

全廠共有史德令鍋爐（Stirling Boiler）三只.其一單立餘二只則建成一座.尋常工作時祗用一爐共附有省熱器（Economizer）一只.進水蒸熱器（Feed water heater）一只.吹式氣流扇（Forced draft fan）一具高八十英尺之烟突一個.其口徑爲六英尺.蒸汽之壓力爲二百五十磅.其高熱（Superheat temperature）爲華氏五百二十度.爐柵爲謀滌式（Murphy type）兩面對坡.自行圜轉.使煤易燃爐之火門（Fire door）前裝一斜式氣流表（Lnclined draft gage）以示爐中氣流之如何.而便開閉其烟門（damper）也其吹式氣流扇乃由一二十五匹馬力之馬達所拖動但亦可應用所備之汽輪機.如圖中所示者.

原動機爲克的司（Curtis）倍利特（Bleeder）式九百三十七 K.V.A. 之汽輪發電機（Turbo-gencrotor）.緣機中之空氣易於發熱而致損害故有空氣洗滌器（Air Washer）之附設.每分鐘所洗之空氣爲五千立方英尺.

凝汽具爲表面式（Surfoce type）.由一離心式之抽水機運冷水.每分鐘爲二千五百加侖此抽水機乃由一四十匹馬力之馬達所曳動.汽凝爲水後.復經一馬達所駛之抽水機而入於蓄熱水筒（Hot water tank）.合外來之冷水.同入於進水抽水機其熱度恆在一百六十度以上.凝汽具中常有空氣混在汽中至此用一蒸汽曳動之空氣抽送機（Air pump）取出之.

水塔之水由二抽水機送入.一爲三程離心式（3 stage Centrifugal type）每分鐘可供水五百加侖水頭之高爲二百三十一英尺.每分鐘行一千四百六十轉.其原動者爲一五十匹馬力之馬達.另一抽水機爲雙層直衝裝式（Duplex directing type）.其能力與前者相等.惟屬蒸汽所駛動耳.水自水塔入濾水器（Filter）以免泥土之入鍋.至此分爲二途.一入蒸熱器而進鍋爐另一小流係至汽輪機軸而洩於溝蓋輪軸之速率甚高藉冷水以減其熱度

也.

蒸汽出鍋亦分二途.一經高熱器(Superheater).再過吸水器(Steam trap)而入於汽輪機.一則不經高熱器.爲尋常之蒸汽(Saturated Steam)用以注入空氣抽送機.進水抽水機.爐柵自動機(Stoker engine,)及汽笛(Whistle)者也.

該廠攷工科之原動部及紡務部之記錄表甚詳.特錄存一份.以資參考.玆舉其原動部之試驗記錄(Dota)於下.並附算法.

日期	民國十五年六月十九日
全日進水量	二萬三千一百加侖
進水熱度	華氏二百七十四度
高熱度 Superheat	華氏五百十二度
蒸汽壓	二百三十磅
耗煤	二十又四分之一噸

演例

每小時進水量 $=23100\div24=962.5$ 加侖

$$=962.5\times\frac{25}{3}\text{磅}=8020\text{磅}$$

每小時耗煤 $=20\frac{1}{4}\div24=0.84$ 噸 $=0.84\times2240$ 磅 $=1880$ 磅

故每磅煤蒸發水汽 $=8020\div1880=4.3$ 磅

由蒸汽表 Steam table 知

$H=1270$　$q_1=274-32=242$

$H-q_1=1270-242=1028$ B.T.U./lb of Steam

$$\text{Factor of evaporation}=\frac{1028}{970.4}=1.28$$

Eguavilent evaporation $=8020\times1.28=8460$ lb of water

B.H.P. $=8460\div34.5=245$

結論　統觀以上三廠規模宏大組織匪易八廠較小設備最完全成績自較他廠爲優.一三兩廠機器太舊.損耗甚鉅是乃亟宜改良者也余於參觀紗廠之餘並得歷觀通邑其他諸廠.如鐵廠麵粉廠油廠.發電廠等.覺該地之實業確爲吾國內地各縣之先進.而其市政.交通.學校.公園及種種公共事業.莫不畢舉汽車道路.尤爲吾國最盛之區百里之遙.瞬息可達.基礎已成方興未艾.實業前程正未可限量也此行得蒙諸廠優予待遇並承諸工程師不避炎威.詳加指示.敬表謝忱並誌於此民國十五年八月記.

奇異公司實習雜記

（續第二期）

陳　章

奇異與西屋學生工程師科之比較　西屋電機製造公司亦爲美國電機製造業中之佼佼者.歷史較奇異爲遠,而規模略遜.所有學生科亦極有名.惟其中情形與奇異學生科略有不同.據余所聞,可作下數點之比較.（一）西屋學生科爲半年製造部,半年試驗部.奇異則無製造部.期間故在西屋對於機器構造必較明澈.而在奇異者則對於機器使用方面,較多習練.（二）西屋學生科年限爲一年.展長不易.故即專在製造或試驗一部,尚覺太短.而奇異則年限甚無一定.若將各部做完,須二年左右.然做一年即去,亦無不可.故年限上較有伸縮餘地,可資有志者多時習練.（三）西屋學生科學生,公司中以另眼看待,不如其他工人之專促出貨,多得時間研究及考詢.奇異學生科,則與普通工人無大異,重在出貨.但因此所有工作,均須負責,不易生苟且之心,得益亦多.以上數點不過大較.以余未進西屋作此比較,本不免有武斷之誚.但所述均爲在西屋做過之同學所言,當無大謬.

斯坎乃克太台（Schenectadv）之情形　奇異總廠所在地爲紐約州之

斯坎乃克太台.該字頗不易發音.據云當初係譯自紅種土人口音.意爲低土.城在紐約州之北部,與我國張家口之緯度相仿.氣候冬寒夏熱.最低温度降至華氏零度下二三十度.因地處低窪,終年陰濕之日爲多.城在紐約中央線幹路之上,故交通運輸,極爲便利.以前尚有伊利運河可通各埠.今則陸路運輸獨盛,運河已成陳跡.惟假期中扁舟一葉,常有遊人蕩漾其間耳.人口凡十萬.而奇異工人及辦事人佔二萬餘,合家族計之.當在七八萬.故此城謂之奇異城可也.除奇異外,工廠之大者爲美國機車公司.工人約三千人.規模尚大,然與奇異抗,則猶大巫遇小巫也.地方風氣,以工人流品複雜,大都來自意大利波蘭匈加利等國,良莠不齊,不如中美同等城之較爲純良.市政極注重,市中街燈尤爲世界有名之一.在奇異廠門前之伊利大道及華盛頓街上,街燈之明亮照耀,點綴之美麗悅目,尤爲特色,宛然奇異公司之廣告也.公園有中央公園,面積尚大,布置亦佳.夏日遊人如織.冬間以滑冰游戲.少長咸集,男女共戲,至爲熱鬧.新落成大西關大橋（Great Western Gate Bridge）爲新英格蘭諸州向西汽車大道必經之路.舊橋殘破不能用.新橋費美金二百五十萬元.長四千四百呎,費時五年,全係鋼骨凝土築成.爲大工程之一.青年會舊址甚小,冬間募款築新所,不一月四十五萬美金溢額.雖云國民富足之由,要亦出於人心之樂助公益,眞可嘆羨也.

電線電纜部試驗實習之情形　余第二部之試驗爲電線電纜部.名雖電線,實際則試驗者止電纜耳.電纜製造成功後.均須加以數種試驗,以測其是否與規則相符.電纜之別,大概因其所用絕緣物質而分.大別爲三種（一）橡皮.（二）Varnished Cambric.（三）紙.三者之中紙類能維持之電壓爲最高,但一浸水氣,作用全失.橡皮則較爲堅固,省去外面鉛皮 Varnished Cambric 則水分不易進而堅固不如橡皮.若以纜內所包導體之數分之,則有單體,雙體,三體,四體,及多體之別.全恃應用情形而定.電纜先自製造部製成後.繞在木架上.成一纜圈.最大者長五百呎,以至最小者長二千呎.每圈均須試驗,結果良美.然後可以送入出運部試驗普通約分三種.一爲高壓試驗.如該纜應用時將爲一千伏脫,則試驗時須加以二倍半之電壓,卽二千五百伏脫試之以保證安全.此種電壓加上時間爲五分鐘或爲十五分鐘.視規定情形而定高壓試驗必須各個導體相互間,及各箇導體與鉛皮間,試過無弊,方得合格.如單體者一次卽足,多體者幾次始畢若有電纜因絕緣體有劣點,不能受此電壓因而破壞者,試驗者須將劣點尋出地點,送回製造部修補,或重造.次爲絕緣耗阻試驗（Insulation Resistance Test）亦爲各箇導體,與鉛皮間之絕緣耗阻.須符規則所有價値,視電纜種類與電壓而異三爲銅耗阻試驗（Copper Resistance Test）試驗電纜內導體之銅耗阻,是否合度,幷便可測其長度,是否準確.此外試驗之特別需要者大多爲高壓紙絕緣電纜.如Hot and Cold Sample Test, Power Factor Test,及 Pending Sample Test 等.其所有試驗方法及理論,不及細述.電纜之發明,愛迪生功亦非淺,至今所用規則,仍有稱爲愛氏 Specifications 者其製造之方法,如絕緣體 Cambric 之製造.紙之種數.紙所浸入之化學液汁,均經過數十年之研究試驗而後成.至今所製電纜電壓已極高,然尙在精進研究,以期改良.其研究向上之精神,至可敬佩.所造之纜,大概均能經過試驗無阻但因電纜大多用於地內,或爲發電廠重要銜接,萬一裝置後發生困難,損失旣大,修理匪易.故甯愼之於先此試驗之所以重要,不惜費人工金錢以辦之也.顧客之謹愼將事者,多雇代表如紐約試驗室（New York Testing Laboratory）雇員.在試驗時監視簽字.其審愼有如此者此試驗每人輪做六星期.工作時一切開機接線,均親自動手,油汚殊甚.所有記錄負責簽字,所得亦不少也.

奇異公司試驗科以外所設之學科　除試驗科以外與之平行者,奇異公司尙設有（一）製造訓練科（Factory Training Course）大多爲機械科畢業出身注重在機器製造及裝配,人數不滿十人,遷調較速,其他待遇與試驗科相仿（二）營商訓練科（Sales Training Course）大概爲商科畢業出身.其遷調練習待遇,與上二科大致相同.所異者,前者在工廠中,後者在公事房耳.此外公司中為鼓勵雇員好學培植公司人材起見,尚人有下列各工餘學科（一）合衆大學（Union College）碩士科專爲試驗科學生之志求高深,而願工讀並進者其辦法則每星期在該大學上課半日,公司照舊給資.大半課程均帶回自行研究豫備如是者二年考試及格,五年內交進論文一篇,授以電工碩士學位如是學者於經濟方面不需預備確是便宜之途但工後往往疲儢,不易潛攻,非體強者難勝任也.（二）合衆大學特別班.此爲合衆大學夜班,專爲廠中雇員夜間求學而設.各種科目皆有,程度並不甚深,所以使失學者有機前進,及專門家之稍學他門學問,以調劑生活耳.取費甚廉.）三）高深工程科(Advanced Engineering Course)此科乃公司專設爲造就本公司將來人才起見者.三年前創辦,每秋於試驗科中招考,取格極嚴.於一年後甄別優劣,五十人左右中選取十餘人再專攻二年第一班將於本夏卒業.大都將服務本公司.其課程注重電機工程製造計劃.及裝置各種問題.大都均係廠中所遇之眞切問題.極爲深奧.而有裨學業.上課時間,爲每星六上午.公司照常給資（四）商業訓練科(Business Training Course)此科專授科目如公司會計學.商法,貨品計價學等.學者大部爲在公司營業部辦事者.但試驗科人員亦得入之.上課時間爲下午五時至七時.每科每星期二次.（五）普通科（General Course）此科專爲試驗科人員而設所授科目爲工程普通問題.及營業要則人數最多.時間與商業訓練科同.（六）工廠職工科.（Factory Vocational Class）科目繁多,如車床,刨床.交流電學,直流電學,鐵心繞法,（Armature Winding）打字速記等等二三十種.學者大都廠中男女工人.上課在夜間.此外尚有（七）豫備試驗科（Preliminary Test Course）與尋常試驗科職務相同,所異者人員均非工科大學卒業.遷調較難,工資較低.（八）學徒科.年份爲六年.學習一二科手藝,同時授以工程常識總觀以上學科凡近十科,人員達千餘人.謂奇異乃一工廠,而不知其中研究學問,絃誦不啻誠工廠而兼學校者也.

萬國工程俱樂部（Cosmopolitan Technical Society） 會爲在奇異公司非美籍雇員而設國際奇異公司擔任協助經費.設會所一室會員大都在試驗科任事約五六十人每兩星期開晚會一次多工程演說演說者皆奇異公司工程師余在廠時所聽之題有如下述『電機在鋼鐵事業之應用』,『無線電眞空管發報機』,『電在林業紙業之應用』,『墨西哥鐵路電化之經過』,『最近蒸汽廠之新趨勢』等等大都演講之外,佐以電影說明.逢佳節如耶誕等,則有 Social Party. 大都例行各種遊藝殿以跳舞余凡會必到,惟於跳舞爲門外漢,未嘗敢問津也.

工業控制板部（Industrial Control Panels）實習之情形 余第三部之實習,爲工業控制板爲期共十星期.此種控制電鑰板,爲控制應用於各種工業之電動機直流交流均有.其最普通者爲 Induction Motor 及 Synchronous Motor Starters. 近來趨勢此種 Starter 之使用方法,均爲自動蓋開關祇須用手按鈕,電動機自起始以至行動各步驟,均能自動,無復人之注意.最普通者爲鋼鐵廠電動機之應用於此業者,在美漸行普遍.鍊鋼所用電之需要,最爲嚴酷電力既巨,動止須迅疾轉換方向又速而今則用自動電鑰板措置裕如.不可謂非電工業界極大之成功此外如升降機, Hoist, 起重機, Shovel 等運動,均須控制又如紗廠絲廠水門汀廠以及各種工業之應用電動機運動者,均須此種 Panel 之設置.可見其繁矣試驗步驟最初先試其局部,是否動作如預期而滿意.如關閉線路之 Contactors, 是否按應關之電壓而關各件 Relay 是否動作如意,及應當 Set 在何價値.最後始將全板試驗.視其步驟.是否按照次序.此種電鑰板線路,大多均甚繁複.往往因一線之誤.全板動作出軌則試驗者必須尋出其癥結所在.而通知出貨部更改之.此試驗爲此間總廠重要試驗之一,頗可得些經驗.十星期中,大概半作助手,半作主試主試時一切負責.部中有工頭（亦係試驗科學生擔任,以半年或一年爲期.）不過於交到出運部前,略爲視察一下而已.

無線電之中國文化宣傳　余在奇異實習時,曾在該公司之廣播無線電站 WGY, 作幾次之中國文化宣傳.第一次爲某音樂家歌唱中國古詩.一爲詩經,一爲唐詩,均譯成英文.邀余往作一小引,略述二詩之源流及中國古今詩體之不同.余於詩歌,素無研究而說來尚滿人意,站中人因倩余作類似此種關於中國文物之演詞.余以此爲宣傳吾國文化之絕妙機會,不能失去,因勉允之第二次余演題爲『中國文化之特點』.第三次演題爲『中國之文字』每次約亘二十分鐘.日後各地聽而生興趣者,有來函稱賞者.第四次爲國際大學晚.(Lnternational Intercollegiate Night)該夜凡奇異工程師中之各大學舊同學,均唱校歌及演其他節目以爲娛樂美國以外,則以國代表之.我中國同學,是時止四人.(吳龐二位適在他分廠.)共有四節目.一爲小引二爲唱『中國男兒』歌三爲魏君之笙獨奏.四爲國歌.人數既少,又素少訓練,欲濫竽而不得.幸預加練習,當場尚差強人意,而尤以魏君之笙爲生色.

以上十五年四月前（待續）

本校機械試驗室述要

張坤賢

本校機械試驗室.落成於交通大學時代建築宏壯設備完善本校機械科開辦未久得有今日成績.實基於此該室前接電機試驗室西連金工廠屋分二部.一爲鍋爐間.一爲機械房.共佔地九千六百方呎鍋爐間復分內外二部外部後方右側安設迴火式火管鍋爐一座.(Return Tubular Boiler)其左安設鍋爐進水機一架.大貯水器兩座.前面左側安設治鋼爐一架.內部安設平式水管鍋爐一座.(B. & W. Horizontal Water-tube Boiler)機械房有樓一層樓之北部爲一二年級機械圖畫教室.樓之南部.有機械科三四年級普

通教室.高等製圖室.及教授預備室各二間樓之西面偏南有試驗水力用之水塔一座.樓下南部東邊.爲儲藏室.西邊爲油及燃料試驗室.北部西邊爲材料試驗室油及燃料試驗室前.有平臺高約丈餘.西邊有梯通之.臺之前面中間有水池一.池面略低於臺.池之前面築一水槽皆供水力試驗之用.水槽之西.安設材料試驗機三架.水力試壓機一架水槽之東安設馬達一座抽水機兩座更東則安設各式蒸汽引擎.凝結器.氣壓機.內燃油引擎.及汽輪機等茲將鍋爐間.及機械房內所安設各種鍋爐及機械分别述之於下.(參照附圖)

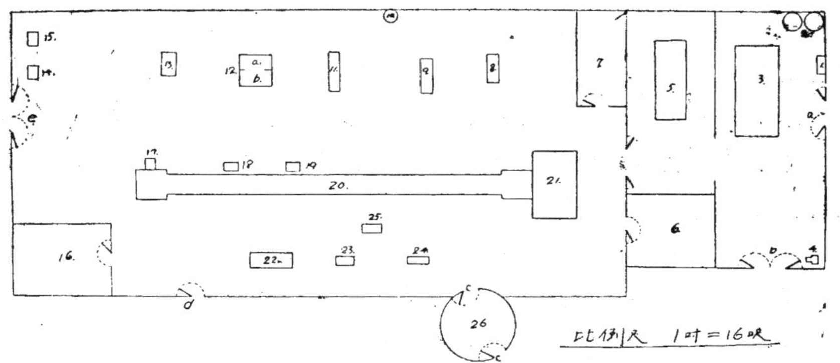

註：上圖比例尺較原圖縮小二分之一所繪各種機械尺寸均以其脚基爲標準
a 爲通電機試驗室之門　b 鍋爐間大門　c 水塔下之小門
d 通金工廠之門　e 機械房大門

(1)鍋鍋進水機　此機用蒸汽力開動.其吸水管與旁之二貯水器相接.水由貯水器吸入機內水房經過水管而至鍋爐內.室內水管及火管鍋爐之水.均由此機供給之.

(2)貯水器　此二貯水器均爲圓形.大小相若.高九呎.口徑四呎自來水管安置其上其水源也.

(3)火管鍋爐　此爲回火式火管鍋爐.火路自爐上起.經迴牆(Baffle

wall）折向而沿鍋壁之外面至後方之燃燒房.然後折入火管前行而至前面之烟囱水路則自進水機.經進水管.而入於火管及鍋壁之間.此鍋爐裝有「內藏單彈簧平安活門」,蒸汽壓力表及水平表等.其鍋爐馬力.爲六十其燃燒面積（Total heating surface）約有七百方呎.

（4）治鋼爐　此爐以煤氣及空氣之混合物爲燃料.下裝小馬達及風箱馬達用以拖動風箱.而空氣與煤氣.在爐後之進氣管混合.然後入爐而燃燒此爐係專爲熱力治鋼而設.（Heat Treatment of Steel）

（5）水管鍋爐　此爲B & W平式水管鍋爐.火路由爐面起沿水管外面.經後方之燃燒房.而至烟囱.水路則由進水機.經進水管.而入於水管內.復沿管壁而流入後面裝置之水鼓.此鍋爐裝有「外表雙彈簧平安活門」及蒸汽壓力表等.其鍋爐馬力爲四十.其燃燒面積約有四百餘方呎.

（6）油及燃料試驗室　此室專爲試驗工程上所用之滑車油及各種燃料而設.內藏各種試驗儀器.

（7）儲藏室　內藏各種機械零件.各種燃料.及應用物品等.

（8）Marshal蒸汽引擎　此爲單缸雙動（Double acting）平臥式引擎.裝置飛球汽制機.（Fly-ball Governor）及平滑D式活門.（Plain D-slide Valve）其速率爲每分鐘二百轉.

（9）氣壓機（Air Compressor）　此機有汽缸二.前缸上方有管突出空際吸取空氣而由缸側裝置之另一氣管壓送至旁置之空氣貯藏器內.

（10）空氣貯藏器（Air Reservoir）　此器高八呎.口徑一呎八吋附裝壓力表.以測驗內藏空氣之壓力器之上端.有管通於氣壓機.空氣即由氣壓機經此管輸入.其旁另有一管.用以通器內所貯之氣至空氣引擎.

（11）凝結器（Condenser）　此爲表面凝結器（Surface Condenser）上部爲橫臥圓筒形.內藏多數薄小氣管.下部一端爲抽水機.一端爲抽氣機其活塞共裝於中部發動機之活塞桿上皆由此發動機動作之抽水機下有管

通水槽.水由水槽吸入機內水房.然後復由水房壓入上部管之外面爲凝結管內蒸汽之用.而蒸汽凝結之後.則由右端之抽氣機抽出.

(12a) Curtis 汽輪機(Curtis Steam Turbine)　此機與旁之直流發電機相連有二十五K.W.其速率爲每分鐘三千六百轉.蒸汽壓力爲一百磅.

(12p)直流發電機　其電力爲二百安培.速率與旁之汽輪機同爲每分鐘三千六百轉.

(13)Leffel蒸汽引擎　此亦爲單缸雙動平臥式引擎.但裝置慣性汽制機(Inertia Governor)及平衡活門(Balanced Valve)

(14)Novo 內燃油引擎　此爲立式四程循環引擎(Four-stroke cycle Engine).用煤油 (Kerosene) 爲燃料.用高壓電氣火花爲燃媒.有六匹馬力.速率爲每分鐘四百五十轉.裝置離心汽制機.(Centrifugal Governor)

(15)Remington 內燃油引擎　此機與Novo內燃油引擎大致相似.

(16)材料試驗室　此室專爲試驗工程上各種應用材料而設.如鋼鐵,木材及水門汀等.內藏各種試驗儀器

(17)及(19)均爲抽水機.

(18)馬達　此馬達用以拖動兩旁抽水機.

(20)水槽　此槽長八十呎.兩端爲方形.闊六呎.中部闊四呎深三呎.

(21)水池　池底高出地面五呎闊九呎.長十四呎深四呎.池之前面中間.有决口.高闊均尺許.裝有水喉及巨管通水塔.當試驗時.水由决口下注水槽.

(22),(23),(24)均爲材料試驗機　其容量一爲十萬磅.一爲二萬磅.一爲三萬磅.皆美國 Reihle 公司所造.十萬磅容量者有變速槓桿二副.能開出六種不同之速率.

(25)水力試壓機　此機利用水力或油.以試驗材料壓力.

(26)水塔　此塔高三十餘呎有管通水池.爲試驗水力之用.

此外電機試驗室內.尚安設內燃煤氣引擎一座.此機為平卧式單缸單動四程循環.機身重大開車時須先用人力轉動飛輪.有六十匹馬力.速率為每分鐘二百轉.裝置飛球式汽制機.

又鍋爐間外尚有火車龍頭式之鍋爐一座.但已破壞不堪.不復能用.

總上所述.可見吾校機械科設備之大概.而年來學校當局.復努力聯絡國內外工程界.得多數廠家公司之信仰.代辦試驗材料.是以此試驗室與社會上工程事業之關係日益密切矣.

機車上各機件之俗稱

T. P.

今夏承鄭保山先生允許.得在甯波機廠實習復承諄諄指導.至為欣感.實習時.得悉廠中工人對於機車上各機件所常呼之名稱茲錄之於下.雅俗姑不論.聊以備讀者之參攷耳.

英文名	工人俗稱
Stack	煙囱
Safety valve	保險凡耳
Steam gauge	汽表或司汀表
Steam pipe	司汀管子
Stay bolts.	司對螺絲
Steam dome	將軍帽(譯書中有譯為汽室者)
Smoke box	煙柜
Water gauge	玻璃管(譯書中有譯為水平計者)
Water leg	爐脚
Tubes (Fire tube)	小煙囱
Tube sheet	格子板

Stop valve	司刀浦凡耳
Oil cup (Lubricator)	自來油杯
Check valve	搖角凡耳
Governor	搿文納
Injector	因搿
Feed pipe	進水管子
Exhaust pipe	回龍汽管子
Drain	特令
Fire door	爐門
Fire box	火箱
Grate	爐篦或爐排
Blow off	白羅
Long seam	直縫
Ring seam	圓縫
Crown sheet	篷頂
Hand hole	小倒門
Man hole	大倒門
Ash pan	灰斗

破舊鍋爐開會記

錢平施

荒野之區,冷僻之地,鍋爐之爆裂不堪復用者,皆被棄於是焉.斷首殘肢,洞胸破腹,或僅存軀殼,或尚遺臟腑,悽慘之狀,目不忍覩.其數日積月累,增加至速,竟有鍋滿之患.每當聚談之頃,鍋首擠擠,擁塞不堪.有名B W (Babcock and Wilcox)者,遍身鐵銹歷年最久,德高望重,衆意所歸.目覩同類之受厄,而慮來者之繼增,恝然憂之,常思所以補救之道.一夕,宣言于衆,共圖良策.衆議僉同,公推B W君主席而正式開會焉.

是夕到者甚衆.有車頭鍋爐,有舶用鍋爐,有直式者,有橫式者,有水管式者,有火管式者,大小皆備,各式俱全.知名之鍋爐如 Stirling, Scotch, Wickes, Keeler, Heine 等,皆列席.會議既開,主席B W君登台致辭曰:『當今科學昌明工業發達,力之供給,遂成重要問題.考力之供給,方法至多,如內燃機器,水電機器等:皆其著者也.然今最盛行者,猶當首推鍋爐.煤燃爐中發出熱力,鍋內貯水,蒸發為氣;以之運送他處,即能轉動各式原動機,如蒸氣機蒸氣輪等.由此觀之,鍋爐之有造于工業者至大,即吾輩之責任至重.乃今之製造與運用吾輩者,學識淺陋,作事疏懶,遂使至重要之鍋爐,時遭爆裂,傷人損物,為害無極.吾輩橫遭殘廢,流落荒野,推原其故,實深痛恨.據近來統計,在一千九百二十年至一千九百廿四年中,我同類之爆裂致命者,共有三千五百六十之多,死傷人類亦有二千.平均每日必有傷亡,至于財產損失之大,更難計數.且照現今情形,損傷之數,將日增無已.若不亟籌補救,後患何堪設想!本會今日開會,旨在考察吾輩爆裂之狀況,研究爆裂之原因,貢諸製造廠與工程師,加以注意.俾得保障吾類之安全,避免生命財產之損失.諸君諒必謂然.今日到會甚衆,鄙人擬請到會諸君,各將一身遭遇,如破裂原因,損失統計,以及防禦方法,詳細說明,共同討論.現依坐位次序,先請A君發言.』

A君乃一直管豎立水管式鍋爐,年十八,起立報告曰,『余係被役于一鋼鐵公司.因施行內部清潔,曾被取下,事畢復位,重行工作.孰知天氣暴冷,保險活塞（Safety valve）冰結不動.余又未與同伴相連合作,遂致受極高之蒸汽壓力而爆裂.計死人三,傷人十二.』主席曰:『此非君之罪,亦非製君者之過,乃用君者疏忽所致.現請B君發言.』

B君性至急,身未起立,即已發言.其言曰:『余乃一橫式水管鍋爐,用于電機公司.因鍋中貯水過少,遂致暴熱而裂.計死人七,傷人十九,損失五萬元.

』某君驚駭曰:『管理疏忽死傷纍纍,家人痛哭.機司可惡.』於是會場空氣,頓爲緊張.主席欲維持秩序,亟轉向C君曰:『請君告吾等以傷身之故.』

C君意似驕矜,蓋製造完固,大部無恙.僅以生鐵泥鼓之不良,遂及于難.計傷三人,死五人,損失無算.主席續詢曰:『君之泥鼓,何以被裂?』C君答曰;『生鐵性質難測,常受壓力溫度之變化,體積增大,能力喪失.遂易破裂若易以鋼製者,則可平安長久,吾亦不至來此矣』

主席轉謂D君曰:『聞君之爆裂曾死四人,損失100,000元,確乎?』D君答曰:『確甚,我雖具彎管,爲狀較險然以視理精細,危機向少.但以鼓首伸縮之故,以致鋼質損壞,余亦遂及于難』.『何以鼓首之伸縮,竟能損壞鋼體,使呈罅凹?』『是因吾鼓之製作,未臻上乘在理應使稍重,而切忌過坦』

E君乃一豎式水管鍋爐,年十七,職司鋼鐵公司之助手鍋爐.其爆裂之故,乃因生火之後已逾一時,蒸汽壓力已大,而汽壓計(Steam gauge)仍指五十磅處.司理人以爲氣壓尙小,未加注意.遂致爆發.計死八七,傷卅六.主席諮詢曰.『何以致此?』E答曰:『汽壓計之不良,或連接汽壓計管之阻塞,與夫安全活塞運用之不便,有以致之.』

主席復曰:『今夕時間有限,請F君卽速發言』F君曰:『吾乃一省煤機.與吾同及于難者,五年中猶有二焉.其致命之由,一爲出口活塞(Outlet valve)之關閉,熱度因之激增;一爲活塞排置之不良,壓力因之過大;一則純由腐蝕所致.』主席曰:『照F君之報告,可知省煤機亦須附以安全活塞,更需時時之視察.五年中爆裂三具,可謂多矣!現請G君報告.』

G君之言曰:『余乃一疊接關節(Lap seam)之橫式火管鍋爐,役于鋸輪工廠.余之破裂,波及三位同伴,且死八人,傷十人.』『請將詳細原因說明.』『主因種于氣管(Steam piping)之波動,因之生鐵出汽緣乃遭損壞.破裂之起,爲頂片之裂縫,不久全身俱爲粉碎.』『據君所言,可知氣管之切忌波動,而生鐵之不能濫用也.』

於時H君起立曰:『余亦一車頭鍋爐,用之已四年,時被修理,並經靜水試驗.工程師在余修理之後,欲求安全活塞之緊袠,將其深埋.及水汽旣升,工程師又因活塞放汽過早,更將活塞螺轉下之,並將彈簧安置過高,俾在預定壓力達到之時弛放.不知活塞因之不能表示高壓,而爆裂成矣.』

I君起立曰:『余乃迴管横式鍋爐遠近馳名,今已十五歲矣.余之運用,具有至大之安全率,並有良好之管理,時施清潔,並加修理.一日修理方竣,從復運用,不意忽遭爆裂,死十三人,傷四十.余因受僱于麵粉廠,故財產損失甚大.至于爆裂之因,似係水槌.』『何謂水槌?』『水槌乃水之在汽管,鍋爐或其他貯水器者強烈之行動.凡帶入水管之水汽遇冷凝結成冰,若任其積貯管中,則其量漸增,終至汽之地位因之減少,不能任意通過.于是水乃被汽驅逐向前,爲力至猛,有如砲彈而爆裂成矣.至于汽爐之有水槌,每由活塞之驟開與夫連接處之斷裂.壓力之驟減,能使水之猛力蒸發,蓋所貯之力皆欲乘此外洩,因之鍋內之水,被擲而上,其力之猛,能致爆裂.』主席曰:『于此可知活塞之驟開,足成水槌,而肇爆裂汽管與鍋爐之禍.』I君曰:『誠然.』

主席向J君曰:『J君能告我等以遇難之歷史乎?』J君起答曰:『余乃一横式水管鍋爐在十八歲時,曾被取出清潔.清潔旣畢,方擬復用,孰知下午十一時生火,翌晨二時,卽遭爆裂,計死三人,傷二人,損失六萬餘.究其原由,乃因貯水過少之故.』主席曰:『此皆疏忽之罪,管理者難逃斥責.現請K君報告.』

K君曰:『余乃火盒式者.役於冰廠,爐裂之時,曾死傷卅餘人.余則全身粉碎,被炸五十餘片.有一片重數百磅,竟飛往數里之遙,爆力可謂大矣.』『其故何在?』『與H君似相彷彿.惟尤有不幸者,余曾數經轉賣,今年已四十矣.腐蝕旣久,汽壓計失效.工程師不察修理之無效,強欲將安全活塞與之合作,于是危險之壓力,遂肇大禍.』

L君報告曰:『余亦一横式迴管鍋爐,年已十四,人皆呼我爲疊接式者,余之工作壓力不滿九十磅,管理亦佳但終被爆裂死五十八人,傷百餘,半皆婦孺,爲狀實慘.』是時全場太息.L君續曰:『肇禍之由乃因疊接關節之分裂』『何謂疊接關節之分裂?』『疊接關節之分裂,常見于疊接式之鍋爐.因關節安置之稍扁,殼板漲縮,遂生彎力(Bending moment,)而致小罅之裂縫,裂縫相連,破損遂成.』『此種弊害能事先發現否?』『當然.近有一鍋爐保險公司之工程師,曾發明橫貫鋼板,足助此種罅隙之發見.爆裂因之減少.』『此種危險能完全免去乎?』『若用抵觸關節(Butt joint,)爲害可以大減,蓋裂縫雖有,然至少也.』

最後M君起立曰:『我初工作于百磅汽壓之下,其後因改爲熱氣鍋爐.壓力減少,竊以爲決無危險矣.不幸安全活塞失效.壓力加高,直至極危險之程度.而余遂爆裂.』『請問有救否?』『惟有工程師之時時試察,與夫工役之勤愼從事,或可稍減其害.』『若壓力低小之鍋爐損失亦若是其大乎?』『亦然.力之貯于水汽中者甚多,蓋水量與汽量皆大故也若壓力驟減則其爆裂之猛,不減於高壓力之鍋爐.』

討論至此,時已不早,主席乃接言曰:『足矣諸君.諸君報告各自遭遇,至詳且盡死傷之衆,何止千百,損失之大何止巨萬.不意區區鍋爐竟有如此影響.綜觀諸君報告,可知爆裂之發生至易且多.但若能稍加注意,大多數可以避免工程師之疏忽誠堪痛恨.玆依諸君之報告,將避免爆裂,保全鍋爐之方法,總括如下.諸君如有異議,望卽提出討論修正;

1. 管理鍋爐之工程師,對于鍋爐之管理,須具眞實之學識.

2. 安全活塞,禁止安置于易致冰凍之處.

3. 鍋爐須忌過熱,並防缺水.

4. 鍋爐各部,皆須時加視察,不可疏忽.

5. 安全活塞,非得工程師之允許,不得旋動.

6. 對于一切鍋爐,皆須爲靜水之試驗(Hydcostatic test)

7. 管理鍋爐之人須時防水槌之發生.（Water hammer）

8. 疊接開節（Lap joint）之鍋爐須加特別之注意.

9. 低壓鍋爐爆發之害,與高壓者等,用者須加防備.

10. 舊鍋爐在使用之先,須加詳細之視察.

11. 新鍋爐之易爆發,與舊者不相上下,用者亦須小心.

12. 鍋爐製造之標準則例,須速行訂定.』

主席宣言既畢,場中掌手雷動,一致贊成主席續言曰:『諸君對于鄙人所言既荷贊同,鄙意擬將議决各項廣告製造廠,工程師等,希望彼輩有所覺悟,加以注意.若是則不特吾輩同類,皆得保全,卽人命之死傷財產之損失,亦可大減.吾輩厥功甚偉,今日之會,爲不虛矣.』

主席言畢,歡聲大作.衆皆喜形于色,相與慰藉旋乃三呼鍋爐萬歲而散.

本校卅週紀念工業展覽會之辦理經過情形

（摘錄淩校長上交通部總次長呈）

為呈報事竊屬校於舉行三十週年紀念開工業展覽會仰蒙 鈞部俯賜贊助獲益至多茲謹將辦理經過情形縷晰陳之查屬校前以成立年屆卅週羣謀慶祝原為紀念既往昭示來茲於是有工業展覽之議校長一面遴選教授若干人組織委員會從事籌商一面呈蒙 鈞部准予文行各路電機關及中外各工廠行家選送出品陳列風聲所播遐邇具瞻惟因時局不靖交通多阻且為時間所限先就電機機械鐵路材料化學工藝等類積極徵集並畫定圖書館為第一會場陳列輕巧電機機件工業材料及其他圖表品物兩操場為第二會場陳列電機及其他巨大機件之開機試用者機械工廠一部分為第三會場專陳各項機械及材料試驗機校西新地一部分為第四會場專陳農用機械實地試驗此外在第二會場之前敷設輕便鐵道開駛小號機車及車輛以資點綴計自五月籌辦起至十月開會止為時共五閱月應徵各行家為輔助教育藉以擴張營業起見多如約自運出品到校佈置不憚煩勞此應行陳明者一也卅週紀念會自十月九日起舉行三天工業展覽會即於同時舉行在紀念會期內來校人數日逾萬人因工業展覽不獨為上海所未有即在我國亦屬創舉所有中西實業界經濟界及教育界人士咸以一覩為快故觀者極形擁擠迨至紀念會期屆滿羣謂籌備為時甚長展覽為時甚短且各行家陳列物品頗費手續自應酌延日期俾來賓從容觀遍藉免向隅特展至十七日閉會據確實統計開會全日者四天半日者五天到場人數共五萬一千九百有奇照會場規定之開放時間計算每小時平均約六百五十人至連日參觀羣衆多為滿意之表示且於會場設備以及所陳物品每多見詢在事人員一一指導與答問極感紛繁具見近日社會人士注重工業同此心理而輿論界對於展覽會逐日均有詳細之記載評許尤為備至此應行陳明者

二也此次應徵各行家及路電機關數凡一百有一計中國四十九家日本十九家英美德奥瑞士瑞典等國三十三家所有陳列物品以各項電機及各種機械爲大宗建築材料五金及農用家用器具次之各種樣本圖表照片雜物又次之此外尚有輕便鐵道駛行引擎機車總計全值約百萬元當屬校徵集之初在滬各行家先行到校參觀考察一切始表示滿意欣然應徵閉會之後經多方接洽各行家有以所陳物品悉數見贈或酌量見贈者惟無重大機件咸云時局孔艱營業未能發展容俟異日情形較佳當贈大宗出品以示贊助至展覽會一切運送佈置均由各廠家自行料理且有開駛發電機供給用電校中耗費少而收效鉅此應行陳明者三也竊維此次工業展覽會原爲發揚教育之精神引起羣衆之觀感幸賴　鈞部主持提倡於上在事人員羣策羣力於下故結果頗稱美滿因念屬校辦理工業教育有年實有賴於社會各方之輔助今茲之舉得使各界人士明悉辦學內容與夫育才宗旨而在校內教學兩方又藉此機會由比較而知吾國工業之尚幼稚及今後應負之責任謀所以積極從事之途校長曾經剴切曉勉諸生互相砥礪毋忘紀念用副　鈞部作育人才之旨屆計閉會時逾兼旬關於應行辦理各項手續業告完畢理合具文呈報並繕具陳列機關及廠家一覽表附呈敬祈　鑒核備案謹呈

南洋大學工業展覽會陳列機關及廠家一覽表

一　中國共四十九家

名稱	地址	物品種類	件數	備註
東省鐵路管理局	哈爾濱	章程圖表	十一件	贈送
吉長鐵路管理局	長春	仝上	五件	仝上
正太鐵路監督局	石家莊	照片書表	九件	仝上
津浦鐵路管理局	天津	圖書	三件	仝上
京漢鐵路管理局	北京	圖書表報	五件	仝上

京奉鐵路管理局	天津	圖表照片	四件	仝上
滬寧 滬杭甬鐵路管理局	上海	仝上	六件	仝上
膠濟鐵路管理局	青島	仝上	四件	仝上
汴洛鐵路局 隴海鐵路營業局	鄭州	圖表	二件	仝上
四洮鐵路工程局	奉天四平街	圖書表報	七件	仝上
揚子江技術委員會	上海廣東路	圖表	一大件	
濬浦局	上海黃浦灘	仝上	一大件	
駐滬電料管理局	上海麥根路	乾電濕電瓶	四件	贈送
中國電氣公司	上海江西路	電機電表	五十件	贈送一件
中國蓄電池廠	上海北西藏路	電機電池	十四件	贈送十三件
同昌電池部	上海雲南路	電池	二件	
譚泮電池廠	上海勞合路	仝上	二件	贈送一件
大華公司	上海博物院路	電機及照片	二件	
益中機器公司	上海江西路	電機及機件	二十九件	贈送二件
新通公司	上海九江路	抽水機	六件	
新中公司	上海長安路	仝上	四件	
中國鐵工廠	上海愛多亞路	紡織機	四件	
合衆機器廠	上海狄思威路歐嘉路	機器照片	四十三件	
華東機器廠有限公司	上海閘北寶通路	印刷機	六件	
列興貿易行	上海昆明路	農用機件	四件	
浙江公立工業專門學校	杭州報國寺	自制機件	六大件	贈送
上海商務印書館	上海寶山路	圖書儀器機件	八十四件	
上海水泥公司	上海四川路	水泥樣品	八件	贈送
中國水泥公司	上海江西路	仝上	一大件	仝上
啓新洋灰公司	上海北京路	洋灰製造品	六大件	贈送一大件

中國製瓷公司	上海四川路	瓷磚	一件	贈送
泰山磚瓦公司	上海勞合路	磚瓦	三十一件	仝上
大豐工業原料公司	上海天后宮橋堍	錳鑛瑩石	三件	仝上
允元實業公司	上海北京路	銅製品	三十五大件	代表天津譚眞製造工廠陳列
上海開灤售品處	上海四川路	礦石	三十件	
和興鋼鐵股份有限公司	上海浦東周家渡	工程材料	一件	贈送
久記木行	上海南市機街	火柴桿枝	一件	仝上
振華油漆廠	上海北蘇州路	油漆	十七件	仝上
金城工藝社	上海西門外來安里	顏料	三件	
龍章造紙廠	上海外日暉橋	紙樣	一件	
天章紙廠	上海北江西路	仝上	一件	
竟成造紙廠	上海新閘路成都路口	仝上	三件	
宜彰帆布公司	天津西關外	布樣	二件	贈送
裕津製革公司	天津	皮樣	一件	仝上
孫吉堂	淮安河下空心街	快鹼	一件	
溥益實業公司	濟南東門外黃台橋北全福莊	糖品	六件	贈送
上海商業儲蓄銀行	上海甯波路	出版品儲蓄盒及鏡框地毯等	五大件	
浙江興業銀行	上海北京路	出版品	五件	
香港國民銀行	上海江西路	仝上	五件	

二 日本共十九家

名稱	地址	物品種類	件數	備註
南滿鐵路	奉天	圖表	一件	贈送
三井洋行	上海四川路	電線及照片	三件	仝上
中華電氣製作所	上海愛多亞路	電線	四十件	
住友洋行	上海九江路	電線及照片	二件	贈送

古河電氣工業株式會社	上海仁記路	電線標本等	二大件	
三菱電機公司	上海支店	仝上	四大件	
日本無線電信電話株式會社	東京市外下澁谷	照片	一件	贈送
日本電池株式會社	京都市新町今出川北	電池標本	一件	仝上
東京電氣公司	上海四川路	電球陳列台	二件	仝上
芝浦製作所	東京芝區於新濱町	玻璃掛燈標本照片電機電扇	二大件	仝上
日立製作所	東京市鞠町正八重州町	照片	一件	仝上
橫河電機製作所	橫濱	電表照片	四件	仝上
松風工業會社	神戶	拒電品	七件	仝上
籐倉電線株式會社	上海支店	電線標本	一件	仝上
安中電機製作所	東京	電機照片	三件	贈送一件
共立電機株式會社	東京	電機電表	三件	贈送
高砂工業會社	東京	電池	四大件	仝上
冲電氣會社	東京	電話聽筒等	三件	仝上
東京報知機會社	東京	報知機	八件	仝上

三　歐美各國　共三十三家

名稱	地址	物品種類	件數	備註
漢運洋行	上海甯波路	百匹馬力道駛引擎車床印字機	二十件	
愼昌洋行	上海圓明園路	各種電機馬達製圖機器	一百件	贈送十件
禪臣洋行	上海江西路	電機馬達礦中所用小鐵路小車頭	五十件	贈送一件
怡和洋行	上海圓明園路	煤氣機氣油模型輪船車床壓氣機	三十件	
茂生洋行	上海廣東路	升降機馬達保險箱皮帶	十五件	
拔伯葛鍋鑪公司	上海黃浦灘	各種鍋鑪模型風箱	十件	
天利洋行	上海江西路	道駛引擎及帮浦	十件	
美通洋行	上海西藏路	犂田機	一件	

物臘兄弟公司		釘錘車刀鋼條鋼片	八十五件	
利商洋行	上海四川路江西路口	留音機油印機計算機	二十件	
中華無線電分公司	上海北京路	無線電圖書	十件	
臺物期洋行	上海南京路	電燈電扇電氣用品	一百件	
鄧祿普橡皮公司	上海愛多亞路	各項橡皮車胎	三十件	
英國鷹立球鍊鋼分廠	上海博物院路	鋼鐵錘車刀鑽鏟	五十件	贈送十三件
維昌洋行	上海江西路	鋼軸軸領馬達帮浦電話機	七十件	
福家中瑞貿易公司	上海愛多亞路	材料試驗機火油機電料電氣用品	二十件	贈送一件
中荷貿易公司	上海江西路	帮浦馬達	十件	
萬泰洋行	上海圓明園路	車床帮浦起重機電表電料	七十件	
英國通用電氣有限公司	上海甯波路	馬達發電機電話機電表	六十件	
開洛公司	上海南京路	無線電收音機	六十件	
羅森德洋行	上海愛多亞路	發電機馬達	三十件	
懋利洋行	上海北京路	無線電收音機及電料	三十件	
英美烟公司 老晉隆洋行	上海博物院路	打字機油印機計算機	二十五件	
瑞鎔機器船廠	上海楊樹浦路	輪船照片	六件	贈送
天和洋行	上海南京路	無線電收音機及應用品	五十件	
西門子洋行	上海江西路	無線電收音機發電機	三十件	贈送一件
蘇爾然兄弟公司	上海愛多亞路	帮浦狄斯爾機氣壓機照片	十件	贈送四件
美孚行	上海廣東路	機器油馬達油柴油	四十七件	贈送
美電洋行	上海黃浦灘	發電機變壓機電扇電表	一百七十件	
約克洋行	上海仁記路	製冰機	一件	
瑞昌機器陳列所	上海北蘇州路	電料物品	一大架	
寬斯洋行	英國倫敦	照片	四十件	贈送

南洋一覽稿(三續)

柴福沅芷湘甫擬

編制(續)

最近四年大學班數增減表

<table>
<tr><th>年級</th><th colspan="3">科 門 班數</th><th>十年度</th><th>十一年度</th><th>十二年度</th><th>十三年度</th></tr>
<tr><td rowspan="2">一年級</td><td colspan="3">工科</td><td>3</td><td>2</td><td>2</td><td>3</td></tr>
<tr><td colspan="3">鐵路管理科</td><td>0</td><td>2</td><td>1</td><td>1</td></tr>
<tr><td rowspan="2">二年級</td><td colspan="3">工科</td><td>3</td><td>3</td><td>2</td><td>2</td></tr>
<tr><td colspan="3">鐵路管理科</td><td>0</td><td>1</td><td>2</td><td>1</td></tr>
<tr><td rowspan="3">三年級</td><td rowspan="2">工科</td><td colspan="2">電機科</td><td>1</td><td>2</td><td>2</td><td>2</td></tr>
<tr><td colspan="2">機械科</td><td>1</td><td>1</td><td>1</td><td>1</td></tr>
<tr><td colspan="3">鐵路管理科</td><td>0</td><td>1</td><td>1</td><td>2</td></tr>
<tr><td rowspan="7">四年級</td><td rowspan="6">工科</td><td rowspan="3">電機科</td><td>電力工程門</td><td rowspan="3">1</td><td>1</td><td>1</td><td>1</td></tr>
<tr><td>有線電信門</td><td>0</td><td>1</td><td rowspan="2">1</td></tr>
<tr><td>無線電信門</td><td>1</td><td>1</td></tr>
<tr><td rowspan="3">機械科</td><td>鐵路機械門</td><td rowspan="3">1</td><td>1</td><td>1</td><td>1</td></tr>
<tr><td>機廠工務門</td><td>1</td><td>1</td><td rowspan="2">1</td></tr>
<tr><td>工業管理門</td><td>0</td><td>1</td></tr>
<tr><td colspan="3">鐵路管理科</td><td>0</td><td>1</td><td>1</td><td>1</td></tr>
<tr><td colspan="4">總計</td><td>10</td><td>17</td><td>18</td><td>18</td></tr>
</table>

十年度仍沿舊制四年級不分門.

十三年度有線電信及無線電信二門合併.名電信門.機廠工務及工業管理二門合併.名工業機械門.

歷年科門因革表

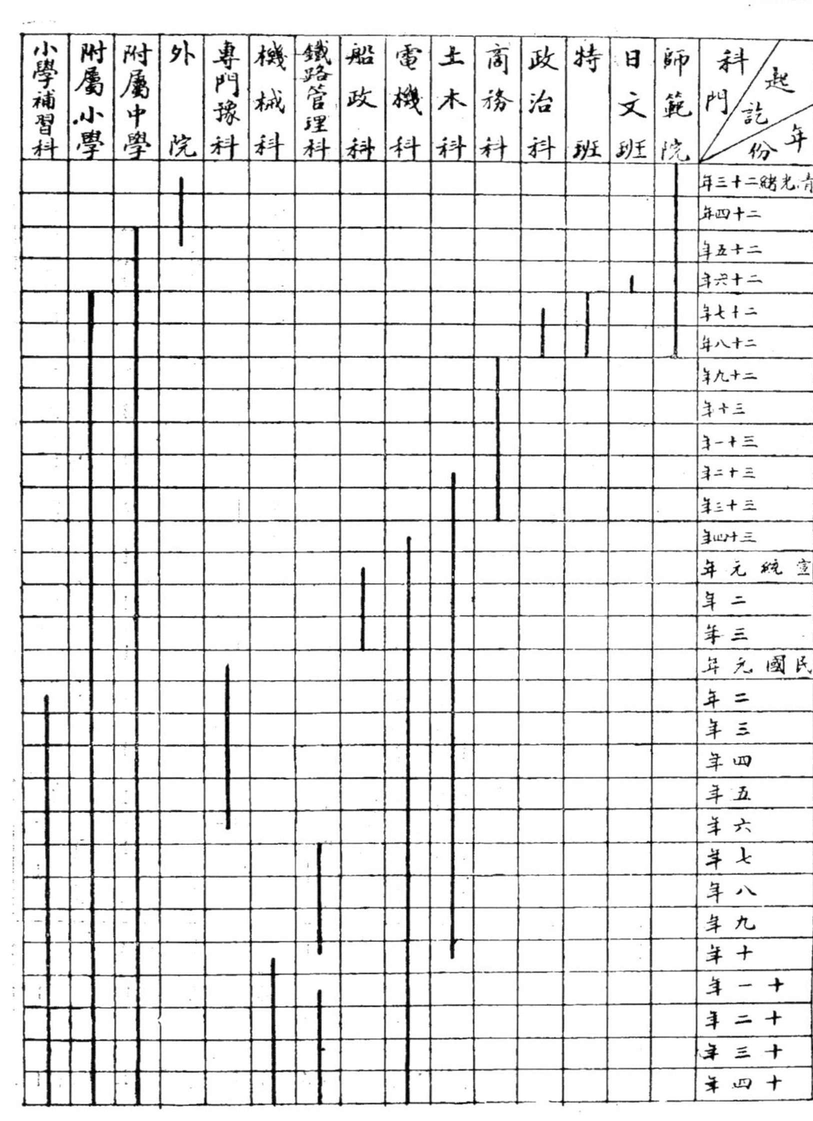

起訖年份 \ 科門	師範院	日文班	特班	政治科	商務科	土木科	電機科	船政科	鐵路管理科	機械科	專門豫科	外院	附屬中學	附屬小學	小學補習科
清光緒二十三年															
二十四年															
二十五年															
二十六年															
二十七年															
二十八年															
二十九年															
三十年															
三十一年															
三十二年															
三十三年															
三十四年															
宣統元年															
二年															
三年															
民國元年															
二年															
三年															
四年															
五年															
六年															
七年															
八年															
九年															
十年															
十一年															
十二年															
十三年															
十四年															

附註 商務科＝商科＝商業科

電機科＝電氣機械科

附屬中學＝高等豫科＝中院

鐵路科→土木科

中學五年級→專門豫科→專科一年級

＝示等於 →示改爲

課程

大學課程.每歐美工科大學相同.

附屬中學課程.如舊制完全中學.注重數理化各科.爲工科之預備.

附屬小學課程.如舊制高等小學.

師範院開辦之始無一定之課程表.教員何時到校.即於何時授課.教授國學之法.乃指定書籍令學生自修.按時呈閱劄記.另設西文西學二部不得兼習西文部.更分英文日本文二種亦不得兼習.西學則數學物理化學等屬之.光緒二十四年.設中院.監院福開森先生始爲之規定學科.按班授課.

商務科船政科課程漸完密每星期授課三十四至三十六小時.普通課程外凡應有之學科咸備並注重實習.土木科原爲鐵路科.故課程初僅限於鐵路工程.及後乃擴充範圍增添科目.專門預科本中學五年級.故課程頗簡單.嗣改作專科一年級乃漸次增高程度.而酌移二年級課程於第一年.

電機機械及鐵路管理三科課程詳見現行學科一覽表.附屬中小學學科表一併附後用便審覽（今略）

經費

部撥款項……每年二十六萬二千圓.
十二年度實支……二十九萬一千餘圓
學生每人每年應繳各費……大學一百五十二圓.中學一百十八圓.小學一百五十一圓.

南洋公學開辦之始經費出自招商及電報二局.本官督商辦性質.清光緒二十二年.督辦盛杏蓀先生商准各股東每年由招商局盈餘項下撥銀六萬兩.電報局盈餘項下撥銀四萬兩.爲南洋公學經費.開辦之後.又特存銀三十萬兩於招商電報二局而取其子金.光緒二十九年.二局改隸北洋.經費驟絀.幸賴存款.得以支持.三十年兩局改隸商部.本校因經費出自兩局亦改隸商部.常年經費.仍照常撥付.存款則因歷年提用.至三十三年僅存六萬兩.是年唐蔚芝先生繼任監督.乃竭力撙節.至次年.又積銀一萬兩.共存七萬兩.革命事起.經費無着.不得已乃提用存款二萬兩.又經部扣二萬兩.僅餘三萬兩.今此僅餘之三萬兩亦疊經提用淨盡矣.

宣統元年經費改由滬寧鐵路局撥付.全年支出數.由十三萬四千餘圓漸增至十九萬餘圓.然此時期內.添建房屋頗多.民國十年.改組交通大學.京奉津浦二鐵路局均有撥款.而全年支出.亦增至三十二萬八千六百餘圓.其後預算雖增.實支轉省.蓋京奉鐵路局撥款雖有成案.從未給領.至十四年五月止.積欠至十五萬餘圓之多.十三年.津浦鐵路因受戰事影響.撥款亦未能如期而至.幸自十三年九月起膠濟鐵路月撥一千元.十四年三月起上海電報局月撥二千元.稍資挹注.錄部撥款項大概如次.

滬寧滬杭甬鐵路局	每年六萬六千圓	膠濟鐵路局	每年一萬二千圓
京奉鐵路局	每年四萬圓	上海電報局	每年二萬四千圓
津浦鐵路局	每年十二萬圓		計共二十六萬二千圓

（本章未完）

南洋季刊第一卷第三期正誤表

消費合作概論

頁數	行數	正	誤
295	10	英國北部	英國北國
295	16	性質	性盾
296	3	合作社出賣	合作出賣

工場委員制

頁數	行數	正	誤
302	13	增進效率	增進功率
303	7	晤面談話	識面談話

孔孟之經濟思想

頁數	行數	正	誤
363	19	壞	壤

中國鐵路管理問題

頁數	行數	正	誤
372	25	浙江	淅江
373	13	開關	開開

贖回中東鐵路財政上應有之準備

頁數	行數	正	誤
377	14	該路對於	該對路於
379	2	第	弟
383	8	全國人士	全國入士

從利權得失觀劃分中國近世交通史之時期

頁數	行數	正	誤
386	1	未爲不可	末爲不可
388	6	急進侵佔	急進侵估

參觀日本大阪合同紗廠記

頁數	行數	正	誤
417	15	梳棉	清花
417	11	紗	細

一年來經濟學會大事記

頁數	行數	正	誤
426	16	之經濟學報	之濟學報

南洋一覽稿

頁數	行數	正	誤
429	11	自機械科之機字起應另作一節	
430	6	自外院之外字起應另作一節	

南洋季刊第一卷第四期機械工程號

版權所有 ◉ 不准翻印

民國十五年十二月出版

編輯處 上海南洋大學出版股

發行處及訂購處 上海南洋大學出版股

印刷者 中國刷印廠

代售處 上海商務印書館 中華書局
北京交通部路政司營業科曹麗順君
青島膠濟鐵路局機務處胡粹士君
南京河海大學吳馥初君

本刊價目表

定價		每期郵費	
每期	大洋二角	本埠	一分
		外埠	二分半
每年	大洋八角	國外	十分

本刊廣告刊例

全面	封面裏頁及底面裏外頁	實洋十五元
	尋常地位	實洋十元
半面	封面裏頁及底面裏外頁	實洋八元
	尋常地位	實洋六元